SAS/OR® User's Guide, Version 6, First Edition

SAS Institute Inc.
SAS Circle □ Box 8000
Cary, NC 27512-8000

The correct bibliographic citation for this manual is as follows: SAS Institute Inc. *SAS/OR® User's Guide, Version 6, First Edition*, Cary, NC: SAS Institute Inc., 1989. 479 pp.

SAS/OR® User's Guide, Version 6, First Edition

1st printing, March 1989
2nd printing, May 1990

Note that text corrections may have been made at each printing.

The SAS® System is an integrated system of software providing complete control over data access, management analysis, and presentation. Base SAS software is the foundation of the SAS System. Products within the SAS System include SAS/ACCESS®, SAS/AF®, SAS/ASSIST®, SAS/CPE®, SAS/DMI®, SAS/ETS®, SAS/FSP®, SAS/GRAPH®, SAS/IML®, SAS/IMS-DL/I®, SAS/OR®, SAS/QC®, SAS/REPLAY-CICS®, SAS/SHARE®, SAS/STAT®, SAS/CONNECT,™ SAS/DB2,™ SAS/SQL-DS,™ and SAS/TOOLKIT™ software. Other SAS Institute products are SYSTEM 2000® Data Management Software, with basic SYSTEM 2000, CREATE,™ Multi-User,™ QueX,™ Screen Writer,™ and CICS interface software; NeoVisuals® software; JMP™ and JMP IN™ software; SAS/RTERM® software; and the SAS/C® Compiler. MultiVendor Architecture™ and MVA™ are trademarks of SAS Institute Inc. *SAS Communications,® SAS Training,® SAS Views,®* and the SASware Ballot® are published by SAS Institute Inc. Plink86® and Plib86® are registered trademarks of Phoenix Technologies Ltd. All other trademarks above are registered trademarks or trademarks, as indicated by their mark, of SAS Institute Inc.

A footnote must accompany the first use of each Institute registered trademark or trademark and must state that the referenced trademark is used to identify products or services of SAS Institute Inc.

The Institute is a private company devoted to the support and further development of its software and related services.

Doc SS1, Ver12.1, 011289

Contents

iv

Illustrations

Figures

Screens

Tables

Credits

Documentation

Composition	Timothy James Cunningham, Gail C. Freeman, Blanche W. Phillips
Graphics Support	Regina C. Luginbuhl
Illustrations	Ginny Matsey
Proofreading	Reid J. Hardin, Philip R. Shelton, Michael H. Smith, Helen F. Weeks, Susan E. Willard
Technical Assistance	Wendy D. Johnson, Radhika V. Kulkarni, Stuart Nisbet
Technical Review	Marcelo Bartroli, Donna Fulenwider, Bill Gjertsen, Edward P. Hughes, Charles B. Kelly, Sandra D. Schlotzhauer
Writing and Editing	Rick Cornell Jr., Regina C. Luginbuhl, Curt Yeo

Software

The procedures in SAS/OR software were implemented by the Operations Research Department of the Applications Division under the leadership of Marc-david Cohen. Contributions and support were given to the project by the members of the Graphics Division, the DPD Division, the Core Division, and the Host Systems Division.

Program development includes design, programming, debugging, support, preliminary documentation, and technical review. Many procedures in SAS/OR software were implemented based on the algorithms used in Version 5 with substantial improvements. In the list below, asterisks follow the names of developers currently supporting the procedure. Other developers listed worked on the procedure previously.

ASSIGN	Marc-david Cohen
CPM	Marc-david Cohen, Radhika V. Kulkarni*
GANTT	Radhika V. Kulkarni
LP	Marc-david Cohen
NETDRAW	Radhika V. Kulkarni
NETFLOW	Marc-david Cohen, Trevor D. Kearney*
TRANS	Marc-david Cohen, Trevor D. Kearney*
Quality Assurance Testing	Marcelo Bartroli, Edward P. Hughes, Charles B. Kelly
Statistical Consulting and Technical Support	Donna Fulenwider

The following staff members made special contributions in the form of leadership and support for the SAS/OR procedure developers: John P. Sall and David M. DeLong.

The PC version of the SAS System was developed on an Apollo domain network, as well as on IBM® personal computers.

Acknowledgments

Many people have been instrumental in the development of SAS/OR software. The individuals acknowledged here have been especially helpful.

Lance Broad	New Zealand Ministry of Forestry
Ken Cruthers	Goodyear Tire & Rubber Company
Patricia Duffy	Auburn University
Paul Hardy	Babcock & Wilcox
Don Henderson	ORI Consulting Group
Vidyadhar G. Kulkarni	University of North Carolina at Chapel Hill
Wayne Maruska	Basin Electric Power Cooperative
Bruce Reed	Auburn University
David Rubin	University of North Carolina at Chapel Hill
John Stone	North Carolina State University

xii

Using This Book

Purpose of This Book

This book documents all of the procedures available in Release 6.03 of SAS/OR software and supersedes the *SAS/OR User's Guide, Version 5 Edition*. To find out which release of SAS/OR software you are using, look at the notes at the beginning of the SAS log.

How This Book Is Organized

Chapters 1 through 3 of this book provide an overview and introduce you to the two groups of procedures (project management and mathematical programming) in SAS/OR software. These introductory chapters briefly describe the procedures available in a given group and compare and contrast procedures.

After the three introductory chapters, the next seven chapters describe individual SAS/OR procedures in alphabetical order. Each procedure description is self-contained; you need to be familiar with only the most basic features of the SAS System and SAS terminology to use most procedures. The statements and syntax necessary to run each procedure are presented in a uniform format throughout this book. You can duplicate the examples by copying the statements and data and running the SAS program. The examples are also useful as models for writing your own programs. The **SAS Sample Library** contains the exact code used to run the examples shown in this book. You can use the SAS Sample Library; consult your SAS Software representative for specific information.

Each procedure description is divided into the following major parts:

ABSTRACT   a short paragraph describing what the procedure does.

INTRODUCTION   introductory and background material, including definitions and occasional introductory examples.

SPECIFICATIONS   a reference section for the syntax for the procedure. The statement syntax is summarized, then the PROC statement is described, and then all other statements are described in alphabetical order. Options for a statement are described in alphabetical order, or they are grouped and described in alphabetical order within each group.

DETAILS   a section with expanded descriptions of features, internal operations, mathematical background, treatment of missing values, computational methods, required computational resources, and input and output data sets.

EXAMPLES   examples using the procedure, including data, SAS statements, and printed output. You can reproduce these examples by copying the statements and data and then running the job.

REFERENCES   a selected bibliography.

Following the chapters that describe SAS/OR procedures, there is one appendix, "Using Macro SASMPSXS to Convert from IBM Format to LP Format." There is a section entitled "Changes and Enhancements" at the front of the book indicating differences between this version of SAS/OR software and Version 5.

How to Use This Book

If you have not used the SAS System before, you should read the *SAS Introductory Guide*. You can also refer to base SAS documentation. Next, read the introductory chapter that corresponds to your area of interest. The introductory chapter will help you choose the procedure that best meets your needs. Once you have chosen the procedure that you will need to use, you can turn to the specific chapter on the procedure. First, read the **ABSTRACT** and **INTRODUCTION** to get an overview of how the procedure works. Next, look at the first part of the **SPECIFICATIONS** section to get a summary of which statements can be used with the procedure and what each statement does. At this point, you may know exactly what statements you need to use for your situation. If not, there may be an example in the **EXAMPLES** section that closely matches your problem and can guide you in selecting statements to use. Otherwise, you may need to read the **SPECIFICATIONS** section in more detail. Finally, the **DETAILS** section contains information on advanced topics and details of analysis.

If you are familiar with the SAS System and with the procedures in SAS/OR software, turn to the section "Changes and Enhancements," which discusses the differences between the present version and previous versions of the SAS/OR procedures. Next, review specific chapters to learn more about the changes to a particular procedure. Many procedures have expanded introductions, new or expanded details sections, and new examples, so even if the procedure has not changed very much, the chapter on the procedure may have new information.

Typographical Conventions

In this book, you will see several type styles used. Style conventions are summarized below:

roman type	is the basic type style used for most text.
italic type	is used to define new terms and to indicate items in statement syntax that you need to supply.
bold type	is used in **SPECIFICATIONS** sections to indicate that you must use the exact spelling and form shown, to refer to matrices and vectors, and to refer you to other sections (either in the same chapter or in other chapters). In addition, sentences of extreme importance are entirely in bold type.
`code`	is used to show examples of SAS statements. In most cases, this book uses lowercase type for SAS code. You can enter your own SAS code in lowercase, uppercase, or a mixture of the two. The SAS System changes your variable names to uppercase, but character variable values remain in lowercase if you have entered them that way. Enter any titles and footnotes exactly as you want them to appear on your output.

How the Output Is Shown

Output from procedures is enclosed in boxes. Within a chapter, the output is numbered consecutively starting with 1, and each output is given a title. Most of the programs in this book were run using the SAS system options LINESIZE=120, PAGESIZE=60, and NODATE. In situations where other options were used, these are usually indicated in the SAS code that accompanies the output. In some cases, if you run the examples, you will get slightly different output. This is a function of whether a floating-point processor is used in your computer, rather than a problem with the software. In all situations, the difference should be very small.

In this book, all graphics and full-screen output is shown on a white background. Because of this, all graphics options specified in the code as using white have been reversed to black in the output.

Changes and Enhancements to SAS/OR® Software

HOW TO USE THIS SECTION

Use this section to get an overview of the major changes and enhancements to procedures in Version 6 of SAS/OR software. All of these changes and enhancements are incorporated into the chapters for the procedures. In all cases, the individual chapters contain more detail on the changes and enhancements. For information on a specific procedure, look at the table of contents at the beginning of the chapter for the procedure. The PROJMAN documentation is listed in its entirety below.

PROJMAN: THE PROJECT MANAGEMENT SHELL

The Project Management Shell is an example of a menu-driven, full-screen facility for project management. It is implemented using the SAS/AF screen control language and serves to tie together several procedures in base SAS software and SAS/OR software.

PROJMAN is designed to provide a basic project management capability. It can schedule projects subject to precedence, resource, and time constraints, and it can be used to track project progress. PROJMAN does not incorporate all the functionality of the CPM, GANTT, and NETDRAW procedures. It does provide enough information to enable you to schedule most of your projects and to serve as a starting point for creating your own project management system using the SAS System. It is designed to be a prototype of a project management application. Because the source code is included, you can take the shell and modify it to suit the particular needs of your application. Note that in order to modify the source code you will need access to PROC BUILD in SAS/AF software.

What the Project Management Shell Can Do

PROJMAN performs three functions for you: it maintains the data sets that contain the project data; it reports the schedule; and it reports the resource usage. The shell is function driven. If you ask for a function, for example to report the schedule, the shell will determine automatically whether the information is available to perform the function. If there is information missing, the shell will request that you enter it and then continue to perform the function. For example, if you request a Gantt chart but have not provided the necessary data, the shell will request that you enter the necessary data. It will then direct you to schedule the project. Finally, it will draw the Gantt chart for you.

Defining the Project Data

The project data are defined in four data sets, the ACTIVITY data set, the CALEN-DAR data set, the HOLIDAY data set, and the RESOURCE data set. Multiple projects can share data by sharing data sets.

The ACTIVITY data identify the tasks that make up the project. The ACTIVITY data also include information about the tasks (for example, the task duration, target dates for the task, resources needed by the task, and the calendar on which to schedule the task).

The other three data sets are optional. The RESOURCE data give the amount of the resources available over the planning horizon of the project. The CALEN-DAR data specify specialized calendars on which the tasks are to be performed. The HOLIDAY data give the dates of holidays over the planning horizon.

PROJMAN automatically maintains a project dictionary. This is a data set that associates the data with the project name. You can rename projects, identify data to projects, and share data (for example, HOLIDAY and RESOURCE data) across projects.

Reporting the Schedule

The schedule consists of the start and finish times of the tasks in the project. The schedule can be reported in a network representation of the project, on a Gantt chart, on a calendar, or in a listing. In addition, the chart or network can be displayed in the default full-screen mode, in the output window of the SAS Display Manager System, or using the graphics mode.

Reporting the Resources

The resource reports show the project's use of resources through the planning horizon. The report can be displayed on a bar chart, on a plot showing cumulative resource use, or printed in the output window of display manager. Both the bar chart and plot can be viewed in either the output window of display manager or using the graphics mode.

INTERACTIVE PROCEDURES

The Version 6 LP and NETFLOW procedures can be run interactively. The NET-DRAW and GANTT procedures are interactive when run in full-screen mode.

You can end an interactive procedure with a DATA step, by invoking another procedure, by submitting an ENDSAS statement, or by submitting a QUIT statement.

For example, using PROC NETFLOW interactively, you can stop NETFLOW before, during, and after optimization and then command NETFLOW to print out all or part of the problem. The amount of information that is displayed can also be controlled. You can save solutions in output data sets or specify into what data sets the current (optimal) solution is to be output. Then you can resume optimization or submit a PIVOT, QUIT, or ENDSAS statement.

The interactive features of the LP procedure enable you to examine intermediate results, and perform sensitivity analysis, parametric programming, and range analysis. You can control the solution processes of PROC LP and PROC NET-FLOW interactively.

THE MACRO FACILITIES

Each procedure in SAS/OR software now has a macro variable available. This variable contains a character string that indicates the status of the procedure. See each specific procedure for details on the macro variable.

THE ASSIGN PROCEDURE

DEC= is a new option on the PROC ASSIGN statement. This option specifies a scaling factor for the input costs data. A section on scaling has been added to the **DETAILS** section. Two new examples using the BY statement have been added to the **EXAMPLES** section. In addition, new memory management schemes enable PROC ASSIGN to solve larger problems with less memory than was possible in Version 5 of SAS/OR software.

THE CPM PROCEDURE

The CPM procedure has several new features.

multiple calendars
> The CPM procedure now allows multiple calendars. PROC CPM enables you to define any number of calendars and associate different activities with each calendar.

modification of work patterns
> You can also change or modify general work patterns with the WORKDAY and CALENDAR data sets. Use these data sets to specify very general patterns of work during any day of the week.

nonstandard relationships
> The LAG= option has been added to the SUCCESSOR statement enabling you to specify nonstandard precedence relationships. For example, you can specify that activity B starts five days after activity A has started.

tracking project progress
> PROC CPM enables you to track your progess using the ACTUAL statement. The ACTUAL statement has been added to enable you to identify variables in the activities data set that contain progress information about the activities in the project.

activity-splitting
> During resource-constrained scheduling, PROC CPM enables non-critical activities to be pre-empted by critical activities. PROC CPM enables you to specify the maximum number of segments into which an activity can be split as well as the minimum duration of any segment of the activity.

Examples have been added to illustrate these new capabilities.

THE LP PROCEDURE

PROC LP can now solve linear goal-programming problems. Special ordered sets can be specified using the TYPE statement and the keywords SOSLE and SOSEQ. All examples in PROC LP are new. **Example 7** illustrates a goal-programming problem; **Example 6** illustrates a problem using special ordered sets. There are variable length differences between the Version 5 and Version 6 LP procedures. In the Version 5 LP procedure you are limited to eight characters, but in the Version 6 LP procedure, using the sparse data input mode, characters can exceed eight. In addition, new memory management schemes enable PROC LP to solve larger problems with less memory than was possible in Version 5 of SAS/OR software.

THE GANTT PROCEDURE

The GANTT procedure now uses a full-screen facility. The procedure now supports multiple calendars. A resource-constrained schedule is plotted on a separate line.

THE NETDRAW PROCEDURE

NETDRAW is a new procedure capable of producing network diagrams. Boxes are used to represent activities, and lines are used to show relationships among the activities. You can use NETDRAW to draw any acyclic network. The diagrams can be produced in line mode, full-screen mode, or, if you have SAS/GRAPH software, in high-resolution graphics mode.

THE NETFLOW PROCEDURE

The NETFLOW procedure has changed extensively from its previous versions (PROC NETFLOW in Version 5 and PROC TNETFLOW in Release 5.16). The Version 6 NETFLOW procedure has many more capabilities and features. In the following section, both the enhancements and the specific code modifications necessary to make Version 6 PROC NETFLOW run in place of Version 5 PROC NETFLOW, and Release 5.16 TNETFLOW, are described.

Listed below are the changes and enhancements to TNETFLOW that appear in the Version 6 NETFLOW procedure.

- Version 6 PROC NETFLOW allows you more flexibility in the way that data are furnished to it. Some of the input data formats of PROC TNETFLOW are not allowed by PROC NETFLOW (for example, numeric node, arc, nonarc, constraint names, and multiple arcs in an observation of ARCDATA. These changes were made to reduce code size). The new data formats are less restrictive. There are many ways that a particular item of the problem's data can be supplied to NETFLOW. This makes problem generation easier and enables you to use the data format that you find most convenient or natural.

- Information on an arc or nonarc variable can be given in more than one observation of ARCDATA and, unlike TNETFLOW, in CONDATA. In the dense format of CONDATA, the data of a constraint do not need to be contained entirely in a single observation. Also, the sparse format of CONDATA now allows a greater variety of observation types. Both CONDATA data formats can include special row names. Arcs have default names in the form TAIL_HEAD, which can be used when data on arcs appear in CONDATA. Steps have been taken to ensure that default names do not cause ambiguity.

- You have extensive control of the optimization process. The way that the pricing strategies are controlled has been improved. Many parts of the optimization algorithm have been changed so that they are more efficient than the corresponding parts of the algorithm of TNETFLOW.

- To an even greater extent than TNETFLOW, NETFLOW was designed to solve large scale problems. PROC NETFLOW's memory management is such that even large problems can be solved on computers that do not have virtual memory facilities. Given a modest amount of memory and an adequate amount of disk space, NETFLOW should solve the problem successfully.

NETFLOW differs from TNETFLOW in many respects. In most instances, you will not be able to delete the *T* of TNETFLOW and have your SAS jobs run. Changes were made to increase solution speed, reduce code size, and enable NETFLOW to improve control and functionality. The changes necessary to your SAS programs may not be extensive and the benefits of using the additional features and greater capabilities of PROC NETFLOW should more than offset the trouble of the conversions.

Converting Version 5 TNETFLOW Programs to Version 6 NETFLOW Programs

The following section describes deletions to, translations of, and changes to Version 5 TNETFLOW options and statements that must be considered while converting programs written for Version 5 TNETFLOW to run with Version 6 NETFLOW.

Deletions

OOK
>   specified use of the *out-of-kilter* algorithm. NETFLOW uses only the primal simplex algorithm.

NSOURCENODE=
NSOURCE=
NSINKNODE=
NSINK=
>   referred to the use of numeric node names, which is prohibited in Version 6 SAS/OR software.

ADDSUPD
ADDD
>   algorithm-supplied supply no longer can be routed directly to otherwise unsatisfied demand nodes. See the THRUNET option of NETFLOW for more information.

MAX1CONSEQS
MAX2CONSEQS
>   anti-cycling devices.

NTYPEOBS
NRHSOBS
>   eliminated due to Version 6 prohibition of numeric values for COLUMN variables in sparse input format.

INVDTYPE=2
>   other option values translated (refer to **Translations**, below).

FLOW
>   used with an OOK warm start.

ABY
CBY
DBY
NBY
   no BY processing is allowed in Version 6 SAS/OR software.

REPORTREDUND
REMOVEREDUND
   options dealing with redundant constraints.

Alias Deletions

ARC
ARCID
   aliases of the NAME statement.

CON
CONID
CONNAME
   aliases of the ROW statement.

CONTYPE
   alias of the TYPE statement.

CONVAR
   alias of the VAR statement.

F1
   alias of the FUTURE1 option.

F2
   alias of the FUTURE2 option.

FROM
   alias of the TAILNODE statement.

HI
HIGH
   aliases of the CAPACITY statement.

LR1
   alias of the LRATIO1 option.

LR2
   alias of the LRATIO2 option.

MAXIMISE
   alias of the MAXIMIZE option.

MI1
   alias of the MAXIT1= option.

MI2
   alias of the MAXIT2= option.

NODEID
NODENAME
   aliases of the NODE statement.

NZT1
   alias of the NOZTOL1 option.

NZT2
   alias of the NOZTOL2 option.

RFF=
   alias of the REFACTFREQ= option.

SCR
   alias of the SCRATCH option.

TAIL
   alias of the TAILNODE statement.

W
   alias of the WARM option.

MAX2CONSEQS
   anti-cycling device.

PRTIBFS
   printed out initial basic feasible solution.

Translations

In the table below, the Version 5 option listed on the left is now invoked with the Version 6 option listed on the right.

Version 5	Version 6
ADDSUPPLY ADDS	THRUNET
KEEPZERO KZ	No specification needed (done as default).
PRICINGx=1	PRICETYPEx=NOQ with PxSCAN=FIRST
PRICINGx=2	PRICETYPEx=NOQ with PxSCAN=BEST
PRICINGx=3 Px	PRICETYPEx=Q
TOTSCANx TSx	QxFILLSCAN=BEST (Version 5 default is QxFILLSCAN=FIRST; Version 6 default is QxFILLSCAN=PARTIAL and QxFILLNPARTIAL=10.)
PRTCONS PC	PRINT CONSTRAINTS, PRINT CON_ARCS, PRINT CON_NONARCS
INVDTYPE=1 IDT=	INVD_2D (This option is no longer the default for <15 side constraints)
IDVDTYPE=2	Deleted.
IDVDTYPE=3	No INVD_2D specification (default for all cases).
PRTNET	PRINT ARCS The solution information may vary, depending on where the statement appears in the program.
PRTNETOP	NETFLOW *procedure call*; RESET ENDPAUSE1; RUN; PRINT ARCS; You can also specify ARCOUT and NODEOUT data sets in the NETFLOW procedure call, and use PROC PRINT to print them.

PRTOPTIM   NETFLOW *procedure call*;
            RUN;
            PRINT ARCS;
            You can also specify CONOUT and DUALOUT data sets
            in the NETFLOW procedure call, and use PROC PRINT
            to print them.

Adjustments and New Restrictions

MAXIT1
  the default has changed from 500 to 1000.

MAXIT2
  the default has changed from 200 to 999999.

DEFCONTYPE
  numeric values are not allowed.

INVFREQ=
  used with INVDTYPE=1 or INVDTYPE=2 in TNETFLOW; use with
  INVD_2D for Version 6. The default has changed from 25 to 50.

REFACTFREQ=
  used with INVDTYPE=3 in TNETFLOW; use with INVD_2D for Version
  6. The default has changed from 15 to 50.

U=
  used with INVDTYPE=3 in TNETFLOW; use with INVD_2D for Version
  6.

DWIA
  used with INVDTYPE=3 for Version 5; use without INVD_2D for
  Version 6.

MAXLUUPDATES=
  used with INVDTYPE=3 for Version 5; use without INVD_2D for
  Version 6.

MAXL=
  used with INVDTYPE=3 for Version 5; use without INVD_2D for
  Version 6.

CAPACITY
  Version 6 allows only a single variable to be listed. The default name
  starts with _CA, _HI, or _UP in Version 5; it must be _CAPAC_,
  UPPER, _UPPERBD, or _HI_ in Version 6.

COST
  Version 6 allows only a single variable to be listed. The default name
  starts with _CO in Version 5; it must be _COST_ or _LENGTH_ in
  Version 6.

DEMAND
  Version 6 allows only a single variable to be listed. The default name
  starts with _DE in Version 5; it must be _DEMAND_ in Version 6.

HEADNODE
  Version 6 allows only a single variable to be listed. No numeric variable
  is allowed. The default name starts with _TO or _HE in Version 5; it
  must be _HEAD_ or _TO_ in Version 6.

LO
  Version 6 allows only a single variable to be listed. The default name
  starts with _LO in Version 5; it must be _LOWER_, _LO_,
  _LOWERBD, or _MINFLOW in Version 6.

NAME
> Version 6 allows only a single variable to be listed. No numeric variable is allowed.

SUPPLY
> the default name starts with _SU in Version 5; it must be _SUPPLY_ in Version 6.

TAILNODE
> no numeric variable is allowed. The default name starts with _TA or _FR in Version 5; it must be _TAIL_ or _FROM_ in Version 6.

NODE
> no numeric variable is allowed. The default name starts with _NO in Version 5; it must be _NODE_ in Version 6.

SUPDEM
> the default name starts with _SD in Version 5; it must be _SUPDEM_ or _SD_ in Version 6.

COLUMN
> no numeric variable is allowed. The default name starts with _COL in Version 5; it must be _COLUMN_ or _COL_ in Version 6.

RHS
> the default name starts with _RHS in Version 5; it must be _RHS_ in Version 6.

ROW
> no numeric variables are allowed.

TYPE
> no numeric variable is allowed. The default name starts with _TYPE in Version 5; it must be _TYPE_ in Version 6.

SPARSECONDATA
> must be specified if constraint data are in sparse format.

Converting Version 5 NETFLOW Programs to Version 6 NETFLOW Programs

This section describes deletions of, translations of, and changes to Version 5 NET-FLOW options and statements that must be considered while converting programs written for Version 5 NETFLOW to run with Version 6 NETFLOW.

Deletions

NSINKNODE=
NSOURCENODE=
> both refer to the use of numeric node names, which is prohibited in Version 6.

BY
> no BY processing is allowed in Version 6.

Translations

In the following table, the Version 5 option listed on the left is now invoked with
with the Version 6 option listed on the right.

Version 5	Version 6
ADDSUPPLY	THRUNET
ASINKNODE=	SINKNODE=
ASOURCENODE=	SOURCENODE=
DATA=	ARCDATA=
MAXIMUM	MAXIMIZE
OUT=	ARCOUT=

Adjustments and New Restrictions

DEFCAPACITY=
> the default is 99999 in Version 5; in Version 6, the default is the value
> of INFINITY=n, (the default value of n is 999999).

DEMAND=
> the default in Version 5 is the minimum of total network supply and the
> sum of capacities of all arcs directed toward the sinknode. In Version 6,
> the default is total network supply.

SUPPLY=
> the default in Version 5 is the minimum of total network demand and
> the sum of capacities of all arcs directed away from the sourcenode. In
> Version 6, the default is total network demand.

CAPACITY
> Version 6 allows only a single variable to be listed.

COST
> Version 6 allows only a single variable to be listed.

DEMAND
> Version 6 allows only a single variable to be listed.

HEADNODE
> no numeric variable is allowed in Version 6.

MINFLOW
> Version 6 allows only a single variable to be listed.

SUPPLY
> Version 6 allows only a single variable to be listed.

TAILNODE
> no numeric variable is allowed in Version 6.

THE TRANS PROCEDURE

The TRANS procedure has several new options available. THRUNET enables you
to force through the network any excess supply, the amount that total supply
exceeds total demand. NOTHRUNET tells PROC TRANS to drain away any
excess supply or excess demand. FLOW= is a new option that lets you specify
the SAS data set containing the initial flows. The Version 5 ADDSUPPLY option
has been replaced by the THRUNET option.

The TAILNODE statement replaces the ID statement, and the HEADNODE statement replaces the VAR statement.

The dual variables are being calculated differently, so the output results will be different from Version 5.

Chapter 1

Introduction to SAS/OR® Software

INTRODUCTION

SAS/OR software is a set of programs for exploring models of distribution networks, production systems, resource allocation problems, and scheduling questions using the tools of operations research.

SAS/OR programs are procedures in the SAS System. If you are familiar with other SAS System procedures, you will find the syntax and use of options very similar. All SAS retrieval, data management, reporting, analysis, and other capabilities can be used with SAS/OR.

Operations research tools are directed toward the solution of management problems. Models in operations research are representations of physical objects or conceptual processes. The structure of the model can be independent of the data for the particular model. For example, a distribution network may connect New York to Washington regardless of the cost of shipping across that link. Using the tools of operations research involves

- defining a structural model of the system under investigation
- collecting the data for the model
- analyzing the model.

A problem is formalized with the construction of a model to represent it. These models, called *mathematical programs*, are represented in SAS data sets and then solved using SAS/OR procedures. The solution and formulation of mathematical programs is called *mathematical programming*. Because mathematical programs are represented in SAS data sets, they can be saved, easily changed, and resolved. The SAS/OR procedures also output SAS data sets containing the solutions. Then, these can be used to produce customized reports. In addition, this structure enables you to build decision support systems using the tools of operations research and other tools in the SAS System as building blocks.

The procedures for scheduling and project management are

CPM   for scheduling projects

GANTT   for plotting Gantt charts

NETDRAW   for drawing network diagrams.

The procedures for general mathematical programming and network flow programming are

ASSIGN	for assignment problems
LP	for linear, integer, and mixed-integer programming
NETFLOW	for network flow programming
TRANS	for transportation problems.

SAS/OR also includes a data conversion macro, SASMPSX, and a project management shell, called PROJMAN, which is a full-screen facility that ties together many procedures for project management. See "Changes and Enhancements to SAS/OR Software" for details on PROJMAN.

Although the SAS/OR procedures are presented as either mathematical programming or project management, there are many project management related problems, including scheduling problems, that can only be solved using mathematical programming procedures. Conversely, there are many problems that are not posed as scheduling problems but can be efficiently solved using the CPM procedure. Production and distribution networks can often be drawn using the NETDRAW procedure.

Project Management

Project management is a broad area of study that involves many disciplines, ranging from employee relations to numerical methods of inventory management. Issues relating to scheduling and resource management are of central concern.

Many of the procedures in SAS/OR software help manage the resources and deadlines of a project. The CPM procedure can be used to find schedules that satisfy the structural relationships among activities and project and activity deadlines while staying within the bounds imposed by resource limitations. The CPM procedure solves this type of scheduling problem and saves the schedule in a SAS data set. Resource use and the progress of the actual schedule can also be monitored with PROC CPM.

The structural relationships among activities can be visualized as a network. If you think of the nodes as activities in the project and the arcs connecting the nodes as indicating the relationship among the activities, then a network drawing can give insight into the scheduling needs of the project. The NETDRAW procedure can draw the project network on line printer, full-screen, and high resolution devices.

A Gantt chart is another tool that is useful for monitoring the progress of a project. The chart graphically displays the calculated schedule and shows the current progress in meeting the schedule. The GANTT procedure can be used to produce line printer, full-screen, and high resolution Gantt charts.

In addition to CPM, NETDRAW, and GANTT, the procedures for solving general mathematical programming models can be used for solving scheduling problems that cannot be solved with CPM. These procedures are also useful for addressing other resource allocation and project management issues.

Mathematical Programming

Problems in distribution and resource allocation arise in many settings, ranging from petro-chemical, manufacturing, and agriculture to finance and economics. Linear, integer, mixed-integer, and network flow programming are optimization techniques that can be applied to many of these problems. SAS/OR software contains procedures for solving these problems that have been specialized for the particular problem in two ways. First, the model input format is specialized for the particular type of problem. When the inherent structure of a model is known, the pertinent data can be represented efficiently. Second, the algorithm used for model solution is specialized for the particular type of problem. The inherent structure of a model also suggests the type of algorithm that should be used to optimize the model efficiently.

There are four procedures in SAS/OR software designed to solve optimization problems: ASSIGN, LP, NETFLOW, and TRANS. The LP procedure solves linear, integer, and mixed-integer programs. It can find optimal solutions and can perform several types of post-optimality analysis including range analysis, sensitivity analysis, and parametric programming. This procedure can also be used interactively. The model is input to PROC LP in either a dense or sparse format. The model specification is robust, so that it is easy to generate models using the tools in the SAS System. The LP procedure can save the solution in one or more SAS data sets. These data sets can then be used to report the results of model solution.

The NETFLOW procedure solves pure network flow problems and network flow problems with linear side constraints. The side constraints can have variables directly related to the network (called arc variables) as well as variables that have nothing to do with the network (called non-arc variables). This procedure accepts the network specification in a format that is particularly suited to networks. The NETFLOW procedure expects the side constraints specified in the same dense or sparse format that the LP procedure uses. Although network problems can be solved by PROC LP, the NETFLOW procedure will generally solve network flow problems more efficiently.

The TRANS procedure solves special types of networks called transportation problems. These are networks in which each node is one of two types, either a supply node or a demand node. This procedure accepts data in a format specialized for this type of problem.

The ASSIGN procedure solves a special type of transportation problem in which the supply at each supply node is one and the demand at each demand node is one. The data format for this procedure is also designed for this type of problem.

ORGANIZATION OF THIS MANUAL

The procedures in this book are arranged in alphabetical order and are preceded by introductory chapters. Chapter 2, "Introduction to Project Management Using SAS/OR Software," provides a discussion of project management using SAS/OR software and illustrates how to use the CPM, GANTT, and NETDRAW procedures. Chapter 3, "Introduction to Mathematical Programming Using SAS/OR Software," provides an overview of the types of problems that can be solved with the mathematical programming procedures in SAS/OR software and highlights issues surrounding model generation, optimization, report writing, and decision support systems. Appendix 1 provides a description of the SASMPSX macro.

Chapter 2

Introduction to Project Management Using SAS/OR® Software

INTRODUCTION

This chapter briefly describes how you can use SAS/OR software for managing your projects. It is not meant to serve as an introduction to project management; several textbooks on project management explain the basic steps involved in defining, planning, and managing projects (Moder, Phillips, and Davis 1983). Briefly, a project is defined as any task comprising a set smaller tasks that need to be done, either sequentially or in parallel. Projects can be small and last only a few minutes (for example, running a set of small computer programs), or they can be mammoth and run for several years (for example, the Apollo space program).

The SAS/OR product has three procedures that can be used for planning, controlling, and monitoring projects: the CPM procedure for scheduling the activities in your project subject to precedence, time, and resource constraints; the GANTT procedure for displaying the computed schedule; and the NETDRAW procedure for displaying the activity network. These procedures integrate with the SAS System enabling you to easily develop a customized project management system suitable for your needs. This chapter illustrates the basic structure of these procedures and shows how you can use them along with various features of the SAS System to manage your projects.

DATA FLOW

This section provides an overview of how project information is transmitted between procedures using the appropriate input and output data sets. Maintaining the project information in SAS data sets enables you to easily merge information from several sources, summarize information, subset a large data set into smaller data sets, and perform a wide variety of other operations using any of the many procedures in the SAS System. Each of the procedures also defines a SAS macro variable that contains a character string indicating whether or not the procedure terminated successfully. This information is useful when the procedure is incorporated as one of the steps in a larger program.

PROC CPM does the project scheduling and forms the core of the project management functionality in SAS/OR software. It uses activity precedence, time and resource constraints, and holiday and calendar information to determine a feasible schedule for the project. The precedence constraints between the activities are described using a network representation, either in Activity-On-Arc or Activity-On-Node notation, and input to PROC CPM using an activity data set. The two different representations are briefly described in Chapter 5, "The CPM Procedure." The activity data set can also specify time constraints on the activities and resource requirement information. The activity data set is required. Resource availability information can be specified using another data set, referred to here as the resource data set. Holiday, workday, and other calendar information is contained in the calendar, workday, and holiday data sets (each of these data sets is described in detail in Chapter 5). The schedule determined by PROC CPM using all the input information and any special scheduling options is saved in an output data set. Further, resource usage information can also be saved in another output data set. **Figure 2.1** illustrates all the input and output data sets that are possible with PROC CPM.

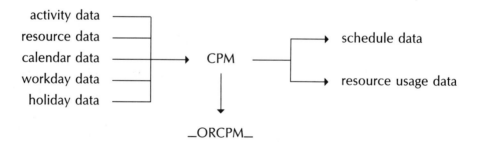

Figure 2.1   Input and Output Data Sets in PROC CPM

In **Figure 2.1**, _ORCPM_ is the macro variable defined by PROC CPM that is available after the completion of the procedure.

   Note: the procedure does not produce any printed output.

   The two output data sets produced by PROC CPM contain all the information about the schedule and the resource usage; these data sets can be used as input to either PROC GANTT or PROC NETDRAW, or any of the several reporting, charting, or plotting procedures in the SAS System. The schedule output data set can also contain additional project information such as project id, department and phase information, target dates, and so on, in the form of ID variables passed to it from the activity input data set via the ID statement. These variables can be used to produce customized reports by reordering, subsetting, summarizing, or condensing the information in the schedule data set in various different ways.

PROC GANTT draws, in line-printer, high-resolution graphics or full-screen mode, a bar chart of the schedules computed by PROC CPM. Such a bar chart is referred to as a Gantt chart in project management terminology. In addition to the schedule data set, PROC GANTT can also use the calendar, workday, and holiday data sets (that were used by PROC CPM to define the calendars used by the activities in the project) to mark holidays and weekends and other non-work periods appropriately on the Gantt chart.

Note: this procedure does not produce an output data set.

As with PROC CPM, PROC GANTT also defines a macro variable named _ORGANTT that has a character string indicating if the procedure terminated successfully. The following figure graphically depicts these relationships:

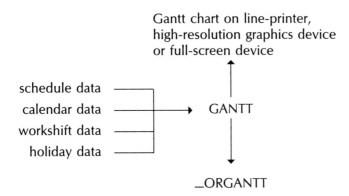

Figure 2.2 Input Data Sets used by PROC GANTT

PROC NETDRAW can be used to draw the networks representing the activity precedence constraints. The procedure automatically places the nodes in the network and draws the arcs connecting them, using the (activity → immediate successor) relationship as specified by the activity data set. If the schedule data set output by PROC CPM is used instead of the activity data set, the network diagram also contains all the schedule times determined by PROC CPM. The procedure can draw the diagram in line-printer as well as high-resolution graphics mode. Further, you can invoke the procedure in full-screen mode, which allows you to scroll around the network to view different parts of it; in this mode, you can also modify the layout of the network by moving the nodes of the network. The procedure also produces an output data set (network data set), which contains the positions of the nodes and the arcs connecting them. This output data set can also be used as an input data set to PROC NETDRAW. As with PROC CPM and PROC GANTT, PROC NETDRAW also defines a macro variable _ORNETDR, which contains a character string indicating if the procedure terminated successfully. **Figure 2.3** illustrates input and output data sets possible with PROC NETDRAW.

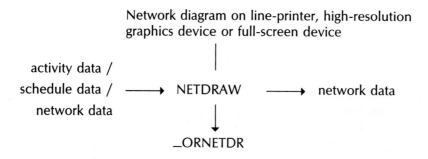

Figure 2.3   Input and Output Data Sets in PROC NETDRAW

Figure 2.1, **Figure 2.2**, and **Figure 2.3** illustrate the data flow going in and out of each of the three procedures: CPM, GANTT, and NETDRAW, respectively. **Figure 2.4** illustrates a typical sequence of steps in a project management system built around the procedures in the SAS System.

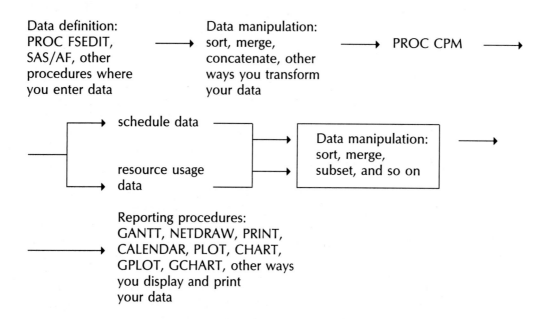

Figure 2.4   Using the SAS System for Project Management

Note: you may want to use PROC NETDRAW to check the logic of the network diagram before scheduling the project using PROC CPM. Further, the above data flow may represent only the first iteration in a continuous scheme for monitoring the progress of a project. As the project progresses, you may update the data sets, including some actual start and finish times for some of the activities, and invoke PROC CPM again, produce updated Gantt charts and network diagrams, and thus continue monitoring the project.

For example, a project management system designed for scheduling and tracking a major outage at a power plant may include the steps illustrated in **Figure 2.5**.

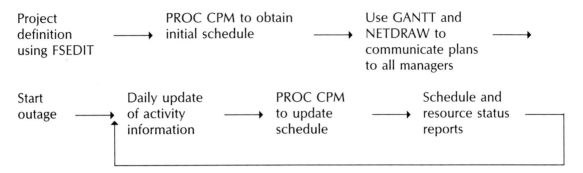

Figure 2.5   Scheduling a Power Plant Outage

Thus, SAS/OR software provides three different procedures designed for performing some of the project management tasks; these procedures can be combined in a variety of different ways to suit your purposes. The rest of this chapter provides a few examples.

EXAMPLES

In this section, a few simple projects are used to illustrate some of the data flow concepts described in the last section. In the graphics examples that follow, the color *white* used in the code has been reversed to black in the example output.

Project Definition

Suppose you want to prepare and conduct a market survey (Moder, Phillips, and Davis 1983) in order to determine the desirability of launching a new product. As a first step, you need to determine the steps involved. Make a list of the tasks that need to be performed and obtain a reasonable estimate of the length of time needed to perform each task. Further, you need to determine the order in which these tasks can be done. The DATA step below creates a SAS data set representing the project. This is the activity data set. The data set contains a variable ACTIVITY listing the basic activities (tasks) involved; a variable DURATION specifying the length of time in days needed to perform the tasks; and, for each task, the variables SUCC1–SUCC3 indicate the immediate successors. An ID variable is also included to provide a more informative description of each task. Thus, the activity Plan Survey takes four days. Once the planning is done, the tasks

Hire Personnel, and Design Questionnaire may begin. The activity data set also contains a variable named PHASE associating each activity with a particular phase of the project.

```
data survey;
   input id          $ 1-20
         activity    $ 24-31
         duration
         succ1       $ 40-47
         succ2       $ 50-57
         succ3       $ 60-67
         phase       $ 70-78;
   cards;
Plan Survey             plan sur   4    hire per  design q            Plan
Hire Personnel          hire per   5    trn per                       Prepare
Design Questionnaire    design q   3    trn per   select h  print q   Plan
Train Personnel         trn per    3    cond sur                      Prepare
Select Households       select h   3    cond sur                      Prepare
Print Questionnaire     print q    4    cond sur                      Prepare
Conduct Survey          cond sur   10   analyze                       Implement
Analyze Results         analyze    6                                  Implement
;
```

The data set SURVEY is an activity data set containing a representation of the project in Activity-On-Node format (a brief discussion of the two types of representations is given in Chapter 5). This data set can be used as an input data set to PROC CPM to determine how long the project will take, given the current estimates of the durations. As an intermediate step, you may want to obtain a graphical representation of the network using PROC NETDRAW. In the initial stages of defining the tasks in a project, it is useful to see how the tasks relate to each other and perhaps modify some of the relationships. The following program invokes PROC NETDRAW; the network diagram is shown in **Output 2.1**.

```
title c=white f=swiss 'Conducting a Market Survey';
pattern1 v=e;

proc netdraw data=survey graphics;
   actnet/act=activity font=simplex
         succ=(succ1-succ3)
         dur=duration
         compress separatearcs
         id=(id) nolabel;
   run;
```

Output 2.1   Network Diagram of SURVEY Project

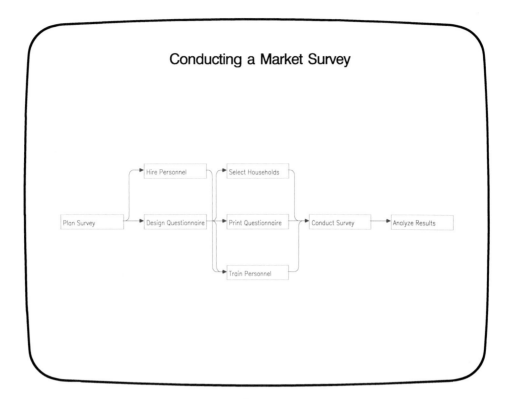

Project Scheduling and Reporting

Having defined the project and ensured that all the relationships have been captured correctly, you can determine a feasible schedule for the activities in the project by invoking PROC CPM. Suppose the activities can be scheduled only on weekdays and there is a holiday on July 4, 1988. Holiday information is passed to PROC CPM using the holiday data set HOLIDATA. The following statements schedule the project to start on July 1, 1988. The early and late start schedules and additional project information are saved in the output data set SURVSCHD. The output data set produced by PROC CPM can then be used to generate a variety of reports. In this example, the data set is first sorted by the variable E_START and then printed using PROC PRINT (see **Output 2.2**). A graphic representation of the schedule is also obtained by invoking PROC GANTT, as shown below. Other procedures that could be used to display the schedule are PROC CALENDAR or PROC NETDRAW. The Gantt chart produced is shown in **Output 2.3**.

```
data holidata;
   format hol date7.;
   hol = '4jul88'd;
run;

proc cpm data=survey date='1jul88'd out=survschd
         interval=weekday holidata=holidata;
   activity   activity;
   successor  succ1-succ3;
   duration   duration;
```

```
        id          id phase;
        holiday     hol;
    run;

    proc sort;
        by e_start;
    run;
    title 'Conducting a Market Survey';
    title2 'Early and Late Start Schedule';
    proc print;
    run;

    pattern1 v=s c=green;
    pattern2 v=e c=green;
    pattern3 v=s c=red;
    pattern4 c=red    v=e;
    pattern5 c=red    v=r2;
    pattern6 c=red    v=12;
    pattern7 c=white v=e;

    title c=white f=swiss 'Conducting a Market Survey';
    title2 c=white f=swiss 'Early and Late Start Schedule';
    proc gantt graphics data=survschd holidata=holidata;
        chart/holiday=(hol) interval=weekday font=simplex ctext=white;
        id    id phase;
    run;
```

Output 2.2   Conducting a Market Survey

```
                              Conducting a Market Survey                                         1
                              Early and Late Start Schedule

        A                                       D                                    E         L
        C                                       U                            E      _F        _F    T  F
        T                                       R                            S      I         S     I  F  F
        I       S        S        S             A                    P       T      N         T     N  F  F
        V       U        U        U             T                    H       A      I         A     I  L  L
    O   I       C        C        C             I                    A       R      S         R     S  O  O
    B   T       C        C        C             O    I               S       T      H         T     H  A  A
    S   Y       1        2        3             N    D               E       T      T         T     T  T  T

  1 plan sur  hire per  design q               4   Plan Survey            Plan      01JUL88  07JUL88  01JUL88  07JUL88  0  0
  2 hire per  trn per                          5   Hire Personnel         Prepare   08JUL88  14JUL88  08JUL88  14JUL88  0  0
  3 design q  trn per   select h  print q      3   Design Questionnaire   Plan      08JUL88  12JUL88  11JUL88  13JUL88  1  0
  4 select h  cond sur                         3   Select Households      Prepare   13JUL88  15JUL88  15JUL88  19JUL88  2  2
  5 print q   cond sur                         4   Print Questionnaire    Prepare   13JUL88  18JUL88  14JUL88  19JUL88  1  1
  6 trn per   cond sur                         3   Train Personnel        Prepare   15JUL88  19JUL88  15JUL88  19JUL88  0  0
  7 cond sur  analyze                         10   Conduct Survey         Implement 20JUL88  02AUG88  20JUL88  02AUG88  0  0
  8 analyze                                    6   Analyze Results        Implement 03AUG88  10AUG88  03AUG88  10AUG88  0  0
```

Output 2.3   Gantt Chart of SURVEY Project

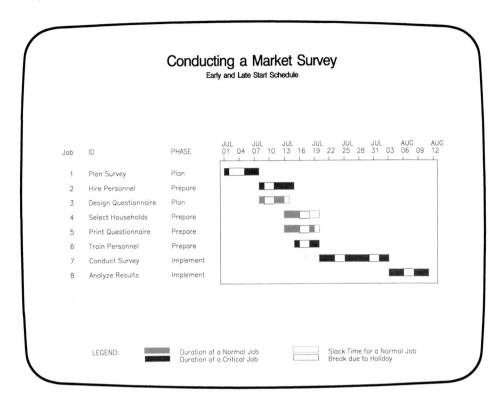

As mentioned in **DATA FLOW**, the output data set can be manipulated in several different ways. Suppose that you want to obtain a condensed report of the project, containing only information about the start and finish times of the three different phases of the project. The following program condenses the information available in the data set SURVSCHD and produces a Gantt chart of the summarized schedule (shown in **Output 2.4**).

```
proc sort data=survschd;
   by phase;
run;

proc summary data=survschd;
   by phase;
   output out=sumsched min(e_start)= max(e_finish)= ;
   var e_start e_finish;
run;

proc sort data=sumsched;
   by e_start;
   format e_start e_finish date7.;
run;

pattern1 v=s c=green;
pattern2 v=e c=green;
pattern3 v=s c=red;
pattern4 c=red    v=e;
pattern5 c=red    v=r2;
pattern6 c=red    v=l2;
pattern7 c=white v=e;
```

```
title c=white f=swiss 'Conducting a Market Survey';
title2 c=white f=swiss 'Summarized Schedule';
proc gantt data=sumsched graphics
     holidata=holidata;
  id phase;
  chart/nojobnum
        nolegend font=swiss ctext=white
        interval=weekday
        holiday=(hol);
run;
```

Output 2.4   Summary Gantt Chart of SURVEY Project

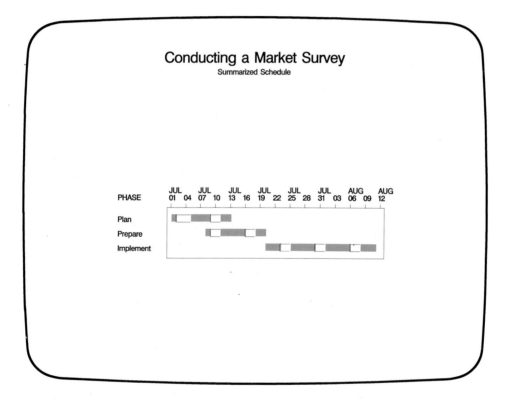

Resource-constrained Scheduling

The previous section illustrated some of the reports that could be generated using the schedule output data set produced by PROC CPM. This section illustrates the use of PROC CPM to obtain a resource usage output data set that can be used to generate reports of resource utilization during the course of a project. A primary concern in data processing centers is the number of processors that need to be used to perform various tasks. Given a series of programming tasks that need to be performed, a common question faced by a data center operator is how to allocate computer resources to various tasks.

Consider a simple job that involves sorting six data sets A, B, C, D, E, and F, merging the first three into one master data set, merging the last three into another comparison data set, and then comparing the two merged data sets. The precedence constraints between the activities (captured by the variables TASK and

SUCC), the time required by the activities (the variable DUR), and the resource required (the variable PROCESR) are shown below:

```
data program;
   input task $ 1-10
         succ $ 11-20
         dur
         procesr ;
   cards;
Sort A    Merge 1    5   1
Sort B    Merge 1    4   1
Sort C    Merge 1    3   1
Sort D    Merge 2    6   1
Sort E    Merge 2    4   1
Sort F    Merge 2    6   1
Merge 1   Compare    5   1
Merge 2   Compare    4   1
Compare              5   1
;
```

If the above project is scheduled (in absolute units) without any resource constraints, it will take 15 time units for completion and will require a maximum availability of six processors. Suppose now that only two processors are available. The RESIN data set sets the availability of the resource to two and PROC CPM is invoked with two input data sets, (activity data set PROGRAM and resource data set RESIN) to produce a resource-constrained schedule. PROC CPM produces two output data sets. The schedule data set (PROGSCHD) contains the resource-constrained schedule (S_START and S_FINISH variables) in addition to the early and late start unconstrained schedules. The resource usage data set (PROGROUT) indicates the number of processors required at every unit of time if the early start schedule or the late start schedule or the resource-constrained schedule were followed. The two output data sets are printed in **Output 2.5**. These two data sets can be used to generate any type of report concerning the schedules or processor usage. In the program below, the unconstrained and constrained schedules are first compared with PROC GANTT (see **Output 2.6**). Then, PROC GPLOT is invoked using the resource usage data set to compare the unconstrained and the constrained usage of the resource (see **Output 2.7**).

```
data resin;
   input per procesr;
   cards;
0   2
;

proc cpm data=program resin=resin
         out=progschd resout=progrout;
   activity  task;
   duration  dur;
   successor succ;
   resource  procesr/per=per;
run;

title 'Scheduling Programming Tasks';
title2 'Data Set PROGSCHD';
proc print data=progschd;
run;
```

```
title2 'Data Set PROGROUT';
proc print data=progrout;
run;

* set up required pattern and symbol statements;
pattern1 c=green v=s;
pattern2 c=green v=e;
pattern3 c=red   v=s;
pattern4 c=red   v=e;
pattern5 c=red   v=r2;
pattern6 c=red   v=l2;
pattern7 c=white v=e;
pattern8 c=cyan  v=s;

title 'Scheduling Programming Tasks';
title2 'Comparison of Schedules';
proc gantt data=progschd graphics;
   chart/ctext=white font=simplex;
   id task;
run;

/* Create a data set for use with PROC GPLOT */
data plotout;
   set progrout;
   label _time_='Time of Usage';
   label procesr='Number of Processors Required';
   label resource='Type of Schedule Followed';
   resource= 'Constrained';
   procesr=rprocesr;
   output;
   resource= 'Early Start';
   procesr=eprocesr;
   output;
run;

axis1 minor=none width=2;
axis2 width=2 length=80 pct;

symbol1 i=steplj w=2 c=red;
symbol2 i=steplj w=2 l=3 c=green;

goptions ctext=white ftext=swiss;
title2 'Comparison of Processor Usage';
proc gplot data=plotout;
   plot procesr * _time_ = resource/vaxis=axis1
                                    haxis=axis2;
run;
```

Output 2.5   Data Sets PROGSCHD and PROGROUT

Scheduling Programming Tasks
Data Set PROGSCHD   1

OBS	TASK	SUCC	DUR	PROCESR	S_START	S_FINISH	E_START	E_FINISH	L_START	L_FINISH
1	Sort A	Merge 1	5	1	0	5	0	5	0	5
2	Sort B	Merge 1	4	1	6	10	0	4	1	5
3	Sort C	Merge 1	3	1	10	13	0	3	2	5
4	Sort D	Merge 2	6	1	0	6	0	6	0	6
5	Sort E	Merge 2	4	1	11	15	0	4	2	6
6	Sort F	Merge 2	6	1	5	11	0	6	0	6
7	Merge 1	Compare	5	1	13	18	5	10	5	10
8	Merge 2	Compare	4	1	15	19	6	10	6	10
9	Compare		5	1	19	24	10	15	10	15

Scheduling Programming Tasks
Data Set PROGROUT   2

OBS	_TIME_	EPROCESR	LPROCESR	RPROCESR	APROCESR
1	0	6	3	2	0
2	1	6	4	2	0
3	2	6	6	2	0
4	3	5	6	2	0
5	4	3	6	2	0
6	5	3	4	2	0
7	6	2	2	2	0
8	7	2	2	2	0
9	8	2	2	2	0
10	9	2	2	2	0
11	10	1	1	2	0
12	11	1	1	2	0
13	12	1	1	2	0
14	13	1	1	2	0
15	14	1	1	2	0
16	15	0	0	2	0
17	16	0	0	2	0
18	17	0	0	2	0
19	18	0	0	1	1
20	19	0	0	1	1
21	20	0	0	1	1
22	21	0	0	1	1
23	22	0	0	1	1
24	23	0	0	1	1
25	24	0	0	0	2

Output 2.6   Gantt Chart Comparing Schedules

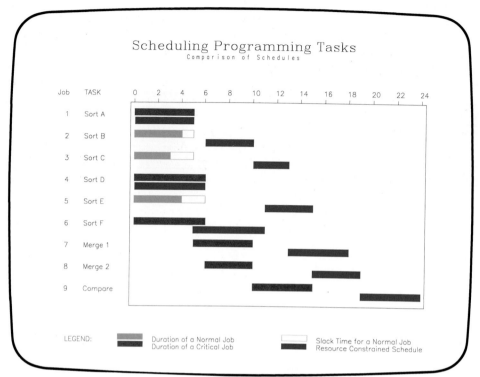

Output 2.7   Plot Comparing Resource Usage

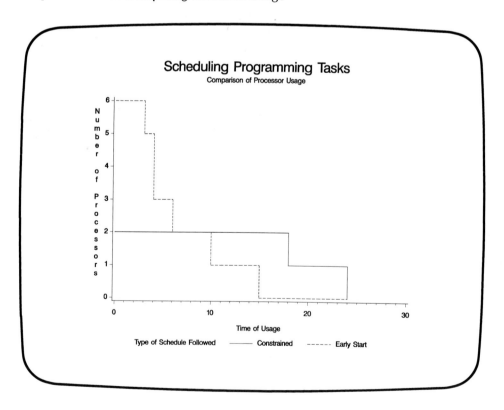

Multiple Projects

Often a project is divided into several subprojects, each of which is then broken into activities with precedence constraints. For purposes of reporting or accounting, it may be essential to group activities into different groups or to aggregate the information pertaining to activities in a given group. Sometimes, totally different projects may use a common pool of resources and you may want to schedule all the projects using the common pool; you may want to vary the priority with which the resources are allotted to the activites on the basis of the projects to which they belong.

Consider a publishing company that accepts manuscripts from different authors for publication. The publication of each book can be treated as a project. Thus, at a given point in time, several projects, almost identical in nature, may be in progress. Some of the resources that may be needed are a technical editor, a copy editor, and a graphic artist. All the books that are currently being published share a common pool of these resources. We shall use a simplified version of such a scenario to illustrate some of the ways in which you can handle multiple projects competing for the same pool of resources.

The following network (**Output 2.8**) represents some of the tasks required for publishing Book 1 and the precedence constraints among them (the durations in the diagram are in weeks).

Output 2.8   Network Diagram for Project Book1

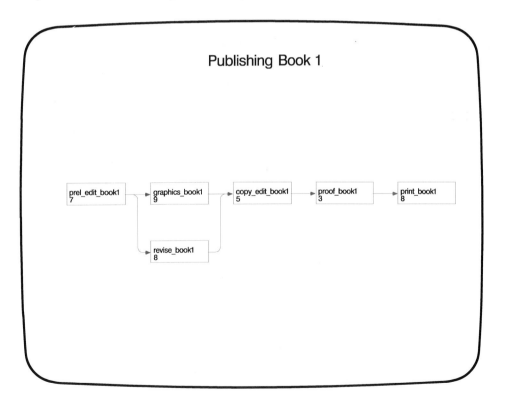

Suppose that the company receives a second book for publishing at the same time as Book 1. The editor and artist now must allocate their time between the two books. Book 1 has priority over Book 2. In the following program, the data sets for the two subprojects are combined to form an activity data set for the entire project. A variable PRIORITY is assigned the value 1 for activities pertaining to the first book and the value 2 for those pertaining to the second one. The RESOURCE data set sets the availability for each of the resources to 1. The input data sets are printed in **Output 2.9**.

```
data books;
   set book1 book2;
   if subproj='Book1' then aprty=1;
   else                     aprty=2;
run;
```

Output 2.9   Input Data Sets for Book Publishing Example

```
                                    Publishing Book 1                                    1

         OBS       TASK          DUR       SUCC          SUBPROJ   EDITOR    ARTIST

          1    prel_edit_book1    1    revise_book1       BOOK1      1         .
          2    prel_edit_book1    1    graphics_book1     BOOK1      1         .
          3    revise_book1       2    copy_edit_book1    BOOK1      1         .
          4    graphics_book1     3    copy_edit_book1    BOOK1      .         1
          5    copy_edit_book1    1    proof_book1        BOOK1      1         .
          6    proof_book1        1    print_book1        BOOK1      1         .
          7    print_book1        2                       BOOK1      .         .
```

```
                                    Publishing Book 2                                    2

         OBS       TASK          DUR       SUCC          SUBPROJ   EDITOR    ARTIST

          1    prel_edit_book2    2    revise_book2       BOOK2      1         .
          2    prel_edit_book2    1    graphics_book2     BOOK2      1         .
          3    revise_book2       2    copy_edit_book2    BOOK2      1         .
          4    graphics_book2     3    copy_edit_book2    BOOK2      .         1
          5    copy_edit_book2    1    proof_book2        BOOK2      1         .
          6    proof_book2        1    print_book2        BOOK2      1         .
          7    print_book2        2                       BOOK2      .         .
```

```
                                 Publishing Books 1 and 2                                 3

      OBS       TASK          DUR       SUCC          SUBPROJ   EDITOR   ARTIST   APRTY

       1    prel_edit_book1    1    revise_book1       BOOK1      1        .        2
       2    prel_edit_book1    1    graphics_book1     BOOK1      1        .        2
       3    revise_book1       2    copy_edit_book1    BOOK1      1        .        2
       4    graphics_book1     3    copy_edit_book1    BOOK1      .        1        2
       5    copy_edit_book1    1    proof_book1        BOOK1      1        .        2
       6    proof_book1        1    print_book1        BOOK1      1        .        2
       7    print_book1        2                       BOOK1      .        .        2
       8    prel_edit_book2    2    revise_book2       BOOK2      1        .        2
       9    prel_edit_book2    1    graphics_book2     BOOK2      1        .        2
      10    revise_book2       2    copy_edit_book2    BOOK2      1        .        2
      11    graphics_book2     3    copy_edit_book2    BOOK2      .        1        2
      12    copy_edit_book2    1    proof_book2        BOOK2      1        .        2
      13    proof_book2        1    print_book2        BOOK2      1        .        2
      14    print_book2        2                       BOOK2      .        .        2
```

```
                                    Resources Available                                  4

             OBS    AVDATE    EDITOR    ARTIST

              1    02JAN89      1         1
```

PROC CPM is then invoked to schedule the project to start on January 2, 1989. The data set BOOKSCHD (printed in **Output 2.10**) contains the schedule for the entire project. Compare the E_START and S_START schedules and note that on January 2, the activity PREL_EDIT_BOOK1 is scheduled to start while the preliminary editing of book 2 has been postponed, due to subproject BOOK1 having priority over subproject BOOK2. On January 23, there is no activity belonging to subproject BOOK1 that demands an editor; thus, the activity PREL-_EDIT_BOOK2 is scheduled to start on that day. As a result, the editor is working on an activity in the second project for two weeks; when COPY_EDIT_BOOK1 is ready to start, the editor is not available, causing a delay in this activity. Thus, even though the first book has priority over the second book, the scheduling algorithm does not keep a resource waiting for activities in the first project. (For details regarding the scheduling algorithm and for options allowing splitting of activities, see Chapter 5.) The entire project finishes on April 2, 1989. The resource usage data set BOOKSOUT is also printed in **Output 2.10**. The following SAS code performs these steps:

```
proc cpm data=books resin=resource
         out=bookschd resout=booksout
         date='2jan89'd interval=week;
     act      task;
     dur      dur;
     succ     succ;
     resource editor artist/per=avdate avp rcp
              rule=actprty actprty=aprty;
run;
```

Output 2.10   Data Sets BOOKSCHD and BOOKSOUT

```
                              Schedule for project BOOKS                                          1

OBS      TASK             SUCC          DUR  EDITOR  ARTIST  S_START   S_FINISH  E_START   E_FINISH  L_START   L_FINISH

 1  prel_edit_book1  revise_book1        1     1       .    02JAN89   08JAN89   02JAN89   08JAN89   09JAN89   15JAN89
 2  prel_edit_book1  graphics_book1      1     1       .    02JAN89   08JAN89   02JAN89   08JAN89   09JAN89   15JAN89
 3  revise_book1     copy_edit_book1     2     1       .    09JAN89   22JAN89   09JAN89   22JAN89   23JAN89   05FEB89
 4  graphics_book1   copy_edit_book1     3     .       1    09JAN89   29JAN89   09JAN89   29JAN89   16JAN89   05FEB89
 5  copy_edit_book1  proof_book1         1     1       .    06FEB89   12FEB89   30JAN89   05FEB89   06FEB89   12FEB89
 6  proof_book1      print_book1         1     1       .    13FEB89   19FEB89   06FEB89   12FEB89   13FEB89   19FEB89
 7  print_book1                          2     .       .    20FEB89   05MAR89   13FEB89   26FEB89   20FEB89   05MAR89
 8  prel_edit_book2  revise_book2        2     1       .    23JAN89   05FEB89   02JAN89   15JAN89   02JAN89   15JAN89
 9  prel_edit_book2  graphics_book2      2     1       .    23JAN89   05FEB89   02JAN89   15JAN89   02JAN89   15JAN89
10  revise_book2     copy_edit_book2     2     1       .    20FEB89   05MAR89   16JAN89   29JAN89   23JAN89   05FEB89
11  graphics_book2   copy_edit_book2     3     .       1    06FEB89   26FEB89   16JAN89   05FEB89   16JAN89   05FEB89
12  copy_edit_book2  proof_book2         1     1       .    06MAR89   12MAR89   06FEB89   12FEB89   06FEB89   12FEB89
13  proof_book2      print_book2         1     1       .    13MAR89   19MAR89   13FEB89   19FEB89   13FEB89   19FEB89
14  print_book2                          2     .       .    20MAR89   02APR89   20FEB89   05MAR89   20FEB89   05MAR89
```

```
                         Resource Usage for project BOOKS                                2

              OBS    _TIME_    REDITOR    AEDITOR    RARTIST    AARTIST

               1    02JAN89       1          0          0          1
               2    09JAN89       1          0          1          0
               3    16JAN89       1          0          1          0
               4    23JAN89       1          0          1          0
               5    30JAN89       1          0          0          1
               6    06FEB89       1          0          1          0
               7    13FEB89       1          0          1          0
               8    20FEB89       1          0          1          0
```

(continued on next page)

(continued from previous page)

```
     9    27FEB89    1        0        0        1
    10    06MAR89    1        0        0        1
    11    13MAR89    1        0        0        1
    12    20MAR89    0        1        0        1
    13    27MAR89    0        1        0        1
    14    03APR89    0        1        0        1
```

Suppose the schedule printed in **Output 2.10** is not acceptable; you want the first book to be finished as soon as possible and do not want resources to be claimed by the second book, causing a delay in the publication of the second book. The structure of the input and output data sets allows you to schedule the two subprojects sequentially. The following program first schedules the subproject BOOK1 using the resources available. The resource usage data set BK1OUT produced by PROC CPM has two variables, AEDITOR and AARTIST, indicating the availability of the editor and the artist on each day of the project, *after* scheduling subproject BOOK1. This data set is used to create the data set REMRES, listing the remaining resources available, which is then used as the resource input data set for scheduling the subproject BOOK2. The two schedules BK1SCHD and BK2SCHD and the two resource usage data sets BK1OUT and BK2OUT are printed in **Output 2.11**. Note that this method of scheduling has ensured that BOOK1 is not delayed; however, the entire project has been delayed by two weeks.

```
/* schedule the higher priority project first */
proc cpm data=book1 resin=resource
         out=bk1schd resout=bk1out
         date='2jan89'd interval=week;
    act       task;
    dur       dur;
    succ      succ;
    resource editor artist/per=avdate avp rcp;
run;


/* Construct the resource availability data set */
/* with proper resource names                   */
data remres;
    set bk1out;
    avdate=_time_;
    editor=aeditor;
    artist=aartist;
    keep avdate editor artist;
    format avdate date7.;
run;

proc cpm data=book2 resin=remres
        out=bk2schd resout=bk2out
        date='2jan89'd interval=week;
    act       task;
    dur       dur;
    succ      succ;
    resource editor artist/per=avdate avp rcp;
run;
```

Output 2.11   Sequential Scheduling of Subprojects

```
                          Schedule for sub-project BOOK1                                    1

 OBS      TASK            SUCC        DUR  EDITOR  ARTIST  S_START   S_FINISH  E_START   E_FINISH  L_START   L_FINISH

  1   prel_edit_book1  revise_book1     1     1      .    02JAN89   08JAN89   02JAN89   08JAN89   02JAN89   08JAN89
  2   prel_edit_book1  graphics_book1   1     1      .    02JAN89   08JAN89   02JAN89   08JAN89   02JAN89   08JAN89
  3   revise_book1     copy_edit_book1  2     1      .    09JAN89   22JAN89   09JAN89   22JAN89   16JAN89   29JAN89
  4   graphics_book1   copy_edit_book1  3     .      1    09JAN89   29JAN89   09JAN89   29JAN89   09JAN89   29JAN89
  5   copy_edit_book1  proof_book1      1     1      .    30JAN89   05FEB89   30JAN89   05FEB89   30JAN89   05FEB89
  6   proof_book1      print_book1      1     1      .    06FEB89   12FEB89   06FEB89   12FEB89   06FEB89   12FEB89
  7   print_book1                       2     .      .    13FEB89   26FEB89   13FEB89   26FEB89   13FEB89   26FEB89

                       Resource Usage for sub-project BOOK1                                 2

                  OBS    _TIME_    REDITOR    AEDITOR    RARTIST    AARTIST

                   1    02JAN89       1          0          0          1
                   2    09JAN89       1          0          1          0
                   3    16JAN89       1          0          1          0
                   4    23JAN89       0          1          1          0
                   5    30JAN89       1          0          0          1
                   6    06FEB89       1          0          0          1
                   7    13FEB89       0          1          0          1
                   8    20FEB89       0          1          0          1
                   9    27FEB89       0          1          0          1
```

```
                          Schedule for sub-project BOOK2                                    3

 OBS      TASK            SUCC        DUR  EDITOR  ARTIST  S_START   S_FINISH  E_START   E_FINISH  L_START   L_FINISH

  1   prel_edit_book2  revise_book2     2     1      .    13FEB89   26FEB89   02JAN89   15JAN89   02JAN89   15JAN89
  2   prel_edit_book2  graphics_book2   2     1      .    13FEB89   26FEB89   02JAN89   15JAN89   02JAN89   15JAN89
  3   revise_book2     copy_edit_book2  2     1      .    27FEB89   12MAR89   16JAN89   29JAN89   23JAN89   05FEB89
  4   graphics_book2   copy_edit_book2  3     .      1    27FEB89   19MAR89   16JAN89   05FEB89   16JAN89   05FEB89
  5   copy_edit_book2  proof_book2      1     1      .    20MAR89   26MAR89   06FEB89   12FEB89   06FEB89   12FEB89
  6   proof_book2      print_book2      1     1      .    27MAR89   02APR89   13FEB89   19FEB89   13FEB89   19FEB89
  7   print_book2                       2     .      .    03APR89   16APR89   20FEB89   05MAR89   20FEB89   05MAR89
```

```
                       Resource Usage for sub-project BOOK2                                 4

                  OBS    _TIME_    REDITOR    AEDITOR    RARTIST    AARTIST

                   1    13FEB89       1          0          0          1
                   2    20FEB89       1          0          0          1
                   3    27FEB89       1          0          1          0
                   4    06MAR89       1          0          1          0
                   5    13MAR89       0          1          1          0
                   6    20MAR89       1          0          0          1
                   7    27MAR89       1          0          0          1
                   8    03APR89       0          1          0          1
                   9    10APR89       0          1          0          1
                  10    17APR89       0          1          0          1
```

Project Cost Control

Cost control and accounting are important aspects of project management. Cost data for a project may be associated with activities or groups of activities, or with resources, such as personnel or equipment. For example, consider a project that consists of several subprojects, each of which is contracted to different companies. From the contracting company's point of view, each subproject can be treated as one cost item; all the company needs to know is how much each subproject is going to cost. On the other hand, another project may contain several activities that each require two types of labor, skilled and unskilled. The cost for each activity in the project may have to be computed on the basis of how much skilled or unskilled labor that activity uses. In this case, activity and project costs are determined from the resources used. Further, for any project, there may be several ways in which costs need to be summarized and accounted for. In addition to determining the cost of each individual activity, you may want to determine periodic budgets for different departments that are involved with the project or compare the actual costs that were incurred with the budgeted costs.

It is easy to set up cost accounting systems using the output data sets produced by PROC CPM, whether costs are associated with activities or with resources. In fact, you can even treat cost as a consumable resource if you can estimate the cost per day for each of the activities (see Chapter 5 for details on resource allocation and types of resources). This section illustrates such a method for monitoring costs and shows how you can compute some of the standard cost performance measures used in project management.

The following three measures can be used to determine if a project is running on schedule and within budget (see Moder, Phillips, and Davis 1983 for a detailed discussion on project cost control):

ACWP or the *actual cost of work performed*
> is the actual costs expended to perform the work accomplished in a given period of time.

BCWP or the *budgeted cost of work performed*
> is the budgeted cost of the work *completed* in a given period of time.

BCWS or the *budgeted cost of work scheduled*
> is the budgeted cost of the work *scheduled* to be accomplished in a given period of time (if a baseline schedule were followed).

Consider the survey example described earlier in this chapter. Suppose that it is possible to estimate the cost per day for each activity in the project. The following data set SURVCOST contains the project data (ACTIVITY, SUCC1–SUCC3, ID, DURATION) and a variable named COST containing the cost per day in dollars. In order to compute the BCWS for the project, you need to establish a baseline schedule. Suppose the early start schedule computed by PROC CPM is chosen as the baseline schedule. The following program invokes PROC CPM with the RESOURCE statement and saves the resource usage data set in SURVROUT. The variable ECOST in this data set contains the daily expense that would need to be incurred for the baseline schedule. This data set can be used to determine the budgeted cumulative cost or BCWS (in the data set BASECOST) for the project.

```
data survcost;
    input id        $ 1-20
          activity  $ 24-31
          duration
          succ1     $ 40-47
          succ2     $ 50-57
          succ3     $ 60-67
          cost;
    cards;
Plan Survey            plan sur   4   hire per  design q          300
Hire Personnel         hire per   5   trn per                     350
Design Questionnaire   design q   3   trn per   select h  print q 100
Train Personnel        trn per    3   cond sur                    500
Select Households      select h   3   cond sur                    300
Print Questionnaire    print q    4   cond sur                    250
Conduct Survey         cond sur  10   analyze                     200
Analyze Results        analyze    6                               500
;
```

```
proc cpm data=survcost date='1jul88'd out=sched
          resout=survrout;
    activity    activity;
    successor   succ1-succ3;
    duration    duration;
    id          id;
    resource    cost;
run;

data basecost (keep=_time_ bcws c_bcws);
    set survrout;
    retain c_bcws 0;
    bcws=ecost;
    c_bcws=c_bcws + bcws;
run;
```

Suppose that the project started as planned on July 1, 1988, but some of the activities took longer than planned and some of the cost estimates were found to be incorrect. The following data set, ACTUAL, contains updated information: the variables AS and AF contain the actual start and finish times of the activities that have been completed or are in progress. The variable ACTCOST contains the revised cost per day for each activity. The following program combines this information with the existing project data and saves the result in the data set UPDATE printed in **Output 2.12**. These data are used by PROC CPM to revise the schedule using the ACTUAL statement to specify the actual start and finish times and by the RESOURCE statement to specify both the budgeted and the actual costs. The resulting schedule is saved in the data set UPDSCHED (printed in **Output 2.12**) and the budgeted and the actual costs for each day of the project (until the current date) are saved in the data set UPDTROUT. The cost data are then used to determine the cumulative costs until the current date (in the data set UPDTCOST). The two data sets BASECOST and UPDTCOST are then merged to create a data set that contains the daily and cumulative values for each of the three types of measures. This data set (also printed in **Output 2.12**) is then used as input to PROC GPLOT to produce a plot of the three cumulative cost measures. The plot is shown in **Output 2.13**.

```
data actual;
    input id $ 1-20 as date9. af date9. actcost;
    format as af date7.;
    cards;
Plan Survey           1JUL88   5JUL88    275
Hire Personnel        6JUL88   10JUL88   350
Design Questionnaire  7JUL88   9JUL88    150
Train Personnel       11JUL88  12JUL88   800
Select Households     10JUL88  12JUL88   450
Print Questionnaire   10JUL88  13JUL88   250
Conduct Survey        14JUL88  .         200
;

data update;
    merge survcost actual;
run;

title 'Updated Project Data';
proc print;
run;
```

```
    proc cpm data=update date='1jul88'd out=updsched
        resout=updtrout;
      activity    activity;
      successor   succ1-succ3;
      duration    duration;
      id          id;
      resource    cost actcost/maxdate='11jul88'D;
      ACTUAL/A_START=AS A_FINISH=AF;
    run;

    title 'Updated Schedule: Data Set UPDSCHED';
    proc print data=updsched;
    run;

    data updtcost (keep=_time_ bcwp acwp c_bcwp c_acwp);
      set updtrout;
      retain c_bcwp 0 c_acwp 0;
      bcwp=ecost;
      acwp=eactcost;
      c_bcwp=c_bcwp + bcwp;
      c_acwp=c_acwp + acwp;
    run;

    /* Create a combined data set to contain the BCWS, BCWP, ACWP */
    /* per day and the cumulative values for these costs.        */
    data costs;
      merge basecost updtcost;
    run;

    title 'Daily and Cumulative BCWS, BCWP, and ACWP';
    proc print data=costs;
    run;

    /* Plot the cumulative costs using GPLOT. */
    data costplot (keep=date dollars id);

      set costs;

      format date date7.;

      date = _time_;
      if c_bcws ¬= . then do;
        dollars = C_BCWS;
        id = 1;
        output;
      end;
      if c_bcwp ¬= . then do;
        dollars = C_BCWP;
        id = 2;
        output;
      end;
      if c_acwp ¬= . then do;
        dollars = C_ACWP;
        id = 3;
        output;
      end;
    run;
```

```
legend1 frame
    value=(f=swiss c=white j=l f=swiss 'BCWS' 'BCWP' 'ACWP')
    label=(f=swiss c=white);

axis1 width=2
    order=('1jul88'd to '1aug88'd by week)
    length=60 pct
    value=(f=swiss c=white)
    label=(f=swiss c=white);
axis2 width=2
    length = 60 pct
    value=(f=swiss c=white)
    label=(f=swiss c=white);


symbol1 i=join v=none c=green w=2 l=1;
symbol2 i=join v=none c=cyan  w=2 l=1;
symbol3 i=join v=none c=red   w=2 l=1;
title f=swiss c=white 'Comparison of Costs';

proc gplot data=costplot;
  plot dollars * date = id / legend=legend1
                  haxis=axis1
                  vaxis=axis2;
run;
```

Output 2.12   Methods for Monitoring Costs and Performance: BCWS, BCWP, ACWP.

```
                                    Updated Project Data                                                  1

OBS   ID                      ACTIVITY   DURATION   SUCC1     SUCC2     SUCC3    COST       AS        AF     ACTCOST

 1    Plan Survey             plan sur       4      hire per  design q           300    01JUL88   05JUL88      275
 2    Hire Personnel          hire per       5      trn per                      350    06JUL88   10JUL88      350
 3    Design Questionnaire     design q      3      trn per   select h  print q   100    07JUL88   09JUL88      150
 4    Train Personnel         trn per        3      cond sur                     500    11JUL88   12JUL88      800
 5    Select Households       select h       3      cond sur                     300    10JUL88   12JUL88      450
 6    Print Questionnaire     print q        4      cond sur                     250    10JUL88   13JUL88      250
 7    Conduct Survey          cond sur      10      analyze                      200    14JUL88      .         200
 8    Analyze Results         analyze        6                                   500       .         .          .
```

```
                                 Updated Schedule: Data Set UPDSCHED                                        2

OBS   ACTIVITY   SUCC1      SUCC2      SUCC3     DURATION    STATUS        A_DUR    ID

 1    plan sur   hire per   design q                 4      Completed        5     Plan Survey
 2    hire per   trn per                             5      Completed        5     Hire Personnel
 3    design q   trn per    select h   print q       3      Completed        3     Design Questionnaire
 4    trn per    cond sur                            3      Completed        2     Train Personnel
 5    select h   cond sur                            3      Completed        3     Select Households
 6    print q    cond sur                            4      Completed        4     Print Questionnaire
 7    cond sur   analyze                            10      In Progress      .     Conduct Survey
 8    analyze                                         6      Pending          .     Analyze Results

OBS   COST    ACTCOST   A_START    A_FINISH    E_START    E_FINISH    L_START    L_FINISH    T_FLOAT    F_FLOAT

 1    300     275       01JUL88    05JUL88     01JUL88    05JUL88     01JUL88    05JUL88       0          0
 2    350     350       06JUL88    10JUL88     06JUL88    10JUL88     06JUL88    10JUL88       0          0
 3    100     150       07JUL88    09JUL88     07JUL88    09JUL88     07JUL88    09JUL88       0          0
```

(continued on next page)

(continued from previous page)

4	500	800	11JUL88	12JUL88	11JUL88	12JUL88	11JUL88	12JUL88	0	0
5	300	450	10JUL88	12JUL88	10JUL88	12JUL88	10JUL88	12JUL88	0	0
6	250	250	10JUL88	13JUL88	10JUL88	13JUL88	10JUL88	13JUL88	0	0
7	200	200	14JUL88	.	14JUL88	23JUL88	14JUL88	23JUL88	0	0
8	500	.	.	.	24JUL88	29JUL88	24JUL88	29JUL88	0	0

Daily and Cumulative BCWS, BCWP, and ACWP   3

OBS	_TIME_	C_BCWS	BCWS	C_BCWP	C_ACWP	BCWP	ACWP
1	01JUL88	300	300	300	275	300	275
2	02JUL88	600	300	600	550	300	275
3	03JUL88	900	300	900	825	300	275
4	04JUL88	1200	300	1200	1100	300	275
5	05JUL88	1650	450	1500	1375	300	275
6	06JUL88	2100	450	1850	1725	350	350
7	07JUL88	2550	450	2300	2225	450	500
8	08JUL88	3450	900	2750	2725	450	500
9	09JUL88	4350	900	3200	3225	450	500
10	10JUL88	5400	1050	4100	4275	900	1050
11	11JUL88	6150	750	5150	5775	1050	1500
12	12JUL88	6650	500	.	.	.	.
13	13JUL88	6850	200	.	.	.	.
14	14JUL88	7050	200	.	.	.	.
15	15JUL88	7250	200	.	.	.	.
16	16JUL88	7450	200	.	.	.	.
17	17JUL88	7650	200	.	.	.	.
18	18JUL88	7850	200	.	.	.	.
19	19JUL88	8050	200	.	.	.	.
20	20JUL88	8250	200	.	.	.	.
21	21JUL88	8450	200	.	.	.	.
22	22JUL88	8650	200	.	.	.	.
23	23JUL88	9150	500	.	.	.	.
24	24JUL88	9650	500	.	.	.	.
25	25JUL88	10150	500	.	.	.	.
26	26JUL88	10650	500	.	.	.	.
27	27JUL88	11150	500	.	.	.	.
28	28JUL88	11650	500	.	.	.	.
29	29JUL88	11650	0	.	.	.	.

Output 2.13   Plot of BCWS, BCWP, and ACWP

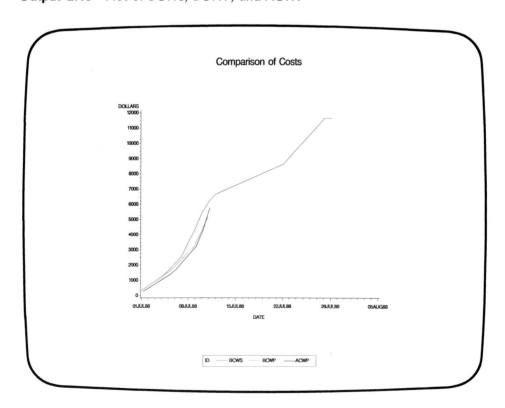

PROJECT MANAGEMENT SYSTEMS

As can be seen from the previous discussion, the procedures of SAS/OR software, when combined with the other parts of the SAS System, provide a rich environment for developing customized project management systems. Every company has its own set of requirements for how project data should be handled and for how costs should be accounted. PROC CPM, PROC GANTT, and PROC NETDRAW, together with the other reporting, summarizing, charting, and plotting procedures, are the basic building blocks that can be combined in several different ways to provide the exact structure that you need. The full-screen editing procedures FSEDIT and FSPRINT can be used to simplify the task of data entry; further, the screen control language (SCL) helps cement the pieces together through its menuing capabilities. You can create easy-to-use applications enabling the user to continually enter information and periodically obtain progress reports.

PROJMAN is an example of such a project management application. A brief discussion of the full-screen interface and the objectives of this application is provided in the section "Changes and Enhancements."

REFERENCES

Moder, J.J., Phillips, C.R., and Davis, E.W. (1983), *Project Management with CPM, PERT and Precedence Diagramming*, New York: Van Nostrand Reinhold Company.

Chapter 3

Introduction to Mathematical Programming Using SAS/OR® Software

INTRODUCTION

The procedures in SAS/OR software solve general linear and mixed-integer mathematical programs. SAS/OR software provides optimizers that exploit the specialized structure in linear programming models, including embedded networks, special ordered sets, pure networks, transportation networks, and assignment networks. The optimizers are the ASSIGN procedure (for the assignment problem), the LP procedure (for mixed-integer programs), the NETFLOW procedure (for network flow models with linear side constraints), and the TRANS procedure (for transportation problems).

Each optimizer is designed to integrate with the SAS System to simplify model building, maintenance, solution, and report writing. This chapter describes how the SAS/OR optimizers are integrated into the SAS System. It shows how the SAS language facilitates handling these types of operations research models and how these techniques can simplify building a decision support system. First, several model types are discussed. Then, the data flow concept as it relates to mathematical programming is considered. Last, issues regarding model building are discussed.

Before exploring these issues, consider some of the types of problems that can be solved using mathematical programming models.

PROBLEM TYPES

Linear programs search for solutions to problems that can be posed by finding the values for a set of variables. These variables are usually called decision variables, and their values optimize (either maximize or minimize) a linear function when subject to a set of linear constraints and possible integer restrictions on the decision variables.

There are a wide variety of problems that fit this description and can be modeled as linear programs. Some of these problems are listed below. In practice, models often contain elements of several types of problems. This list is not meant to be exhaustive but is meant to suggest application areas. There are many introductory texts on the subject of mathematical programming (see Wagner 1975 and Hillier and Lieberman 1967). These references contain both descriptions of model types and details about model formulation that can be helpful when you are faced with novel applications.

- *Product-mix* problems find the mix that generates the largest return when there are several products that compete for limited resources.
- *Blending* problems find the mix of ingredients to be used in a product so that it meets minimum standards at minimum cost.
- *Network flow* problems find the optimal flow of material through a network. The network may have supply and demand at nodes, costs and capacities on arcs, and multiple products flowing through the arcs. The optimal flow may be the minimum cost flow or the maximum flow.
- *Transportation* problems find the optimal flow from supply points to demand points.
- *Assignment* problems find the optimal assignment of source nodes to demand nodes.
- *Time-staged* problems are models whose structure repeats as a function of time. Production and inventory models are classic examples of time-staged problems. In each period, production plus inventory minus current demand equals inventory carried to the next period.
- *Scheduling* problems assign people to times and places so as to optimize peoples' preferences while satisfying the demands of the schedule.
- *Multiple objective* problems have multiple, possibly conflicting, objectives. Typically, the objectives are prioritized and the problems are solved sequentially in a priority order.
- *Capital budgeting* and *project selection* problems ask for the project or set of projects that will yield the greatest return.

- *Location* problems seek the set of locations that meet the distribution needs at minimum cost.
- *Cutting stock* problems find the partition of raw material that minimizes waste and satisfies demand.

DATA FLOW

Each of the optimization procedures in SAS/OR software takes a model that has been saved in one or more SAS data sets, solves it, and saves the solution in other SAS data sets. This is the data flow concept. Because of the intimate relationship between the model and the SAS data set, the ability to manipulate and build models easily depends on the data formats that the optimization procedures require. Similarly, the ability to report solutions easily depends on the data formats in which the optimization procedures save the solution. This section provides an overview of the relationship between the SAS data sets containing the model and the optimization procedures.

The optimization procedures in the SAS/OR product also define SAS macro variables. Each of these variables contains a character string that describes the status of the optimizer on termination of the procedure.

Mixed-Integer Programming

The LP procedure can be used to solve general linear and mixed-integer programs. PROC LP requires a problem data set that contains the model. In addition, a primal and active data set can be used for warm starting a problem that has only been partially solved previously.

Figure 3.1 illustrates all the input and output data sets that are possible with PROC LP. It also shows the macro variable _ORLP_ that PROC LP defines.

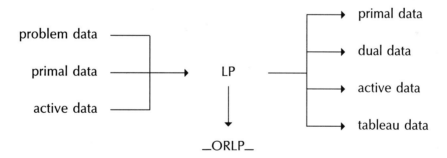

Figure 3.1   PROC LP: Input and Output Data Sets

The problem data describing the model may be in one of two formats: a dense format or a sparse format. The dense format represents the model as a rectangular matrix. The sparse format represents only the nonzero elements of a rectangular matrix. Because the models are in SAS data sets, you can concatenate and merge problem data that may represent pieces of a larger model. You cannot combine data sets in sparse data format with data sets in dense data format. The sparse and dense input formats are described in more detail later in this chapter.

Network Flow Programming

Network flow problems, for example, finding the minimum cost flow in a network, require model representation in a format that is simpler than that required by PROC LP. The network is represented in two data sets: a node data set and an arc data set. A node data set names the nodes in the network and gives supply and demand information for them. An arc data set defines the arcs in the network using the node names and gives the arc costs and capacities. In addition, a side-constraint data set gives any side constraints that apply to the flow through the network. Examples of these data sets appear later in this chapter. **Figure 3.2** illustrates all the input and output data sets possible with PROC NETFLOW, as well as _ORNETFL, the macro variable.

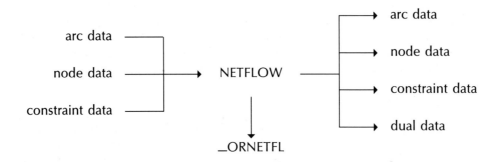

Figure 3.2   PROC NETFLOW: Input and Output Data Sets

The constraint data contain constraints that are not implicit network constraints, although they may involve arc variables. These can be specified in either the sparse or dense input formats. This is the same format that is used by the LP procedure. Because of this, any of the model building techniques that apply to models for PROC LP also apply for network flow models having side constraints.

The NETFLOW procedure saves solutions in four data sets. Arc data sets and node data sets store solutions for the pure network model, ignoring the restrictions imposed by the side constraints. On the other hand, the constraint data sets and dual data sets contain the solutions to the network flow problem when the side contraints apply.

Transportation Networks

Transportation networks are a special type of network, called *bipartite networks*. Bipartite networks have only supply and demand nodes and arcs directed from supply nodes to demand nodes. For these networks, data can be given most efficiently in a rectangular or matrix form. The TRANS procedure takes cost, capacity, and lower-bound data in this form. The observations in these data sets correspond to supply nodes and the variables correspond to demand nodes. **Figure 3.3** illustrates the input data sets and the output data set used with PROC TRANS, as well as _ORTRANS, the macro variable defined by PROC TRANS.

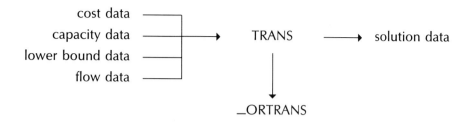

Figure 3.3 PROC TRANS: Input and Output Data Sets

The TRANS procedure puts the solution in a single output data set. The details are described in Chapter 10, "The TRANS Procedure." As with the other optimization procedures, the TRANS procedure defines a macro variable, named _ORTRANS, that has a character string that describes the solution status.

Assignment Networks

The assignment problem is a special type of transportation problem that has only unit supply and demand values. As with the transportation problem, the cost data for this type of problem are saved in a SAS data set in rectangular form. **Figure 3.4** illustrates the input data set and output data set used with PROC ASSIGN. _ORASSIG is the macro variable defined by PROC ASSIGN.

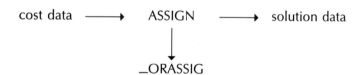

Figure 3.4 PROC ASSIGN: Input and Output Data Sets

The ASSIGN procedure also saves the solution in a SAS data set and defines a macro variable, _ORASSIG.

MODEL FORMATS

Model generation and maintenance are often difficult and expensive aspects of applying mathematical programming techniques. The flexible input formats for the optimization procedures in SAS/OR software simplify this task.

A simple product mix problem serves as a starting point for a discussion of different types of model formats supported in SAS/OR software.

A small candy manufacturer makes two products: chocolates and gum drops. The company's president asks the question, "What combination of chocolates and gum drops should we produce in a day in order to maximize the company's profit?" He knows that chocolates contribute $0.25 per pound to profit and gum drops $0.75 per pound. The variables *chocolates* and *gum drops* are the decision variables.

The following four processes are used to manufacture the candy:

1. Process 1 combines and cooks the basic ingredients for both chocolates and gum drops.
2. Process 2 adds colors and flavors to the gum drops and then cools and shapes the drops.
3. Process 3 chops and mixes nuts and raisins, adds them to the chocolates, then cools and shapes the candies.
4. Process 4 is packaging: chocolates are placed in individual paper shells; gum drops are wrapped in cellophane packages.

During the day there are seven and one-half hours (27,000 seconds) available for each process.

Firm time standards have been established for each process. Process 1 takes 15 seconds for each pound of chocolate and 40 seconds for each pound of gum drops. Process 2 takes 56.25 seconds per pound of gum drops. For Process 3, 18.75 seconds are required for each pound of chocolate. In packaging, Process 4, a pound of chocolates can be wrapped in 12 seconds, whereas 50 seconds are required for a pound of gum drops. These data are summarized below:

| | | available time | time required per pound | |
| | | | chocolates | gum drops |
process	activity	(seconds)	(seconds)	(seconds)
1	cooking	27,000	15	40
2	color/flavor	27,000	-	56.25
3	condiments	27,000	18.75	-
4	packaging	27,000	12	50

The object is to maximize the company's total profit:

$$0.25(\text{chocolates}) + 0.75(\text{gum drops}) \;.$$

The production of the candy is limited by the time available for each process. The limits placed on production by Process 1 are expressed by the inequality

$$15(\text{chocolates}) + 40(\text{gum drops}) \leq 27,000 \;.$$

Process 1 can handle any combination of chocolates and gum drops that satisfies this inequality.

The limits on production by other processes generate constraints described by these inequalities:

Process 2 $56.25(\text{gum drops}) \leq 27,000$
Process 3 $18.75(\text{chocolates}) \leq 27,000$
Process 4 $12(\text{chocolates}) + 50(\text{gum drops}) \leq 27,000 \;.$

This simple linear program illustrates the type of problem known as a product mix example. Its solution tells you what mix of products maximizes the objective without violating the constraints. There are two formats that can be used to represent this model.

Dense Format

The DATA step below creates a SAS data set for the problem described above. Notice that the values of CHOCO and GUMDR in the data set are the coefficients of those variables in the equations corresponding to the objective function and constraints. The variable _ID_ contains a character string that names the rows in the problem data set. The variable _TYPE_ is a character variable that contains keywords that describe the type of each row in the problem data set. And the variable _RHS_ contains the right-hand-side values.

```
data factory;
   input _id_ $ choco gumdr _type_ $ _rhs_;
   cards;
object      .25     .75    MAX    .
process1  15.00   40.00    LE   27000
process2   0.00   56.25    LE   27000
process3  18.75    0.00    LE   27000
process4  12.00   50.00    LE   27000
;
```

Optimization with PROC LP

The problem can be solved using the LP procedure. You invoke the procedure with the PROC LP statement. Because the special variables _ID_, _TYPE_, and _RHS_ are used in the problem data set, you do not need to identify them to the LP procedure.

```
proc lp;
```

The output from the LP procedure is printed in four sections. The first section is the PROBLEM SUMMARY (**Output 3.1**). It describes the problem giving the number and type of variables in the model and the number and type of constraints.

Output 3.1   PROC LP: The PROBLEM SUMMARY

```
                                                         1

     L I N E A R   P R O G R A M M I N G   P R O C E D U R E
                     PROBLEM  SUMMARY

          Max object              Objective Function
          _RHS_                   Rhs Variable
          _TYPE_                  Type Variable
          Problem Density             0.166667

          Variable Type               Number

          Non-negative                   2
          Slack                          4

          Total                          6

          Constraint Type             Number

          LE                             4
          Objective                      2

          Total                          6
```

The PROBLEM SUMMARY shows, for example, that there are two non-negative decision variables, namely CHOCO and GUMDR. It also shows that there are four constraints of type LE.

After the procedure prints this information, it solves the problem and then prints the SOLUTION SUMMARY (**Output 3.2**). This section gives information about the solution that was found.

Output 3.2   PROC LP: The SOLUTION SUMMARY

```
                                                                        1
         L I N E A R   P R O G R A M M I N G   P R O C E D U R E

                          SOLUTION  SUMMARY

                        Terminated Successfully

         Objective value                              475

         Phase 1 iterations                             0
         Phase 2 iterations                             4
         Phase 3 iterations                             0
         Integer iterations                             0
         Integer solutions                              0
         Initial basic feasible variables               6
         Time used (secs)                              16
         Number of inversions                           2

         Machine epsilon                              1E-8
         Machine infinity               1.7976931349E308
         Maximum phase 1 iterations                   100
         Maximum phase 2 iterations                   100
         Maximum phase 3 iterations            2147483646
         Maximum integer iterations                   100
         Time limit (secs)                            120
```

You can see that the procedure terminated successfully at an optimal objective value of 475 and that it took four phase 2 iterations.

The next section is the VARIABLE SUMMARY (**Output 3.3**). The variable summary gives the value for each variable. It also tells you its objective function coefficient, its status in the solution, and its reduced cost.

Output 3.3   PROC LP: The VARIABLE SUMMARY

```
                                                                        1
         L I N E A R   P R O G R A M M I N G   P R O C E D U R E

                          VARIABLE  SUMMARY

         Variable                                          Reduced
     Col Name    Status Type      Price   Activity           Cost

       1 CHOCO    BASIC NON-NEG    0.25 1000.000000         0.000
       2 GUMDR    BASIC NON-NEG    0.75  300.000000         0.000
       3 process1       SLACK            0.000            -0.013
       4 process2 BASIC SLACK         10125.000000         0.000
       5 process3 BASIC SLACK          8250.000000         0.000
       6 process4       SLACK            0.000            -0.005
```

The last section is the CONSTRAINT SUMMARY (**Output 3.4**). This output gives the value of the objective function, the value of each constraint, and the dual activities.

Output 3.4   PROC LP: The CONSTRAINT SUMMARY

```
                                                                              1
          L I N E A R   P R O G R A M M I N G   P R O C E D U R E

                         CONSTRAINT  SUMMARY

      Constraint            S/S                              Dual
      Row Name      Type    Col       Rhs     Activity     Activity


        1 object    OBJECT                    475.000000    -1.000
        2 process1  LE       3      27000   27000.000000     0.013
        3 process2  LE       4      27000   16875.000000     0.000
        4 process3  LE       5      27000   18750.000000     0.000
        5 process4  LE       6      27000   27000.000000     0.005
```

For a complete description of the output from PROC LP, see Chapter 7, "The LP Procedure."

Sparse Format

Typically, mathematical programming models are sparse. That is, very few of the coefficients in the constraint matrix are nonzero. The dense problem format shown in the last section would be an inefficient way to represent sparse models. The LP procedure also accepts data in a sparse input format. With this format, only the nonzero coefficients need to be specified. The format is robust and very flexible. It simplifies matrix generation using elements in the SAS language. In addition, the sparse input format is consistent with the standard MPS sparse format and much more flexible. For this reason, models using the MPS format can be easily converted to the LP format. The Appendix, "Using Macro SASMPSXS to Convert from IBM Format to LP Format," describes a SAS macro for conversion.

Although the factory example of the last section is not very sparse, it can be used to illustrate the form of the sparse input format. The sparse problem data set has four variables: a row type identifying variable, a row name variable, a column name variable, and a coefficient variable.

```
data factory;
    format _type_ $8. _row_ $16. _col_ $16.;
    input _type_ $ _row_ $ _col_ $ _coef_;
    cards;
max       object       .            .
.         object       chocolate    .25
.         object       gum_drops    .75
le        process1     .            .
.         process1     chocolate    15
.         process1     gum_drops    40
.         process1     _rhs_        27000
le        process2     .            .
.         process2     gum_drops    56.25
.         process2     _rhs_        27000
le        process3     .            .
.         process3     chocolate    18.75
.         process3     _rhs_        27000
```

```
le        process4    .           .
.         process4    chocolate   12
.         process4    gum_drops   50
.         process4    _rhs_       27000
;
```

Notice in the input statement that the _TYPE_ variable contains keywords as for the dense format, the _ROW_ variable contains the row names in the model, the _COL_ variable contains the column names in the model, and the _COEF_ variable contains the coefficients for that particular row and column. Because the row and column names are the values of variables in a SAS data set, they are not limited to eight characters. This feature, as well as the absence of order restrictions on the records in the data set, simplifies matrix generation.

Optimization with PROC LP

The SPARSEDATA option in the PROC LP statement tells the LP procedure that the model in the problem data set is in the sparse format. This example also illustrates how the solution of the linear program is saved in two output data sets: the primal data set and the dual data set.

```
proc lp sparsedata primalout=primal dualout=dual;
```

The primal data set contains the information that is printed in the VARIABLE SUMMARY plus additional information about the bounds on the variables. The dual data set contains information that is printed in the CONSTRAINT SUMMARY plus additional information about the constraints (**Output 3.5**).

Output 3.5   Printout of the Primal and Dual Solutions

```
                                                                                                        1

OBS  _OBJ_ID_  _RHS_ID_  _VAR_              _TYPE_   _STATUS_  _LBOUND_  _VALUE_  _UBOUND_    _PRICE_  _R_COST_

 1   object    _rhs_     chocolate          NON-NEG  _BASIC_      0       1000   1.7977E308    0.25   -0.000000
 2   object    _rhs_     gum_drops          NON-NEG  _BASIC_      0        300   1.7977E308    0.75   -0.000000
 3   object    _rhs_     process1           SLACK                0          0   1.7977E308    0.00   -0.012963
 4   object    _rhs_     process2           SLACK    _BASIC_      0      10125   1.7977E308    0.00    0.000000
 5   object    _rhs_     process3           SLACK    _BASIC_      0       8250   1.7977E308    0.00    0.000000
 6   object    _rhs_     process4           SLACK                0          0   1.7977E308    0.00   -0.004630
 7   object    _rhs_     PHASE_1_OBJECTIV   OBJECT   _DEGEN_      0          0   1.7977E308    0.00    0.000000
 8   object    _rhs_     object             OBJECT   _BASIC_      0        475   1.7977E308    0.00    0.000000
```

```
                                                                                                        2

OBS  _OBJ_ID_  _RHS_ID_  _ROW_ID_   _TYPE_   _RHS_    _L_RHS_   _VALUE_   _U_RHS_    _DUAL_

 1   object    _rhs_     object     OBJECT       0       475       475       475   -1.00000
 2   object    _rhs_     process1   LE       27000     27000     27000     27000    0.01296
 3   object    _rhs_     process2   LE       27000     27000     16875     27000    0.00000
 4   object    _rhs_     process3   LE       27000     27000     18750     27000    0.00000
 5   object    _rhs_     process4   LE       27000     27000     27000     27000    0.00463
```

Network Format

Network flow problems can be described by specifying the nodes in the network and their supplies and demands, and by specifying the arcs in the network and their costs, capacities, and lower flow bounds. Consider a simple transshipment problem as an illustration.

Suppose you have two factories, two warehouses, and three customers. The two factories each have a production capacity of 500 widgets. The three customers have demands of 100, 200, and 50 widgets, respectively. The following data set describes the supplies (positive values for the SUPDEM variable) and the demands (negative values for the SUPDEM variable) at each of the customers and factories:

```
data nodes;
   format node $16.;
   input node $  supdem;
   cards;
customer_1   -100
customer_2   -200
customer_3    -50
factory_1     500
factory_2     500
;
```

Suppose that you have two warehouses that are used to store the widgets before shipment to your customers and that there are different costs for shipping widgets between each factory, warehouse, and customer.

What is the minimum cost routing for supplying the customers?

The following data set describes the arcs in the network. Each record defines a new arc in the network and gives data about the arc. For example, there is an arc between the node FACTORY_1 and the node WAREHOUSE_1. Each unit of flow on that arc costs 10 dollars. Although this example does not include them, you can also have lower and upper bounds on the flow across that arc.

```
data network;
   format from $16. to $16.;
   input from $ to $ cost;
   cards;
factory_1     warehouse_1  10
factory_2     warehouse_1   5
factory_1     warehouse_2   7
factory_2     warehouse_2   9
warehouse_1   customer_1    3
warehouse_1   customer_2    4
warehouse_1   customer_3    4
warehouse_2   customer_1    5
warehouse_2   customer_2    5
warehouse_2   customer_3    6
;
```

Optimization with PROC NETFLOW

To find the minimum cost routing, you can use the NETFLOW procedure. This procedure will take the model as defined in the NETWORK and NODES data sets and find the minimum cost flow.

```
proc netflow arcout=arc_sav nodeout=nod_sav
            arcdata=network nodedata=nodes;
   node node;        /* node data set information */
   supdem supdem;

   tail from;        /* arc data set information */
   head to;
   cost cost;

   run;
```

The solution saved in the ARC_SAV data set tells you, among other things, the optimal number of widgets to send across each arc in the network. Thus, it tells you how many units to ship from each factory to each warehouse and from each warehouse to each customer.

Notice which arcs have positive flow (_FLOW_ is greater than 0). These arcs send widgets from FACTORY_2 to WAREHOUSE_1 and from there on to the three customers. The model indicates no production at FACTORY_1 and no use of WAREHOUSE_2 (**Output 3.6**).

Output 3.6   Minimum Cost Routing using PROC NETFLOW

OBS	_FROM_	_TO_	_COST_	_CAPAC_	_LO_	_SUPPLY_	_DEMAND_	_FLOW_	_FCOST_	_RCOST_	_ANUMB_	_TNUMB_	_STATUS_	
1	warehouse_1	customer_1	3	999999	0	.	100	100	300	.	5	2	KEY_ARC	BASIC
2	warehouse_2	customer_1	5	999999	0	.	100	0	0	4	6	4	LOWERBD	NONBASIC
3	warehouse_1	customer_2	4	999999	0	.	200	200	800	.	7	2	KEY_ARC	BASIC
4	warehouse_2	customer_2	5	999999	0	.	200	0	0	3	8	4	LOWERBD	NONBASIC
5	warehouse_1	customer_3	4	999999	0	.	50	50	200	.	9	2	KEY_ARC	BASIC
6	warehouse_2	customer_3	6	999999	0	.	50	0	0	4	10	4	LOWERBD	NONBASIC
7	factory_1	warehouse_1	10	999999	0	500	.	0	0	5	1	1	LOWERBD	NONBASIC
8	factory_2	warehouse_1	5	999999	0	500	.	350	1750	.	2	3	KEY_ARC	BASIC
9	factory_1	warehouse_2	7	999999	0	500	.	0	0	.	3	1	KEY_ARC	BASIC
10	factory_2	warehouse_2	9	999999	0	500	.	0	0	2	4	3	LOWERBD	NONBASIC

Drawing the Network with PROC NETDRAW

The network can be drawn using the NETDRAW procedure. This procedure expects the network to be specified in the same format as PROC NETFLOW.

```
proc netdraw graphics;
   actnet / activity=from successor=(to) separatearcs rectilinear;
```

The NETDRAW procedure can be used to display the network on either a full-screen device, a graphics device, or a printer (**Output 3.7**). See **Example 8** in chapter 8, "The NETDRAW Procedure," for further discussion of node placement.

Output 3.7 A Graph of the Network using PROC NETDRAW

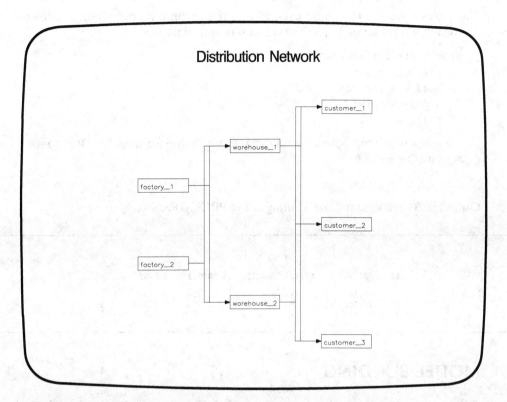

Transportation and Assignment Formats

The transportation and assignment models are described simply in rectangular data sets. Suppose that, instead of sending the widgets from factories to warehouses and then to the customers, widgets are sent directly from the factories to the customers.

Finding the minimum cost routing could be done using the NETFLOW procedure. However, because the network represents a transportation problem, the data for the problem can be represented more simply.

```
data transprt;
   input source $ supply cust_1 cust_2 cust_3;
   cards;
demand          .    250    200    50
factory1       250    10     9      7
factory2       250     9    10      8
;
```

This DATA step shows the source names as the values for the SOURCE variable, the supply at each source node as the values for the SUPPLY variable, and the unit shipping cost for source to sink as the values for the sink variables CUST_1 to CUST_3. Notice that the first record contains the demands at each of the sink nodes.

Optimization with PROC TRANS

The TRANS procedure can be used to find the minimum cost routing. It solves the problem and saves the solution in an output data set.

```
proc trans cost=transprt nothrunet;
   tailnode source
   headnode cust_1--cust_3;
   supply supply;
   run;
```

The solution printed below shows the amount to ship from each factory to each customer (**Output 3.8**).

Output 3.8   Minimum Cost Routing using PROC TRANS

```
                                                                              1

       OBS    SOURCE    CUST_1    CUST_2    CUST_3    SUPPLY    _DUAL_

        1     _DUAL_      -9        -9        -7         .         .
        2     factory1     0       200        50        250        0
        3     factory2   250         0         0        250        0
```

MODEL BUILDING

Often you want to keep the data separate from the structure of the model. This is particularly useful for large models with numerous identifiable components. The data are best organized in rectangular tables that can be easily examined and modified. Then, before the problem is solved, the model is built using the stored data. This process of model building is known as matrix generation. In conjunction with the sparse format, the SAS DATA step provides a good matrix generation language.

For example, consider the candy manufacturing example introduced above. Suppose that for the user interface it is more convenient to have the data so that each record describes the information related to each product (namely, the contribution to the objective function and the unit amount needed for each process needed by each product). A DATA step for saving these data might look like this:

```
data manfg;
   input product $16. object process1 - process4 ;
   cards;
chocolate          .25   15.00  0.00 18.75 12.00
gum_drops          .75   40.00 56.25  0.00 50.00
licorice          1.00   29.00 30.00 20.00 20.00
jelly_beans        .85   10.00  0.00 30.00 10.00
_rhs_               .   27000 27000 27000 27000
;
```

Notice that there is a special record at the end that has the product _RHS_. This record gives the amounts of time available for each of the processes. You could have just as easily had this information stored in another data set. The next example illustrates a model in which the data are stored in separate data sets.

Building the model involves adding the data to the structure. There are as many ways to do this as there are programmers and problems. The following DATA step

shows one way to take the candy data and build a sparse format model to solve
the product mix problem:

```
data model;
    array process object process1-process4;
    format _type_ $8. _row_ $16. _col_ $16.;
    keep _type_ _row_ _col_ _coef_;

    /* read the manufacturing data */

    set manfg;

    /* build the object function */

    if _n_=1 then do;
        _type_='max'; _row_='object'; _col_=' '; _coef_=.; output;
        end;

    /* build the constraints */

    do over process;
        if _i_>1 then do;
            _type_='le'; _row_='process'||put(_i_-1,1.);
            end;
        else            _row_='object';
        _col_=product; _coef_=process;
        output;
        end;

    proc print;
    run;
```

The sparse format data set is produced (**Output 3.9**).

Output 3.9 Sparse Format Data Set

OBS	_TYPE_	_ROW_	_COL_	_COEF_
1	max	object		.
2	max	object	chocolate	0.25
3	le	process1	chocolate	15.00
4	le	process2	chocolate	0.00
5	le	process3	chocolate	18.75
6	le	process4	chocolate	12.00
7		object	gum_drops	0.75
8	le	process1	gum_drops	40.00
9	le	process2	gum_drops	56.25
10	le	process3	gum_drops	0.00
11	le	process4	gum_drops	50.00
12		object	licorice	1.00
13	le	process1	licorice	29.00
14	le	process2	licorice	30.00
15	le	process3	licorice	20.00
16	le	process4	licorice	20.00
17		object	jelly_beans	0.85
18	le	process1	jelly_beans	10.00
19	le	process2	jelly_beans	0.00
20	le	process3	jelly_beans	30.00
21	le	process4	jelly_beans	10.00

(continued on next page)

(continued from previous page)

```
          22                   object              _rhs_                       .
          23    le             process1            _rhs_                 27000.00
          24    le             process2            _rhs_                 27000.00
          25    le             process3            _rhs_                 27000.00
          26    le             process4            _rhs_                 27000.00
```

The model data set looks a little different from the sparse representation of the candy model shown earlier. It not only includes the additional products, LICORICE and JELLY_BEANS, but it also defines the model in a different order. Because the sparse format is robust, you can generate the model in ways that are convenient for the DATA step program and your data handling needs.

If the problem you wanted to solve had 300 products, all you would need to do is increase the size of the MANFG data set to include the new product data. Also, if the problem had more than four processes, all you would have to do is add the new process variables to the MANFG data set and increase the size of the PROCESS array in the model data set. With these two simple changes and your new data, you could solve a product mix problem having hundreds of processes and products.

Matrix Generation

Often you want to keep data in separate tables and then automate model building and reporting. This example illustrates a problem that has elements of a product mix problem and a blending problem. Suppose you make four kinds of ties: all silk, all polyester, a 50-50 polyester-cotton blend, and a 30-70 cotton-polyester blend.

The data you have include cost and supplies of raw material: selling price, minimum contract sales, maximum demand of the finished products, and the proportions of raw materials that go into each product. Assume that you want to identify the product mix that maximizes profit.

The data are saved in three SAS data sets. The following program demonstrates one way for these data to be saved. Alternatively, you might want to use the full-screen editor PROC FSEDIT to store and edit these data.

```
data material;
    input descpt $char20.  cost  supply;
    cards;
silk_material             .21   25.8
polyester_material        .6    22.0
cotton_material           .9    13.6
;

data tie;
    input descpt $char20. price contract demand;
    cards;
all_silk                  6.70   6.0    7.00
all_polyester             3.55  10.0   14.00
poly_cotton_blend         4.31  13.0   16.00
cotton_poly_blend         4.81   6.0    8.50
;
```

```
data manfg;
   input descpt $char20.  silk  poly cotton;
   cards;
all_silk                   100     0      0
all_polyester                0   100      0
poly_cotton_blend            0    50     50
cotton_poly_blend            0    30     70
;
```

The following program takes the raw data from the three data sets and builds a linear program model in the data set called MODEL. Although it is designed for the three-resource, four-product problem described here, this program can be extended easily to include more resources and products. The model building DATA step remains essentially the same; all that changes are the dimensions of loops and arrays. Of course, the data tables must increase to accommodate the new data.

```
data model;
  array  raw_mat {3} $ 20;
  array  raw_comp {3} silk poly cotton;
  length _type_ $ 8 _col_ $ 20 _row_ $ 20 _coef_ 8;
  keep   _type_      _col_        _row_        _coef_;

  /* define the objective, lower, and upper bound rows */

  _row_='profit'; _type_='max';      output;
  _row_='lower';  _type_='lowerbd'; output;
  _row_='upper';  _type_='upperbd'; output;
  _type_=' ';

  /* the object and upper rows for the raw materials */

  do i=1 to 3;
     set material;
     raw_mat i =descpt;  _col_=descpt;
     _row_='profit';    _coef_=-cost;  output;
     _row_='upper';     _coef_=supply; output;
     end;

  /* the object, upper, and lower rows for the products */

  do i=1 to 4;
     set tie;
     _col_=descpt;
     _row_='profit'; _coef_=price;    output;
     _row_='lower';  _coef_=contract; output;
     _row_='upper';  _coef_=demand;   output;
     end;
```

```
        /* the coefficient matrix for manufacturing */

    _type_='eq';
    do i=1 to 4;                    /* loop for each raw material */
       set manfg;
       do j=1 to 3;                 /* loop for each product       */


          _col_=descpt;/* % of material in product    */
          _row_  = raw_mat j;
          _coef_ = raw_comp j /100;
          output;
          _col_  = raw_mat j;  _coef_ = -1;
          output;

          /* the right-hand-side */

          if i=1 then do; _col_='_rhs_'; _coef_=0; output;  end;
          end;
       _type_=' ';
       end;
    stop;
run;
```

Next, solve the model using PROC LP and save the solution in the primalout data
set named SOLUTION.

```
proc lp sparsedata primalout=solution;

proc print ;
   id _var_;
   var _lbound_--_r_cost_;
run;
```

Output 3.10 is then produced by the PRINT procedure.

Output 3.10   A Simple Report of the Solution

VAR	_LBOUND_	_VALUE_	_UBOUND_	_PRICE_	_R_COST_
all_polyester	10	11.800	14.0	3.55	0.000
all_silk	6	7.000	7.0	6.70	6.490
cotton_material	0	13.600	13.6	-0.90	4.170
cotton_poly_blend	6	8.500	8.5	4.81	0.196
poly_cotton_blend	13	15.300	16.0	4.31	0.000
polyester_material	0	22.000	22.0	-0.60	2.950
silk_material	0	7.000	25.8	-0.21	0.000
PHASE_1_OBJECTIVE	0	0.000	1.7977E308	0.00	0.000
profit	0	168.708	1.7977E308	0.00	0.000

The solution shows that you should produce 11.8 units of polyester ties, 7 units of silk ties, 8.5 units of the cotton-polyester blend, and 15.3 units of the polyester-cotton blend. It also shows the amounts of raw materials that go into this product mix to generate a total profit of 168.708 dollars.

Exploiting Model Structure

For network models, you can further simplify model handling problems and exploit the structure in the model by using the NETFLOW procedure.

Recall the transshipment problem discussed earlier. The solution required no production at FACTORY_1 and no storage at WAREHOUSE_2. Suppose this solution, although optimal, is unacceptable. You impose an additional constraint requiring balancing the production at the two factories. Now, you want the production at the two factories to differ by, at most, 100 units while satisfying the customers demand at minimum cost. Such a constraint might look like

$$-100 \leq \text{FACTORY\_1\_WAREHOUSE\_1} + \text{FACTORY\_1\_WAREHOUSE\_2}$$
$$- \text{FACTORY\_2\_WAREHOUSE\_1} - \text{FACTORY\_2\_WAREHOUSE\_2} \leq 100$$

You save the network and supply and demand information in the two data sets as was done earlier.

```
data network;
   format from $16. to $16.;
   input  from $ to $ cost;
   cards;
factory_1  warehouse_1  10
factory_2  warehouse_1   5
factory_1  warehouse_2   7
factory_2  warehouse_2   9
warehouse_1 customer_1   3
warehouse_1 customer_2   4
warehouse_1 customer_3   4
warehouse_2 customer_1   5
warehouse_2 customer_2   5
warehouse_2 customer_3   6
;

data nodes;
   format node $16.;
   input node $  supdem;
   cards;
customer_1 -100
customer_2 -200
customer_3  -50
factory_1   500
factory_2   500
;
```

The factory balancing constraint is not a part of the network. It is represented in the sparse format in a data set for side constraints.

```
data side_con;
   format _type_ $8. _row_ $16. _col_ $21. _coef_ 8.;
   input _type_      _row_       _col_       _coef_;
```

```
          cards;
   eq          balance    .                          .
   .           balance    factory_1_warehouse_1      1
   .           balance    factory_1_warehouse_2      1
   .           balance    factory_2_warehouse_1     -1
   .           balance    factory_2_warehouse_2     -1
   .           balance    diff                      -1
   lo          lowerbd    diff                    -100
   up          upperbd    diff                     100
   ;
```

This format constrains an equality constraint that sets the value of DIFF to be the amount that FACTORY_1 production exceeds FACTORY_2 production. It also contains implicit bounds on the DIFF variable. Note that the DIFF variable is a non-arc variable.

This problem is solved using the NETFLOW procedure. Indicate the NETWORK, NODES, and SIDE_CON data sets on the PROC NETFLOW statement.

```
proc netflow sparsecondata conout=arc_sav
             arcdata=network nodedata=nodes condata=side_con;
   node node;
   supdem supdem;
   tail from;
   head to;
   cost cost;
   column _col_;

   run;
```

The solution is saved in the ARC_SAV data set. Notice that the solution now has production balanced across the factories; the production at FACTORY_2 exceeds that at FACTORY_1 by 100 units (**Output 3.11**).

Output 3.11   Problem Solution Using PROC NETFLOW

OBS	FROM	TO	COST	CAPAC	LO	NAME	SUPPLY	DEMAND	FLOW	FCOST	RCOST	ANUMB	TNUMB	STATUS	
1	warehouse_1	customer_1	3	999999	0	.	100	100	300	.	5	2	KEY_ARC	BASIC
2	warehouse_2	customer_1	5	999999	0	.	100	0	0	1.0	6	4	LOWERBD	NONBASIC
3	warehouse_1	customer_2	4	999999	0	.	200	75	300	.	7	2	KEY_ARC	BASIC
4	warehouse_2	customer_2	5	999999	0	.	200	125	625	.	8	4	NONKEY ARC	BASIC
5	warehouse_1	customer_3	4	999999	0	.	50	50	200	.	9	2	KEY_ARC	BASIC
6	warehouse_2	customer_3	6	999999	0	.	50	0	0	1.0	10	4	LOWERBD	NONBASIC
7	factory_1	warehouse_1	10	999999	0	500	.	0	0	2.0	1	1	LOWERBD	NONBASIC
8	factory_2	warehouse_1	5	999999	0	500	.	225	1125	.	2	3	KEY_ARC	BASIC
9	factory_1	warehouse_2	7	999999	0	500	.	125	875	.	3	1	KEY_ARC	BASIC
10	factory_2	warehouse_2	9	999999	0	500	.	0	0	5.0	4	3	LOWERBD	NONBASIC
11			0	100	-100	diff	.	.	-100	0	1.5	0	.	LOWERBD	NONBASIC

REPORT WRITING

The reporting of the solution is also an important aspect of modeling. Because the optimization procedures save the solution in one or more SAS data sets, report writing can be accomplished with any of the tools in the SAS language.

The DATA Step

You can use the DATA step and PROC PRINT to produce reports. For example, you can print a simple table showing the revenue generated from the production of ties followed by the cost of material with the following program:

```
data product(keep= _var_ _value_ _price_ revenue)
     material(keep=_var_ _value_ _price_ cost);
  set solution;
  if _price_>0 then do;
     revenue=_price_*_value_; output product;
     end;
  else if _price_<0 then do;
     _price_=-_price_;
     cost = _price_*_value_; output material;
     end;
run;

/* print the product report */

proc print data=product;
   id _var_;
   var _value_ _price_ revenue;
   sum revenue;
   title 'Revenue Generated from Tie Sales';
run;

/* print the materials report */

proc print data=material;
   id _var_;
   var _value_ _price_ cost;
   sum cost;
   title 'Cost of Raw Materials';
run;
```

This DATA step reads the SOLUTION data set saved by PROC LP and segregates the records based on whether they correspond to materials or products, namely whether the contribution to profit is positive or negative. Each of these is then printed to produce the summary table in **Output 3.12**.

Output 3.12   Producing a Revenue Report using PROC LP

```
                                                                          1
                    Revenue Generated from Tie Sales

           _VAR_           _VALUE_     _PRICE_     REVENUE

           all_polyester     11.8       3.55       41.890
           all_silk           7.0       6.70       46.900
           cotton_poly_blend  8.5       4.81       40.885
           poly_cotton_blend 15.3       4.31       65.943
                                                  =======
                                                  195.618


                       Cost of Raw Materials

           _VAR_           _VALUE_     _PRICE_      COST

           cotton_material   13.6       0.90       12.24
           polyester_material 22.0      0.60       13.20
           silk_material      7.0       0.21        1.47
                                                  =====
                                                  26.91
```

Other Reporting Procedures

The CHART procedure can be a useful tool for displaying the solution to mathematical programming models. The ARC_SAV data set that contains the solution
to the balanced transshipment problem can be displayed effectively using PROC
CHART. You can see graphically the amount that is shipped from each factory
and warehouse with the following statements:

```
proc chart data=arc_sav;
   hbar from / sumvar=_flow_;
run;
```

Output 3.13 displays the horizontal bar chart that is produced.

Output 3.13   A Bar Chart Showing the Solution to the Balanced
                   Transshipment Problem

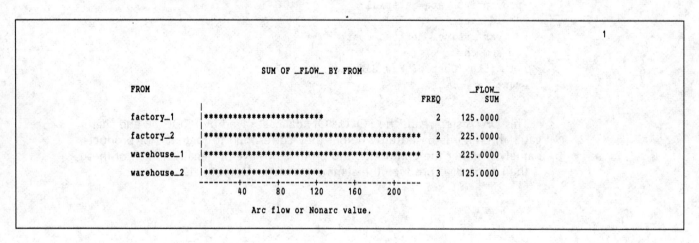

The horizontal bar chart is just one way of displaying the solution to a mathematical program. The solution to the tie product mix problem that was solved
using PROC LP can also be illustrated using PROC CHART. Here, a pie chart

shows the relative contribution of each product to total revenues. The following program produces **Output 3.14**:

```
proc chart data=product;
  pie _var_ / sumvar=revenue;
  title 'Projected Tie Sales Revenue';
run;
```

Output 3.14   Producing a Pie Chart using PROC LP and PROC CHART

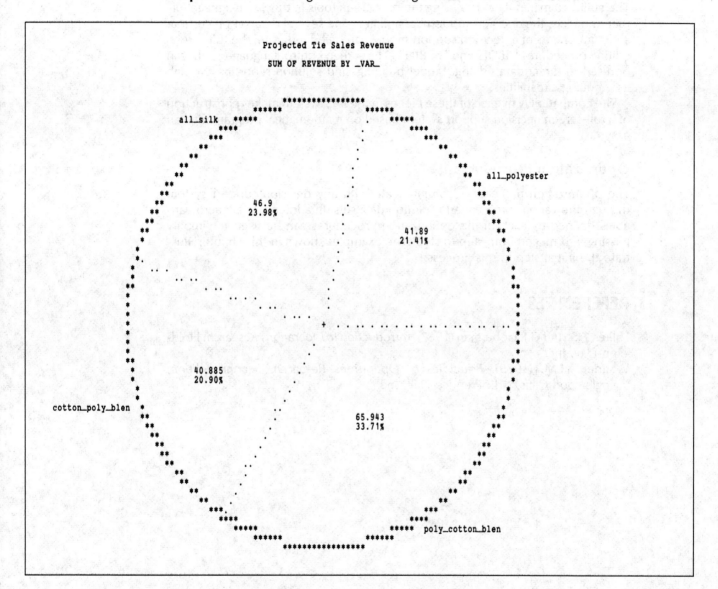

The TABULATE procedure is another procedure that can help automate solution reporting. There are several examples in Chapter 7 that illustrate its use.

DECISION SUPPORT SYSTEMS

The close relationship between a SAS data set and the representation of the mathematical model facilitates the building of decision support systems. This is particularly apparent when you consider the ability to segregate data as a function of information content, handle the data in this form, and build the mathematical program just prior to model solution.

The Full-Screen Interface

The ability to manipulate data using the full-screen tools in the SAS language further enhances the decision support capabilities. The several data set pieces that are components of a decision support model can be edited using the full-screen editing procedures FSEDIT and FSPRINT. The screen control language (SCL) can be used to direct data editing, model building, and solution reporting through its menuing capabilities.

The compatibility of each of these pieces in the SAS System makes construction of a full-screen decision support system based on mathematical programming an easy task.

Optimization Procedures

The optimization procedures communicate with any decision support system through the various problem and solution data sets. In addition, the macro variables defined by each of the optimization procedures can be used to simplify passing information from step to step. The examples shown in this chapter illustrate the initial step in this process.

REFERENCES

Hillier, F.S. and G.J. Lieberman (1967), *Introduction to Operations Research*, Holden-Day, Inc.

Wagner, H.M. (1975), *Principles of Operations Research, Second Edition*, Englewood Cilffs, N.J.: Prentice-Hall, Inc.

Chapter 4

The ASSIGN
Procedure

ABSTRACT

The ASSIGN procedure finds the minimum or maximum cost assignment of m sink nodes to n source nodes. The procedure can handle problems where $m=n$, $m<n$, or $m>n$.

INTRODUCTION

The ASSIGN procedure finds the minimum or maximum cost assignment of sink nodes to source nodes. Many practical problems can be formulated in a way that is solvable by PROC ASSIGN.

Introductory Example

Consider assigning five programmers to five programming jobs. Each programmer prefers specific programming jobs over others. You can use PROC ASSIGN to assign jobs to programmers in such a way that the total preferences of the group are maximized. Suppose you ask each programmer to rank the jobs according to preference (using 1 for the most preferred job and 5 for the least preferred job). PROC ASSIGN maximizes the total preference of the group by minimizing the sum of the preferences. In the matrix that follows, each row of the matrix represents a programmer and each column represents a programming job. Each entry in the matrix is a preference ranking each programmer gave each programming job.

PRGMER	JOB1	JOB2	JOB3	JOB4	JOB5
PRGMER1	4	1	3	5	2
PRGMER2	2	1	3	4	5
PRGMER3	3	2	4	1	5
PRGMER4	2	3	4	5	1
PRGMER5	4	2	3	1	5

To solve this problem using PROC ASSIGN, the data must be in a SAS data set; the solution is output to a SAS data set. Each observation corresponds to a programmer and contains the programming job assigned to it. In this way, the procedure identifies the assignment of the five jobs to the five programmers. To solve this assignment problem, place the preference data into a SAS data set (PREFER). Then, call PROC ASSIGN, identifying the cost variables in the input data set. The solution is output by PROC ASSIGN to a SAS data set (PREFER1) and printed with the PRINT procedure. The following statements produce **Output 4.1**:

```
title 'Assigning Programming Jobs to Programmers';

data prefer;                    * STORE THE DATA;
   input  prgmer $ job1-job5;
   cards;
PRGMER1 4 1 3 5 2
PRGMER2 2 1 3 4 5
PRGMER3 3 2 4 1 5
PRGMER4 2 3 4 5 1
PRGMER5 4 2 3 1 5
;
proc assign data=prefer out=prefer1;   * SOLVE THE PROBLEM;
   cost job1-job5;
   id prgmer;
run;

proc print data=prefer1;               * PRINT THE SOLUTION;
   sum _fcost_;
run;
```

The following note is printed on the SAS log:

```
NOTE: The minimum cost assignment costs 8.
```

Output 4.1   Assigning Programming Jobs to Programmers

```
                    Assigning Programming Jobs to Programmers                        1

 OBS    PRGMER    JOB1    JOB2    JOB3    JOB4    JOB5    _ASSIGN_    _FCOST_

  1     PRGMER1     4       1       3       5       2      JOB2          1
  2     PRGMER2     2       1       3       4       5      JOB1          2
  3     PRGMER3     3       2       4       1       5      JOB4          1
  4     PRGMER4     2       3       4       5       1      JOB5          1
  5     PRGMER5     4       2       3       1       5      JOB3          3
                                                                    ========
                                                                        8
```

The solution, given in column _ASSIGN_, shows how each programming job should be assigned to each worker in order to minimize the assignment cost, which is equivalent to maximizing the worker preferences. _FCOST_ expresses in units of preference the cost of the assignment. The SUM statement in the PRINT procedure is used to total the assignment cost.

Formulation

The formal statement of the problem solved by the ASSIGN procedure is as follows:

If $n = m$ then: $\min (\max) \sum_{j=1}^{m} \sum_{i=1}^{n} c_{ij} x_{ij}$

subject to: $\sum_{j=1}^{m} x_{ij} = 1$ for $i = 1, \ldots, n$

$\sum_{i=1}^{n} x_{ij} = 1$ for $j = 1, \ldots, m$

where $x = 0$ or 1 for $i = 1, \ldots n$ and $j = 1, \ldots m$.

If $n < m$ then: $\min (\max) \sum_{j=1}^{m} \sum_{i=1}^{n} c_{ij} x_{ij}$

subject to: $\sum_{j=1}^{m} x_{ij} = 1$ for $i = 1, \ldots, n$

$\sum_{i=1}^{n} x_{ij} \leq 1$ for $j = 1, \ldots, m$

where $x = 0$ or 1 for $i = 1, \ldots n$ and $j = 1, \ldots m$.

If $n > m$ then: $\min (\max) \sum_{j=1}^{m} \sum_{i=1}^{n} c_{ij} x_{ij}$

subject to: $\sum_{j=1}^{m} x_{ij} \leq 1$ for $i = 1, \ldots, n$

$\sum_{i=1}^{n} x_{ij} = 1$ for $j = 1, \ldots, m$

where $x = 0$ or 1 for $i = 1, \ldots n$ and $j = 1, \ldots m$.

SPECIFICATIONS

The following statements are used in PROC ASSIGN:

PROC ASSIGN options;
   BY variables;
   COST variables;
   ID variables;

PROC ASSIGN Statement

PROC ASSIGN *options*;

The options below can appear in the PROC ASSIGN statement.

Data Set Options

DATA=*SASdataset*
:   names the SAS data set that contains the network specification. If DATA= is omitted, the most recently created SAS data set is used.

OUT=*SASdataset*
:   specifies a name for the output data set. If OUT= is omitted, the SAS System creates a data set and automatically names it according to the DATA*n* naming convention. See "SAS Files" in base SAS documentation for more information.

Optimization Control Options

DEC=*n*
:   specifies a scaling factor for the input cost data. The input data are scaled by 10^n. The default value of *n* is 3. For more information, see the discussion on scaling in the **DETAILS** section.

MAXIMUM
:   specifies that the objective is to find an assignment that maximizes the sum of the costs. By default, PROC ASSIGN minimizes the sum of the costs.

BY Statement

BY *variables*;

A BY statement can be used with PROC ASSIGN to obtain separate solutions on problems in groups defined by the BY variables. When you use a BY statement, the procedure expects the input data to be sorted in ascending order of the BY variables. If your input data set is not sorted, use the SORT procedure with a similar BY statement to sort the data, or, if appropriate, use the BY statement options NOTSORTED or DESCENDING. See **Example 4:   Using PROC ASSIGN with a BY Statement**. For more information, see the discussion of the BY statement in base SAS documentation.

COST Statement

COST *variables*;

The COST statement identifies the variables in the input data set that contain the costs of assigning each sink node to each source node. If the value of a COST variable is missing, then that particular assignment between source and sink node is infeasible. If you do not use a COST statement, then all numeric variables not specified in the ID or BY statements are assumed to be cost variables.

To find an assignment that maximizes profit instead of minimizing cost, include the MAXIMUM option in the PROC ASSIGN statement and let the COST variables represent profit instead of cost. The COST variables must be numeric. See **Example 1:   Assigning Subcontractors to Construction Jobs** for an illustration of the COST statement.

ID Statement

ID *variables*;

The ID statement identifies variables in the input data set that are to be included in the output data set. ID variables can be character or numeric.

Note: variables specified in the BY and COST statements are automatically included in the output data set.

DETAILS

Missing Values

Because the value of a cost variable is interpreted as the cost of an assignment, a missing value for a cost variable is assumed to mean that the assignment is not allowed. Refer to **Example 1** for an illustration of a data set with missing values.

Output Data Set

The output data set contains the *m* cost variables in the input data set, any variables identified in the ID statement, and two new variables named _ASSIGN_ and _FCOST_. The variable named _ASSIGN_ is a character variable containing the names of the sink nodes (variables) assigned to the source nodes (observations). The variable named _FCOST_ is a numeric variable containing the costs of assigning the sink nodes to the source nodes. Note that the values of the *m* cost variables in the output data set reflect any effects of scaling performed by PROC ASSIGN.

The Objective Value

If the problem is infeasible, an error message is printed on the SAS log. Otherwise, the value of the objective function

$$\sum_{j=1}^{m} \sum_{i=1}^{n} c_{ij} x_{ij}$$

under the optimal assignment is reported on the SAS log.

Macro Variable _ORASSIG

On termination, the ASSIGN procedure defines a macro variable named _ORASSIG. This variable contains a character string that indicates the status of the procedure on termination and gives the objective value at termination. The form of the _ORASSIG character string is

STATUS=*xxx*   **OBJECTIVE=***yyy*

where *xxx* can be any one of the following:

- SUCCESSFUL
- INFEASIBLE
- MEMORY_ERROR
- IO_ERROR
- SYNTAX_ERROR
- SEMANTIC_ERROR
- BADDATA_ERROR
- UNKNOWN_ERROR

This information is useful when PROC ASSIGN comprises one step in a larger program that needs to identify just how the ASSIGN procedure terminated.

Because _ORASSIG is a standard SAS macro variable it can be used in the ways that all macro variables can be used. See the *SAS Guide to Macro Processing, Version 6 Edition* for more information. **Example 2:   Assigning Construction Jobs to Subcontractors** illustrates one method to print the _ORASSIG variable on the log.

Scaling

PROC ASSIGN uses a variant of the out-of-kilter algorithm. Integral cost data are important for maintaining a rapid rate of convergence with this algorithm. To assure integrality, the cost data are automatically scaled by DEC decimal places on input to PROC ASSIGN. If this scaling results in loss of accuracy in the input data, a warning is printed on the log indicating a nonzero fractional component in the data after scaling. The output data set produced by PROC ASSIGN contains the scaled input cost data rescaled to its original order of magnitude. You can use these data to analyze the effects of scaling.

EXAMPLES

Example 1:   Assigning Subcontractors to Construction Jobs

This example shows how PROC ASSIGN can be used to maximize an objective function. Consider a construction project that consists of nine jobs. Because of the nature of the project, each job must be performed by a different subcontractor. Each job is bid upon by twelve subcontractors. The matrix that follows shows the expected profit to the contractor if each job is given to each subcontractor. Each row in the matrix represents a different job, and each column represents a different subcontractor.

SUBCONTRACTOR	1	2	3	4	5	6	7	8	9	10	11	12
JOB1	79	24	13	53	47	66	85	17	92	47	46	13
JOB2	43	59	33	95	55	97	34	55	84	94	26	56
JOB3	29	52	0	27	13	33	0	11	71	86	6	76
JOB4	88	83	64	72	0	67	27	47	83	62	35	38
JOB5	65	90	56	62	53	91	48	23	6	89	49	33
JOB6	44	79	86	93	71	7	86	59	0	56	45	59
JOB7	35	51	-9	91	39	32	3	12	79	25	79	81
JOB8	50	12	59	32	23	64	20	94	97	14	11	97
JOB9	25	17	39	.	38	63	87	14	4	18	11	45

The negative profit in the third column means that if job 7 is awarded to subcontractor 3, the contractor loses money. The missing value in the fourth column means that subcontractor 4 did not bid on job 9. PROC ASSIGN treats a missing value differently from the way it treats a 0. While it is possible that an optimal assignment could include a 0 (or even a negative) contribution to profit, the missing value is never included in an assignment. In this case, subcontractor 4 is never awarded job 9, regardless of the profit structure.

You can use PROC ASSIGN to find how the contractor should award the jobs to the subcontractors to maximize his profit. First, put the data in a SAS data set. Then, call PROC ASSIGN using the MAXIMUM option.

The following statements produce **Output 4.2**:

```
title 'Assigning Subcontractors to Construction Jobs';

data profit;                         * READ THE DATA;
   input job $ subcon1-subcon12;
   cards;
JOB1 79 24 13 53 47 66 85 17 92 47 46 13
JOB2 43 59 33 95 55 97 34 55 84 94 26 56
JOB3 29 52  0 27 13 33  0 11 71 86  6 76
JOB4 88 83 64 72  0 67 27 47 83 62 35 38
JOB5 65 90 56 62 53 91 48 23  6 89 49 33
JOB6 44 79 86 93 71  7 86 59  0 56 45 59
JOB7 35 51 -9 91 39 32  3 12 79 25 79 81
JOB8 50 12 59 32 23 64 20 94 97 14 11 97
JOB9 25 17 39  . 38 63 87 14  4 18 11 45
;
proc assign maximum data=profit;     * SOLVE THE PROBLEM;
   cost subcon1-subcon12;
   id job;
run;

proc print;                          * PRINT THE SOLUTION;
   sum _fcost_;
run;
```

The cost of the optimal assignment printed on the SAS log is

```
NOTE: The maximum return assignment yields 814.
```

This means that the contractor can expect a profit of $814 if he follows the optimal assignment.

Output 4.2   Assigning Subcontractors to Construction Jobs

OBS	JOB	SUBCON1	SUBCON2	SUBCON3	SUBCON4	SUBCON5	SUBCON6	SUBCON7	SUBCON8	SUBCON9	SUBCON10	SUBCON11	SUBCON12	_ASSIGN_	_FCOST_
1	JOB1	79	24	13	53	47	66	85	17	92	47	46	13	SUBCON9	92
2	JOB2	43	59	33	95	55	97	34	55	84	94	26	56	SUBCON6	97
3	JOB3	29	52	0	27	13	33	0	11	71	86	6	76	SUBCON10	86
4	JOB4	88	83	64	72	0	67	27	47	83	62	35	38	SUBCON1	88
5	JOB5	65	90	56	62	53	91	48	23	6	89	49	33	SUBCON2	90
6	JOB6	44	79	86	93	71	7	86	59	0	56	45	59	SUBCON3	86
7	JOB7	35	51	-9	91	39	32	3	12	79	25	79	81	SUBCON4	91
8	JOB8	50	12	59	32	23	64	20	94	97	14	11	97	SUBCON12	97
9	JOB9	25	17	39	.	38	63	87	14	4	18	11	45	SUBCON7	87
															===
															814

Note that three subcontractors, SUBCON5, SUBCON8, and SUBCON11, are not assigned to any jobs.

Example 2: Assigning Construction Jobs to Subcontractors

Suppose the data from **Example 1** are transposed so that variables are jobs. Then each observation contains the profit from awarding each job to a single subcontractor. The following program finds the maximum profit assignment and produces **Output 4.3**:

```
title 'Assigning Construction Jobs to Subcontractors';

data profit;                          *READ THE DATA;
   input subcont $ job1-job9;
   cards;

SUBCON1     79    43    29    88    65    44    35    50    25
SUBCON2     24    59    52    83    90    79    51    12    17
SUBCON3     13    33     0    64    56    86    -9    59    39
SUBCON4     53    95    27    72    62    93    91    32     .
SUBCON5     47    55    13     0    53    71    39    23    38
SUBCON6     66    97    33    67    91     7    32    64    63
SUBCON7     85    34     0    27    48    86    32     0    87
SUBCON8     17    55    11    47    23    59    12    94    14
SUBCON9     92    84    71    83     6     0    79    97     4
SUBCON10    47    94    86    62    89    56    25    14    18
SUBCON11    46    26     6    35    49    45    79    11    11
SUBCON12    13    56    76    38    33    59    81    97    45
;

proc assign maximum data=profit;  * SOLVE THE PROBLEM;
   cost job1-job9;
   id subcont;
run;

proc print;                        * PRINT THE SOLUTION;
   sum _fcost_;
run;
```

The cost of the optimal assignment printed on the SAS log is

```
NOTE: The maximum return assignment yields 814.
```

This means that the contractor can expect a profit of $814 if the optimal assignment is followed. The output data set includes the same results as in **Example 1**.

Output 4.3 Assigning Construction Jobs to Subcontractors

```
                        Assigning Construction Jobs to Subcontractors                                    1

  OBS   SUBCONT    JOB1   JOB2   JOB3   JOB4   JOB5   JOB6   JOB7   JOB8   JOB9   _ASSIGN_   _FCOST_

    1   SUBCON1     79     43     29     88     65     44     35     50     25    JOB4         88
    2   SUBCON2     24     59     52     83     90     79     51     12     17    JOB5         90
    3   SUBCON3     13     33      0     64     56     86     -9     59     39    JOB6         86
    4   SUBCON4     53     95     27     72     62     93     91     32      .    JOB7         91
    5   SUBCON5     47     55     13      0     53     71     39     23     38                  0
    6   SUBCON6     66     97     33     67     91      7     32     64     63    JOB2         97
```

(continued on next page)

(continued from previous page)

7	SUBCON7	85	34	0	27	48	86	32	0	87	JOB9	87
8	SUBCON8	17	55	11	47	23	59	12	94	14		0
9	SUBCON9	92	84	71	83	6	0	79	97	4	JOB1	92
10	SUBCON10	47	94	86	62	89	56	25	14	18	JOB3	86
11	SUBCON11	46	26	6	35	49	45	79	11	11		0
12	SUBCON12	13	56	76	38	33	59	81	97	45	JOB8	97
												=======
												814

The macro variable _ORASSIG defined by PROC ASSIGN contains information regarding the termination of the procedure. This information can be useful when you use PROC ASSIGN as part of a larger SAS program. For example, the following information is printed on the log using the macro language with the statement:

```
%put  &_orassig;
```

On the log the following appears:

```
STATUS=SUCCESSFUL  OBJECTIVE=814.
```

Example 3:   Minimizing Swim Times

A swim coach needs to assign male and female swimmers to each stroke of a medley relay team. The swimmers' best times for each stroke are stored in a SAS data set. The ASSIGN procedure is used to evaluate the times and to match strokes and swimmers to minimize the total relay swim time. The following statements produce **Output 4.4**:

```
title 'Assigning Strokes Using the BY Statement';

data relay;
   input name $ sex $ back breast fly free;
   cards;
SUE      F 35.1 36.7 28.3 36.1
KAREN    F 34.6 32.6 26.9 26.2
JAN      F 31.3 33.9 27.1 31.2
ANDREA   F 28.6 34.1 29.1 30.3
CAROL    F 32.9 32.2 26.6 24.0
ELLEN    F 27.8 32.5 27.8 27.0
JIM      M 26.3 27.6 23.5 22.4
MIKE     M 29.0 24.0 27.9 25.4
SAM      M 27.2 33.8 25.2 24.1
CLAYTON  M 27.0 29.2 23.0 21.9
;

proc assign out=fast;
   cost back--free;
   id name;
   by sex;

proc print;
   by sex;
   sum _fcost_;
run;
```

Output 4.4   Assigning Swimmers using the BY Statement

```
                        Assigning Strokes Using the BY Statement                                  1
-------------------------------------------- SEX=F --------------------------------------------
        OBS    NAME      BACK     BREAST     FLY      FREE     _ASSIGN_    _FCOST_

          1    SUE       35.100   36.700    28.300    36.100                  0.0
          2    KAREN     34.600   32.600    26.899    26.199    BREAST       32.6
          3    JAN       31.300   33.899    27.100    31.199    FLY          27.1
          4    ANDREA    28.600   34.100    29.100    30.300                  0.0
          5    CAROL     32.899   32.200    26.600    24.000    FREE         24.0
          6    ELLEN     27.800   32.500    27.800    27.000    BACK         27.8
                                                                          --------
        SEX                                                                111.5


-------------------------------------------- SEX=M --------------------------------------------
        OBS    NAME      BACK     BREAST     FLY      FREE     _ASSIGN_    _FCOST_

          7    JIM       26.300   27.600    23.500    22.399    FREE         22.399
          8    MIKE      29.000   24.000    27.899    25.399    BREAST       24.000
          9    SAM       27.199   33.799    25.199    24.100    BACK         27.199
         10    CLAYTON   27.000   29.199    23.000    21.899    FLY          23.000
                                                                          --------
        SEX                                                                96.598
                                                                          ========
                                                                          208.098
```

On the basis of this solution, Jim will swim freestyle, Mike will swim breast stroke, Sam will swim back stroke, and Clayton will swim butterfly. For the women's team, Karen will swim breast stroke, Jan will swim butterfly, Carol will swim freestyle, and Ellen will swim back stroke.

Example 4:   Using PROC ASSIGN with a BY Statement

A major beverage company wants to assign TV commercials to television commercial time slot openings in a way that maximizes the overall effectiveness of its television advertising. The time slots in this example begin at 7:00 on a Saturday morning and run hourly through 3:00 p.m. A combination of Nielsen TV ratings and market research testing produces an effectiveness rating for each time slot and commercial combination. The commercials are of three types: children, lifestyle, and sports. The company is willing to show up to three commercials in each time slot as long as the commercials are of different types. Which commercials should be assigned to which time slots in order to maximize the total effectiveness of its television advertising campaign? Data are missing for those time slots where certain programs are not available; for instance, no sports shows are presented during the 7:00 a.m. time slot.

The following statements produce **Output 4.5**:

```
title 'Assigning Televison Commercials Using the BY Statement';

data beverage;
   input commercl $ type $ slot1-slot9;
   cards;
COMM1  KIDS   27.2 32.8  30.4   31.5    20.9    19.8     .       .     .
COMM2  KIDS   37.4 33.5  38.4   32.4    25.6    27.2     .       .     .
COMM3  KIDS   32.5 31.9  34.6   34.5    26.7    28.3     .       .     .
COMM4  LIFEST  .   22.6  25.9   25.3    26.4    28.3    29.1    22.2  20.2
COMM5  LIFEST  .   25.1  36.6   36.8    38.2    33.5    33.2    33.1  30.1
COMM6  LIFEST  .   20.2  31.3   29.3    24.6    25.1    20.0    22.4  23.1
```

```
COMM7  SPORTS  .   .    25.1  26.1  28.3  36.1  29.4  31.7  34.5
COMM8  SPORTS  .   .    24.7  27.2  36.4  31.2  28.7  33.2  33.1
COMM9  SPORTS  . 20.2  20.4  20.2  25.6  37.8  35.6  32.4  34.3
;
proc assign maximum out=newslots;
   cost slot1-slot9;
   id commercl;
   by type;
run;
proc print;
   by type;
   sum _fcost_;
run;
```

Output 4.5   Assigning Television Commercials using the BY Statement

```
                  Assigning Television Commercials Using the BY Statement                        1
---------------------------------------------------- TYPE=KIDS ----------------------------------------------------

 OBS   COMMERCL   SLOT1    SLOT2    SLOT3    SLOT4    SLOT5    SLOT6    SLOT7    SLOT8    SLOT9    _ASSIGN_   _FCOST_

  1     COMM1    27.199   32.799   30.399   31.500   20.899   19.800     .        .        .       SLOT2     32.799
  2     COMM2    37.399   33.500   38.399   32.399   25.600   27.199     .        .        .       SLOT3     38.399
  3     COMM3    32.500   31.899   34.600   34.500   26.699   28.300     .        .        .       SLOT4     34.500
                                                                                                           -------
 TYPE                                                                                                       105.698

--------------------------------------------------- TYPE=LIFEST ---------------------------------------------------

 OBS   COMMERCL   SLOT1    SLOT2    SLOT3    SLOT4    SLOT5    SLOT6    SLOT7    SLOT8    SLOT9    _ASSIGN_   _FCOST_

  4     COMM4      .      22.600   25.899   25.300   26.399    28.3     29.1   22.199   20.199     SLOT7      29.1
  5     COMM5      .      25.100   36.600   36.799   38.200    33.5     33.2   33.100   30.100     SLOT5      38.2
  6     COMM6      .      20.199   31.300   29.300   24.600    25.1     20.0   22.399   23.100     SLOT3      31.3
                                                                                                           -------
 TYPE                                                                                                        98.6

--------------------------------------------------- TYPE=SPORTS ---------------------------------------------------

 OBS   COMMERCL   SLOT1    SLOT2    SLOT3    SLOT4    SLOT5    SLOT6    SLOT7    SLOT8    SLOT9    _ASSIGN_   _FCOST_

  7     COMM7      .        .      25.100   26.100   28.300   36.100   29.399   31.699   34.500     SLOT9     34.500
  8     COMM8      .        .      24.699   27.199   36.399   31.199   28.699   33.200   33.100     SLOT5     36.399
  9     COMM9      .      20.199   20.399   20.199   25.600   37.799   35.600   32.399   34.299     SLOT6     37.799
                                                                                                           -------
 TYPE                                                                                                       108.698
                                                                                                           =======
                                                                                                           312.996
```

On the basis of this survey, this company has decided to drop commercial advertising from the 7:00 a.m. (slot1) and 2:00 p.m. (slot8) time slots.

REFERENCES

Minieka, E. (1978), *Optimization Algorithms for Networks and Graphs*, New York: Marcel Dekker, Inc.

Papadimitriov, C. M. and Steiglitz, K. (1982), *Combinatorial Optimization Algorithms and Complexity*, Englewood Cliffs, N.J.: Prentice-Hall, Inc.

66

Chapter 5
The CPM
Procedure

ABSTRACT

The CPM procedure schedules activities in a project subject to precedence, resource, and time constraints. The schedule obtained by PROC CPM is saved in an output data set. Resource utilization can be summarized and saved in an output data set.

INTRODUCTION

The CPM procedure is a tool that can be used for planning, controlling, and monitoring a project. This introduction provides you with a brief overview of some of the prominent features of CPM and the definitions of a few terms used in this chapter.

A typical project consists of several activities. These activities may have precedence and time constraints. Some of them may already be in progress; some of them may follow different work schedules. All of the activities may compete for scarce resources. PROC CPM allows you to schedule activities subject to all of these constraints.

For example, consider a software project in which an applications developer has her software finished and ready for preliminary testing. In order to complete the project, several activities must take place. Certain activities cannot start until other activites have finished. For instance, the preliminary documentation must be written before it can be revised and edited or before QA (Quality Assurance) can test the software. Such constraints among the activities (namely, activity B can start after activity A has finished) are referred to as *precedence constraints*. Given the precedence constraints and estimated durations of the activities, you can use the *critical path method* to determine the shortest completion time for the project.

The first step towards determining project completion time is to capture the relationships between the activities in a convenient representation. This is done by using a network diagram. Two types of network diagrams are popular for representing a project.

- Activity-On-Arc (AOA) or Activity-On-Edge (AOE) diagrams show the activities on the arcs or edges of the network. For the software project referred to above, the AOA representation is shown in **Figure 5.1**. This method of representing a project is also known as the *arrow diagramming method* (ADM).
- Activity-On-Node (AON) or Activity-On-Vertex (AOV) diagrams show the activities on nodes or vertices of the network. **Figure 5.2** shows the AON representation of the project. This method is also known as the *precedence diagramming method* (PDM). The Activity-On-Node (AON) representation is more flexible because it allows you to specify nonstandard precedence relationships between the activities (for example, you can specify that activity B starts five days after the start of activity A).

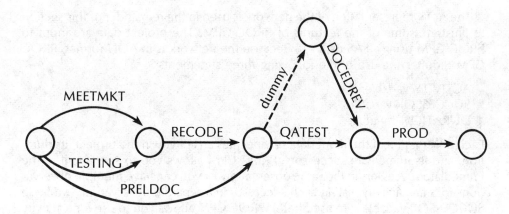

Figure 5.1 Activity-On-Arc Network

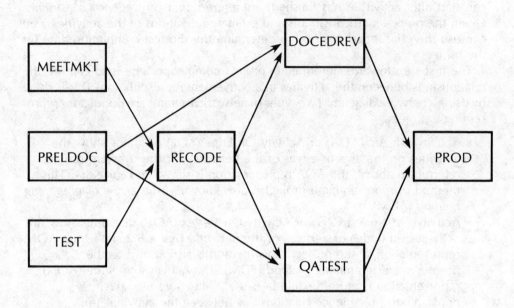

Figure 5.2 Activity-On-Node Network

The AON representation of the network is used in the remainder of this section to illustrate some of the features of PROC CPM. The project data are input to PROC CPM using a SAS data set. Because the network is in AON format, PROC CPM requires the use of the following three statements:

ACTIVITY *variable*;
SUCCESSOR *variables*;
DURATION *variable*;

Each observation of the input data set specifies an activity in the project, its duration, and its immediate successors. PROC CPM allows you to specify all of the immediate successors in the same observation, or you can have multiple observations for each activity, listing each successor in a separate observation. (Multiple SUCCESSOR variables are used here). PROC CPM allows you to use long activity names. In this example, shorter names are used for the activities to facilitate data entry; a variable DESCRPT is used to contain a longer description for each activity.

The procedure determines, among other things,

- the minimum time in which the project can be completed
- the set of activities that is critical to the completion of the project in the minimum amount of time.

No printed output is produced. However, the results are saved in an output data set that is shown in **Output 5.1**.

The code for the entire program is as follows:

```
data software;
    input descrpt  $char20.
          duration 23-24
          activity $ 27-34
          succesr1 $ 37-44
          succesr2 $ 47-54;
    cards;
Initial Testing       20  TESTING   RECODE
Prel. Documentation   15  PRELDOC   DOCEDREV  QATEST
Meet Marketing         1  MEETMKT   RECODE
Recoding               5  RECODE    DOCEDREV  QATEST
QA Test Approve       10  QATEST    PROD
Doc. Edit and Revise  10  DOCEDREV  PROD
Production             1  PROD
;

proc cpm data=software
         out=intro1
         interval=weekdays
         date='01mar88'd;
    id descrpt;
    activity activity;
    duration duration;
    successor succesr1 succesr2;
run;

proc print data=intro1 noobs;
    id descrpt;
run;
```

Output 5.1   Software Production Project Plan

DESCRPT	ACTIVITY	SUCCESR1	SUCCESR2	DURATION	E_START	E_FINISH	L_START	L_FINISH	T_FLOAT	F_FLOAT
Initial Testing	TESTING	RECODE		20	01MAR88	28MAR88	01MAR88	28MAR88	0	0
Prel. Documentation	PRELDOC	DOCEDREV	QATEST	15	01MAR88	21MAR88	15MAR88	04APR88	10	10
Meet Marketing	MEETMKT	RECODE		1	01MAR88	01MAR88	28MAR88	28MAR88	19	19
Recoding	RECODE	DOCEDREV	QATEST	5	29MAR88	04APR88	29MAR88	04APR88	0	0
QA Test Approve	QATEST	PROD		10	05APR88	18APR88	05APR88	18APR88	0	0
Doc. Edit and Revise	DOCEDREV	PROD		10	05APR88	18APR88	05APR88	18APR88	0	0
Production	PROD			1	19APR88	19APR88	19APR88	19APR88	0	0

The output data set contains some new variables that are described below.

E_START   early start, the earliest time an activity can begin subject to any time constraints and the completion time of the preceding activity

E_FINISH   early finish, the earliest time an activity can be finished, assuming it starts at E_START

L_START   late start, the latest time an activity can begin so that the project is not delayed

L_FINISH   late finish, the latest time an activity can be finished without delaying the project

T_FLOAT   total float, the amount of flexibility in the starting of a specific activity without delaying the project (T_FLOAT = L_START−E_START = L_FINISH−E_FINISH)

F_FLOAT   free float, the difference between the early finish time of the activity and the early start time of the activity's immediate successors.

In **Output 5.1** the majority of the tasks have a total float of 0. These events are *critical*, that is, any delay in these activities will cause the project to be delayed. The activity MEETMKT has a slack period of 19 days because there are 19 workdays between 01MAR88 and 28MAR88. The INTERVAL= option in the PROC CPM statement allows you to specify the durations of the activities in one of several possible units, including days, weeks, months, hours, minutes. In addition, you can schedule activities around weekends and holidays. You can also choose different patterns of work during a day or a week (holidays on Friday and Saturday) and different sets of holidays for the different activities in the project. A CALENDAR consists of a set of work schedules for a typical week and a set of holidays. PROC CPM allows you to define any number of calendars and associate different activities with different calendars.

You saw that you could schedule your project by choosing a project start date. You can also specify a project finish date, if you have a deadline that is to be met and you need to determine the latest start times for the different activities in the project. You can also set constraints on start or finish dates for specific activites within a given project as well. For example, the testing of the software may have to be delayed until the testing group finishes a project with a higher priority. PROC CPM can schedule the project subject to such restrictions through the use of the ALIGNDATE and ALIGNTYPE statements. See **Example 10** for more information on the use of the ALIGNDATE and ALIGNTYPE statements.

For a project that is already in progress, you can incorporate the ACTUAL schedule of the activities (some activities may already be completed while others are still in progress) to obtain a progress update.

Quite often the resources needed to perform the activities in a project are available only in limited quantities and may cause certain activities to be postponed due to unavailability of the required resources. You can use PROC CPM to schedule the activities in a project subject to resource constraints. In addition to obtaining a resource-constrained schedule in an output data set, you can save the resource utilization summary in another output data set, the ROUT= data set. A wide range of options allows you to control the scheduling process. **Table 5.1** and **Table 5.2** show you specific statements and options and their uses.

SPECIFICATIONS

The following statements are used in PROC CPM:

> **PROC CPM** *options;*
>   **ACTIVITY** *variable;*
>   **ACTUAL** */ actual options;*
>   **ALIGNDATE** *variable;*
>   **ALIGNTYPE** *variable;*
>   **CALID** *variable;*
>   **DURATION** *variable;*
>   **HEADNODE** *variable;*
>   **HOLIDAY** *variable / holiday options;*
>   **ID** *variables;*
>   **RESOURCE** *variables / resource options;*
>   **SUCCESSOR** *variables / lag option;*
>   **TAILNODE** *variable;*

Table 5.1 lists the statements according to their functionality. It also indicates whether each statement is required or optional.

Table 5.1   CPM Statements and Descriptions for Use

Function	Statement/Option Name	If Required
AON representation	**ACTIVITY** statement	required in AON
	SUCCESSOR statement	required in AON
	LAG option	
AOA representation	**HEADNODE** statement	required in AOA
	TAILNODE statement	required in AOA
Duration of activity	**DURATION** statement	required
Time constraints	**ALIGNDATE** statement	not required
	ALIGNTYPE statement	not required
Resource constraints	**RESOURCE** statement	required if activities use limited resources
Additional project information	**ID** statement	not required
Progress reporting	**ACTUAL** statement	not required
Holidays	**HOLIDAY** statement	not required
Multiple calendars	**CALID** statement	not required

PROC CPM Statement

   PROC CPM *options*;

The options that can appear in the PROC CPM statement are grouped according to their functions and described briefly under different section headings. **Table 5.2** lists the options alphabetically and indicates the name of the section under which each option is described.

Table 5.2   PROC CPM Statement Options and Related Sections

Option	Section
CALEDATA	Data set option
COLLAPSE	Miscellaneous option
DATA	Data set option
DATE	Time constraint option
DAYLENGTH	Duration control option
DAYSTART	Duration control option
FINISHBEFORE	Time constraint option
HOLIDATA	Data set option
INTERVAL	Duration control option
INTPER	Duration control option
OUT	Data set option
RESOURCEIN	Data set option
RESOURCEOUT	Data set option
WORKDATA	Data set option

Data Set Options

This section briefly describes all the input and output data sets used by PROC CPM. **Table 5.3** follows this section, showing the association between specific input data sets, variables, and statements.

   CALEDATA=*SASdataset*
   CALENDAR=*SASdataset*
      identifies a SAS data set that specifies the work pattern during a standard week for each of the calendars that are to be used in the project. Each observation of this data set (also referred to as the calendar data set) contains the name or the number of the calendar being defined in that observation, the names of the shifts or work patterns used each day, and, optionally, a standard workday length in hours. For information on the structure of this data set see **Multiple Calendars** in **DETAILS**. The work shifts referred to in the CALEDATA data set are defined in the WORKDATA data set.

   DATA=*SASdataset*
      names the SAS data set that contains the network specification and activity information. If DATA= is omitted, the most recently created SAS data set is used. This data set (also referred to in this chapter as the

activities data set) contains all of the information that is associated with each activity in the network.

HOLIDATA=*SASdataset*

identifies a SAS data set that specifies holidays. These holidays can be associated with specific calendars that are also identified in the HOLIDATA data set (also referred to as the holidays data set). HOLIDATA= must be used with a HOLIDAY statement that specifies the variable in the SAS data set that contains the start time of holidays. Optionally, the data set may include a variable that specifies the length of each holiday or a variable that identifies the finish time of each holiday (if the holidays are longer than one day). For projects involving multiple calendars, this data set may also include the variable specified by the CALID statement that identifies the calendar to be associated with each holiday.

OUT=*SASdataset*

specifies a name for the output data set that contains the schedule determined by PROC CPM. This data set contains all of the variables that were specified in the DATA= input data set to define the project. Every observation in the activities input data set has a corresponding observation in the output data set. If PROC CPM is used to determine a schedule that is not subject to any resource constraints, then this output data set contains the early and late start schedules; otherwise, it also contains the resource-constrained schedule. See **OUT= Output Data Set** in the **DETAILS** section for information about the names of the new variables in the data set. If OUT= is omitted, the SAS System still creates a data set and names it according to the DATA*n* convention. See "SAS Files" in base SAS documentation for more information.

RESOURCEIN=*SASdataset*
RESIN=*SASdataset*
RIN=*SASdataset*
RESLEVEL=*SASdataset*

names the SAS data set that contains the levels available for the different resources used by the activities in the project. This data set also contains information about the type of resource (replenishable or consumable) and the priority for each resource. The specification of the RESIN= data set (also referred to as the resources data set) indicates to PROC CPM that the schedule of the project is to be determined subject to resource constraints. For further information about the format of this data set, see **RESOURCEIN= Input Data Set** in the **DETAILS** section.

If this option is specified, you must also use the RESOURCE statement to identify the variable names for the resources to be used for resource-constrained scheduling. In addition, you must specify the name of the variable in this data set (using the PERIOD= option in the RESOURCE statement) that contains the dates from which the resource availabilities in each observation are valid. Further, the data set must be sorted in order of increasing values of this period variable.

RESOURCEOUT=*SASdataset*
RESOUT=*SASdataset*
ROUT=*SASdataset*
RESUSAGE=*SASdataset*

names the SAS data set in which you can save resource usage profiles for each of the resources specified in the RESOURCE statement. In this data set, you can save the resource usage by time period for the early start, late start, and resource-constrained schedules and for the surplus level of resources remaining after resource allocation is performed. By default, it provides the usage profiles for the early and late start schedules if resource allocation is not performed.

If resource allocation is performed, this data set also provides usage profiles for the resource-constrained schedule and a profile of the level of remaining resources.

You can control the types of profiles to be saved by using the ESPROFILE (early start usage), LSPROFILE (late start usage), RCPROFILE (resource-constrained usage), or AVPROFILE (resource availability after resource allocation) options in the RESOURCE statement. Any combination of these four options can be specified. You can also specify the option ALL to indicate that all four options (ESPROFILE, LSPROFILE, RCPROFILE, AVPROFILE) are to be in effect. For details about variable names and the interpretation of the values in this data set, see **RESOURCEOUT= Data Set** in the **DETAILS** section.

WORKDATA=*SASdataset*
WORKDAY=*SASdataset*
identifies a SAS data set that defines the work pattern during a standard working day. Each numeric variable in this data set (also referred to as the workday data set) is assumed to denote a unique shift pattern during one working day. The variables must be formatted as SAS time values and the observations are assumed to specify, alternately, the times when consecutive shifts start and end.

Table 5.3 lists all of the variables associated with each input data set and the statements in which they are to be specified.

Table 5.3   PROC CPM Input Data Sets and Associated Variables

Data Set	Variable Name	Statement	Denotation
CALEDATA	CALID	CALID	Calendar name or number
	SUN, . . . _SAT_	Default names	Work pattern on day of week, valid values: WORKDAY, HOLIDAY, or one of the numeric variables in the WORKDATA data set
	D_LENGTH	Default name	Length of standard work day
DATA	ACTIVITY	ACTIVITY	Activity in AON format
	SUCCESSOR	SUCCESSOR	Immediate successor in AON format
	LAG	SUCCESSOR	Nonstandard precedence relationship

(continued)

Table 5.3   (continued)

Data Set	Variable Name	Statement	Denotation
	HEADNODE	HEADNODE	Head of arrow in AOA format
	TAILNODE	TAILNODE	Tail of arrow in AOA format
	DURATION	DURATION	Duration of activity
	ID	ID	Additional project information
	CALID	CALID	Calendar followed by activity
	ALIGNDATE	ALIGNDATE	Time constraint on activity
	ALIGNTYPE	ALIGNTYPE	Type of time constraint, valid values: SGE, SEQ, SLE, FGE, FEQ, FLE, MS, MF
	RESOURCE	RESOURCE	Amount of resource required
	ACTPRTY	RESOURCE	Activity priority
	MAXNSEGMT	RESOURCE	Maximum number of segments allowed
	MINSEGMTDUR	RESOURCE	Minimum duration of a segment
	A_START	ACTUAL	Actual start time of activity
	A_FINISH	ACTUAL	Actual finish time of activity
	REMDUR	ACTUAL	Remaining duration
	PCTCOMP	ACTUAL	Percentage of work completed
HOLIDATA	HOLIDAY	HOLIDAY	Start of holiday
	HOLIDUR	HOLIDAY	Duration of holiday
	HOLIFIN	HOLIDAY	End of holiday
	CALID	CALID	Calendar to which holiday applies

(continued)

Table 5.3   (continued)

Data Set	Variable Name	Statement	Denotation
RESOURCEIN	OBSTYPE	RESOURCE	Type of observation; valid values: RESLEVEL, RESTYPE, SUPLEVEL, RESPRTY
	PERIOD	RESOURCE	Time from which resource is available
	RESOURCE	RESOURCE	Resource type, availability, priority information
WORKDATA	Any numeric variable		On-off pattern of work

Duration Control Options

DAYLENGTH=*daylength*
specifies the length of the workday. On each day, work is scheduled starting at the beginning of the day as specified in the DAYSTART= option and ending *daylength* hours later. The DAYLENGTH= value should be a SAS time value. The default value of daylength is 24 hours if the INTERVAL= option is specified as DTDAY, DTHOUR, DTMINUTE, or DTSECOND, and the default value of *daylength* is eight hours if the INTERVAL= option is specified as WORKDAY or DTWRKDAY; for other values of the INTERVAL parameter, the DAYLENGTH parameter is ignored.

DAYSTART=*daystart*
specifies the start of the workday. The DAYSTART= value should be a SAS time value. This parameter is to be specified only when the INTERVAL parameter is one of the following: DTDAY, WORKDAY, DTWRKDAY, DTHOUR, DTMINUTE, or DTSECOND. The default value of DAYSTART is 9 a.m. if INTERVAL is WORKDAY; otherwise, the value of DAYSTART is equal to the time part of the SAS datetime value specifed for the DATE parameter.

INTERVAL=*interval*
requests that each unit of duration be measured in *interval* units. Possible values for *interval* are DAY, WEEK, WEEKDAYS, WORKDAY, MONTH, QTR, YEAR, HOUR, MINUTE, SECOND, DTDAY, DTWRKDAY, DTWEEK, DTMONTH, DTQTR, DTYEAR, DTHOUR, DTMINUTE, and DTSECOND. If the DATE= option is specified, then the default is DAY. See **Using the INTERVAL= Option** in the **DETAILS** section for further information regarding this option.

INTPER=*period*
requests that each unit of duration be equivalent to *period* units of duration. The default is 1.

Time Constraint Options

DATE=*d*
specifies the SAS date, time, or datetime *d* that is to be used as an alignment date for the project. If neither the FINISHBEFORE option nor any other alignment options are specified, then CPM schedules the

project to start on *d*. If *d* is a SAS time value, the INTERVAL parameter should be HOUR, MINUTE, or SECOND; if it is a SAS date value, INTERVAL should be DAY, WEEKDAY, WORKDAY, WEEK, MONTH, QTR, or YEAR; and if it is a SAS datetime value, INTERVAL should be DTWRKDAY, DTDAY, DTHOUR, DTMINUTE, DTSECOND, DTWEEK, DTMONTH, DTQTR, or DTYEAR.

FINISHBEFORE
specifies that the project be scheduled to complete before the date given in the DATE= option.

Miscellaneous Option

COLLAPSE
creates only one observation per activity in the output data set when the input data set for a network in Activity-On-Node format contains multiple observations for the same activity. Note that this option is allowed only if the network is in Activity-On-Node format.

Often, the input data set may have more than one observation per activity (especially if the activity has several successors). If you are interested only in the schedule information about the activity, there is no need for multiple observations in the output data set for this activity. Use the COLLAPSE option in this case.

ACTIVITY Statement

ACTIVITY *variable*;

The ACTIVITY statement is required when data are input in an Activity-On-Node format, and this statement identifies the variable that contains the names of the nodes in the network. The activity associated with each node has a duration equal to the value of the DURATION variable. The ACTIVITY variable can be character or numeric because it is treated symbolically. Each node in the network must be uniquely defined.

ACTUAL Statement

ACTUAL / *actual options*;

The ACTUAL statement identifies variables in the activities data set that contain progress information about the activities in the project. For a project that is already in progress, you can describe the actual status of any activity by specifying the activity's actual start, actual finish, remaining duration, or percent of work completed. You can also specify options in the ACTUAL statement that control the updating of the project schedule. The use of the ACTUAL statement causes the addition of four new variables (A_START, A_FINISH, A_DUR, and STATUS) in the OUT= output data set; these variables are defined in the **OUT= Output Data Set** section. See **Progress Updating** in the **DETAILS** section for more information.

The following options are available with the ACTUAL statement.

Progress Variables Specifications

At least one of the four variables (A_START, A_FINISH, REMDUR, PCTCOMP) needs to be specified on the ACTUAL statement. The TIMENOW parameter in this statement is used in conjunction with the values of these variables to check for consistency and to determine default values, if necessary.

A_START=*variable*

identifies a variable in the DATA=input data set that specifies the actual start times of activities that are in progress or that are already completed. Note that the actual start time of an activity must be less than TIMENOW.

A_FINISH=*variable*

identifies a variable in the DATA=input data set that specifies the actual finish time of activities that are already completed. The actual finish time of an activity must be less than TIMENOW.

PCTCOMP=*variable*

identifies a variable in the DATA=input data set that specifies the percentage of the work that has been completed for the current activity. The values for this variable must be between 0 and 100. A value of zero for this variable means that the current activity has not yet started. A value of 100 means that the activity is already complete. Once again, the TIMENOW parameter is used as a reference point to resolve the values specified for the PCTCOMP variable. See **Progress Updating** in the **DETAILS** section for more information.

REMDUR=*variable*

identifies a variable in the activities data set that specifies the remaining duration of activities that are in progress. The values of this variable must be non-negative: a value of zero for this variable means that the activity in that observation is completed, while a value greater than or equal to the duration means that the activity is not completed (the remaining duration is used to revise the estimate of the original duration). The value of the TIMENOW parameter is used to determine an actual start time or an actual finish time or both for activities based on the value of the remaining duration. See **Progress Update** in the **DETAILS** section for further information.

Updating Options

AUTOUPDT

requests that PROC CPM should assume automatic completion (or start) of activities that are predecessors to activities already completed (or in progress). For example, if activity B is a successor of activity A, and B has an actual start time (or actual finish time or both) specified while A has missing values for both actual start and actual finish times, then AUTOUPDT causes PROC CPM to assume that A must have already finished. PROC CPM then assigns activity A an actual start time and an actual finish time consistent with the precedence constraints. AUTOUPDT is the default.

NOAUTOUPDT

requests that PROC CPM should not assume automatic completion of activities. (NOAUTOUPDT is the reverse of AUTOUPDT.) In other words, only those activities that have nonmissing actual start or nonmissing actual finish times or both (either specified as values for A_START and A_FINISH variables, or computed on the basis of REMDUR or PCTCOMP and TIMENOW) are assumed to have started; all other activities have an implicit start time that is greater than or equal to TIMENOW. This option requires you to enter the progress information for all the activities that have started or are complete; an activity is assumed to be *pending* until one of the progress variables indicates that it has started.

TIMENOW=*timenow*
CURRDATE=*timenow*

specifies the SAS date, time, or datetime value that is used as a reference point to resolve the values of the remaining duration and percent completion times when the ACTUAL statement is used. It can be thought of as the instant at the *beginning of the specified date*, when a "snapshot" of the project is taken; the actual start times or finish times or both are specified for all activities that have started or been completed by the *end of the previous day*. If an ACTUAL statement is used without specification of the TIMENOW parameter, the default value is set to be the time period following the maximum of all the actual start and finish times that have been specified; if there are no actual start or finish times, then TIMENOW is set to be equal to the current date. See **Progress Updating** in the **DETAILS** section for further information regarding the TIMENOW parameter and the ACTUAL statement.

TIMENOWSPLT

indicates that activities that are in progress at TIMENOW can be split at TIMENOW if they cause resource infeasibilities. During resource allocation, any activities with E_START less than TIMENOW are scheduled even if there are not enough resources (a warning message is issued to the log if this is the case). This is true even for activities that are in progress. The TIMENOWSPLT option permits an activity to be split into two segments at TIMENOW, allowing the second segment of the activity to be scheduled later when resource levels permit. See **Activity Splitting** in the **DETAILS** section for information regarding activity segments. Note that activities with an alignment type of *MS* or *MF* are not allowed to be split; also, activities without resource requirements will not be split.

ALIGNDATE Statement

ALIGNDATE *variable*;

The ALIGNDATE statement identifies the variable in the DATA= input data set that specifies the dates to be used to constrain each activity to start or finish on a particular date. The ALIGNDATE statement is used in conjunction with the ALIGNTYPE statement, which specifies the type of alignment. A missing value for the ALIGNDATE variable indicates that the particular activity has no restriction imposed on it.

PROC CPM requires that if the ALIGNDATE statement is used, then all start activities (activities with no predecessors) have nonmissing values for the ALIGNDATE variable. If any start activity has a missing ALIGNDATE value, it is assumed to start on the date specified in the PROC CPM statement (if such a date is given) or, if no date is given, on the earliest specified start date of all start activities. If none of the start activities has a start date specified and a project start date is not specified in the PROC CPM statement, the input data are in error and the procedure stops execution and returns an error message.

ALIGNTYPE Statement

> ALIGNTYPE *variable*;

This statement is used to specify whether the date value in the ALIGNDATE statement is the earliest start date, the latest finish date, and so forth, for the activity in the observation. The allowed values of the variable specified are SEQ, SGE, SLE, FEQ, FGE, FLE, MS, and MF. These values stand for *start equal*, *start greater than or equal to*, *start less than or equal to*, *finish equal to*, *finish greater than or equal to*, *finish less than or equal to*, *mandatory start*, and *mandatory finish*, respectively. If an ALIGNDATE statement is specified and no ALIGNTYPE statement is given, all of the activities are assumed to have an aligntype of SGE. If an activity has a nonmissing value for the ALIGNDATE variable and a missing value for the ALIGNTYPE variable, then the aligntype is assumed to be SGE. See **Time-Constrained Scheduling** in the **DETAILS** section for information on how the ALIGNDATE and ALIGNTYPE variables affect the schedule of the project.

CALID Statement

> CALID *variable*;

The CALID statement specifies the name of a SAS variable that is used in the DATA, the HOLIDATA, and the CALEDATA data sets to identify the name or number of the calendar that each observation refers to. This variable can be either numeric or character depending on whether the different calendars are identified by unique numbers or names. If this variable is not found in any of the three data sets, PROC CPM looks for a default variable named _CAL_ in that data set (a warning message is then issued to the log). In the activities data set, this variable specifies the calendar used by the activity in the given observation. Each calendar in the project is defined using the WORKDATA, CALEDATA, and the HOLIDATA data sets. Each observation of the CALEDATA data set defines a standard work week through the shift patterns as defined by the WORKDATA data set and a standard day length; these values are associated with the calendar identified by the value of the calendar variable in that observation. Likewise, each observation of the HOLIDATA data set defines a holiday for the calendar identified by the value of the calendar variable.

If there is no calendar variable in the activities data set, all activities are assumed to follow the default calendar. If there is no calendar variable in the HOLIDATA data set, all of the holidays specified are assumed to occur in all the calendars. If there is no calendar variable in the CALEDATA data set, the first observation is assumed to define the default work week (which is also followed by any calendar that might be defined in the HOLIDATA data set) and all subsequent observations are ignored. See **Multiple Calendars** in the **DETAILS** section for further information.

DURATION Statement

> DURATION *variable*;

The DURATION statement identifies the variable in the input data set that contains the length of time necessary to complete the activity. If the network is input in Activity-On-Arc format, then the variable identifies the duration of the activity denoted by the arc joining the TAILNODE and the HEADNODE. If the network is input in Activity-On-Node format, then the variable identifies the duration of the activity at the node specified in the ACTIVITY statement. The variable specified must be numeric. The DURATION statement must be specified. The values of the DURATION variable are assumed to be in *interval* units, where *interval* is the value of the INTERVAL parameter.

HEADNODE Statement

> HEADNODE *variable*;

or

> TO *variable*;

The HEADNODE statement is required when data are input in Activity-On-Arc format. This statement specifies the variable in the input data set that contains the name of the node on the head of an arrow in the project network. This node is identified with the event that signals the end of an activity on that arc. The variable specified can be either a numeric or character variable because the procedure treats this variable symbolically. Each node must be uniquely defined.

HOLIDAY Statement

> HOLIDAY *variable* / HOLIDUR = *variable*
>   HOLIFIN = *variable*;

The HOLIDAY statement specifies the names of variables used to describe non-workdays in a SAS data set. PROC CPM accounts for holidays only when the INTERVAL= option has one of the following values: DAY, WORKDAY, WEEKDAY, DTDAY, DTWRKDAY, DTHOUR, DTMINUTE, or DTSECOND. The HOLIDAY statement must be used with the HOLIDATA= option in the PROC CPM statement. Recall that the HOLIDATA= option identifies the SAS data set that contains a list of the holidays and non-workdays around which you schedule your project. Holidays are defined by specifying the start of the holiday (the HOLIDAY variable) and either the length of the holiday (the HOLIDUR variable) or the finish time of the holiday (the HOLIFIN variable). The HOLIDAY variable is mandatory with the HOLIDAY statement; the HOLIDUR and HOLIFIN variables are optional. The HOLIDAY and the HOLIFIN variables must be formatted as SAS date or datetime variables.

The INTERVAL= option specified on the PROC CPM statement is used to interpret the value of the duration and the holiday duration variables. Thus, if the duration of a holiday is specified as 2 and the INTERVAL= value is WEEKDAY, the length of the holiday is interpreted as two weekdays.

If no format is associated with a HOLIDAY variable, it is assumed to be formatted as a SAS date value. If the schedule of the project is computed as datetime values (which is the case if INTERVAL is DTDAY, WORKDAY, and so on), the holiday variables are interpreted as follows:

- if the HOLIDAY variable is formatted as a date value, then the holiday is assumed to start at the value of DAYSTART on the day specified in the observation and end *d* units of *interval* later (where *d* is the value of the HOLIDUR variable and *interval* is the value of the INTERVAL= option)
- if the HOLIDAY variable is formatted as a datetime value, then the holiday is assumed to start at the date and time specified and end *d* units of *interval* later.

If a particular observation contains both the duration as well as the finish time of the holiday, only the finish time is used; the duration is ignored.

ID Statement

> ID *variables*;

The ID statement identifies variables not specified in the TAILNODE, HEADNODE, ACTIVITY, SUCCESSOR, or DURATION statements that are to be included in the OUT= output data set. This statement is useful to carry any relevant information about each activity from the input data set to the output data set.

RESOURCE Statement

RESOURCE *variables / resource options;*

The RESOURCE statement identifies the variables in the DATA= input data set, which contains the levels of the various resources required by the different activities. This statement is necessary if the procedure is required to summarize resource utilization for various resources.

This statement is also required when the activities in the network use limited resources and a schedule is to be determined subject to resource constraints in addition to precedence constraints. The levels of the various resources available are obtained from the RESOURCEIN= data set, which need not contain all of the variables listed in the RESOURCE statement. If any resource variable specified in the RESOURCE statement is not also found in the RESOURCEIN= data set, it is assumed to be available in unlimited quantity and is not used in determining the constrained schedule.

The options listed below are available with the RESOURCE statement to help control scheduling the activities subject to resource constraints. Some control the scheduling heuristics, some control the amount of information to be output to the RESOURCEOUT data set, and so on.

Resource Allocation Control Options

ACTIVITYPRTY=*variable*
ACTPRTY=*variable*
    required if resource-constrained scheduling is to be performed and the scheduling rule specified is ACTPRTY. This option identifies the variable in the input data set that contains the priority of each activity. If SCHEDRULE=ACTPRTY, then all activities waiting for resources are ordered by increasing values of the ACTPRTY variable. Missing values of the priority variable are treated as +INFINITY.

DELAY=*delay*
    specifies the maximum amount by which an activity can be delayed due to lack of resources. If E_START of an activity is 1JUN88 and L_START is 5JUN88 and DELAY is specified as 2, CPM first tries to schedule the activity to start on 1JUN88. If there are not enough resources to schedule the activity, CPM postpones the activity's start time. However, it does not postpone it beyond 7JUN88 (because DELAY=2 and L_START=5JUN88).
    If the activity cannot be scheduled even on 7JUN88, then CPM tries to schedule it by using supplementary levels of resources, if available. If resources are still not sufficient, the procedure stops with an error message. The default value of DELAY is assumed to be +INFINITY.

INFEASDIAGNOSTIC
    requests PROC CPM to continue scheduling even when resources are insufficient. When PROC CPM schedules the project subject to resource constraints, the scheduling process is stopped when the procedure cannot find sufficient resources for an activity before the activity's latest possible start time (accounting for the DELAY option and using supplementary resources if necessary and if allowed). The INFEASDIAGNOSTIC option can be used to override this default action.

(Sometimes, you may want to know the level of resources needed to schedule a project to completion even if resources are insufficient.) This option is equivalent to specifying infinite supplementary levels for all the resources under consideration; the DELAY= value is assumed to equal the default value of + INFINITY, unless it is specified as otherwise.

OBSTYPE=*variable*

specifies a character variable in the RESOURCEIN= data set that contains the type identifier for each observation. Valid values for this variable are RESLEVEL, RESTYPE, RESPRTY, or SUPLEVEL. If OBSTYPE= is not specified, then all observations in the data set are assumed to denote the levels of the resources, and all resources are assumed to be replenishable.

PERIOD=*variable*

specifies the variable in the RESOURCEIN= data set that specifies the date from which a specified level of the resource is available for each observation containing levels of the resources. It is an error if the PERIOD= variable has a missing value for any observation specifying the levels of the resources or if the RESOURCEIN= data set is not sorted in increasing order of the PERIOD= variable.

SCHEDRULE=*rule*

RULE=*rule*

specifies the rule to be used to order the list of activities whose predecessor activities have been completed while scheduling activities subject to resource constraints. Valid values for *rule* are LST, LFT, SHORTDUR, ACTPRTY, and RESPRTY. (See **Scheduling Rules** in **DETAILS** for more information.) The default value of SCHEDRULE is LST. If a wrong specification is given for the SCHEDRULE= option, the default value is used, and a message is printed on the log to this effect.

Options Controlling Activity Splitting

By default, PROC CPM assumes that any activity, once started, cannot be stopped until it is completed (except for breaks due to holidays or weekends). Thus, even during resource-constrained scheduling, an activity is scheduled only if enough resources can be found for it throughout its *entire* duration. Sometimes, you may want to allow pre-emption of activities already in progress; thus, a more *critical* activity could cause another activity to be split into two or more segments. However, you may not want a particular activity to be split into too many segments, nor may you want an activity to be split too many times. The following three options enable you to control the splitting of activities during resource allocation:

MAXNSEGMT=*variable*

specifies a variable in the activities data set that indicates the maximum number of segments that the current activity can be split into. A missing value for this variable is set to a default value that depends on the duration of the activity and the value of the MINSEGMTDUR variable.

MINSEGMTDUR=*variable*

specifies a variable in the activities data set that indicates the minimum duration of any segment of the current activity. A missing value for this variable is set to a value one fifth of the activity's duration.

SPLITFLAG

indicates that activities are allowed to be split into segments during resource allocation. This option can be used instead of specifying either

the MAXNSEGMT or the MINSEGMTDUR variables; PROC CPM
assumes that the activity can be split into no more than five segments.

Options Controlling RESOURCEOUT= Data Set

ALL

is equivalent to specifying the ESPROFILE and LSPROFILE options when
an unconstrained schedule is obtained and equivalent to specifying all
four options, AVPROFILE (AVP), ESPROFILE (ESP), LSPROFILE (LSP), and
RCPROFILE (RCP), when a resource-constrained schedule is obtained. If
none of these four options are specified and a RESOUT= data set is
specified, by default the ALL option is assumed to be in effect.

AVPROFILE

AVP

AVL

creates one variable in the RESOURCEOUT= data set corresponding to
each variable in the RESOURCE statement. These new variables denote
the amount of resources remaining after resource allocation. This option
is ignored if resource allocation is not done.

ESPROFILE

ESP

ESS

creates one variable in the RESOURCEOUT= data set corresponding to
each variable in the RESOURCE statement. Each new variable denotes
the resource usage based on the early start schedule for the
corresponding resource variable.

LSPROFILE

LSP

LSS

creates one variable in the RESOURCEOUT= data set corresponding to
each variable in the RESOURCE statement. Each new variable denotes
the resource usage based on the late start schedule for the
corresponding resource variable.

MAXDATE=*maxdate*

specifies the maximum value of the _TIME_ variable in the
RESOURCEOUT data set. The default value of *maxdate* is the maximum
finish time for all of the schedules for which a usage profile was
requested.

MAXOBS=*max*

specifies an upper limit on the number of observations that the
RESOURCEOUT= data set can contain. If the values specified for
ROUTINTERVAL= and ROUTINTPER= are such that the data set will
contain more than *max* observations, then CPM does not create the
output data set; it stops with an error message.

   The MAXOBS= option is useful as a check to ensure that a very large
data set (with several thousands of observations) is not created due to a
wrong specification of the ROUTINTERVAL= parameter. For example, if
INTERVAL=DTYEAR and ROUTINTERVAL=DTHOUR and the project
extends over 2 years, the number of observations would exceed 15,000.
The default value of MAXOBS= is 1000.

MINDATE=*mindate*

specifies the minimum value of the _TIME_ variable in the
RESOURCEOUT data set. The default value of *mindate* is the minimum

start time for all of the schedules for which a usage profile was requested.

Thus, the RESOURCEOUT data set has observations containing the resource usage and availability information starting from *mindate* through *maxdate*.

RCPROFILE
RCP
RCS

creates one variable in the RESOURCEOUT= data set corresponding to each variable in the RESOURCE statement. Each new variable denotes the resource usage based on the resource-constrained schedule for the corresponding resource variable. This option is ignored if resource allocation is not done.

ROUTINTERVAL=*routinterval*
STEPINT=*routinterval*

specifies the units to be used to determine the time interval between two successive values of the variable _TIME_ in the RESOURCEOUT= data set. It can be used in conjunction with the ROUTINTPER= option to control the amount of information to be presented in the data set. Valid values for ROUTINTERVAL= are DAY, WORKDAY, WEEK, MONTH, WEEKDAY, QTR, YEAR, DTDAY, DTWRKDAY, DTWEEK, DTMONTH, DTQTR, DTYEAR, DTSECOND, DTMINUTE, DTHOUR, SECOND, MINUTE, or HOUR. The value of this parameter must be chosen carefully; a massive amount of data could be generated by a bad choice. If this parameter is not specified, it is set to be the same as the INTERVAL parameter.

ROUTINTPER=*number*
STEPSIZE=*number*
STEP=*number*

specifies the number of *routinterval* units between successive observations in the RESOURCEOUT= data set when ROUTINTERVAL= *routinterval* is specified. For example, if ROUTINTERVAL=MONTH and ROUTINTPER=2, the time interval between each pair of observations in the RESOURCEOUT= data set is two months. The default value of ROUTINTPER is 1. If the value of ROUTINTERVAL is ' ', then ROUTINTPER can be used to specify the exact numeric interval between two successive values of the variable _TIME_ in the RESOURCEOUT= data set. Note that ROUTINTPER is only allowed to have integer values when *routinterval* is specified as one of the following: WEEK, MONTH, QTR, YEAR, DTWEEK, DTMONTH, DTQTR, or DTYEAR.

Options Controlling OUT= Data Set

NOE_START

requests that the E_START and E_FINISH variables, namely the variables specifying the early start schedule, be dropped from the OUT= data set. Note that if resource allocation is not done, these variables are always included in the output data set.

NOL_START

requests that the OUT= data set does not include the late start schedule, namely, the L_START and L_FINISH variables. Note that if resource allocation is not done, these variables are always included in the output data set.

NORESOURCEVARS
NORESVARSOUT
NORESVARS

requests that the variables specified in the RESOURCE statement be dropped from the OUT= data set. By default all of the resource variables specified on the RESOURCE statement are also included in the output data set.

SUCCESSOR Statement

SUCCESSOR *variables* / LAG =(variables);

The SUCCESSOR statement is required when data are input in an Activity-On-Node format. This statement specifies the variables that contain the names of the immediate successor nodes (activities) to the ACTIVITY node. These variables must be of the same type and length as those defined in the ACTIVITY statement.

If the precedence constraints among the activities have some nonstandard relationships, you can specify these using the LAG= option. The LAG variables must be character type variables. You can specify as many LAG variables as there are SUCCESSOR variables; each SUCCESSOR variable is matched with the corresponding LAG variable. You must specify the LAG variables enclosed in parentheses. In a given observation, the *i*th LAG variable specifies the type of relation between the current activity (as specified by the ACTIVITY variable) and the activity specified by the *i*th SUCCESSOR variable. In addition to the type of relation, you can also specify any lag between the two activities in the same variable. The relation_lag information is expected to be specified as:

keyword_duration

where *keyword* is ' ', FS, SS, SF, or FF, and *duration* is a number specifying the duration of the lag (in interval units). A value of ' ' for the keyword is assumed to mean the same as FS, which is the standard relation of *finish-to-start*. The other three keywords, SS, SF, and FF, denote relations of the type *start-to-start*, *start-to-finish*, and *finish-to-finish*, respectively. If there are no LAG variables, all relationships are assumed to be of the type *finish-to-start* with no lag duration. Note that the LAG variables are matched one-to-one with the SUCCESSOR variables. If there are more LAG variables than SUCCESSOR variables, the extra LAG variables are ignored; conversely, if there are fewer LAG variables, the extra SUCCESSOR variables are all assumed to indicate successors with a *normal* (finish-to-start) relationship. Below are some examples of lag specifications:

Activity	SUCCESSR	LAG	Interpretation
A	B	SS_3	Start to start lag of 3 units
A	B	_5.5	Finish to start lag of 5.5 units
A	B	FF_4	Finish to finish lag of 4 units
A	B	_SS	Invalid and ignored (with warning)
A		SS_3	Ignored

The statement used in an invocation of PROC CPM with the above data is

SUCCESSOR *SUCCESSR*/**LAG=** (lag);

TAILNODE Statement

TAILNODE *variable*;

or

FROM *variable*;

The TAILNODE statement is required when data are input in Activity-On-Arc (arrow notation) format. It specifies the variable that contains the name of each node on the tail of an arc in the project network. This node is identified with the event that signals the *start* of the activity on that arc. The variable specified can be either a numeric or character variable since the procedure treats this variable symbolically. Each node must be uniquely defined.

DETAILS

Introduction

This section provides a detailed outline of the use of the procedure. The material is organized in subsections that describe different aspects of the procedure. They have been placed in increasing order of functionality. The first section describes how to use PROC CPM to schedule a project subject only to precedence constraints. Succeeding sections describe some of the features that enable you to control the units of duration and specify nonstandard precedence constraints. Next, the statements needed to place time constraints on the activities are introduced. The next section describes the format of the output data set. The **Multiple Calendars** section deals with an advanced topic that may not be of much interest unless you wish to use complicated calendar specifications for the different activities.

The **Progress Updating** section describes how to incorporate the actual start and finish times for a project that is already in progress. The next section pertains to resource usage and resource-constrained scheduling and describes how to specify information about the resources and the resource requirements for the activities. The scheduling algorithm is also described in this section, and some advanced features are discussed under separate subsections. The **RESOURCEOUT= Data Set** section describes the format of the resource usage output data set and explains how to interpret the variables in it.

PROC CPM also defines a macro variable that is described in the **Macro Variable _ORCPM_** section. Finally, a table in the **Missing Values in Input Data Sets** section lists all of the variables in the different input data sets and describes how PROC CPM treats missing values corresponding to each of them.

Scheduling Subject to Precedence Constraints

The basic function of PROC CPM is to determine a schedule of the activities in a project, subject to precedence constraints among the activities. The minimum amount of information that is required for a successful invocation of PROC CPM is the network information specified either in AON or AOA formats and the duration of each activity in the network. The INTERVAL parameter specifies the units of duration and the DATE parameter specifies a start date for the project. If a start date is not specified for the project, the schedule is computed as pure numbers with a project start date of zero. The DATE parameter can be a SAS date, time, or datetime value and can be used to specify a start date or a finish date for the project. Recall that the FINISHBEFORE option causes the DATE parameter to be interpreted as a finish time for the project.

PROC CPM computes an early start schedule as well as a late start schedule of the project. The early start time (E_START) for all *start* activities (those activities with no predecessors) in the project is set to be equal to the value of the DATE parameter (if there is no FINISHBEFORE option). The early finish time (E_FINISH) for each start activity is computed as E_START + DUR, where DUR is the activity's duration. For each of the other activities in the network, the early start time is computed as the maximum of the early finish time of all its immediate predecessors. The project finish time is equal to the value of the DATE parameter if a FINISHBEFORE option was specified; otherwise, it is computed as the maximum of the early finish time of all the *finish* activities (those activities with no successors) in the network. The late finish (L_FINISH) time for all the finish activities in the project is set to be equal to the project finish time. The late start (L_START) time is computed as L_FINISH−DUR. For each of the other activities in the network, the late finish time is computed as the minimum of the late start time of all its immediate successors.

Once the early and late start schedules have been computed, the procedure computes the free and total float times for each activity. Free float is defined as the maximum delay that can be allowed in an activity without delaying a successor activity; total float is the difference between the activity's late finish time and early finish time.

Using the INTERVAL= Option

The INTERVAL= option enables you to define the units of the DURATION variable; that is, you can indicate whether the durations are specified as hours, minutes, days, or in terms of workdays, and so on. In addition to specifying the units, the INTERVAL option also indicates whether the schedule is to be output as SAS time, date, or datetime values, or as unformatted numeric values. The prefix *DT* in the value of the INTERVAL parameter (as in DTDAY, DTWEEK, and so on) indicates to PROC CPM that the schedule is output as SAS datetime values and the DATE parameter is expected to be a SAS datetime value. Thus, use DTYEAR, DTMONTH, DTQTR, or DTWEEK instead of the corresponding YEAR, MONTH, QTR, or WEEK if DATE is specified as a SAS datetime value.

The start and finish times for the different schedules computed by PROC CPM denote the first and last *day* of work, respectively, when the values are formatted as SAS *date* values. If the times are SAS *time* or *datetime* values, they denote the first and last *second* of work, respectively.

If INTERVAL is specified as WORKDAY, the procedure schedules work on weekdays and non-holidays starting at 9 a.m. and ending at 5 p.m. If you use INTERVAL=DTWRKDAY, the procedure also schedules work only on weekdays and non-holidays. In this case, however, the procedure assumes the DATE= option is a SAS datetime value, and the procedure interprets the start of the workday from the time portion of that option. To change the length of the workday, use the DAYLENGTH= option in conjunction with INTERVAL=DTWRKDAY.

Table 5.4 lists various valid combinations of the INTERVAL parameter and the type of the DATE parameter (number, SAS time, date or datetime value) and the resulting interpretation of the duration units and the format type of the schedule variables (numbers, SAS time, date or datetime) output to the OUT= data set.

Table 5.4 PROC CPM INTERVAL and DATE Parameters and Units of Duration

DATE Type	INTERVAL	Units of Duration	Format of Schedule Variables
number		period	unformatted
SAS time	HOUR	hour	SAS time
	MINUTE	minute	SAS time
	SECOND	second	SAS time
SAS date	DAY	day	SAS date
	WEEKDAY	day (5-day week)	SAS date
	WORKDAY	day (5-day week: 9-5 day)	SAS datetime
	WEEK	week	SAS date
	MONTH	month	SAS date
	QTR	qtr	SAS date
	YEAR	year	SAS date
SAS datetime	DTSECOND	second	SAS datetime
	DTMINUTE	minute	SAS datetime
	DTHOUR	hour	SAS datetime
	DTDAY	day (7-day week)	SAS datetime
	DTWRKDAY	day (5-day week)	SAS datetime
	DTWEEK	week	SAS datetime
	DTMONTH	month	SAS datetime
	DTQTR	qtr	SAS datetime
	DTYEAR	year	SAS datetime

Note: for the first five specifications of the INTERVAL parameter in the last section (DTSECOND, . . . , DTWRKDAY), day starts at DAYSTART and is DAYLENGTH hours long.

Nonstandard Precedence Relationships

A *standard* precedence constraint between two activities (for example, activity A and an immediate successor B) implies that the second activity is ready to start as soon as the first activity has finished. Such a relationship is called a *finish-to-start* relationship with a time lapse of zero. Often, you may want to allow other types of relationships between activities, for example,

- activity B can start five days after activity A has started: start-to-start lag of five days
- activity B can start three days after activity A has finished: finish-to-start lag of three days.

The AON representation of the network allows you to specify such relationships between activities: use the LAG= option in the SUCCESSOR statement. This allows you to use variables in the activities data set that specify the type of relationship between two activities and the time lag between the two events involved. See the **SUCCESSOR Statement** section earlier in this chapter for information on the specification. **Example 5: Nonstandard Relationships** in the **EXAMPLES** section uses a nonstandard precedence relationship.

This section briefly describes how nonstandard relationships are treated internally by PROC CPM. Any nonstandard precedence constraint is handled by introducing dummy activities between the two relevant activities. Suppose A is the preceding activity and B is its immediate successor, lag is the duration of the lag, and dur(A) and dur(B) are the durations of A and B, respectively. The duration of the dummy activity is calculated as follows for the four different cases:

LAG Type	Definition	Duration of Dummy Activity
FS	finish-to-start	lag
SS	start-to-start	lag − dur(A)
SF	start-to-finish	lag − dur(A) − dur(B)
FF	finish-to-finish	lag − dur(B)

Note that the dummy activity is assumed to follow the default calendar (see **Multiple Calendars** in the **DETAILS** section for a definition of the default calendar).

Time-Constrained Scheduling

You can use the DATE= parameter in the PROC CPM statement and the FINISHBEFORE option to impose start or finish dates on the project as a whole. Often, you may wish to impose start or finish constraints on individual activities within the project. The ALIGNDATE and ALIGNTYPE statements allow you to do so. For each activity in the project, you can specify a particular date (as the value of the ALIGNDATE variable) and whether you want the activity to start on or finish before that date (by specifying one of several *alignment types* as the value of the ALIGNTYPE variable). PROC CPM uses all these dates in the computation of the early and late start schedules.

The following explanation best illustrates the restrictions imposed on the start or finish times of an activity by the different types of alignment allowed. Let D denote the value of the ALIGNDATE variable for a particular activity and let DUR be its duration. If MINSDATE and MAXFDATE are used to denote the earliest allowed start date and the latest allowed finish date, respectively, for the activity, then **Table 5.5** illustrates the values of MINSDATE and MAXFDATE as a function of the value of the ALIGNTYPE variable.

Table 5.5 Determining Alignment Date Values with the ALIGNTYPE
Statement in PROC CPM

Keywords	Aligntype	MINSDATE	MAXFDATE
SEQ	start equal	D	D + DUR
SGE	start greater than or equal	D	+ INFINITY
SLE	start less than or equal	− INFINITY	D + DUR

(continued)

Table 5.5   (*continued*)

Keywords	Aligntype	MINSDATE	MAXFDATE
FEQ	finish equal	D − DUR	D
FGE	finish greater than or equal	D − DUR	+ INFINITY
FLE	finish less than or equal	− INFINITY	D
MS	mandatory start	D	D + DUR
MF	mandatory finish	D − DUR	D

Once the above dates have been calculated for all of the activities in the project, the values of MINSDATE are used in the computation of the early start schedule and the values of MAXFDATE are used in the computation of the late start schedule.

For the first six alignment types, the value of MINSDATE specifies a lower bound on the early start time and the value of MAXFDATE specifies an upper bound on the late finish time of the activity. The early start time (E_START) of an activity is computed as the maximum of its MINSDATE and the early finish times (E_FINISH) of all its predecessors (E_FINISH = E_START + DUR). If a target completion date is not specified (using the FINISHBEFORE option), the project completion time is determined as the maximum value of E_FINISH over all of the activities in the project. The late finish time (L_FINISH) for each of the finish activities (those with no successors) is computed as the minimum of its MAXFDATE and the project completion date; late start time (L_START) is computed as L_FINISH − DUR. L_FINISH for each of the other activities in the network is computed as the minimum of its MAXFDATE and the L_START times of all its successors.

Note that the precedence constraints of the network are always respected. Thus, it is possible that an activity that has an alignment constraint of the type SEQ, constraining it to start on a particular date, say D, may not start on the specified date D due to its predecessors not being finished before D. During resource-constrained scheduling, a further slippage in the start date could occur due to insufficient resources. In other words, the precedence constraints and resource constraints have priority over the time constraints (as imposed by the ALIGNDATE and ALIGNTYPE statements) in the determination of the schedule of the activities in the network.

The last two alignment types, MS and MF, however, specify *mandatory dates* for the start and finish times of the activities for both the early and late start schedules. These alignment types can be used to schedule activities to start or finish on a given date disregarding precedence and resource constraints. Thus, an activity with the ALIGNTYPE variable's value equal to MS and the ALIGNDATE variable's value equal to D is scheduled to start on D (for the early, late, as well as the resource-constrained schedules) irrespective of whether its predecessors are finished or not or whether there are enough resources or not.

Note that it is possible for the L_START time of an activity to be less than its E_START time if there are constraints on the start times of certain activities in the network that make the target completion date (or constraints on the finish times of some successor activities) infeasible. In such cases, some of the activities in the network have negative values for T_FLOAT, indicating that these activities are super-critical. See **Example 10:   Time Constraints** for a demonstration of this situation.

OUT= Output Data Set

The output data set always contains the variables in the input data set that are listed in the TAILNODE, HEADNODE, ACTIVITY, SUCCESSOR, DURATION, or ID statements. If the INTPER= option is specified in the PROC CPM statement, then the values of the DURATION variable in the output data set are obtained by multiplying the corresponding values in the input data set by INTPER. Thus, the values in the output data set are the durations used by PROC CPM to compute the schedule. If the procedure was used without specifying a RESOURCEIN= data set and only the unconstrained schedule was obtained, then the output data set contains six new variables named E_START, L_START, E_FINISH, L_FINISH, T_FLOAT, and F_FLOAT.

If a resource-constrained schedule was obtained, however, the output data set contains two new variables named S_START and S_FINISH; the T_FLOAT and F_FLOAT variables are omitted. You can request the omission of the E_START and E_FINISH variables by specifying NOE_START and the omission of the L_START and L_FINISH variables by specifying NOL_START in the RESOURCE statement. The variables listed in the RESOURCE statement are also included in the output data set; to omit them, use the NORESOURCEVARS option in the RESOURCE statement.

If an ACTUAL statement was specified, the output data set contains four more new variables: A_START, A_FINISH, A_DUR, and STATUS. The format of the schedule variables in this data set (namely, E_START, E_FINISH, L_START, and so on) is consistent with the format of the DATE= option in the PROC CPM statement.

Definitions of Variables in the OUT= Data Set

Each observation in the output data set is associated with an activity with the variables having the following meanings:

A_DUR
   the actual duration of the activity. This value is missing unless the activity is completed and may be different from the duration of the activity, as specified by the DURATION variable. It is based on the values of the progress variables. See **Progress Updating** for further details.

A_FINISH
   the actual finish time of the activity, either as specified in the input data set or as computed by PROC CPM on the basis of the progress variables specified.

A_START
   the actual start time of the activity, either as specified in the input data set or as computed by PROC CPM on the basis of the progress variables specified.

E_FINISH
   the completion time if the activity is started at the early start time.

E_START
   the earliest time the activity can be started. This is the maximum of the maximum early finish time of all predecessor activities and any lower

bound placed on the start time of this activity by the alignment constraints.

F_FLOAT

the free float time, which is the difference between the early finish time of the activity and the early start time of the activity's immediate successors. Consequently, it is the maximum delay that can be tolerated in the activity without affecting the scheduling of a successor activity.

L_FINISH

the latest completion time of the activity. This is the minimum of the minimum late start time of any successor activities and any upper bound placed on the finish time of the activity by the alignment constraints.

L_START

the latest time the activity can be started. This is computed from the activity's latest finish time.

S_FINISH

the completion time for the activity under the resource-constrained schedule.

S_START

the resource-constrained start time of the activity.

STATUS

the current status of the activity. This is a character valued variable. Possible values for the status of an activity are *pending, in progress,* or *completed*; the meanings are self-evident. If the project is scheduled subject to resource constraints, activities that are *pending* are classified as *pending* or *infeasible* depending on whether or not PROC CPM was able to determine a resource-constrained schedule for the activity.

T_FLOAT

the total float time, which is the difference between the activity late finish time and early finish time. Consequently, it is the maximum delay that can be tolerated in performing the activity and still complete the project on schedule. If the activity is on the critical path, then T_FLOAT=0.

If activity splitting is allowed during resource-constrained scheduling, the output data set may contain more than one observation corresponding to each observation in the activities data set. It will also contain new variables that are explained in the **Activity Splitting** section.

Multiple Calendars

Work pertaining to a given activity is assumed to be done according to a particular *calendar*. A calendar is defined here in terms of a work pattern for each day and a work week structure for each week. In addition, each calendar may have holidays during a given year.

PROC CPM allows you to define very general calendars using the WORKDATA, CALEDATA, and HOLIDATA data sets and options in the PROC CPM statement. The WORKDATA (or workdays) data set specifies distinct shift patterns during a day. The CALEDATA (or calendar) data set specifies a typical work week for any given calendar; for each day of a typical week, it specifies the shift pattern that is followed. The HOLIDATA (or holidays) data set specifies a list of holidays and the calendars that they refer to; holidays are defined either by specifying the start of the holiday and its duration in INTERVAL units or by specifying the start and end of the holiday period. The activities data set (the DATA= input data set) then specifies the calendar that is used by each activity in the project through the CALID variable (or a default variable _CAL_). Each of the three data sets used to define calendars is described in greater detail later in this section.

Each new value for the CALID variable in either the CALEDATA data set or the HOLIDATA data set defines a new calendar. If a calendar value appears on the CALEDATA data set and not on the HOLIDATA data set, it is assumed to have the same holidays as the default calendar (the default calendar is defined below). If a calendar value appears on the HOLIDATA data set and not on the CALEDATA data set, it is assumed to have the same work pattern structures (for each week and within each day) as the default calendar. In the activities data set, valid values for the CALID variable are those that are already defined in either the CALEDATA data set or the HOLIDATA data set.

Cautions

The HOLIDATA, CALEDATA, and WORKDATA data sets and the processing of holidays and different calendars are supported only when the INTERVAL parameter is DAY, WEEKDAY, DTDAY, WORKDAY, DTWRKDAY, DTHOUR, DTMINUTE, or DTSECOND. PROC CPM uses default specifications whenever some information required to define a calendar is missing or invalid. The defaults have been chosen to allow for consistency among different types of specifications and to correct for errors in input, while maintaining compatibility with earlier versions of PROC CPM. You get a wide range of control over the calendar specifications, from letting PROC CPM define a single calendar entirely from defaults, to defining several calendars of your choice with precisely defined work patterns for each day of the week and for each week. If the CALEDATA, WORKDATA and HOLIDATA data sets are used along with multiple calendar specifications, it is important to remember how all of the data sets and the various options interact to form the work patterns for the different calendars.

Default Calendar

The default calendar is a special calendar that is defined by PROC CPM; its definition and uses are explained in this subsection.

If there is no CALID variable and no CALEDATA or WORKDATA data sets, the default calendar is defined by the INTERVAL and the DAYSTART and DAYLENGTH parameters on the PROC CPM statement. If INTERVAL is DAY, DTDAY, DTHOUR, DTMINUTE or DTSECOND, work is done on all seven days of the week; otherwise, Saturday and Sunday are considered to be nonworking days. Further, if the schedule is computed as SAS datetime values, the length of the working day is determined by the values of the DAYSTART and DAYLENGTH parameters. All of the holidays specified in the HOLIDATA data set refer to this default calendar, and all of the activities in the project follow it. Thus, if there is no CALID variable, the default calendar is the only calendar that is used for all of the activities in the project.

If there is a CALID variable that identifies distinct calendars, you can use an observation in the CALEDATA data set to define the work week structure for the default calendar. Use the value 0 (if CALID is a numeric variable) or the value DEFAULT (if CALID is a character variable) to identify the default calendar. In the absence of such an observation, the default calendar is defined by the INTERVAL, DAYSTART, and DAYLENGTH parameters, as before. The default calendar is used to substitute default work patterns for missing values in the calendar data set or to set default work week structures for newly defined calendars in the HOLIDAYS data set.

WORKDATA Data Set

All numeric variables in the data set are assumed to denote unique shift patterns during one working day. For each variable the observations specify, alternately, the times when consecutive shifts start and end. Suppose S1, S2, and S3 are numeric variables formatted as TIME6. Consider the following data:

S1	S2	S3	
7:00	.	7:00	(start)
11:00	08:00	11:00	(end)
12:00	.	.	(start)
16:00	.	.	(end)

The above data set defines three different work patterns. A missing value in the first observation is assumed to be 0 (or 12:00 a.m.); a missing value in any other observation is assumed to denote 24:00. Thus, the workday in S1 starts at 7:00 a.m. and continues until 4:00 p.m. with an hour off for lunch from 11:00 a.m. until 12:00 p.m. S2 defines a workday from 12:00 a.m. to 8:00 a.m., and S3 defines a workday from 7:00 a.m. to 11:00 a.m. The last two values for the variables S2 and S3 (both values are 24:00) are effectively ignored.

This data set can be used to define all of the unique shift patterns that occur in any of the calendars in the project. These shift patterns are tied to the different calendars in which they occur using the CALEDATA data set.

CALEDATA Data Set

This data set defines specific calendars using the names of the shift variables in the WORKDATA data set. Use the variable specified in the CALID statement or a variable named _CAL_ to give the calendar name or number. Character variables named _SUN_, _MON_, _TUE_, _WED_, _THU_, _FRI_, and _SAT_ are used to indicate the work pattern that is followed on each day of the week. Valid values for these variables are any shift variable name defined in the WORKDATA data set, HOLIDAY, or WORKDAY.

Note: a missing value for any of these variables is assumed to denote that the work pattern for the corresponding day is the same as for the default calendar.

When the INTERVAL parameter is specified as DTDAY, WORKDAY, or DTWRKDAY, it is necessary to know the length of a *standard* working day in order to be able to compute the schedules consistently. For example, a given calendar may have an eight-hour day on Monday, Tuesday, and Wednesday and a seven-hour day on Thursday and Friday. If a given activity following that calendar has a duration of four days, does it mean that its duration is equal to 8*4 = 32 hours or 7*4 = 28 hours? To avoid ambiguity, a numeric variable named D_LENGTH can be specified in the CALEDATA data set to define the length of a standard working day for the specified calendar. If this variable is not found in the CALEDATA data set, all calendars for the project are assumed to have a standard daylength as defined by the default calendar.

For example, consider the following data:

CAL	_SUN_	_MON_	_TUE_	_FRI_	_SAT_	D_LENGTH
1	HOLIDAY	S1	S1	S2	S3	8:00
2	HOLIDAY	.	.	.	HOLIDAY	.

The above data define two calendars, 1 and 2. The values S1, S2, and S3 refer to the shift variables defined above. Activities in the project can follow either of these two calendars or the default calendar.

Suppose the DAYSTART parameter has been specified as 9:00 a.m. and the DAYLENGTH parameter is eight hours. Further, suppose that INTERVAL=DTDAY. Using these parameter specifications, PROC CPM defines the default calendar as having a seven-day week with each day being an eight-hour day (from 9:00 a.m. to 5:00 p.m.). Recall that the default calendar is defined to have seven or five working days depending on whether INTERVAL is DTDAY or WORKDAY, respectively. For calendar 1, work on Monday and Tuesday is done from 7:00 a.m. to 11:00 a.m. and then from 12:00 p.m. to 4:00 p.m., work on Friday is from 12:00 a.m. to 8:00 a.m., work on Saturday is from 7:00 a.m. to 11:00 a.m., and Sunday is a holiday; on other days work is from 9:00 a.m. to 5:00 p.m., as defined by the default calendar. The D_LENGTH value specifies the number of hours in a standard work day; when durations of activities are specified in terms of number of workdays, then the D_LENGTH value is used as a multiplier to convert workdays to the appropriate number of hours. Calendar 2 has holidays on Saturday and Sunday, and on the remaining days, it follows the standard working day as defined by the default calendar.

If there are multiple observations in the CALENDAR data set identifying the same calendar, all except the first occurrence are ignored. The value 0 (if CALID is a numeric variable) or the value DEFAULT (if CALID is a character variable) refers to the default calendar. So the same data set can be used to define the default calendar also.

Note: a missing value for the CALID variable is assumed to refer to the default calendar.

HOLIDATA Data Set

This data set defines holidays for the different calendars that may be used in the project. Holidays are specified by using the HOLIDAY statement. See the **HOLIDAY Statement** earlier in this chapter for a description of the syntax. This data set must contain a variable (the HOLIDAY variable) whose values specify the start of each holiday. Optionally, the data set may also contain a variable (the HOLIDUR variable) used to specify the length of each holiday or another variable (the HOLIFIN variable) specifying the finish time of each holiday. The variable specified by the CALID statement (or a variable named _CAL_) can be used in this data set to identify the calendar that each holiday refers to. A missing value for the HOLIDAY variable in an observation causes that observation to be ignored. If both the HOLIDUR and the HOLIFIN variables have missing values in a given observation, the holiday is assumed to start at the date/time specified for the HOLIDAY variable and last one unit of *interval* where the INTERVAL option has been specified as *interval*. If a given observation has valid values for both the HOLIDUR and the HOLIFIN variables, only the HOLIFIN variable is used so that the holiday is assumed to start and end as specified by the HOLIDAY and HOLIFIN variables, respectively. A missing value for the CALID variable causes the holiday to be included in all of the calendars, including the default.

The HOLIDUR variable is a natural way of expressing vacation times as *n workdays*, and the HOLIFIN variable is more useful for defining standard holiday periods, such as the CHRISTMAS holiday from 23DEC87 to 25DEC87 (both days inclusive). Note that the HOLIDUR variable is assumed to be in units of the INTERVAL parameter and also refers to the particular work pattern structure for the given calendar.

For example, consider the following data:

HOLISTA	HOLIDUR	HOLIFIN	_CAL_
23DEC87	.	25DEC87	.
01JAN88	1	.	1

18JAN88	.	.	2
28JAN88	3	.	2
28JAN88	3	.	3

Suppose calendars 1 and 2 and the default calendar have been defined as described earlier in the description of the CALEDATA and WORKDATA data sets. Recall that in this example INTERVAL=DTDAY, DAYSTART='09:00'T, and DAYLENGTH='08:00'T. Because the schedule is computed as SAS datetime values, the holiday values (specified here as SAS date values) are converted to SAS datetime values. The HOLIDATA data set, given above, defines a new calendar, calendar 3, which follows the same work pattern as the default calendar. The first observation has a missing value for _CAL_ and, hence, the holiday in this observation pertains to all the calendars. As defined by the above data, the holiday lists for the different calendars are as follows:

CALENDAR	HOLISTART	HOLIEND
0	23DEC87:09:00	25DEC87:17:00
1	23DEC87:09:00	25DEC87:08:00
	01JAN88:00:00	01JAN88:08:00
2	23DEC87:09:00	25DEC87:17:00
	18JAN88:09:00	18JAN88:17:00
	28JAN88:09:00	01FEB88:17:00
3	23DEC87:09:00	25DEC87:17:00
	28JAN88:09:00	30JAN88:17:00

Note that, even though both calendars 2 and 3 have the same specifications for HOLISTA and HOLIDUR, the actual holiday periods are different for the two calendars. For calendar 2, the three days starting from Thursday, January 28, imply that the holidays are on Thursday, Friday, and Monday (because Saturday and Sunday are already holidays). For calendar 3 (all seven days are working days), the holidays are on Thursday, Friday, and Saturday.

Progress Updating

Once a project has been defined with all of its activities and their relationships, the durations, the resources needed, and so on, it is often useful to periodically monitor its progress. During resource-constrained scheduling, it is useful to schedule only activities that are in the future, taking into consideration the activities that have already been completed or scheduled and the resources that have already been used by them or allotted for them. The ACTUAL statement is used in PROC CPM to convey information about the current status of a project. As information about the activities becomes available, it can be incorporated into the schedule of the project through the specification of the actual start or finish times or both, the duration that is still remaining for the activity, or the percentage of work that has been completed on an activity. The specification of the progress variables and the options on the ACTUAL statement have been described earlier in this chapter. This section describes how the options work together and how some default values are determined.

The options that are discussed together in this section are

- the TIMENOW parameter
- the AUTOUPDT and NOAUTOUPDT options
- the TIMENOWSPLT option
- the progress variables (A_START, A_FINISH, REMDUR, and PCTCOMP variables).

The TIMENOW parameter is specified in the ACTUAL statement. This parameter is used as a reference point to resolve the values of the remaining duration and percent completion times. All actual start and finish times specified are checked to ensure that they are less than TIMENOW. If there is some inconsistency, a warning message is issued to the log.

If the ACTUAL statement is used, at least one of the four progress variables must be specified. PROC CPM uses the nonmissing values for the progress variables in any given observation to determine the information that is to be used for the activity. It is possible that there are some inconsistencies in the specification of the values relating to the progress information. For example, an activity may have valid values for both the A_START and the A_FINISH variables and also have the value of the PCTCOMP variable to be less than 100. PROC CPM looks at the values in a specific order, resolving inconsistencies in a reasonable manner. Further, PROC CPM determines revised estimates of the durations of the activities on the basis of the actual and progress information.

Suppose that for a given activity, AS is the actual start, AF is the actual finish, REMDUR is the remaining duration, PCTC is the percent complete, and DURN is the duration of the activity as specified by the values of the corresponding variables in the activities data set. (If a particular variable is not specified, assume that the corresponding value is missing.) The *elapsed duration* of an activity in progress is the time lapse between its actual start and TIMENOW. Recall that the output data set contains new variables called A_START, A_FINISH, and A_DUR. Below is a list of some of the conventions followed by PROC CPM.

- If both AS and AF are specified, the revised duration is computed as the time lapse between AS and AF; in the output data set, the variable A_DUR is also set to this value; A_START is set to AS and A_FINISH to AF.
- If AS is specified without AF, PROC CPM uses REMDUR to compute the revised duration as the sum of the elapsed duration and the remaining duration.
- If AS is specified and both AF and REMDUR are missing, the revised duration is computed on the basis of the elapsed duration and PCTC.
- If AS is given and none of AF, REMDUR and PCTC is specified, the duration is not revised. If the time lapse between AS and TIMENOW is greater than or equal to the duration of the activity, it is assumed to have finished at the appropriate time (AS+DURN) and the output data set has the appropriate values for A_START, A_FINISH and A_DUR.
- If AS is missing and AF is valid, PROC CPM determines AS on the basis of AF and the specified duration. (REMDUR and PCT, if specified, are ignored.)
- If AS and AF are both missing, the revised duration is determined on the basis of REMDUR and PCTC. If the activity has started (if PCTC>0), AS is set appropriately, and if it has also finished (which is the case if PCTC=100), AF is also set.

Using the above rules, PROC CPM attempts to determine actual start and finish times for as many activities as possible using the information given for each activity. The next question is: what about activities that have missing values for the actual start and finish times? Suppose a given activity has a valid value for A_START and is currently in progress. It seems logical for successors of this activity to have missing values for A_START. But how about predecessors of the activity? If they have missing values for A_START and A_FINISH, does it mean that there was an error in the input of the actual dates or an error in the precedence constraints? The options AUTOUPDT and NOAUTOUPDT allow you to control the answer to this question. AUTOUPDT instructs CPM to automatically fill in appropriate A_START and A_FINISH values for all activities that precede already started activities. NOAUTOUPDT implies that only those activities are to be assumed to be in progress or completed that have explicit progress information confirming their status; all other activities have an implicit start date that is greater than or equal to TIMENOW. The default option is AUTOUPDT.

The scheduling algorithm treats the actual start and finish times as follows:

- If A_START is not missing, during the forward pass the E_START time is set equal to A_START and the E_FINISH time is set to E_START+the revised duration.
- If A_START is missing, the E_START time is computed as before.
- If A_FINISH is not missing, in the backward pass the L_FINISH time is set equal to A_FINISH and the L_START time is computed on the basis of L_FINISH and the revised duration.
- If E_START is less than TIMENOW in an activity, the activity is scheduled during resource allocation even if there are not enough resources (a warning message is issued to the log if this is the case). Thus, resource allocation is done only for the period starting from TIMENOW.
- If resource-constrained scheduling is being performed, the TIMENOWSPLT option can be used. This option affects those activities that are currently in progress that cause resource infeasibilities. The TIMENOWSPLT option causes such activities to be split at TIMENOW into segments; the first segment is assumed to be complete before TIMENOW, and the second segment is delayed until sufficient resources are freed.

The output data set contains the actual start times for all activities that are in progress or completed and the actual finish and duration times for all those activities that are completed. Some of these values may have been derived from the percent completion or remaining duration times in the activities data set or may have been implicitly determined through the AUTOUPDT option. Also included in the output data set is a variable named STATUS describing the status of each activity. The possibilities are *completed*, *in progress*, or *pending*.

Resource Usage/Allocation

Often the activities in a project use several resources. If you assume that these resources are available in unlimited quantities, then the only restrictions on the start and finish times of the activities in the project are those imposed by precedence constraints and dates specified for alignment of the activities. In most practical situations, however, there are limitations on the availability of resources; as a result, neither the early start schedule nor the late start schedule (nor any intermediate schedule for that matter) may be feasible. In such cases, the project manager is faced with the task of scheduling the activities in the project subject to constraints on resource availability, in addition to precedence constraints and constraints on the start and finish times of certain activities in the project. This problem is known as *resource allocation*.

You can use PROC CPM to schedule the activities in a project subject to resource constraints. To perform resource allocation, you must specify the resource requirements for each activity in the project and also specify the amount of resources available on each day under consideration. The resource requirements are specified in the activities data set, with the variable names identified to PROC CPM through the RESOURCE statement. The levels of resources available on different dates, as well as other information regarding the resources, such as the type of resource, the priority of the resource, and so forth, are obtained from the RESOURCEIN= data set.

Specifying resource requirements is described in detail in **Specification of Resource Requirements**, and the description of the format of the RESOURCEIN= data set is given in **RESOURCEIN= Input Data Set**. **Scheduling Method** describes how you can use the SCHEDRULE= and DELAY= options in conjunction with certain special observations in the RESOURCEIN= data set to control the process of resource allocation to suit your needs.

RESOURCEIN= Input Data Set

This data set contains all of the necessary information about the resources that are to be used by PROC CPM to schedule the project. Typically, the RESOURCEIN= data set contains the resource variables (numeric), a type identifier variable (character) that identifies the type of information in each observation, and a period variable (numeric and usually a SAS time, date, or datetime variable). The value of the type identifier variable in each observation tells CPM how to interpret that observation. Valid values for this variable are RESLEVEL, RESTYPE, RESPRTY, and SUPLEVEL. If the value of the type identifier variable in a particular observation is RESLEVEL, then that observation contains the levels available for each resource from the time specified in the period variable. Missing values are not allowed for the period variable in an observation containing the levels of the resources.

Each resource can be classified as either consumable or replenishable. A consumable resource is one that is used up by the job (such as bricks or money), while a replenishable resource becomes available again once a job using it is over (such as manpower or machinery). If the value of the type identifier variable is RESTYPE, then that observation identifies the nature (consumable or replenishable) of the resource. The observation contains a value 1 for a replenishable resource and a value 2 for a consumable one. A missing value in this observation is treated as 1. In fact, if there is no observation in the RESOURCEIN= data set with the type identifier variable equal to RESTYPE, then all resources are assumed to be replenishable.

One of the scheduling rules that can be specified in the SCHEDRULE= option is RESPRTY, which requires ordering the resources according to some priority (details are given in **Scheduling Rules**). If this option is used, there must be an observation in the RESOURCEIN= data set with the type identifier variable taking the value RESPRTY. This observation specifies the ordering of the resources.

If the type identifier variable is given as SUPLEVEL, the observation denotes the amount of extra resource that is available for use throughout the duration of the project. This extra resource is used only if the activity cannot be scheduled without delaying it beyond its late start time. See **Secondary Levels of Resources** for details about the use of supplementary levels of resources.

The period variable must have nonmissing values for observations specifying the levels of the resources (that is, with type identifier equal to RESLEVEL). However, the period variable does not have any meaning when the type identifier variable has values RESTYPE, RESPRTY, or SUPLEVEL; if the period variable has nonmissing values in these observations, it is ignored. It is assumed that the data set is sorted in order of increasing values of the period variable. Specify only one observation of each of the types RESTYPE, RESPRTY, and SUPLEVEL.

A resource is available at the specified level from the time given in the first observation with a nonmissing value for the level of the resource. Its level changes to a new one whenever a new observation is encountered with a nonmissing value of level for this resource, and the date of change to this new level is the date specified in this new observation.

The following example illustrates the details about the RESOURCEIN= data set. Consider the following data:

OBSTYPE	DATE	WORKERS	BRICKS
RESTYPE	.	1	2
RESPRTY	.	10	10
SUPLEVEL	.	1	.
RESLEVEL	1JUL88	.	1000
RESLEVEL	5JUL88	4	.
RESLEVEL	9JUL88	.	1500

In this example there are two resources, WORKERS and BRICKS. The variable named OBSTYPE is the type identifier, and the variable named DATE is the period variable. The first observation (because OBSTYPE has value RESTYPE) indicates that WORKERS is a replenishable resource and BRICKS is a consumable resource. The second observation indicates that both resources have equal priority. In the third observation, a 1 under WORKERS indicates that a supplementary level of 1 worker is available if necessary, while no reserve is available for the resource BRICKS.

The next three observations indicate the resource availability profile. The resource WORKERS is unavailable until July 5, 1988, when the level jumps from zero to 4 and remains at that level through the end of the project. The resource BRICKS is available from July 1, 1988, at level 1000. On July 9, an additional 500 bricks are made available to increase the total availability to 1500. Note that missing values in observations 5 and 6 indicate that there is no change in the availability for the respective resources.

Specification of Resource Requirements

To perform resource allocation or to summarize the resource utilization, it is necessary to specify the amount of resources required by each activity. In this section, the format for this specification is described. The amount required by each activity, for each of the resources listed in the RESOURCE statement, is specified in the DATA= input data set. The requirements for each activity are assumed to be constant throughout the activity's duration. A missing value for a resource variable in the input data set indicates that the particular resource is not required for the activity in that observation.

The interpretation of the specification depends on whether or not the resource is replenishable. Suppose that the value for a given resource variable in a particular observation is x. If the resource is *replenishable*, it indicates that x units of the resource are required throughout the duration of the activity specified in that observation. On the other hand, if the resource is *consumable*, it indicates that the specified resource is consumed at the rate of x units per unit *interval*, where *interval* is the value specified in the INTERVAL= option in the PROC CPM statement. For example, consider the following specification:

ACTIVITY	DUR	WORKERS	BRICKS
A	5	.	100
B	4	2	.

Here, ACTIVITY denotes the activity under consideration, DUR is the duration in days (that is, INTERVAL=DAY), and the resource variables are WORKERS and BRICKS. A missing value for WORKERS in observation 1 indicates that activity A does not need the resource WORKERS while the same is true for the resource BRICKS and activity B. It is assumed that the resource WORKERS has been identified as replenishable, and the resource BRICKS has been identified as consumable in a RESOURCEIN= data set. Thus, a value 100 for the consumable resource BRICKS indicates that 100 bricks per day are required for each of the 5 days of the duration of activity A, and a value 2 for the replenishable resource WORKERS indicates that 2 workers are required throughout the duration (4 days) of activity B.

Scheduling Method

PROC CPM uses the serial-parallel (serial in time and parallel in activities) method of scheduling. In this section, the basic scheduling algorithm is described. (Modifications to the algorithm if an ACTUAL statement is used or if activity splitting is allowed are described later.) The basic algorithm proceeds through the following steps:

Step 1
>   An initial tentative schedule describing the early and late start and finish times is determined without taking any resource constraints into account. This schedule does, however, reflect any restrictions placed on the start and finish times by the use of the ALIGNDATE and ALIGNTYPE statements. As far as possible, PROC CPM tries to schedule each activity to start at its E_START time (as calculated in this step). Set TIME=min(E_START), where the minimum is taken over all activities in the network.

Step 2
>   All of the activities whose E_START coincide with TIME are arranged in a waiting list that is sorted according to the rule specified in the SCHEDRULE= option. (See **Scheduling Rules** below for details on the valid values of this option.) PROC CPM tries to schedule the activities in the same order as on this list. For each activity the procedure checks to see if the required amount of each resource will be available throughout the activity's duration; if enough resources are available, the activity is scheduled to start at TIME. The resource availability profile is examined to see if there is likely to be an increase in resources in the future. If none is perceived until L_START+DELAY, the procedure tries to schedule the activity to start at TIME using supplementary levels of the resources (if there was an observation in the RESOURCEIN= data set specifying supplementary levels of resources); otherwise, it is postponed. If TIME is equal to or greater than the value of L_START+DELAY and the activity cannot be scheduled (even using supplementary resources), PROC CPM stops with an error message, giving a partial schedule.
>
>   Note that once an activity that uses a supplementary level of a replenishable resource is over, the supplementary level that was used is returned to the reservoir and is not used again until needed. For consumable resources, if supplementary levels were used on a particular date, PROC CPM attempts to bring the reservoir back to the original level at the earliest possible time. In other words, the next time the primary availability of the resource increases, the reservoir is first used to replenish the supplementary level of the resource (see **Example 14: Using Supplementary Resources**). Adjustment is made to the resource

availability profile to account for any activity that is scheduled to start at TIME.

Step 3

All of the activities in the waiting list that were unable to be scheduled in Step 2 are postponed and are tentatively scheduled to start at the time when the next change takes place in the resource availability profile (that is, their E_START is set to the next change date in the availability of resources). TIME is advanced to the minimum E_START time of all unscheduled activities, and Steps 1, 2, and 3 are repeated until all activities are scheduled or the procedure stops with an error message.

Some important points to keep in mind are

- Holidays and other nonworking times are automatically accounted for in the process of resource allocation. Do not specify zero availabilities for the resources on holidays; PROC CPM skips holidays and weekends if needed during resource allocation just as in the unrestricted case.
- It is assumed that the activities cannot be interrupted once they are started, unless one of the splitting options is used.

Scheduling Rules

The SCHEDRULE= option specifies the criterion to use for determining the order in which activities are to be considered while scheduling them subject to resource constraints. As described in **Scheduling Method**, at a time given by TIME, all activities whose tentative E_START coincides with TIME are arranged in a list ordered according to *rule*. The five valid values of *rule* are listed below along with a brief description of their respective effects.

LST

specifies that the activities in the waiting list are sorted in the order of increasing L_START time. Thus, this option causes activities that are closer to being critical to be scheduled first.

LFT

specifies that the activities in the waiting list are sorted in the order of increasing L_FINISH time.

SHORTDUR

specifies that the activities in the waiting list are sorted in the order of increasing durations. Thus, PROC CPM tries to schedule activities with shorter durations first.

ACTPRTY

specifies that PROC CPM should sort the activities in the waiting list in the order of increasing values of the variable specified in the ACTIVITYPRTY= option in the RESOURCE statement. This variable specifies a user-assigned priority to each activity in the project (low value of the variable indicates high priority).

Note: if SCHEDRULE is specified as ACTPRTY, the RESOURCE statement must contain the specification of the variable in the input data set that assigns priorities to the activities; if the variable name is not specified through the ACTIVITYPRTY= option, then CPM ignores the specification for the SCHEDRULE= option and uses the default scheduling rule of LST instead.

RESPRTY

specifies that PROC CPM should expect an observation in the RESOURCEIN= data set identified by the value RESPRTY for the type identifier variable and specifying priorities for the resources. PROC CPM uses these priority values (once again, low values indicate high priority) to order the activities; the activities are ordered according to the highest priority resource that they use. In other words, the CPM procedure uses the resource priorities to assign priorities to the activities in the project; these activity priorities are then used to order the activities in the waiting list (in increasing order). If this option is specified and there is no observation in the RESOURCEIN= data set specifying the resource priorities, PROC CPM ignores the specification for the SCHEDRULE= option and uses the default scheduling rule of LST instead.

Secondary Levels of Resources and the DELAY= Option

These are two features that you can use to control the process of scheduling subject to resource constraints. In some applications, time is an important factor, and you may be willing to use extra resources in order to meet project deadlines; on the other hand, there may be cases where you are willing to allow the project completion to be delayed by an arbitrary amount if insufficient resources warrant doing so. In the first case, specify the availability of supplementary resources in the RESOURCEIN= data set and set DELAY=0. In the latter case, set DELAY equal to some very large number or leave it unspecified (in which case it is assumed to be +INFINITY). You can achieve a combination of both effects (using supplementary levels and setting a limit on the delay allowed) by specifying an intermediate value for the DELAY= option and including an observation in the RESOURCEIN= data set with supplementary levels.

Activity Splitting

As mentioned in **Scheduling Method**, PROC CPM assumes that activities cannot be pre-empted once they have already been started. Thus, an activity is scheduled only if it can be assured of enough resources throughout its entire duration. Sometimes, you may be able to make better use of the resources by allowing activities to be *split*. PROC CPM allows you to specify the maximum number of segments that an activity can be split into as well as the minimum duration of any segment of the activity. Suppose that for a given activity, d is its duration, *maxn* is the maximum number of segments allowed, and *dmin* is the minimum duration allowed for a segment. If one or the other of these values is not given, it is calculated appropriately based on the duration of the activity.

The scheduling algorithm described earlier is modified as below:

- In Step 2, the procedure tries to schedule the entire activity (call it A) if it is critical. Otherwise, PROC CPM schedules, if possible, only the first part (say A1) of the activity (of length *dmin*). The remainder of the activity (call it A2, of length $d-dmin$) is added to the waiting list to be scheduled later. When it is A2's turn to be scheduled, it is again a candidate for splitting if the values of *maxn* and *dmin* allow it, and if it is not critical. This process is repeated until the entire activity has been scheduled.
- While ordering the activities in the waiting list, in case of a tie, the split segments of an activity are given priority over unsplit activities. Note that some scheduling rules could lead to more splitting than others.
- Activities that have an alignment type of MS or MF imposed on them by the ALIGNTYPE variable will not be split.

If activity splitting is allowed, a new variable is included in the OUT= output data set called SEGMT_NO (label=*segment part number*). If splitting does occur, the output data set has more observations than the DATA= input data set. Activities that are not split are treated as before, except that the value of the variable SEGMT_NO is set to missing. For split activities, the number of observations output is equal to 1 plus the number of disjoint segments created. The first observation corresponding to such an activity has SEGMT_NO set to missing and the S_START and S_FINISH times are set to be equal to the start and finish times, respectively, of the entire activity. That is, S_START is equal to the scheduled start time of the first segment and S_FINISH is equal to the scheduled finish time of the last segment that the activity is split into. Following this observation are created as many observations as the number of disjoint segments in the activity. All values for these segments are the same as the first observation for this activity, except SEGMT_NO, S_START, S_FINISH, and the duration. SEGMT_NO is the index of the segment, S_START and S_FINISH are the resource-constrained start and finish times for this segment, and duration is the duration of this segment.

Actual Dates and Resource Allocation

The resource-constrained scheduling algorithm uses the early start schedule as the base schedule to determine possible start times for activities in the project. If an ACTUAL statement is used in the invocation of PROC CPM, the early start schedule (as well as the late start schedule) reflects the progress information that was specified for activities in the project, and thus affects the resource-constrained schedule also. Further, activities that are already completed or in progress are scheduled at their actual start without regard to resource constraints. If the resource usage profile for such activities indicates that the resources are insufficient, a warning is issued to the log, but the activities are not postponed beyond their actual start time. The RESOURCEOUT data set contains negative values for the availability of the insufficient resources. These extra amounts are assumed to have come from the supplementary levels of the resources (if such a reservoir existed); for details on supplementary resources, see **Secondary Levels of Resources and the DELAY= Option**. If activity splitting is allowed (either through the specification of the MINSEGMTDUR or MAXNSEGMT variables or the SPLITFLAG or TIMENOWSPLT options), activities that are currently in progress may be split at TIMENOW if resources are insufficient; then the second segment of the split activity is added to the list of activities that need to be scheduled subject to resource constraints. Starting from TIMENOW, all activities that are still unscheduled are treated as described in **Scheduling Method**.

RESOURCEOUT= Data Set

This data set contains information about the resource usage for the resources specified in the RESOURCE statement. The options ALL, AVPROFILE, ESPROFILE, LSPROFILE, and RCPROFILE (each is defined earlier in **RESOURCE Statement**) control the number of variables that are to be created in this data set. The options ROUTINTERVAL and ROUTINTPER control the number of observations that this data set is to contain. Of the options listed above, AVPROFILE and RCPROFILE are allowed only if the procedure is used to obtain a resource-constrained schedule.

The data set always contains a variable named _TIME_ that specifies the date for which the resource usage or availability in the observation is valid. For each of the variables specified in the RESOURCE statement, one, two, three, or four new variables are created depending on how many of the four possible options (AVPROFILE, ESPROFILE, LSPROFILE, and RCPROFILE) are in effect. If none of these four options is specified, the ALL option is assumed to be in effect. Recall that the ALL option is equivalent to specifying ESPROFILE and LSPROFILE when PROC CPM is used to obtain an unconstrained schedule and is equivalent to specifying all four options when PROC CPM is used to obtain a resource-constrained schedule.

The new variables are named according to the following convention:

- the prefix A is used for the variable describing the resource availability profile
- the prefix E is used for the variable denoting the early start usage
- the prefix L is used for the variable denoting the late start usage
- the prefix R is used for the variable denoting the resource-constrained usage.

The suffix is the name of the resource variable if the name is less than eight characters. If the name is eight characters long, the suffix is formed by concatenating the first four and last three characters of the variable name. The user must ensure that this naming convention results in unique variable names in the RESOURCEOUT= data set.

ROUTINTERVAL=*routinterval* and ROUTINTPER=*routintper* specify that two successive values of the _TIME_ variable differ by *n* number of *routinterval* units. If the value of ROUTINTERVAL is not specified, PROC CPM chooses a default value depending on the format of the start and finish variables in the OUT= data set. The value of ROUTINTERVAL (STEPINT) used is indicated in a message written to the SAS log.

MINDATE=*mindate* and MAXDATE=*maxdate* specify the minimum and maximum values of the _TIME_ variable, respectively. Thus, the RESOURCEOUT data set has observations containing the resource usage information starting from *mindate* to *maxdate* with the time interval between the values of the _TIME_ variable in two successive observations being equal to *routintper* units of *routinterval*.

For example, if ROUTINTERVAL=month and ROUTINTPER=3, then the time interval between each pair of observations in the RESOURCEOUT= data set is three months.

Interpretation of New Variables

The availability profile indicates the amount of resources available at the beginning of the time interval specified in the _TIME_ variable after accounting for the resources used through the previous time period. For replenishable resources, the usage profiles indicate the amount of resource used, while for consumable resources they indicate the rate of usage per unit *routinterval* at the start of the time interval specified in the _TIME_ variable. The following example illustrates the interpretation.

Suppose that for the data given earlier, activities A and B have S_START equal to 1JUL88 and 5JUL88, respectively. If the RESOURCE statement has the options AVPROFILE and RCPROFILE, the RESOURCEOUT= data set has these five variables, _TIME_, RWORKERS, AWORKERS, RBRICKS, and ABRICKS. Suppose further that ROUTINTERVAL=DAY and ROUTINTPER=1. The RESOURCEOUT= data set contains the following observations:

TIME	RWORKERS	AWORKERS	RBRICKS	ABRICKS
1JUL88	0	0	100	1000
2JUL88	0	0	100	900
3JUL88	0	0	100	800
4JUL88	0	0	100	700
5JUL88	2	2	100	600
6JUL88	2	2	0	500
7JUL88	2	2	0	500

8JUL88	2	2	0	500
9JUL88	0	4	0	1000

On each day of activity A's duration, the resource BRICKS is consumed at the rate of 100 bricks per day. At the beginning of the first day (July 1, 1988), all 1000 bricks are still available. Note that each day the availability drops by 100 bricks, which is the rate of consumption. On July 5, activity B is scheduled to start. On the four days starting with July 5, the value of RWORKERS is 2, indicating that 2 workers are used on each of those days leaving an available supply of 2 workers (AWORKERS is equal to 2 on all 4 days). If, in this example, ROUTINTPER is set to 2, then the observations would be as below:

TIME	RWORKERS	AWORKERS	RBRICKS	ABRICKS
1JUL88	0	0	100	1000
3JUL88	0	0	100	800
5JUL88	2	2	100	600
7JUL88	2	2	0	500
9JUL88	0	4	0	1000

Note that the value of RBRICKS remains 100 in the first three observations because RBRICKS denotes the rate of consumption of the resource BRICKS per day on the days specified by the variable _TIME_ in the respective observations.

On a day when supplementary levels of resources were used through the beginning of the day, the value for the availability profile for the relevant resources is negative. The absolute magnitude of this value denotes the amount of supplementary resource that was used through the beginning of the day. For instance, if ABRICKS is −100 on 11JUL88, it indicates that 100 bricks from the supplementary reservoir were used through the end of July 10, 1988. See **Example 14: Using Supplementary Resources** and **Example 15: Use of the INFEASDIAGNOSTIC Option**.

Macro Variable _ORCPM_

The CPM procedure defines a macro variable named _ORCPM_. This variable contains a character string that indicates the status of the procedure. It is set at procedure termination. The form of the _ORCPM_ character string is STATUS= REASON= , where STATUS is either SUCCESSFUL or ERROR_EXIT and REASON (if PROC CPM terminated unsuccessfully) can be one of the following:

CYCLE
RES_INFEASIBLE
BADDATA_ERROR
MEMORY_ERROR
IO_ERROR
SEMANTIC_ERROR
SYNTAX_ERROR
CPM_BUG
UNKNOWN_ERROR

This information can be used when PROC CPM is one step in a larger program that needs to determine whether the procedure terminated successfully or not. Because _ORCPM_ is a standard SAS macro variable, it can be used in the ways that all macro variables can be used (see *SAS Guide to Macro Processing, Version 6 Edition*).

Missing Values in Input Data Sets

The following table summarizes the treatment of missing values for variables in the input data sets used by PROC CPM.

Table 5.6 Treatment of Missing Values in the CPM Procedure

Data Set	Variable	Value Used / Assumption Made / Action Taken
CALEDATA	CALID	Default Calendar (0 or DEFAULT)
	SUN,. . . _SAT_	Corresponding shift for default calendar
	D_LENGTH	DAYLENGTH, if available 8:00; if INTERVAL=WORKDAY, DTWRKDAY; 24:00, otherwise
DATA	ACTIVITY	Input error: procedure stops with error message
	SUCCESSOR	Missing
	LAG	FS_0: if corresponding successor variable value is not missing
	HEADNODE	Input error: procedure stops with error message
	TAILNODE	Input error: procedure stops with error message
	DURATION	Input error: procedure stops with error message
	ID	Missing
	CALID	Default Calendar (0 or DEFAULT)
	ALIGNDATE	Project start date: if it is a start activity
	ALIGNTYPE	SGE: if ALIGNDATE is not missing
	RESOURCE	0
	ACTPRTY	Infinity (that is, activity has lowest priority)
	MAXNSEGMT	Calculated from MINSEGMTDUR
	MINSEGMTDUR	0.2 * DURATION

(continued)

Table 5.6   (*continued*)

Data Set	Variable	Value Used / Assumption Made / Action Taken
	A_START A_FINISH REMDUR PCTCOMP	See **Progress Updating** for details. A hierarchy of rules is used to resolve missing values for these four variables.
HOLIDATA	HOLIDAY	Observation ignored
	HOLIDUR	Ignored, if HOLIFIN is not missing; else, 1.0
	HOLIFIN	Ignored, if HOLIDUR is not missing; else, HOLIDAY + (1 unit of INTERVAL)
	CALID	Holiday applies to all calendars defined
RESOURCEIN	OBSTYPE	RESLEVEL
	PERIOD	Input error, if OBSTYPE is RESLEVEL Ignored, otherwise
	RESOURCE	1.0, if OBSTYPE is RESTYPE INFINITY, if OBSTYPE is RESPRTY 0.0, if OBSTYPE is SUPLEVEL 0.0, if OBSTYPE is RESLEVEL and this is first observation of this type (otherwise, value in previous observation)
WORKDATA	Any numeric variable	00:00, if first observation 24:00, otherwise

FORMAT Specification

As can be seen from the description of all of the statements and options used by PROC CPM, the procedure handles SAS date, time, and datetime values in several ways: as time constraints on the activities, holidays specified as date or datetime values, periods of resource availabilities, actual start and finish times, and several other options that control the scheduling of the activities in time. The procedure tries to reconcile any differences that may exist in the format specifications for the different variables. For example, if holidays are formatted as SAS date values, while alignment constraints are specified in terms of SAS datetime values, PROC CPM will convert all of the holidays to SAS datetime values suitably. However, the procedure needs to know how the variables are to be interpreted (as SAS date, datetime, or time values) in order for this reconciliation to be correct. Thus, it is important for you to always explicitly use a FORMAT statement for each SAS date, time, or datetime variable that is used in the invocation of PROC CPM.

EXAMPLES

Introduction

This section contains sixteen examples that illustrate several of the features of PROC CPM. The following table lists features of these examples.

Table 5.7 Examples Used to Illustrate Features of CPM

Example	Illustrates use of
Example 1	CPM with AOA and AON format.
Example 2	CPM with a calendar.
Example 3	CPM with PROC GANTT.
Example 4	CPM to combine three estimates of a project's duration.
Example 5	LAG variables to describe nonstandard relationships.
Example 6	the options INTERVAL, DAYSTART, DAYLENGTH to control work pattern.
Example 7	the HOLIDATA= option to schedule work around holidays.
Example 8	the CALEDATA and WORKDATA data sets to schedule a job over a nonstandard work week.
Example 9	multiple calendars by modifying the calendar data set.
Example 10	the ALIGNDATE and ALIGNTYPE statements to impose time constraints on activities.
Example 11	the ACTUAL statement to incorporate progress information.
Example 12	the RESOURCEOUT= option with the RESOURCE statement to summarize resource utilization.
Example 13	the RESOURCEIN= option with the RESOURCE statement to perform resource allocation.
Example 14	the DELAY= option to illustrate the use of a supplementary level of resources.
Example 15	the INFEASDIAGNOSTIC option to check for infeasibilities.
Example 16	the MINSEGMTDUR= option to allow non-critical activities to be pre-empted during resource-constrained scheduling.

Example 1: Scheduling a Construction Project

This example shows how to use PROC CPM to find the critical path in a small network when data are input in both the Activity-On-Arc format and the Activity-On-Node format. The problem is one of scheduling the times to begin several tasks in a construction project. Because of the nature of the project, some of the tasks must be completed before others can be started.

Table 5.8 summarizes the relationship among the tasks and gives the duration in days to complete each task. The table shows the relationship among tasks by listing the immediate successors to each task (the activities that can be started only upon completion of the predecessor task). For example, because the well must be drilled before the pump house can be constructed, the task DRILL WELL has as its immediate successor the task PUMP HOUSE.

Table 5.8 Summary of Task Relationships and Task Completion Times

Task	Duration	Immediate Successors
DRILL WELL	4	PUMP HOUSE
PUMP HOUSE	3	INSTALL PIPE
POWER LINE	3	INSTALL PIPE
EXCAVATE	5	INSTALL PIPE, INSTALL PUMP, FOUNDATION
DELIVER MATERIAL	2	ASSEMBLE TANK
ASSEMBLE TANK	4	ERECT TOWER
FOUNDATION	4	ERECT TOWER
INSTALL PIPE	2	
INSTALL PUMP	6	
ERECT TOWER	6	

The INSTALL PIPE, INSTALL PUMP, and ERECT TOWER tasks have no activities as successors because completion of these tasks completes the project. These activities are included in this list in order to specify their durations.

The relationship among the tasks can be represented by the network illustrated in **Figure 5.3**.

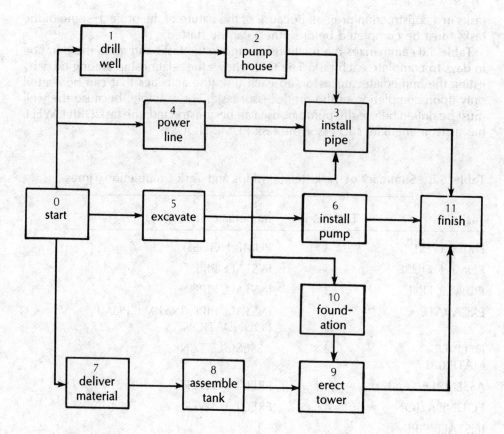

Figure 5.3 Network Showing Task Relationships as Represented in Activity-On-Node Format

The project is represented in Activity-On-Node format. The following DATA step reads the network in this Activity-On-Node format into a SAS data set; call it EXMP1.

```
data exmp1;
   input task    $ 1-16
         duration
         succesr1 $ 21-35
         succesr2 $ 36-50
         succesr3 $ 51-65;
   cards;
drill well        4   pump house
pump house        3   install pipe
power line        3   install pipe
excavate          5   install pipe    install pump    foundation
deliver material  2   assemble tank
assemble tank     4   erect tower
foundation        4   erect tower
install pump      6
install pipe      2
erect tower       6
;
```

To find the critical path for this network, call PROC CPM with the following statements:

```
title 'Scheduling a Construction Project';
title2 'Activity-On-Node Format';
proc cpm;
   activity task;
   duration duration;
   successor succesr1 succesr2 succesr3;
run;

proc print;
run;
```

CPM produces the data set in **Output 5.2**.

Output 5.2   Using PROC CPM to Schedule Problems in Activity-On-Node Format

```
                           Scheduling a Construction Project                              1
                                Activity-On-Node Format

OBS TASK             SUCCESR1       SUCCESR2    SUCCESR3    DURATION E_START E_FINISH L_START L_FINISH T_FLOAT F_FLOAT

 1 drill well        pump house                               4       0        4        6      10       6       0
 2 pump house        install pipe                             3       4        7       10      13       6       0
 3 power line        install pipe                             3       0        3       10      13      10       4
 4 excavate          install pipe   install pump foundation   5       0        5        0       5       0       0
 5 deliver material  assemble tank                            2       0        2        3       5       3       0
 6 assemble tank     erect tower                              4       2        6        5       9       3       3
 7 foundation        erect tower                              4       5        9        5       9       0       0
 8 install pump                                               6       5       11        9      15       4       4
 9 install pipe                                               2       7        9       13      15       6       6
10 erect tower                                                6       9       15        9      15       0       0
```

The data set output by PROC CPM contains the solution in days. It shows that the early start time for the DRILL WELL task is the beginning of day 0, and the early finish time is the beginning of day 4. Alternatively, if you know that the project is to start on the first of July 1988, then you might want to solve the problem using the following statements:

```
proc cpm date='1jul88'd;
   activity task;
   duration duration;
   successor succesr1 succesr2 succesr3;
   title2 'Dated Schedule';
run;

proc print;
run;
```

The additional specification of the DATE= parameter results in the output data set shown in **Output 5.3**.

Output 5.3   Finding the Critical Path in a Small Network with the DATE=
Parameter Specified

```
                          Scheduling a Construction Project                        1
                                   Dated Schedule

OBS  TASK            SUCCESR1        SUCCESR2        SUCCESR3   DURATION E_START  E_FINISH L_START  L_FINISH T_FLOAT F_FLOAT

  1  drill well      pump house                                    4    01JUL88  04JUL88  07JUL88  10JUL88     6       0
  2  pump house      install pipe                                  3    05JUL88  07JUL88  11JUL88  13JUL88     6       0
  3  power line      install pipe                                  3    01JUL88  03JUL88  11JUL88  13JUL88    10       4
  4  excavate        install pipe    install pump foundation       5    01JUL88  05JUL88  01JUL88  05JUL88     0       0
  5  deliver material assemble tank                                2    01JUL88  02JUL88  04JUL88  05JUL88     3       0
  6  assemble tank   erect tower                                   4    03JUL88  06JUL88  06JUL88  09JUL88     3       3
  7  foundation      erect tower                                   4    06JUL88  09JUL88  06JUL88  09JUL88     0       0
  8  install pump                                                  6    06JUL88  11JUL88  10JUL88  15JUL88     4       4
  9  install pipe                                                  2    08JUL88  09JUL88  14JUL88  15JUL88     6       6
 10  erect tower                                                   6    10JUL88  15JUL88  10JUL88  15JUL88     0       0
```

In this case, the early start time for the DRILL WELL task is the beginning of
01JUL88, and the early completion time is the end of 04JUL88.

Suppose, next, that instead of starting work on July 1, 1988, you want to schedule the project for completion before that date. To do so, use the FINISHBEFORE
option:

```
proc cpm date='1jul88'd finishbefore;
   activity task;
   duration duration;
   successor succesr1 succesr2 succesr3;
   title2 'Use of the FINISHBEFORE Option';
run;

proc print;
run;
```

PROC CPM produces the data set in **Output 5.4**. Note that all of the activities
are completed before July 1, 1988.

Output 5.4   Finding the Critical Path in a Small Network with a Project Finish Date Specified

```
                          Scheduling a Construction Project                           1
                              Use of the FINISHBEFORE Option

OBS TASK            SUCCESR1       SUCCESR2       SUCCESR3    DURATION E_START E_FINISH L_START L_FINISH T_FLOAT F_FLOAT

  1 drill well      pump house                                  4     16JUN88 19JUN88  22JUN88 25JUN88    6       0
  2 pump house      install pipe                                3     20JUN88 22JUN88  26JUN88 28JUN88    6       0
  3 power line      install pipe                                3     16JUN88 18JUN88  26JUN88 28JUN88   10       4
  4 excavate        install pipe   install pump foundation      5     16JUN88 20JUN88  16JUN88 20JUN88    0       0
  5 deliver material assemble tank                              2     16JUN88 17JUN88  19JUN88 20JUN88    3       0
  6 assemble tank   erect tower                                 4     18JUN88 21JUN88  21JUN88 24JUN88    3       3
  7 foundation      erect tower                                 4     21JUN88 24JUN88  21JUN88 24JUN88    0       0
  8 install pump                                                6     21JUN88 26JUN88  25JUN88 30JUN88    4       4
  9 install pipe                                                2     23JUN88 24JUN88  29JUN88 30JUN88    6       6
 10 erect tower                                                 6     25JUN88 30JUN88  25JUN88 30JUN88    0       0
```

The same problem can be described in an Activity-On-Arc format. This network representation is shown in **Figure 5.4**.

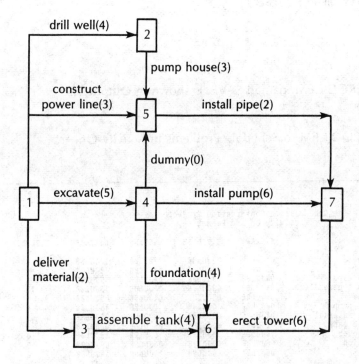

Figure 5.4   Network Showing Task Relationships as Represented in Activity-On-Arc Format

The number in brackets following each activity is the activity's duration in days. The arc labeled DUMMY is used to capture the precedence relationship between the tasks EXCAVATE and INSTALL PIPE. Dummy arcs are often needed when representing scheduling problems in Activity-On-Arc format. The following DATA statement saves the network description in a SAS data set:

```
data const1;
   input activity $ 1-20 tail 22 dur 24 head 26;
   cards;
drill well          1 4 2
```

```
pump house          2 3 5
install pipe        5 2 7
construct power line 1 3 5
excavate            1 5 4
install pump        4 6 7
deliver material    1 2 3
assemble tank       3 4 6
erect tower         6 6 7
foundation          4 4 6
dummy               4 0 5
;
```

To find the critical path for this network when you know that the project is to start on July 1, 1988, invoke PROC CPM with these statements:

```
proc cpm date='1jul88'd out=save;
    tailnode tail;
    duration dur;
    headnode head;
    id activity;
    title2 'Activity-On-Arc Format';
run;


proc print;
run;
```

The data set from PROC CPM, named SAVE, is shown in **Output 5.5**.

Output 5.5   Using PROC CPM to Schedule Problems in Activity-On-Arc Format

```
                        Scheduling a Construction Project                              1
                              Activity-On-Arc Format

OBS   TAIL   HEAD   DUR   ACTIVITY            E_START   E_FINISH   L_START   L_FINISH   T_FLOAT   F_FLOAT

 1     1      2      4    drill well          01JUL88   04JUL88    07JUL88   10JUL88       6         0
 2     2      5      3    pump house          05JUL88   07JUL88    11JUL88   13JUL88       6         0
 3     5      7      2    install pipe        08JUL88   09JUL88    14JUL88   15JUL88       6         6
 4     1      5      3    construct power line 01JUL88  03JUL88    11JUL88   13JUL88      10         4
 5     1      4      5    excavate            01JUL88   05JUL88    01JUL88   05JUL88       0         0
 6     4      7      6    install pump        06JUL88   11JUL88    10JUL88   15JUL88       4         4
 7     1      3      2    deliver material    01JUL88   02JUL88    04JUL88   05JUL88       3         0
 8     3      6      4    assemble tank       03JUL88   06JUL88    06JUL88   09JUL88       3         3
 9     6      7      6    erect tower         10JUL88   15JUL88    10JUL88   15JUL88       0         0
10     4      6      4    foundation          06JUL88   09JUL88    06JUL88   09JUL88       0         0
11     4      5      0    dummy               06JUL88   06JUL88    14JUL88   14JUL88       8         2
```

Example 2:   Printing the Schedules on Calendars

This example shows how you can use the output from PROC CPM to print calendars containing the critical path schedule, the late start schedule, and the early start schedule. The example uses the network described in the last example and assumes that the data set SAVE contains the solution as printed above. The following statements print the three calenders:

```
data crit;
   set save;
   if t_float>0 then delete;  /* keep only the critical activities */

proc sort data=crit;
   by e_start;
run;

title 'Calendar of Critical Activities';
proc calendar schedule;       /* print the critical act. calendar  */
   id e_start;
   var activity;
   dur dur;
run;

proc sort data=save;          /* sort data for late start calendar */
   by l_start;

title 'Late Start Calendar';
proc calendar schedule;       /* print the late start calendar     */
   id l_start;
   var activity;
   dur dur;
run;

proc sort data=save;          /* sort data for early start calendar*/
   by e_start;


title 'Early Start Calendar';
proc calendar schedule;       /* print the early start calendar    */
   id e_start;
   var activity;
   dur dur;
run;
```

This program produces the calendars in **Output 5.6.**

Output 5.6 Printing Schedule Calendars

```
                            Calendar of Critical Activities                                    1
 -------------------------------------------------------------------------------------------
|                                                                                           |
|                                    July  1988                                             |
|                                                                                           |
|-------------------------------------------------------------------------------------------|
|   Sunday    |   Monday    |   Tuesday   |  Wednesday  |  Thursday   |   Friday    |  Saturday   |
|-------------+-------------+-------------+-------------+-------------+-------------+-----------|
|             |             |             |             |             |      1      |      2      |
|             |             |             |             |             |             |           |
|             |             |             |             |             |             |           |
|             |             |             |             |             |+===========excavate============>|
|-------------+-------------+-------------+-------------+-------------+-------------+-----------|
|      3      |      4      |      5      |      6      |      7      |      8      |      9      |
|             |             |             |             |             |             |           |
|             |             |             |             |             |             |           |
|<===================excavate===================+|+===================  ========foundation=============================+|
|-------------+-------------+-------------+-------------+-------------+-------------+-----------|
|     10      |     11      |     12      |     13      |     14      |     15      |     16      |
|             |             |             |             |             |             |           |
|             |             |             |             |             |             |           |
|+========================================erect tower=======================================+||
|-------------+-------------+-------------+-------------+-------------+-------------+-----------|
|     17      |     18      |     19      |     20      |     21      |     22      |     23      |
|             |             |             |             |             |             |           |
|             |             |             |             |             |             |           |
|             |             |             |             |             |             |           |
|-------------+-------------+-------------+-------------+-------------+-------------+-----------|
|     24      |     25      |     26      |     27      |     28      |     29      |     30      |
|             |             |             |             |             |             |           |
|             |             |             |             |             |             |           |
|             |             |             |             |             |             |           |
|-------------+-------------+-------------+-------------+-------------+-------------+-----------|
|     31      |             |             |             |             |             |           |
|             |             |             |             |             |             |           |
|             |             |             |             |             |             |           |
|             |             |             |             |             |             |           |
 -------------------------------------------------------------------------------------------
```

```
                              Late Start Calendar                              2
|------------------------------------------------------------------------------|
|                                                                              |
|                                  July 1988                                   |
|                                                                              |
|------------------------------------------------------------------------------|
|   Sunday   |   Monday   |  Tuesday   | Wednesday  |  Thursday  |   Friday   |  Saturday  |
|------------------------------------------------------------------------------|
|            |            |            |            |            |     1      |     2      |
|            |            |            |            |            |            |            |
|            |            |            |            |            |            |            |
|            |            |            |            |            |+===========excavate============>|
|------------------------------------------------------------------------------|
|     3      |     4      |     5      |     6      |     7      |     8      |     9      |
|            |            |            |            |            |            |            |
|            |            |            |            |+==================drill well==============>|
|            |+======deliver material========+|+===========================foundation======================+|
|<====================excavate====================+|+============================assemble tank============================+|
|------------------------------------------------------------------------------|
|     10     |     11     |     12     |     13     |     14     |     15     |     16     |
|            |+================construct power line==============+|            |
|+=============================erect tower==============================+|
|+=============================install pump==============================+|
|<=drill well==+|+====================pump house===================+|+=========install pipe=========+|
|------------------------------------------------------------------------------|
|     17     |     18     |     19     |     20     |     21     |     22     |     23     |
|            |            |            |            |            |            |            |
|            |            |            |            |            |            |            |
|            |            |            |            |            |            |            |
|------------------------------------------------------------------------------|
|     24     |     25     |     26     |     27     |     28     |     29     |     30     |
|            |            |            |            |            |            |            |
|            |            |            |            |            |            |            |
|            |            |            |            |            |            |            |
|------------------------------------------------------------------------------|
|     31     |            |            |            |            |            |            |
|            |            |            |            |            |            |            |
|            |            |            |            |            |            |            |
|            |            |            |            |            |            |            |
|------------------------------------------------------------------------------|
```

```
                                 Early Start Calendar                                    3
 ------------------------------------------------------------------------------------------
|                                                                                          |
|                                     July  1988                                           |
|------------------------------------------------------------------------------------------|
|  Sunday    |   Monday   |  Tuesday   | Wednesday  |  Thursday  |   Friday   |  Saturday  |
|------------------------------------------------------------------+------------+----------|
|            |            |            |            |          1 |          2 |
|            |            |            |            |            |            |
|            |            |            |            |+=====construct power line======>|
|            |            |            |            |+==========drill well===========>|
|            |            |            |            |+=======deliver material========+|
|            |            |            |            |+==========excavate============>|
|------------+------------+------------+------------+------------+------------+------------|
|          3 |          4 |          5 |          6 |          7 |          8 |          9 |
|            |            |            |            |            |            |            |
|+===========================assemble tank===========================+|            |
|<constructpower|            |            |+===============================install pump==============================>|
|<========drill well==========+|+====================pump house===================+|+=========install pipe==========+|
|<==================excavate==================+|+===============================foundation===============================+|
|------------+------------+------------+------------+------------+------------+------------|
|         10 |         11 |         12 |         13 |         14 |         15 |         16 |
|            |            |            |            |            |            |            |
|            |            |            |            |            |            |            |
|+=================================erect tower================================+|            |
|<========install pump=========+|            |            |            |            |
|------------+------------+------------+------------+------------+------------+------------|
|         17 |         18 |         19 |         20 |         21 |         22 |         23 |
|            |            |            |            |            |            |            |
|            |            |            |            |            |            |            |
|            |            |            |            |            |            |            |
|------------+------------+------------+------------+------------+------------+------------|
|         24 |         25 |         26 |         27 |         28 |         29 |         30 |
|            |            |            |            |            |            |            |
|            |            |            |            |            |            |            |
|            |            |            |            |            |            |            |
|------------+------------+------------+------------+------------+------------+------------|
|         31 |            |            |            |            |            |            |
|            |            |            |            |            |            |            |
|            |            |            |            |            |            |            |
|            |            |            |            |            |            |            |
 ------------------------------------------------------------------------------------------
```

Example 3:   Printing a Gantt Chart

This example prints a Gantt chart of the schedule obtained from PROC CPM. The example uses the network described in **Example 1** (Activity-On-Arc format) and assumes that the data set SAVE contains the schedule sorted by the variable E_START. First, the dummy activity is deleted in a DATA step and PROC GANTT is invoked to print the Gantt chart in **Output 5.7**.

```
    data;
        set save;
        if dur=0 then delete;

    title 'Gantt Chart of the Schedule';
    proc gantt;
        id activity;
    run;
```

Output 5.7 Printing a Gantt Chart

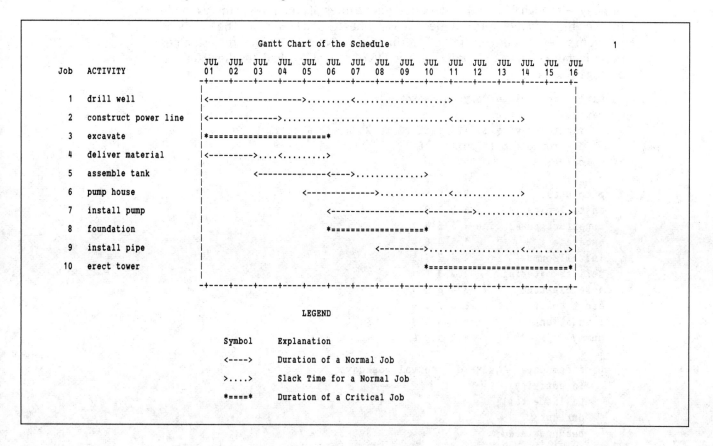

Example 4: Scheduling Only on Weekdays with PERT

This example uses PROC CPM to perform program evaluation review technique (PERT) analysis on a project. The PERT technique is used to include uncertainty about durations in scheduling.

You must provide three estimates of project duration: a pessimistic estimate (TP), an optimistic estimate (TO), and a median estimate (TM). The PERT approach uses a weighted average of these estimates as the activity duration. The average usually used is

$$(TP + (4 * TM) + TO) / 6$$

This average may result in nonintegral durations, where some jobs take part of a day. Although PROC CPM does not require integral durations, in this example the weighted durations are rounded off using the ROUND function. The following program saves the network (in AON format) from **Example 1** with three estimates of project duration in a SAS data set. The DATA step also calculates the weighted average duration.

```
title 'Scheduling Only on Weekdays';
data;
   input activity $ 1-20 tail 22 tm 24 head 26 tp 28 to 30;
   dur=round((tp+(4*tm)+to)/6,1);
   cards;
drill well             1 4 2 5 2
pump house             2 3 5 5 2
install pipe           5 2 7 3 1
construct power line   1 3 5 6 1
excavate               1 5 4 6 4
install pump           4 6 7 7 5
deliver material       1 2 3 4 1
assemble tank          3 4 6 6 1
erect tower            6 6 7 9 4
foundation             4 4 6 5 3
dummy                  4 0 5 0 0
;
proc cpm date='1jul88'd interval=weekdays;
   id activity;
   tailnode tail;
   dur dur;
   headnode head;

proc sort;
   by e_start;

title2 'Calendar of Schedule';
proc calendar schedule weekdays;
   id e_start;
   var activity;
   dur dur;
run;
```

Note that specifying INTERVAL=WEEKDAYS in the PROC CPM statement tells the CPM procedure to schedule activities only on weekdays. Similarly, the WEEKDAYS option in the PROC CALENDAR statement produces the calendar with only weekdays in **Output 5.8**.

Output 5.8 Scheduling Only on Weekdays with PERT

```
                    Scheduling Only on Weekdays                                1
                      Calendar of Schedule
-------------------------------------------------------------------------------
|                                                                             |
|                              July  1988                                     |
|                                                                             |
|-----------------------------------------------------------------------------|
|    Monday      |    Tuesday     |   Wednesday    |    Thursday    |   Friday    |
|----------------+----------------+----------------+----------------+----------------|
|                |                |                |                |    1        |
|                |                |                |                |             |
|                |                |                |                |             |
|                |                |                |                |+==deliver material==>|
|                |                |                |                |+======excavate======>|
|                |                |                |                |+construct power line>|
|                |                |                |                |+=====drill well=====>|
|----------------+----------------+----------------+----------------+----------------|
|    4           |    5           |    6           |    7           |    8        |
|                |                |                |                |             |
|                |                |                |                |             |
|<==deliver material==+|+==================================assemble tank=========================================+|
|<======================================excavate========================================+|+=====foundation====>|
|<==========construct power line============+|                     |+====install pump====>|
|<============================drill well===================================+|+================pump house================>|
|----------------+----------------+----------------+----------------+----------------|
|    11          |    12          |    13          |    14          |    15       |
|                |                |                |                |             |
|                |                |                |                |             |
|<==============================foundation===========================+|             |
|<====================================install pump=======================================+|
|<=====pump house=====+|+===============install pipe================+|+==============erect tower================>|
|----------------+----------------+----------------+----------------+----------------|
|    18          |    19          |    20          |    21          |    22       |
|                |                |                |                |             |
|                |                |                |                |             |
|<=====================================erect tower=================================+|             |
|----------------+----------------+----------------+----------------+----------------|
|    25          |    26          |    27          |    28          |    29       |
|                |                |                |                |             |
|                |                |                |                |             |
|                |                |                |                |             |
|                |                |                |                |             |
|                |                |                |                |             |
-------------------------------------------------------------------------------
```

Example 5: Nonstandard Relationships

This example shows the use of LAG variables to describe nonstandard relationships. Consider the network in AON format from **Example 1**; the data set is called EXMP1. Suppose that after laying the foundation, at least two days are required to elapse before the tower can be erected. The pair of activities FOUNDATION and ERECT TOWER have a nonstandard relationship that can be conveyed to PROC CPM using a LAG variable. Because there are three successor variables, you can specify three LAG variables to be matched one-for-one with the corresponding successor variables. However, because there is only one nonstandard relationship that is between the task FOUNDATION and an activity in the first successor variable, only one LAG variable will be used. The following DATA step modifies the data set EXMP1 by adding a new variable called LAG1, containing the nonstandard relationship. PROC CPM is then invoked, as in **Example 1**, but with the additional LAG option on the SUCCESSOR statement. The output data set produced is printed in **Output 5.9**. Compare it with the data set printed in

Output 5.3 to note that the activity ERECT TOWER has been postponed by two days; this also results in an increase in the slack time (T_FLOAT and F_FLOAT) for several activities in the project.

```
data exmplag;
   set exmp1;
   if task = 'foundation' & succesr1 = 'erect tower'
      then  lag1 = 'fs_2';
run;

proc cpm data=exmplag date='1jul88'd;
   activity task;
   duration duration;
   successor succesr1 succesr2 succesr3 / lag = (lag1);
run;

proc print;
   title 'Nonstandard Relationships';
run;
```

Output 5.9 Nonstandard Relationships

```
                            Nonstandard Relationships                                          1

OBS TASK              SUCCESR1        SUCCESR2       SUCCESR3     DURATION E_START E_FINISH L_START L_FINISH T_FLOAT F_FLOAT

  1 drill well        pump house                                    4      01JUL88 04JUL88 09JUL88 12JUL88    8       0
  2 pump house        install pipe                                  3      05JUL88 07JUL88 13JUL88 15JUL88    8       0
  3 power line        install pipe                                  3      01JUL88 03JUL88 13JUL88 15JUL88   12       4
  4 excavate          install pipe    install pump   foundation     5      01JUL88 05JUL88 01JUL88 05JUL88    0       0
  5 deliver material  assemble tank                                 2      01JUL88 02JUL88 06JUL88 07JUL88    5       0
  6 assemble tank     erect tower                                   4      03JUL88 06JUL88 08JUL88 11JUL88    5       5
  7 foundation        erect tower                                   4      06JUL88 09JUL88 06JUL88 09JUL88    0       0
  8 install pump                                                    6      06JUL88 11JUL88 12JUL88 17JUL88    6       6
  9 install pipe                                                    2      08JUL88 09JUL88 16JUL88 17JUL88    8       8
 10 erect tower                                                     6      12JUL88 17JUL88 12JUL88 17JUL88    0       0
```

Example 6:   Controlling the Project Calendar

This example illustrates the use of the options INTERVAL, DAYSTART, and DAYLENGTH to control the project calendar, namely, the work pattern during a standard week and, if the schedule is computed as SAS datetime values, the start and length of the workday. In **Example 1**, none of these three options were specified; hence, the durations were assumed to be days (INTERVAL=DAY), and work was scheduled on all seven days of the week. In **Example 4**, the specification of INTERVAL=WEEKDAYS caused the schedule to skip weekends. The present example shows further ways of controlling the project calendar.

You can schedule only on weekdays during a part of the day; for example, you can schedule only on weekdays from 9:00 a.m. to 5:00 p.m. To do this, you specify the option INTERVAL=WORKDAY. If all of the activity durations are in integral units of days, then INTERVAL=WORKDAY is equivalent to INTERVAL=WEEKDAYS, except that the start and finish times in the output data set are in SAS datetime values. However, if some of the activity durations require fractions of days and you want to schedule only during a portion of the workday, you should use INTERVAL=WORKDAY when the DATE parameter is a SAS date value and INTERVAL=DTWRKDAY when DATE= is a SAS datetime value.

Suppose you want to schedule the job specified in **Example 1**, but you have revised the durations of two activities. You plan for DRILL WELL to take 3.5 days and EXCAVATE to take 4.75 days. To schedule this job, use the INTERVAL=WORKDAY option rather than the default INTERVAL=DAY (assume that the data is saved in the data set EXMP6). The default setting would schedule work only on a daily basis. The workday option causes PROC CPM to schedule only on weekdays from 9:00 a.m. to 5:00 p.m. One unit of duration is interpreted as eight hours of work. To schedule the construction project to start on July 1, you can call PROC CPM with the following program:

```
title 'Scheduling on Workdays';
title2 'Day Starts at 9 A.M.';
proc cpm interval=workday
         data=exmp6 date='1jul88'd;
   activity task;
   duration duration;
   successor succesr1 succesr2 succesr3;
run;

proc print;
run;
```

The schedule is printed in **Output 5.10**.

Output 5.10   Workday Scheduling

```
                            Scheduling on Workdays                                    1
                            Day Starts at 9 A.M.

  OBS   TASK              SUCCESR1          SUCCESR2       SUCCESR3     DURATION         E_START

   1    drill well        pump house                                    3.50      01JUL88:09:00:00
   2    pump house        install pipe                                  3.00      06JUL88:13:00:00
   3    power line        install pipe                                  3.00      01JUL88:09:00:00
   4    excavate          install pipe      install pump   foundation   4.75      01JUL88:09:00:00
   5    deliver material  assemble tank                                 2.00      01JUL88:09:00:00
   6    assemble tank     erect tower                                   4.00      05JUL88:09:00:00
   7    foundation        erect tower                                   4.00      07JUL88:15:00:00
   8    install pump                                                    6.00      07JUL88:15:00:00
   9    install pipe                                                    2.00      11JUL88:13:00:00
  10    erect tower                                                     6.00      13JUL88:15:00:00

  OBS      E_FINISH           L_START            L_FINISH      T_FLOAT    F_FLOAT

   1    06JUL88:12:59:59   11JUL88:11:00:00   14JUL88:14:59:59   6.25      0.00
   2    11JUL88:12:59:59   14JUL88:15:00:00   19JUL88:14:59:59   6.25      0.00
   3    05JUL88:16:59:59   14JUL88:15:00:00   19JUL88:14:59:59   9.75      3.50
   4    07JUL88:14:59:59   01JUL88:09:00:00   07JUL88:14:59:59   0.00      0.00
   5    04JUL88:16:59:59   05JUL88:09:00:00   07JUL88:14:59:59   2.75      0.00
   6    08JUL88:16:59:59   07JUL88:15:00:00   13JUL88:14:59:59   2.75      2.75
   7    13JUL88:14:59:59   07JUL88:15:00:00   13JUL88:14:59:59   0.00      0.00
   8    15JUL88:14:59:59   13JUL88:15:00:00   21JUL88:14:59:59   4.00      4.00
   9    13JUL88:12:59:59   19JUL88:15:00:00   21JUL88:14:59:59   6.25      6.25
  10    21JUL88:14:59:59   13JUL88:15:00:00   21JUL88:14:59:59   0.00      0.00
```

If you want to change the length of the workday, use the DAYLENGTH= option in the PROC CPM statement. For example, if you want an 8.5-hour

workday instead of the 8-hour default workday, you should include
DAYLENGTH='08:30'T in the PROC CPM statement as shown below:

```
proc cpm daylength='08:30't
         interval=workday data=exmp6 date='1jul88'd;
   activity task;
   duration duration;
   successor succesr1 succesr2 succesr3;
   title2 'Day Starts at 9 A.M. and is 8.5 Hours Long';
run;
```

The output produced is shown in **Output 5.11**.

You might also want to change the start of the workday. By default the workday
starts at 9:00 a.m. To change the default, you use the DAYSTART= option. The
example below schedules the project to start at 7:00 a.m. on July 1. The project
is scheduled on 8.5-hour workdays each starting at 7:00 a.m. The schedule produced by PROC CPM is also shown in **Output 5.11**.

```
proc cpm daylength='08:30't daystart='07:00't
         interval=workday data=exmp6 date='1jul88'd;
   activity task;
   duration duration;
   successor succesr1 succesr2 succesr3;
   title2 'Day Starts at 7 A.M. and is 8.5 Hours Long';
run;

proc print;
run;
```

Output 5.11   Scheduling on Workdays with Nonstandard Hours

```
                              Scheduling on Workdays                                    1
                        Day Starts at 9 A.M. and is 8.5 Hours Long

    OBS    TASK              SUCCESR1         SUCCESR2        SUCCESR3     DURATION        E_START

     1     drill well        pump house                                    3.50      01JUL88:09:00:00
     2     pump house        install pipe                                  3.00      06JUL88:13:15:00
     3     power line        install pipe                                  3.00      01JUL88:09:00:00
     4     excavate          install pipe     install pump    foundation   4.75      01JUL88:09:00:00
     5     deliver material  assemble tank                                 2.00      01JUL88:09:00:00
     6     assemble tank     erect tower                                   4.00      05JUL88:09:00:00
     7     foundation        erect tower                                   4.00      07JUL88:15:22:30
     8     install pump                                                    6.00      07JUL88:15:22:30
     9     install pipe                                                    2.00      11JUL88:13:15:00
    10     erect tower                                                     6.00      13JUL88:15:22:30

    OBS       E_FINISH           L_START          L_FINISH      T_FLOAT    F_FLOAT

     1     06JUL88:13:14:59   11JUL88:11:07:30   14JUL88:15:22:29    6.25       0.00
     2     11JUL88:13:14:59   14JUL88:15:22:30   19JUL88:15:22:29    6.25       0.00
     3     05JUL88:17:29:59   14JUL88:15:22:30   19JUL88:15:22:29    9.75       3.50
     4     07JUL88:15:22:29   01JUL88:09:00:00   07JUL88:15:22:29    0.00       0.00
     5     04JUL88:17:29:59   05JUL88:15:22:30   07JUL88:15:22:29    2.75       0.00
     6     08JUL88:17:29:59   07JUL88:15:22:30   13JUL88:15:22:29    2.75       2.75
     7     13JUL88:15:22:29   07JUL88:15:22:30   13JUL88:15:22:29    0.00       0.00
     8     15JUL88:15:22:29   13JUL88:15:22:30   21JUL88:15:22:29    4.00       4.00
     9     13JUL88:13:14:59   19JUL88:15:22:30   21JUL88:15:22:29    6.25       6.25
    10     21JUL88:15:22:29   13JUL88:15:22:30   21JUL88:15:22:29    0.00       0.00
```

```
                              Scheduling on Workdays                              2
                         Day Starts at 7 A.M. and is 8.5 Hours Long

    OBS   TASK              SUCCESR1        SUCCESR2       SUCCESR3    DURATION        E_START

     1    drill well        pump house                                  3.50     01JUL88:07:00:00
     2    pump house        install pipe                                3.00     06JUL88:11:15:00
     3    power line        install pipe                                3.00     01JUL88:07:00:00
     4    excavate          install pipe    install pump   foundation   4.75     01JUL88:07:00:00
     5    deliver material  assemble tank                               2.00     01JUL88:07:00:00
     6    assemble tank     erect tower                                 4.00     05JUL88:07:00:00
     7    foundation        erect tower                                 4.00     07JUL88:13:22:30
     8    install pump                                                  6.00     07JUL88:13:22:30
     9    install pipe                                                  2.00     11JUL88:11:15:00
    10    erect tower                                                  6.00     13JUL88:13:22:30

    OBS        E_FINISH            L_START            L_FINISH       T_FLOAT     F_FLOAT

     1    06JUL88:11:14:59    11JUL88:09:07:30    14JUL88:13:22:29     6.25       0.00
     2    11JUL88:11:14:59    14JUL88:13:22:30    19JUL88:13:22:29     6.25       0.00
     3    05JUL88:15:29:59    14JUL88:13:22:30    19JUL88:13:22:29     9.75       3.50
     4    07JUL88:13:22:29    01JUL88:07:00:00    07JUL88:13:22:29     0.00       0.00
     5    04JUL88:15:29:59    05JUL88:13:22:30    07JUL88:13:22:29     2.75       0.00
     6    08JUL88:15:29:59    07JUL88:13:22:30    13JUL88:13:22:29     2.75       2.75
     7    13JUL88:13:22:29    07JUL88:13:22:30    13JUL88:13:22:29     0.00       0.00
     8    15JUL88:13:22:29    13JUL88:13:22:30    21JUL88:13:22:29     4.00       4.00
     9    13JUL88:11:14:59    19JUL88:13:22:30    21JUL88:13:22:29     6.25       6.25
    10    21JUL88:13:22:29    13JUL88:13:22:30    21JUL88:13:22:29     0.00       0.00
```

An alternate way of specifying the start of each working day is to use INTERVAL=DTWRKDAY and specify a SAS datetime value for the project start date. Using INTERVAL=DTWRKDAY tells PROC CPM that the DATE= option is a SAS datetime value and that the time given is the start of the workday. For the present example, you could have used DATE='1JUL88:07:00'DT.

Example 7:   Scheduling around Holidays

This example shows how you can schedule around holidays with PROC CPM. First, save a list of holidays in a SAS data set as SAS date variables. Then, use the HOLIDATA= option in the PROC CPM statement to identify the data set, and list the names of the variables in the data set in a HOLIDAY statement. For example, suppose you want to schedule the project in **Example 1** to start on July 1, 1988.

Suppose in your scheduling plans you want to assign work on all days of the week, allowing a day off on July 4, 1988, and on July 8, 1988. The following DATA step saves these days in a SAS data set. The variable VACTNDUR is used later in this example.

```
data holidays;
    format vactn date7.;
    vactn='4jul88'd;
    output;
    vactn='8jul88'd;
    vactndur=3;
    output;
```

Using PROC CPM, you can schedule the project to start on July 1, as follows:

```
title 'Scheduling Around Holidays';
proc cpm data=exmp1 out=save
         holidata=holidays date='1jul88'd;
   holiday vactn;
   activity task;
   duration duration;
   successor succesr1 succesr2 succesr3;
run;

proc print data=save;
run;
```

The resulting schedule is shown in **Output 5.12**.

Output 5.12   Holiday Scheduling

```
                                      Scheduling Around Holidays                                              1

OBS TASK              SUCCESR1        SUCCESR2       SUCCESR3       DURATION E_START E_FINISH  L_START L_FINISH T_FLOAT F_FLOAT

  1 drill well        pump house                                      4     01JUL88 05JUL88  09JUL88 12JUL88    6      0
  2 pump house        install pipe                                    3     06JUL88 09JUL88  13JUL88 15JUL88    6      0
  3 power line        install pipe                                    3     01JUL88 03JUL88  13JUL88 15JUL88   10      4
  4 excavate          install pipe    install pump foundation         5     01JUL88 06JUL88  01JUL88 06JUL88    0      0
  5 deliver material  assemble tank                                   2     01JUL88 02JUL88  05JUL88 06JUL88    3      0
  6 assemble tank     erect tower                                     4     03JUL88 07JUL88  07JUL88 11JUL88    3      3
  7 foundation        erect tower                                     4     07JUL88 11JUL88  07JUL88 11JUL88    0      0
  8 install pump                                                      6     07JUL88 13JUL88  12JUL88 17JUL88    4      4
  9 install pipe                                                      2     10JUL88 11JUL88  16JUL88 17JUL88    6      6
 10 erect tower                                                       6     12JUL88 17JUL88  12JUL88 17JUL88    0      0
```

You can specify longer holiday periods by using the HOLIDUR option on the HOLIDAY statement. Recall that holiday duration is also assumed to be in *interval* units where *interval* is the value specified for the INTERVAL parameter. Suppose that in addition to the holiday on July 4, 1988, a vacation period for the entire project starts on July 8, 1988, with duration specified as 3. First the project is scheduled with INTERVAL=DAY so that the holidays are on July 4, and on July 8, 9, and 10, 1988.

```
proc cpm interval=day out=save1
         date='1jul88'd data=exmp1
         holidata=holidays;
   holiday vactn / holidur=(vactndur);
   activity task;
   duration duration;
   successor succesr1 succesr2 succesr3;
run;
```

The schedule, sorted in order of E_START, is printed in **Output 5.13**.

Output 5.13   Variable Length Holidays: INTERVAL=DAY

```
                         Scheduling Around Holidays                              1
                     Variable Length Holidays : Interval=Day

 OBS    TASK            DURATION   E_START   E_FINISH   L_START   L_FINISH   T_FLOAT   F_FLOAT

  1     drill well          4      01JUL88   05JUL88    11JUL88   14JUL88       6         0
  2     power line          3      01JUL88   03JUL88    15JUL88   17JUL88      10         4
  3     excavate            5      01JUL88   06JUL88    01JUL88   06JUL88       0         0
  4     deliver material    2      01JUL88   02JUL88    05JUL88   06JUL88       3         0
  5     assemble tank       4      03JUL88   07JUL88    07JUL88   13JUL88       3         3
  6     pump house          3      06JUL88   11JUL88    15JUL88   17JUL88       6         0
  7     foundation          4      07JUL88   13JUL88    07JUL88   13JUL88       0         0
  8     install pump        6      07JUL88   15JUL88    14JUL88   19JUL88       4         4
  9     install pipe        2      12JUL88   13JUL88    18JUL88   19JUL88       6         6
 10     erect tower         6      14JUL88   19JUL88    14JUL88   19JUL88       0         0
```

Now suppose that work on the project is to be scheduled only on weekdays. The INTERVAL= option is set to WEEKDAY. Then, the value 3 specified for the variable VACTNDUR is interpreted as 3 weekdays. Thus, the holidays are on July 4, and on July 8, 11, and 12, 1988, because July 9 and 10 (Saturday and Sunday) are nonworking days anyway. The statements below schedule the project to start on July 1, 1988, with INTERVAL=WEEKDAY. The resulting schedule is printed in **Output 5.14**.

```
title2 'Variable Length Holidays : Interval=Weekday';

proc cpm interval=weekday out=save2
         date='1jul88'd data=exmp1
         holidata=holidays;
   holiday vactn / holidur=(vactndur);
   activity task;
   duration duration;
   successor succesr1 succesr2 succesr3;
run;
```

Output 5.14   Variable Length Holidays: INTERVAL=WEEKDAY

```
                         Scheduling Around Holidays                              1
                    Variable Length Holidays : Interval=Weekday

 OBS    TASK            DURATION   E_START   E_FINISH   L_START   L_FINISH   T_FLOAT   F_FLOAT

  1     drill well          4      01JUL88   07JUL88    15JUL88   20JUL88       6         0
  2     power line          3      01JUL88   06JUL88    21JUL88   25JUL88      10         4
  3     excavate            5      01JUL88   13JUL88    01JUL88   13JUL88       0         0
  4     deliver material    2      01JUL88   05JUL88    07JUL88   13JUL88       3         0
  5     assemble tank       4      06JUL88   14JUL88    14JUL88   19JUL88       3         3
  6     pump house          3      13JUL88   15JUL88    21JUL88   25JUL88       6         0
  7     foundation          4      14JUL88   19JUL88    14JUL88   19JUL88       0         0
  8     install pump        6      14JUL88   21JUL88    20JUL88   27JUL88       4         4
  9     install pipe        2      18JUL88   19JUL88    26JUL88   27JUL88       6         6
 10     erect tower         6      20JUL88   27JUL88    20JUL88   27JUL88       0         0
```

Next, the same project is scheduled to start on July 1, 1988, with INTERVAL=WORKDAY. The resulting data set is printed in **Output 5.15**. Note that this time the vacation period starts at 9:00 a.m. on July 8 and ends at 9:00 a.m. on July 13, 1988.

```
title2 'Variable Length Holidays : Interval=Workday';

proc cpm interval=workday out=save3
         date='1jul88'd data=exmp1
         holidata=holidays;
    holiday vactn / holidur=(vactndur);
    activity task;
    duration duration;
    successor succesr1 succesr2 succesr3;
run;
```

Output 5.15 Variable Length Holidays: INTERVAL=WORKDAY

```
                              Scheduling Around Holidays
                        Variable Length Holidays : Interval=Workday

OBS TASK            DURATION      E_START          E_FINISH         L_START          L_FINISH  T_FLOAT F_FLOAT

  1 drill well         4     01JUL88:09:00:00 07JUL88:16:59:59 15JUL88:09:00:00 20JUL88:16:59:59    6       0
  2 power line         3     01JUL88:09:00:00 06JUL88:16:59:59 21JUL88:09:00:00 25JUL88:16:59:59   10       4
  3 excavate           5     01JUL88:09:00:00 13JUL88:16:59:59 01JUL88:09:00:00 13JUL88:16:59:59    0       0
  4 deliver material   2     01JUL88:09:00:00 05JUL88:16:59:59 07JUL88:09:00:00 13JUL88:16:59:59    3       0
  5 assemble tank      4     06JUL88:09:00:00 14JUL88:16:59:59 14JUL88:09:00:00 19JUL88:16:59:59    3       3
  6 pump house         3.    13JUL88:09:00:00 15JUL88:16:59:59 21JUL88:09:00:00 25JUL88:16:59:59    6       0
  7 foundation         4     14JUL88:09:00:00 19JUL88:16:59:59 14JUL88:09:00:00 19JUL88:16:59:59    0       0
  8 install pump       6     14JUL88:09:00:00 21JUL88:16:59:59 20JUL88:09:00:00 27JUL88:16:59:59    4       4
  9 install pipe       2     18JUL88:09:00:00 19JUL88:16:59:59 26JUL88:09:00:00 27JUL88:16:59:59    6       6
 10 erect tower        6     20JUL88:09:00:00 27JUL88:16:59:59 20JUL88:09:00:00 27JUL88:16:59:59    0       0
```

Example 8:   CALEDATA and WORKDATA Data Sets

This example shows how you can schedule the job over a nonstandard day and a nonstandard week. In the first part of the example, the calendar followed is a six-day week with an 8.5-hour workday starting at 7:00 a.m. The project data is the same as was used in **Example 6**, (data set is EXMP6). The 4th and 8th of July are still treated as holidays (use the data set HOLIDAYS). To indicate that work is to be done on all days of the week except Sunday, use INTERVAL=DTDAY and define a calendar data set with a single variable, _SUN_, and a single observation identifying Sunday as a holiday. The DATA step creating CALENDAR and the invocation of PROC CPM follows:

```
data calendar;
    _sun_='holiday';
run;

title 'Scheduling on the 6-Day Week';
proc cpm daylength='08:30't interval=dtday
         date='1jul88:07:00'dt data=exmp6
         calendar=calendar
         holidata=holidays;
    holiday vactn;
    activity task;
    duration duration;
```

```
                  successor succesr1 succesr2 succesr3;
              run;


              proc print;
              run;
```

The resulting schedule is printed in **Output 5.16**.

Output 5.16 Scheduling on the Six-Day Week

```
                              Scheduling on the 6-Day Week                                1

  OBS    TASK                 SUCCESR1            SUCCESR2         SUCCESR3      DURATION         E_START

    1    drill well           pump house                                         3.50     01JUL88:07:00:00
    2    pump house           install pipe                                       3.00     06JUL88:11:15:00
    3    power line           install pipe                                       3.00     01JUL88:07:00:00
    4    excavate             install pipe        install pump     foundation    4.75     01JUL88:07:00:00
    5    deliver material     assemble tank                                      2.00     01JUL88:07:00:00
    6    assemble tank        erect tower                                        4.00     05JUL88:07:00:00
    7    foundation           erect tower                                        4.00     07JUL88:13:22:30
    8    install pump                                                            6.00     07JUL88:13:22:30
    9    install pipe                                                            2.00     11JUL88:11:15:00
   10    erect tower                                                             6.00     13JUL88:13:22:30

  OBS       E_FINISH            L_START            L_FINISH       T_FLOAT     F_FLOAT

    1    06JUL88:11:14:59    11JUL88:09:07:30    14JUL88:13:22:29    6.25        0.00
    2    11JUL88:11:14:59    14JUL88:13:22:30    18JUL88:13:22:29    6.25        0.00
    3    05JUL88:15:29:59    14JUL88:13:22:30    18JUL88:13:22:29    9.75        3.50
    4    07JUL88:13:22:29    01JUL88:07:00:00    07JUL88:13:22:29    0.00        0.00
    5    02JUL88:15:29:59    05JUL88:13:22:30    07JUL88:13:22:29    2.75        0.00
    6    09JUL88:15:29:59    07JUL88:13:22:30    13JUL88:13:22:29    2.75        2.75
    7    13JUL88:13:22:29    07JUL88:13:22:30    13JUL88:13:22:29    0.00        0.00
    8    15JUL88:13:22:29    13JUL88:13:22:30    20JUL88:13:22:29    4.00        4.00
    9    13JUL88:11:14:59    18JUL88:13:22:30    20JUL88:13:22:29    6.25        6.25
   10    20JUL88:13:22:29    13JUL88:13:22:30    20JUL88:13:22:29    0.00        0.00
```

Suppose now that you want to schedule work on a five-and-one-half-day week (five full working days starting on Monday and half a working day on Saturday). A full work day is from 8:00 a.m. to 4:00 p.m. The data set WORKDAT is used to define the work pattern for a full day (in the shift variable FULLDAY) and a half-day (in the shift variable HALFDAY). The CALDAT data set specifies the appropriate work pattern for each day of the week. Both these data sets are shown in **Output 5.17**, which also contains the schedule produced by PROC CPM using the following statements:

```
title 'Scheduling on a Five-and-a-Half-Day Week';
proc cpm out=save4
        date='1jul88'd data=exmp6
        holidata=holidays
        workday=workdat
        calendar=caldat;
    holiday vactn;
    activity task;
    duration duration;
    successor succesr1 succesr2 succesr3;
run;
```

Output 5.17   Scheduling on a Five-and-One-Half-Day Week

```
                     Scheduling on a Five-and-a-Half-Day Week                            1
                               Workdays Data Set

                          OBS    FULLDAY    HALFDAY

                           1      8:00       8:00
                           2     16:00      12:00
                     Scheduling on a Five-and-a-Half-Day Week
                               Calendar Data Set

    OBS    _SUN_      _MON_      _TUE_      _WED_      _THU_      _FRI_      _SAT_     D_LENGTH

     1     holiday   fullday    fullday    fullday    fullday    fullday    halfday     8:00
```

```
                     Scheduling on a Five-and-a-Half-Day Week                            2
                              Schedule Produced by CPM

  OBS    TASK              SUCCESR1          SUCCESR2          SUCCESR3       DURATION         E_START

   1    drill well        pump house                                          3.50      01JUL88:08:00:00
   2    pump house        install pipe                                        3.00      07JUL88:08:00:00
   3    power line        install pipe                                        3.00      01JUL88:08:00:00
   4    excavate          install pipe      install pump      foundation      4.75      01JUL88:08:00:00
   5    deliver material  assemble tank                                       2.00      01JUL88:08:00:00
   6    assemble tank     erect tower                                         4.00      05JUL88:12:00:00
   7    foundation        erect tower                                         4.00      09JUL88:10:00:00
   8    install pump                                                          6.00      09JUL88:10:00:00
   9    install pipe                                                          2.00      12JUL88:12:00:00
  10    erect tower                                                           6.00      14JUL88:14:00:00

  OBS        E_FINISH            L_START            L_FINISH      T_FLOAT    F_FLOAT

   1    06JUL88:15:59:59    12JUL88:10:00:00    15JUL88:13:59:59    6.25       0.00
   2    12JUL88:11:59:59    15JUL88:14:00:00    20JUL88:09:59:59    6.25       0.00
   3    06JUL88:11:59:59    15JUL88:14:00:00    20JUL88:09:59:59    9.75       3.50
   4    09JUL88:09:59:59    01JUL88:08:00:00    09JUL88:09:59:59    0.00       0.00
   5    05JUL88:11:59:59    06JUL88:10:00:00    09JUL88:09:59:59    2.75       0.00
   6    11JUL88:15:59:59    09JUL88:10:00:00    14JUL88:13:59:59    2.75       2.75
   7    14JUL88:13:59:59    09JUL88:10:00:00    14JUL88:13:59:59    0.00       0.00
   8    18JUL88:09:59:59    14JUL88:14:00:00    22JUL88:09:59:59    4.00       4.00
   9    14JUL88:11:59:59    20JUL88:10:00:00    22JUL88:09:59:59    6.25       6.25
  10    22JUL88:09:59:59    14JUL88:14:00:00    22JUL88:09:59:59    0.00       0.00
```

Note that, in this case, it was not necessary to specify DAYLENGTH, DAYSTART, or INTERVAL in the PROC CPM statement. The default value of INTERVAL=DAY was assumed, and the CALDAT and WORKDAT data sets defined the workday and workweek completely. The length of a standard working day was also included in the calendar data set, completing all of the necessary specifications.

Example 9:   Multiple Calendars

This example illustrates the use of multiple calendars within a project. Suppose that the company that was contracted to do the excavation has a six-day work week; thus, the activity EXCAVATE has a six-day week while all the other actvities follow the five-and-one-half-day workweek described in the last example. The same workdays data set is used, but the calendar data set is modified to include a variable named _CAL_ to identify two different calendars, say CAL1 and CAL2. CAL1 is the five-and-one-half-day week calendar and CAL2 is the six-day week calendar. Let the new calendar data set be CALDAT2. In this example, the PROC CPM statement is used to set several of the default values, so the calendar data set is more concise than in the previous example. A new holidays data set (HOL-DAT2) is created that defines July 4, 1988, to be a holiday in both the calendars, using the variable _CAL_. To associate activities with the appropriate calendar, include a variable named _CAL_ in the activities data set to refer to the appropriate calendar. The new data set, EXMP9, is created from EXMP6, by a simple DATA step shown below. The statements used to invoke PROC CPM are also shown below. The data sets HOLDAT2 and CALDAT2 and the output produced by PROC CPM are shown in **Output 5.18**. Note that CAL1 follows the same work-week as the five-and-one-half-day calendar used in **Example 8**, though it is defined in a different manner. Compare the schedule in **Output 5.18** with that in **Output 5.17**.

```
data exmp9;
   set exmp6;
   if task = 'excavate' then _cal_ = 'cal2 ';
   else                      _cal_ = 'cal1';
run;

proc cpm date='1jul88'd data=exmp9
     holidata=holdat2
     workday=workdat
     calendar=caldat2
     interval=workday
     daystart='08:00't
     daylength='08:00't;
   holiday vactn;
   activity task;
   duration duration;
   successor succesr1 succesr2 succesr3;
run;
```

Output 5.18 Multiple Calendars

```
                         Multiple Calendars
                         Holidays Data Set
                                                            1

                 OBS      VACTN      _CAL_

                  1      04JUL88     cal1
                  2      04JUL88     cal2
```

```
                         Multiple Calendars
                         Calendar Data Set

              OBS     _SUN_      _SAT_      _CAL_
                                                            2
               1     holiday    halfday    cal1
               2     holiday    fullday    cal2
```

```
                         Multiple Calendars
                         Output Data Set

 OBS   TASK              SUCCESR1        SUCCESR2       SUCCESR3    DURATION         E_START        3

  1    drill well        pump house                                 3.50     01JUL88:08:00:00
  2    pump house        install pipe                               3.00     07JUL88:08:00:00
  3    power line        install pipe                               3.00     01JUL88:08:00:00
  4    excavate          install pipe    install pump   foundation  4.75     01JUL88:08:00:00
  5    deliver material  assemble tank                              2.00     01JUL88:08:00:00
  6    assemble tank     erect tower                                4.00     05JUL88:12:00:00
  7    foundation        erect tower                                4.00     07JUL88:14:00:00
```

(continued on next page)

```
(continued from previous page)

        8     install pump                                  6.00    07JUL88:14:00:00
        9     install pipe                                  2.00    11JUL88:12:00:00
        10    erect tower                                   6.00    13JUL88:10:00:00

      OBS          E_FINISH            L_START            L_FINISH       T_FLOAT    F_FLOAT

       1      06JUL88:15:59:59    09JUL88:10:00:00    14JUL88:09:59:59     5.75       0.00
       2      11JUL88:11:59:59    14JUL88:10:00:00    18JUL88:13:59:59     5.75       0.00
       3      06JUL88:11:59:59    14JUL88:10:00:00    18JUL88:13:59:59     9.25       3.50
       4      07JUL88:13:59:59    01JUL88:08:00:00    07JUL88:13:59:59     0.00       0.00
       5      05JUL88:11:59:59    05JUL88:14:00:00    07JUL88:13:59:59     2.25       0.00
       6      09JUL88:11:59:59    07JUL88:14:00:00    13JUL88:09:59:59     2.25       2.25
       7      13JUL88:09:59:59    07JUL88:14:00:00    13JUL88:09:59:59     0.00       0.00
       8      15JUL88:09:59:59    13JUL88:10:00:00    20JUL88:13:59:59     4.00       4.00
       9      13JUL88:11:59:59    18JUL88:14:00:00    20JUL88:13:59:59     5.75       5.75
       10     20JUL88:13:59:59    13JUL88:10:00:00    20JUL88:13:59:59     0.00       0.00
```

Example 10:   Time Constraints

Suppose that for the construction project of the previous examples, restrictions are imposed on two of the activities: DRILL WELL has to start on July 1, and DELIVER MATERIAL cannot start before July 5, 1988. The data set EXMP10, printed below, has two variables, ADATE and ATYPE, which allow you to specify these restrictions. DRILL WELL has ATYPE equal to SEQ for *start equal to*, and DELIVER MATERIAL has ATYPE equal to SGE for *start greater than or equal to*. Suppose also that you want the project to be completed by the end of July 15, 1988.

The statements needed to schedule the project subject to these restrictions are shown below. The resulting data set is printed using PROC PRINT and shown in **Output 5.19**. Note that the floats corresponding to the activities are different from the unconstrained schedule. In particular, some of the activities have negative values for T_FLOAT, indicating that if the project deadline has to be met, these activities must be started earlier. Examining the constraints indicates that the activity DELIVER MATERIAL is responsible for the negative floats because it is constrained to start on or after July 5, 1988; however, for the project to be completed on time, it must start no later than July 4.

```
title2 'Aligned Schedule';
proc cpm data=exmp10 date='16jul88'd FINISHBEFORE;
    tailnode tail;
    duration dur;
    headnode head;
    aligndate adate;
    aligntype atype;
    id activity;
run;


proc print;
run;
```

Output 5.19   Time Constraints on the Activities

```
                    Time Constraints on the Activities                              1
                              Data Exmp10

        OBS    ACTIVITY              TAIL    DUR    HEAD    ADATE    ATYPE

          1    drill well             1      4       2     01JUL88   seq
          2    pump house             2      3       5       .
          3    install pipe           5      2       7       .
          4    construct power line   1      3       5       .
          5    excavate               1      5       4       .
          6    install pump           4      6       7       .
          7    deliver material       1      2       3     05JUL88   sge
          8    assemble tank          3      4       6       .
          9    erect tower            6      6       7       .
         10    foundation             4      4       6       .
         11    dummy                  4      0       5       .
```

```
                    Time Constraints on the Activities                              2
                              Aligned Schedule

OBS  TAIL  HEAD  DUR  ACTIVITY             E_START   E_FINISH   L_START   L_FINISH   T_FLOAT   F_FLOAT

  1    1     2    4   drill well           01JUL88   04JUL88    01JUL88   04JUL88      0         0
  2    2     5    3   pump house           05JUL88   07JUL88    11JUL88   13JUL88      6         0
  3    5     7    2   install pipe         08JUL88   09JUL88    14JUL88   15JUL88      6         6
  4    1     5    3   construct power line 01JUL88   03JUL88    11JUL88   13JUL88     10         4
  5    1     4    5   excavate             01JUL88   05JUL88    01JUL88   05JUL88      0         0
  6    4     7    6   install pump         06JUL88   11JUL88    10JUL88   15JUL88      4         4
  7    1     3    2   deliver material     05JUL88   06JUL88    04JUL88   05JUL88     -1         0
  8    3     6    4   assemble tank        07JUL88   10JUL88    06JUL88   09JUL88     -1         0
  9    6     7    6   erect tower          11JUL88   16JUL88    10JUL88   15JUL88     -1        -1
 10    4     6    4   foundation           06JUL88   09JUL88    06JUL88   09JUL88      0         1
 11    4     5    0   dummy                06JUL88   06JUL88    14JUL88   14JUL88      8         2
```

Example 11:   Progress Update

This example shows the use of the ACTUAL statement to track a project's progress. Consider the data in **Example 1** for the network in AOA format. Suppose that the project has started as scheduled on July 1, 1988, and that the current date is July 7, 1988. You may wish to enter the actual dates for the activities that are already in progress or complete and have the CPM procedure determine the schedule of activities that are still undone based on the current information. You can do so by specifying actual start (and finish) times for activities that have already started (are complete). Assume that current information has been incorporated into an UPDATE data set, shown in **Output 5.20**. The variables AS and AF contain the actual start and finish times of the activities. The following statements invoke PROC CPM. The option NOAUTOUPDT is specified so that only those activities that have explicit progress information are assumed to have started. The resulting output data set contains the new variables A_START, A_FINISH, A_DUR, and STATUS; this data set is printed in **Output 5.20**.

```
proc cpm date='1jul88'd data=update;
    tailnode tail;
    duration dur;
    headnode head;
    id activity;
    actual / a_start=as a_finish=af noautoupdt
         timenow='7jul88'd;
run;

proc print;
    title2 'Updated Schedule';
run;
```

Output 5.20 Progress Update

```
                              Progress Update                                    1
                             Data Set Update

          OBS    ACTIVITY              TAIL   DUR   HEAD      AS        AF

           1    drill well              1      4     2     01JUL88   05JUL88
           2    pump house              2      3     5     06JUL88      .
           3    install pipe            5      2     7        .         .
           4    construct power line    1      3     5     01JUL88   03JUL88
           5    excavate                1      5     4     02JUL88   05JUL88
           6    install pump            4      6     7        .         .
           7    deliver material        1      2     3     01JUL88   02JUL88
           8    assemble tank           3      4     6     04JUL88      .
           9    erect tower             6      6     7        .         .
          10    foundation              4      4     6     06JUL88      .
          11    dummy                   4      0     5        .         .
```

```
                              Progress Update                                    2
                             Updated Schedule

                         A                                                 L
                     S   C                  A        A        E    E   L    _   T  F
                     T   T            A      _        F        _    _   _    F   _  _
                T H  A   I            S      F        S        F    L   F    I   F  F
             T  A E  T   V            T      S        T        I    S   S    N   L  L
          O  A  I A  U   I            A      T        A        N    T   T    I   O  O
          B  I  L D  S   T            R      A        R        I    A   A    S   A  A
          S  L  D R  _   Y            T      R        T        S    R   R    H   T  T
                                             T        T        H    T   T

          1  1  2 4 Completed  5 drill well            01JUL88 05JUL88  01JUL88 05JUL88  01JUL88 05JUL88  0  0
          2  2  5 3 In Progress . pump house    06JUL88         .       06JUL88 08JUL88  06JUL88 08JUL88  0  0
          3  5  7 2 Pending     . install pipe                  .       09JUL88 10JUL88  14JUL88 15JUL88  5  5
          4  1  5 3 Completed   3 construct power line 01JUL88 03JUL88  01JUL88 03JUL88  01JUL88 03JUL88  0  0
          5  1  4 5 Completed   4 excavate    02JUL88 05JUL88   02JUL88 05JUL88  02JUL88 05JUL88  0  0
          6  4  7 6 Pending     . install pump                  .       07JUL88 12JUL88  10JUL88 15JUL88  3  3
          7  1  3 2 Completed   2 deliver material 01JUL88 02JUL88  01JUL88 02JUL88  01JUL88 02JUL88  0  0
          8  3  6 4 In Progress . assemble tank  04JUL88         .       04JUL88 07JUL88  04JUL88 07JUL88  0  2
          9  6  7 6 Pending     . erect tower                   .       10JUL88 15JUL88  10JUL88 15JUL88  0  0
         10  4  6 4 In Progress . foundation    06JUL88         .       06JUL88 09JUL88  06JUL88 09JUL88  0  0
         11  4  5 0 Pending     . dummy                         .       07JUL88 07JUL88  14JUL88 14JUL88  7  2
```

Example 12:   Summarizing Resource Utilization

This example shows how you can use the RESOURCE statement in conjunction with the RESOURCEOUT= option to summarize resource utilization. The following data set, EXMP12, sets up the project network and activity costs and is the basis of the SAS program used in this example:

```
obs activity            tail dur head cost

 1 drill well              1    4    2    1.5
 2 pump house              2    3    5    2.3
 3 install pipe            5    2    7    2.1
 4 construct power line    1    3    5    1.1
 5 excavate                1    5    4    5.3
 6 install pump            4    6    7    1.2
 7 deliver material        1    2    3    0.5
 8 assemble tank           3    4    6    3.2
 9 erect tower             6    6    7   15.0
10 foundation              4    4    6    1.2
11 dummy                   4    0    5     .
```

The following program saves the cost information in a data set named ROUT, which is printed using PROC PRINT. Two variables, ECOST and LCOST, denote the usage of the resource COST corresponding to the early and late start schedules, respectively. The summary information is then presented in two ways: on a calendar and in a chart. Charts, as shown in **Output 5.21**, can be used to compare different schedules with respect to resource usage.

```
title 'Summarizing Resource Utilization';
proc cpm date='1jul88'd resourceout=rout data=exmp12;
   id activity;
   tailnode tail;
   duration dur;
   headnode head;
   resource cost;
run;

proc format;                    /* format the cost variables */
   picture efmt other='009.99 e' (prefix='$');
   picture lfmt other='009.99 l' (prefix='$');

proc calendar legend;          /* print the costs on a calendar */
   id _time_;
   var  ecost lcost;
   format ecost efmt.
      lcost lfmt.;
   label ecost='e = early start costs'
      lcost='l = late start costs';
run;

proc chart;                      /* plot the costs in a bar chart */
   hbar _time_/sumvar=ecost discrete;
   hbar _time_/sumvar=lcost discrete;
run;
```

Output 5.21 Summarizing Resource Utilization

```
                      Summarizing Resource Utilization                        1
    ----------------------------------------------------------------------
   |                                                                      |
   |                            July  1988                                |
   |                                                                      |
    ----------------------------------------------------------------------
   | Sunday  |  Monday | Tuesday |Wednesday | Thursday |  Friday | Saturday |
   +---------+---------+---------+----------+----------+---------+---------+
   |         |         |         |          |          |    1    |    2    |
   |         |         |         |          |          |         |         |
   |         |         |         |          |          | $8.40 e | $8.40 e |
   |         |         |         |          |          | $5.30 l | $5.30 l |
    ----------------------------------------------------------------------
   |    3    |    4    |    5    |    6     |    7     |    8    |    9    |
   |         |         |         |          |          |         |         |
   | $11.10 e| $10.00 e| $10.80 e|  $7.90 e |  $4.70 e | $4.50 e | $4.50 e |
   |  $5.30 l|  $5.80 l|  $5.80 l|  $4.40 l |  $5.90 l | $5.90 l | $5.90 l |
    ----------------------------------------------------------------------
   |   10    |   11    |   12    |   13     |   14     |   15    |   16    |
   |         |         |         |          |          |         |         |
   | $16.20 e| $16.20 e| $15.00 e| $15.00 e | $15.00 e | $15.00 e| $0.00 e |
   | $17.70 l| $19.60 l| $19.60 l| $19.60 l | $18.30 l | $18.30 l| $0.00 l |
    ----------------------------------------------------------------------
   |   17    |   18    |   19    |   20     |   21     |   22    |   23    |
   |         |         |         |          |          |         |         |
   |         |         |         |          |          |         |         |
    ----------------------------------------------------------------------
   |   24    |   25    |   26    |   27     |   28     |   29    |   30    |
   |         |         |         |          |          |         |         |
   |         |         |         |          |          |         |         |
    ----------------------------------------------------------------------
   |   31    |         |         |          |          |         |         |
   |         |         |         |          |          |         |         |
   |         |         |         |          |          |         |         |
    ----------------------------------------------------------------------

                      ---------------------
                     |       Legend        |
                     | e = early start costs |
                     | l = late start costs  |
                      ---------------------
```

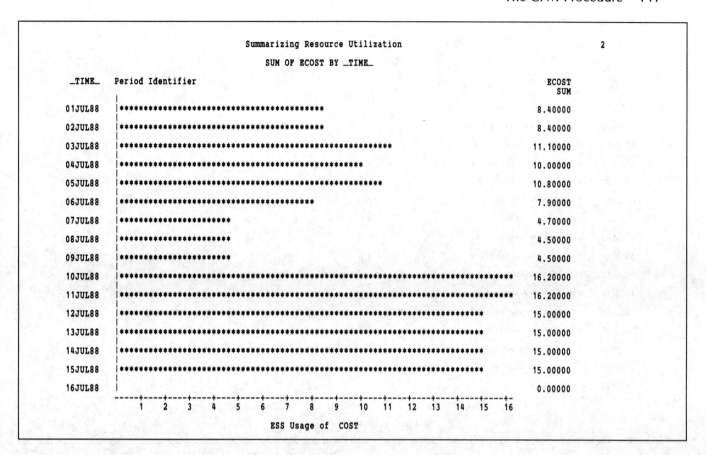

```
                        Summarizing Resource Utilization                          2

                           SUM OF ECOST BY _TIME_

    _TIME_    Period Identifier                                            ECOST
                                                                            SUM
              |
    01JUL88   |**********************************************             8.40000
    02JUL88   |**********************************************             8.40000
    03JUL88   |************************************************************  11.10000
    04JUL88   |********************************************************    10.00000
    05JUL88   |***********************************************************   10.80000
    06JUL88   |*******************************************                 7.90000
    07JUL88   |*************************                                   4.70000
    08JUL88   |************************                                    4.50000
    09JUL88   |************************                                    4.50000
    10JUL88   |************************************************************************************  16.20000
    11JUL88   |************************************************************************************  16.20000
    12JUL88   |*****************************************************************************  15.00000
    13JUL88   |*****************************************************************************  15.00000
    14JUL88   |*****************************************************************************  15.00000
    15JUL88   |*****************************************************************************  15.00000
    16JUL88   |                                                           0.00000
              ----+----+----+----+----+----+----+----+----+----+----+----+----+----+----+-
                  1    2    3    4    5    6    7    8    9   10   11   12   13   14   15   16
                                  ESS Usage of  COST
```

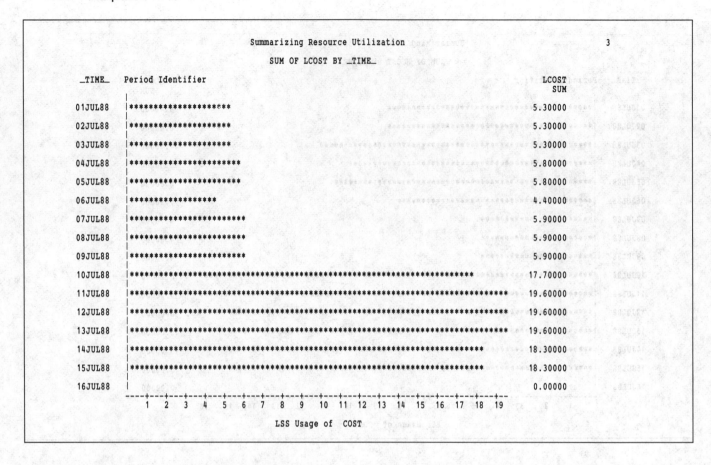

```
                              Summarizing Resource Utilization                               3

                                  SUM OF LCOST BY _TIME_

       _TIME_   Period Identifier                                                   LCOST
                |                                                                    SUM

     01JUL88    |*********************                                             5.30000
                |
     02JUL88    |*********************                                             5.30000
                |
     03JUL88    |*********************                                             5.30000
                |
     04JUL88    |***********************                                           5.80000
                |
     05JUL88    |***********************                                           5.80000
                |
     06JUL88    |******************                                                4.40000
                |
     07JUL88    |***********************                                           5.90000
                |
     08JUL88    |***********************                                           5.90000
                |
     09JUL88    |***********************                                           5.90000
                |
     10JUL88    |*********************************************************         17.70000
                |
     11JUL88    |**************************************************************    19.60000
                |
     12JUL88    |**************************************************************    19.60000
                |
     13JUL88    |**************************************************************    19.60000
                |
     14JUL88    |*********************************************************         18.30000
                |
     15JUL88    |*********************************************************         18.30000
                |
     16JUL88    |                                                                  0.00000
                ----+---+---+---+---+---+---+---+---+---+---+---+---+---+---+---+---+---+---+--
                    1   2   3   4   5   6   7   8   9  10  11  12  13  14  15  16  17  18  19
                                      LSS Usage of  COST
```

Example 13: Resource Allocation

In the previous example, a summary of the resource utilization was obtained. Suppose that you want to schedule the project subject to constraints on the availability of money. The data, as in **Example 12**, are assumed to be in a data set named EXMP12. The resource variable, COST, specifies the rate of consumption of dollars per day by each activity in the project. Now, suppose that the availability of money is saved in a data set named RESINF printed below:

```
         obs      per       otype      cost

          1        .        restype       2
          2        .        suplevel     40
          3     01JUL88     reslevel     40
          4     06JUL88     reslevel     90
          5     11JUL88     reslevel    130
          6     16JUL88     reslevel    180
```

In the data set RESINF, the first observation indicates that COST is a consumable resource, and the second observation indicates that a supplementary level of forty dollars is available, if necessary. The remaining observations indicate the availability profile from July 1, 1988. PROC CPM is then used to schedule the project to start on July 1, 1988, subject to the availability, as specified. Here, the DELAY= option is not specified and, therefore, the supplementary level of resource is not used because the primary levels of resources are found to be sufficient if some of the activities are delayed.

The data set contains the resource-constrained start and finish times in the variables S_START and S_FINISH. Note that the project is delayed by three days due to lack of sufficient resources (the maximum value of S_FINISH is 18JUL88, while the maximum value of E_FINISH is 15JUL88). The data set ROUT contains variables RCOST and ACOST; RCOST denotes the usage of the resource COST corresponding to the resource-constrained schedule, and ACOST denotes the remaining level of the resource after resource allocation. Both output data sets are printed below using PROC PRINT.

```
proc cpm data=exmp12 date='1jul88'd resourcein=resinf
    out=sched resourceout=rout;
  tailnode tail;
  duration dur;
  headnode head;
  resource cost / period=per obstype=otype rcp avp;
  id activity;
run;

proc print data=sched;
  title 'Resource Constrained Schedule';
run;

proc print data=rout;
  title 'RCprofile and AVprofile for Constrained Schedule';
run;
```

Output 5.22 Scheduling a Project Subject to Availability of Resources

				Resource Constrained Schedule							1
OBS	TAIL	HEAD	DUR	ACTIVITY	COST	S_START	S_FINISH	E_START	E_FINISH	L_START	L_FINISH
1	1	2	4	drill well	1.5	01JUL88	04JUL88	01JUL88	04JUL88	07JUL88	10JUL88
2	2	5	3	pump house	2.3	06JUL88	08JUL88	05JUL88	07JUL88	11JUL88	13JUL88
3	5	7	2	install pipe	2.1	09JUL88	10JUL88	08JUL88	09JUL88	14JUL88	15JUL88
4	1	5	3	construct power line	1.1	01JUL88	03JUL88	01JUL88	03JUL88	11JUL88	13JUL88
5	1	4	5	excavate	5.3	01JUL88	05JUL88	01JUL88	05JUL88	01JUL88	05JUL88
6	4	7	6	install pump	1.2	06JUL88	11JUL88	06JUL88	11JUL88	10JUL88	15JUL88
7	1	3	2	deliver material	0.5	01JUL88	02JUL88	01JUL88	02JUL88	04JUL88	05JUL88
8	3	6	4	assemble tank	3.2	05JUL88	08JUL88	03JUL88	06JUL88	06JUL88	09JUL88
9	6	7	6	erect tower	15.0	13JUL88	18JUL88	10JUL88	15JUL88	10JUL88	15JUL88
10	4	6	4	foundation	1.2	06JUL88	09JUL88	06JUL88	09JUL88	06JUL88	09JUL88
11	4	5	0	dummy	0.0	06JUL88	06JUL88	06JUL88	06JUL88	14JUL88	14JUL88

```
                RCprofile and AVprofile for Constrained Schedule                2

                OBS      _TIME_    RCOST    ACOST

                  1      01JUL88     8.4     40.0
                  2      02JUL88     8.4     31.6
                  3      03JUL88     7.9     23.2
                  4      04JUL88     6.8     15.3
                  5      05JUL88     8.5      8.5
                  6      06JUL88     7.9     50.0
                  7      07JUL88     7.9     42.1
                  8      08JUL88     7.9     34.2
                  9      09JUL88     4.5     26.3
                 10      10JUL88     3.3     21.8
                 11      11JUL88     1.2     58.5
                 12      12JUL88     0.0     57.3
                 13      13JUL88    15.0     57.3
                 14      14JUL88    15.0     42.3
                 15      15JUL88    15.0     27.3
                 16      16JUL88    15.0     62.3
                 17      17JUL88    15.0     47.3
                 18      18JUL88    15.0     32.3
                 19      19JUL88     0.0     17.3
```

Example 14:   Using Supplementary Resources

In this example, the same project as in **Example 13** is scheduled with a specification of DELAY=0. This indicates to PROC CPM that a supplementary level of resources is to be used if an activity cannot be scheduled to start on or before its latest start time (as computed in the unrestrained case). Once again, the RCPROFILE and AVPROFILE options are used to save the resource-constrained usage profile and the resource availability profile in a data set named ROUT1.

The negative values for RCOST in observation numbers 14 and 15 of the data set ROUT1 indicate the amount of supplementary resource that was used through the beginning of the day specified in the respective observations. Thus, ACOST=−2.7 in observation 14, indicating that the primary level fell to 0 and 2.7 dollars were used from the supplementary level through the end of July 13, 1988.

Similarly, by the beginning of July 15, the supplementary level was depleted by 17.7 dollars. Because the rate of consumption is 15 dollars per day on July 15, the level is further depleted by 15 dollars so that ACOST at the end of July 15 is −32.7. At the beginning of July 16, the value of ACOST increases to 17.3 dollars because 50 dollars are added to the primary availability on this day (see DATA RESINF), of which 32.7 dollars are allotted to bring the supplementary level back to 40 dollars.

```
    title 'Use of Supplementary Resources';
    proc cpm data=exmp12 date='1jul88'd resourcein=resinf
        out=sched1 resourceout=rout1;
      tailnode tail;
      duration dur;
      headnode head;
      resource cost / delay=0 period=per obstype=otype rcp avp;
      id activity;
    run;

    proc print data=sched1;
    run;

    proc print data=rout1;
    run;
```

Output 5.23   Using Supplementary Resources

```
                          Use of Supplementary Resources                              1

 OBS  TAIL  HEAD  DUR  ACTIVITY           COST   S_START   S_FINISH  E_START   E_FINISH  L_START   L_FINISH

  1     1     2    4   drill well          1.5   01JUL88   04JUL88   01JUL88   04JUL88   07JUL88   10JUL88
  2     2     5    3   pump house          2.3   06JUL88   08JUL88   05JUL88   07JUL88   11JUL88   13JUL88
  3     5     7    2   install pipe        2.1   09JUL88   10JUL88   08JUL88   09JUL88   14JUL88   15JUL88
  4     1     5    3   construct power line 1.1   01JUL88   03JUL88   01JUL88   03JUL88   11JUL88   13JUL88
  5     1     4    5   excavate            5.3   01JUL88   05JUL88   01JUL88   05JUL88   01JUL88   05JUL88
  6     4     7    6   install pump        1.2   06JUL88   11JUL88   06JUL88   11JUL88   10JUL88   15JUL88
  7     1     3    2   deliver material    0.5   01JUL88   02JUL88   01JUL88   02JUL88   04JUL88   05JUL88
  8     3     6    4   assemble tank       3.2   05JUL88   08JUL88   03JUL88   06JUL88   06JUL88   09JUL88
  9     6     7    6   erect tower        15.0   10JUL88   15JUL88   10JUL88   15JUL88   10JUL88   15JUL88
 10     4     6    4   foundation          1.2   06JUL88   09JUL88   06JUL88   09JUL88   06JUL88   09JUL88
 11     4     5    0   dummy               0.0   06JUL88   06JUL88   06JUL88   06JUL88   14JUL88   14JUL88
```

```
          Use of Supplementary Resources                   2

            OBS    _TIME_    RCOST    ACOST

             1    01JUL88     8.4     40.0
             2    02JUL88     8.4     31.6
             3    03JUL88     7.9     23.2
             4    04JUL88     6.8     15.3
             5    05JUL88     8.5      8.5
             6    06JUL88     7.9     50.0
             7    07JUL88     7.9     42.1
             8    08JUL88     7.9     34.2
             9    09JUL88     4.5     26.3
            10    10JUL88    18.3     21.8
            11    11JUL88    16.2     43.5
            12    12JUL88    15.0     27.3
            13    13JUL88    15.0     12.3
            14    14JUL88    15.0     -2.7
            15    15JUL88    15.0    -17.7
            16    16JUL88     0.0     17.3
```

Example 15:   Use of the INFEASDIAGNOSTIC Option

The option INFEASDIAGNOSTIC instructs PROC CPM to continue scheduling even when resources are insufficient. When PROC CPM schedules subject to resource constraints, it stops the scheduling process when it cannot find sufficient resources for an activity before the activity's latest possible start time. In this case, you may want to determine which resources are needed to schedule a project and when the deficiencies occur. The INFEASDIAGNOSTIC option is equivalent to specifying infinite supplementary levels for all the resources under consideration. The DELAY= value is assumed to equal the default value of +INFINITY, unless it is specified as otherwise.

The same activities data set, EXMP12, is used as in the previous few examples. The resource availability is saved in the data set RESINF2, printed in **Output 5.24**. If PROC CPM is invoked without the INFEASDIAGNOSTIC option, PROC CPM terminates with an error message because the resources are insufficient to schedule the project.

If you add the option INFEASDIAGNOSTIC to the RESOURCE statement, PROC CPM assumes that there is an infinite supply of supplementary levels for all of the relevant resources. Thus, if at any point in the scheduling process it finds that an activity does not have enough resources and it cannot be postponed any further, then it schedules the activity ignoring the insufficiency of the resources. The availability profile in the RESOURCEOUT data set contains negative values for all of the resources that were insufficient on any given day. This feature is useful for diagnosing the level of insufficiency of any resource; you can determine the problem areas by examining the availability profile for the different resources. The following PROC step uses the INFEASDIAGNOSTIC option, and the resulting data sets are printed using PROC PRINT and displayed in **Output 5.24**.

```
proc cpm data=exmp12 date='1jul88'd resourcein=resinf2
          out=infsched resourceout=infrout;
    tailnode tail;
    duration dur;
    headnode head;
    resource cost / period=per obstype=otype
                    infeasdiagnostic;
    id activity ;
run;
```

Output 5.24   Infeasible Diagnostics

```
                              Insufficient Resources                              1
                                  Data Resinf2

                 OBS       PER      OTYPE      COST

                  1         .       restype      2
                  2      01JUL88    reslevel    40
                  3      06JUL88    reslevel    90
                  4      11JUL88    reslevel   130
```

```
                              Insufficient Resources                              2
                  Resource Constrained Schedule with INFEASDIAGNOSTIC Option

OBS  TAIL  HEAD  DUR  ACTIVITY             COST   S_START   S_FINISH  E_START   E_FINISH  L_START   L_FINISH

 1    1     2    4   drill well           1.5   01JUL88   04JUL88   01JUL88   04JUL88   07JUL88   10JUL88
 2    2     5    3   pump house           2.3   06JUL88   08JUL88   05JUL88   07JUL88   11JUL88   13JUL88
 3    5     7    2   install pipe         2.1   09JUL88   10JUL88   08JUL88   09JUL88   14JUL88   15JUL88
 4    1     5    3   construct power line 1.1   01JUL88   03JUL88   01JUL88   03JUL88   11JUL88   13JUL88
 5    1     4    5   excavate             5.3   01JUL88   05JUL88   01JUL88   05JUL88   01JUL88   05JUL88
 6    4     7    6   install pump         1.2   06JUL88   11JUL88   06JUL88   11JUL88   10JUL88   15JUL88
 7    1     3    2   deliver material     0.5   01JUL88   02JUL88   01JUL88   02JUL88   04JUL88   05JUL88
 8    3     5    4   assemble tank        3.2   05JUL88   08JUL88   03JUL88   06JUL88   06JUL88   09JUL88
 9    6     7    6   erect tower         15.0   10JUL88   15JUL88   10JUL88   15JUL88   10JUL88   15JUL88
10    4     6    4   foundation           1.2   06JUL88   09JUL88   06JUL88   09JUL88   06JUL88   09JUL88
11    4     5    0   dummy                0.0   06JUL88   06JUL88   06JUL88   06JUL88   14JUL88   14JUL88
```

```
                              Insufficient Resources                              3
                               Infeasible Diagnostics

                 OBS    _TIME_    ECOST    LCOST    RCOST    ACOST

                  1    01JUL88     8.4      5.3      8.4     40.0
                  2    02JUL88     8.4      5.3      8.4     31.6
                  3    03JUL88    11.1      5.3      7.9     23.2
                  4    04JUL88    10.0      5.8      6.8     15.3
                  5    05JUL88    10.8      5.8      8.5      8.5
                  6    06JUL88     7.9      4.4      7.9     50.0
                  7    07JUL88     4.7      5.9      7.9     42.1
                  8    08JUL88     4.5      5.9      7.9     34.2
                  9    09JUL88     4.5      5.9      4.5     26.3
                 10    10JUL88    16.2     17.7     18.3     21.8
                 11    11JUL88    16.2     19.6     16.2     43.5
                 12    12JUL88    15.0     19.6     15.0     27.3
                 13    13JUL88    15.0     19.6     15.0     12.3
                 14    14JUL88    15.0     18.3     15.0     -2.7
                 15    15JUL88    15.0     18.3     15.0    -17.7
                 16    16JUL88     0.0      0.0      0.0    -32.7
```

Note that the data set INFROUT contains negative values for the ACOST variable in the last three observations indicating that at the beginning of July 14, 15, and 16, 1988 (that is, at the end of July 13, 14, and 15) the resource levels are insufficient. This information could be useful for increasing the availability on those days.

Example 16:   Activity Splitting

This example illustrates the use of the MINSEGMTD variable to allow activity splitting. The data are the same as in the data set EXMP12, except that the resource under consideration is WORKERS and not COST; a new variable called MINSEG is included (call the new data set EXMP16), which specifies the minimum length of any segment. A simple rule is followed for specifying this duration: if an activity's duration is longer than three days, allow it to be split, and let the minimum duration of any segment be two days. The data set EXMP16 and the resource availability data set (RESINF16) are printed in **Output 5.25**. Note that the resource under consideration is a replenishable one. The project is first scheduled without the splitting option. When splitting is allowed, some of the activities are split into disjoint segments and a shorter project duration is obtained; an additional benefit is that the resource usage is more uniform. (Note that splitting may not always give you an earlier project completion time.) The two different schedules, with and without splitting, as well as the resource usage profiles are also printed in **Output 5.25**.

```
title 'Activity Splitting';
proc cpm data=exmp16 date='1jul88'd resourcein=resinf16
    out=sched16  resourceout=rout16;
   tailnode tail;
   duration dur;
   headnode head;
   resource workers / period=per obstype=otype;
   id activity;
run;

proc cpm data=exmp16 date='1jul88'd resourcein=resinf16
    out=spltschd  resourceout=spltrout;
   tailnode tail;
   duration dur;
   headnode head;
   resource workers / period=per obstype=otype
                      minsegmtdur=minseg;
   id activity;
run;

proc print data=sched16;
   title2 'Resource Constrained Schedule: No Splitting';
run;

proc print data=spltschd;
   title2 'Resource Constrained Schedule: Splitting Allowed';
run;

proc print data=rout16;
   title2 'Resource Usage Profile: No Splitting';
run;

proc print data=spltrout;
   title2 'Resource Usage Profile: Splitting Allowed';
run;
```

Output 5.25   Activity Splitting

```
                              Activity Splitting                                    1
                           Activity Data Set EXMP16

        OBS      ACTIVITY              TAIL    DUR    HEAD    WORKERS    MINSEG

          1      drill well             1       4      2        2          2
          2      pump house             2       3      5        2          .
          3      install pipe           5       2      7        2          .
          4      construct power line   1       3      5        1          .
          5      excavate               1       5      4        3          2
          6      install pump           4       6      7        2          2
          7      deliver material       1       2      3        1          .
          8      assemble tank          3       4      6        2          .
          9      erect tower            6       6      7        4          2
         10      foundation             4       4      6        2          .
         11      dummy                  4       0      5        0          .
```

```
                              Activity Splitting                                    2
                    Resource Availability Data Set RESINF16

        OBS        PER        OTYPE         WORKERS

          1         .         restype          1
          2      01JUL88      reslevel         6
```

```
                              Activity Splitting                                    3
                   Resource Constrained Schedule: No Splitting

BS   TAIL  HEAD  DUR   ACTIVITY              WORKERS   S_START   S_FINISH   E_START   E_FINISH   L_START   L_FINISH

 1     1     2    4    drill well               2      01JUL88   04JUL88    01JUL88   04JUL88    07JUL88   10JUL88
 2     2     5    3    pump house               2      09JUL88   11JUL88    05JUL88   07JUL88    11JUL88   13JUL88
 3     5     7    2    install pipe             2      12JUL88   13JUL88    08JUL88   09JUL88    14JUL88   15JUL88
 4     1     5    3    construct power line     1      03JUL88   05JUL88    01JUL88   03JUL88    11JUL88   13JUL88
 5     1     4    5    excavate                 3      01JUL88   05JUL88    01JUL88   05JUL88    01JUL88   05JUL88
 6     4     7    6    install pump             2      06JUL88   11JUL88    06JUL88   11JUL88    10JUL88   15JUL88
 7     1     3    2    deliver material         1      01JUL88   02JUL88    01JUL88   02JUL88    04JUL88   05JUL88
 8     3     6    4    assemble tank            2      05JUL88   08JUL88    03JUL88   06JUL88    06JUL88   09JUL88
 9     6     7    6    erect tower              4      12JUL88   17JUL88    10JUL88   15JUL88    10JUL88   15JUL88
10     4     6    4    foundation               2      06JUL88   09JUL88    06JUL88   09JUL88    06JUL88   09JUL88
11     4     5    0    dummy                    0      06JUL88   06JUL88    06JUL88   06JUL88    14JUL88   14JUL88
```

```
                              Activity Splitting                                    4
                   Resource Constrained Schedule: Splitting Allowed

OBS  TAIL  HEAD  SEGMT_NO  DUR   ACTIVITY              WORKERS   S_START   S_FINISH   E_START   E_FINISH   L_START   L_FINISH

  1    1     2      .       4    drill well               2      01JUL88   07JUL88    01JUL88   04JUL88    07JUL88   10JUL88
  2    1     2      1       2    drill well               2      01JUL88   02JUL88    01JUL88   04JUL88    07JUL88   10JUL88
  3    1     2      2       2    drill well               2      06JUL88   07JUL88    01JUL88   04JUL88    07JUL88   10JUL88
  4    2     5      .       3    pump house               2      08JUL88   11JUL88    05JUL88   07JUL88    11JUL88   13JUL88
  5    2     5      1       2    pump house               2      08JUL88   09JUL88    05JUL88   07JUL88    11JUL88   13JUL88
  6    2     5      2       1    pump house               2      11JUL88   11JUL88    05JUL88   07JUL88    11JUL88   13JUL88
  7    5     7      .       2    install pipe             2      14JUL88   15JUL88    08JUL88   09JUL88    14JUL88   15JUL88
  8    1     5      .       3    construct power line     1      03JUL88   05JUL88    01JUL88   03JUL88    11JUL88   13JUL88
  9    1     4      .       5    excavate                 3      01JUL88   05JUL88    01JUL88   05JUL88    01JUL88   05JUL88
 10    4     7      .       6    install pump             2      07JUL88   13JUL88    06JUL88   11JUL88    10JUL88   15JUL88
 11    4     7      1       4    install pump             2      07JUL88   10JUL88    06JUL88   11JUL88    10JUL88   15JUL88
 12    4     7      2       2    install pump             2      12JUL88   13JUL88    06JUL88   11JUL88    10JUL88   15JUL88
 13    1     3      .       2    deliver material         1      01JUL88   02JUL88    01JUL88   02JUL88    04JUL88   05JUL88
 14    3     6      .       4    assemble tank            2      03JUL88   06JUL88    03JUL88   06JUL88    06JUL88   09JUL88
 15    6     7      .       6    erect tower              4      10JUL88   15JUL88    10JUL88   15JUL88    10JUL88   15JUL88
 16    4     6      .       4    foundation               2      06JUL88   09JUL88    06JUL88   09JUL88    06JUL88   09JUL88
 17    4     5      .       0    dummy                    0      06JUL88   06JUL88    06JUL88   06JUL88    14JUL88   14JUL88
```

```
                        Activity Splitting                              5
                  Resource Usage Profile: No Splitting

        OBS     _TIME_   EWORKERS   LWORKERS   RWORKERS   AWORKERS

          1    01JUL88      7          3          6          0
          2    02JUL88      7          3          6          0
          3    03JUL88      8          3          6          0
          4    04JUL88      7          4          6          0
          5    05JUL88      7          4          6          0
          6    06JUL88      8          4          6          0
          7    07JUL88      6          6          6          0
          8    08JUL88      6          6          6          0
          9    09JUL88      6          6          6          0
         10    10JUL88      6          8          4          2
         11    11JUL88      6          9          4          2
         12    12JUL88      4          9          6          0
         13    13JUL88      4          9          6          0
         14    14JUL88      4          8          4          2
         15    15JUL88      4          8          4          2
         16    16JUL88      0          0          4          2
         17    17JUL88      0          0          4          2
         18    18JUL88      0          0          0          6
```

```
                        Activity Splitting                              6
                Resource Usage Profile: Splitting Allowed

        OBS     _TIME_   EWORKERS   LWORKERS   RWORKERS   AWORKERS

          1    01JUL88      7          3          6          0
          2    02JUL88      7          3          6          0
          3    03JUL88      8          3          6          0
          4    04JUL88      7          4          6          0
          5    05JUL88      7          4          6          0
          6    06JUL88      8          4          6          0
          7    07JUL88      6          6          6          0
          8    08JUL88      6          6          6          0
          9    09JUL88      6          6          6          0
         10    10JUL88      6          8          6          0
         11    11JUL88      6          9          6          0
         12    12JUL88      4          9          6          0
         13    13JUL88      4          9          6          0
         14    14JUL88      4          8          6          0
         15    15JUL88      4          8          6          0
         16    16JUL88      0          0          0          6
```

REFERENCES

Clough, R. and Sears, G. (1979), *Construction Project Management*, New York: John Wiley & Sons, Inc.

Davis, E.W. (1973), "Project Scheduling under Resource Constraints: Historical Review and Categorization of Procedures," *AIIE Transactions*, 5, 297–313.

Elmaghraby, S.E. (1977), *Activity Networks: Project Planning and Control by Network Models*, New York: John Wiley & Sons, Inc.

Horowitz, E. and Sahni, S. (1976), *Fundamentals of Data Structures*, Potomac, MD: Computer Science Press, Inc.

Minieka, E. (1978), *Optimization Algorithms for Networks and Graphs*, New York: Marcel Dekker, Inc.

Moder, J.J., Phillips, C.R., and Davis, E.W. (1983), *Project Management with CPM, PERT and Precedence Diagramming*, New York: Van Nostrand Reinhold Company.

Wiest, J.D. (1967), "A Heuristic Model for Scheduling Large Projects with Limited Resources," *Management Science*, 13, 359–377.

ABSTRACT

The GANTT procedure represents graphically the progress of activities in a project such as may be scheduled by the CPM procedure. In addition to the early and late start schedules, PROC GANTT can plot the actual schedule and depict, on the chart, other important times associated with a project, such as project deadlines and other important days during the duration of the project. The resource-constrained schedule for each activity can also be plotted on a separate line. It is a useful tool for monitoring projects as they progress.

The chart produced by PROC GANTT can be of high resolution quality rather than line-printer quality if you specify the GRAPHICS option in the PROC GANTT statement.

Note: you must have SAS/GRAPH software if you want to produce Gantt charts of high resolution quality using the GRAPHICS option. See **Specifications for the Graphics Version of PROC GANTT** for more information on producing high quality Gantt charts.

In addition to sending the output to either a plotter or a printer, you can view the Gantt chart of the project at the terminal in full-screen mode by specifying the FULLSCREEN option in the PROC GANTT statement. See **Specifications for the Full-Screen Version of PROC GANTT** for more information.

INTRODUCTION

The GANTT procedure recognizes several options and statements for tailoring Gantt charts to suit your needs. Each option and statement is explained in detail in the **SPECIFICATIONS** section, and examples illustrate most features. There are several distinctive features in the GANTT procedure. These features are listed below.

- The input data set is expected to be similar to the OUT= output data set produced by PROC CPM, with each observation representing an activity in the network.
- It is possible to obtain a detailed Gantt chart by specifying the single statement

  ```
  proc gantt data = SASdataset;
  ```

  where the data set specified is the output data set from PROC CPM.
- Each observation in the data set is plotted on a separate line of the chart, unless activity splitting during resource-constrained scheduling has caused an activity to split into disjoint segments; for details regarding the output format in this case, see **Printed Output**.
- The horizontal axis represents time, and the vertical axis represents the sequence of observations in the data set.

- Both axes can be plotted across more than one page.
- The procedure automatically provides extensive labeling of the time axis allowing you to determine easily the exact time of events plotted on the chart. The labels are determined on the basis of the formats of the times being plotted.
- The procedure produces Gantt charts of line-printer quality by default. You can specify the GRAPHICS option in the PROC GANTT statement to obtain high resolution quality Gantt charts. To obtain the full-screen version of the procedure, use the FULLSCREEN (FS) option in the PROC GANTT statement.
- Calendar information that was used by PROC CPM can also be passed to PROC GANTT so that relevant holiday/weekend information for each activity is plotted on the Gantt chart.

SPECIFICATIONS

The following statements are used in PROC GANTT:

PROC GANTT *options*;
    BY *variables*;
    CHART *specifications / options*;
    ID *variables*;

PROC GANTT Statement

PROC GANTT *options*;

The following options can appear in the PROC GANTT statement:

CALEDATA= *SASdataset*
CALENDAR= *SASdataset*
    identifies a SAS data set that specifies the work pattern during a standard week for each of the calendars that are to be used in the project. Each observation of this data set (also referred to as the calendar data set) contains the name or the number of the calendar being defined in that observation, the names of the shifts or work patterns used each day, and, optionally, a standard workday length in hours. For details on the structure of this data set see **Multiple Calendars and Holidays**. The work shifts referred to in the CALEDATA data set are defined in the WORKDATA data set.

DATA=*SASdataset*
    names the SAS data set to be used by PROC GANTT. If DATA= is omitted, the most recently created SAS data set is used. This data set contains all the time variables (early, late, actual, and resource-constrained start and finish times and any other variables to be specified on a CHART statement) that are to be plotted on the chart. For projects that use multiple calendars, this data set also identifies the calendar that is used by each activity.

HOLIDATA=*SASdataset*
    names the SAS data set that specifies holidays. These holidays can be associated with specific calendars that are also identified in the HOLIDATA data set (also referred to as the holidays data set). HOLIDATA= must be used with the HOLIDAYS= option in the CHART statement, which specifies the variable in the SAS data set that contains the start time of holidays. Optionally, the data set may include a variable

that specifies the length of each holiday or a variable that identifies the finish time of each holiday (if the holidays are longer than one day). For projects involving multiple calendars, this data set may also include the variable specified by the CALID= option that identifies the calendar to be associated with each holiday.

MAXDEC=*n*
M=*n*

indicates the maximum number of decimal positions printed for a number. A decimal specification in a format overrides a MAXDEC= specification. The default value of MAXDEC is 2.

SPLIT=*'splitchar'*

splits labels used as column headings where the split character appears. When you define the value of the split character, you must enclose it in single quotes. In PROC GANTT, column headings for ID variables consist of either variable labels (if they are present and space permits) or variable names. If the variable label is used as the column heading, then the split character determines where the column heading is to be split.

WORKDATA=*SASdataset*
WORKDAY=*SASdataset*

identifies a SAS data set that defines the work pattern during a standard working day. Each numeric variable in this data set (also referred to as the workday data set) is assumed to denote a unique shift pattern during one working day. The variables must be formatted as SAS time values, and the observations are assumed to specify, alternately, the times when consecutive shifts start and end.

BY Statement

BY *variable*;

A BY statement can be used with PROC GANTT to obtain separate Gantt charts for observations in groups defined by the BY variables. When a BY statement appears, the procedure expects the input data to be sorted in order of the BY variables. If your input data set is not sorted, use the SORT procedure with a similar BY statement to sort the data. The chart for each BY group is formatted separately based only on the observations within that group.

CHART Statement

CHART *specifications / options*;

The CHART statement controls the format of the Gantt chart and specifies additional variables (other than the early, late, actual, and resource-constrained start and finish times) to be plotted on the chart. This statement is not needed if default options are to be used for plotting the Gantt chart. For example, a variable that can be specified in the CHART statement is one that contains the target finish date for each activity in a project. That is, if FDATE is a variable in the input data set containing the desired finish date for each activity, the CHART statement can be used to mark the value of FDATE on the chart for each activity. A CHART specification can be one of the following types:

variable1. . .variablen
variable1=symbol1. . .variablen=symboln
(variables)=symbol1. . .(variables)=symboln.

variable1. . .variablen

indicates that each variable is to be plotted using the default symbol, the first character of the variable name. For example, the statement

```
CHART SDATE FDATE;
```

causes the values of SDATE to be plotted with an S and the values of FDATE with an F.

variable1=symbol1. . .variablen=symboln

indicates that each variable is to be plotted using the symbol specified. The symbol must be a single character enclosed in quotes.

(variables)=symbol1. . .(variables)=symboln

indicates that each variable within the parentheses is to be plotted using the symbol associated with that group. The symbol must be a single character enclosed in single quotes. For example, the statement

```
CHART (ED SD)='*'
      (FD LD)='+';
```

plots the values of the variables in the first group using an asterisk and the values of the variables in the second group using a plus sign.

A single CHART statement can contain specifications in more than one of these forms. Also, each CHART statement produces a separate Gantt chart.

Note: it is not necessary to specify a CHART statement if default values are to be used to draw the Gantt chart.

The following options can appear in the CHART statement:

A_FINISH=*variable*
AF=*variable*

specifies the variable containing the actual finish time of each activity in the input data set. This option is not required if the default variable name A_FINISH is used.

A_START=*variable*
AS=*variable*

specifies the variable containing the actual start time of each activity in the input data set. This option is not required if the default variable name A_START is used.

BETWEEN= *number*

specifies the number of columns between two consecutive ID variable columns. This option gives you greater flexiblity in spacing the ID columns. The default value of BETWEEN is 3.

CALID= *name*

specifies the name of a SAS variable that is used in the DATA=, the HOLIDATA=, and the CALEDATA= data sets to identify the name or number of the calendar that each observation refers to. This variable can be either numeric or character depending on whether the different calendars are identified by unique numbers or names. If this variable is not found in any of the three data sets, PROC CPM looks for a default variable named _CAL_ in that data set (a warning message is issued to the log). For each activity in the DATA= input data set, this variable identifies the calendar followed by the activity that is used to mark the appropriate holidays and weekends for the activity. See **Multiple Calendars and Holidays** for details.

CRITFLAG
FLAG
   indicates that critical jobs be flagged as being critical or 'super_critical'.
   An activity is said to be critical if its total float is zero. If the total float is
   negative, the activity is said to be supercritical. Critical activities are
   marked 'CR', and supercritical activities are marked 'SC' on the left side
   of the chart.

DAYLENGTH=*daylength*
   specifies the length of the workday. On each day, work is scheduled
   starting at the beginning of the day as specified in the DAYSTART=
   option and ending *daylength* hours later. The DAYLENGTH= value
   should be a SAS time value. The default value of daylength is 24 hours
   if the INTERVAL= option is specified as DTDAY, DTHOUR,
   DTMINUTE, or DTSECOND, and it is 8 hours if the INTERVAL= option
   is specified as WORKDAY or DTWRKDAY; for other values of the
   INTERVAL parameter, the DAYLENGTH parameter is ignored.
      Note: the DAYLENGTH parameter is needed to mark the non-
   worked periods within a day correctly (if the MARKBREAK option is in
   effect). The DAYLENGTH parameter is also used to determine the start
   and end of a weekend precisely (to the nearest second). The accuracy is
   needed if you want to depict on a Gantt chart the exact time (for
   example, to within the nearest hour) for the start and finish of holidays
   or weekends. This option is used only if the times being plotted are SAS
   datetime values.

DAYSTART= *daystart*
   specifies the start of the workday; the end of the day *dayend* is
   computed as *daylength* seconds after *daystart*. The DAYSTART= value
   should be a SAS time value. This parameter is to be specified only when
   the INTERVAL parameter is one of the following: DTDAY, WORKDAY,
   DTWRKDAY, DTHOUR, DTMINUTE, or DTSECOND. For purposes of
   denoting on the Gantt chart, the weekend is assumed to start at *dayend*
   on Friday and end at *daystart* on Monday morning. Of course, if the
   SCALE and MININTERVAL values are such that the resolution is not very
   high, you will be unable to discern the start and end of holidays and
   weekends to the nearest hour. The default value of *daystart* is 9:00 a.m.
   if INTERVAL=WORKDAY or DTWRKDAY and midnight otherwise.

DUPOK
   causes duplicate values of ID variables to *not be skipped*. As described
   later in the **ID Statement** section, if two or more consecutive
   observations have the same combination of values for all the ID
   variables, only the first of these observations is plotted. The option
   DUPOK overrides this behavior and causes *all* the observations to be
   plotted.

E_FINISH=*variable*
EF=*variable*
   specifies the variable containing the early finish time of each activity in
   the input data set. This option is not required if the default variable
   name E_FINISH is used.

E_START=*variable*
ES=*variable*
   specifies the variable containing the early start time of each activity in
   the input data set. This option is not required if the default variable
   name E_START is used.

FILL

causes each page of the Gantt chart to be filled as completely as possible before a new page is started (when the size of the project requires the Gantt chart to be split across several pages). If the FILL option is not specified, the pages are constrained to contain an approximately equal number of activities.

FORMCHAR[*index list*]=*'string'*

defines the characters to be used for constructing the table outlines and dividers. The value is a string 11 characters long defining the two bar characters, vertical and horizontal, and the nine corner characters: upper left, upper middle, upper right, middle left, middle middle (cross), middle right, lower left, lower middle, and lower right. The default value of FORMCHAR is '|----|+|---'. Any character or hexadecimal string can be substituted to customize the table appearance. Use an index list to specify which default form character each supplied character replaces; or replace the entire default string by specifying the full 11 character replacement string with no index list. For example, change the four corners to asterisks by using

```
formchar(3 5 9 11)= '****'   .
```

Specifying

```
formchar='           '  (11 blanks)
```

produces tables with no outlines or dividers. If you have your printout routed to an IBM 6670 printer using an extended font (typestyle 27 or 225) with input character set 216, it is recommended that you specify

```
formchar='FABFACCCBCEB8FECABCBBB'X   .
```

If you are printing on a printer with a TN (text) print train, it is recommended that you specify

```
formchar='4FBFACBFBC4F8F4FABBFBB'X   .
```

See "SAS System Options" and "The CALENDAR Procedure" in base SAS documentation for an illustration of these characters.

HCONCHAR= 'c'

specifies the symbol to be used for drawing the connecting line described in the HCONNECT option. The default character is '-'. This is a line-printer option and is not valid in conjunction with the GRAPHICS option. For corresponding graphics options, see the options LHCON= and CHCON=, described in **Specifications for the Graphics Version of PROC GANTT**.

HCONNECT

causes a line to be drawn for each activity from the left boundary of the chart to the beginning of the bar for the activity. This feature is particularly useful when the Gantt chart is drawn on a large page. In this case, the schedule bars for some of the activities may not start close enough to the left boundary of the chart; the connecting lines help identify the activity that each bar refers to.

HOLICHAR= 'c'

indicates the character to print for holidays. Note that PROC GANTT prints only those holidays that fall within the duration or the slack time of an activity. The default symbol used for holidays is '!'.

HOLIDAY=*(variable)*
HOLIDAYS=*(variable)*
   specifies the variable in the HOLIDATA data set that identifies holidays
   to be marked on the schedule. If there is no end time nor duration
   specified for the holiday, it is assumed to start at the time specified by
   the HOLIDAY variable and last one unit of *interval*, where *interval* is the
   value of the INTERVAL parameter.

HOLIDUR=*(variable)*
HDURATION=*(variable)*
   specifies the variable in the HOLIDATA data set that identifies the
   durations of the holidays that are to be marked on the schedule.

HOLIEND=*(variable)*
HOLIFIN=*(variable)*
   specifies the variable in the HOLIDATA data set that identifies the finish
   times of the holidays that are to be marked on the schedule.

INCREMENT=*increment*
   specifies the increment for labeling the time axis of the Gantt chart. If
   INCREMENT= is not specified, a value is chosen that provides the
   maximum possible labeling.

INTERVAL=*interval*
HOLINTERVAL=*interval*
   specifies the units for the values of the HOLIDUR variables. Valid values
   for this option are DAY, DTDAY, WEEKDAY, WORKDAY, DTWRKDAY,
   DTHOUR, DTMINUTE, and DTSECOND. If INTERVAL has been
   specified as WEEKDAY, WORKDAY, or DTWRKDAY, weekends are also
   marked on the Gantt chart with the same symbol as holidays for line-
   printer quality charts. Graphics quality Gantt charts use the same
   PATTERN statement as the one used for marking holidays. The default
   value of INTERVAL is DAY if the times being plotted are SAS date values
   and DTDAY if the times are SAS datetime values. See **Specifying the
   INTERVAL= Option** for further details regarding this option.

JOINCHAR=*'string'*
   defines a string 7 characters long, identifying nonblank characters to be
   used for drawing the schedule. The first two symbols are used to plot
   the schedule of an activity with positive total float. The first symbol
   denotes the duration of such an activity while the second symbol
   denotes the slack present in the activity's schedule. The third symbol is
   used to plot the duration of a *critical* activity (with zero total float).
      The next two symbols are used to plot the schedule of a *super_critical*
   activity (one with negative float). Thus, the fourth symbol is used to plot
   the negative slack of such an activity starting from the late start time (to
   early start time), and the fifth symbol is used to plot the duration of the
   activity (from early start to early finish). The sixth symbol is used to plot
   the actual schedule of an activity if the A_START and A_FINISH
   variables are specified. The seventh symbol is used to plot the resource-
   constrained schedule of an activity if the S_START and S_FINISH
   variables are specified. The default value of JOINCHAR is '-.=-*-*'.

L_FINISH=*variable*
LF=*variable*
   specifies the variable containing the late finish time of each activity in
   the input data set. This option is not required if the default variable
   name L_FINISH is used.

L_START=*variable*
LS=*variable*
    specifies the variable containing the late start time of each activity in the input data set. This option is not required if the default variable name L_START is used.

MARKBREAK
    causes all breaks (nonworked periods) during a day to be marked on the Gantt chart. The symbol used for marking the breaks is the same as the HOLICHAR symbol. This option may not be of much use unless the chart has been plotted with a scale that allows you to discern the different hours within a day on the Gantt chart. For instance, if the chart is in terms of days, there is no point in trying to show the breaks within a day; on the other hand, if it is in terms of hours or seconds, you may want to see the start and end of the various shifts within a day. This option turns on the MARKWKND option.

MARKWKND
    causes all weekends (or nonworked days during a week) to be marked on the Gantt chart. The symbol used for marking weekends is the same as the HOLICHAR symbol. Note that weekends are marked on the chart also if the INTERVAL parameter is specified as WEEKDAY, WORKDAY, or DTWRKDAY.

MAXDATE=*maxdate*
    specifies the end time for the time axis of the chart. The default value is the largest value of the times being plotted.

MINDATE=*mindate*
    specifies the starting time for the time axis of the chart. The default value is the smallest value of the times being plotted.

MININTERVAL=*mininterval*
    specifies the smallest interval to be identified on the chart. For example, if MININTERVAL=*day*, then one day is represented on the chart by *scale* (see the SCALE= option) number of columns. The default value of MININTERVAL is chosen on the basis of the formats of the times being plotted, as explained in **Specifying the Mininterval= Option**. See also **Page Format** for further explanation on how to use the MININTERVAL= option in conjunction with the SCALE= option.

NOJOBNUM
    suppresses printing of an identifying job number for each activity; by default, the job number is printed to the left of the Gantt chart.

NOLEGEND
    suppresses printing the concise default legend at the end of each page of the Gantt chart.

OVERLAPCH='c'
OVLPCHAR='c'
    indicates the overprint character to be printed when more than one of the early, late, or actual times (that is, the AF, AS, EF, ES, LS, LF, SS, SF variables) are to be plotted in the same column. The default character is '*'.

OVPCHAR='c'
    indicates the character to be printed if one of the variables specified in the CHART statement is to be plotted in the same column as one of the start or finish times. If no OVPCHAR= option is given, @ is used. Note that if one of the E_START, E_FINISH, L_START, L_FINISH, A_START,

A_FINISH, S_START, or S_FINISH times coincides with another, the overprint character to be printed can be specified separately using the OVERLAPCH= option.

PADDING=*padding*
FINPAD=*padding*

requests that finish times on the chart be increased by one *padding* unit. This allows the procedure to mark the finish times as the end of the last time period instead of the beginning. Possible values for *padding* are NONE, DTSECOND, DTMINUTE, DTHOUR, DTWEEK, DTMONTH, DTQTR, DTYEAR, SECOND, MINUTE, HOUR, DAY, WEEK, MONTH, QTR, or YEAR. The default value is chosen on the basis of the format of the times being plotted. See **Specifying the PADDING= Option** for further explanation of this option.

PAGELIMIT=*pages*
PAGES=*pages*

specifies an upper limit on the number of pages allowed for the Gantt chart. The default value of *pages* is 100. This option is useful for preventing a voluminous amount of output being generated by a wrong specification of the MININTERVAL= or SCALE= options.

REF=*values*

indicates the position of one or more vertical reference lines in the chart section. The values allowed are constant values. Only those reference lines that fall within the scope of the chart are printed. The reference lines are printed using the character specified in the REFCHAR= option (or |, if none is specified). If a time variable value is to be printed in the column where a REF= value goes, the plotting symbol for the time variable is printed instead of the REFCHAR= value. Similarly, the HOLICHAR= symbol has precedence over the REFCHAR= value.

   Example 2, **Example 4**, and **Example 5** show some of the ways to specify a list of values for reference lines.

REFCHAR='*c*'

indicates the character to print for reference lines. If no REFCHAR= option is given, the vertical bar (|) is used.

REFLABEL

specifies that the reference lines are to be labeled. The labels are formatted in the same way as the time axis and are placed along the bottom border of the Gantt chart at the appropriate points. If the reference lines are too numerous and the scale does not allow all the labels to be nonoverlapping, then some of the labels are dropped.

S_FINISH=*variable*
SF=*variable*

specifies the variable containing the resource-constrained finish time of each activity in the input data set. This option is not required if the default variable name S_FINISH is used.

S_START=*variable*
SS=*variable*

specifies the variable containing the resource-constrained start time of each activity in the input data set. This option is not required if the default variable name S_START is used.

SCALE=*scale*

requests that *scale* number of columns on the chart be equal to one unit of *mininterval*. The default value of SCALE is 1 if the time axis of the chart is too wide to fit on one page. If the time axis fits on less than one page, then a default value is chosen that expands the time axis as much as possible but still fits the time axis on one page.

SKIP=*skip*

S=*skip*

requests that *skip* number of lines be skipped between the plots of the schedules of two activities. The SKIP= option is allowed to take integer values between 0 and 4, inclusive. The default value of SKIP is 1.

SUMMARY

requests that a detailed description of all symbols and joining characters used in the Gantt chart be printed before the first page of the chart. This description includes examples of some strings that could occur in the body of the Gantt chart.

SYMCHAR='*string*'

defines the symbols to be used for plotting the early start, late start, early finish, late finish, actual start, actual finish, and the resource-constrained start and finish times, in that order. The default value is '<<>>**<>'. If any of the above times coincide, the symbol plotted is the one specified in the OVERLAPCH= option (or *, if none is specified). If the actual times and the resource-constrained schedules are not plotted on the chart, you can specify only the first four symbols. If fewer than the required number of symbols are specified, nonspecified symbols are obtained from the default string.

Specifying the INTERVAL= Option

The INTERVAL= option is needed only if you want holidays and breaks or both during a week or day to be indicated on the Gantt chart. The value of the INTERVAL parameter is used to compute the start and end of holiday periods to be compatible with the way they were computed and used by PROC CPM. Further, if the MARKWKND or MARKBREAK option is in effect, the INTERVAL parameter, in conjunction with the DAYSTART and DAYLENGTH options and the WORKDATA=, HOLIDATA=, and CALENDAR= data sets, helps identify the breaks during a standard week or day as well as the holidays that are to be marked on the chart. Valid values for the INTERVAL parameter are DAY, DTDAY, WEEKDAY, WORKDAY, DTWRKDAY, DTHOUR, DTMINUTE, and DTSECOND. If you specify INTERVAL as WEEKDAY or WORKDAY, the MARKWKND option is assumed to be in effect; otherwise, breaks during a week are indicated only if MARKWKND is specified and breaks within a day are marked only if MARKBREAK is specified.

Specifying the MININTERVAL= Option

If the time values being plotted are SAS date values, the valid values for MININTERVAL are DAY, WEEK, QTR, or YEAR. If the values are SAS datetime values, valid values for the option are DTDAY, DTWEEK, DTMONTH, DTQTR, DTYEAR, DTHOUR, DTMINUTE, or DTSECOND. If they are SAS time values, then valid values for MININTERVAL are HOUR, MINUTE, or SECOND.

Note: if the times being plotted are SAS datetime values and MININTERVAL is specified as DTHOUR, DTMINUTE, or DTSECOND, the output generated could run into several thousands of pages. Therefore, be careful when choosing the value of MININTERVAL.

Table 6.1 shows the default values of MININTERVAL corresponding to different values of the format of the times being plotted on the chart.

Table 6.1 Default Values of the MININTERVAL= Option

Format	MININTERVAL
DATEw.	DAY
DATETIMEw.d	DTDAY
HHMMw.d	HOUR
MONYYw.	MONTH
TIMEw.d	HOUR
YYMMDDw.	MONTH
YYQw.	MONTH

Specifying the PADDING= Option

As explained in **Input Data Set**, the finish times in the output data set from PROC CPM denote the final time unit of an activity's duration; that is, the activity finishes at the end of the day/second specified as the finish time. A plot of the activity's duration should continue through the end of the final time unit. Thus, if the E_FINISH time is specified as June 4, 1988, the early finish time for the activity is plotted at the end of June 4, 1988 (or the beginning of June 5, 1988).

In other words, the finish times are *padded* by a day (second) if the finish time variables are formatted as SAS date (SAS time or datetime) values. This treatment is consistent with the meaning of the variables as output by PROC CPM.

Default values of *padding* corresponding to different format types are shown in **Table 6.2**.

Table 6.2 Default Values of the PADDING= Option Corresponding to Format Type

Format	PADDING
SAS date value	DAY
SAS datetime value	DTSECOND
SAS time value	SECOND
other	NONE

The PADDING= option is provided to override the default padding explained above. Valid values of this option are NONE, SECOND, MINUTE, HOUR, DAY, WEEK, MONTH, QTR, YEAR, DTSECOND, DTMINUTE, DTHOUR, DTWEEK, DTMONTH, DTQTR, and DTYEAR. Use the value NONE if you do not want the finish times to be adjusted.

Since finish times are adjusted by the value of the PADDING= option, it is recommended that activities with 0 duration be deleted from the data set input to PROC GANTT. If this is not done, an activity with 0 duration is shown on the chart as having a positive duration because finish times are padded to show the end of the last time unit.

ID Statement

ID *variables*;

The ID statement specifies the variables to be printed that further identify each activity. If two or more consecutive observations have the same combination of values for all the ID variables, only the first of these observations is plotted. If the ID variables do not all fit on one page, they are omitted and a message explaining the omission is printed on the log.

Specifications for the Full-Screen Version of PROC GANTT

You can invoke PROC GANTT in full-screen mode by specifying FS (or FULLSCREEN) in the PROC statement. The full-screen mode offers you a convenient way to browse the Gantt chart for the project. For large projects, where the chart could span several pages, the full-screen mode is especially convenient because you can scroll around the output using commands on the command line or function keys. You can scroll to a given point on the chart by specifying a job number or a given point in time along the time axis. You can optionally display the title or the legend.

The specifications for the full-screen version of PROC GANTT and the output format are the same as those for the line-printer version. There are a few minor differences, however, that are listed below:

- The FILL option is not relevant in this case because all of the activities are plotted on one logical page.
- The NOLEGEND option is not effective. The screen always displays only the body of the chart along with the ID columns. To see what the symbols mean, you can use the SHOW LEGEND command, which causes the legend to be displayed at the bottom of the chart. To delete the legend, use the DELETE LEGEND command.
- The SUMMARY option is not supported in full-screen mode.
- The SCALE parameter works the same way as in the line-printer version, except for its default behavior. The default value is always 1, unlike in the line-printer case where, if the time axis fits on less than one page, the default value is chosen so that the time axis fills as much of the page as possible.

Full-Screen Commands

Table 6.3 lists the commands that can be used in the full-screen version of PROC GANTT.

Table 6.3 Full-Screen Commands and Their Purpose

Scrolling	Controlling Display	Exiting
BACKWARD	SHOW	END
FORWARD	DELETE	CANCEL
LEFT	FIND	
RIGHT		
TOP		
BOTTOM		
VSCROLL		
HSCROLL		

These commands are explained in greater detail below and demonstrated in **Example 12**.

BACKWARD

scrolls towards the top of the Gantt chart by the VSCROLL amount. BACKWARD MAX scrolls to the top of the chart. You can also specify the vertical scroll amount for the current command as BACKWARD PAGE | HALF | n. Note that during vertical scrolling, the column headings are not scrolled.

BOTTOM

scrolls to the bottom of the Gantt chart.

DELETE LEGEND | TITLE

deletes the legend or the title on the screen. DELETE LEGEND deletes the legend from the current display; DELETE TITLE deletes the current title (titles) from current display.

END

ends the current invocation of the procedure.

FIND

scrolls to the specified position on the chart. The format of the command is FIND JOB n or FIND TIME t. FIND JOB n scrolls backward or forward and positions the activity with job number n at the top of the chart. FIND TIME t scrolls left or right and positions the time t on the time axis at the left boundary of the chart area displayed.

FORWARD

scrolls towards the bottom of the Gantt chart by the VSCROLL amount. FORWARD MAX scrolls to the bottom of the chart. You can also specify the vertical scroll amount for the current command as FORWARD PAGE | HALF | n. Note that during vertical scrolling, the column headings are not scrolled.

HELP

displays a HELP screen listing all the full-screen commands specific to PROC GANTT.

HOME

moves the cursor to the command line.

HSCROLL

sets the amount that information scrolls horizontally when you execute the LEFT or RIGHT command. The format is HSCROLL PAGE | HALF | n. The specification is assumed to be in number of columns. HSCROLL PAGE sets the scroll amount to be number of columns in the part of the screen displaying the plot of the schedules. HSCROLL HALF is half that amount; HSCROLL n sets the horizontal scroll amount to n columns. The default setting is PAGE.

KEYS

displays current function key settings.

LEFT

scrolls towards the left boundary of the Gantt chart by the HSCROLL amount. LEFT MAX scrolls to the left boundary. You can also specify the horizontal scroll amount for the current command as LEFT PAGE | HALF | n. Note that during horizontal scrolling, the ID columns are not scrolled.

RIGHT

scrolls towards the right boundary of the network by the HSCROLL amount. RIGHT MAX scrolls to the right boundary. You can also specify the horizontal scroll amount for the current command as RIGHT PAGE | HALF | n. Note that during horizontal scrolling, the ID columns are not scrolled.

SHOW LEGEND | TITLE

displays the legend or the title on the screen. SHOW LEGEND displays the legend in the bottom portion of the current display; SHOW TITLE displays the current title (titles) in the top portion of the current display.

TOP

scrolls to the top of the Gantt chart.

VSCROLL

sets the amount that information scrolls vertically when you execute the BACKWARD or FORWARD command. The format is VSCROLL PAGE | HALF | n. The specification is assumed to be in number of rows. VSCROLL PAGE sets the scroll amount to be number of rows in the part of the screen displaying the plot of the schedules. VSCROLL HALF is half that amount; VSCROLL n sets the vertical scroll amount to n rows. The default setting is PAGE.

Specifications for the Graphics Version of PROC GANTT

This section describes the options that can be used in conjunction with the GRAPHICS option in a PROC GANTT statement to obtain high resolution quality Gantt charts. Most of the options described earlier for line-printer quality charts are also valid with the GRAPHICS option, with similar interpretations.

Table 6.7 in **Valid and Invalid Options for Line-Printer and Graphics Charts** shows valid options and lists any change in interpretation for the graphics version. **Table 6.8** lists the line-printer options that are invalid with the GRAPHICS option; for each such option, the corresponding option for high resolution charts is listed, where applicable. **Table 6.9** lists, for each GRAPHICS option described in this section, the corresponding line-printer option, if one exists. Refer to **DETAILS** for these tables.

Graphics Options in the PROC GANTT Statement

PROC GANTT *options*;

The options in the PROC GANTT statement listed below are specifically for graphics quality Gantt charts.

ANNOTATE=*SASdataset*
ANNO=*SASdataset*

specifies the input data set that must be an ANNOTATE= type data set containing the appropriate ANNOTATE variables. See the "ANNOTATE= Data Sets" chapter in your appropriate SAS/GRAPH documentation for details regarding annotate data sets. See **Example 17:   Using the SAS/GRAPH ANNOTATE= Option** for an illustration of this.

GOUT=*graphics catalog*

specifies the name of the graphics catalog used to save the output produced by PROC GANTT for later replay. See the "SAS/GRAPH Graphics Output" chapter in your appropriate SAS/GRAPH documentation for more details.

GRAPHICS

indicates that the Gantt chart produced be of high resolution quality. If you specify the GRAPHICS option but you do not have SAS/GRAPH software at your site, the procedure stops and issues an error message.

Graphics Options in the CHART Statement

CHART *specifications/options*;

As before, the CHART statement controls the format of the Gantt chart and speci-fies additional variables (other than the early, late, actual, and resource-constrained start and finish times) to be plotted on the chart. The same forms for the specification of CHART variables (as in the line-printer version) are allowed although the interpretation is somewhat different. Each form of specification is repeated here with a corresponding description of the interpretation. Note that the symbols for any activity are plotted on a line above the one corresponding to that activity. In addition to plotting the required symbol, PROC GANTT draws a vertical line below the symbol in the same color as the symbol. The length of the line is the same as the height of the bars (referred to as bar height) that repre-sent the durations of the activities on the Gantt chart. This line helps identify the exact position of the plotted value.

variable1. . .variablen
> indicates that each variable is to be plotted using symbols specified in SYMBOL statements. The *i*th variable in the list is plotted using the plot symbol, color, and font specified in the *i*th SYMBOL statement. The height specified in the SYMBOL statement is multiplied by the bar height to obtain the height of the symbol that is plotted. Thus, if H=0.5 in the first SYMBOL statement and the bar height is 5 percent of the screen area, then the first symbol is plotted with a height of 2.5 percent. For example, suppose the following two SYMBOL statements are in effect:

```
SYMBOL1 V=STAR C=RED   H=1;
SYMBOL2 V=V    C=GREEN H=0.5 F=GREEK;
```

Then, the statement

```
CHART SDATE FDATE;
```

> causes values of SDATE to be plotted with a red star that is as high as each bar and the values of FDATE with an inverted green triangle that is half as high as the bar height. See **SYMBOL Statement Specification** for details regarding SYMBOL statement specifications.

variable1=symbol1. . .variablen=symboln
> indicates that each variable is to be plotted using the symbol specified. The symbol must be a single character enclosed in quotes. The font used for the symbol is the same as the font used for the text.

(variables)=symbol1. . .(variables)=symboln
> indicates that each variable in parentheses is to be plotted using the symbol associated with that group. The symbol must be a single character enclosed in single quotes. For example, the statement

```
CHART (ED SD)='*'
      (FD LD)='+';
```

> plots the values of variables in the first group using an asterisk and the values of variables in the second group using a plus sign.

A single CHART statement can contain requests in more than one of these forms.

Note: it is not necessary to specify a CHART statement if only default values are to be used to draw the Gantt chart.

The options listed below can appear in the CHART statement specifically for the production of high resolution quality Gantt charts.

ANNOTATE=*SASdataset*
ANNO=*SASdataset*

specifies the input data set that must be an ANNOTATE= type data set containing the appropriate ANNOTATE variables. See the "ANNOTATE= Data Sets" chapter in your appropriate SAS/GRAPH documentation for details regarding annotate data sets. See **Example 17** for further illustration.

CAXIS=*color*
CAXES=*color*
CA=*color*

specifies the color to use for printing axes for the Gantt chart. If CAXIS= is omitted, the first color in the COLORS= list of the GOPTIONS statement is used.

CFRAME=*color*
CFR=*color*

specifies the color to use for filling the axis area. This option is ignored if the NOFRAME option is specified.

CHCON=*color*

specifies the color to use for drawing the horizontal connecting lines. If CHCON= is not specified, the axis color is used.

CREF=*color*

specifies the color to use for drawing vertical lines on the chart requested by the REF= option. If CREF= is not specified, the axis color is used.

CTEXT=*color*
CT=*color*

specifies the color to use for printing text that appears on the chart, including variable names or labels, tick mark values, values of ID variables, and so on. If CTEXT= is omitted, PROC GANTT uses the first color in the COLORS= list of the GOPTIONS statement.

DESCRIPTION=*'string'*
DES=*'string'*

specifies a descriptive string, up to 40 characters in length, that appears in the description field of PROC GREPLAY's master menu. If DESCRIPTION= is omitted, the description field contains a description assigned by PROC GANTT.

FONT=*name*

specifies the font to use for printing job numbers, ID variables, legend, labels on the time axis, and so forth. If this option is not specified, the hardware character set for your device is used to draw the text.

LHCON=*linetype*

specifies the line style (1-46) to be used for drawing the connecting line described in the option HCONNECT (described earlier in the **CHART Statement** section). Possible values for *linetype* are

    1   solid line (the default value when LHCON= is omitted)

  2—46 various dashed lines. See **Figure 6.1**.

For the corresponding line-printer option, see the HCONCHAR= option, described earlier.

LREF=*linetype*

specifies the line style (1-46) used for drawing the reference lines. The default line style is 1, a solid line. See **Figure 6.1** for examples of the various line styles.

NAME=*'string'*

where *'string'* specifies a descriptive string, up to eight characters long, that appears in the Name field of PROC GREPLAY's master menu. If you omit the NAME= option, the Name field of PROC GREPLAY's master menu contains the name of the procedure.

NOFRAME
NOFR

suppresses drawing the vertical boundaries to the left and right of the Gantt chart; only the top axis and a parallel line at the bottom are drawn. If this option is not specified, the entire chart area is framed.

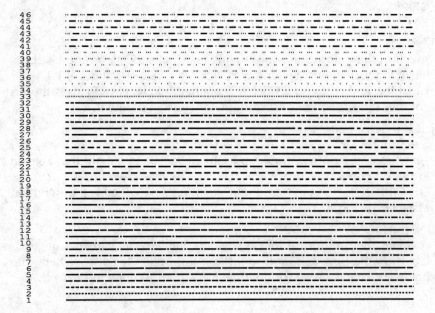

Figure 6.1   Valid Line Styles

DETAILS

Input Data Set

Often, the input data set that is used with PROC GANTT is the SCHEDULE output data set (the OUT= data set) produced by PROC CPM, sometimes with some additional variables added. Typically, this data set contains the start and finish times for the early and late start schedules (E_START, E_FINISH, L_START, and L_FINISH variables). For projects that are already in progress, this data set also contains the actual start and finish times (A_START and A_FINISH) of activities that have been completed. If PROC CPM has been used to perform resource-constrained scheduling, the SCHEDULE output data set also contains the resource-constrained start and finish times of the activities (specified by variables named S_START and S_FINISH). When such a data set is used as the input data set to PROC GANTT, the procedure draws a Gantt chart showing three different schedules for each activity: the predicted schedule using E_START, E_FINISH, L_START, and L_FINISH on the first line for the activity, the actual schedule using A_START and A_FINISH on the second line, and the resource-constrained schedule using S_START and S_FINISH on the third line.

Normally, each observation of the data set causes one set of bars to be plotted corresponding to the activity in that observation. If activity splitting has occurred during resource-constrained scheduling, the SCHEDULE output data set contains more than one observation for each activity. It also contains a variable named SEGMT_NO. For activities that are not split, this variable has a missing value. For split activities, the number of observations in the output data set is equal to (1 + the number of disjoint segments that the activity is split into). The first observation corresponding to such an activity has SEGMT_NO equal to missing and the S_START and S_FINISH times are equal to the start and finish times, respectively, of the entire activity. Following this observation, there are as many observations as the number of disjoint segments in the activity. All values for these segments are the same as the first observation for this activity, except SEGMT_NO, S_START, S_FINISH, and the duration. SEGMT_NO is the index of the segment, S_START and S_FINISH are the resource-constrained start and finish times for this segment, and duration is the duration of this segment. See **Printed Output** for details on how PROC GANTT treats the observations in this case.

Note: for a given observation in the output data set from PROC CPM, the finish times (E_FINISH, L_FINISH, and S_FINISH) denote the last *day* of work when the variables are formatted as SAS *date* values; if they are formatted as SAS *time* or *datetime* values, they denote the last *second* of work. For instance, if an activity has E_START=2JUN88 and E_FINISH=4JUN88, then the earliest start time for the activity is the beginning of June 2, 1988, and the earliest finish time is the end of June 4, 1988. Thus, PROC GANTT assumes that the early, late, or actual finish time of an activity is at the end of the time interval specified for the respective variable.

All start and finish times and additional variables specified in the CHART statement must be numeric and have the same formats. The ID and BY variables can be either numeric or character. Although the data set does not have to be sorted, the output may be more meaningful if the data are in order of increasing early start time. Further, if the data set contains segments of split activities, the data should also be sorted by SEGMT_NO for each activity.

Missing Values in Input Data Sets

Table 6.4 summarizes the treatment of missing values for variables in the input data sets used by PROC GANTT.

Table 6.4 Treatment of Missing Values in PROC GANTT

Data Set	Variable	Value used / Assumption made / Action taken
CALEDATA	CALID	default calendar (0 or "DEFAULT")
	SUN,. . ._SAT_	corresponding shift for default calendar
	D_LENGTH	DAYLENGTH, if available; else, 8:00, if INTERVAL=WORKDAY or DTWRKDAY; 24:00, otherwise
DATA	CHART	value ignored
	E_START	value ignored
	E_FINISH	value ignored
	L_START	value ignored
	L_FINISH	value ignored
	A_START	value ignored
	A_FINISH	value ignored
	S_START	value ignored
	S_FINISH	value ignored
	ID	missing
	CALID	default calendar (0 or "DEFAULT")
	SEGMT_NO	if SEGMT_NO is missing, all variables in this observation except S_START and S_FINISH are used; S_START and S_FINISH are used only if SEGMT_NO is not missing.
HOLIDATA	HOLIDAY	observation ignored
	HOLIDUR	ignored, if HOLIFIN is not missing; else, 1.0
	HOLIFIN	ignored, if HOLIDUR is not missing; else, HOLIDAY + (1 unit of INTERVAL)
	CALID	holiday applies to all calendars defined
WORKDATA	any numeric variable	00:00, if first observation; 24:00, otherwise

Page Format

The GANTT procedure divides the observations (activities) into a number of subgroups of approximately equal numbers. The size of each group is determined by the PAGESIZE system option. Similarly, the time axis is divided into a number of approximately equal divisions depending on the LINESIZE system option.

If the FILL option is specified, however, each page is filled as completely as possible before plotting on a new page. If both axes are split, the pages are ordered with the chart for each group of activities being plotted completely (the time axis occupying several consecutive pages, if needed) before proceeding to the next group.

If a BY statement is used, each BY group is formatted separately.

Two options that can be used effectively to control the format of the chart are the MININTERVAL= and SCALE= options. MININTERVAL is the smallest time interval unit to be identified on the chart, and SCALE is the number of columns to be used to denote one unit of MININTERVAL. For example, if MININTERVAL=MONTH and SCALE=10, the chart is formatted so that 10 columns denote the period of one month. The first of these 10 columns denotes the start of the month and the last denotes the end, with each column representing approximately three days. Further, the INCREMENT= option can be used to control the labeling. In the above example, if INCREMENT=2, then the time axis would have labels for alternate months.

Labeling on the Time Axis

If the variables being plotted in the chart are unformatted numeric values, the time axis is labeled by the corresponding numbers in increments specified by the INCREMENT= option. However, if the variables have DATE, DATETIME, or TIME formats, then the time axis is labeled with two or three lines. Each line is determined by the value of MININTERVAL, which in turn is determined by the format. **Table 6.5** illustrates the label corresponding to different values of MININTERVAL.

Table 6.5 Label Corresponding to MININTERVAL Values

MININTERVAL	First Line	Second Line	Third Line
DAY, WEEKDAY, WEEK, DTWEEK	month	day	
MONTH, QTR, YEAR, DTMONTH, DTQTR, DTYEAR	year	month	
DTHOUR, DTMINUTE, DTSECOND, DTDAY	month	day	time
HOUR, MINUTE, SECOND	time		

Note that the labeling on the time axis has been changed from the Version 5 labels.

Multiple Calendars and Holidays

Work pertaining to a given activity is assumed to be done according to a particular *calendar*. A calendar is defined in terms of a *work pattern* for each day and a *work-week structure* for each week. In addition, each calendar may have holidays during a given year. The **Multiple Calendars** section in Chapter 5, "The CPM Procedure," describes in great detail how calendars are defined and how all the options work together. In this chapter, a less detailed description is provided. PROC GANTT uses the same structure as PROC CPM for defining calendars with some minor differences. These differences in syntax are listed below.

- The HOLIDAY variable is specified as an option in the CHART statement and is not a separate statement as in PROC CPM.
- The CALID variable is also specified as an option in the CHART statement.
- The HOLIDUR and HOLIFIN variables are also specified as options in the CHART statement.
- The INTERVAL parameter is specified in the CHART statement and not in the PROC statement as in PROC CPM.

The WORKDATA (or workdays) data set specifies distinct shift patterns during a day. The CALEDATA (or calendar) data set specifies a typical workweek for any given calendar; for each day of a typical week, it specifies the shift pattern that is followed. The HOLIDATA (or holidays) data set specifies a list of holidays and the calendars that they refer to; holidays are defined either by specifying the start of the holiday and its duration in INTERVAL units or by specifying the start and end of the holiday period. If both the HOLIDUR and the HOLIFIN variables have missing values in a given observation, the holiday is assumed to start at the date/ time specified for the HOLIDAY variable and last one unit of *interval* where the INTERVAL option has been specified as *interval*. If a given observation has valid values for both the HOLIDUR and the HOLIFIN variables, only the HOLIFIN variable is used so that the holiday is assumed to start and end as specified by the HOLIDAY and HOLIFIN variables, respectively. The activities data set (the DATA= input data set) then specifies the calendar that is used by each activity in the project through the CALID variable (or a default variable _CAL_). Each of the three data sets used to define calendars is described in greater detail in the **Multiple Calendars** section in Chapter 5.

Each new value for the CALID variable in either the CALEDATA or the HOLIDATA data sets defines a new calendar. If a calendar value appears on the CALEDATA data set and not on the HOLIDATA data set, it is assumed to have the same holidays as the default calendar (the default calendar is defined in the PROC CPM chapter). If a calendar value appears on the HOLIDATA data set and not on the CALEDATA data set, it is assumed to have the same work pattern structures (for each week and within each day) as the default calendar. In the activities data set, valid values for the CALID variable are those that are already defined in either the CALEDATA or the HOLIDATA data sets.

All the holiday and workday and workweek information is used by PROC GANTT only for display; in particular, the weekend and shift information is used only if the MARKWKND or MARKBREAK options are in effect. The INTERVAL parameter, which has a greater scope in PROC CPM, is used here only to determine the end of holiday periods appropriately. Further, the HOLIDATA, CALEDATA, and WORKDATA data sets and the processing of holidays and different calendars are supported only when the INTERVAL parameter is DAY, WEEKDAY, DTDAY, WORKDAY, DTWRKDAY, DTHOUR, DTMINUTE, or DTSECOND.

Macro Variable _ORGANTT

The GANTT procedure defines a macro variable named _ORGANTT. This variable contains a character string that indicates the status of the procedure. It is set at procedure termination. The form of the _ORGANTT character string is STATUS= REASON=, where STATUS is either SUCCESSFUL or ERROR_EXIT and REASON can be one of the following:

- BADDATA_ERROR
- MEMORY_ERROR
- IO_ERROR
- SEMANTIC_ERROR
- SYNTAX_ERROR
- GANTT_BUG
- UNKNOWN_ERROR

This information can be used when PROC GANTT is one step in a larger program that needs to determine whether the procedure terminated successfully or not. Because _ORGANTT is a standard SAS macro variable, it can be used in the ways that all macro variables can be used (see the *SAS Guide to Macro Processing, Version 6 Edition*).

Full-Screen Version

Output Format

The output format is similar to the line-printer version of PROC GANTT. When PROC GANTT is invoked with the FS option, the screen is filled with a display of the Gantt chart. The display consists of column headings at the top and ID values (if an ID statement is used to specify ID variables) at the left. The body of the chart occupies the bottom right portion of the display. The column headings can be scrolled left or right, the ID values can be scrolled up or down, and the body of the chart can scroll along both directions. The display does not include the TITLES or LEGEND. Use the SHOW TITLE (SHOW LEGEND) commands to see the titles (the legend), as in **Example 12**.

In addition to using the symbols and joining characters as described for the line-printer version of PROC GANTT, the full-screen version also uses different colors to distinguish between the different types of activities and the associated bars.

You can use the FIND command to locate a particular job (by job number) or a particular time along the time axis. The format of the FIND command is FIND JOB n or FIND TIME t. All the commands that are specific to PROC GANTT are described in detail in **Specifications for the Full-Screen Version of PROC GANTT**. Most of the global commands used in SAS/FSP software are also valid with PROC GANTT; some of the relevant ones are described in the following section, **Full-Screen Global Commands**.

Full-Screen Global Commands

Most of the global commands used in SAS/FSP software are also valid with PROC GANTT; these commands are described in greater detail in Appendix 2, "Command Reference," in your appropriate SAS/FSP documentation. Some of the commands used for printing screens are described in the current section.

SAS/FSP software provides you with a set of printing commands that allow you to take pictures of windows and to route those pictures to a printer or a file. Whether you choose to route these items directly to a printer queue or to a print file, SAS/FSP software provides you with a means of supplying printing instructions. The following is an overview of these related commands and their functions:

FREE
  releases items in print queue to a printer.

PRTFILE
  specifies file destination for printed items.

SPRINT
  takes a picture of a window.

FREE
  releases all items in the print queue to the printer. This includes pictures taken with the SPRINT command as well as items sent to the print queue with the SEND command. All items in the print queue are also automatically sent to the printer when you exit the procedure, send an item that uses a different form, or send an item to a print file. Items are also sent automatically when internal buffers have been filled.
  Items sent to a file: if you have routed pictures taken with the SPRINT command to a file rather than to a printer, the file is closed when you execute a FREE command. It is also closed when you send an item that uses a different form, send items to a different print file or to the print queue, or exit the procedure.

Note: any items sent to the same print file after it has been closed will replace the current contents.

PRTFILE [*fileref* | *'actualfilename'* | CLEAR]

specifies a file to which the procedure sends letters or pictures taken with the SPRINT command instead of sending them to the default printer. You can specify a previously assigned fileref or an actual filename.

Using a filename: to specify a file named *destination-file*, execute

```
prtfile 'destination-file'
```

where *destination-file* follows you system's conventions. Note that quotes are required when you specify an actual filename rather than a fileref.

Using a fileref: you can also specify a previously assigned fileref.*

Return to the default: specify PRTFILE CLEAR to prompt the procedure to route information once again to the queue for the default printer.

Identify the current print file: specify PRTFILE to prompt the procedure to identify the current print file.

SPRINT [NOBORDER] [NOCMD]

takes a picture of the current window exactly as you see it, including window contents, border, and command line. By default, the picture is sent to the queue for the default printer.

Border and command line: by default, both the window border and command line are included in the picture you take with the SPRINT command. You can capture a picture of the window contents that excludes either the window border, the command line, or both. Specify NOBORDER to exclude the border and NOCMD to exclude the command line. Taking a picture of the window contents without the border and command line is a convenient way to print text for a report.

Destination: the destination of the picture captured with the SPRINT command is determined by the PRTFILE command. By default, the picture goes to the default printer. Use the PRTFILE command if you want it sent to a file instead. Each time you execute the SPRINT command, the picture you take is appended to the current print file; it does not write over the current file. See the PRTFILE command for further explanation.

Graphics Version

Formatting the Chart

If necessary, PROC GANTT divides the Gantt chart into several pages. The amount of information contained on each page is determined by the values of the global parameters HPOS and VPOS. The height of each bar of the Gantt chart is computed as $(1/v)\%$ of the screen height where VPOS=v. Thus, the larger the value of VPOS, the narrower the bar. The height of the characters in the text is the same as the height of each bar. The value of HPOS determines the width of the chart. The screen is assumed to be divided into h columns where HPOS=h; thus, each column is assumed to be as wide as $(1/h)\%$ of the screen width. Hence, SCALE=10 and MININTERVAL=WEEK imply that a duration of one week is denoted by a bar of length $(10/h)\%$ of the screen width.

---

* For a discussion of assigning filerefs to external files, see the FILENAME statement in base SAS documentation.

PROC GANTT uses hardware text whenever possible, unless the global option NOCHARACTERS is in effect, in which case the SIMPLEX font is used. You can specify any other font for the text and the labeling of the time axis by using the FONT= option in the CHART statement. Global PATTERN statements are used to control the fill pattern to be used for the bars depending on whether the activity is critical or not. See the following section, **Using PATTERN Statements**, for details.

Using PATTERN Statements

PROC GANTT uses those patterns that are available with PROC GCHART. PROC GANTT uses a maximum of eight different patterns to denote various phases in an activity's duration and the various types of schedules that are plotted. Patterns are specified in PATTERN statements which can be used anywhere in your SAS program. **Table 6.6** lists the use of each of the first eight PATTERN statements that are used by PROC GANTT.

Table 6.6 PATTERN Statements used by PROC GANTT

PATTERN Statement	Used to denote
1	duration of a noncritical activity
2	slack time for a noncritical activity
3	duration of a critical activity
4	slack time for a supercritical activity
5	duration of a supercritical activity
6	actual duration of an activity
7	break due to a holiday
8	resource-constrained duration of an activity

Any PATTERN statements that you specify are used. If more are needed, default PATTERN statements are used. The **PATTERN Statements** section in the "Enhancing Your Graphics Output Designs" chapter in your appropriate SAS/GRAPH documentation contains a detailed description of PATTERN Statements. Most of the relevant information from that section is reproduced here for the sake of completeness.

PATTERN Statement Specification

The general form of a PATTERN statement is

PATTERN*n options*;

where

n

is a number ranging from 1 to 255. If you do not specify a number after the keyword PATTERN, PATTERN1 is assumed.

options

allows you to specify the colors and patterns used to fill the bars in your output.

PATTERN statements are additive; if you specify a C= or V= option in a PATTERN statement and then omit that option in a later PATTERN statement ending in the same number, the option remains in effect. To turn off options specified in a previous PATTERN*n* statement, either specify all options in a new PATTERN*n* statement, or use the keyword PATTERN*n* followed by a semicolon. For example, the following statement turns off any C= or V= option specified in previous PATTERN3 statements:

```
pattern3;
```

You can reset options in PATTERN statements to their default values by specifying a null value. A comma can be used (but is not required) to separate a null parameter from the next option.

For example, the following statements both cause C= to assume its default value (the value of the CPATTERN= option or the first color in the COLORS= list):

```
pattern c=, v=solid;
```

or

```
pattern c= v=solid;
```

In the following statement, both options are reset to their default values:

```
pattern2 c= v=;
```

You can also turn off options by specifying the RESET= option in a GOPTIONS statement. Refer to "The GOPTIONS Statement" chapter in your appropriate SAS/GRAPH documentation for details.

You can specify the following options in a PATTERN statement:

COLOR=*color*
C=*color*

specifies the color to use for a bar or other area to be filled. If you do not specify C= in a PATTERN statement, the procedure uses the value you specified for the CPATTERN= option in a GOPTIONS statement. If you omitted the CPATTERN= option, the procedure uses the pattern specified by V= (see below) with each color in the COLORS= list before it uses the next PATTERN statement.

REPEAT=*n*
R=*n*

specifies the number of times the PATTERN statement is to be reused. For example, the following statement represents one pattern to be used by SAS/GRAPH software:

```
pattern1 v=x3 c=red;
```

You can use the REPEAT= option in the statement to repeat the pattern before going to the next pattern. For example, if you specify the following statements, PATTERN1 is repeated ten times before PATTERN2 is used:

```
pattern1 v=x3 c=red   r=10;
pattern2 v=s  c=blue r=10;
```

Remember that if you omit the COLOR= option from the PATTERN statement and you do not specify the CPATTERN= option, SAS/GRAPH software repeats the pattern for each color in the current COLORS= list. If you specify the R= option in a PATTERN statement from which the

C= option is omitted, the statement cycles through the COLORS= list the number of times given by R=.

For example, if the current device has seven colors, then the following statement results in seventy patterns because each group of seven patterns generated by cycling through the COLORS= list is repeated ten times:

```
pattern v=x3 r=10;
```

VALUE=*value*
V=*value*

specifies the pattern to use for a bar or other area to be filled.

The valid values you can use depend on what procedure you are using and the type of graph you are producing. In PROC GANTT, which produces bars, you must use one of the pattern values shown in **Figure 6.2**.

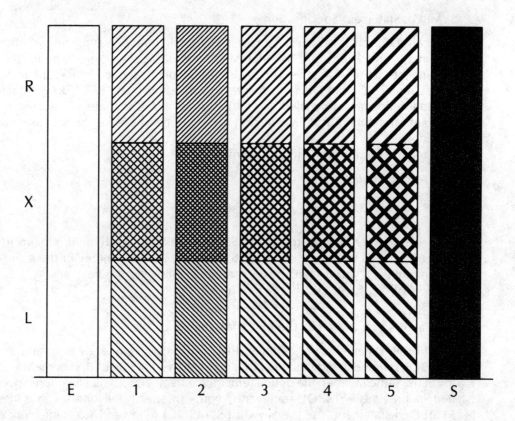

Figure 6.2 Pattern Selection Guide

In a PATTERN statement, if you specify a value for V= but not for C=, the procedure uses the value you specified for the CPATTERN= option in a GOPTIONS statement. If you omitted the CPATTERN= option, the procedure uses the pattern specified for V= with each color in the COLORS= list before it uses the next PATTERN statement. Thus, if you specify the following statements, the PATTERN1 statement is used for the first type of bar, namely, for the duration of a noncritical activity:

```
pattern1 c=red    v=x3;
pattern2          v=s;
pattern3 c=blue   v=l3;
pattern4 c=green v=r4;
proc gantt data=sched;
```

The PATTERN2 statement is used for the second type of bar, namely, for the slack time of a noncritical activity. Because a C= value is not specified in the PATTERN2 statement, SAS/GRAPH software uses the PATTERN2 statement and cycles through the colors in the COLORS= list for the device to obtain as many patterns as there are colors in the list. If needed, the PATTERN3 and PATTERN4 values are then used for any remaining types of bars.

SYMBOL Statement Specification

You can specify a SYMBOL statement anywhere in your SAS program. SYMBOL statements give PROC GANTT information about the characters to be used for plotting the CHART variables. The **SYMBOL Statements** section in the "Enhancing Your Graphics Output Designs" chapter in your appropriate SAS/GRAPH documentation contains a detailed description of SYMBOL statements. Most of the relevant information from that section is reproduced here for the sake of completeness.

The general form of a SYMBOL statement is

SYMBOL*n options*;

where

n

is a number ranging from 1 to 255. Each SYMBOL statement remains in effect until you specify another SYMBOL statement ending in the same number. If you do not specify a number following the keyword SYMBOL, SYMBOL1 is assumed.

options

allows you to specify the plot characters and color.

SYMBOL statements are additive; that is, if you specify a given option in a SYMBOL statement and then omit that option in a later SYMBOL statement ending in the same number, the option remains in effect. To turn off all options specified in previous SYMBOL statements, you can specify all options in a new SYMBOL*n* statement, use the keyword SYMBOL*n* followed by a semicolon, or specify a null value. A comma can be used (but is not required) to separate a null parameter from the next option.

For example, the following statements both cause C= to assume its default value (the value of the CSYMBOL= option or the first color in the COLORS= list):

```
symbol1 c=, v=plus;
```

and

```
symbol1 c= v=plus;
```

In the following statement, both options are reset to their default values:

```
symbol4 c= v=;
```

You can also turn off options by specifying the RESET= option in a GOPTIONS statement. Refer to "THE GOPTIONS Statement" in your appropriate SAS/GRAPH documentation for details.

General options   You can specify the following options in the SYMBOL statement:

COLOR=*color*
C=*color*
  specifies the color to use for the corresponding plot specification. Both the points and the line will have this color.
    If you do not specify the C= option in a SYMBOL statement, the procedure uses the value you specified for the CSYMBOL= option in a GOPTIONS statement. If you omit the CSYMBOL= option, the procedure uses the value specified by the V= option with each color in the COLORS= list before it uses the next SYMBOL statement.

F=*font*
H=*height*
  F= specifies the font from which the value specified with V= is to be drawn. H= specifies the height of the characters.
    For example, this SYMBOL statement

```
symbol1 c=green v=k f=special h=2;
```

  indicates that the symbol at each data point is the letter K from the SPECIAL font (a filled square), drawn in green, the height being twice the bar height.

REPEAT=*n*
R=*n*
  specifies the number of times the SYMBOL statement is to be reused.

V=*symbol*
  gives the plot character for the corresponding plot specifications. Possible V= values are the letters A through W, the numbers 0 through 9, and the special symbols shown in **Figure 6.3**.

Note that if you use the special symbol comma (,) with V=, you must enclose the comma in quotes. Here is an example:

```
symbol1 v=',';
```

If you omit the V= value, V=NONE is used.

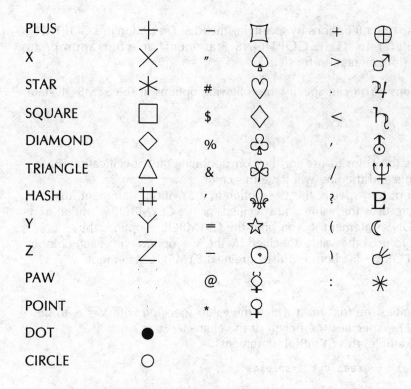

PLUS	+	–	⬠	+	⊕
X	×	"	♠	>	♂
STAR	✳	#	♡	.	♃
SQUARE	□	$	◇	<	♄
DIAMOND	◇	%	♣	'	☉
TRIANGLE	△	&	✿	/	Ψ
HASH	♯	'	⚜	?	♇
Y	Y	=	☆	(	☾
Z	Z	–	☉	)	♀
PAW		@	☿	:	✳
POINT	.	*	♀		
DOT	●				
CIRCLE	○				

Figure 6.3 Values for the V= Option

Valid and Invalid Options for Line-Printer and Graphics Charts

All the options that are valid for both line-printer and graphics Gantt charts are explained in detail in the **SPECIFICATIONS** section for the line-printer case. With few exceptions these options have the same interpretation for the graphics version.

The following options in the GANTT statement have the same effect in both line-printer and graphics versions of PROC GANTT:

- CALEDATA=*SASdataset*
- DATA=*SASdataset*
- HOLIDATA=*SASdataset*
- MAXDEC=*n*
- SPLIT='*splitchar*'
- WORKDATA=*SASdataset*

The following options in the CHART statement have the same effect in both line-printer and graphics versions of PROC GANTT:

- A_FINISH=*variable*
- A_START=*variable*
- BETWEEN=*number*
- CALID=*name*
- CRITFLAG
- DAYLENGTH=*daylength*
- DAYSTART=*daystart*
- DUPOK
- E_FINISH=*variable*
- E_START=*variable*

- FILL
- HCONNECT
- HOLIDAY=(*variable*)
- HOLIDUR=(*variable*)
- HOLIEND=(*variable*)
- INCREMENT=*increment*
- INTERVAL=*interval*
- L_FINISH=*variable*
- L_START=*variable*
- MARKBREAK
- MARKWKND
- MAXDATE=*maxdate*
- MINDATE=*mindate*
- MININTERVAL=*mininterval*
- NOJOBNUM
- NOLEGEND
- PADDING=*padding*
- PAGES=*pages*
- REF=*values*
- REFLABEL
- S_FINISH=*variable*
- S_START=*variable*

Table 6.7 lists those line-printer options that have a different interpretation for the graphics version of PROC GANTT.

Table 6.7   Line-Printer Options and the Corresponding Graphics Interpretation

Line-Printer Option	Corresponding Graphics Interpretation
SCALE=*scale*	one column is denoted by $(1/h)\%$ of the screen width where HPOS=h
SKIP=*skip*	*skip* number of bar heights are skipped between the bars for two consecutive activities. 0 is not a valid value in the graphics case
SUMMARY	all the patterns and symbols that are used with the corresponding interpretation are listed.

Table 6.8 lists options, in alphabetical order, that are valid only in conjunction with the GRAPHICS option. When applicable, the corresponding line-printer option is also listed. **Table 6.9** lists options specific for line-printer charts and, where applicable, the corresponding graphics option.

Table 6.8 Graphics Options Not Valid for a Line-Printer Chart

Graphics Option/Statement	Corresponding Line-Printer Option
ANNOTATE=*SASdataset*	n/a
CAXIS=*color*	n/a
CFRAME=*color*	n/a
CHCON=*color*	n/a
CREF=*color*	n/a
CTEXT=*color*	n/a
DESCRIPTION=*string*	n/a
FONT=*name*	n/a
GOUT=*graphics catalog*	n/a
GRAPHICS	line-printer chart is the default
LHCON=*linetype*	HCONCHAR='*c*'
LREF=*linetype*	REFCHAR='*c*'
NAME='*string*'	n/a
NOFRAME	FORMCHAR='*string*'
PATTERN statement	JOINCHAR='*string*' and SYMCHAR='*string*'
SYMBOL statement	first character of variable name is plotted (See description of CHART specifications)

Table 6.9 Line-Printer Options Not Valid with the GRAPHICS Option

Line-Printer Option	Corresponding Graphics Option
FORMCHAR='*string*'	NOFRAME
HCONCHAR='*c*'	LHCON=*linetype* & CHCON=*color*
HOLICHAR='*c*'	PATTERN statement number 7 is used
JOINCHAR='*string*'	PATTERN statement numbers 1–6 and 8 are used
OVERLAPCH='*c*'	n/a
OVPCHAR='*c*'	n/a
REFCHAR='*c*'	LREF=*linetype* & CREF=*color*
SYMCHAR='*string*'	PATTERN statement numbers 1–6 and 8 are used

Printed Output

PROC GANTT produces one or more pages of printed values and a plot of the schedule. If the SUMMARY option is specified, the chart is preceded by a detailed description of the symbols used. A legend is printed at the foot of the chart on each page unless suppressed by the NOLEGEND option. The main body of the output consists of columns of the ID values and the Gantt chart of the schedule. For each activity in the project, PROC GANTT prints the values of the ID variables in the ID columns and plots one, two, or all three of the following schedules: the schedule as specified by the early and late start and finish times, the actual schedule as specified by the actual start and finish times, and the resource-constrained schedule as specified by the resource-constrained start and finish times. The procedure looks for default variable names for each of these times (E_START for early start, E_FINISH for early finish, S_START for resource-constrained start times, and so on), or you may explicitly specify the names of the appropriate variables using the ES, EF, LS, . . . options. Normally, each observation in the data set is assumed to denote a new activity, and a new set of ID values are printed and the schedules corresponding to this activity are plotted on the chart. There are two exceptions to this rule:

- If the ID values for two or more succeeding observations are identical, only the first such observation is used.
- If there is a variable named SEGMT_NO in the input data set, PROC GANTT assumes that the data set contains observations for segments of activities that were split during resource-constrained scheduling. In accordance with the conventions used by PROC CPM, recall that only observations with a missing value for SEGMT_NO are assumed to denote a new activity. Further, the data are assumed to be sorted by SEGMT_NO for each activity. For each activity, PROC GANTT plots the schedules corresponding to the ES, EF, LS, LF, AS, and AF variables on the basis of the first observation for this activity, namely, the observation with a missing value for the SEGMT_NO. This observation is also the one used for printing values for the ID variables for this activity. If the activity is not split, this same observation is used to plot the resource-constrained schedule also. However, if the activity is split, then all the observations for this activity with integer values for the variable SEGMT_NO are used to plot the resource-constrained schedule as disjoint segments on the line used for plotting the S_START and S_FINISH times.

In addition to the schedules that are plotted, the Gantt chart also displays any variables specified in the CHART statement. Holidays, weekends, breaks within a day, and reference lines are also marked appropriately. For details on how to specify holidays, weekends, and breaks within a day, see **Multiple Calendars and Holidays**. It is important to note that all times are plotted at the start of the appropriate time period. Thus, if the chart starts on June 1, 1988, in column 15 of the page and the value of E_START is 2JUN88, MININTERVAL=DAY and SCALE=5, then the early start time is plotted in column 20. Each activity is identified by a job number (unless the NOJOBNUM option is used), which by default is printed to the left of the ID values. If the time axis of the chart is very wide, causing it to be divided across more than one page, this job number is printed to the left of the respective activity on succeeding pages. ID values are not printed on continuation pages.

Column headings for ID variables consist of either variable labels (if they are present and if space permits) or variable names. To suppress variable labels in column headings, use the NOLABEL system option. (See the OPTIONS statement in "SAS Statements Used Anywhere," in base SAS documentation, for a description of the NOLABEL option.) If the ID variable is formatted, the value is printed using that format. If the ID variables occupy too much space, leaving no room for the chart to be started on the first page, they are omitted and a warning message is printed on the log.

If the CRITFLAG option is specified, a flag is printed to the right of the ID values that indicates how critical the activity is. This flag is also repeated on continuation pages if the time axis occupies more than one page. The body of the chart starts to the right of this flag.

LINE-PRINTER AND FULL-SCREEN EXAMPLES

The first 11 examples illustrate several of the line-printer options available with PROC GANTT. **Example 1** shows how to obtain a basic Gantt chart using the default options. **Example 2** demonstrates how to use various options to customize the Gantt chart for the same project. In **Example 3**, an extra input data set containing holiday information is used to mark the holidays used in computing the schedule by PROC CPM. The same example also illustrates the use of the CHART statement to specify additional variables to be plotted on the chart. **Example 4** illustrates the use of the MININTERVAL= and SCALE= options to control the width of the chart; this also shows how the chart is divided and continued on the succeeding page when the time axis extends beyond one page. In **Example 5**, the MINDATE= and MAXDATE= options are used to permit viewing of only the desired portion of the schedule in greater detail. **Example 6** uses the HOLIDUR= option in conjunction with the INTERVAL= option to mark holidays of varying lengths on the Gantt chart. **Example 7** illustrates the use of the CALENDAR and WORKDAY data sets to mark holiday information from different calendars on the chart.

In **Example 8**, the actual schedule for each activity is plotted on a separate line, in addition to the early and late start schedules. **Example 9** shows the resource-constrained schedule containing split segments of activities. **Example 10** illustrates the use of the BY statement to obtain Gantt charts for different projects in a multiproject environment. In **Example 11**, PROC GANTT is used after some data manipulation steps to produce Gantt charts for individuals, each working on different subsets of activities in the project. **Example 12** illustrates the use of full-screen PROC GANTT.

Example 1:   Printing a Gantt Chart

This example shows how to use the GANTT procedure to obtain a basic Gantt chart using the default options. The data shown below describe the precedence relationships among the tasks involved in the construction of a typical floor in a multistory building. The first step saves the precedence relationships in a SAS data set. The variable ACTIVITY names each task, the variable DUR specifies the time it takes to complete the task in days, and the variables SUCCESS1 to SUCCESS4 specify tasks that are immediate successors to the task identified by the ACTIVITY variable.

PROC CPM determines the shortest schedule for the project that finishes before September 1, 1988. The solution schedule, saved in a SAS data set, is sorted before PROC GANTT plots the schedule. Because the DATA= option is not specified, PROC GANTT uses the latest data set, which happens to be the sorted version of the output data set from PROC CPM. The Gantt chart is plotted on two pages because there are too many observations (29) to fit on one page. Note that the observations are split into two groups containing 15 and 14 observations, respectively, so that the chart size on each page is approximately equal. The time axis is labeled from June 21, 1988, to September 1, 1988, because these are the minimum and maximum dates in the input data set. A legend is printed at the bottom of the chart on each page.

```
title 'Gantt Example 1';
title2 'Printing a Gantt Chart';

data;
   format activity $20. success1 $20. success2 $20. success3 $20.
                    success4 $20.;
```

```
      input activity dur success1-success4;
      cards;
form                    4 pour . . .
pour                    2 core . . .
core                   14 strip spray_fireproof insulate_walls .
strip                   2 plumbing curtain_wall risers doors
strip                   2 electrical_walls balance_elevator . .
curtain_wall            5 glaze_sash . . .
glaze_sash             5 spray_fireproof insulate_walls . .
spray_fireproof         5 ceil_ducts_fixture . . .
ceil_ducts_fixture     5 test . . .
plumbing               10 test . . .
test                    3 insulate_mechanical . . .
insulate_mechanical     3 lath . . .
insulate_walls          5 lath . . .
risers                 10 ceil_ducts_fixture . . .
doors                   1 port_masonry . . .
port_masonry            2 lath finish_masonry . .
electrical_walls       16 lath . . .
balance_elevator        3 finish_masonry . . .
finish_masonry          3 plaster marble_work . .
lath                    3 plaster marble_work . .
plaster                 5 floor_finish tiling acoustic_tiles .
marble_work             3 acoustic_tiles . . .
acoustic_tiles          5 paint finish_mechanical . .
tiling                  3 paint finish_mechanical . .
floor_finish            5 paint finish_mechanical . .
paint                   5 finish_paint . . .
finish_mechanical       5 finish_paint . . .
finish_paint            2 caulking_cleanup . . .
caulking_cleanup        4 finished . . .
;

* invoke cpm to find the optimal schedule;

proc cpm finishbefore date='1sep88'd;
   activity activity;
   duration dur;
   successors success1-success4;

* sort the schedule by the early start date;

proc sort; by e_start;

* invoke proc gantt to print the schedule;

proc gantt;
run;
```

Output 6.1   Printing a Gantt Chart

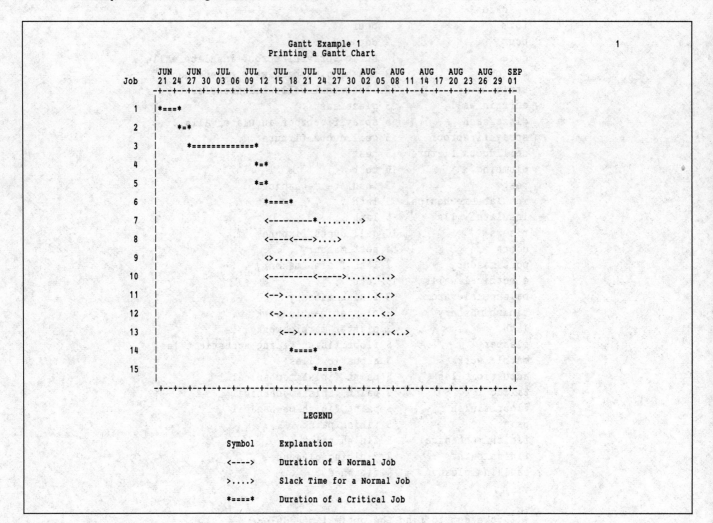

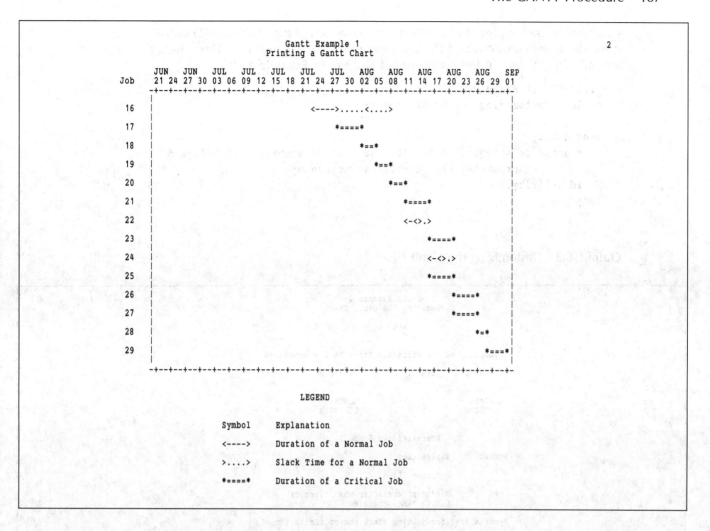

Example 2: Customizing the Gantt Chart

This example shows how to control the format of the Gantt chart using CHART statement options. The input data set used by PROC GANTT is the same as that used in **Example 1**. The output is on four pages; the first two pages contain a detailed description of the various symbols used by the procedure to plot the schedule. This description is produced by using the SUMMARY option. The next two pages contain the chart. The FILL option causes the first page to be filled as completely as possible before the second page is started. Thus, the first page of the chart contains 17 activities while the second page contains only 11 activities.

The SKIP=2 option causes 2 lines to be skipped between observations. The NOLEGEND option suppresses printing of the legend while the NOJOBNUM option causes job numbers to be omitted. The CRITFLAG option is used to produce the flag to the left of the main chart indicating if an activity is critical. The REF= option produces the reference lines shown on the chart on the specified dates. INCREMENT=5 indicates to the procedure that labels are to be printed in increments of 5 units of MININTERVAL, which, by default, is DAY. The ID

statement is used to print the activity names to the left of the chart. The ID statement also causes the activity, STRIP, to appear only once in the chart. Thus, there
are only 28 activities in this chart instead of 29 as in **Example 1**.

```
title 'Gantt Example 2';
title2 'Customizing the Gantt Chart';

proc gantt;
   chart / ref='10jun88'd to '30aug88'd by 15 summary fill nolegend
           increment=5 skip=2 critflag nojobnum;
   id activity;
run;
```

Output 6.2   Customizing the Gantt Chart

```
                         Gantt Example 2                              1
                     Customizing the Gantt Chart

                             Summary


        Symbols used for different times on the schedule

        Variable      Symbol         Variable      Symbol


        E_START         <            L_START         <
        E_FINISH        >            L_FINISH        >


                        Miscellaneous Symbols

        Symbol     Explanation

          |        Reference Line

          *        Overprint character when start or
                   finish times coincide

        Symbols used for joining start and/or finish times

        Symbol     Explanation

          -        Duration of non-critical job

          .        Slack time for non-critical job

          =        Duration of critical job

          -        Slack time(neg.) for supercritical job

          *        Duration of supercritical job
```

```
                         Gantt Example 2                              2
                     Customizing the Gantt Chart

                          Summary (Contd.)


                Some examples of typical strings

        String          Description

        <--->...<...>    Duration followed by slack time:
                         early finish before late start

        <---<--->...>    Duration followed by slack time:
                         early finish after late start

        <---*...>        Duration followed by slack time:
                         early finish equals late start
```

(continued on next page)

(continued from previous page)

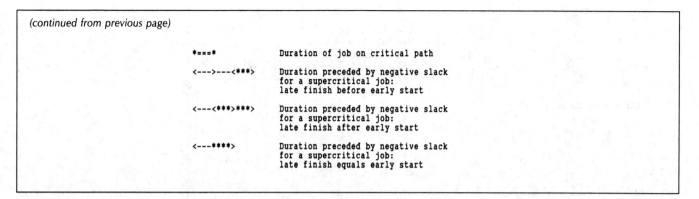

```
        *====*                  Duration of job on critical path

        <--->---<***>           Duration preceded by negative slack
                                for a supercritical job:
                                late finish before early start

        <---<***>***>           Duration preceded by negative slack
                                for a supercritical job:
                                late finish after early start

        <---****>               Duration preceded by negative slack
                                for a supercritical job:
                                late finish equals early start
```

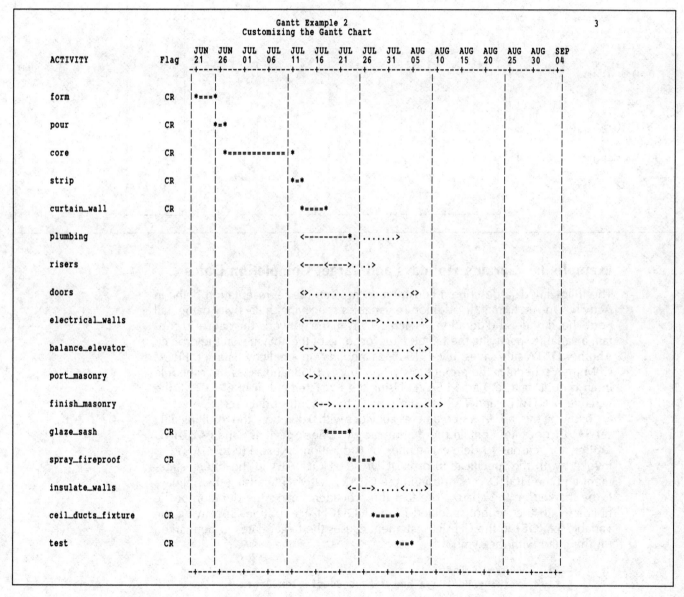

```
                                Gantt Example 2                                         3
                            Customizing the Gantt Chart

                    JUN  JUN  JUL  JUL  JUL  JUL  JUL  JUL  JUL  AUG  AUG  AUG  AUG  AUG  AUG  SEP
 ACTIVITY      Flag  21   26   01   06   11   16   21   26   31   05   10   15   20   25   30   04
                   -+----+----+----+----+----+----+----+----+----+----+----+----+----+----+----+-
                    |    |         |                   |                   |                   |

 form          CR  |*====*        |                   |                   |                   |

 pour          CR  |    *=*       |                   |                   |                   |

 core          CR  |    *=============|*               |                   |                   |

 strip         CR  |              *=*                  |                   |                   |

 curtain_wall  CR  |              *=====*              |                   |                   |

 plumbing          |              <----------*........>|                   |                   |

 risers            |              <----<---->.|..>     |                   |                   |

 doors             |              <>.........|.........<>                  |                   |

 electrical_walls  |              <----------<-|--->........>|            |                   |

 balance_elevator  |              <-->.......|.........<.>|               |                   |

 port_masonry      |               <->.......|.........<.>|               |                   |

 finish_masonry    |               <-->.....|.............<|.>            |                   |

 glaze_sash    CR  |    |         |         *=====*|                   |                   |

 spray_fireproof CR |    |         |         *=|==*               |                   |

 insulate_walls    |    |         |         <-|-->.....<.....>|                            |

 ceil_ducts_fixture CR|  |         |                   *=====*                             |

 test          CR  |    |         |                   *==*                                 |

                    |    |         |                   |                   |                   |
                   -+----+----+----+----+----+----+----+----+----+----+----+----+----+----+----+-
```

```
                                   Gantt Example 2                                    4
                                Customizing the Gantt Chart

                       JUN  JUN  JUL  JUL  JUL  JUL  JUL  JUL  JUL  AUG  AUG  AUG  AUG  AUG  AUG  SEP
ACTIVITY           Flag  21   26   01   06   11   16   21   26   31   05   10   15   20   25   30   04
                       -+----+----+----+----+----+----+----+----+----+----+----+----+----+----+----+-

insulate_mechanical  CR   |    |         |    |    |    |    |    |  *==*|                   |         |

lath                 CR   |    |         |    |    |    |    |    |    *| =*                 |         |

plaster              CR   |    |         |    |    |    |    |    |  *====*                  |         |

marble_work               |    |         |    |    |    |    |    |  <-<>.>                  |         |

acoustic_tiles       CR   |    |         |    |    |    |    |    |    *====*                |         |

tiling                    |    |         |    |    |    |    |    |    <-<>.>                |         |

floor_finish         CR   |    |         |    |    |    |    |    |    *====*                |         |

paint                CR   |    |         |    |    |    |    |    |         *==| =*          |         |

finish_mechanical    CR   |    |         |    |    |    |    |    |         *==| =*          |         |

finish_paint         CR   |    |         |    |    |    |    |    |                   *=*    |         |

caulking_cleanup     CR   |    |         |    |    |    |    |    |                   *====*            |

                       -+----+----+----+----+----+----+----+----+----+----+----+----+----+----+----+-
```

Example 3:   Marking Holidays and Target Completion Dates

The following data describe a construction project, the representation being in
Activity-On-Arc format. In addition to variables specifying the activity name, tail
node, head node, and duration of each activity in the network, the data also contain a variable specifying the target dates for some of the activities in the project.
Another DATA step saves July 4, 1988, as a holiday in a holiday data set. PROC
CPM then schedules the project to start on July 1, 1988, and saves the schedule
in an output data set named SAVE. Using the ID statement in PROC CPM, the
variables ACTIVITY and TARGET are passed to the output data set.

Following this, a DATA step deletes activities with 0 duration; the resulting data
set SAVE1 does not contain the dummy activity. (See **Specifying the PADDING
Option** for reasons to delete activities of 0 duration.) Next, PROC GANTT is
invoked with the specification of HOLIDATA=HOLDATA in the PROC statement and the HOLIDAY= option in the CHART statement causing the holidays
to be marked on the chart. Note that the procedure marks the duration of the
holiday with the symbol specified in the HOLICHAR= option. Specifying the
variable TARGET in the CHART statement causes the target dates to be marked
on the chart with the symbol 'T'.

```
title 'Gantt Example 3';
title2 'Marking Holidays and Target Completion Dates';

data const1;
   format target date9.;
   input activity $ 1-20 tail 22 dur 24 head 26
         target date9.;
   cards;
```

```
     Drill Well            1 4 2 .
     Pump House            2 3 5 .
     Install Pipe          5 2 7 10jul88
     Construct Power Line  1 3 5  7jul88
     Excavate              1 5 4  9jul88
     Install Pump          4 6 7 .
     Deliver Material      1 2 3 .
     Assemble Tank         3 4 6 .
     Erect Tower           6 6 7 .
     Foundation            4 4 6 12jul88
     Dummy                 4 0 5 .
     ;

   data holdata;
      format hol date7.;
      input hol date7.;
      cards;
4jul88
;

   * schedule the project subject to holidays;

   proc cpm data=const1 date='1jul88'd holidata=holdata out=save;
      tailnode tail;
      duration dur;
      headnode head;
      id activity target;
      holiday hol;

   * delete activities with 0 duration;

   data save1;
      set save;
      if dur=0 then delete;

   * sort the schedule by the early start date;

   proc sort out=sched; by e_start;

   * plot the schedule;

   proc gantt holidata=holdata data=sched;
      chart target='T' / holichar='H' holiday=(hol)
                         scale=4;
      id activity;
   run;
```

Output 6.3   Marking Holidays and Target Completion Dates on the Gantt
Chart

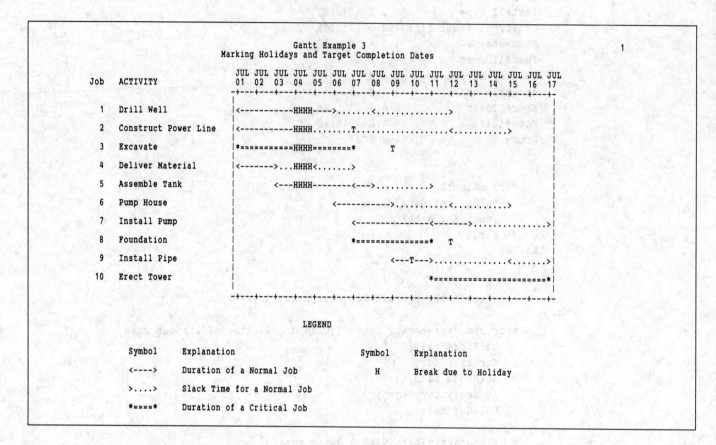

```
                              Gantt Example 3                                  1
                    Marking Holidays and Target Completion Dates

                    JUL JUL JUL JUL JUL JUL JUL JUL JUL JUL JUL JUL JUL JUL JUL JUL JUL
 Job   ACTIVITY      01  02  03  04  05  06  07  08  09  10  11  12  13  14  15  16  17
                    -+---+---+---+---+---+---+---+---+---+---+---+---+---+---+---+---+-
                     |                                                             |
  1    Drill Well    |<----------HHHH---->.......<...............>                 |
                     |                                                             |
  2    Construct Power Line |<----------HHHH.......T..................<...........>|
                     |                                                             |
  3    Excavate      |*==========HHHH=======*        T                            |
                     |                                                             |
  4    Deliver Material |<------->...HHHH<.......>                                 |
                     |                                                             |
  5    Assemble Tank |      <---HHHH--------<--->...........>                      |
                     |                                                             |
  6    Pump House    |              <----------->...........<...........>         |
                     |                                                             |
  7    Install Pump  |                  <---------------<------->...............>  |
                     |                                                             |
  8    Foundation    |              *===============*    T                        |
                     |                                                             |
  9    Install Pipe  |                  <---T--->...............<.......>          |
                     |                                                             |
 10    Erect Tower   |                      *=======================*             |
                     |                                                             |
                    -+---+---+---+---+---+---+---+---+---+---+---+---+---+---+---+---+-


                                  LEGEND


         Symbol     Explanation                Symbol     Explanation
         <---->     Duration of a Normal Job      H       Break due to Holiday
         >....>     Slack Time for a Normal Job
         *====*     Duration of a Critical Job
```

Example 4:   Using the MININTERVAL= and SCALE= Options

The construction project described in **Example 3** is scheduled using PROC CPM
with INTERVAL=WEEK so that durations are in units of weeks instead of days.
The start date for the project is specified as June 30, 1988.

The specifications MININTERVAL=WEEK and SCALE=10 cause PROC
GANTT to use 10 columns to denote one week. Note that this choice also causes
the chart to become too wide to fit on one page. Thus, PROC GANTT splits the
chart into two pages. The first page contains the ID variable as well as the job
number while the second page contains only the job number. The chart is split
so that the printed area on each page is approximately equal.

The specification REF='1JUL88'D TO '15OCT88'D BY MONTH causes PROC
GANTT to draw reference lines at the start of every month. Further, the reference
lines are labeled using the REFLABEL option.

```
title 'Gantt Example 4';
title2 'Use of MININTERVAL and SCALE Options';

* schedule using interval=week;

proc cpm data=const1 date='30jun88'd interval=week
        out=save;
```

```
      tailnode tail;
      duration dur;
      headnode head;
      id activity;

   *delete activities with 0 duration;

   data save;
      set save;
      if dur=0 then delete;

   proc sort data=save; by e_start;

   proc gantt data=save;
      chart / mininterval=week scale=10 nolegend
             ref='1jul88'd to '15oct88'd by month
             reflabel;
      id activity;
   run;
```

Output 6.4   Using the MININTERVAL= and SCALE= Options on a Gantt Chart

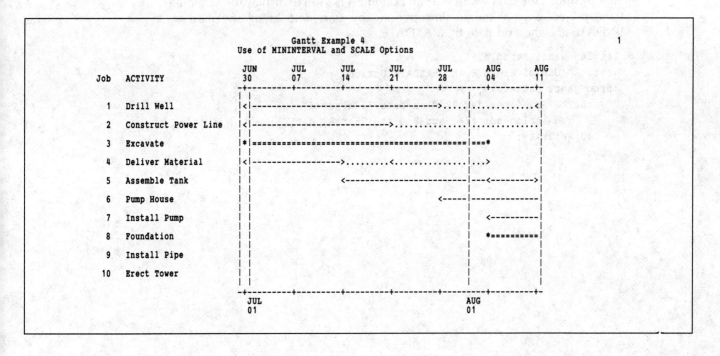

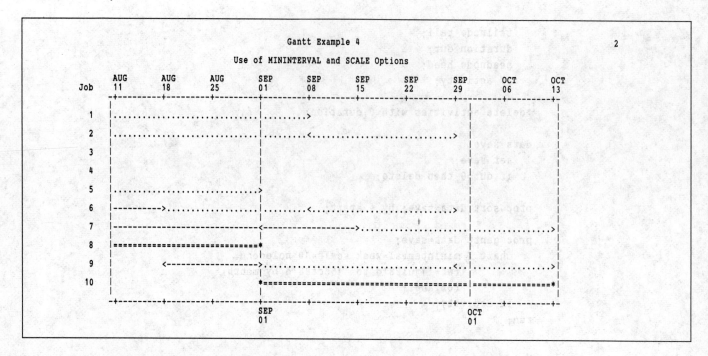

Example 5:   Using the MINDATE= and MAXDATE= Options

In this example, the data set SAVE from **Example 4** is used to display the schedule of the project over a limited time period, the start date being specified by MINDATE and the end date by MAXDATE.

```
title 'Gantt Example 5';
title2 'Use of MINDATE and MAXDATE Options';
proc gantt data=save;
   chart / mindate='1aug88'd maxdate='31aug88'd
           nolegend ref='5aug88'd to '25aug88'd by 5;
   id activity;
run;
```

Output 6.5 Using the MINDATE= and MAXDATE= Options on a Gantt Chart

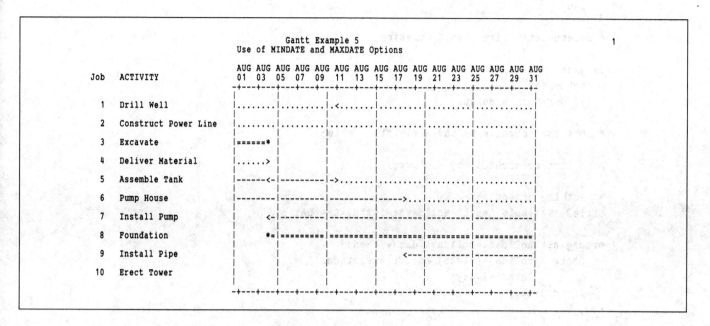

Example 6: Variable Length Holidays

This example shows how you can mark vacation periods that last longer than one day on the Gantt chart. This can be done by using the HOLIDUR= option. Recall that holiday duration is assumed to be in *interval* units where *interval* is the value specified for the INTERVAL parameter. The project data for this example are the same as the data used in the previous example. Suppose that in your scheduling plans you want to assign work on all days of the week, allowing a day off on July 4, 1988, and a vacation period starting on July 8, 1988, with duration specified as three. The data set HOLIDAYS contains the holiday information for the project. First, the project is scheduled with INTERVAL=DAY so that the holidays are on July 4, 1988, and on July 8, 9, and 10, 1988. PROC GANTT is invoked with INTERVAL= DAY to correspond to the invocation of PROC CPM. The resulting output is shown in **Output 6.6**.

```
title 'Gantt Example 6';

data holidays;
    format vactn date 7.;
    vactn= '4jul88'd; output;
    vactn= '8jul88'd; vactndur=3; output;
    run;

* schedule the project subject to holidays;

proc cpm data=const1 date='1jul88'd holidata=holidays out=save
        interval=day;
    tailnode tail;
    duration dur;
    headnode head;
```

```
      id activity target;
      holiday vactn / holidur=(vactndur);
      run;

* delete activities with 0 duration;

data save1;
   set save;
   if dur=0 then delete;

* sort the schedule by the early start date;

proc sort out=sched1; by e_start;

* plot the schedule;
title2 'Variable Length Holidays: INTERVAL = DAY';

proc gantt holidata=holidays data=sched1;
   chart / holiday=(vactn) holidur=(vactndur)
           interval=day;
   id activity;
run;
```

Output 6.6 Variable Length Holidays: INTERVAL=DAY

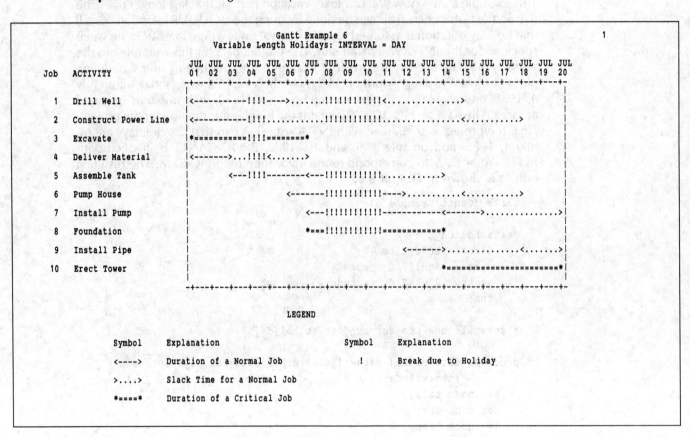

Next, consider the same project and holidays data set, but invoke PROC CPM with INTERVAL=WEEKDAY. Then, the value 3 specified for the variable VACTNDUR is interpreted as 3 weekdays. The holidays are on July 4 and July 8, July 11, and July 12, 1988, because July 9 and July 10 (Saturday and Sunday) are nonworking days anyway. The same steps are used as above, except that INTERVAL is set to WEEKDAY instead of DAY in both PROC CPM and PROC GANTT. Suppose that the resulting data set is saved as SCHED2. The following invocation of PROC GANTT produces **Output 6.7**. Note that the use of INTERVAL= WEEKDAY causes weekends to be also marked on the chart.

```
title2 'Variable Length Holidays: INTERVAL = WEEKDAY';

proc gantt holidata=holidays data=sched2;
   chart / holiday=(vactn) holidur=(vactndur)
           interval=weekday;
   id activity;
run;
```

Output 6.7   Variable Length Holidays: INTERVAL=WEEKDAY

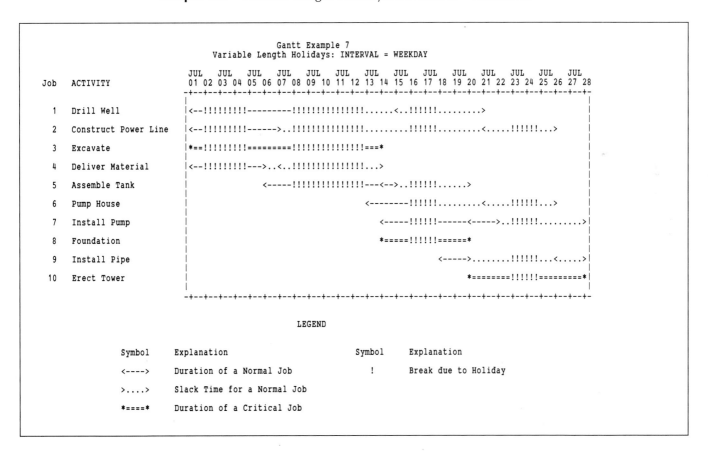

Finally, when the INTERVAL= option is specified as WORKDAY, the workday is assumed to be from 9:00 a.m. to 5:00 p.m. and the holiday period starts from 9:00 a.m. on July 8 and ends at 9:00 a.m. on July 13, 1988. PROC GANTT is invoked with the MARKBREAK option and MININTERVAL=DTHOUR so that all

breaks during a day can be seen. Because SCALE is not specified, this means that each column denotes one hour of the schedule. Because the project duration is several days long, the entire Gantt chart would be spread across many pages. Here, only a portion of the Gantt chart is shown (in **Output 6.8**) using the MINDATE= and MAXDATE= options. Note that the Gantt chart is labeled with the date as well as the time values on the time axis.

```
title2 'Variable Length Holidays: INTERVAL = WORKDAY';

proc gantt holidata=holidays data=sched3;
   chart / holiday=(vactn) holidur=(vactndur)
           interval=weekday mininterval=dthour
           markbreak
           mindate='1jul88:09:00'dt
           maxdate='7jul88:09:00'dt;
   id activity;
run;
```

Output 6.8   Variable Length Holidays: INTERVAL=WORKDAY

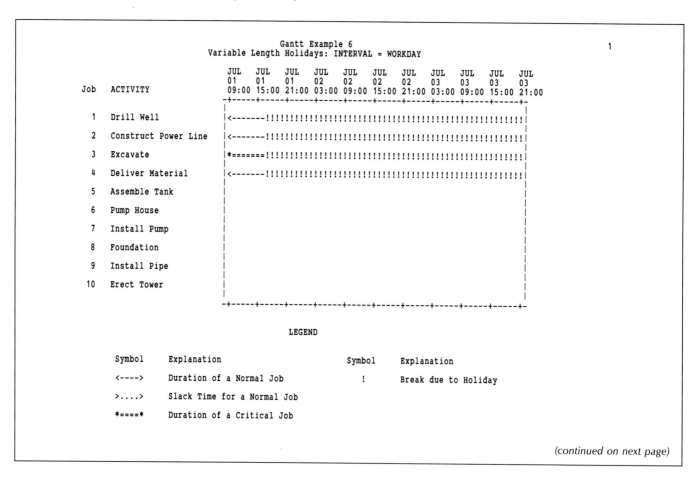

(continued from previous page)

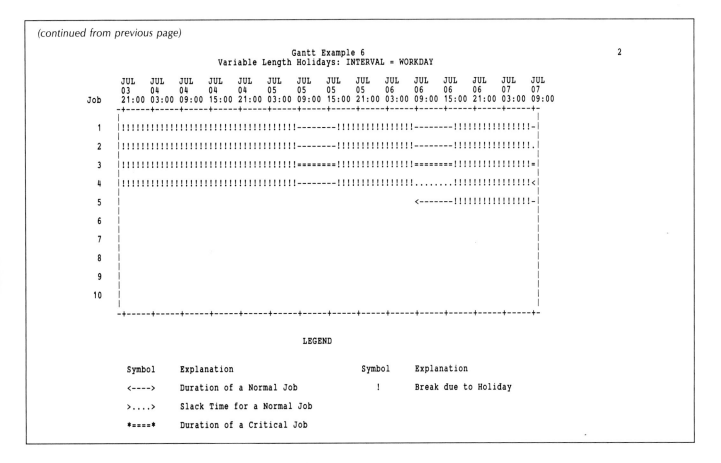

Example 7: Multiple Calendars

This example illustrates the use of multiple calendars within a project. The data for this example are the same as the data used in **Example 9** in Chapter 5, "The CPM Procedure." Suppose that the company that was contracted to do the excavation has a six-day workweek; thus, the activity EXCAVATE has a six-day week while all the other activities follow a five-and-one-half-day workweek. The workdays data set defines the work pattern for a full day (in the shift variable FULLDAY) and a half-day (in the shift variable HALFDAY). The CALDAT2 data set includes a variable named _CAL_ that identifies two different calendars, CAL1 and CAL2. CAL1 is the five-and-one-half-day week calendar and CAL2 is the six-day week calendar. The holidays data set (HOLDAT2) defines July 4, 1988, to be a holiday in both the calendars, via the variable _CAL_. To associate activities with the appropriate calendar, a variable named _CAL_ in the activities data set identifies the appropriate calendar. The input data sets to PROC CPM are printed in **Output 6.9**. The program used to invoke PROC CPM and PROC GANTT is shown below. The Gantt chart is shown in **Output 6.10**.

Output 6.9   Multiple Calendars: Data Sets

```
                              Multiple Calendars
                              Project Data Set

    OBS     TASK            DURATION     SUCCESR1         SUCCESR2       SUCCESR3      _CAL_

     1      Drill Well        3.50       Pump House                                   CAL1
     2      Pump House        3.00       Install Pipe                                 CAL1
     3      Power Line        3.00       Install Pipe                                 CAL1
     4      Excavate          4.75       Install Pipe     Install Pump   Foundation   CAL2
     5      Deliver Material  2.00       Assemble Tank                                CAL1
     6      Assemble Tank     4.00       Erect Tower                                  CAL1
     7      Foundation        4.00       Erect Tower                                  CAL1
     8      Install Pump      6.00                                                    CAL1
     9      Install Pipe      2.00                                                    CAL1
    10      Erect Tower       6.00                                                    CAL1
```

```
                              Multiple Calendars                                         2
                              Holidays Data Set

                    OBS        VACTN     _CAL_

                     1        04JUL88    CAL1
                     2        04JUL88    CAL2
```

```
                              Multiple Calendars                                         3
                              Workdays Data Set

                    OBS      FULLDAY    HALFDAY

                     1        8:00       8:00
                     2       16:00      12:00
```

```
                              Multiple Calendars                                         4
                              Calendar Data Set

                  OBS      _SUN_       _SAT_     _CAL_

                   1      HOLIDAY     HALFDAY    CAL1
                   2      HOLIDAY     FULLDAY    CAL2
```

```
proc cpm date='1jul88'd data=project out=sched5
     holidata=holdat2
     workday=workdat
     calendar=caldat2
     interval=workday
     daystart='08:00't
     daylength='08:00't;
  holiday vactn;
  activity task;
  duration duration;
  successor succesr1 succesr2 succesr3;
  id _cal_;
run;

title 'Example 7';
title2 'Multiple Calendars';
```

```
proc gantt data=sched5
    holidata=holdat2
    workday=workdat
    calendar=caldat2;
  chart / holiday=(vactn)
          interval=workday
          daystart='08:00't
          daylength='08:00't
          markbreak
          mindate='1jul88:08:00'dt
          maxdate='7jul88:08:00'dt;
    id task;
run;
```

Output 6.10 Multiple Calendars

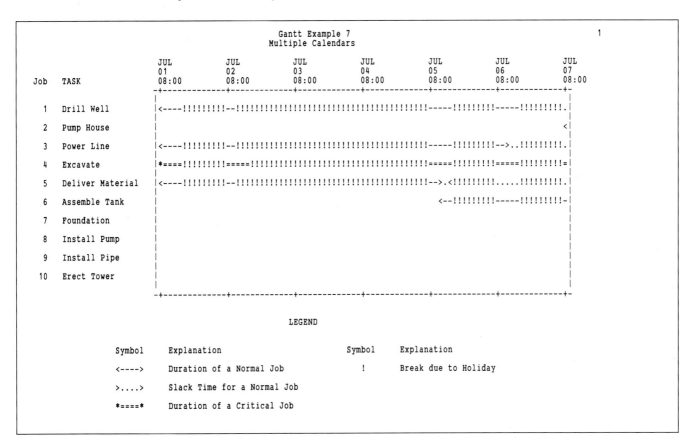

Example 8:   Plotting the Actual Schedule

Suppose that the project is complete and you wish to compare the actual progress of the activities with the schedule computed by PROC CPM. The following DATA step stores actual start and finish times of each activity in a data set named ACTUAL. A data set named UPDATE is then created that contains both the schedule obtained from PROC CPM (the data set SAVE1 from **Example 3** is used because it does not contain the dummy activity) and the actual schedule. The resulting data set is sorted by early start time.

PROC GANTT is then used to plot computed and actual schedules for each activity on separate lines. The A_START= and A_FINISH= options in the CHART statement specify the variables containing the actual start and finish times for each activity. SYMCHAR='<<>>SF' causes the symbols 'S' and 'F' to be used to print actual start and finish times instead of the default symbol '*'. OVERLAPCH='@' indicates that the symbol '@' is to be used when any of the start or finish times coincide.

```
title 'Gantt Example 8';
title2 'Plotting Actual Start and Finish Times on the Chart';

data actual;
   format fdate date9. sdate date9.;
   input activity $ 1-20 fdate date9. sdate date9.;
   cards;
Drill Well            5jul88    1jul88
Pump House            9jul88    7jul88
Install Pipe          12jul88   10jul88
Construct Power Line  5jul88    1jul88
Excavate              7jul88    2jul88
Install Pump          12jul88   8jul88
Deliver Material      5jul88    2jul88
Assemble Tank         7jul88    5jul88
Erect Tower           17jul88   13jul88
Foundation            12jul88   8jul88
;

* merge the computed schedule with the actual schedule;

data update;
   merge save1 actual;

* sort the data;

proc sort;
   by e_start;

* plot the computed and actual schedules using proc gantt;

proc gantt data=update holidata=holdata;
   chart / symchar='<<>>SF' overlapch='@' holiday=(hol)
           a_start=sdate a_finish=fdate;
   id activity;

run;
```

Output 6.11   Plotting the Actual Schedule on the Gantt Chart

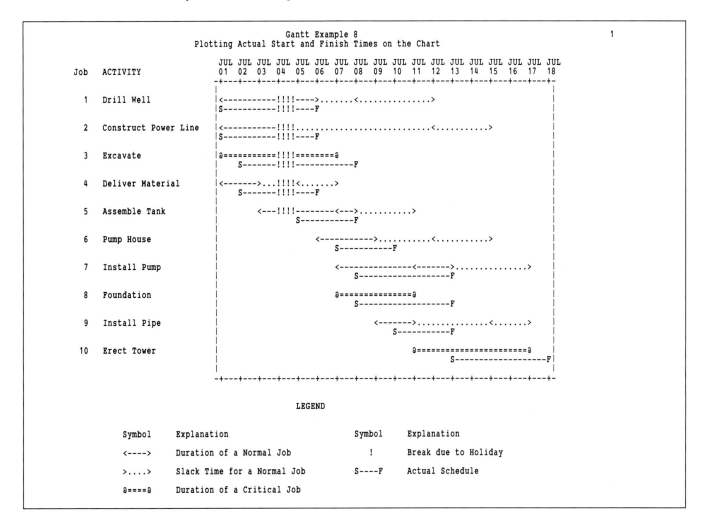

```
                                   Gantt Example 8                                    1
                      Plotting Actual Start and Finish Times on the Chart

                    JUL JUL JUL JUL JUL JUL JUL JUL JUL JUL JUL JUL JUL JUL JUL JUL JUL JUL
                    01  02  03  04  05  06  07  08  09  10  11  12  13  14  15  16  17  18
   Job   ACTIVITY   -+---+---+---+---+---+---+---+---+---+---+---+---+---+---+---+---+---+-
                    |
    1    Drill Well |<-----------!!!!---->.......<..............>                    |
                    |S-----------!!!!----F                                          |
                    |                                                               |
    2    Construct Power Line  |<-----------!!!!............................<...........>    |
                    |S-----------!!!!----F                                          |
                    |                                                               |
    3    Excavate   |a===========!!!!========a                                      |
                    |     S-------!!!!------------F                                  |
                    |                                                               |
    4    Deliver Material  |<------->...!!!!<.......>                               |
                    |     S-------!!!!----F                                         |
                    |                                                               |
    5    Assemble Tank  |      <---!!!!--------<--->..........>                     |
                    |             S-----------F                                     |
                    |                                                               |
    6    Pump House  |               <---------->...........<...........>           |
                    |               S-----------F                                   |
                    |                                                               |
    7    Install Pump  |             <---------------<------->..............>        |
                    |               S------------------F                            |
                    |                                                               |
    8    Foundation  |             a===============a                                |
                    |               S------------------F                            |
                    |                                                               |
    9    Install Pipe  |               <------->..............<.......>             |
                    |               S-----------F                                   |
                    |                                                               |
   10    Erect Tower  |                       a=====================a               |
                    |                         S-------------------F|                |
                    |                                                               |
                    -+---+---+---+---+---+---+---+---+---+---+---+---+---+---+---+---+---+-


                                      LEGEND


           Symbol      Explanation                    Symbol      Explanation

           <---->      Duration of a Normal Job         !         Break due to Holiday

           >....>      Slack Time for a Normal Job    S----F       Actual Schedule

           a====a      Duration of a Critical Job
```

Example 9:   Plotting the Resource-Constrained Schedule

This example illustrates the plotting of the resource-constrained schedule on the Gantt chart. The schedule used is the one produced in **Example 16** of Chapter 5, "The CPM Procedure." The output data set from PROC CPM is printed in **Output 6.12**.

Output 6.12   Resource-Constrained Schedule

```
                              Gantt Example 9                                      1
                         Resource Constrained Schedule

OBS  TAIL  HEAD  SEGMT_NO  DUR  ACTIVITY            WORKERS  S_START  S_FINISH  E_START  E_FINISH  L_START  L_FINISH
  1    1     2      .       4   Drill Well             2     01JUL88  07JUL88   01JUL88  04JUL88   07JUL88  10JUL88
  2    1     2      1       2   Drill Well             2     01JUL88  02JUL88   01JUL88  04JUL88   07JUL88  10JUL88
  3    1     2      2       2   Drill Well             2     06JUL88  07JUL88   01JUL88  04JUL88   07JUL88  10JUL88
  4    2     5      .       3   Pump House             2     08JUL88  11JUL88   05JUL88  07JUL88   11JUL88  13JUL88
  5    2     5      1       2   Pump House             2     08JUL88  09JUL88   05JUL88  07JUL88   11JUL88  13JUL88
  6    2     5      2       1   Pump House             2     11JUL88  11JUL88   05JUL88  07JUL88   11JUL88  13JUL88
  7    5     7      .       2   Install Pipe           2     14JUL88  15JUL88   08JUL88  09JUL88   14JUL88  15JUL88
  8    1     5      .       3   Construct Power Line   1     03JUL88  05JUL88   01JUL88  03JUL88   11JUL88  13JUL88
  9    1     4      .       5   Excavate               3     01JUL88  05JUL88   01JUL88  05JUL88   01JUL88  05JUL88
 10    4     7      .       6   Install Pump           2     07JUL88  13JUL88   06JUL88  11JUL88   10JUL88  15JUL88
 11    4     7      1       4   Install Pump           2     07JUL88  10JUL88   06JUL88  11JUL88   10JUL88  15JUL88
 12    4     7      2       2   Install Pump           2     12JUL88  13JUL88   06JUL88  11JUL88   10JUL88  15JUL88
 13    1     3      .       2   Deliver Material       1     01JUL88  02JUL88   01JUL88  02JUL88   04JUL88  05JUL88
 14    3     6      .       4   Assemble Tank          2     03JUL88  06JUL88   03JUL88  06JUL88   06JUL88  09JUL88
 15    6     7      .       6   Erect Tower            4     10JUL88  15JUL88   10JUL88  15JUL88   10JUL88  15JUL88
 16    4     6      .       4   Foundation             2     06JUL88  09JUL88   06JUL88  09JUL88   06JUL88  09JUL88
```

PROC GANTT is invoked with all default options and an ID statement. Note that even though the input data set to PROC GANTT contains 16 observations, the Gantt chart shows only 10 activities. The observations corresponding to the split segments of each activity have been combined to produce the plot of the resource-constrained schedule for that activity.

```
title 'Example 9';
title2 'Plotting the Resource Constrained Schedule';
proc gantt data=spltschd;
   id activity;
run;
```

Output 6.13   Resource-Constrained Schedule

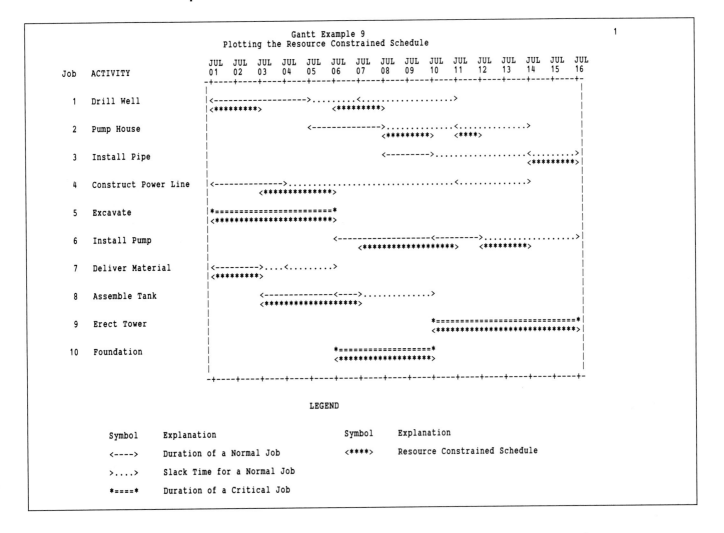

Example 10:   BY Processing

Suppose that the construction is divided into three subprojects, A, B, and C, and you want separate Gantt charts for each project. The data set CONST2, printed below, contains project information in a variable named PROJECT. After scheduling the master project using PROC CPM with ACTIVITY and PROJECT as ID variables, the output data set is sorted by project name and early start time. Then PROC GANTT is invoked with the variable PROJECT specified in the BY statement to obtain individual Gantt charts for each project.

```
title 'Gantt Example 10';
title2 'BY Processing';

proc cpm data=const2 date='1jul88'd;
   tailnode tail;
   duration dur;
   headnode head;
   id activity project;
```

```
data proj;
   set _last_;
   if dur=0 then delete;

proc sort;
   by project e_start;

proc gantt data=proj;
   chart / scale=4 increment=2;
   by project;
   id activity;
run;
```

Output 6.14   Using BY Processing for Separate Gantt Charts

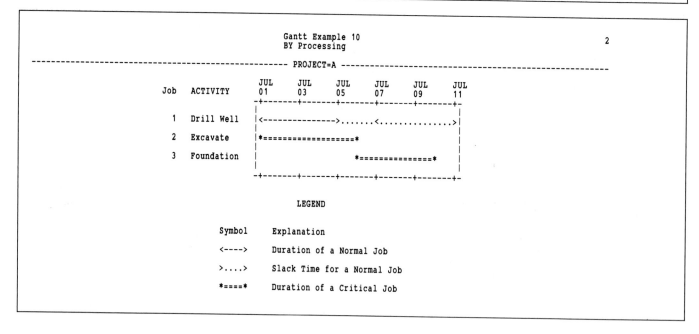

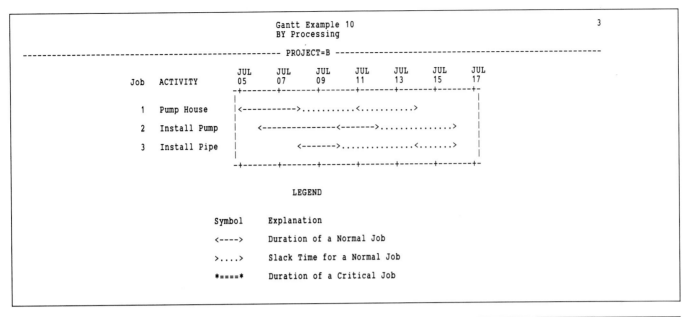

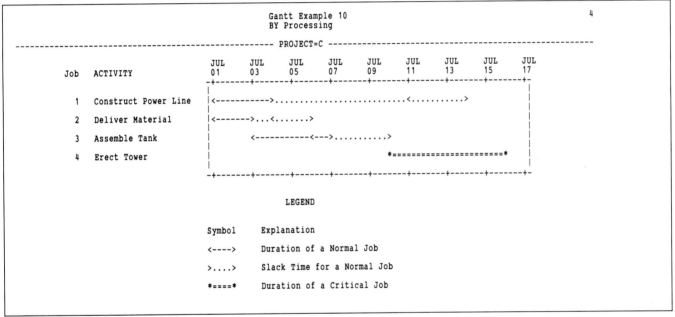

Example 11:   Gantt Charts by Persons

Now suppose that you want to obtain individual Gantt charts for two people (Thomas and William) working on the construction project. The data set CONST3, printed in **Output 6.15**, contains two new variables, Thomas and William. Each variable has a value 1 for activities in which the person is involved. (Each value has a missing value otherwise.) Thus, a value 1 for the variable Thomas in observation number 1 indicates that Thomas is working on the activity DRILL WELL.

PROC CPM is used to schedule the project to start on July 1, 1988. A data set named PERSONS is created containing one observation per activity per person working on that activity and a new variable named PERSON containing the name of the person to which the observation pertains. For example, this new data set contains two observations for the activity INSTALL PUMP, one with PERSON='Thomas' and the other with PERSON='William', and no observation

for the activity CONSTRUCT POWER LINE. This data set is printed in order by
PERSON and E_START, also in **Output 6.15**. Then, PROC GANTT is used to
obtain individual charts for each person. The resulting output is shown in
Output 6.16.

```
proc cpm data=const3 date='1jul88'd;
    tailnode tail;
    duration dur;
    headnode head;
    id activity thomas william;
run;
data persons;
    set _last_;
    if dur=0 then delete;
    if William^=. then do;
      person='William';
      output;
      end;
    if Thomas^=. then do;
      person='Thomas';
      output;
      end;
    drop Thomas William;
run;
proc sort data=persons;
    by person e_start;
run;
```

Output 6.15 Gantt Charts by Persons

```
                              Gantt Example 11                                    1
                              Data CONST3

        OBS    ACTIVITY            TAIL   DUR   HEAD   THOMAS   WILLIAM

          1    Drill Well            1     4     2      1         .
          2    Pump House            2     3     5      .         .
          3    Install Pipe          5     2     7      1         1
          4    Construct Power Line  1     3     5      .         .
          5    Excavate              1     5     4      .         1
          6    Install Pump          4     6     7      1         1
          7    Deliver Material      1     2     3      1         1
          8    Assemble Tank         3     4     6      .         1
          9    Erect Tower           6     6     7      1         .
         10    Foundation            4     4     6      1         .
         11    Dummy                 4     0     5      .         .
```

```
                              Gantt Example 11                                    2
                              Data PERSONS

 OBS  TAIL  HEAD  DUR  ACTIVITY          E_START   E_FINISH   L_START   L_FINISH   T_FLOAT   F_FLOAT   PERSON

  1     1     2    4   Drill Well        01JUL88   04JUL88    07JUL88   10JUL88       6         0      Thomas
  2     1     3    2   Deliver Material  01JUL88   02JUL88    04JUL88   05JUL88       3         0      Thomas
  3     4     7    6   Install Pump      06JUL88   11JUL88    10JUL88   15JUL88       4         4      Thomas
  4     4     6    4   Foundation        06JUL88   09JUL88    06JUL88   09JUL88       0         0      Thomas
  5     5     7    2   Install Pipe      08JUL88   09JUL88    14JUL88   15JUL88       6         6      Thomas
  6     6     7    6   Erect Tower       10JUL88   15JUL88    10JUL88   15JUL88       0         0      Thomas
  7     1     4    5   Excavate          01JUL88   05JUL88    01JUL88   05JUL88       0         0      William
  8     1     3    2   Deliver Material  01JUL88   02JUL88    04JUL88   05JUL88       3         0      William
  9     3     6    4   Assemble Tank     03JUL88   06JUL88    06JUL88   09JUL88       3         3      William
 10     4     7    6   Install Pump      06JUL88   11JUL88    10JUL88   15JUL88       4         4      William
 11     5     7    2   Install Pipe      08JUL88   09JUL88    14JUL88   15JUL88       6         6      William
```

The following statements produce **Output 6.16**:

```
title 'Gantt Example 11';
title2 'Personalized Gantt Charts';
proc gantt data=persons;
    chart / scale=4 increment=2;
    by person;
    id activity;
run;
```

Output 6.16   Gantt Charts by Person

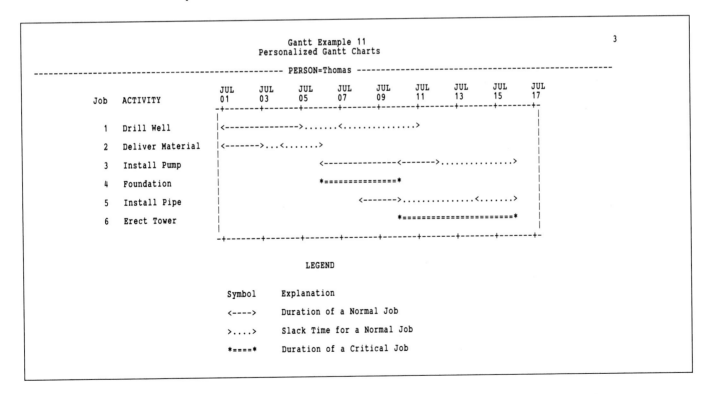

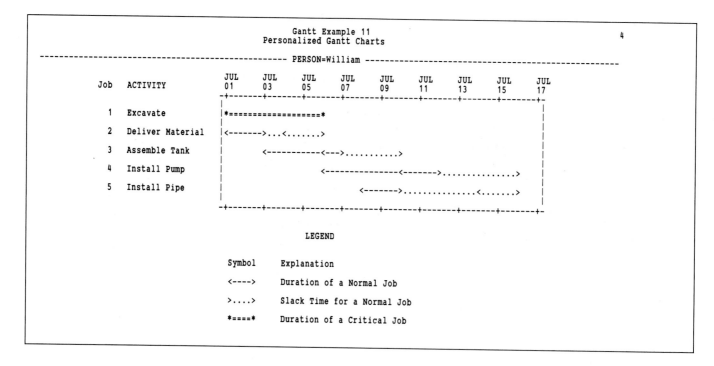

```
                            Gantt Example 11                                    4
                          Personalized Gantt Charts
------------------------------------------- PERSON=William -------------------------------------------

                   JUL    JUL    JUL    JUL    JUL    JUL    JUL    JUL    JUL
                   01     03     05     07     09     11     13     15     17
          Job  ACTIVITY  -+------+------+------+------+------+------+------+------+-
                          |                                                      |
           1   Excavate   |*=================*                                   |
                          |                                                      |
           2   Deliver Material |<------->...<.......>                           |
                          |                                                      |
           3   Assemble Tank    |    <-----------<--->...........>               |
                          |                                                      |
           4   Install Pump     |            <--------------<------->.............>  |
                          |                                                      |
           5   Install Pipe     |                 <------->.............<.......>   |
                          |                                                      |
                          -+------+------+------+------+------+------+------+------+-


                                   LEGEND


                   Symbol      Explanation

                   <---->      Duration of a Normal Job

                   >....>      Slack Time for a Normal Job

                   *====*      Duration of a Critical Job
```

Example 12:   Full-Screen Gantt Chart

The project and schedule data from **Example 1** and **Example 2** above are used here to illustrate the full-screen version of PROC GANTT. The program used to invoke PROC GANTT in full-screen mode is shown below. The extended character set for the PC is used to choose symbols and joining characters for the schedule bars. The initial screen is shown in **Screen 6.1**. The rest of this section shows the screens produced by issuing various commands in full-screen mode. Each screen is captioned appropriately.

```
title 'Gantt Example 12';
title2 'Full-Screen Gantt Chart';

data ex  ;
   format activity $20. success1 $20. success2 $20. success3 $20.
                   success4 $20.;
   input activity dur success1-success4;
   cards;
form               4 pour . . .
pour               2 core . . .
core               14 strip spray_fireproof insulate_walls .
strip              2 plumbing curtain_wall risers doors
strip              2 electrical_walls balance_elevator . .
curtain_wall       5 glaze_sash . . .
glaze_sash         5 spray_fireproof insulate_walls . .
spray_fireproof    5 ceil_ducts_fixture . . .
ceil_ducts_fixture 5 test . . .
plumbing           10 test . . .
test               3 insulate_mechanical . . .
insulate_mechanical 3 lath . . .
insulate_walls     5 lath . . .
risers             10 ceil_ducts_fixture . . .
doors              1 port_masonry . . .
```

```
port_masonry            2 lath finish_masonry . .
electrical_walls       16 lath . . .
balance_elevator        3 finish_masonry . . .
finish_masonry          3 plaster marble_work . .
lath                    3 plaster marble_work . .
plaster                 5 floor_finish tiling acoustic_tiles .
marble_work             3 acoustic_tiles . . .
acoustic_tiles          5 paint finish_mechanical . .
tiling                  3 paint finish_mechanical . .
floor_finish            5 paint finish_mechanical . .
paint                   5 finish_paint . . .
finish_mechanical       5 finish_paint . . .
finish_paint            2 caulking_cleanup . . .
caulking_cleanup        4 finished . . .
;
proc cpm finishbefore date='1sep88'd out=sched12;
   activity activity;
   duration dur;
   successors success1-success4;
run;
proc sort;
   by e_start;
run;


proc gantt data=sched12  fs;
   chart /
           increment=5 critflag
           formchar='bacdc9cdbbbacebac8cdbc'x
           joinchar='fec4fec4fefefe'x
           symchar ='fefefefefefefefefe'x
           overlapch='fe'x;
   id activity;
run;
```

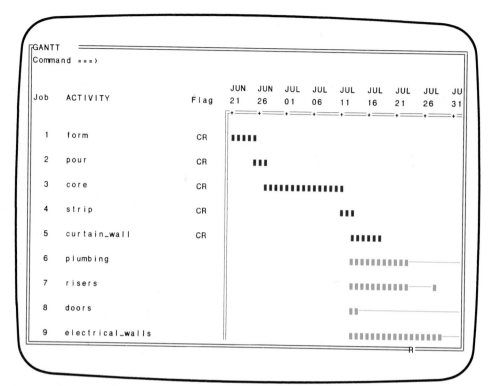

Screen 6.1   Initial Screen

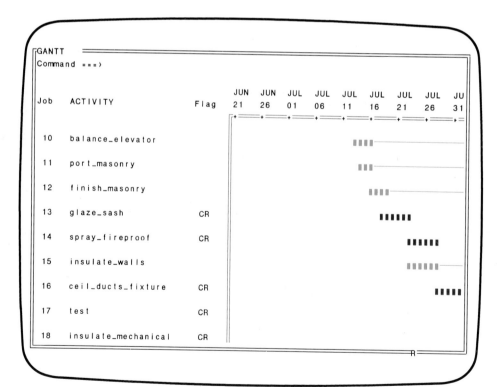

Screen 6.2   After **FORWARD** Command in **Screen 6.1**

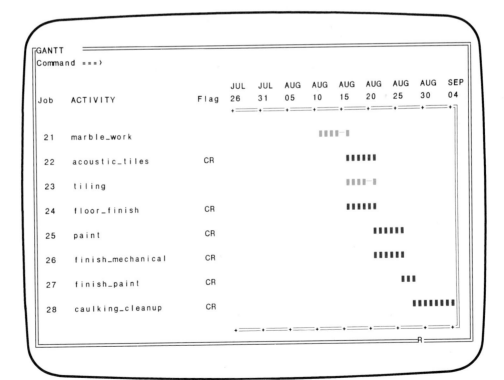

Screen 6.3   After **RIGHT MAX** Command in **Screen 6.2**

Screen 6.4   After **BOTTOM** Command in **Screen 6.3**

Screen 6.5   After **FIND JOB 5** Command in **Screen 6.4**

Screen 6.6   After **FIND TIME '16JUL88'D** Command in **Screen 6.5**

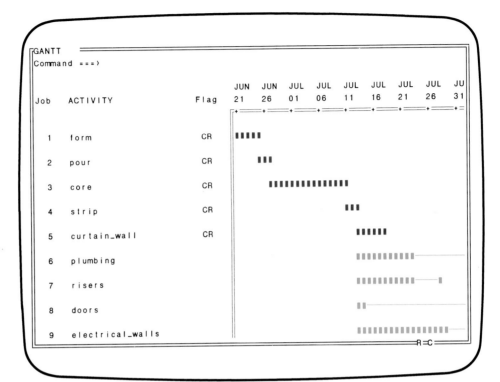

Screen 6.7   After **TOP; LEFT MAX** Commands in **Screen 6.6**

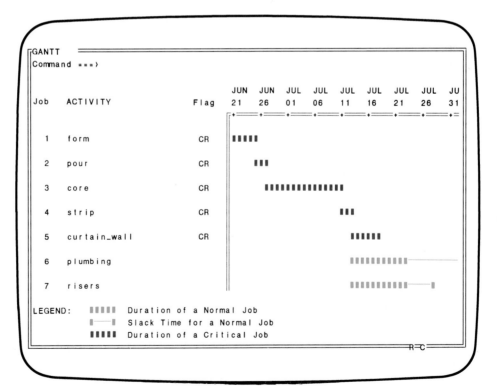

Screen 6.8   After **SHOW LEGEND** Command in **Screen 6.7**

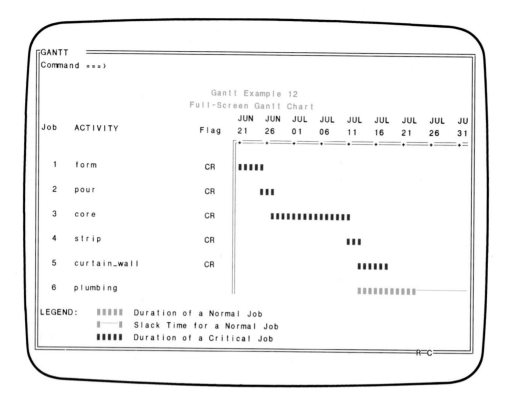

Screen 6.9 After **SHOW TITLE** Command in **Screen 6.8**

GRAPHICS EXAMPLES

The code in **Examples 3**, **6**, **8**, and **9** is repeated in **Examples 13**, **14**, **15**, and **16** to illustrate the use of PATTERN and SYMBOL statements and other graphics options to produce a graphics quality Gantt chart. **Example 17** uses the ANNOTATE= option and also illustrates a nonstandard use of PROC GANTT.

In all the examples presented, the early and late start schedules are specified in the data set by means of the variables, E_START, E_FINISH, L_START, and L_FINISH; hence, the ES=, EF=, LS=, and LF= options are not needed in the CHART statement. In the graphics examples that follow, the color *white* used in the code has been reversed to black in the example output.

Example 13: Marking Holidays and Target Completion Dates

The data set for the Gantt chart is created in the same manner as in **Example 3**. Here, only the statements required to generate the Gantt chart are shown. Before invoking PROC GANTT, you specify the required fill patterns and symbols using PATTERN and SYMBOL statements. Next, PROC GANTT is invoked with the GRAPHICS option. You specify the HOLIDATA=HOLDATA option in the PROC statement and the HOLIDAY= option in the CHART statement, causing the holidays to be marked on the chart. Note that the procedure marks the *duration* of the holiday with the fill pattern specified in the seventh PATTERN statement. Specifying the variable TARGET in the CHART statement causes target dates to be marked on the chart with the symbol specified in the SYMBOL statement, a PLUS symbol in red. The duration and slack time of the activities are indicated by the use of the appropriate fill patterns as explained in the legend.

Colors for the axis, text, and frame fill are specified using the options CAXIS=, CTEXT=, and CFRAME=, respectively. The global options HPOS= and VPOS= are set to 100 and 40, respectively. The SIMPLEX font is used for all text.

```
title c=white f= Simplex 'Gantt Example 13';
title2 c=white f=simplex
               'Marking Holidays and Target Completion Dates';


* specify the device on which you want the chart printed;

goptions vpos=40 hpos=100;

* set up required pattern and symbol statements;

pattern1 c=green v=s;
pattern2 c=green v=e;
pattern3 c=red   v=s;
pattern4 c=red   v=e;
pattern5 c=red   v=r2;
pattern6 c=red   v=l2;
pattern7 c=cyan  v=e;

symbol   c=red v=plus;

* plot the schedule;

proc gantt graphics holidata=holdata data=sched;
   chart target / holiday=(hol) cframe=white font=simplex
                 caxis=white ctext=white;
   id activity;
run;
```

Output 6.17   Using the GRAPHICS Option to Mark Holidays and Target Completion Dates

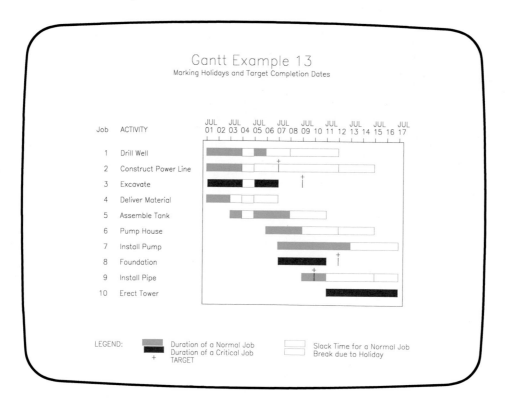

Example 14:   Plotting the Actual Schedule

As in **Example 13**, fill patterns are specified using PATTERN statements. PROC GANTT is used with the GRAPHICS option to plot computed as well as actual schedules on separate lines for each activity. The A_START= and A_FINISH= options in the CHART statement are used to specify the variables containing the actual start and finish times for each activity. The actual schedule is plotted with the fill pattern specified in the sixth PATTERN statement.

The value of VPOS= is set to 50 using a GOPTIONS statement to enable PROC GANTT to draw the entire chart on one page. This example also illustrates the use of the HCONNECT option which causes a connecting line (in default line style) to be drawn from the left boundary of the chart to the early start time for each activity.

```
title c=white f=simplex 'Gantt Example 14';
title2 c=white f=simplex
        'Plotting Actual Start and Finish Times on the Chart';

* set vpos to 50 and hpos to 100;

goptions vpos=50 hpos=100;

* set up required pattern statements;

pattern1 c=green v=s;
pattern2 c=green v=e;
pattern3 c=red   v=s;
pattern4 c=red   v=e;
```

```
pattern5 c=red    v=r2;
pattern6 c=cyan   v=s;
pattern7 c=white  v=e;

* plot the computed and actual schedules using proc gantt;

proc gantt graphics data=update holidata=holdata;
   chart / holiday=(hol) font=simplex
           a_start=sdate a_finish=fdate
           caxis=white ctext=white hconnect;
   id activity;

run;
```

Output 6.18 Using the GRAPHICS Option to Plot Actual Schedules

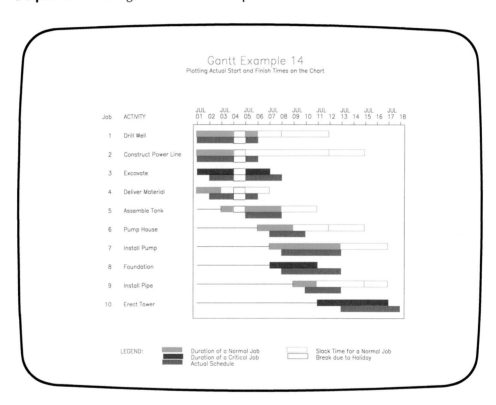

Example 15:   Using the MININTERVAL= and SCALE= Options

This example uses the same data as **Example 8** of the line-printer section. The PATTERN statements are the same as in **Example 14**. Here the SCALE= option is set to 7 so that the chart fits on two pages. Because MININTERVAL=WEEK and SCALE=7, PROC GANTT uses $(7/h)\%$ of the screen width to denote one week, where h is the value of POS.

```
* schedule using interval=week;

proc cpm data=const1 date='30jun88'd interval=week
         out=save;
   tailnode tail;
```

```
      duration dur;
      headnode head;
      id activity;

*delete activities with 0 duration;

data save;
   set save;
   if dur=0 then delete;

*sort the schedule by the early start date;

proc sort;
   by e_start;

title f=swiss c=white 'Gantt Example 15';
title2 f=swiss c=white 'Use of Mininterval and Scale Options';


goptions vpos=40 hpos=85;

proc gantt graphics;
   chart / mininterval=week scale=7 nolegend
           ref='1jul88'd to '15oct88'd by month
           font=swiss caxis=white ctext=white;
   id activity;
run;
```

Output 6.19   Using the GRAPHICS Option to Produce a Gantt Chart Using the MININTERVAL= and SCALE= Options

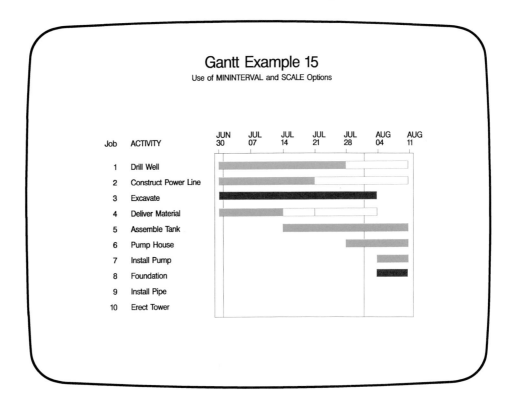

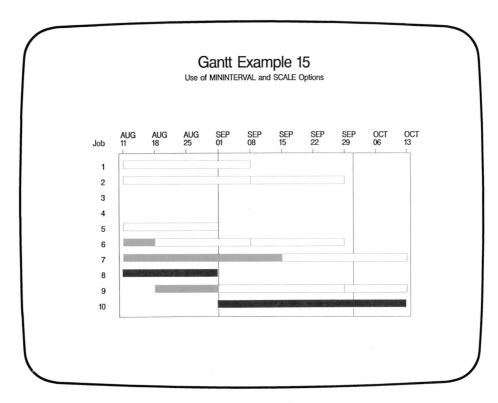

Example 16:   Using the MINDATE= and MAXDATE= Options

This example uses the same data as **Example 5** and also illustrates the LREF= option. Further, the option INCREMENT= is set to 3 resulting in a different placement of tick marks than in **Example 13** and **Example 14**.

```
title c=white f=simplex 'Gantt Example 16';
title2 c=white f=simplex 'Use of Mindate and Maxdate Options';

goptions vpos=40 hpos=100;

proc gantt graphics data=save;
   chart / increment=3 mindate='1aug88'd maxdate='31aug88'd
           nolegend ref='5aug88'd to '25aug88'd by 5
           ctext=white caxis=white font=simplex
           cref=white lref=2;
   id activity;
run;
```

Output 6.20   Using the GRAPHICS Option to Produce a Gantt Chart Using the MINDATE= and MAXDATE= Options

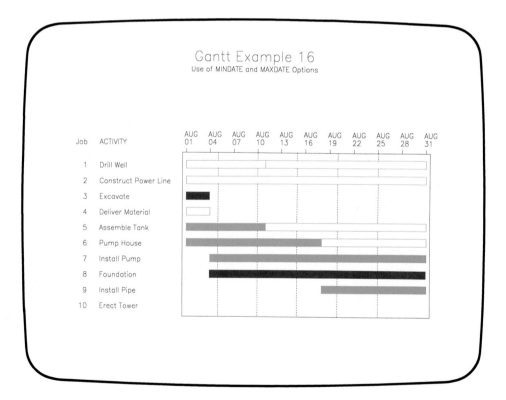

Example 17:   Using the SAS/GRAPH ANNOTATE= Option

This example illustrates a nonstandard use of PROC GANTT; it also uses the ANNOTATE= option to add text to the body of the chart. Suppose that the construction project is in progress and the activities have so far been progressing according to plan. The data set CONST17 contains the network data as well as the actual start and finish times and a variable PCTCOMP, which specifies the percent of work that has been completed. PROC CPM is first used to schedule this project with all the given information. Instead of plotting the actual start and finish times on a separate line, suppose now that you want to plot the actual schedule and the early start schedule on the same line. The DATA step shown below uses the calculated values of the start and finish times and creates new variables ES, EF, LS, and LF that will be used as input to PROC GANTT. For completed activites, set both early and late schedules to be the same as the actual schedule. For activities in progress, set the early start and finish times to denote the completed portion of the activity's duration and the late start and finish times to denote the remaining portion of the activity's duration. For activities not yet started, use only the early start schedule. Suppose also that you want to label the chart with the percent completion time to the right of the bar for each activity. An ANNOTATE= data set is created with the appropriate labels which is then used in the call to PROC GANTT.

```
data const17;
    format a_start a_finish date7.;
    input activity $ 1-20 tail 22 dur 24 head 26 a_start date9.
        a_finish date9. pctcomp;
    cards;
Drill Well           1 4 2 1jul88 .       75
Pump House           2 3 5 .      .       .
Install Pipe         5 2 7 .      .       .
Construct Power Line 1 3 5 1jul88 3jul88  100
Excavate             1 5 4 1jul88 .       60
Install Pump         4 6 7 .      .       .
Deliver Material     1 2 3 1jul88 2jul88  100
Assemble Tank        3 4 6 3jul88 .       25
Erect Tower          6 6 7 .      .       .
Foundation           4 4 6 .      .       .
Dummy                4 0 5 .      .       .
;


proc cpm data=const17 date='1jul88'd out=save;
    tailnode tail;
    duration dur;
    headnode head;
    id activity pctcomp;
    actual / pctcomp=pctcomp
             as=a_start
             af=a_finish
             timenow='5jul88'd;
run;

/* remove dummy acitivity and sort */
data save;
    set save;
    if dur^=0;
run;
proc sort;
    by e-start;
run;
```

```
data stfin;
   set save;
   format es ef ls lf date7.;
   if a_start ^=. then do;
      es=a_start;
      if a_finish ^=. then do;
         ef=a_finish;
         ls=a_start;
         lf=a_finish;
         end;

      else do;
         ef='4jul88'd;
         ls='5jul88'd;
         lf=e_finish;
         end;
      end;
   else do;
       es=e_start;
       ef=e_finish;
       end;
   drop e_start e_finish l_start l_finish a_start a_finish;
run;


/* The following data set is used to annotate the Gantt chart to
   specify the amount of work done on each activity */

data anno;
   /* set up required variable lengths, etc. */
   length function color style   $8;
   length xsys ysys hsys         $1;
   length when position          $1;

   set save;

   xsys      = '2';
   ysys      = '2';
   hsys      = '4';
   when      = 'a';

   if pctcomp ^= . then text = put (pctcomp,f3.) || ' pct';
   else              text = ' ';

   /* place above text at the appropriate position */
   function = 'label   ';
   style='swiss    ';
   x = floor(l_finish +2);
   y = _n_;
   color = 'white';
   angle = 0;
   rotate = 0;
   size = 1;
   position = '6';
   run;
```

```
pattern1 c=green v=e;
pattern2 c=green v=e;
pattern3 c=red   v=s;

title c=white f=swiss 'Construction Project: Progress Report';
proc gantt graphics data=stfin;
   chart / es=es ef=ef ls=ls lf=lf
           ref='5jul88'd font=swiss
           ctext=white caxis=white
           anno=anno
           nojobnum nolegend;
   id activity status;
run;
```

Output 6.21 Using the ANNOTATE= Option

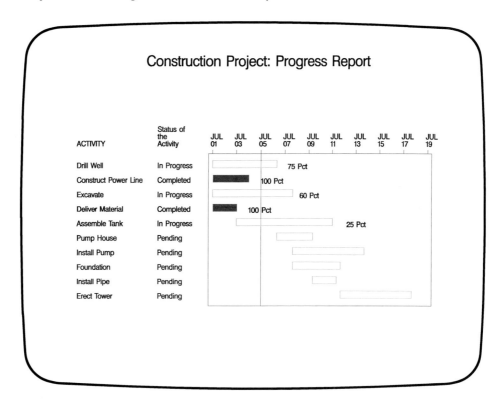

Chapter 7

The LP
Procedure

ABSTRACT

The LP procedure solves linear programs, integer programs, and mixed-integer programs. It also performs parametric programming, range analysis, and reports on solution sensitivity to changes in the right-hand-side constants and price coefficients.

The LP procedure can be used interactively. You can tell the procedure to stop at intermediate stages in the iterative solution process. When one of these stopping points is reached, the procedure waits for further input. Then, intermediate results can be printed, options reset, and the procedure instructed to continue execution.

INTRODUCTION

The LP procedure is used to optimize a linear function subject to linear and integer constraints. Specifically, the LP procedure solves the general mixed-integer program of the form

$$\max\,(\min)\ \mathbf{c'x}$$
$$\text{subject to:}\ \ \mathbf{Ax} \overset{\leq}{\underset{\geq}{=}} \mathbf{b} \qquad\qquad (mip)$$

$$\ell_i \leq x_i\ \leq u_i \text{ for } i = 1, \ldots, n$$

$$x_i \text{ is integer for } i \varepsilon \mathbf{S}$$

where

    $\mathbf{A}$ is an $m \times n$ matrix of technological coefficients.

    $\mathbf{b}$ is an $m \times 1$ matrix of right-hand-side (rhs) constants.

    $\mathbf{c}$ is an $n \times 1$ matrix of price coefficients.

    $\mathbf{x}$ is an $n \times 1$ matrix of structural variables.

    ℓ_i is a lower bound on x_i.

    u_i is an upper bound on x_i.

    $\mathbf{S}$ is a subset of the set of indices $\{\,1, \ldots, n\,\}$.

Linear programs (when $\mathbf{S}$ is empty) are denoted by (lp). For these problems, the procedure employs the two-phase revised simplex method, which uses the Bartels-Golub update of the LU decomposed basis matrix to pivot between feasible solutions (see Bartels 1971). In phase 1, PROC LP finds a basic feasible solution to (lp), while in phase 2, PROC LP finds an optimal solution, $\mathbf{x}^{opt}$. The procedure implicitly handles unrestricted variables, lower-bounded variables, upper-bounded variables, and ranges on constraints. When no explicit lower bounds are specified, PROC LP assumes that all variables are bounded below by zero.

When a variable is specified as an integer variable, $\mathbf{S}$ has at least one element. Then, the procedure uses the branch and bound technique for optimization. The relaxed problem (the problem with no integer constraints) is solved initially using the primal algorithm described above. Constraints are added in defining the subsequent descendent problems in the branch and bound tree. These problems are then solved using the dual simplex algorithm. Dual pivots are referred to as phase 3 pivots.

The procedure can also analyze the sensitivity of the solution $\mathbf{x}^{opt}$ to changes in both the objective function and the right-hand-side constants. There are three techniques available for this analysis: sensitivity analysis, parametric programming, and range analysis. Sensitivity analysis enables you to examine the size of a perturbation to the right-hand-side or objective vector by an arbitrary change vector for which the basis of the current optimal solution remains optimal.

Parametric programming, on the other hand, enables you to specify the size of the perturbation beforehand, then examine how the optimal solution changes as the desired perturbation is realized. With this technique, the procedure pivots to maintain optimality as the right-hand-side or objective vector is perturbed beyond the point for which the current solution is optimal. Range analysis is used to examine the range of each right-hand-side value or objective coefficient for which the basis of the current optimal solution remains optimal.

The LP procedure can also save both primal and dual solutions, the current tableau, and the branch and bound tree in SAS data sets. This enables you to generate solution reports and perform additional analyses with the SAS System. Although PROC LP reports solutions, this feature is particularly useful for reporting solutions in formats tailored to your specific needs. Saving computational results in a data set also enables you to continue executing a problem not solved because of insufficient time or other computational problems.

Introductory Example

PROC LP expects the definition of one or more linear, integer, or mixed-integer programs in an input data set (in this example, this data set is referred to as the problem data set). There are two formats, a dense format and a sparse format, for this data set.

In the dense format, each variable in the data set is one of the following: a structural variable, an id variable, a right-hand-side constant, a type identifier, a constant for right-hand-side sensitivity analysis, or a range variable. The value of the type identifier variable named in the TYPE statement in each observation tells PROC LP how to interpret the observation as a part of the mathematical programming problem. PROC LP recognizes the following keywords as values for the type identifier variable: MAX, MIN, EQ, LE, GE, SOSLE, SOSEQ, UNRSTRCT, UPPERBD, LOWERBD, BASIC, PRICESEN, FREE, INTEGER, and BINARY. **Example 1:   An Oil Blending Problem** describes how the procedure interprets an observation having some of these keywords.

The sparse input format to PROC LP is designed to enable you to specify only the nonzero coefficients in the description of linear programs, integer programs, and mixed-integer programs. The SAS data set that describes the sparse model must contain at least four SAS variables: a type variable, a column variable, a row variable, and a coefficient variable. Each observation in the data set defines one or more rows, columns, or coefficients in the model. The value of the type variable is a keyword that tells PROC LP how to interpret the observation. The values of the row and column variables name the rows and columns in the model, and the values of the coefficient variables give the coefficients. The SAS data set can contain multiple pairs of row and coefficient variables. In this way, more information about the model can be specified in each observation in the data set.

With both the dense and sparse formats for model specification, the observation order is not important. This feature is particularly useful when using the sparse model input.

A simple blending problem illustrates the dense and sparse input formats and the use of PROC LP. A step in refining crude oil into finished oil products involves a distillation process that splits crude into various streams. Suppose there are three types of crude available: Arabian light, Arabian heavy, and Brega. These types of crude are distilled into light naphtha, intermediate naphtha, and heating oil. These in turn are blended into jet fuel using one of two recipes. What amounts of the three crudes maximize the profit from producing jet fuel? A formulation to answer this question is as follows:

$$\text{max}\quad -175 * \text{a\_light} - 165 * \text{a\_heavy} - 205 * \text{brega} + 300 * \text{jet\_1} + 300 * \text{jet\_2}$$

$$
\begin{aligned}
\text{st.}\quad &.035 * \text{a\_light} + .030 * \text{a\_heavy} + .045 * \text{brega} = \text{naphthal} \\
&.100 * \text{a\_light} + .075 * \text{a\_heavy} + .135 * \text{brega} = \text{naphthai} \\
&.390 * \text{a\_light} + .300 * \text{a\_heavy} + .430 * \text{brega} = \text{heatingo} \\
&.3 * \text{naphthai} + .7 * \text{heatingo} = \text{jet\_1} \\
&.2 * \text{naphthal} + .8 * \text{heatingo} = \text{jet\_2} \\
&\text{a\_light} <= 110 \\
&\text{a\_heavy} <= 165 \\
&\text{heatingo} <= 80 \\
\end{aligned}
$$

a_light, a_heavy, brega, naphthai, naphthal, heatingo, jet_1, and jet_3 >= 0

The following data set gives the representation of this formulation. Notice that the variable names are the structural variables, the rows are the constraints, and that the coefficients are given as the values for the structural variables.

```
data;
   input _id_ $14.
         a_light a_heavy brega naphthal naphthai heatingo jet_1 jet_2
         _type_ $ _rhs_;
   cards;
profit          -175 -165 -205   0  0  0  300  300  max      .
naphtha_l_conv  .035 .030 .045  -1  0  0    0    0  eq       0
naphtha_i_conv  .100 .075 .135   0 -1  0    0    0  eq       0
heating_o_conv  .390 .300 .430   0  0 -1    0    0  eq       0
recipe_1           0    0    0   0 .3 .7   -1    0  eq       0
recipe_2           0    0    0  .2  0 .8    0   -1  eq       0
available        110  165   80   .  .  .    .    .  upperbd  .
;
```

The same model may be specified in the sparse format as follows. This format enables you to omit the zero coefficients.

```
data;
   input _type_ $ a10 _col_ $13. a24 _row_ $16. _coef_;
   cards;
max        .              profit             .
eq         .              napha_l_conv       .
eq         .              napha_i_conv       .
eq         .              heating_oil_conv   .
eq         .              recipe_1           .
eq         .              recipe_2           .
upperbd    .              available          .
.          a_light        profit           -175
.          a_light        napha_l_conv      .035
.          a_light        napha_i_conv      .100
.          a_light        heating_oil_conv  .390
.          a_light        available         110
.          a_heavy        profit           -165
.          a_heavy        napha_l_conv      .030
.          a_heavy        napha_i_conv      .075
.          a_heavy        heating_oil_conv  .300
```

.	a_heavy	available	165
.	brega	profit	-205
.	brega	napha_l_conv	.045
.	brega	napha_i_conv	.135
.	brega	heating_oil_conv	.430
.	brega	available	80
.	naphthal	napha_l_conv	-1
.	naphthal	recipe_2	.2
.	naphthai	napha_i_conv	-1
.	naphthai	recipe_1	.3
.	heatingo	heating_oil_conv	-1
.	heatingo	recipe_1	.7
.	heatingo	recipe_2	.8
.	jet_1	profit	300
.	jet_1	recipe_1	-1
.	jet_2	profit	300
.	jet_2	recipe_2	-1
.	_rhs_	profit	0
;			

Because the input order of the model into PROC LP is unimportant, this model can be specified in sparse input in arbitrary row order. **Example 2:   A Sparse View of the Oil Blending Problem** in the **EXAMPLES** section demonstrates this.

The dense and sparse forms of model input give you flexibility to generate models using the SAS language. The dense form of the model is solved with the statement

```
proc lp;    .
```

The sparse form is solved with the statement

```
proc lp sparsedata;    .
```

Example 1 and **Example 2** in the **EXAMPLES** section continue with this problem.

The interactive use of the procedure is best understood by considering the types of statements that are used with PROC LP. The COL, COEF, ROW, VAR, RHS, TYPE, RHSSEN, and RANGE statements are problem definition statements. They tell PROC LP how to interpret the variables in the input data set in terms of the mathematical program defined there. After you have entered these statements, you can enter a QUIT, PIVOT, (IPIVOT if the problem has integer variables), or a RUN statement. These statements cause an immediate action: QUIT terminates the LP procedure; PIVOT (IPIVOT) executes one simplex (branch and bound) pivot; and RUN is the usual RUN statement. Because of options you may have set, an error condition, or a control break, the procedure can return control to you before completing execution. When this happens, you can reset options using the RESET statement, examine the current solution with the PRINT and SHOW statements, and continue execution of the procedure using the PIVOT (IPIVOT) or RUN statements. In addition, whenever the procedure is iterating and you press the CTRL-BREAK key combination, the procedure returns control to you at the end of the next pivot.

SPECIFICATIONS

Below is a list of statements used in PROC LP, in alphabetical order as they appear in the text that follows. **Table 7.1** shows you specific statements and options and where you use them.

PROC LP *options;*
   COEF *variables;*
   COL *variable;*
   IPIVOT;
   PIVOT;
   PRINT *options;*
   QUIT *option;*
   RANGE *variable;*
   RESET *options;*
   RHS *variables;*
   RHSSEN *variables;*
   ROW *variables;*
   SHOW *options;*
   TYPE *variable;*
   VAR *variables;*

Table 7.1 LP Statements and Descriptions for Use

Format	Statements
sparse input format problem definition statements	COEF statement
	COL statement
	RANGE statement
	RHS statement
	RHSSEN statement
	ROW statement
	TYPE statement
dense input format problem definition statements	TYPE statement
	RANGE statement
	RHS statement
	RHSSEN statement
	ROW statement
	VAR statement
interactive statements	IPIVOT statement
	PIVOT statement
	PRINT statement
	QUIT statement
	RESET statement
	SHOW statement
	RUN statement

The COEF, COL, TYPE, and ROW statements are used for identifying variables in the problem data set when the model is in the sparse input format. Each of these statements can be omitted if there are variables in the problem data set with names _COEF, _COL, _TYPE, and _ROW. Otherwise, they must be used.

The ROW, TYPE, RHS, RHSSEN, RANGE, and VAR statements are used for identifying variables in the problem data set when the model is in the dense input format. The RHS and TYPE statements are not needed if the input data set contains variables _RHS_ and _TYPE_; otherwise, they must be used. The VAR statement is optional. When it is not specified, PROC LP uses as structural variables all numeric variables not explicitly or implicitly included in statement lists.

The RHS, RHSSEN, and RANGE statements can also be used when the model is in the sparse format. Then, they would identify how to interpret columns given in the model.

The SHOW, PRINT, PIVOT, IPIVOT, QUIT, and RESET statements are useful when executing PROC LP interactively. However, they can also be used in batch mode.

PROC LP Statement

   PROC LP *options*;

The options below can appear in the PROC LP statement.

Data Set Options

   ACTIVEIN=*SASdataset*
      names the SAS data set containing the active nodes in a branch and bound tree that is to be used to restart an integer program.

   ACTIVEOUT=*SASdataset*
      names the SAS data set in which to save the current branch and bound tree of active nodes.

   DATA=*SASdataset*
      names the SAS data set containing the problem data. If DATA= is not specified, PROC LP uses the most recently created SAS data set.

   DUALOUT=*SASdataset*
      names the SAS data set that contains the current dual solution (shadow prices) on termination of the LP procedure. This data set contains the current dual solution only if PROC LP terminates successfully.

   PRIMALIN=*SASdataset*
      names the SAS data set that contains a feasible solution to the problem defined by the DATA= data set. The data set specified in the PRIMALIN= option should have the same format as a data set saved using the PRIMALOUT= option. Specifying PRIMALIN= is particularly useful for continuing iteration on a problem previously attempted. It is also useful for performing sensitivity analysis on a previously solved problem.

   PRIMALOUT=*SASdataset*
      names the SAS data set that contains the current primal solution when LP terminates.

   SPARSEDATA
      tells PROC LP that the data are in the sparse input data format. If this option is not specified, PROC LP assumes that the data are in the dense format. See **DETAILS** for information about the sparse input format.

TABLEAUOUT=*SASdataset*
names the SAS data set in which to save the final tableau.

Print Control Options

FLOW
requests that a journal (the ITERATION LOG) of pivot information be printed at each PRINTFREQ= iteration. This includes the number of the columns entering and leaving the basis, the reduced cost of the entering column, and the current objective value.

FUZZ=*f*
prints all numbers within *f* of zero as zeros. The default value is 1.0E−10.

NOFLOW
is the inverse of the FLOW option.

NOPARAPRINT
is the inverse of the PARAPRINT option.

NOPRINT
suppresses printing of the VARIABLE, CONSTRAINT, and SENSITIVITY ANALYSIS SUMMARIES. This option is equivalent to the PRINTLEVEL=0 option.

NOTABLEAUPRINT
is the inverse of the TABLEAUPRINT option.

PARAPRINT
indicates that the solution be printed at each pivot when performing parametric programming.

PRINT
is the inverse of the NOPRINT option.

PRINTFREQ=*i*
indicates that at each *i*th iteration a line in the (INTEGER) ITERATION LOG be printed.

PRINTLEVEL=*i*
indicates the amount of printing that the procedure should perform. When *i*=−2, only messages to the SAS log are printed. When *i*=−1, the option is equivalent to NOPRINT unless the problem is infeasible. If it is infeasible, the infeasible rows are printed in the CONSTRAINT SUMMARY along with the INFEASIBLE INFORMATION SUMMARY. When *i*=0, this option is identical to NOPRINT. When *i*=1, all output is printed. The default value is 1.

TABLEAUPRINT
indicates that the final tableau be printed.

Interactive Control Options

ENDPAUSE
requests that PROC LP pause before printing the solution. When this pause occurs, you can enter the RESET, SHOW, or PRINT statements.

FEASIBLEPAUSE
requests that PROC LP pause after a feasible (not necessarily integer feasible) solution has been found.

IFEASIBLEPAUSE=*m*
requests that PROC LP pause after every *m* integer feasible solutions. The default value is 99999999.

IPAUSE=*n*

requests that PROC LP pause after every *n* integer iterations. At a pause, you can enter the RESET, SHOW, PRINT, IPIVOT, QUIT, and PIVOT statements. The default value is 99999999.

NOENDPAUSE

is the inverse of the ENDPAUSE option.

NOFEASIBLEPAUSE

is the inverse of the FEASIBLEPAUSE option.

PAUSE=*n*

requests that PROC LP pause after every *n* iterations. At a pause, you can enter the RESET, SHOW, PRINT, IPIVOT, QUIT, and PIVOT statements. The default value is 99999999.

READPAUSE

requests that PROC LP pause after the data have been read and the initial basis inverted.

Branch and Bound Algorithm Control Options

BACKTRACK=LIFO, FIFO, OBJ, PROJECT, PSEUDOC, ERROR

specifies the rule used to choose the next active problem when backtracking is required. The default value is OBJ. See **DETAILS** for further discussion.

CANSELECT=LIFO, FIFO, OBJ, PROJECT, PSEUDOC, ERROR

specifies the rule used to choose the next active problem when solving an integer or mixed-integer program. The default value is LIFO. See **DETAILS** for further discussion.

DOBJECTIVE=*d*

specifies that PROC LP should discard active nodes unless the node will lead to an integer solution with objective at least as large (or as small for minimizations) as the objective of the relaxed problem minus (plus) *d*. The default value is + infinity.

IEPSILON=*e*

requests that PROC LP consider an integer variable *x* as having an integer value if *x* is within *e* units of an integer. The default value is 1.0E−7.

IMAXIT=*m*

performs at most *m* integer iterations. The default value is 100.

IOBJECTIVE=*o*

specifies that PROC LP should discard active nodes unless the node could lead to an integer solution with objective at least as large (or as small for minimizations) as *o*. The default value is −infinity (+infinity).

PENALTYDEPTH=*n*

requests that PROC LP examine *n* variables as branching candidates when VARSELECT=PENALTY. If PENALTYDEPTH is not specified when VARSELECT=PENALTY, then all of the variables are considered branching candidates. The default is the number of integer variables. See **DETAILS** for a more complete description.

POBJECTIVE=*p*

specifies that PROC LP should discard active nodes unless the node could lead to an integer solution with objective at least as large as $r-p|r|$ for maximizations (at least as small as $r+p|r|$ for minimizations) where r is the objective of the relaxed non-integer constrained problem. The default value is $+$infinity.

VARSELECT=CLOSE, PRIOR, PSEUDOC, FAR, PRICE, PENALTY

specifies the rule used to choose the branching variable on an integer iteration. Default is FAR. See **DETAILS** for further discussion.

WOBJECTIVE=w

specifies that PROC LP should delay examination of active nodes unless the node could lead to an integer solution with objective at least as large (or as small for minimizations) as w, until all such active nodes have been explored. The default is $r-.3\,|\,r\,|$ for maximization and $r+.3\,|\,r\,|$ for minimizations where r is the objective of the relaxed non-integer constrained problem.

Sensitivity/Parametric/Ranging Control Options

NORANGEPRICE

is the inverse of the RANGEPRICE option.

NORANGERHS

is the inverse of the RANGERHS option.

PRICEPHI=Φ

specifies the limit for parametric programming when perturbing the price vector. See **DETAILS** for a more complete description. See **Example 5** for an illustration of this option.

RANGEPRICE

indicates that range analysis is to be performed on the price coefficients. See **DETAILS** for further discussion.

RANGERHS

indicates that range analysis is to be performed on the right-hand-side vector. See **DETAILS** for further discussion.

RHSPHI=Φ

specifies the limit for parametric programming when perturbing the right-hand-side vector. See **DETAILS** for further discussion.

Simplex Algorithm Control Options

DEVEX

indicates that the devex method of weighting the reduced costs be used in pricing (Harris 1975).

EPSILON=e

specifies a positive number close to zero. It is used in the following instances:

During phase 1, if the sum of the basic artificial variables is within e of 0, the current solution is considered feasible. If this sum is not exactly zero, then there are artificial variables within e of zero in the current solution. In this case, a note is printed on the SAS log.

During phase 1, if all reduced costs are $\le e$ for nonbasic variables at their lower bounds and $\ge e$ for nonbasic variables at their upper bounds and the sum of infeasibilities is greater than e, then the problem is considered infeasible. If the maximum reduced cost is within e of 0, a note is printed on the SAS log.

During phase 2, if all reduced costs are $\le e$ for nonbasic variables at their lower bounds and $\ge e$ for nonbasic variables at their upper bounds, then the current solution is considered optimal.

During phases 1, 2, and 3, e is also used to test if the denominator is different from zero before performing the ratio test to determine which basic variable should leave the basis.

The default value of EPSILON is 1.0E−8.

GOALPROGRAM

specifies that multiple objectives in the input data set are to be treated as sequential objectives in a goal-programming model. The value of the right-hand-side variable in the objective row gives the priority of the objective. Lower numbers have higher priority.

INFINITY=s

specifies the largest number PROC LP uses in computation. INFINITY= is used to determine when a problem has an unbounded variable value. The default value is 7.2E75.*

INVFREQ=m

reinverts the current basis matrix after m major and minor iterations. The default value is 50.

INVTOL=t

reinverts the current basis matrix if the largest element in absolute value in the decomposed basis matrix is greater than t. If after reinversion this condition still holds, then INVTOL is increased by a factor of 10 and a note indicating this modification is printed on the SAS log. When INVTOL is frequently exceeded, this may be an indication of a numerically unstable problem. The default value is 1000.

MAXIT1=m

performs at most $m \geq 0$ phase 1 iterations. The default value is 100.

MAXIT2=m

performs at most $m \geq 2$ phase 2 iterations. If $m=0$, then only phase 1 is entered so that on successful termination PROC LP will have found a feasible, but not necessarily optimal, solution. The default value is 100.

MAXIT3=m

performs at most $m \geq 0$ phase 3 iterations. All dual pivots are counted as phase 3 pivots. The default value is 99999999.

NODEVEX

is the inverse of the DEVEX option.

PRICETYPE=COMPLETE, DYNAMIC, NONE, PARTIAL

specifies the type of multiple pricing to be performed. If this option is specified and the PRICE= option is not specified, then PRICE= is assumed to be 10. The default value is PARTIAL. See **DETAILS** for a description of this process.

PRICE=k

specifies the number of columns to subset when multiple pricing is used in selecting the column to enter the basis (Greenberg 1978). The type of suboptimization used is determined by the PRICETYPE= option. See **DETAILS** for a description of this process.

REPSILON=e

specifies a positive number close to zero. REPSILON is used in the ratio test to determine which basic variable is to leave the basis. The default value is 1.0E−14.

---

* This value is system dependent.

SCALE=ROW, COLUMN, BOTH, or NONE
> specifies the type of scaling to be used. See **Scaling** in **DETAILS** for further discussion. The default value is COLUMN.

TIME=t
> checks at each iteration to see if t seconds have elapsed since PROC LP began. If more than t seconds have elapsed, the procedure pauses and prints the current solution. The default value is 120 seconds.

U=u
> allows the user to control the choice of pivots during **LU** decomposition and updating the basis matrix. The variable u should take values between EPSILON and 1.0 because small values of u bias the algorithm toward maintaining sparsity at the expense of numerical stability and vice versa. The more sparse the decomposed basis, the less time each iteration takes. The default value is .1. See **Memory Management** in **DETAILS** for further discussion.

COEF Statement

> COEF *variables*;

For the sparse input format, the COEF statement specifies the numeric variables in the problem data set that contain the coefficients in the model. The value of the coefficient variable in a given observation is the value of the coefficient in the column and row specified in the COLUMN and ROW variables in that observation. For multiple ROW variables, the LP procedure maps the ROW variables to the COEF variables on the basis of their order in the COEF and ROW statements. There must be the same number of COEF variables as ROW variables. If the COEF statement is omitted, PROC LP looks for the default variable names that have the prefix _COEF.

COL Statement

> COL *variable*;

For the sparse input format, the COL statement specifies a character variable in the problem data set that contains the names of the columns in the model. Columns in the model are either structural variables, right-hand-side vectors, right-hand-side change vectors, or a range vector. The COL variable must be a character variable. If the COL statement is omitted, PROC LP looks for the default variable name having the prefix _COL.

IPIVOT Statement

> IPIVOT;

The IPIVOT statement causes the LP procedure to execute one integer branch and bound pivot and pause.

PIVOT Statement

> PIVOT;

The PIVOT statement causes the LP procedure to execute one simplex pivot and pause.

PRINT Statement

PRINT *print options*;

The PRINT statement is useful for printing part of a solution summary, examining intermediate tableaus, performing sensitivity analysis, and parametric programming. The options that can be used with this statement are

BEST
    prints a SOLUTION, VARIABLE, and CONSTRAINT SUMMARY for the best integer solution found.

COLUMN(*colnames*)/SENSITIVITY
    prints a VARIABLE SUMMARY containing the logical and structural variables listed in the *colnames* list. If the /SENSITIVITY option is included, then sensitivity analysis is performed on the price coefficients for the listed *colnames* structural variables.

MATRIX(*rownames,colnames*)/PICTURE
    prints the submatrix of the matrix of constraint coefficients defined by the *rownames* and *colnames* lists. If the /PICTURE option is included, then the formatted submatrix is printed. The format used is summarized in **Table 7.2**.

Table 7.2 Format Summary

Condition on the Coefficient x				Symbols Printed
	ABS(x)	=	0	" "
0	< ABS(x) <		.000001	SGN(x) "Z"
.000001	≤ ABS(x) <		.00001	SGN(x) "Y"
.00001	≤ ABS(x) <		.0001	SGN(x) "X"
.0001	≤ ABS(x) <		.001	SGN(x) "W"
.001	≤ ABS(x) <		.01	SGN(x) "V"
.01	≤ ABS(x) <		.1	SGN(x) "U"
.1	≤ ABS(x) <		1	SGN(x) "T"
	ABS(x)	=	1	SGN(x) "1"
1	≤ ABS(x) <		10	SGN(x) "A"
10	≤ ABS(x) <		100	SGN(x) "B"
100	≤ ABS(x) <		1000	SGN(x) "C"
1000	≤ ABS(x) <		10000	SGN(x) "D"
10000	≤ ABS(x) <		100000	SGN(x) "E"
100000	≤ ABS(x) <		1.0E06	SGN(x) "F"
.			.	
.			.	
.			.	

INTEGER
    prints a VARIABLE SUMMARY containing only the integer variables.

NONINTEGER
: prints a VARIABLE SUMMARY containing only the continuous variables.

PRICESEN
: prints the results of parametric programming for the current value of PRICEPHI, the price coefficients, and all of the price change vectors.

RANGEPRICE
: performs range analysis on the price coefficients.

RANGERHS
: performs range analysis on the right-hand-side vector.

RHSSEN
: prints the results of parametric programming for the current value of RHSPHI, the right-hand-side coefficients, and all of the right-hand-side change vectors.

ROW(*rownames*)/SENSITIVITY
: prints a CONSTRAINT SUMMARY containing the rows listed in the rowname list. If the /SENSITIVITY option is included, then sensitivity analysis is performed on the right-hand-side coefficients for the listed *rownames*.

SOLUTION
: prints the SOLUTION SUMMARY, including the VARIABLE SUMMARY and the CONSTRAINT SUMMARY.

TABLEAU
: prints the current tableau.

QUIT Statement

QUIT/*option*;

The QUIT statement causes the LP procedure to terminate processing immediately. No further printing is performed and no output data sets are created. To save the output data sets defined in the PROC LP statement or in the RESET statement, use the option /SAVE, which causes the procedure to save data in the output data sets and then causes the procedure to terminate.

RANGE Statement

RANGE *variable*;

For the dense input format, the RANGE statement identifies the variable in the problem data set that contains the range coefficients. These coefficients enable you to specify the feasible range of a row. For example, if the *i*th row is

$$a'x \leq b_i$$

and the range coefficient for this row is $r_i > 0$, then all values of x that satisfy

$$b_i - r_i \leq a'x \leq b_i$$

are feasible for this row. **Table 7.3** shows the bounds on a row as a function of the row type and the sign on a nonmissing range coefficient r.

Table 7.3 Interpretation of the Range Coefficient

		Bounds	
r	_TYPE_	Lower	Upper
$\neq 0$	LE	$b - \lvert r \rvert$	b
$\neq 0$	GE	b	$b + \lvert r \rvert$
> 0	EQ	b	$b + r$
< 0	EQ	$b + r$	b

If you include a range variable in the model and have a missing value or zero for it in a constraint row, then that constraint is treated as if no range variable had been included.

If the RANGE statement is omitted, PROC LP assumes that the variable named _RANGE_ contains the range coefficients.

For the sparse input format, the RANGE statement gives the name of a column in the problem data set that contains the range constants. If the RANGE statement is omitted, then PROC LP assumes that the column named _RANGE_ in the sparse problem data set contains the range constants. See **Sparse Data Input Format** later in this chapter.

RESET Statement

RESET *options*;

The RESET statement is used to change options after the procedure has started execution. All of the options that can be set in the PROC LP statement can also be reset with the RESET statement, except for the DATA=, the PRIMALIN=, and the ACTIVEIN= options. In addition to the options available with the PROC LP statement, the following two options can be used:

LOWER(*colnames*)=n;
   during phase 3, this sets the lower bound on all of the structural variables listed in the *colnames* list to n. This may contaminate the branch and bound tree. All nodes that descend from the current problem will have lower bounds that may be different from those input in the problem data set.

UPPER(*colnames*)=n;
   during phase 3, this sets the upper bound on all of the structural variables listed in the *colnames* list to n. This may contaminate the branch and bound tree. All nodes that descend from the current problem will have upper bounds that may be different from those input in the problem data set.

RHS Statement

RHS *variables*;

For the dense input format, the RHS statement identifies variables in the problem data set that contain the constant right-hand side of the linear program. Only numeric variables can be specified. If more than one variable is included in the RHS statement, the procedure assumes that problems for several linear programs are defined by the problem data set. A new linear program is defined for each variable in the RHS list. If the RHS statement is omitted, PROC LP assumes that the variable named _RHS_ contains the right-hand-side constants.

For the sparse input format, the RHS statement gives the names of one or more columns in the problem data set that are to be considered as right-hand-side constants. If the RHS statement is omitted, then PROC LP assumes that the column named _RHS_ in the sparse problem data set contains the right-hand-side constants. See **Sparse Data Input Format** later in this chapter.

RHSSEN Statement

RHSSEN *variables*;

For the dense input format, the RHSSEN statement identifies variables in the problem data set that define change vectors for examining the sensitivity of the optimal solution to changes in the RHS constants.

For the sparse input format, the RHSSEN statement gives the names of one or more columns in the problem data set that are to be considered as change vectors. If the RHSSEN statement is omitted, then PROC LP assumes that the column named _RHSSEN_ in the sparse problem data set contains the right-hand-side change vector. See the **Sparse Data Input Format**, **Right-Hand-Side Sensitivity Analysis**, and **Right-Hand-Side Parametric Programming** sections later in this chapter.

ROW Statement

ROW *variables*;

For the dense input format, the ROW statement specifies a variable in the problem data set that contains a name for each row of constraint coefficients and for each row of objective coefficients. If ROW is not included, the LP procedure looks for the default variable name, _ROW_. If this is not a variable in the problem data set, PROC LP uses the default name _OBSxx_, where xx specifies the number of the observation in the problem data set.

For the sparse input format, the ROW statement specifies the character variables in the problem data set that contain the names of the rows in the model. Rows in the model are one of the following types: constraints, objective functions, bounding rows, or variable describing rows. The ROW variables must be character variables. There must be the same number of ROW variables as variables specified in the COEF statement. If the ROW statement is omitted, PROC LP looks for the default variable names having the prefix _ROW.

SHOW Statement

SHOW *options*;

The SHOW statement specifies that PROC LP print either the current options or the current solution status on the SAS log.

OPTIONS   requests that the options be printed on the SAS log.

STATUS   requests that the status of the current solution be printed on the SAS log.

TYPE Statement

TYPE *variables*;

For the sparse and dense input formats, the TYPE statement specifies a character variable in the problem data set that contains the type identifier for each observation. This variable has keyword values that specify how the LP procedure should interpret the observation. If the TYPE statement is omitted, PROC LP assumes that the variable named _TYPE_ contains the type keywords.

The following are valid values for the TYPE variable in an observation:

MAX   contains the price coefficients of an objective row, for example, **c** in the problem *(mip)*, to be maximized.

MIN   contains the price coefficients of an objective row, for example, **c** to be minimized.

EQ (=)   contains coefficients of an equality constrained row.

LE (≤)   contains coefficients of an inequality, less than or equal to, constrained row.

GE (≥)   contains coefficients of an inequality, greater than or equal to, constrained row.

SOSLE   identifies the row as specifying a special ordered set. The variables flagged in this row are members of a set **at most one** of which can be above its lower bound in the optimal solution.

SOSEQ   identifies the row as specifying a special ordered set. The variables flagged in this row are members of a set **exactly one** of which must be above its lower bound in the optimal solution. Note that variables in this type of special ordered set must be integer.

UNRSTRCT   identifies those structural variables to be considered as unrestricted variables. These are variables for which $\ell_i = -$INFINITY and $u_i = +$INFINITY. Any variable that has a one in this observation is considered an unrestricted variable.

UPPERBD   identifies upper bounds u_i on the structural variables. For each structural variable that is to have an upper bound $u_i = +$INFINITY, the observation must contain a missing value or the current value of INFINITY. All other values are interpreted as upper bounds, including 0. Upper bounds can also be specified explicitly in constraint rows. However; using the UPPERBD keyword and implicitly specifying upper bounds on the structural variables is more efficient computationally.

LOWERBD   identifies lower bounds on the structural variables. If all structural variables are to be nonnegative, that is $\ell_i = 0$, then do not include an observation with the LOWERBD keyword in a variable specified in the TYPE statement. Using LOWERBD causes PROC LP to treat implicitly the lower bounds on the structural variables, which results in computational efficiencies that could not be realized when explicitly defining the lower bounds in constraint rows. Missing values for variables in a lower-bound row indicate that the variable has zero lower bound.

Note: a variable with lower or upper bounds cannot also be unrestricted.

INTEGER   identifies variables that are integer-constrained. In a feasible solution, these variables must have integer values. A missing value in a row with INTEGER type keyword indicates that that variable is not integer constrained. The value of variables in the INTEGER row gives an ordering to the integer-constrained variables that is used when the VARSELECT= option equals PRIOR.

Note: every integer-constrained variable must have an upper bound defined in a row with type UPPERBD (see **Controlling the Branch and Bound Search** later in this chapter).

BINARY   identifies variables that are constrained to be either 0 or 1. This is equivalent to specifying that the variable is an integer variable and has a lower bound of 0 and an upper bound of 1. A missing value in a row with BINARY type keyword indicates that that variable is not constrained to be 0 or 1. The value of variables in the BINARY row gives an ordering to the integer-constrained variables that is used when the VARSELECT= option equals PRIOR. (See **Controlling the Branch and Bound Search** later in this chapter.)

BASIC   identifies variables that form an initial basic feasible solution.

PRICESEN   identifies a vector that is used to evaluate the sensitivity of the optimal solution to changes in the objective function.

FREE   identifies a nonbinding constraint. Any number of FREE constraints can appear in a problem data set.

VAR Statement

   VAR *variables*;

For the dense input format, the VAR statement identifies variables in the problem data set that are to be interpreted as structural variables, x, in the linear program. Only numeric variables can be specified. If no VAR statement is specified, the procedure uses as structural variables all numeric variables not included in an RHS or RHSSEN statement.

DETAILS

Missing Values

The LP procedure treats missing values as missing in all rows except those that identify either upper or lower bounds on structural variables. If the row is an upper-bound row, then the type identifier is UPPERBD and PROC LP treats missing values as +INFINITY. If the row is a lower-bound row, then the type identifier is LOWERBD and PROC LP treats the missing values as 0.

Sparse Data Input Format

Table 7.4 shows the keywords that are recognized by PROC LP and in which variables they can appear in the problem data set. The SAS data set that describes the sparse model must contain at least four SAS variables: a type variable, a column variable, a row variable, and a coefficient variable. Each observation in the data set defines one or more rows, columns, or coefficients in the model. The value of the type variable is a keyword that tells PROC LP how to interpret the observation. The values of the row and column variables name the rows and columns in the model, and the values of the coefficient variables give the coefficients.

Table 7.4 Variable Keywords Used in the Problem Data Set

TYPE (_TYPE_)	COL (_COLxxxx)	ROW (_ROWxxxx)	COEF (_COEFxxx)
'MAX'			
'MIN'			
'LE'			
'GE'			
'EQ'			
'SOSLE'			
'SOSEQ'			
'LOWERBD'			
'UPPERBD'			
'UNRSTRCT'			
'BINARY'			
'INTEGER'			
'BASIC'			
'FREE'			
'PRICESEN'	'_RHS_'		
	'_RHSSEN_'		
	'_RANGE_'		
' '			
'*xxxxxxx'			

Follow these rules for sparse data input:

- The order of the observations is unimportant.
- Each unique column name appearing in the COL variable defines a unique column in the model.
- Each unique row name appearing in the ROW variable defines a unique row in the model.
- The type of the row is identified when an observation in which the row name appears (in a ROW variable) has type MIN, MAX, LE, GE, EQ, SOSLE, SOSEQ, UNRSTRCT, UPPERBD, LOWERBD, INTEGER, BINARY, BASIC, FREE, or PRICESEN.

- The type of each row must be identified at least once. If a row is given a type more than once, the multiple definitions must be identical.
- When there are multiple rows named in an observation (that is, when there are multiple ROW variables), the TYPE variable applies to each row named in the observation.
- Each column is assumed to be a structural column in the model unless the column is identified as a right-hand-side vector, a right-hand-side change vector, or a range vector. A column can also be identified as one of these types using the special column names _RHS_, _RHSSEN_, or _RANGE_, or the RHS, RHSSEN, or RANGE statements following the PROC LP statement.
- A TYPE variable beginning with the character * causes the observation to be interpreted as a comment.

When the column names appear in the VARIABLE summary in the PROC LP output, they are listed in alphabetical order. The row names appear in the order in which they appear in the problem data set.

Memory Management

Memory usage is affected by a great many factors including the density of the technological coefficient matrix, the model structure, and the density of the decomposed basis matrix. The algorithm requires that the decomposed basis fit completely in memory. Any additional memory is used for nonbasic columns. The partition between the decomposed basis and the nonbasic columns is dynamic so that as the inverse grows, which typically happens as iterations proceed, more memory is available to it and less is available for the nonbasic columns.

The LP procedure determines the initial size of the decomposed basis matrix. If the area used is too small, PROC LP must spend time compressing this matrix, which degrades performance. If PROC LP must compress the decomposed basis matrix on the average more than 15 times per iteration, then the size of the memory devoted to the basis is increased. If the work area cannot be made large enough to invert the basis, an error return occurs. On the other hand, if PROC LP compresses the decomposed basis matrix on the average once every other iteration, then memory devoted to the decomposed basis is decreased, freeing memory for the nonbasic columns.

For many models, memory constraints will not be a problem because both the decomposed basis and all the nonbasic columns will have no problem fitting. However, when the models become large relative to the available memory, the algorithm tries to adjust memory distribution in order to solve the problem. In the worst cases, only one nonbasic column will fit in memory with the decomposed basis matrix.

The size of the decomposed basis is affected by the value of the option U. The option U ranges between EPSILON and 1. When searching for a pivot in updating and inverting, any element less than U times the largest element in its row is excluded. A small U biases the algorithm toward maintaining sparsity at the expense of numerical stability and vice versa. Values of 0.1 and .01 have been reported in the literature as satisfactory (Reid 1976). However, because a satisfactory value depends on the problem data, the LP procedure's default (=.1) is to opt for numerical stability at the expense of sparsity.

Problems involving memory use can also occur when solving mixed-integer problems. Data associated with each node in the branch and bound tree must be kept in memory. As the tree grows, competition for memory by the decomposed basis, the nonbasic columns, and the branch and bound tree may become critical. If the situation becomes critical, the procedure will automatically switch to branching strategies that use less memory. However, it is possible to reach a point where no further processing is possible. In this case, PROC LP terminates on a memory error.

The Reduced Costs, Dual Activities, and CURRENT TABLEAU

The evaluation of reduced costs and the dual activities are independent of problem structure. For a basic solution, let **B** be the matrix composed of the basic columns of **A** and let **N** be the matrix composed of the nonbasic columns of **A**. The reduced cost associated with the ith variable is

$$(c' - c_B' B^{-1} A)_i$$

and the dual activity of the jth row is

$$(c_B' B^{-1})_j \ .$$

The CURRENT TABLEAU is a section printed when you specify either the TABLEAUPRINT option in the PROC LP statement or you specify the TABLEAU option in the PRINT statement. The output contains a row for each basic variable and a column for each nonbasic variable. In addition, there is a row for the reduced costs and a column for the product

$$B^{-1} b \ .$$

This column is labeled INV(B)*R. The body of the tableau contains the matrix

$$B^{-1} N \ .$$

Macro Variable _ORLP_

The LP procedure defines a macro variable named _ORLP_. This variable contains a character string that indicates the status of the procedure. It is set whenever the user gets control, at break points, and at procedure termination. The form of the _ORLP_ character string is STATUS= PHASE= OBJECTIVE= P_FEASIBLE= D_FEASIBLE= INT_ITERATION= INT_FEASIBLE= ACTIVE= ITERATION= TIME=. The terms are interpreted as follows:

STATUS=	the status of the current solution
PHASE=	the phase the procedure is in
OBJECTIVE=	the current objective value
P_FEASIBLE=	whether the current solution is primal feasible
D_FEASIBLE=	whether the current solution is dual feasible
INT_ITERATION=	
	the number of integer iterations performed
INT_FEASIBLE=	the number of integer feasible solutions found
ACTIVE=	the number of active nodes in the current branch and bound tree
ITERATION=	the number of iterations performed in the current phase.
TIME=	the time thus far.

Table 7.5 shows the possible values for the nonnumeric terms in the string.

Table 7.5 Possible Values for Nonnumeric Terms

STATUS	P_FEASIBLE	D_FEASIBLE
SUCCESSFUL	YES	YES
UNBOUNDED	NO	NO
INFEASIBLE		
MAX_TIME		
MAX_ITER		
PIVOT		
BREAK		
INT_FEASIBLE		
INT_INFEASIBLE		
INT_MAX_ITER		
ACTIVE		
RELAXED		
FATHOMED		
IPIVOT		
UNSTABLE		
SINGULAR		
MEMORY_ERROR		
IO_ERROR		
SYNTAX_ERROR		
SEMANTIC_ERROR		
BADDATA_ERROR		
UNKNOWN_ERROR		

This information can be used when PROC LP is one step in a larger program that needs to identify how the LP procedure terminated. Because _ORLP_ is a standard SAS macro variable, it can be used in the ways that all macro variables can be used (see the *SAS Guide to Macro Processing, Version 6 Edition*).

Pricing

PROC LP performs multiple pricing when determining which variable will enter the basis at each pivot (see Greenberg 1978). This heuristic can shorten execution time in many problems. The specifics of the multiple pricing algorithm depend on the value of the PRICETYPE= option. However, in general, when some form of multiple pricing is used, during the first iteration PROC LP places the PRICE=k nonbasic columns yielding the greatest marginal improvement to the objective function in a candidate list. This list identifies a subproblem of the original. On subsequent iterations, only the reduced costs for the nonbasic variables in the candidate list are calculated. This accounts for the potential time savings. When either the candidate list is empty or the subproblem is optimal, a new candidate list must be identified and the process repeats. Because identification of the subproblem requires pricing the complete problem, an iteration in which this occurs is called a *major iteration*. A *minor iteration* is an iteration in which only the sub-problem is to be priced.

The value of the PRICETYPE= option determines the type of multiple pricing that is to be used. The types of multiple pricing include partial suboptimization (PRICETYPE=PARTIAL), complete suboptimization (PRICETYPE=COMPLETE), and complete suboptimization with dynamically varying k (PRICE-TYPE=DYNAMIC).

When partial suboptimization is used, in each minor iteration the nonbasic column in the subproblem yielding the greatest marginal improvement to the objective is brought into the basis and removed from the candidate list. The candidate list now has one less entry. At each subsequent iteration, another column from the subproblem is brought into the basis and removed from the candidate list. When there are either no remaining candidates or the remaining candidates do not improve the objective, the subproblem is abandoned and a major iteration is performed. If the objective cannot be improved on a major iteration, the current solution is optimal and PROC LP terminates.

Complete suboptimization is identical to partial suboptimization with one exception. When a nonbasic column from the subproblem is brought into the basis, it is replaced in the candidate list by the basic column that is leaving the basis. As a result, the candidate list does not diminish at each iteration.

When PRICETYPE=DYNAMIC, complete suboptimization is performed, but the value of k changes so that the ratio of minor to major iterations is within two units of k.

These heuristics can shorten execution time for small values of k. Care should be exercised in choosing k because too large a value can use more time than if pricing were not used.

Scaling

Before iterating, the procedure scales the rows and columns of both the constraints and objective rows. They are scaled so that the largest element in absolute value in each row or column equals 1. They are scaled by rows first and then by columns. This technique can improve the numerical stability of an ill-conditioned problem. If you want to modify the default matrix scaling used, which is COLUMN, use the SCALE=NONE, ROW, or BOTH option in the PROC LP statement.

Integer Programming

Formulations of mathematical programs often require that some of the decision variables take only integer values. Consider the formulation of (*mip*) presented in the **INTRODUCTION**:

$$\max (\min) \ \mathbf{c'x}$$
$$\text{subject to: } \mathbf{Ax} \begin{array}{c} \leq \\ = \\ \geq \end{array} \mathbf{b} \qquad\qquad (mip)$$

$$\ell_i \leq x_i \leq u_i \quad \text{for } i = 1, \ldots, n$$

$$\{x_i \mid i\varepsilon S\} \ \text{are integer} \ .$$

The set of indices **S** identifies those variables that must only take integer values. When **S** does not contain all of the integers between 1 and n, inclusive, problem (mip) is called a mixed-integer program. Otherwise, it is known as an integer program. Let $x^{opt}(mip)$ denote an optimal solution to (mip).

Specifying the Problem

An integer or mixed-integer problem can be solved with PROC LP. To solve this problem, you must identify the integer variables. You can do this with a row in the input data set that has the keyword INTEGER for the type variable. Any variable that has a nonmissing and nonzero value for this row is interpreted as an integer variable. It is important to note that integer variables must have upper bounds explicitly defined using the UPPERBD keyword. The values in the INTEGER row not only identify those variables that must be integral, but they also give an ordering to the integer variables that can be used in the solution technique.

The Branch and Bound Technique

The branch and bound approach is used to solve integer and mixed-integer problems. The following discussion outlines the approach and explains how to use several options to control the procedure.

The branch and bound technique solves an integer program by solving a sequence of linear programs. The sequence can be represented by a tree, with each node in the tree being identified with a linear program that is derived from the problems on the path leading to the root of the tree. The root of the tree is identified with a linear program that is identical to (mip) except that S is empty. This relaxed version of (mip) can be written as

$$\max (\min) \; c'x$$
$$\text{subject to:} \quad Ax \; \overset{\leq}{\underset{\geq}{=}} \; b \qquad\qquad (lp(0))$$

$$\ell_i \leq x_i \leq u_i \;\; \text{for } i = 1, \ldots, n \;\; .$$

The branch and bound approach generates linear programs along the nodes of the tree using the following schema. Consider $x^{opt}(0)$, the optimal solution to $lp(0)$. If $x^{opt}(0)_i$ is integer for all $i \varepsilon S$, then $x^{opt}(0)$ is optimal in (mip). Suppose for some $i \varepsilon S$, $x^{opt}(0)_i$ is nonintegral. In that case, define two new problems $(lp(1))$ and $(lp(2))$, descendents of the parent problem $(lp(0))$. The problem $(lp(1))$ is identical to $(lp(0))$ except for the additional constraint $x_i \leq \lfloor x^{opt}(0)_i \rfloor$, and the problem $(lp(2))$ is identical to $(lp(0))$ except for the additional constraint $x_i \geq \lceil x^{opt}(0)_i \rceil$. The notation $\lceil y \rceil$ means the smallest integer greater than or equal to y, and the notation $\lfloor y \rfloor$ means the largest integer less than or equal to y. Note that the two new problems do not have $x^{opt}(0)$ as a feasible solution, but because the solution to (mip) must satisfy one of the above constraints, $x^{opt}(mip)_i$ must satisfy one of the new constraints. The two problems thus defined are called *active nodes* in the branch and bound tree, and the variable i is called the *branching variable*.

Next, the algorithm chooses one of the problems associated with an active node and attempts to solve it using the dual algorithm. The problem may be infeasible, in which case the problem is dropped. If it can be solved, and it in turn does not have an integer solution (that is a solution for which x_i is integer for all $i \varepsilon S$), then it defines two new problems. These new problems contain all of the constraints of the parent problems plus the appropriate additional one.

Branching continues in this manner until either there are no active nodes or an integer solution is found. When an integer solution is found, its objective value provides a bound for the objective of *(mip)*. In particular, if **z** is the objective value of the current best integer solution, then any active problems whose parent problem has objective $\leq$**z** can be discarded (assuming that the problem is a maximization). This can be done because all problems that descend from this parent will also have objective $\leq$**z**. This technique is known as fathoming.

When there are no active nodes remaining to be solved, the current integer solution is optimal in *(mip)*. If no integer solution has been found, then *(mip)* is infeasible.

It is important to realize that integer programs are NP-complete. Roughly speaking, this means that the effort required to solve them grows exponentially with the size of the problem. For example, a problem with 10 binary variables can, in the worst case, generate $2^{10} = 1024$ nodes in the branch and bound tree. A problem with 20 binary variables can, in the worst case, generate $2^{20} = 1048576$ nodes in the branch and bound tree. Although the algorithm is unlikely to have to generate every single possible node, the need to explore even a small fraction of the number of nodes in a large problem can be resource intensive.

The INTEGER ITERATION LOG

To help monitor the growth of the branch and bound tree, the LP procedure reports on the status of each problem that is solved. The report, printed in the INTEGER ITERATION LOG, can be used to reconstruct the branch and bound tree. Each row in the report describes the results of the attempted solution of the linear program at a node in the tree. In the following discussion, a problem on a given line in the log is called the current problem. The following eight columns are printed in the report:

ITER
identifies the number of the branch and bound iteration.

PROBLEM
identifies how the current problem fits in the branch and bound tree.

CONDITION
reports the result of the attempted solution of the current problem. Values for CONDITION are

ACTIVE
the current problem was solved successfully

INFEASIBLE
the current problem is infeasible

FATHOMED
the current problem cannot lead to an improved integer solution so it is dropped

SUBOPTIMAL
the current problem has an integer feasible solution.

OBJECTIVE
reports the objective value of the current problem.

BRANCHED
names the variable that is branched in subtrees defined by the descendents of this problem.

VALUE
gives the current value of the variable named in the column labeled BRANCHED.

SINFEAS
gives the sum of the integer infeasibilities in the current problem.

ACTIVE
reports the total number of nodes currently active in the branch and bound tree.

To reconstruct the branch and bound tree from this report, consider the interpretation of iteration j. If ITER=j and PROBLEM=k, then the problem solved on iteration j is identical to the problem solved on iteration $|k|$ with an additional constraint. If $k>0$ then the constraint is an upper bound on the variable named in the BRANCH column on iteration j. On the other hand, if $k<0$ then the constraint is a lower bound on that variable. The value of the bound can be obtained from the value of VALUE in iteration $|k|$ as described in the previous section. **Example 8:   A Simple Integer Program** shows an INTEGER ITERATION LOG in its output (**Output 7.12**).

Controlling the Branch and Bound Search

There are several options you can use to control branching. This is accomplished by controlling the program's choice of the branching variable and of the next active node. In the discussion that follows, let

$$f_i(k) = x^{opt}(k)_i - \lfloor x^{opt}(k)_i \rfloor$$

where $\mathbf{x}^{opt}(k)$ is the optimal solution to the problem solved on iteration k.

The CANSELECT= option directs the choice of next active node. Valid keywords for this option include LIFO, FIFO, OBJ, PROJECT, PSEUDOC, and ERROR. The following list describes the action that each of these causes when the procedure must choose for solution a problem from the list of active nodes.

LIFO   chooses the last problem added to the tree of active nodes. This search has the effect of a depth first search of the branch and bound tree. If at the current node the two descendent problems are not added to the active tree, then the procedure must backtrack. The BACKTRACK= option controls the search for the next problem. This option can take the same values as the CANSELECT= option.

FIFO   chooses the first nodes added to the tree of active nodes. This search has the effect of a breadth first search of the branch and bound tree.

OBJ   chooses the problem whose parent has the largest (least if the problem is a minimization) objective value.

PROJECT   chooses the problem with the largest (least if the problem is a minimization) projected objective value. The projected objective value is evaluated using the sum of integer infeasibilities, $s(k)$, associated with an active node $(lp(k))$, defined by

$$s(k) = \Sigma_{i \in S} \, min \, \{f_i(k), \, (1 - f_i(k))\} \quad .$$

An empirical measure of the rate of decrease (increase) in the objective value is defined as

$$\lambda = (z(0) - \mathbf{z}^{\bullet}) \, / \, s(0)$$

where

z(k)   is the optimal objective value for (lp(k)), and

z*   is the objective value of the current best integer solution.

The projected objective value for problems (lp(k+1)) and (lp(k+2)) is defined as

$$z(k) - \lambda s(k) \quad .$$

PSEUDOC   chooses the problem with the largest (least if the problem is a minimization) projected pseudocost. The projected pseudocost is evaluated using the weighted sum of infeasibilities $s_w(k)$ associated with an active problem (lp(k)), defined by

$$s_w(k) = \Sigma_{i \in S} \min \ \{d_i f_i(k), \ u_i(1 - f_i(k))\} \quad .$$

The weights u_i and d_i are initially equal to the absolute value of the ith objective coefficient and are updated whenever an integer feasible solution is encountered. They are modified by examining the empirical marginal change in the objective as additional constraints are placed on the variables in S along the path from (lp(0)) to the node associated with the integer feasible solution. In particular, if the definition of problems (lp(k+1)) and (lp(k+2)) from parent (lp(k)) involve the addition of constraints $x_i \leq \lfloor x^{opt}(k)_i \rfloor$ and $x_i \geq \lceil x^{opt}(k)_i \rceil$, respectively. and one of them is on the path to an integer feasible solution, then either

$$d_i = (z(k) - z(k + 1)) / f_i(k)$$

or

$$u_i = (z(k) - z(k + 2)) / (1 - f_i(k)) \quad .$$

Note the similarity between $s_w(k)$ and $s(k)$. The weighted quantity $s_w(k)$ accounts to some extent for the influence of the objective function. The projected pseudocost for problems (lp(k+1)) and (lp(k+2)) is defined as

$$z_w(k) \equiv z(k) - s_w(k) \quad .$$

ERROR   chooses the problem with the largest (least if the problem is a minimization) error. The error associated with problems (lp(k+1)) and (lp(k+2)) is defined as

$$(z_w(k) - z^*) / (z(k) - z^*) \quad .$$

The VARSELECT= option directs the choice of branching variable. Valid keywords for this option include CLOSE, FAR, PRIOR, PSEUDOC, PRICE, and

PENALTY. The following list describes the action that each of these causes when $x^{opt}(k)$, an optimal solution of problem $(lp(k))$, is used to define active problems $(lp(k+1))$ and $(lp(k+2))$.

CLOSE   chooses as branching variable the variable $x^{opt}(k)_i$ such that i minimizes

$$\{\min\ \{f_j(k),\ (1-f_j(k))\}\ |\ j\varepsilon S\ \text{and}$$
$$\text{IEPSILON} \le f_j(k) \le 1 - \text{IEPSILON}\}\ \ .$$

FAR   chooses as branching variable the variable $x^{opt}(k)_i$ such that i maximizes

$$\{\min\ \{f_j(k),\ (1-f_j(k))\}\ |\ j\varepsilon S\ \text{and}$$
$$\text{IEPSILON} \le f_j(k) \le 1 - \text{IEPSILON}\ \}\ \ .$$

PRIOR   chooses as branching variable i such that $i\varepsilon S$ $x^{opt}(k)_i$ nonintegral, and variable i has the minimum value in the INTEGER row in the input data set. This choice for VARSELECT= is recommended when you have enough insight into the model to identify those integer variables that have the most significant effect on the objective value.

PENALTY   chooses as branching variable $x^{opt}(k)_i$ such that $i\varepsilon S$ and a bound on the decrease in the objective of $(lp(k))$ (penalty) resulting from adding the constraint $x_i \le \lfloor x^{opt}(k)_i \rfloor$ or $x_i \ge \lceil x^{opt}(k)_i \rceil$ is maximized. The bound is calculated without pivoting using techniques of sensitivity analysis (Garfinkel and Nemhauser 1972). Because the cost of calculating the maximum penalty can be large if **S** is large, you may want to limit the number of variables in **S** for which the penalty is calculated. The penalty is calculated for PENALTYDEPTH= variables in **S**.

PRICE   chooses as branching variable i such that $i\varepsilon S$, $x^{opt}(k)_i$ is nonintegral, and variable i has the maximum price coefficient.

PSEUDOC   chooses as branching variable the variable $x^{opt}(k)_i$ such that i maximizes

$$\{\min\ \{d_j f_j(k),\ u_j(1-f_j(k))\}\ |\ j\varepsilon S\ \text{and}$$
$$\text{IEPSILON} \le f_j(k) \le 1 - \text{IEPSILON}\}\ \ .$$

The weights u_j and d_j are initially equal to the absolute value of the jth objective coefficient and are updated whenever an integer feasible solution is encountered. See the discussion on the CANSELECT= option for details on the method of updating the weights.

Customizing Search Heuristics

Often a good heuristic for searching the branch and bound tree of a problem can be found. You are tempted to continue using this heuristic when the problem data changes but the problem structure remains constant. The ability to reset procedure options interactively enables you to experiment with search techniques in an attempt to identify approaches that perform well. Then you can easily reapply these techniques to subsequent problems.

For example, the PIP branch and bound strategy (Crowder, Johnson, and Padberg 1983) describes one such heuristic. The following program uses a similar strategy. Here the OBJ rule (choose the active node with largest parent objective function in the case of a maximization problem) is used for selecting the next active node to be solved until an integer feasible solution is found. Once such a solution is found, the search procedure is changed to the LIFO rule: choose the problem most recently placed in the list of active nodes.

```
proc lp canselect=obj ifeasiblepause=1;
run;
   reset canselect=lifo ifeasiblepause=9999999;
run;
```

Saving and Restoring the List of Active Nodes

The list of active nodes can be saved in a SAS data set for use at a subsequent invocation of PROC LP. The ACTIVEOUT= option in the PROC LP statement names the data set into which the current list of active nodes is saved when the procedure terminates due to an error termination condition. Examples of such conditions are time limit exceeded, integer iterations exceeded, or phase 3 iterations exceeded. The ACTIVEIN= option in the PROC LP statement names a data set that can be used to initialize the list of active nodes. To achieve the greatest benefit when restarting PROC LP, use the PRIMALOUT= and PRIMALIN= options in conjunction with the ACTIVEOUT= and ACTIVEIN= options. See **Example 10:   Restarting an Integer Program** for an illustration.

Sensitivity Analysis

Sensitivity analysis is a technique for examining the effect of changes in model parameters on the optimal solution. The analysis enables you to examine the size of a perturbation to the right-hand-side or objective vector by an arbitrary change vector for which the basis of the current optimal solution remains optimal. When sensitivity analysis is performed on integer constrained problems, the integer variables are fixed at the value they obtained in the integer solution. Care must be used when interpreting the results of such analyses.

Right-Hand-Side Sensitivity Analysis

Consider the problem

$$\max\ (\min)\ \mathbf{c}'\mathbf{x}$$
$$\text{subject to:}\ \ \mathbf{Ax} \overset{\leq}{\underset{\geq}{=}} \mathbf{b} + \varphi\mathbf{r} \hspace{3cm} (lpr(\varphi))$$

$$\ell_i \leq x_i \leq u_i\ \text{ for } i = 1, \ldots, n\ .$$

Let $\mathbf{x}^{opt}(\varphi)$ denote an optimal basic feasible solution to $(lpr(\varphi))$. PROC LP can be used to examine the effects of changes in φ on the solution $\mathbf{x}^{opt}(0)$ of problem $(lpr(0))$. For the basic solution $\mathbf{x}^{opt}(0)$, let $\mathbf{B}$ be the matrix composed of the basic columns of $\mathbf{A}$ and let $\mathbf{N}$ be the matrix composed of the nonbasic columns of $\mathbf{A}$.

For the basis matrix $\mathbf{B}$, the basic components of $\mathbf{x}^{opt}(0)$, written as $\mathbf{x}^{opt}(0)_\mathbf{B}$, can be expressed as

$$\mathbf{x}^{opt}(0)_\mathbf{B} = \mathbf{B}^{-1}(\mathbf{b} - \mathbf{N}\mathbf{x}^{opt}(0)_\mathbf{N}) \quad .$$

Furthermore, because $\mathbf{x}^{opt}(0)$ is feasible

$$\ell_\mathbf{B} \leq \mathbf{B}^{-1}(\mathbf{b} - \mathbf{N}\mathbf{x}^{opt}(0)_\mathbf{N}) \leq \mathbf{u}_\mathbf{B}$$

where $\ell_\mathbf{B}$ is a column vector of the lower bounds on the structural basic variables, and $\mathbf{u}_\mathbf{B}$ is a column vector of the upper bounds on the structural basic variables.

For each right-hand-side change vector $\mathbf{r}$ identified in the RHSSEN statement, PROC LP finds an interval $[\varphi_{min}, \varphi_{max}]$ such that

$$\ell_\mathbf{B} \leq \mathbf{B}^{-1}(\mathbf{b} + \varphi\mathbf{r} - \mathbf{N}\mathbf{x}^{opt}(0)_\mathbf{N}) \leq \mathbf{u}_\mathbf{B}$$

for $\varphi\varepsilon[\varphi_{min}, \varphi_{max}]$. Furthermore, because changes in the right-hand side do not affect the reduced costs, for $\varphi\varepsilon[\varphi_{min}, \varphi_{max}]$

$$\mathbf{x}^{opt}(\varphi)' = (\ (\mathbf{B}^{-1}(\mathbf{b} + \varphi\mathbf{r} - \mathbf{N}\mathbf{x}^{opt}(0)_\mathbf{N}))', \mathbf{x}^{opt}(0)_\mathbf{N}'\ )$$

is optimal in $(lpr(\varphi))$.

For $\varphi = \varphi_{min}$ and $\varphi = \varphi_{max}$, PROC LP reports the following:

- the name of the leaving variables
- the value of the optimal objective in the modified problems
- the optimal solution in the modified problems.

The leaving variable identifies the basic variable i that first reaches either the lower bound ℓ_i or the upper bound u_i as φ reaches φ_{min} or φ_{max}. This is the basic variable that would leave the basis to maintain primal feasibility.

Multiple RHSSEN variables can appear in a problem data set.

Price Sensitivity Analysis

Consider the problem

$$\begin{aligned}
&\max\ (\min)\ \mathbf{c}'\mathbf{x} \\
&\text{subject to:}\quad \mathbf{A}\mathbf{x} \overset{\leq}{\underset{\geq}{=}} \mathbf{b} \qquad\qquad\qquad (lpp(\varphi)) \\
&\qquad\qquad \ell_i \leq x_i \leq u_i \ \text{ for } i = 1, \ldots, n \quad .
\end{aligned}$$

Let $\mathbf{x}^{opt}(\varphi)$ denote an optimal basic feasible solution to $(lpp(\varphi))$. PROC LP can be used to examine the effects of changes in φ on the solution $\mathbf{x}^{opt}(0)$ of problem $(lpp(0))$. For the basic solution $\mathbf{x}^{opt}(0)$, let $\mathbf{B}$ be the matrix composed of the basic columns of $\mathbf{A}$ and let $\mathbf{N}$ be the matrix composed of the nonbasic columns of $\mathbf{A}$. For basis matrix $\mathbf{B}$, the reduced cost associated with the ith variable can be written as

$$rc_i(\varphi) = ((\mathbf{c} + \varphi\mathbf{r})_\mathbf{N}' - (\mathbf{c} + \varphi\mathbf{r})_\mathbf{B}'\mathbf{B}^{-1}\mathbf{N})_i$$

where $(c+\phi r)_N$ and $(c+\phi r)_B$ is a partition of the vector of price coefficients into nonbasic and basic components. Because $x^{opt}(0)$ is optimal in $(lpp(0))$, the reduced costs satisfy

$$rc_i(0) \geq (\leq) \, 0$$

if the nonbasic variable in column i is at its upper bound and

$$rc_i(0) \leq (\geq) \, 0$$

if the nonbasic variable in column i is at its lower bound.

For each price coefficient change vector r identified with the keyword PRICESEN in the TYPE variable, PROC LP finds an interval $[\phi_{min}, \phi_{max}]$ such that for $\phi \varepsilon [\phi_{min}, \phi_{max}]$

$$rc_i(\phi) \geq (\leq) \, 0$$

if the nonbasic variable in column i is at its upper bound and

$$rc_i(\phi) \leq (\geq) \, 0$$

if the nonbasic variable in column i is at its lower bound. Because changes in the price coefficients do not affect feasibility, for $\phi \varepsilon [\phi_{min}, \phi_{max}]$, $x^{opt}(0)$ is optimal in $(lpp(\phi))$. For $\phi = \phi_{min}$ and $\phi = \phi_{max}$, PROC LP reports the following:

- name of entering variables
- value of the optimal objective in the modified problems
- price coefficients in the modified problems
- reduced costs in the modified problems.

The entering variable identifies the variable whose reduced costs first go to zero as ϕ reaches ϕ_{min} or ϕ_{max}. This is the nonbasic variable that would enter the basis to maintain optimality (dual feasibility).

Multiple PRICESEN variables may appear in a problem data set.

Range Analysis

Range analysis is sensitivity analysis for specific change vectors. When range analysis is performed on integer-constrained problems, integer variables are fixed at the value they obtained during the branch and bound iterations. Care must be used in interpreting the results of such analyses.

Right-Hand-Side Range Analysis

The effects on the optimal solution of changes in each right-hand-side value can be studied using the RANGERHS option in the PROC LP or RESET statements. This option results in sensitivity analysis for the **m** right-hand-side change vectors specified by the columns of the **m**x**m** identity matrix.

Price Range Analysis

The effects on the optimal solution of changes in each price coefficient can be studied using the RANGEPRICE option in the PROC LP or RESET statements. This option results in sensitivity analysis for the **n** price change vectors specified by the columns of the **n**x**n** identity matrix.

Parametric Programming

Sensitivity analysis and range analysis examine how the optimal solution behaves with respect to perturbations of model parameter values. These approaches assume that the basis at optimality will not be allowed to change. When greater flexibility is desired and a change of basis is acceptable, parametric programming can be used.

When parametric programming is performed on integer-constrained problems, integer variables are fixed at the value they obtained during the branch and bound iterations. Care must be used in interpreting the results of such analyses.

Right-Hand-Side Parametric Programming

As discussed in **Right-Hand-Side Sensitivity Analysis**, for each right-hand-side change vector **r**, PROC LP finds an interval $[\varphi_{min},\varphi_{max}]$ such that for $\varphi\varepsilon[\varphi_{min},\varphi_{max}]$

$$\mathbf{x}^{opt}(\varphi)' = ((\mathbf{B}^{-1}(\mathbf{b} + \varphi\mathbf{r} - \mathbf{N}\mathbf{x}^{opt}(0)_{\mathbf{N}}))', \mathbf{x}^{opt}(0)_{\mathbf{N}}')$$

is optimal in $(lpr(\varphi))$ for the fixed basis **B**. Leaving variables that inhibit further changes in φ without a change in the basis **B** are associated with the quantities φ_{min} and φ_{max}. By specifying RHSPHI=Φ in either the PROC LP statement or in the RESET statement, you can examine the solution $\mathbf{x}^{opt}(\varphi)$ as φ increases or decreases from 0 to Φ.

When RHSPHI=Φ is specified, the procedure first finds the interval $[\varphi_{min},\varphi_{max}]$ as described above. Then, if $\Phi\varepsilon[\varphi_{min},\varphi_{max}]$, no further investigation is needed. However, if $\Phi>\varphi_{max}$ or $\Phi<\varphi_{min}$, then the procedure attempts to solve the new problem $(lpr(\Phi))$. To accomplish this, it pivots the leaving variable out of the basis while maintaining dual feasibility. If this new solution is primal feasible in $(lpr(\Phi))$, no further investigation is needed; otherwise, the procedure identifies the new leaving variable and pivots it out of the basis, again maintaining dual feasibility. Dual pivoting continues in this manner until a solution that is primal feasible in $(lpr(\Phi))$ is identified. Because dual feasibility is maintained at each pivot, the $(lpr(\Phi))$ primal feasible solution is optimal.

At each pivot, the procedure reports on the variables that enter and leave the basis, the current range of φ, and the objective value. When $\mathbf{x}^{opt}(\Phi)$ is found, it is printed. If you want the solution $\mathbf{x}^{opt}(\varphi)$ at each pivot, then specify the PARAPRINT option in either the PROC LP or RESET statement.

Price Parametric Programming

As discussed in **Price Sensitivity Analysis**, for each price change vector **r**, PROC LP finds an interval $[\varphi_{min},\varphi_{max}]$ such that for each $\varphi\varepsilon[\varphi_{min},\varphi_{max}]$

$$rc_i(\varphi) = ((\mathbf{c} + \varphi\mathbf{r})'_{\mathbf{N}} - (\mathbf{c} + \varphi\mathbf{r})'_{\mathbf{B}}\mathbf{B}^{-1}\mathbf{N})_i$$

satisfies the conditions for optimality in $(lpp(\varphi))$ for the fixed basis **B**. Entering variables that inhibit further changes in φ without a change in the basis **B** are associated with the quantities φ_{min} and φ_{max}. By specifying PRICEPHI=Φ in either the PROC LP statement or the RESET statement, you can examine the solution $\mathbf{x}^{opt}(\varphi)$ as φ increases or decreases from 0 to Φ.

When PRICEPHI=Φ is specified, the procedure first finds the interval $[\varphi_{min},\varphi_{max}]$ as described above. Then, if $\Phi\varepsilon[\varphi_{min},\varphi_{max}]$, no further investigation is needed. However, if $\Phi>\varphi_{max}$ or $\Phi<\varphi_{min}$, the procedure attempts to solve the new problem $(lpp(\Phi))$. To accomplish this it pivots the leaving variable out of the basis while maintaining primal feasibility. If this new solution is dual feasible in $(lpp(\Phi))$, no further investigation is needed; otherwise, the procedure identifies the new leaving variable and pivots it out of the basis, again maintaining primal feasibility. Pivoting continues in this manner until a solution that is dual feasible in $(lpp(\Phi))$ is identified. Because primal feasibility is maintained at each pivot, the $(lpp(\Phi))$ dual feasible solution is optimal.

At each pivot, the procedure reports on the variables that enter and leave the basis, the current range of φ, and the objective value. When $\mathbf{x}^{opt}(\Phi)$ is found, it is printed. If you want the solution $\mathbf{x}^{opt}(\varphi)$ at each pivot, then specify the PARAPRINT option in either the PROC LP or RESET statement.

Interactive Facilities

The interactive features of the LP procedure allow you to examine intermediate results, perform sensitivity analysis, parametric programming, and range analysis, and control the solution process.

Controlling Interactive Features

You can gain control of the LP procedure for interactive processing by pressing the CTRL-BREAK key combination when the procedure is executing phase 1, 2, or 3, when certain error conditions are encountered, or by setting a break point

- when a feasible solution is found
- at each pivot of the simplex algorithm
- at each integer pivot of the branch and bound algorithm
- after the data are read but before iteration begins
- after the problem has been solved but before results are printed.

When an error condition is encountered, the procedure enables you to gain control. Error conditions include time limit exceeded, phase 1 iterations exceeded, phase 2 iterations exceeded, phase 3 iterations exceeded, and integer iterations exceeded. At these points you can enter any of the interactive statements including RESET, PIVOT, IPIVOT, PRINT, QUIT, SHOW, and RUN. You can use the RESET statement to reset the option that caused the error condition.

Break points are set using the options FEASIBLEPAUSE, PAUSE, IFEASIBLEPAUSE, IPAUSE, READPAUSE, and ENDPAUSE. The LP procedure prints a message on the SAS log when it gives you control because of encountering one of these break points. At that point you can enter any of the interactive statements. Break points can also be generated by typing the control break keys during phases one, two, or three.

Some statements result in immediate execution. PIVOT, IPIVOT, QUIT, PRINT, and SHOW are examples of these. The PIVOT and IPIVOT statements result in control being returned to you after a single simplex algorithm pivot and integer pivot, respectively. On the other hand, the QUIT statement requests that you leave the LP procedure immediately. If you want to quit but save output data sets, then type QUIT/SAVE. The PRINT and SHOW statements print current solution information before returning control to you.

Printing Intermediate Results

Once you have control of the procedure you can examine the current values of the options and the status of the problem being solved using the SHOW statement. All printing done by the SHOW statement goes to the SAS log.

Details about the current status of the solution are obtained using the PRINT statement. The various print options enable you to examine parts of the variable and constraint summaries, print the current tableau, perform sensitivity analysis on the current solution, and perform range analysis.

Interactive Facilities in Batch Mode

All of the interactive statements can be used when processing in batch mode. This is particularly convenient when the interactive facilities are used to control the search of the branch and bound tree when you are solving integer problems.

Sensitivity Analysis

Two features that enhance the ability to perform sensitivity analysis need further explanation. When you specify /SENSITIVITY with the print options in the PRINT statement the procedure defines a new change row (change column if /SENSITIVITY is in a PRINT ROW (rowname) statement) to use in sensitivity analysis and parametric programming. This new change row (change column) has a +1 entry for each variable (right-hand-side coefficient) listed in the PRINT statement. This enables you to define new change rows interactively.

In addition, you can interactively change the RHSPHI= and PRICEPHI= options using the RESET statement. This enables you to perform parametric programming interactively.

Computer Resources

Memory

The memory requirements for PROC LP vary with the size of the problem. In addition to the memory that the code of the LP procedure takes, significant portions of memory are needed for the supervisor and problem data. The memory requirement for data is, at a minimum, approximately $(7*m*\text{sizeof}(double))$ + $(6*n*\text{sizeof}(double))$ bytes where n is the number of variables in the model, m is the number of constraints in the model, and $double$ refers to a double precision number.

CPU Time

The time needed to solve a problem of a given size varies significantly with problem structure, pricing strategy, and other parameter settings. It is strictly data dependent and cannot be predicted.

Problem Size Limitations

The number of constraints and variables in a problem that PROC LP can solve depend on the host platform, the available memory, and the available space for utility data sets.

Output Data Sets

The procedure can optionally produce four output data sets. These are the ACTIVEOUT, PRIMALOUT, DUALOUT, and TABLEAUOUT data sets. Each contains two variables that identify the particular problem in the input data set. These variables are

> _OBJ_ID_   identifies the objective function ID.
>
> _RHS_ID_   identifies the right-hand-side variable.

Additionally, each data set contains other variables, which are discussed below.

ACTIVEOUT= Data Set

The ACTIVEOUT= data set contains a representation of the current active branch and bound tree. You can use this data set to initialize the branch and bound tree to continue iterations on an incompletely solved problem. Each active node in the tree generates two observations in this data set. The first is a LOWERBD observation that is used to reconstruct the lower-bound constraints on the currently described active node. The second is an UPPERBD observation that is used to reconstruct the upper-bound constraints on the currently described active node. In addition to these, an observation that describes the current best integer solution is included. The data set contains the following variables:

STATUS
: contains the keywords LOWERBD, UPPERBD, and INTBEST for identifying the type of observation.

PROB
: contains the problem number for the current observation.

OBJECT
: contains the objective value of the parent problem that generated the current problem.

SINFEA
: contains the sum of the integer infeasibilities of the current problem.

PROJEC
: contains the data needed for CANSELECT=PROJECT when the branch and bound tree is read using the ACTIVEIN= option.

PSEUDO
: contains the data needed for CANSELECT=PSEUDOC when the branch and bound tree is read using the ACTIVEIN= option.

the integer constrained structural variables
: integer-constrained structural variables are also included in the ACTIVEOUT= data set. For each observation, these variables contain values for defining the active node in the branch and bound tree.

PRIMALOUT= Data Set

The PRIMALOUT= data set contains the current primal solution . If the problem has integer-constrained variables, the PRIMALOUT= data set contains the current best integer feasible solution. If none have been found, the PRIMALOUT= data set contains the relaxed solution. In addition to _OBJ_ID_ and _RHS_ID_, the data set contains:

VAR
: identifies the variable name.

TYPE
: identifies the type of variable as specified in the input data set. Artificial variables are labeled as type ARTIFCL.

STATUS
: identifies whether the variable is basic, nonbasic, or at an upper bound in the current solution.

LBOUND
: contains the input lower bound on the variable unless an integer solution is given. In this case, _LBOUND_ contains the lower bound on the variable needed to realize the integer solution on subsequent calls to PROC LP when using the PRIMALIN= option.

VALUE
: identifies the value of the variable in the current solution.

UBOUND
: contains the input upper bound on the variable unless an integer solution is given. In this case, _UBOUND_ contains the upper bound on the variable needed to

realize the integer solution on subsequent calls to PROC LP when using the PRIMALIN= option.

PRICE   contains the input price coefficient of the variable.

_R_COST_   identifies the value of the reduced cost in the current solution.

Example 3: Analyzing the Sensitivity of the Solution to Changes in the Objective Coefficients in **EXAMPLES** shows a typical data set. Note that it is necessary to include the information on objective function and right-hand side in order to distinguish problems in multiple problem data sets.

DUALOUT= Data Set

The DUALOUT= data set contains the dual solution for the current solution. In addition to _OBJ_ID_ and _RHS_ID_, it contains the following variables:

_ROW_ID_   identifies the row or constraint name.

TYPE   identifies the type of row as specified in the input data set.

RHS   gives the value of the right-hand side on input.

_L_RHS_   gives the lower bound for the row evaluated from the input right-hand-side value, the TYPE of the row, and the value of the RANGE variable for the row.

VALUE   gives the value of the row at optimality, excluding logical variables.

_U_RHS_   gives the upper bound for the row evaluated from the input right-hand-side value, the TYPE of the row, and the value of the RANGE variable for the row.

DUAL   gives the value of the dual variable associated with the row.

TABLEAUOUT= Data Set

The TABLEAUOUT= data set contains the current tableau. The tableau is output so that the variables in the model are variables in the data set and each observation, except for the first, corresponds to a basic variable in the solution. The observation labeled R_COSTS contains the reduced costs $c'_N - c'_B B^{-1}N$. In addition to _OBJ_ID_ and _RHS_ID_, it contains the following variables:

BASIC
    the names of the basic variables in the solution

INV(B)*R
    the values of $B^{-1}r$, where r is the right-hand-side vector

the variables in the model
    the values in the tableau, namely $B^{-1}A$.

Input Data Sets

In addition to the DATA= input data set, PROC LP recognizes the ACTIVEIN= and the PRIMALIN= data sets.

ACTIVEIN= Data Set

The ACTIVEIN= data set contains a representation of the current active tree. The format is identical to the ACTIVEOUT= data set.

PRIMALIN= Data Set

The PRIMALIN= data set's format is identical to the PRIMALOUT= data set. PROC LP uses the PRIMALIN= data set to identify variables at their upper bounds in the current solution and variables that are basic in the current solution.

You can add observations to the end of the problem data set if they define cost sensitivity change vectors and have TYPE=PRICESEN. You can also add variables that define right-hand-side sensitivity change vectors. This enables you to solve a problem, save the solution in a SAS data set, and perform sensitivity analysis later. You can also use the PRIMALIN= data set to restart problems that have not been completely solved or to which new variables have been added.

Printed Output

The output from the LP procedure is discussed below in five sections:

- PROBLEM SUMMARY
- SOLUTION SUMMARY including a VARIABLE SUMMARY and a CONSTRAINT SUMMARY
- INFEASIBLE INFORMATION SUMMARY
- RHS SENSITIVITY ANALYSIS SUMMARY (the RHS RANGE ANALYSIS SUMMARY not discussed below)
- PRICE SENSITIVITY ANALYSIS SUMMARY (the PRICE RANGE ANALYSIS SUMMARY not discussed below).

For integer-constrained problems, the procedure also prints an INTEGER ITERATION LOG. The description of this LOG can be found in the **DETAILS** section under **Integer Programming**.

When you request that the tableau be printed, the procedure prints the CURRENT TABLEAU. The description of this can be found in the **DETAILS** section under **The Reduced Costs, Dual Activities, and CURRENT TABLEAU**.

A problem data set can contain a set of constraints with several right-hand sides and several objective functions. PROC LP considers each combination of right-hand side and objective function as defining a new linear programming problem and solves each, performing all sensitivity analysis on each problem. For each problem defined, PROC LP prints a new sequence of output sections. **Example 1** in **EXAMPLES** discusses each of these elements.

Note: circled numbers in the output in the **EXAMPLES** section correspond to the numbered list below. The LP procedure produces the following printed output by default.

The PROBLEM SUMMARY

The problem summary includes the following:

1. type of optimization and the name of the objective row (as identified by the ID variable)
2. name of the SAS variable that contains the right-hand-side constants
3. name of the SAS variable that contains the type keywords
4. density of the coefficient matrix (the ratio of the number of nonzero elements to the number of total elements) after the slack and surplus variables have been appended
5. number of each type of variable in the mathematical program
6. number of each type of constraint in the mathematical program.

The SOLUTION SUMMARY

The solution summary includes the following:

7. termination status of the procedure
8. objective value of the current solution
9. number of phase 1 iterations that were completed
10. number of phase 2 iterations that were completed
11. number of phase 3 iterations that were completed
12. number of initial basic feasible variables identified
13. time used in solving the problem excluding reading the data and printing the solution
14. number of inversions of the basis matrix
15. current value of several of the options.

The VARIABLE SUMMARY

The variable summary includes the following:

16. column number associated with each structural and logical variable in the problem.
17. name of each structural and logical variable in the problem. (PROC LP gives the logical variables the name of the constraint ID for which the logical variable is either the slack or surplus. If no ID variable is specified, the procedure names the logical variable _OBSn_, where n is the observation that describes the constraint.)
18. variable's status in the current solution. The status can be BASIC, DEGEN, or ALTER, depending upon whether the variable is a basic variable, a degenerate variable, or can be brought into the basis to define an alternate optimal solution.
19. kind of variable (whether it is logical or structural, and, if structural, its bound type).
20. value of the objective coefficient associated with each variable.
21. activity of the variable in the current solution.
22. variable's reduced costs in the current solution.

The CONSTRAINT SUMMARY

The constraint summary includes the following:

23. constraint row number and its ID
24. the kind of constraint (whether it is an OBJECTIVE, LE, EQ, GE, RANGELE, RANGEEQ, RANGEGE, or FREE row)
25. number of the slack or surplus variable associated with the constraint row
26. value of the right-hand-side constant associated with the constraint row
27. current activity of the row (excluding logical variables)
28. current activity of the dual variable (shadow price) associated with the constraint row.

The INFEASIBLE INFORMATION SUMMARY

The infeasible information summary includes the following:

29. name of the infeasible row
30. right-hand side and current activity for the row
31. name of each nonzero and nonmissing variable in the row
32. activity and upper and lower bounds for the variable.

The RHS SENSITIVITY ANALYSIS SUMMARY

The RHS sensitivity analysis summary includes the following:

33. value of φ_{min}
34. leaving variable when $\varphi = \varphi_{min}$
35. objective value when $\varphi = \varphi_{min}$
36. value of φ_{max}
37. column number and name of each logical and structural variable
38. activity of the variable when $\varphi = \varphi_{min}$
39. activity of the variable when $\varphi = \varphi_{max}$.

The PRICE SENSITIVITY ANALYSIS SUMMARY

The price sensitivity analysis summary includes the following:

40. value of φ_{min}
41. entering variable when $\varphi = \varphi_{min}$
42. objective value when $\varphi = \varphi_{min}$
43. value of φ_{max}
44. entering variable when $\varphi = \varphi_{max}$
45. objective value when $\varphi = \varphi_{max}$
46. column number and name of each logical and structural variable
47. price of the variable when $\varphi = \varphi_{min}$
48. variable's reduced cost when $\varphi = \varphi_{min}$
49. price of the variable when $\varphi = \varphi_{max}$
50. variable's reduced cost when $\varphi = \varphi_{max}$.

EXAMPLES

Introduction

This section contains fourteen examples that illustrate several of the features of PROC LP. **Table 7.6** lists each example and a short description.

Table 7.6 Examples Used to Illustrate Features of PROC LP

Example	Illustrates the use of
1	dense input format
2	sparse input format
3	the RANGEPRICE option to show you the range over which each objective coefficient can vary without changing the variables in the basis
4	more sensitivity analysis and restarting a problem
5	parametric programming
6	special ordered sets
7	goal programming
8	integer programming
9	numerical stability and scaling
10	restarting integer programs
11	controlling the search of the branch and bound tree
12	matrix generation and report writing for an assignment problem
13	matrix generation and report writing for a scheduling problem
14	a multi-commodity transshipment problem

Example 1:   An Oil Blending Problem

The blending problem presented in the introduction is a good example for demonstrating some of the features of the LP procedure. Recall that a step in refining crude oil into finished oil products involves a distillation process that splits crude into various streams. Suppose that there are three types of crude available, Arabian light, Arabian heavy, and Brega. These are distilled into light naphtha, intermediate naphtha, and heating oil. Using one of two recipes, these in turn are blended into jet fuel. Assume that you can sell as much fuel as is produced. What production strategy maximizes the profit from jet fuel sales? The following SAS code demonstrates a way of answering this question using linear programming. The SAS data set is a representation of the formulation for this model given in the introductory section.

```
data;
   input _row_ $14.
         a_light a_heavy brega naphthal naphthai heatingo jet_1 jet_2
         _type_ $ _rhs_;
   cards;
profit          -175 -165 -205   0   0   0  300  300  max      .
naphtha_l_conv  .035 .030 .045  -1   0   0    0    0  eq       0
naphtha_i_conv  .100 .075 .135   0  -1   0    0    0  eq       0
heating_o_conv  .390 .300 .430   0   0  -1    0    0  eq       0
recipe_1           0    0    0   0  .3  .7   -1    0  eq       0
recipe_2           0    0    0  .2   0  .8    0   -1  eq       0
available        110  165   80   .   .   .    .    .  upperbd  .
;

proc lp;
run;
```

The _ROW_ variable contains the names of the rows in the model; the variables A_LIGHT to JET_2 are the names of the structural variables in the model; the _TYPE_ variable contains the keywords that tell the LP procedure how to interpret each row in the model; and the _RHS_ variable gives the value of the right-hand-side constants.

The structural variables are interpreted as the quantity of each type of constituent or finished product. For example, the value of A_HEAVY in the solution is the amount of Arabian heavy crude to buy while the value of JET_1 in the solution is the amount of recipe 1 jet fuel that is produced. As discussed above, the values given in the model data set are the technological coefficients whose interpretation depends on the model. In this example, the coefficient −175 in the PROFIT row for the variable A_LIGHT gives a cost coefficient (because the row with _ROW_=PROFIT has _TYPE_=MAX) for the structural variable A_LIGHT. This means that for each unit of Arabian heavy crude purchased, a cost of 175 units is incurred.

The coefficients .035, .100, and .390 for the A_LIGHT variable give the percentages of each unit of Arabian light crude that is distilled into the light naphtha, intermediate naphtha, and heating oil components. The 110 value in the row _ROW_=AVAILABLE gives the quantity of Arabian light that is available.

PROC LP produces the following page of PROBLEM SUMMARY output. Included in the summary is an identification of the objective, defined by the first observation of the problem data set; the right-hand-side variable, defined by the variable _RHS_; and the type identifier, defined by the variable _TYPE_. See **Output 7.1.**

Output 7.1 PROBLEM SUMMARY for the Oil Blending Problem

```
                                                                    1
          L I N E A R   P R O G R A M M I N G   P R O C E D U R E
                          PROBLEM  SUMMARY

          Max profit              Objective Function
          _RHS_                   Rhs Variable
          _TYPE_                  Type Variable
          Problem Density                       0.45

          Variable Type           Number

          Non-negative                          5
          Upper Bounded                         3

          Total                                 8

          Constraint Type         Number

          EQ                                    5
          Objective                             1

          Total                                 6
```

The next section of output contains the SOLUTION SUMMARY, which indicates whether or not an optimal solution was found. In this example, the procedure terminates successfully (with an optimal solution), with 1544 as the value of the objective function. Also included in this section of output is the number of phase 1 and phase 2 iterations, the number of variables used in the initial basic feasible solution, and the time used to solve the problem. For several options specified in the PROC LP statement, the current option values are also printed. See **Output 7.2**.

Output 7.2 SOLUTION SUMMARY for the Oil Blending Problem

```
                                                                    2
          L I N E A R   P R O G R A M M I N G   P R O C E D U R E
                          SOLUTION  SUMMARY
                        Terminated Successfully

          Objective value                       1544

          Phase 1 iterations                    0
          Phase 2 iterations                    7
          Phase 3 iterations                    0
          Integer iterations                    0
          Integer solutions                     0
          Initial basic feasible variables      3
          Time used (secs)                      8
          Number of inversions                  2

          Machine epsilon                       1E-8
          Machine infinity        1.7976931349E308
          Maximum phase 1 iterations            100
          Maximum phase 2 iterations            100
          Maximum phase 3 iterations       99999999
          Maximum integer iterations            100
          Time limit (secs)                     120
```

The next section of output contains the VARIABLE SUMMARY, which is part of the SOLUTION SUMMARY. A line is printed for each variable in the mathematical program with the variable name, the status of the variable in the solution, the type of variable, the variable's price coefficient, the activity of the variable in the solution, and the reduced cost for the variable. The status of a variable can be

BASIC   if the variable is a basic variable in the solution

DEGEN   if the variable is a basic variable whose activity is at its lower bound

ALTER   if the variable is nonbasic and can be used to define an alternate optimal solution.

The TYPE column shows how PROC LP interprets the variable in the problem data set. Types include the following:

NON-NEG   if the variable is a nonnegative variable with lower bound 0 and upper bound +INFINITY.

LOWERBD   if the variable has a lower bound specified in a LOWERBD observation and upper bound +INFINITY.

UPPERBD   if the variable has an upper bound that is less than +INFINITY and lower bound 0. This upper bound is specified in an UPPERBD observation.

UPLOWBD   if the variable has a lower bound specified in a LOWERBD observation and an upper bound specified in an UPPERBD observation.

INTEGER   if the variable is constrained to take integer values. If this is the case, then it must also be upper and lower bounded.

BINARY   if the variable is constrained to take values 0 or 1.

UNRSTRCT   if the variable is an unrestricted variable having bounds of −INFINITY and +INFINITY.

SLACK   if the variable is a slack variable that PROC LP has appended to a LE constraint. For variables of this type, the variable name is the same as the name of the constraint (given in the ROW variable) for which this variable is the slack. A nonzero slack variable indicates that the constraint is not tight. The slack is the amount by which the right-hand side of the constraint exceeds the left-hand side.

SURPLUS   if the variable is a surplus variable that PROC LP has appended to a GE constraint. For variables of this type, the variable name is the same as the name of the constraint (given in the ROW variable) for which this variable is the surplus. A nonzero surplus variable indicates that the constraint is not tight. The surplus is the amount by which the left-hand side of the constraint exceeds the right-hand side.

The VARIABLE SUMMARY gives the value of the structural variables at optimality. In this example, it tells you how to produce the jet fuel to maximize your profit. You should buy 110 units of A_LIGHT and 80 units of BREGA. These are used to make 7.45 units of NAPHTHAL, 21.8 units of NAPHTHAI, and 77.3 units of HEATINGO. These in turn are used to make 60.65 units of JET_1 using recipe 1 and 63.33 units of JET_2 using recipe 2.

Output 7.3   VARIABLE SUMMARY for the Oil Blending Problem

```
                                                                        3
          L I N E A R   P R O G R A M M I N G   P R O C E D U R E

                          VARIABLE  SUMMARY

            Variable                                          Reduced
      Col  Name          Status   Type     Price   Activity     Cost

        1  A_LIGHT                UPPERBD   -175    110.000   11.600000
        2  A_HEAVY                UPPERBD   -165      0.000  -21.450000
        3  BREGA                  UPPERBD   -205     80.000    3.350000
        4  NAPHTHAL      BASIC  NON-NEG        0      7.450000  0.000000
        5  NAPHTHAI      BASIC  NON-NEG        0     21.800000  0.000000
        6  HEATINGO      BASIC  NON-NEG        0     77.300000  0.000000
        7  JET_1         BASIC  NON-NEG      300     60.650000  0.000000
        8  JET_2         BASIC  NON-NEG      300     63.330000  0.000000
```

The reduced cost associated with each nonbasic variable is the marginal value of that variable if it is brought into the basis. In other words, the objective function value would (assuming no constraints were violated) increase by the reduced cost of a nonbasic variable if that variable's value is increased by one. Similarly, the objective function value would (assuming no constraints were violated) decrease by the reduced cost of a nonbasic variable if that variable's value is decreased by one. Basic variables always have a zero reduced cost. At optimality, for a maximization problem, nonbasic variables that are not at an upper bound have nonpositive reduced costs, for example A_HEAVY. The objective would decrease if they were to increase beyond their optimal value. Nonbasic variables at upper bounds have nonnegative reduced costs, showing that increasing the upper bound (if the reduced cost is not zero) increases the objective. For nonbasic variables at their upper bound, the reduced cost is the marginal value of increasing the upper bound, often called the *shadow price*. In this example, although A_HEAVY is a nonbasic upper-bounded variable, it is at its lower bound. Its negative reduced cost tells you that increasing it would decrease the objective.

For minimization problems, the definition of reduced costs remain the same but the conditions for optimality change. For example, at optimality the reduced costs of all nonupper-bounded variables are nonnegative, and the reduced costs of upper-bounded variables at their upper bound are nonpositive.

The next section of output contains the CONSTRAINT SUMMARY. For each constraint row, free row, and objective row, a line is printed in the CONSTRAINT SUMMARY. Included on the line are the constraint name, the row type, the slack or surplus variable associated with the row, the right-hand-side constant associated with the row, the activity of the row (not including the activity of the slack and surplus variables), and the dual activity (shadow prices).

A dual variable is associated with each constraint row. At optimality the value of this variable, the dual activity, tells you the marginal value of the right-hand-side constant. For each unit increase in the right-hand-side constant, the objective changes by this amount. This quantity is also known as the *shadow price*. For example, the marginal value for the right-hand-side constant of constraint HEATING_O_CONV is −450.0. See **Output 7.4**.

Output 7.4   CONSTRAINT SUMMARY for the Oil Blending Problem

```
                                                                    4

          LINEAR  PROGRAMMING  PROCEDURE

                    CONSTRAINT  SUMMARY

Constraint                 S/S                              Dual
Row Name          Type     Col      Rhs     Activity      Activity

     1 profit     OBJECT                     1544.000    -1.000000
     2 naphtha_l_conv EQ            0        0.000000   -60.000000
     3 naphtha_i_conv EQ            0        0.000000   -90.000000
     4 heating_o_conv EQ            0        0.000000    -450.000
     5 recipe_1   EQ               0        0.000000    -300.000
     6 recipe_2   EQ               0        0.000000    -300.000
```

Example 2:   A Sparse View of the Oil Blending Problem

Typically, mathematical programming models are very sparse. This means that only a small percentage of the coefficients are nonzero. The sparse problem input is ideal for these models. The **Introductory Example** showed the oil blending problem in a sparse form. Here, we show the same problem in a sparse form with the data given in a different order. In addition to representing the problem in a concise form, the sparse format

- allows long column names and row names.
- enables easy matrix generation. (See **Examples 12, 13,** and **14.**)
- is compatible with MPSX sparse format. (See **Appendix 1** for details.)

The model in the sparse format is solved by invoking PROC LP with the SPARSEDATA option as shown below.

```
data oil;
    input _type_ $ a10 _col_ $13. a24 _row_ $16. _coef_;
    cards;
max     .               profit              .
.       arabian_light   profit            -175
.       arabian_heavy   profit            -165
.       brega           profit            -205
.       jet_1           profit             300
.       jet_2           profit             300
eq      .               napha_l_conv        .
.       arabian_light   napha_l_conv      .035
.       arabian_heavy   napha_l_conv      .030
.       brega           napha_l_conv      .045
.       naphtha_light   napha_l_conv       -1
eq      .               napha_i_conv        .
.       arabian_light   napha_i_conv      .100
.       arabian_heavy   napha_i_conv      .075
.       brega           napha_i_conv      .135
.       naphtha_inter   napha_i_conv       -1
eq      .               heating_oil_conv    .
.       arabian_light   heating_oil_conv  .390
.       arabian_heavy   heating_oil_conv  .300
.       brega           heating_oil_conv  .430
.       heating_oil     heating_oil_conv   -1
```

```
eq            .              recipe_1                  .
.             naphtha_inter  recipe_1                  .3
.             heating_oil    recipe_1                  .7
eq            .              recipe_2                  .
.             jet_1          recipe_1                 -1
.             naphtha_light  recipe_2                  .2
.             heating_oil    recipe_2                  .8
.             jet_2          recipe_2                 -1
.             _rhs_          profit                    0
upperbd       .              available                .
.             arabian_light  available               110
.             arabian_heavy  available               165
.             brega          available                80
;

proc lp SPARSEDATA;
run;
```

The output from PROC LP follows.

Output 7.5   Output for the Sparse Oil Blending Problem

```
                                                                      1
          L I N E A R   P R O G R A M M I N G   P R O C E D U R E

                          PROBLEM SUMMARY

          Max profit                 Objective Function
          _rhs_                      Rhs Variable
          _TYPE_                     Type Variable
          Problem Density                 0.45

          Variable Type              Number

          Non-negative                    5
          Upper Bounded                   3

          Total                           8

          Constraint Type            Number

          EQ                              5
          Objective                       1

          Total                           6
```

```
                                                                      2
          L I N E A R   P R O G R A M M I N G   P R O C E D U R E

                          SOLUTION  SUMMARY

                       Terminated Successfully

          Objective value                 1544

          Phase 1 iterations                0
          Phase 2 iterations                7
          Phase 3 iterations                0
          Integer iterations                0
          Integer solutions                 0
          Initial basic feasible variables  3
          Time used (secs)                  9
          Number of inversions              2

                                          (continued on next page)
```

(continued from previous page)

```
                    Machine epsilon                              1E-8
                    Machine infinity                1.7976931349E308
                    Maximum phase 1 iterations                    100
                    Maximum phase 2 iterations                    100
                    Maximum phase 3 iterations               99999999
                    Maximum integer iterations                    100
                    Time limit (secs)                             120
```

```
                L I N E A R   P R O G R A M M I N G   P R O C E D U R E                    3

                              VARIABLE  SUMMARY

            Variable                                                    Reduced
       Col  Name             Status   Type      Price     Activity         Cost

         1  arabian_heavy             UPPERBD    -165     0.000000    -21.450000
         2  arabian_light             UPPERBD    -175     110.000      11.600000
         3  brega                     UPPERBD    -205     80.000000     3.350000
         4  heating_oil      BASIC  NON-NEG         0     77.300000     0.000000
         5  jet_1            BASIC  NON-NEG       300     60.650000     0.000000
         6  jet_2            BASIC  NON-NEG       300     63.330000     0.000000
         7  naphtha_inter    BASIC  NON-NEG         0     21.800000     0.000000
         8  naphtha_light    BASIC  NON-NEG         0      7.450000     0.000000
```

```
                                                                                          4
                L I N E A R   P R O G R A M M I N G   P R O C E D U R E

                              CONSTRAINT  SUMMARY

       Constraint              S/S                                     Dual
       Row  Name        Type   Col      Rhs      Activity           Activity

         1  profit      OBJECT                   1544.000          -1.000000
         2  napha_l_conv  EQ           0         0.000000         -60.000000
         3  napha_i_conv  EQ           0         0.000000         -90.000000
         4  heating_oil_conv EQ        0         0.000000        -450.000
         5  recipe_1      EQ           0         0.000000        -300.000
         6  recipe_2      EQ           0         0.000000        -300.000
```

Example 3: Analyzing the Sensitivity of the Solution to Changes in the Objective Coefficients

Simple solution of a linear program is often not enough. A manager needs to evaluate how sensitive the solution is to changing assumptions. The LP procedure provides several tools that are useful for "what if", or sensitivity, analysis. One tool studies the effects of changes in the objective coefficients.

For example, in the oil blending problem the cost of crude and the selling price of jet fuel can be highly variable. If you wanted to know the range over which each objective coefficient can vary without changing the variables in the basis, you would use the RANGEPRICE option in the PROC LP statement.

```
proc lp sparsedata RANGEPRICE PRIMALOUT=SOLUTION;
run;
```

In addition to the PROBLEM and SOLUTION summaries, the LP procedure produces a PRICE RANGE SUMMARY shown in **Output 7.6**. For each structural variable, the upper and lower ranges of the price (objective function coefficients) and the objective value is shown. The blocking variables, those variables that would enter the basis if the objective coefficient were perturbed further, are also given. For example, the output shows that if the cost of ARABIAN_LIGHT crude were to increase from 175 to 186.6 per unit (remember that you are maximizing profit so the ARABIAN_LIGHT objective coefficient would decrease from −175 to −186.6), then it would become optimal to use less of this crude for any fractional increase in its cost. Increasing the unit cost to 186.6 would drive its reduced cost to zero. Any additional increase would drive its reduced cost negative and would destroy the optimality conditions, thus, you would want to use less of it in your processing. The output shows that at the point where the reduced cost is zero you would only be realizing a profit of 268=1544−(110*11.6) and that ARABIAN_LIGHT enters the basis, that is, leaves its upper bound. On the other hand, if the cost of ARABIAN_HEAVY were to decrease to 143.55, you would want to stop using the formulation of 110 units of ARABIAN_LIGHT and 80 units of BREGA and switch to a production scheme which included ARABIAN_HEAVY, in which case the profit would increase from the 1544 level.

Output 7.6   PRICE RANGE SUMMARY for the Oil Blending Problem

```
                                                                                  1
                 L I N E A R   P R O G R A M M I N G   P R O C E D U R E

                             PRICE RANGE SUMMARY

            Variable      --------------Min Phi--------------  --------------Max Phi--------------
     Col    Name           Price Entering       Objective       Price Entering       Objective

      1  arabian_heavy        -INF  .                -INF  -143.550 arabian_heavy    1544.000
      2  arabian_light    -186.600  arabian_light  268.000    +INF  .                  +INF
      3  brega            -208.350  brega          1276.000    +INF  .                  +INF
      4  heating_oil        -7.79070 brega          941.779  71.50000 arabian_heavy   7070.950
      5  jet_1             290.190  brega          949.044  392.258 arabian_heavy   7139.452
      6  jet_2             290.510  brega          942.993  387.195 arabian_heavy   7066.067
      7  naphtha_inter     -24.8148 brega          1003.037  286.000 arabian_heavy   7778.800
      8  naphtha_light     -74.4444 brega          989.389  715.000 arabian_heavy   6870.750
```

Note that in the PROC LP statement the PRIMALOUT=SOLUTION option was given. This caused the procedure to save the optimal solution in a SAS data set named SOLUTION. This data set can be used to perform further analysis on the problem without having to resolve it from scratch. **Example 4** shows how this is done. A printout of the data set follows.

Output 7.7   The PRIMALOUT= Data Set for the Oil Blending Problem

```
BS  _OBJ_ID_  _RHS_ID_  _VAR_          _TYPE_    _STATUS_  _LBOUND_  _VALUE_   _UBOUND_    _PRICE_  _R_COST_

 1  profit    _rhs_     arabian_heavy  UPPERBD             0         0.00      165        -165     -21.45
 2  profit    _rhs_     arabian_light  UPPERBD   _UPPER_   0       110.00      110        -175      11.60
 3  profit    _rhs_     brega          UPPERBD   _UPPER_   0        80.00       80        -205       3.35
 4  profit    _rhs_     heating_oil    NON-NEG   _BASIC_   0        77.30     1.7977E308    0        0.00
 5  profit    _rhs_     jet_1          NON-NEG   _BASIC_   0        60.65     1.7977E308  300        0.00
 6  profit    _rhs_     jet_2          NON-NEG   _BASIC_   0        63.33     1.7977E308  300        0.00
 7  profit    _rhs_     naphtha_inter  NON-NEG   _BASIC_   0        21.80     1.7977E308    0        0.00
 8  profit    _rhs_     naphtha_light  NON-NEG   _BASIC_   0         7.45     1.7977E308    0        0.00
 9  profit    _rhs_     PHASE_1_OBJECTIV OBJECT  _DEGEN_   0         0.00     1.7977E308    0        0.00
10  profit    _rhs_     profit         OBJECT    _BASIC_   0      1544.00     1.7977E308    0        0.00
```

Example 4: Additional Analysis of the Sensitivity of the Solution to Changes in the Objective Coefficients

The objective coefficient ranging analysis, discussed in the last example, is useful for accessing the effects of changing costs and returns on the optimal solution if each objective function coefficient is modified in isolation. However, this is often not the case.

Suppose that you anticipate that the cost of crude will be increasing and you want to examine how that will impact your optimal production plans. Furthermore, you estimate that if the price of ARABIAN_LIGHT goes up by 1 unit, then the price of ARABIAN_HEAVY will rise by 1.2 units and the price of BREGA will increase by 1.5 units. However, you plan on passing some of your increased overhead on to your jet fuel customers, and you decide to increase the price of jet fuel 1 unit for each unit of increase cost of ARABIAN_LIGHT. An examination of the solution sensitivity to changes in the cost of crude is a two-step process. First, add the information on the proportional rates of change in the crude costs and the jet fuel price to the problem data set. Then, invoke the LP procedure. The following program accomplishes this. First, it adds a new row, named CHANGE, to the model. It gives this row a type of PRICESEN. That tells PROC LP to perform objective function coefficient sensitivity analysis using the given rates of change. The program then invokes PROC LP to perform the analysis. Notice that the PRIMALIN=SOLUTION option is used in the PROC LP statement. This tells the LP procedure to use the saved solution. Although it is not necessary to do this, it will eliminate the need for PROC LP to resolve the problem and can save computing time.

```
data sen;
    input _type_ $ a10 _col_ $13. a24 _row_ $16. _coef_;
    cards;
pricesen .             change              .
.        arabian_light change              1
.        arabian_heavy change              1.2
.        brega         change              1.5
.        jet_1         change              -1
.        jet_2         change              -1
;

data;
    set oil sen;

proc lp sparsedata primalin=solution;
run;
```

The output shows the range over which the current basic solution remains optimal so that the current production plan need not change. The objective coefficients can be modified by adding PHI times the change vector given in the SEN data set, where PHI ranges from a minimum of -4.15891 to a maximum of 29.72973. At the minimum value of PHI the profit would have decreased to 1103.073. This value of PHI corresponds to an increase in the cost of ARABIAN_HEAVY to 169.99 (namely, $-175+PHI*1.2$), ARABIAN_LIGHT to 179.158 ($= -175+PHI*1$), and BREGA to 211.23 ($= -205+PHI*1.5$), and corresponds to an increase in the price of JET_1 and JET_2 to 304.15 ($=300+PHI*-1$). These values can be found in the PRICE column under the section labeled MINIMUM PHI.

Output 7.8 The PRICE SENSITIVITY ANALYSIS SUMMARY for the Oil Blending Problem

```
          L I N E A R   P R O G R A M M I N G   P R O C E D U R E                1

                      PRICE SENSITIVITY ANALYSIS SUMMARY
                            Sensitivity Vector change

                   Minimum Phi                    -4.15891
                   Entering Variable                 brega
                   Optimal Objective              1103.073

                   Maximum Phi                    29.72973
                   Entering Variable         arabian_heavy
                   Optimal Objective              4695.946

             Variable        ------Minimum Phi--------  ------Maximum Phi--------
      Col    Name              Price    Reduced Cost       Price    Reduced Cost

        1  arabian_heavy     -169.991    -24.450652      -129.324     0.000000
        2  arabian_light     -179.159     10.027933      -145.270    22.837838
        3  brega             -211.238      0.000000      -160.405    27.297297
        4  heating_oil          0.000000   0.000000         0.000000   0.000000
        5  jet_1              304.159      0.000000       270.270     0.000000
        6  jet_2              304.159      0.000000       270.270     0.000000
        7  naphtha_inter        0.000000   0.000000         0.000000   0.000000
        8  naphtha_light        0.000000   0.000000         0.000000   0.000000
```

The PRICE SENSITIVITY ANALYSIS SUMMARY also shows the effects of lowering the cost of crude and lowering the price of jet fuel. In particular, at the maximum phi of 29.72973, the current optimal production plan yields a profit of 4695.946. Any increase or decrease in PHI beyond the limits given will result in a change in the production plan. More precisely, the columns that constitute the basis will change.

Example 5: Parametric Programming for the Oil Blending Problem

This example continues to examine the effects of a change in the cost of crude and the selling price of jet fuel. Suppose that you know the cost of ARABIAN_LIGHT crude is likely to increase 30 units, with the effects on oil and fuel prices as described in **Example 4**. The analysis in the last example only accounted for an increase of a little over 4 units (because the minimum PHI was −4.15891). Because an increase in the cost of ARABIAN_LIGHT beyond 4.15891 units requires a change in the optimal basis, it may require a change in the optimal production strategy as well. This type of analysis, where you want to find how the solution changes with changes in the objective function coefficients or right-hand-side vector, is called parametric programming.

You can answer this question by using the PRICEPHI= option in the PROC LP statement. The following program instructs PROC LP to continually increase the cost of the crudes and the return from jet fuel using the ratios given above, until the cost of ARABIAN_LIGHT increases at least 30 units.

```
proc lp sparsedata primalin=solution PRICEPHI=-30;
run;
```

The PRICEPHI= option in the PROC LP statement tells PROC LP to perform parametric programming on any price change vectors specified in the problem data set. The value that the PRICEPHI= option takes tells PROC LP how far to change the value of PHI and in what direction. PRICEPHI=−30 tells PROC LP to continue pivoting until the problem with objective function equal to the original objective function −30* change vector.

The output in **Output 7.9** shows the result of this analysis. The first page is the PRICE SENSITIVITY ANALYSIS SUMMARY as discussed in **Example 4**. The next page is an accounting for the change in basis as a result of decreasing PHI beyond −4.1589. It shows that BREGA left the basis at an upper bound and entered the basis at a lower bound. The interpretation of these basis changes can be difficult (see Hadley 1962, Dantzig 1963).

The last page of output shows the optimal solution at the printed value of PHI, namely −30.6878. At an increase of 30.6878 units in the cost of ARABIAN_LIGHT and the related changes to the other crudes and the jet fuel it is optimal to modify the production of jet fuel as shown in the activity column. Although this plan is optimal, it results in a profit of 0. This may suggest that the ratio of a unit increase in the price of jet fuel for unit increase in the cost of ARABIAN_LIGHT may be lower than desirable.

Output 7.9   Parametric Programming for the Oil Blending Problem

```
        L I N E A R   P R O G R A M M I N G   P R O C E D U R E

             PRICE SENSITIVITY ANALYSIS SUMMARY
                  Sensitivity Vector change

             Minimum Phi                -4.15891
             Entering Variable              brega
             Optimal Objective           1103.073

             Maximum Phi                 29.72973
             Entering Variable      arabian_heavy
             Optimal Objective           4695.946

      Variable      ------Minimum Phi-------- ------Maximum Phi--------
Col   Name           Price  Reduced Cost       Price  Reduced Cost

  1  arabian_heavy  -169.991   -24.450652     -129.324    0.000000
  2  arabian_light  -179.159    10.027933     -145.270   22.837838
  3  brega          -211.238     0.000000     -160.405   27.297297
  4  heating_oil       0.000000   0.000000        0.000000  0.000000
  5  jet_1           304.159     0.000000      270.270    0.000000
  6  jet_2           304.159     0.000000      270.270    0.000000
  7  naphtha_inter     0.000000   0.000000        0.000000  0.000000
  8  naphtha_light     0.000000   0.000000        0.000000  0.000000
```

```
        L I N E A R   P R O G R A M M I N G   P R O C E D U R E

             PRICE SENSITIVITY ANALYSIS SUMMARY
                  Sensitivity Vector change

      Leaving          Entering                    Current
      Variable         Variable      Objective       Phi

      brega            brega         1103.073      -4.1589
```

```
        L I N E A R   P R O G R A M M I N G   P R O C E D U R E

             PRICE SENSITIVITY ANALYSIS SUMMARY
                  Sensitivity Vector change

             Minimum Phi                -30.6878
             Entering Variable      arabian_light
             Optimal Objective               0
```

(continued on next page)

(continued from previous page)

```
                  Variable        ------------At Pricephi----------------
              Col Name                  Price    Activity Reduced Cost

                1 arabian_heavy       -201.825    0.000000   -43.591270
                2 arabian_light       -205.688    110.000      0.000000
                3 brega               -251.032    0.000000   -21.369048
                4 heating_oil            0.000000 42.900000     0.000000
                5 jet_1                 330.688   33.330000     0.000000
                6 jet_2                 330.688   35.090000     0.000000
                7 naphtha_inter          0.000000 11.000000     0.000000
                8 naphtha_light          0.000000  3.850000     0.000000
```

You may ask what is the optimal return if PHI is exactly -30. Because the change in the objective is linear as a function of PHI, you can calculate the objective for any value of PHI between those given. For example, for any PHI between -4.1589 and -30.6878, the optimal objective value is

$$PHI * (1103.0726 - 0) / (-4.589 - -30.6878) + b$$

where

$$b = 30.6878 * (1103.0726 - 0) / (-4.589 - -30.6878) \quad .$$

For PHI $= -30$, this is 28.5988.

Example 6:   Special Ordered Sets and the Oil Blending Problem

Often a manager wants to evaluate the cost of making a choice among alternatives. And in particular, he wants to make the most profitable choice. Suppose that at most one oil crude can be used in the production process. This identifies a set of variables of which at most one can be above its lower bound. This additional restriction could be included in the model by adding a binary integer variable for each of the three crudes. Constraints would be needed that would drive the appropriate binary variable to 1 whenever the corresponding crude is used in the production process. Then a constraint limiting the total of these variables to at most one would be added. A similar formulation for a fixed charge problem is shown in **Example 8**.

The SOSLE type implicitly does this. The data step below adds a row to the model that identifies which variables are in the set. The SOSLE type tells the LP procedure that *at most one* of the variables in this set can be above its lower bound. If you use the SOSEQ type, it tells PROC LP that exactly one of the variables in the set must be above its lower bound. Only integer variables can be in an SOSEQ set.

```
data special;
   input _type_ $ @10 _col_ $13. @24 _row_ $16. _coef_;
   cards;
SOSLE      .              special         .
   .       arabian_light  special         1
   .       arabian_heavy  special         1
   .       brega          special         1
;
data;
   set oil special;
proc lp sparsedata;
run;
```

The output includes an INTEGER ITERATION LOG. This log shows the progress that PROC LP is making in solving the problem. This is discussed in some detail in **Example 8**.

Output 7.10   The Oil Blending Problem with a Special Ordered Set

```
                                                                              1
              LINEAR  PROGRAMMING  PROCEDURE
                         PROBLEM  SUMMARY

              Max profit              Objective Function
              _rhs_                   Rhs Variable
              _TYPE_                  Type Variable
              Problem Density              0.45

              Variable Type               Number

              Non-negative                    5
              Upper Bounded                   3

              Total                           8

              Constraint Type             Number

              EQ                              5
              Objective                       1

              Total                           6
```

```
                                                                              2
              LINEAR  PROGRAMMING  PROCEDURE
                      INTEGER ITERATION LOG

    Iter Problem  Condition Objective Branched Value Sinfeas Active

       1       0    ACTIVE      1544 brega      80      0     2
       2      -1 SUBOPTIMAL      268    .        .      .     1
       3       1 SUBOPTIMAL     1276    .        .      .     0
```

```
                                                                              3
              LINEAR  PROGRAMMING  PROCEDURE

                        SOLUTION  SUMMARY

                   Integer Optimal Solution

       Objective value                       1276.000

       Phase 1 iterations                           0
       Phase 2 iterations                           6
       Phase 3 iterations                           0
       Integer iterations                           3
       Integer solutions                            2
       Initial basic feasible variables             3
       Time used (secs)                             9
       Number of inversions                         4

       Machine epsilon                           1E-8
       Machine infinity           1.7976931349E308
       Maximum phase 1 iterations                 100
       Maximum phase 2 iterations                 100
       Maximum phase 3 iterations            99999999
       Maximum integer iterations                 100
       Time limit (secs)                          120
```

```
                                                                    4

              L I N E A R   P R O G R A M M I N G   P R O C E D U R E

                            VARIABLE  SUMMARY

         Variable                                          Reduced
     Col Name          Status   Type    Price    Activity    Cost

       1 arabian_heavy          UPPERBD  -165    0.000000  -21.450000
       2 arabian_light          UPPERBD  -175    110.000    11.600000
       3 brega                  UPPERBD  -205    0.000000    3.350000
       4 heating_oil    BASIC NON-NEG       0   42.900000    0.000000
       5 jet_1          BASIC NON-NEG     300   33.330000    0.000000
       6 jet_2          BASIC NON-NEG     300   35.090000    0.000000
       7 naphtha_inter  BASIC NON-NEG       0   11.000000    0.000000
       8 naphtha_light  BASIC NON-NEG       0    3.850000    0.000000
```

```
                                                                    5


              L I N E A R   P R O G R A M M I N G   P R O C E D U R E

                           CONSTRAINT  SUMMARY

         Constraint           S/S                          Dual
     Row Name         Type    Col     Rhs     Activity    Activity

       1 profit        OBJECT                  1276.000   -1.000000
       2 napha_1_conv  EQ               0      0.000000  -60.000000
       3 napha_i_conv  EQ               0      0.000000  -90.000000
       4 heating_oil_conv EQ            0      0.000000  -450.000
       5 recipe_1      EQ               0      0.000000  -300.000
       6 recipe_2      EQ               0      0.000000  -300.000
```

The solution shows that only the ARABIAN_LIGHT crude is purchased. The requirement that only one crude be used in the production is met, and the profit is 1276. This tells you that the value of purchasing crude from an additional source, namely BREGA, is worth 1544−1276=268.

Example 7: Goal-Programming a Product Mix Problem.

The next example shows how to use PROC LP to solve a linear goal-programming problem. PROC LP has the ability to solve a series of linear programs each with a new objective function. These objective functions are ordered by priority. The first step is to solve a linear program with the highest priority objective function constrained only by the formal constraints in the model. Then, the next highest priority objective function is solved, constrained by the formal constraints in the model and by the value that the highest priority objective function realized. That is, the second problem optimizes the second highest priority objective function among the alternate optimal solutions to the first optimization problem. The process continues until a linear program is solved for each of the objectives.

This technique is useful for differentiating among alternate optimal solutions to a linear program. It also fits into the formal paradigm presented in goal programming. In goal programming, the objective functions typically take on the role of driving a linear function of the structural variables to meet a target level as closely as possible. The details of this can be found in many books on the subject including Ignizio (1976).

Consider the following problem taken from Ignizio (1976). A small paint company manufactures two types of paint, latex and enamel. In production, the company uses 10 hours of labor to produce 100 gallons of latex and 15 hours of labor to produce 100 gallons of enamel. Without hiring outside help or requiring overtime, the company has 40 hours of labor available each week. Furthermore, each paint generates a profit at the rate of $1.00 per gallon. The company has the following objectives listed in decreasing priority:

- avoid the use of overtime
- achieve a weekly profit of $1000
- produce at least 700 gallons of enamel paint each week.

The program to solve this problem follows.

```
data object;
   input _row_ $ latex enamel n1 n2 n3 p1 p2 p3 _type_ $ _rhs_;
   cards;
overtime   .    .    .    .    1  .    .    . min    1
profit     .    .    .    1    .  .    .    . min    2
enamel     .    .    .    .    1  .    .    . min    3
overtime  10   15    1    .    .  -1   .    . eq    40
profit   100  100    .    1    .  .    -1   . eq  1000
enamel     .    1    .    .    1  .    .    -1 eq    7
;

proc lp GOALPROGRAM;
run;
```

The data set called OBJECT contains the model. Its first three observations are the objective rows, and the next three observations are the constraints. The values in the right-hand-side variable _RHS_ in the objective rows, give the priority of the objectives. So, the objective in the first observation with _ROW_=OVERTIME has the highest priority, the objective named PROFIT the next highest, and the objective named ENAMEL the lowest. Note that the value of the right-hand-side variable determines the priority, not the order, in the data set.

Because this example is set in the formal goal-programming scheme, the model has structural variables representing negative (n1, n2, and n3) and positive (p1, p2, and p3) deviations from target levels. For example, n1+p1 is the deviation from the objective of avoiding the use of overtime and underusing the normal work time, namely using exactly 40 work hours. The other objectives are handled similarly.

Notice that the PROC LP statement includes the GOALPROGRAM option. Without this option, the procedure would solve three separate problems: one for each of the three objective functions. In that case, however, the procedure would not constrain the second and third programs using the results of the first and second programs, respectively; also, the values 1, 2, and 3 for _RHS_ in the objective rows would have no effect.

Output 7.11 shows the solution of the goal program, apparently as three linear program outputs. However, examination of the CONSTRAINT SUMMARIES in the second and third problems show that the constraints labeled by the objectives OVERTIME and PROFIT have type FIXEDOBJ. This indicates that these objective rows have become constraints in the subsequent problems.

Output 7.11   Goal Programming

```
                                                                            1
        L I N E A R   P R O G R A M M I N G   P R O C E D U R E
                        PROBLEM  SUMMARY

        Min overtime                 Objective Function
        _RHS_                        Rhs Variable
        _TYPE_                       Type Variable
        Problem Density                         0.458333

        Variable Type                           Number

        Non-negative                                   8

        Total                                          8

        Constraint Type                         Number

        EQ                                             3
        Objective                                      3

        Total                                          6
```

```
                                                                            2
        L I N E A R   P R O G R A M M I N G   P R O C E D U R E
                        SOLUTION  SUMMARY

                     Terminated Successfully

        Objective value                      0.000000

        Phase 1 iterations                          0
        Phase 2 iterations                          0
        Phase 3 iterations                          0
        Integer iterations                          0
        Integer solutions                           0
        Initial basic feasible variables            7
        Time used (secs)                            0
        Number of inversions                        1

        Machine epsilon                          1E-8
        Machine infinity             1.7976931349E308
        Maximum phase 1 iterations                100
        Maximum phase 2 iterations                100
        Maximum phase 3 iterations           99999999
        Maximum integer iterations                100
        Time limit (secs)                         120
```

```
                                                                            3
        L I N E A R   P R O G R A M M I N G   P R O C E D U R E

                        VARIABLE  SUMMARY

             Variable                                        Reduced
        Col  Name    Status  Type     Price    Activity       Cost

          1  LATEX   ALTER NON-NEG       0     0.000000      0.000000
          2  ENAMEL  ALTER NON-NEG       0     0.000000      0.000000
          3  N1      BASIC NON-NEG       0    40.000000      0.000000
          4  N2      BASIC NON-NEG       0     1000.000      0.000000
          5  N3      BASIC NON-NEG       0     7.000000      0.000000
          6  P1            NON-NEG       1     0.000000      1.000000
          7  P2      ALTER NON-NEG       0     0.000000      0.000000
          8  P3      ALTER NON-NEG       0     0.000000      0.000000
```

```
L I N E A R   P R O G R A M M I N G   P R O C E D U R E

                    CONSTRAINT  SUMMARY

Constraint              S/S                              Dual
Row Name      Type      Col      Rhs     Activity      Activity

  1 overtime  OBJECT                     0.000000     -1.000000
  2 profit    FREE_OBJ                   1000.000      0.000000
  3 enamel    FREE_OBJ                   7.000000      0.000000
  4 overtime  EQ          40   40.000000      0.000000
  5 profit    EQ        1000   1000.000      0.000000
  6 enamel    EQ           7   7.000000      0.000000
```

```
                                                              5

L I N E A R   P R O G R A M M I N G   P R O C E D U R E

                     PROBLEM  SUMMARY

    Min profit              Objective Function
    _RHS_                      Rhs Variable
    _TYPE_                    Type Variable
    Problem Density              0.458333

    Variable Type                 Number

    Non-negative                     8

    Total                            8

    Constraint Type               Number

    EQ                               3
    Objective                        3

    Total                            6
```

```
                                                              6

L I N E A R   P R O G R A M M I N G   P R O C E D U R E

                    SOLUTION  SUMMARY

                 Terminated Successfully

    Objective value                600.000

    Phase 1 iterations                   0
    Phase 2 iterations                   2
    Phase 3 iterations                   0
    Integer iterations                   0
    Integer solutions                    0
    Initial basic feasible variables     7
    Time used (secs)                    17
    Number of inversions                 3

    Machine epsilon                   1E-8
    Machine infinity    1.7976931349E308
    Maximum phase 1 iterations         100
    Maximum phase 2 iterations         100
    Maximum phase 3 iterations    99999999
    Maximum integer iterations         100
    Time limit (secs)                  120
```

```
        L I N E A R   P R O G R A M M I N G   P R O C E D U R E

                        VARIABLE   SUMMARY

        Variable                                         Reduced
   Col  Name      Status   Type      Price    Activity   Cost

    1   LATEX     BASIC  NON-NEG      0      4.000000    0.000000
    2   ENAMEL           NON-NEG      0      0.000000   50.000000
    3   N1               NON-NEG      0      0.000000   10.000000
    4   N2        BASIC  NON-NEG      1    600.000       0.000000
    5   N3        BASIC  NON-NEG      0      7.000000    0.000000
    6   P1        DEGEN  NON-NEG      0      0.000000    0.000000
    7   P2               NON-NEG      0      0.000000    1.000000
    8   P3        ALTER  NON-NEG      0      0.000000    0.000000
```

```
                                                              8

        L I N E A R   P R O G R A M M I N G   P R O C E D U R E

                       CONSTRAINT   SUMMARY

    Constraint            S/S                              Dual
   Row  Name     Type     Col     Rhs     Activity    Activity

    1   overtime FIXEDOBJ                0.000000   -10.000000
    2   profit   OBJECT                600.000       -1.000000
    3   enamel   FREE_OBJ               7.000000      0.000000
    4   overtime EQ               40   40.000000    -10.000000
    5   profit   EQ             1000  1000.000        1.000000
    6   enamel   EQ                7    7.000000      0.000000
```

```
                                                              9

        L I N E A R   P R O G R A M M I N G   P R O C E D U R E

                        PROBLEM   SUMMARY

      Min enamel               Objective Function
      _RHS_                           Rhs Variable
      _TYPE_                         Type Variable
      Problem Density                    0.458333

      Variable Type                      Number

      Non-negative                          8

      Total                                 8

      Constraint Type                    Number

      EQ                                    3
      Objective                             3

      Total                                 6
```

```
                                                             10

        L I N E A R   P R O G R A M M I N G   P R O C E D U R E

                        SOLUTION   SUMMARY

                     Terminated Successfully

      Objective value                    7.000000

      Phase 1 iterations                    0
      Phase 2 iterations                    1
      Phase 3 iterations                    0
      Integer iterations                    0
      Integer solutions                     0
      Initial basic feasible variables      7
      Time used (secs)                     17
      Number of inversions                  5
```

(continued on next page)

(continued from previous page)

```
           Machine infinity             1.7976931349E308
           Maximum phase 1 iterations               100
           Maximum phase 2 iterations               100
           Maximum phase 3 iterations          99999999
           Maximum integer iterations               100
           Time limit (secs)                        120
```

```
                                                                    11
           L I N E A R   P R O G R A M M I N G   P R O C E D U R E

                           VARIABLE  SUMMARY

             Variable                                          Reduced
      Col  Name      Status  Type     Price    Activity          Cost

        1  LATEX     BASIC  NON-NEG      0     4.000000       0.000000
        2  ENAMEL    DEGEN  NON-NEG      0     0.000000       0.000000
        3  N1               NON-NEG      0     0.000000       0.200000
        4  N2        BASIC  NON-NEG      0      600.000       0.000000
        5  N3        BASIC  NON-NEG      1     7.000000       0.000000
        6  P1        DEGEN  NON-NEG      0     0.000000       0.000000
        7  P2               NON-NEG      0     0.000000       0.020000
        8  P3               NON-NEG      0     0.000000       1.000000
```

```
                                                                    12
           L I N E A R   P R O G R A M M I N G   P R O C E D U R E

                          CONSTRAINT  SUMMARY

      Constraint          S/S                                    Dual
      Row  Name    Type    Col      Rhs     Activity         Activity

        1  overtime FIXEDOBJ               0.000000       -0.200000
        2  profit   FIXEDOBJ                600.000       -0.020000
        3  enamel   OBJECT                 7.000000       -1.000000
        4  overtime EQ            40      40.000000       -0.200000
        5  profit   EQ          1000        1000.000       0.020000
        6  enamel   EQ             7       7.000000        1.000000
```

The solution to the last linear program shows a value of 4 for the variable LATEX and a value of 0 for the variable ENAMEL. This tells you that the solution to the linear goal program is to produce 400 gallons of latex and no enamel paint.

The values of the objective functions in the three linear programs tell you whether you can achieve the three objectives. The activities of the constraints labeled OVERTIME, PROFIT, and ENAMEL tell you values of the three linear program objectives. Because the first linear programming objective OVERTIME is 0, the highest priority objective, which is to avoid using additional labor, is accomplished. However, because the second and third objectives are nonzero, the second and third priority objectives are not satisfied completely. The PROFIT objective is 600. Because the PROFIT objective is to minimize the negative deviation from the profit constraint this means that only a profit of $400 = 1000 - 600$ is realized. Similarly, the ENAMEL objective is 7 indicating that there is a negative deviation from the ENAMEL target of 7 units.

Example 8:   A Simple Integer Program

Recall the linear programming problem presented in Chapter 3, "Introduction to Mathematical Programming." In that problem, a firm produces two products, chocolates and gumdrops, that are processed by four processes: cooking, color/flavor, condiments, and packaging. The objective is to determine the product mix that maximizes the profit to the firm while not exceeding manufacturing capacities. The problem is extended to demonstrate a use of integer-constrained variables.

Suppose that you must manufacture only one of the two products and you must decide which one. In addition, there is a setup cost of 100 if you make the chocolates and 75 if you make the gumdrops. To identify which product will maximize profit, you define two zero-one integer variables, ICHOCO and IGUMDR, and you also define two new constraints, CHOCOLATE and GUM. The constraint labeled CHOCOLATE forces ICHOCO to equal one when chocolates are manufactured. Similarly, the constraint labeled GUM forces IGUMDR to equal one when gumdrops are manufactured. Also, you should include a constraint labeled ONLY_ONE that requires the sum of ICHOCO and IGUMDR to equal one. Since ICHOCO and IGUMDR are integer variables, this constraint eliminates the possibility of both products being manufactured. Notice the coefficients -10000 which are used to force ICHOCO and IGUMDR whenever CHOCO and GUMDR are nonzero. This technique, which is often used in integer programming, can cause severe numerical problems. If this driving coefficient is too large, then arithmetic overflows and underflow may result. If the driving coefficient is too small, then the integer variable may not be driven to one as desired by the modeler. **Example 9** demonstrates the problem.

The objective coefficients of the integer variables ICHOCO and IGUMDR are the negatives of the setup costs for the two products. The following is the data set that describes this problem and the call to PROC LP to solve it:

```
data;
   input _row_ $10. choco gumdr ichoco igumdr _type_ $ _rhs_;
   cards;
object        .25     .75    -100     -75 max      .
cooking        15      40       0       0 le    27000
color           0   56.25       0       0 le    27000
package     18.75       0       0       0 le    27000
condiments     12      50       0       0 le    27000
chocolate       1       0  -10000       0 le        0
gum             0       1       0  -10000 le        0
only_one        0       0       1       1 eq        1
binary          .       .       1       2 binary    .
;

proc lp;
run;
```

The solution shows that gumdrops are produced. See **Output 7.12**.

Output 7.12   Summaries and an Integer Programming Iteration Log

```
                                                                          1
        L I N E A R   P R O G R A M M I N G   P R O C E D U R E
                        PROBLEM  SUMMARY

            Max object              Objective Function
            _RHS_                   Rhs Variable
            _TYPE_                  Type Variable
            Problem Density             0.257143

            Variable Type               Number

            Non-negative                    2
            Binary                          2
            Slack                           6

            Total                          10

            Constraint Type             Number

            LE                              6
            EQ                              1
            Objective                       1

            Total                           8
```

```
                                                                          2
        L I N E A R   P R O G R A M M I N G   P R O C E D U R E
                        INTEGER ITERATION LOG

     Iter Problem  Condition Objective Branched Value Sinfeas Active

       1      0      ACTIVE    397.5   ICHOCO   0.1    0.2      2
       2     -1   SUBOPTIMAL   260        .      .      .       1
       3      1   SUBOPTIMAL   285        .      .      .       0
```

```
                                                                          3
        L I N E A R   P R O G R A M M I N G   P R O C E D U R E
                        SOLUTION SUMMARY

                   Integer Optimal Solution

        Objective value                    285.000

        Phase 1 iterations                       1
        Phase 2 iterations                       6
        Phase 3 iterations                       5
        Integer iterations                       3
        Integer solutions                        2
        Initial basic feasible variables         8
        Time used (secs)                        11
        Number of inversions                     6

        Machine epsilon                       1E-8
        Machine infinity          1.7976931349E308
        Maximum phase 1 iterations             100
        Maximum phase 2 iterations             100
        Maximum phase 3 iterations        99999999
        Maximum integer iterations             100
        Time limit (secs)                      120
```

```
                 L I N E A R   P R O G R A M M I N G   P R O C E D U R E          4

                           VARIABLE   SUMMARY

         Variable                                          Reduced
     Col Name      Status  Type      Price     Activity      Cost

       1 CHOCO     DEGEN NON-NEG      0.25      0.000000    0.000000
       2 GUMDR     BASIC NON-NEG      0.75    480.000000    0.000000
       3 ICHOCO          BINARY       -100      0.000000  2475.000
       4 IGUMDR    BASIC BINARY        -75      1.000000    0.000000
       5 cooking   BASIC SLACK               7800.000      0.000000
       6 color           SLACK                  0.000000   -0.013333
       7 package   BASIC SLACK              27000.000      0.000000
       8 condiments BASIC SLACK              3000.000      0.000000
       9 chocolate       SLACK                  0.000000   -0.250000
      10 gum       BASIC SLACK               9520.000      0.000000
```

```
                 L I N E A R   P R O G R A M M I N G   P R O C E D U R E          5

                           CONSTRAINT   SUMMARY

      Constraint          S/S                              Dual
      Row Name    Type    Col      Rhs     Activity      Activity

        1 object    OBJECT                  285.000     -1.000000
        2 cooking   LE      5     27000   19200.000      0.000000
        3 color     LE      6     27000   27000.000      0.013333
        4 package   LE      7     27000       0.000000   0.000000
        5 condiments LE     8     27000   24000.000      0.000000
        6 chocolate LE      9         0       0.000000   0.250000
        7 gum       LE     10         0   -9520.000      0.000000
        8 only_one  EQ                1       1.000000 -75.000000
```

Output 7.12 shows an integer iteration log. The branch and bound tree can be reconstructed from the information contained in this log. The column labeled ITER numbers the integer iterations. The column labeled PROBLEM identifies the ITER number of the parent problem from which the current problem is defined. For example, ITER=2 has PROBLEM=−1. This means that problem 2 is a direct descendent of problem 1. Furthermore, because problem 1 BRANCHED on ICHOCO, you know that problem 2 is identical to problem 1 with an additional constraint on variable ICHOCO. The minus sign in the PROBLEM=−1 in ITER=2 tells you that the new constraint on variable ICHOCO is a lower bound. Moreover, because VALUE=.1 in ITER=1, you know that ICHOCO=.1 in ITER=1 so that the added constraint in ITER=2 is ICHOCO≥⌈.1⌉. In this way the information in the log can be used to reconstruct the branch and bound tree. In fact, when you save an ACTIVEOUT= data set, it contains information in this format that is used to reconstruct the tree when you restart a problem using the ACTIVEIN= data set. See **Example 10**.

Note that by defining a SOSLE special ordered set containing the variables CHOCO and GUMDR, the integer variable ICHOCO and IGUMDR and the three associated constraints would not have been needed.

Example 9:   Numerical Stability

The modeling technique used in the last example to drive an integer variable to one whenever a specific continuous variable is nonzero is a technique that is often needed in integer programming formulations. In particular if ICHOCO is to be driven to one whenever CHOCO is nonzero, you add the constraint

$$CHOCO - \mathbf{M} * ICHOCO \leq 0 \quad .$$

When CHOCO is 0, then ICHOCO will also be 0 because ICHOCO has a negative objective function coefficient and the problem is a maximization. If CHOCO is positive, then ICHOCO must also be positive to satisfy the above constraint and, in fact, must be 1 because it is an integer variable with an upper bound of 1.

The choice of how large **M** is can be critical (**M** is positive). A value of **M** too small can result in an incorrect formulation. A value of **M** too large leads to problems with the numerical stability of the model. In this example, you can see how an injudicious choice of **M** results in numerical problems. For example, suppose that instead of **M**=10000, as in **Example 8**, you used **M**=1.0e18. This number appears to be large, but it is clearly not astronomical in terms of the capability of most computers.

```
data;
   input _row_ $10. choco gumdr ichoco igumdr _type_ $ _rhs_;
   cards;
object        .25     .75    -100     -75 max         .
cooking        15      40       0       0 le      27000
color           0   56.25      0       0 le      27000
package     18.75       0       0       0 le      27000
condiments     12      50       0       0 le      27000
chocolate       1       0   -1e18       0 le          0
gum             0       1       0   -1e18 le          0
only_one        0       0       1       1 eq          1
binary          .       .       1       2 binary      .
;


proc lp;
run;
```

By default, the LP procedure scales the problem matrix so that the largest element in absolute value in each noninteger column is 1. In this case it will identify infeasibilities when printing the solution.

The output is shown in **Output 7.13**.

Output 7.13 The Solution of a Numerically Unstable Problem

```
                                                                        1
        L I N E A R   P R O G R A M M I N G   P R O C E D U R E

                        PROBLEM  SUMMARY

        Max object              Objective Function
        _RHS_                   Rhs Variable
        _TYPE_                  Type Variable
        Problem Density               0.257143

        Variable Type                 Number

        Non-negative                     2
        Binary                           2
        Slack                            6

        Total                           10

        Constraint Type               Number

        LE                               6
        EQ                               1
        Objective                        1

        Total                            8
```

```
                                                                        2
        L I N E A R   P R O G R A M M I N G   P R O C E D U R E

                        SOLUTION  SUMMARY

                   Integer Optimal Solution

        Objective value                 645.000

        Phase 1 iterations                    1
        Phase 2 iterations                    5
        Phase 3 iterations                    0
        Integer iterations                    1
        Integer solutions                     1
        Initial basic feasible variables      8
        Time used (secs)                      9
        Number of inversions                  3

        Machine epsilon                      1E-8
        Machine infinity          1.7976931349E308
        Maximum phase 1 iterations            100
        Maximum phase 2 iterations            100
        Maximum phase 3 iterations       99999999
        Maximum integer iterations            100
        Time limit (secs)                     120
```

```
                                                                        3
        L I N E A R   P R O G R A M M I N G   P R O C E D U R E

                        VARIABLE  SUMMARY

            Variable                                        Reduced
        Col Name       Status Type     Price   Activity       Cost

         1 CHOCO       BASIC  NON-NEG   0.25   1440.000     0.000000
         2 GUMDR       BASIC  NON-NEG   0.75    480.000     0.000000
         3 ICHOCO      BASIC  BINARY    -100      0.000     0.000000
         4 IGUMDR      BASIC  BINARY     -75      1.000     0.000000
         5 cooking     BASIC  SLACK          -13800.000     0.000000
         6 color              SLACK              0.000    -0.013333
         7 package            SLACK              0.000    -0.013333
         8 condiments  BASIC  SLACK          -14280.000     0.000000
         9 chocolate          SLACK              0.000     0.000000
        10 gum         BASIC  SLACK              1E18       0.000000
```

```
              L I N E A R   P R O G R A M M I N G   P R O C E D U R E              4

                          CONSTRAINT  SUMMARY

       Constraint              S/S                                 Dual
       Row Name       Type     Col      Rhs      Activity        Activity

           1 object   OBJECT                      645.000       -1.000000
       *****cooking   LE         5     27000    40800.000        0.000000
           3 color    LE         6     27000    27000.000        0.013333
           4 package  LE         7     27000    27000.000        0.013333
       *****condiments LE        8     27000    41280.000        0.000000
           6 chocolate LE        9         0        0.000000     0.000000
           7 gum      LE        10         0       -1E18         0.000000
           8 only_one EQ                   1        1.000000   -75.000000
```

Notice that the constraints labeled COOKING and CONDIMENTS are flagged. Examination shows that even though the solution appears to be optimal these constraints have been violated. The solution that is given is not feasible. The solution is feasible in the scaled coordinates because a coefficient has effectively become zero. However, when scaling is removed, the infeasibility becomes apparent. The following ERROR message is printed on the LOG:

```
ERROR: The problem seems to be numerically unstable. A feasible
       solution before rescaling becomes infeasible after rescaling.
       Check the CONSTRAINT SUMMARY for flagged problem constraints.
```

Note that this is only one example where numerical instabilities result from model formulation and the extended range of coefficients. Other cases which PROC LP cannot identify are also possible. The prudent analyst must take care to avoid these types of problem in model formulations and identify them in the examination of solutions.

Example 10: Restarting an Integer Program

The following example is attributed to Haldi (Garfinkel and Nemhauser 1972) and is used in the literature as a test problem. Notice that the ACTIVEOUT= and the PRIMALOUT= options are used when invoking PROC LP. These cause the LP procedure to save the primal solution in the data set named P and the active tree in the data set named A. If the procedure fails to find an optimal integer solution on the initial call, it can be called later using the A and P data sets as starting information.

```
data haldi10;
   input x1-x12 _type_ $ _rhs_;
   cards;
   0   0   0   0   0   0   1   1   1   1   1   1  MAX  .
   9   7  16   8  24   5   3   7   8   4   6   5  LE  110
  12   6   6   2  20   8   4   6   3   1   5   8  LE   95
  15   5  12   4   4   5   5   5   6   2   1   5  LE   80
  18   4   4  18  28   1   6   4   2   9   7   1  LE  100
 -12   0   0   0   0   0   1   0   0   0   0   0  LE    0
   0 -15   0   0   0   0   0   1   0   0   0   0  LE    0
   0   0 -12   0   0   0   0   0   1   0   0   0  LE    0
   0   0   0 -10   0   0   0   0   0   1   0   0  LE    0
   0   0   0   0 -11   0   0   0   0   0   1   0  LE    0
```

```
   0   0   0   0   0 -11   0    0    0    0    0    0   1 LE      0
   1   1   1   1   1   1  1000 1000 1000 1000 1000 1000 UPPERBD .
   1   2   3   4   5   6   7    8    9   10   11   12   INTEGER .
;
```

```
proc lp ACTIVEOUT=a PRIMALOUT=p;
run;
```

The output from the call to PROC LP is shown in **Output 7.14**. Notice that the procedure performed 100 iterations and then terminated on maximum integer iterations. This is because by default IMAXIT=100. The procedure reports the current best integer solution.

Output 7.14   Output from the HALDI10 Problem

1

```
            L I N E A R   P R O G R A M M I N G   P R O C E D U R E

                            PROBLEM  SUMMARY

                    Max _OBS1_            Objective Function
                    _RHS_                 Rhs Variable
                    _TYPE_                Type Variable
                    Problem Density             0.318182

                    Variable Type               Number

                    Integer                         12
                    Slack                           10

                    Total                           22

                    Constraint Type             Number

                    LE                              10
                    Objective                        1

                    Total                           11
```

2

```
            L I N E A R   P R O G R A M M I N G   P R O C E D U R E
                            INTEGER ITERATION LOG

   Iter Problem  Condition Objective Branched Value Sinfeas Active
      1      0     ACTIVE  18.709524  X9      1.543 1.11905    2
      2     -1     ACTIVE  18.676973  X11     0.487 1.96707    3
      3     -2     ACTIVE  18.642641  X9      2.482 1.49839    4
      4     -3     ACTIVE  18.402785  X12     7.379 1.62351    5
      5     -4     ACTIVE  17.894108  X4      0.575 1.43847    6
      6     -5     ACTIVE  17.044781  X6      0.727 0.86313    6
      7     -6     ACTIVE  15.681818  X10     3.682 0.65909    6
      8      7     ACTIVE  15.194805  X3      0.266 0.55195    7
      9     -8   INFEASIBLE 11.181818          .      .        6
     10      8   INFEASIBLE 14.236364          .      .        5
     11      1     ACTIVE  18.467723  X12     9.371 0.88948    6
     12      3     ACTIVE   18.42787  X12     8.326 1.21835    7
     13      2     ACTIVE  18.556848  X12     8.598  1.0323    8
     14     13     ACTIVE  18.449188  X8      0.711 1.26379    9
     15    -14     ACTIVE  18.405426  X10     7.649 1.35788   10
     16    -15     ACTIVE  15.277778  X6      0.389    1.1     11
     17    -16     ACTIVE  14.666667  X12     3.667 0.76667   11
     18     17     ACTIVE  14.285714  X9      2.286 0.74286   12
     19    -18     ACTIVE  13.333333  X12     1.333   0.85    12
     20    -11     ACTIVE  16.439394  X10     6.439 0.88636   12
     21     14     ACTIVE   18.39619  X9      2.481 1.25385   13
     22    -21     ACTIVE  18.222868  X12     7.355 1.28101   14
     23    -22     ACTIVE  17.401515  X10     6.402 1.28409   14
     24     23     ACTIVE  17.154182  X4       0.6  1.08976   15
     25    -24     ACTIVE  16.681818  X10     5.682 0.84091   15
```

(continued on next page)

(continued from previous page)

26	25	ACTIVE	16.218182	X6	0.727	0.75909	15
27	-26	ACTIVE	16	X3	0.25	0.25	15
28	-27	ACTIVE	11.5	X10	0.5	0.5	15
29	-12	ACTIVE	14.19697	X4	0.22	0.85606	16
30	11	ACTIVE	18.460133	X8	0.539	1.04883	17
31	-30	ACTIVE	18.453638	X12	8.683	1.12993	18
32	-31	ACTIVE	18.078095	X4	0.792	0.70511	19
33	-32	ACTIVE	17.662338	X10	7.505	0.91299	20
34	-33	INFEASIBLE	16.249351	.	.	.	19
35	33	ACTIVE	17.301299	X9	0.301	0.57489	20
36	31	ACTIVE	18.439678	X10	7.448	1.20125	21
37	36	ACTIVE	18.403728	X6	0.645	1.3643	22
38	-37	ACTIVE	18.048289	X4	0.7	1.18395	23
39	-38	ACTIVE	17.679087	X8	1.833	0.52644	24
40	-39	ACTIVE	17.655399	X12	7.721	0.56127	25
41	-40	ACTIVE	17.342857	X9	0.343	0.50476	26
42	-41	ACTIVE	15.7	X10	4.7	0.51667	26
43	42	ACTIVE	15.14	X7	0.14	0.36833	27
44	-36	ACTIVE	17.25974	X6	0.727	0.82078	28
45	12	ACTIVE	18.421212	X8	0.473	1.39121	29
46	-45	ACTIVE	18.413786	X12	7.637	1.5385	30
47	-46	ACTIVE	16.136364	X4	0.414	1.14697	31
48	-47	ACTIVE	14.963636	X6	0.727	0.63333	31
49	46	ACTIVE	18.38408	X10	6.418	1.84271	32
50	49	ACTIVE	18.276233	X7	0.488	2.42793	33
51	-50	ACTIVE	18.200716	X4	0.597	1.44575	34
52	-51	ACTIVE	17.395517	X6	0.636	1.18597	35

L I N E A R   P R O G R A M M I N G   P R O C E D U R E
INTEGER ITERATION LOG

Iter	Problem	Condition	Objective	Branched	Value	Sinfeas	Active
53	-52	ACTIVE	17.047421	X12	6.687	1.09635	36
54	-53	ACTIVE	15.781818	X10	3.782	0.62576	36
55	54	ACTIVE	15.156364	X3	0.167	0.57697	36
56	-55	INFEASIBLE	11.305556	.	.	.	35
57	4	ACTIVE	18.296842	X6	0.636	1.94504	36
58	-49	ACTIVE	16.427778	X6	0.493	1.54545	37
59	15	ACTIVE	18.088704	X6	0.545	1.22222	38
60	45	ACTIVE	18.340673	X4	0.667	1.57882	39
61	30	ACTIVE	18.368316	X10	7.602	1.20052	40
62	-61	ACTIVE	18.193131	X4	0.8	0.67438	40
63	-62	ACTIVE	17.077922	X6	0.818	0.26623	41
64	-63	SUBOPTIMAL	17	.	.	.	40
65	50	ACTIVE	18.101151	X4	0.6	1.77832	39
66	61	ACTIVE	18.198323	X7	1.506	1.85351	40
67	66	ACTIVE	18.069847	X12	8.517	1.67277	41
68	-67	ACTIVE	17.910909	X4	0.7	0.73015	41
69	-68	FATHOMED	17.790909	.	.	.	40
70	67	ACTIVE	17.694684	X10	6.369	1.6177	41
71	-57	ACTIVE	18.056766	X4	0.687	0.99534	42
72	-13	ACTIVE	18.045455	X4	0.705	0.68939	42
73	22	ACTIVE	18.127619	X6	0.636	1.29593	42
74	21	ACTIVE	18.226936	X10	7.547	1.51448	43
75	-74	ACTIVE	18.027475	X6	0.727	0.66916	43
76	-75	FATHOMED	17.933333	.	.	.	42
77	74	ACTIVE	17.890182	X4	0.7	0.92339	42
78	-59	ACTIVE	17.773333	X4	0.7	0.76	42
79	-66	ACTIVE	18.044048	X12	8.542	1.71158	43
80	79	ACTIVE	17.954536	X11	0.477	1.90457	44
81	-80	FATHOMED	17.723058	.	.	.	43
82	80	ACTIVE	17.875084	X4	0.678	1.16624	43
83	-73	ACTIVE	17.88381	X3	0.251	0.61524	43
84	-83	FATHOMED	16.474006	.	.	.	42
85	-82	ACTIVE	17.231221	X6	0.727	0.76182	42
86	-65	ACTIVE	17.649903	X6	0.636	1.09381	42
87	-77	FATHOMED	17.698182	.	.	.	41
88	-60	ACTIVE	17.674343	X7	0.672	0.91603	42
89	71	FATHOMED	16.82685	.	.	.	41
90	-70	FATHOMED	17.611746	.	.	.	40
91	59	FATHOMED	16.896354	.	.	.	39
92	40	ACTIVE	17.519375	X10	6.56	0.76125	40
93	37	FATHOMED	16.87688	.	.	.	39
94	88	FATHOMED	17.56229	.	.	.	38
95	-78	ACTIVE	17.533333	X12	7.533	0.7	39
96	-95	FATHOMED	16.833333	.	.	.	38

(continued on next page)

(continued from previous page)

```
 97     95    ACTIVE 17.494369 X8    1.503 0.77252   39
 98     39    ACTIVE    17.52  X10   6.667 0.70111   40
 99    -79  FATHOMED 16.378788  .       .     .      39
100     98    ACTIVE 17.190085 X12   7.551 1.37615   39
```

L I N E A R   P R O G R A M M I N G   P R O C E D U R E   4

SOLUTION   SUMMARY

Terminated on Maximum Integer Iterations
Integer Feasible Solution

Objective value	17.000000

Phase 1 iterations	0
Phase 2 iterations	8
Phase 3 iterations	173
Integer iterations	100
Integer solutions	1
Initial basic feasible variables	12
Time used (secs)	84
Number of inversions	49

Machine epsilon	1E-8
Machine infinity	1.7976931349E308
Maximum phase 1 iterations	100
Maximum phase 2 iterations	100
Maximum phase 3 iterations	99999999
Maximum integer iterations	100
Time limit (secs)	120

L I N E A R   P R O G R A M M I N G   P R O C E D U R E   5

VARIABLE   SUMMARY

Col	Variable Name	Status	Type	Price	Activity	Reduced Cost
1	X1	DEGEN	INTEGER	0	0.000000	0.000000
2	X2	DEGEN	INTEGER	0	0.000000	0.000000
3	X3	DEGEN	INTEGER	0	0.000000	0.000000
4	X4		INTEGER	0	1.000000	-7.714286
5	X5	DEGEN	INTEGER	0	0.000000	0.000000
6	X6		INTEGER	0	1.000000	-0.428571
7	X7		INTEGER	1	0.000000	-2.214286
8	X8		INTEGER	1	0.000000	-0.828571
9	X9	DEGEN	INTEGER	1	0.000000	0.000000
10	X10		INTEGER	1	8.000000	-2.857143
11	X11		INTEGER	1	0.000000	-3.090909
12	X12		INTEGER	1	9.000000	0.571429
13	_OBS2_	BASIC	SLACK		20.000000	0.000000
14	_OBS3_	BASIC	SLACK		5.000000	0.000000
15	_OBS4_	BASIC	SLACK		10.000000	0.000000
16	_OBS5_		SLACK		0.000000	-0.428571
17	_OBS6_		SLACK		0.000000	-0.642857
18	_OBS7_		SLACK		0.000000	-0.114286
19	_OBS8_		SLACK		0.000000	-0.142857
20	_OBS9_	BASIC	SLACK		2.000000	0.000000
21	_OBS10_		SLACK		0.000000	-1.090909
22	_OBS11_	BASIC	SLACK		2.000000	0.000000

```
      L I N E A R   P R O G R A M M I N G   P R O C E D U R E                    6
                         CONSTRAINT  SUMMARY

      Constraint              S/S                              Dual
      Row Name     Type       Col       Rhs     Activity      Activity
         1 _OBS1_   OBJECT                       17.000000    -1.000000
         2 _OBS2_   LE         13       110      90.000000     0.000000
         3 _OBS3_   LE         14        95      90.000000     0.000000
         4 _OBS4_   LE         15        80      70.000000     0.000000
         5 _OBS5_   LE         16       100     100.000000     0.428571
         6 _OBS6_   LE         17         0       0.000000     0.642857
         7 _OBS7_   LE         18         0       0.000000     0.114286
         8 _OBS8_   LE         19         0       0.000000     0.142857
         9 _OBS9_   LE         20         0      -2.000000     0.000000
        10 _OBS10_  LE         21         0       0.000000     1.090909
        11 _OBS11_  LE         22         0      -2.000000     0.000000
```

To continue with the solution of this problem, invoke PROC LP with the ACTIVEIN= and PRIMALIN= options.

```
proc lp data=haldi10 ACTIVEIN=a PRIMALIN=p;
run;
```

The procedure picks up iterating where it left off.

Output 7.15 Continuation of the Output from the HALDI10 Problem

```
      L I N E A R   P R O G R A M M I N G   P R O C E D U R E                    1
                         PROBLEM  SUMMARY

      Max _OBS1_                    Objective Function
      _RHS_                         Rhs Variable
      _TYPE_                        Type Variable
      Problem Density                0.318182

      Variable Type                 Number

      Integer                           12
      Slack                             10

      Total                             22

      Constraint Type               Number

      LE                                10
      Objective                          1

      Total                             11
```

```
      L I N E A R   P R O G R A M M I N G   P R O C E D U R E                    2
                         INTEGER ITERATION LOG

      Iter Problem  Condition Objective Branched Value Sinfeas Active

       101     -92  FATHOMED  17.03125      .       .      .      38
       102      97  ACTIVE    17.404249 X7  0.217 0.67127         38
       103     -72  FATHOMED  17.454545     .       .      .      37
       104     -98  ACTIVE    17.453333 X7  0.453 0.64111         37
       105     -86  ACTIVE    17.400909 X8  1.441 0.83455         38
       106     -71  ACTIVE    17.429872 X3  0.25  0.78606         38
       107      70  ACTIVE    17.475338 X4  0.6   1.55316         38
```

(continued on next page)

(continued from previous page)

108	102	ACTIVE	17.380952 X9	2.381	0.64603	38
109	92	ACTIVE	17.256874 X2	0.265	0.67388	38
110	-105	ACTIVE	17.195122 X12	6.438	1.07118	38
111	-107	FATHOMED	16.988889	.	.	37
112	41	ACTIVE	17.2225 X7	0.16	0.37333	37
113	112	ACTIVE	17.1875 X8	2.188	0.33333	37
114	113	FATHOMED	17.153651	.	.	36
115	104	ACTIVE	17.35619 X11	0.356	0.53857	36
116	-97	FATHOMED	17.350388	.	.	35
117	105	FATHOMED	17.159365	.	.	34
118	109	INFEASIBLE	17.167622	.	.	33
119	35	ACTIVE	17.210909 X7	0.211	0.47697	33
120	-85	FATHOMED	17.085714	.	.	32
121	-44	FATHOMED	17.142857	.	.	31
122	-88	ACTIVE	17.58954 X6	0.713	1.03852	31
123	-122	FATHOMED	17.30239	.	.	30
124	-108	FATHOMED	17.133333	.	.	29
125	-106	FATHOMED	15.933194	.	.	28
126	-110	FATHOMED	14.381818	.	.	27
127	-100	FATHOMED	17.02	.	.	26
128	60	FATHOMED	16.585187	.	.	25
129	119	FATHOMED	17.164773	.	.	24
130	115	ACTIVE	17 X5	0.121	0.27143	24
131	130	ACTIVE	17 X1	0.189	0.33889	24
132	131	ACTIVE	17 X3	0.083	0.15	24
133	-132	FATHOMED	15.944444	.	.	23

LINEAR PROGRAMMING PROCEDURE   3

SOLUTION SUMMARY

Integer Optimal Solution

Objective value	17.000000
Phase 1 iterations	0
Phase 2 iterations	0
Phase 3 iterations	115
Integer iterations	133
Integer solutions	0
Initial basic feasible variables	12
Time used (secs)	48
Number of inversions	31

LINEAR PROGRAMMING PROCEDURE   4

VARIABLE SUMMARY

Col	Variable Name	Status	Type	Price	Activity	Reduced Cost
1	X1	DEGEN	INTEGER	0	0.000000	0.000000
2	X2	DEGEN	INTEGER	0	0.000000	0.000000
3	X3	DEGEN	INTEGER	0	0.000000	0.000000
4	X4		INTEGER	0	1.000000	-7.714286
5	X5	DEGEN	INTEGER	0	0.000000	0.000000
6	X6		INTEGER	0	1.000000	-0.428571
7	X7		INTEGER	1	0.000000	-2.214286
8	X8		INTEGER	1	0.000000	-0.828571
9	X9	DEGEN	INTEGER	1	0.000000	0.000000
10	X10		INTEGER	1	8.000000	-2.857143
11	X11		INTEGER	1	0.000000	-3.090909
12	X12		INTEGER	1	9.000000	0.571429
13	_OBS2_	BASIC	SLACK		20.000000	0.000000
14	_OBS3_	BASIC	SLACK		5.000000	0.000000
15	_OBS4_	BASIC	SLACK		10.000000	0.000000
16	_OBS5_		SLACK		0.000000	-0.428571
17	_OBS6_		SLACK		0.000000	-0.642857
18	_OBS7_		SLACK		0.000000	-0.114286
19	_OBS8_		SLACK		0.000000	-0.142857
20	_OBS9_	BASIC	SLACK		2.000000	0.000000
21	_OBS10_		SLACK		0.000000	-1.090909
22	_OBS11_	BASIC	SLACK		2.000000	0.000000

```
                                                                        5
        L I N E A R   P R O G R A M M I N G   P R O C E D U R E

                         CONSTRAINT  SUMMARY

    Constraint           S/S                              Dual
    Row Name    Type     Col      Rhs     Activity      Activity

     1 _OBS1_   OBJECT                    17.000000     -1.000000
     2 _OBS2_   LE        13      110     90.000000      0.000000
     3 _OBS3_   LE        14       95     90.000000      0.000000
     4 _OBS4_   LE        15       80     70.000000      0.000000
     5 _OBS5_   LE        16      100    100.000000      0.428571
     6 _OBS6_   LE        17        0      0.000000      0.642857
     7 _OBS7_   LE        18        0      0.000000      0.114286
     8 _OBS8_   LE        19        0      0.000000      0.142857
     9 _OBS9_   LE        20        0     -2.000000      0.000000
    10 _OBS10_  LE        21        0      0.000000      1.090909
    11 _OBS11_  LE        22        0     -2.000000      0.000000
```

Example 11: Alternative Search of the Branch and Bound Tree

In this example, the HALDI10 problem is solved. However, here the default strategy for searching the branch and bound tree is modified. By default, the search strategy has VARSELECT=FAR. This means that when searching for an integer variable to branch on the procedure, use the one that has value farthest from an integer value. An alternative strategy has VARSELECT=PENALTY. This strategy causes PROC LP to look at the cost, in terms of the objective function, of branching on an integer variable. The procedure looks at PENALTYDEPTH= integer variables before choosing the one with the largest cost. This is a much more expensive strategy (in terms of execution time) than the VARSELECT=FAR strategy, but it can be beneficial if fewer integer iterations must be done to find an optimal solution.

```
proc lp VARSELECT=PENALTY;
run;
```

Compare the number of integer iterations needed to solve the problem using this heuristic with the default strategy used in **Example 10**. Although in this example the difference is profound, solution times can vary significantly with the search technique. See **Output 7.16**.

Output 7.16 Summaries and an Integer Programming Iteration Log: Using VARSELECT=PENALTY

```
                                                                        1
        L I N E A R   P R O G R A M M I N G   P R O C E D U R E

                          PROBLEM  SUMMARY

        Max _OBS1_                  Objective Function
        _RHS_                       Rhs Variable
        _TYPE_                      Type Variable
        Problem Density                  0.318182

        Variable Type                      Number

        Integer                             12
        Slack                               10

        Total                               22
```

(continued on next page)

(continued from previous page)

Constraint Type	Number
LE	10
Objective	1
Total	11

2

L I N E A R   P R O G R A M M I N G   P R O C E D U R E
INTEGER ITERATION LOG

Iter	Problem	Condition	Objective	Branched	Value	Sinfeas	Active
1	0	ACTIVE	18.709524	X4	0.8	1.11905	2
2	-1	ACTIVE	18.309524	X3	0.129	1.31905	3
3	-2	ACTIVE	16.547134	X6	0.816	0.78733	4
4	-3	ACTIVE	16.363499	X12	8.796	0.78733	5
5	-4	SUBOPTIMAL	16	.	.	.	4
6	4	ACTIVE	16.220741	X9	0.782	0.86074	5
7	1	FATHOMED	16.585187	.	.	.	4
8	2	ACTIVE	17.67723	X6	0.886	0.43662	5
9	-8	ACTIVE	17.56338	X10	7.93	0.43662	6
10	-9	SUBOPTIMAL	17	.	.	.	5
11	9	FATHOMED	17.225962	.	.	.	4
12	8	FATHOMED	16.421875	.	.	.	3

3

L I N E A R   P R O G R A M M I N G   P R O C E D U R E
SOLUTION SUMMARY
Integer Optimal Solution

Objective value	17.000000
Phase 1 iterations	0
Phase 2 iterations	8
Phase 3 iterations	20
Integer iterations	12
Integer solutions	2
Initial basic feasible variables	12
Time used (secs)	20
Number of inversions	8
Machine epsilon	1E-8
Machine infinity	1.7976931349E308
Maximum phase 1 iterations	100
Maximum phase 2 iterations	100
Maximum phase 3 iterations	99999999
Maximum integer iterations	100
Time limit (secs)	120

4

L I N E A R   P R O G R A M M I N G   P R O C E D U R E
VARIABLE SUMMARY

Col	Variable Name	Status	Type	Price	Activity	Reduced Cost
1	X1		INTEGER	0	0.000000	-18.000000
2	X2		INTEGER	0	0.000000	-4.000000
3	X3		INTEGER	0	0.000000	-4.000000
4	X4		INTEGER	0	1.000000	-18.000000
5	X5	DEGEN	INTEGER	0	0.000000	0.000000
6	X6		INTEGER	0	1.000000	-1.000000
7	X7		INTEGER	1	0.000000	-5.000000
8	X8		INTEGER	1	0.000000	-3.000000
9	X9		INTEGER	1	0.000000	-1.000000
10	X10		INTEGER	1	8.000000	-8.000000
11	X11		INTEGER	1	0.000000	-8.545455
12	X12	BASIC	INTEGER	1	9.000000	0.000000

(continued on next page)

(continued from previous page)

```
13 _OBS2_    BASIC   SLACK              20.000000    0.000000
14 _OBS3_    BASIC   SLACK               5.000000    0.000000
15 _OBS4_    BASIC   SLACK              10.000000    0.000000
16 _OBS5_            SLACK               0.000000   -1.000000
17 _OBS6_    DEGEN   SLACK               0.000000    0.000000
18 _OBS7_    DEGEN   SLACK               0.000000    0.000000
19 _OBS8_    DEGEN   SLACK               0.000000    0.000000
20 _OBS9_    BASIC   SLACK               2.000000    0.000000
21 _OBS10_           SLACK               0.000000   -2.545455
22 _OBS11_   BASIC   SLACK               2.000000    0.000000
```

```
                                                                        5

          L I N E A R   P R O G R A M M I N G   P R O C E D U R E

                        CONSTRAINT  SUMMARY

        Constraint            S/S                                 Dual
        Row Name     Type     Col     Rhs     Activity          Activity

          1 _OBS1_   OBJECT                    17.000000        -1.000000
          2 _OBS2_   LE        13     110      90.000000         0.000000
          3 _OBS3_   LE        14      95      90.000000         0.000000
          4 _OBS4_   LE        15      80      70.000000         0.000000
          5 _OBS5_   LE        16     100     100.000000         1.000000
          6 _OBS6_   LE        17       0       0.000000         0.000000
          7 _OBS7_   LE        18       0       0.000000         0.000000
          8 _OBS8_   LE        19       0       0.000000         0.000000
          9 _OBS9_   LE        20       0      -2.000000         0.000000
         10 _OBS10_  LE        21       0       0.000000         2.545455
         11 _OBS11_  LE        22       0      -2.000000         0.000000
```

Although the VARSELECT=PENALTY strategy works well in this example, there is no guarantee that it will work well with your model. Experimentation with various strategies is necessary to find the one that works well with your model and data, particularly if a model is solved repeatedly with few changes to either the structure or the data.

Example 12:   An Assignment Problem

This example departs somewhat from the emphasis of previous ones. Typically, linear programming models are large, have considerable structure, and are solved with some regularity. Some form of automatic model building, or matrix generation as it is commonly called, is a useful aid. The sparse input format provides a great deal of flexibility in model specification so that, in many cases, the DATA step can be used to generate the matrix.

The following assignment problem illustrates some techniques in matrix generation. In this example, you have four machines that can produce any of six grades of cloth, and you have five customers that demand various amounts of each grade of cloth. The return from supplying a customer with a demanded grade depends on the machine on which the cloth was made. In addition, the machine capacity depends both upon the specific machine used and the grade of cloth made.

To formulate this problem, let i denote customer, j denote grade, and k denote machine. Then let x_{ijk} denote the amount of cloth grade j made on machine k for customer i; let r_{ijk} denote the return from selling one unit of grade j cloth made on machine k to customer i; let d_{ij} denote the demand for grade j cloth by customer i; let c_{jk} denote the number of units of machine k required to produce one unit of grade j cloth; and let a_k denote the number of units of machine k available. Then, we want to

$$\text{max } \Sigma_{ijk} r_{ijk} x_{ijk}$$

subject to:

$$\Sigma_k x_{ijk} = d_{ij} \qquad \text{for all } i \text{ and } j,$$
$$\Sigma_{ij} c_{jk} x_{ijk} \leq a_k \qquad \text{for all } k,$$
$$x_{ijk} \geq 0 \qquad \text{for all } i, j, \text{ and } k.$$

The data are saved in three data sets. The OBJECT data set contains the returns for satisfying demand, the DEMAND data set contains the amounts demanded, and the RESOURCE data set contains the conversion factors for each grade and the total amounts of machine resources available.

```
title 'An Assignment Problem';

data object;
   input machine customer
         grade1 grade2 grade3 grade4 grade5 grade6;
   cards;
1 1 102 140 105  105 125 148
1 2 115 133 118  118 143 166
1 3  70 108  83   83  88  86
1 4  79 117  87   87 107 105
1 5  77 115  90   90 105 148
2 1 123 150 125  124 154   .
2 2 130 157 132  131 166   .
2 3 103 130 115  114 129   .
2 4 101 128 108  107 137   .
2 5 118 145 130  129 154   .
3 1  83   .   .   97 122 147
3 2 119   .   .  133 163 180
3 3  67   .   .   91 101 101
3 4  85   .   .  104 129 129
3 5  90   .   .  114 134 179
4 1 108 121  79    . 112 132
4 2 121 132  92    . 130 150
4 3  78  91  59    .  77  72
4 4 100 113  76    . 109 104
4 5  96 109  77    . 105 145
;

data demand;
   input customer
         grade1 grade2 grade3 grade4 grade5 grade6;
   cards;
1 100 100 150  150 175 250
2 300 125 300  275 310 325
3 400   0 400  500 340   0
4 250   0 750  750   0   0
5   0 600 300    0 210 360
;
```

```
data resource;
   input machine
         grade1 grade2 grade3 grade4 grade5 grade6 avail;
   cards;
1 .250 .275 .300  .350  .310  .295  744
2 .300 .300 .305  .315  .320  .     244
3 .350 .    .     .320  .315  .300  790
4 .280 .275 .260  .     .250  .295  672
;
```

The linear program is built using the DATA step. The model is saved in a SAS data set in the sparse input format for PROC LP. Each section of the following DATA step generates a piece of the linear program. The first section generates the objective function; the next section generates the demand constraints; and the last section generates the machine resource availability constraints.

```
/*  build the linear programming model */

data model;
   array grade{6} grade1-grade6;
   length _type_ $ 8 _row_ $ 8 _col_ $ 8;
   keep _type_ _row_ _col_ _coef_;

   ncust=5;
   nmach=4;
   ngrade=6;

   /* generate the objective function */

   _type_='MAX';
   _row_='OBJ';
   do k=1 to nmach;
      do i=1 to ncust;
         link readobj;       /* read the objective coefficient data */
         do j=1 to ngrade;
            if grade{j}¬=. then do;
               _col_='X'||put(i,1.)||put(j,1.)||put(k,1.);
               _coef_=grade{j};
               output;
            end;
         end;
      end;
   end;


   /* generate the demand constraints */

   do i=1 to ncust;
      link readdmd;          /* read the demand data */
      do j=1 to ngrade;
         if grade{j}¬=. then do;
            _type_='EQ';
            _row_='DEMAND'||put(i,1.)||put(j,1.);
```

```
                  _col_='_RHS_';
                  _coef_=grade(j);
                  output;
                  _type_=' ';
                  do k=1 to nmach;
                     _col_='X'||put(i,1.)||put(j,1.)||put(k,1.);
                     _coef_=1.0;
                     output;
                  end;
               end;
            end;
         end;

      /* generate the machine constraints */

      do k=1 to nmach;
         link readres;          /* read the machine data */
         _type_='LE';
         _row_='MACHINE'||put(k,1.);
         _col_='_RHS_';
         _coef_=avail;
         output;
         _type_=' ';
         do i=1 to ncust;
            do j=1 to ngrade;
               if grade(j)¬=. then do;
                  _col_='X'||put(i,1.)||put(j,1.)||put(k,1.);
                  _coef_=grade(j);
                  output;
                  end;
               end;
            end;
         end;


   readobj: set object;
   return;
   readdmd: set demand;
   return;
   readres: set resource;
   return;
   run;
```

With the model built and saved in a data set, it is ready for solution using PROC LP. The following program solves the model and saves the solution in the data set called PRIMAL:

```
/* solve the linear program */

proc lp data=model sparsedata noprint primalout=primal;
run;
```

The solution is prepared for reporting using the DATA step, and a report is written using PROC TABULATE.

```
/* report the solution */

data solution;
   set primal;
   keep customer grade machine amount;
   if substr(_var_,1,1)='X' then do;
     if _value_¬=0 then do;
       customer = substr(_var_,2,1);
       grade    = substr(_var_,3,1);
       machine  = substr(_var_,4,1);
       amount   = _value_;
       output;
     end;
   end;
run;

proc tabulate data=solution;
   class customer grade machine;
   var   amount;
   table (machine*customer), (grade*amount);
run;
```

The report shown in **Output 7.17** gives the assignment of customer, grade of cloth, and machine that maximizes the return and does not violate the machine resource availability.

Output 7.17   An Assignment Problem

```
                           An Assignment Problem                               1
              L I N E A R   P R O G R A M M I N G   P R O C E D U R E
                           PROBLEM  SUMMARY

        Max OBJ                        Objective Function
        _RHS_                                 Rhs Variable
        _TYPE_                               Type Variable
        Problem Density                          0.053131

        Variable Type                              Number

        Non-negative                                  120
        Slack                                           4

        Total                                         124

        Constraint Type                            Number

        LE                                              4
        EQ                                             30
        Objective                                       1

        Total                                          35
```

```
                          An Assignment Problem                                2
                   L I N E A R   P R O G R A M M I N G   P R O C E D U R E

                              SOLUTION  SUMMARY

                            Terminated Successfully

           Objective value                     871426.03763

           Phase 1 iterations                           10
           Phase 2 iterations                           65
           Phase 3 iterations                            0
           Integer iterations                            0
           Integer solutions                             0
           Initial basic feasible variables             26
           Time used (secs)                             40
           Number of inversions                          4

           Machine epsilon                            1E-8
           Machine infinity               1.7976931349E308
           Maximum phase 1 iterations                  100
           Maximum phase 2 iterations                  100
           Maximum phase 3 iterations             99999999
           Maximum integer iterations                  100
           Time limit (secs)                           120
```

```
                          An Assignment Problem                                3
```

		GRADE					
		1	2	3	4	5	6
		AMOUNT	AMOUNT	AMOUNT	AMOUNT	AMOUNT	AMOUNT
		SUM	SUM	SUM	SUM	SUM	SUM
MACHINE	CUSTOMER						
1	1	.	100.00	150.00	150.00	175.00	250.00
	2	.	.	300.00	.	.	.
	3	.	.	256.72	210.31	.	.
	4	.	.	750.00	.	.	.
	5	.	92.27	.	.	.	.
2	3	.	.	143.28	.	340.00	.
	5	.	.	300.00	.	.	.
3	2	.	.	.	275.00	310.00	325.00
	3	.	.	.	289.69	.	.
	4	.	.	.	750.00	.	.
	5	.	.	.	.	210.00	360.00
4	1	100.00	.	.	.	.	.
	2	300.00	125.00	.	.	.	.
	3	400.00	.	.	.	.	.
	4	250.00	.	.	.	.	.
	5	.	507.73	.	.	.	.

Example 13:   A Scheduling Problem

Scheduling problems is an application area where techniques in model generation can be valuable. Problems involving scheduling are often solved with integer
programming and are similar to assignment problems. In the following example,
you have eight one-hour time slots in each of five days. You have to assign four

people to these time slots so that each slot is covered on every day. You allow the people to specify preference data for each slot on each day. In addition, there are constraints that must be satisfied:

- each person has some slots for which they are unavailable
- each person must have either slot 4 or 5 off for lunch
- each person can work at most two time slots in a row
- each person can work at most a specified number of hours in the week.

To formulate this problem, let i denote person, j denote time slot, and k denote day. Then, let $x_{ijk} = 1$ if person i is assigned to time slot j on day k, and 0 otherwise; let p_{ijk} denote the preference of person i for slot j on day k; and let h_i denote the number of hours in a week that person i will work. Then, we want to

$$\max \ \Sigma_{ijk} \ p_{ijk} \ x_{ijk}$$

subject to:

$\Sigma_i \, x_{ijk} = 1$	for all j and k,
$x_{i4k} + x_{i5k} \leq 1$	for all i and k,
$x_{i,l,k} + x_{i,l+1,k} + x_{i,l+2,k} \leq 2$	for all i and k, and $l = 1, \ldots, 6$
$\Sigma_{jk} x_{ijk} \leq h_i$	for all i,
$x_{ijk} = 0$ or 1	for all i, and k such that $p_{ijk} > 0$, otherwise $x_{ijk} = 0$.

To solve this problem, create a data set that has the hours and preference data for each individual, time slot, and day. A 10 represents the most desirable time slot and a 1 represents the least desirable time slot. In addition, a 0 indicates that the time slot is not available.

```
title 'A Scheduling Problem';

data raw;
    input name $ hour slot mon tue wed thu fri;
    cards;
marc  20    1      10 10 10 10 10
marc  20    2       9  9  9  9  9
marc  20    3       8  8  8  8  8
marc  20    4       1  1  1  1  1
marc  20    5       1  1  1  1  1
marc  20    6       1  1  1  1  1
marc  20    7       1  1  1  1  1
marc  20    8       1  1  1  1  1
mike  20    1      10  9  8  7  6
mike  20    2      10  9  8  7  6
mike  20    3      10  9  8  7  6
mike  20    4      10  3  3  3  3
mike  20    5       1  1  1  1  1
mike  20    6       1  2  3  4  5
mike  20    7       1  2  3  4  5
mike  20    8       1  2  3  4  5
bill  20    1      10 10 10 10 10
bill  20    2       9  9  9  9  9
bill  20    3       8  8  8  8  8
bill  20    4       0  0  0  0  0
bill  20    5       1  1  1  1  1
bill  20    6       1  1  1  1  1
```

```
bill  20   7        1   1   1   1   1
bill  20   8        1   1   1   1   1
bob   20   1       10   9   8   7   6
bob   20   2       10   9   8   7   6
bob   20   3       10   9   8   7   6
bob   20   4       10   3   3   3   3
bob   20   5        1   1   1   1   1
bob   20   6        1   2   3   4   5
bob   20   7        1   2   3   4   5
bob   20   8        1   2   3   4   5
;
```

These data are read by the following DATA step, and an integer program is built to solve the problem. The model is saved in the data set named MODEL. First, the objective function is built using the data saved in the RAW data set. Then, the constraints requiring a person to be working in each time slot are built. Next, the constraints allowing each person time for lunch are added. Then, the constraints restricting people to at most two consecutive hours are added. Next, the constraints limiting the time that any one person works in a week are added. Finally, the constraints allowing a person to be assigned only to a time slot for which he is available are added. The code to build each of these constraints follows the formulation closely.

```
data model;
    array week{5} mon tue wed thu fri;
    array hours{4} hours1 hours2 hours3 hours4;
    retain hours1-hours4;

    set raw end=eof;

    length _type_ $ _col_ $ _row_ $;
    keep _type_ _col_ _row_ _coef_;

    if      name='marc' then i=1;
    else if name='mike' then i=2;
    else if name='bill' then i=3;
    else if name='bob'  then i=4;

    hours{i}=hour;

    /* build the objective function */

    do k=1 to 5;
       _col_='x'||put(i,1.)||put(slot,1.)||put(k,1.);

       _row_='object';
       _coef_=week{k} * 1000;
       output;
       _row_='upper';
       if week{k}^=0 then _coef_=1;
       output;
       _row_='integer';
       _coef_=1;
       output;
    end;
```

```
/* build the rest of the model */

if eof then do;
   _coef_=.;
   _col_=' ';
   _type_='upper';
   _row_='upper';
   output;
   _type_='max';
   _row_='object';
   output;
   _type_='int';
   _row_='integer';
   output;

   /* every hour 1 person working */

   do j=1 to 8;
      do k=1 to 5;
         _row_='work'||put(j,1.)||put(k,1.);
         _type_='eq';
         _col_='_RHS_';
         _coef_=1;
         output;
         _coef_=1;
         _type_=' ';
         do i=1 to 4;
            _col_='x'||put(i,1.)||put(j,1.)||put(k,1.);
            output;
         end;
      end;
   end;

   /* each person has a lunch */

   do i=1 to 4;
      do k=1 to 5;
         _row_='lunch'||put(i,1.)||put(k,1.);
         _type_='le';
         _col_='_RHS_';
         _coef_=1;
         output;
         _coef_=1;
         _type_=' ';
         _col_='x'||put(i,1.)||'4'||put(k,1.);
         output;
         _col_='x'||put(i,1.)||'5'||put(k,1.);
         output;
      end;
   end;
```

```
                    /* work at most 2 slots in a row */

                    do i=1 to 4;
                      do k=1 to 5;
                        do l=1 to 6;
                        _row_='seq'||put(i,1.)||put(k,1.)||put(l,1.);
                        _type_='le';
                        _col_='_RHS_';
                        _coef_=2;
                         output;
                        _coef_=1;
                        _type_=' ';
                           do j=0 to 2;
                              _col_='x'||put(i,1.)||put(l+j,1.)||put(k,1.);
                              output;
                           end;
                        end;
                      end;
                    end;


                    /* work at most n hours in a week */

                    do i=1 to 4;
                      _row_='capacit'||put(i,1.);
                      _type_='le';
                      _col_='_RHS_';
                      _coef_=hours(i);
                      output;
                      _coef_=1;
                      _type_=' ';
                      do j=1 to 8;
                        do k=1 to 5;
                           _col_='x'||put(i,1.)||put(j,1.)||put(k,1.);
                           output;
                        end;
                      end;
                    end;


                  end;

         run;
```

The model saved in the data set named MODEL is in the sparse format. The constraint that requires one person to work in time slot 1 on day 2 is named WORK12; it is:

$$\sum_i x_{i12} = 1 \quad .$$

It looks like

TYPE	_COL_	_ROW_	_COEF_
eq	_RHS_	work12	1
	x112	work12	1
	x212	work12	1
	x312	work12	1
	x412	work12	1

in the MODEL data set.

The model is solved using the LP procedure. The option PRIMALOUT=SOLUTION causes PROC LP to save the primal solution in the data set named SOLUTION.

```
/* solve the linear program */

proc lp sparsedata noprint PRIMALOUT=solution
   time=1000 maxit1=1000 maxit2=1000;
run;
```

The DATA step below takes the solution data set SOLUTION and generates a report data set named REPORT. It translates the variable names x_{ijk} so that a more meaningful report can be written. Then, PROC TABULATE is used to print a schedule showing how the eight time slots are covered for the week.

```
/* report the solution */
title 'Reported Solution';

data report;
   set solution;
   keep name slot mon tue wed thu fri;
   if substr(_var_,1,1)='x' then do;
     if _value_>0 then do;
        n=substr(_var_,2,1);
        slot=substr(_var_,3,1);
        d=substr(_var_,4,1);
        if      n='1' then name='marc';
        else if n='2' then name='mike';
        else if n='3' then name='bill';
        else               name='bob';
        if      d='1' then mon=1;
        else if d='2' then tue=1;
        else if d='3' then wed=1;
        else if d='4' then thu=1;
        else               fri=1;
        output;
     end;
   end;
run;

proc format;
   value xfmt 1='  xxx  ';
run;
```

```
proc tabulate data=report;
   class name slot;
   var mon--fri;
   table (slot * name), (mon tue wed thu fri)*sum=' '*f=xfmt.
         /misstext=' ';
run;
```

The output from PROC TABULATE summarizes the schedule. Notice that the constraint requiring that a person be assigned to each possible time slot on each day is satisfied.

Output 7.18   A Scheduling Problem

```
                        A Scheduling Problem                              1
            L I N E A R   P R O G R A M M I N G   P R O C E D U R E

                           PROBLEM  SUMMARY

          Max object                Objective Function
          _RHS_                            Rhs Variable
          _TYPE_                          Type Variable
          Problem Density                     0.015446

          Variable Type                         Number

          Integer                                  160
          Slack                                    144

          Total                                    304

          Constraint Type                       Number

          LE                                       144
          EQ                                        40
          Objective                                 1

          Total                                    185
```

```
                        A Scheduling Problem                              2
            L I N E A R   P R O G R A M M I N G   P R O C E D U R E

                           SOLUTION  SUMMARY

                        Integer Optimal Solution

          Objective value                       211000

          Phase 1 iterations                        96
          Phase 2 iterations                        57
          Phase 3 iterations                         0
          Integer iterations                         1
          Integer solutions                          1
          Initial basic feasible variables         146
          Time used (secs)                         129
          Number of inversions                       5

          Machine epsilon                         1E-8
          Machine infinity            1.7976931349E308
          Maximum phase 1 iterations              1000
          Maximum phase 2 iterations             10000
          Maximum phase 3 iterations          99999999
          Maximum integer iterations               100
          Time limit (secs)                       1000
```

```
                              A Scheduling Problem                              3
      -----------------------------------------------------------------
      |                     |   MON  |   TUE  |   WED  |   THU  |   FRI  |
      |-------------+-------+--------+--------+--------+--------+--------|
      |SLOT         |NAME   |        |        |        |        |        |
      |-------------+-------+--------+--------+--------+--------+--------|
      |1            |bill   |        |        |   xxx  |   xxx  |   xxx  |
      |             |-------+--------+--------+--------+--------+--------|
      |             |marc   |   xxx  |   xxx  |        |        |        |
      |-------------+-------+--------+--------+--------+--------+--------|
      |2            |marc   |        |   xxx  |   xxx  |   xxx  |   xxx  |
      |             |-------+--------+--------+--------+--------+--------|
      |             |mike   |   xxx  |        |        |        |        |
      |-------------+-------+--------+--------+--------+--------+--------|
      |3            |bob    |   xxx  |        |        |        |        |
      |             |-------+--------+--------+--------+--------+--------|
      |             |marc   |        |        |   xxx  |   xxx  |   xxx  |
      |             |-------+--------+--------+--------+--------+--------|
      |             |mike   |        |   xxx  |        |        |        |
      |-------------+-------+--------+--------+--------+--------+--------|
      |4            |mike   |   xxx  |   xxx  |   xxx  |   xxx  |   xxx  |
      |-------------+-------+--------+--------+--------+--------+--------|
      |5            |marc   |   xxx  |   xxx  |   xxx  |   xxx  |   xxx  |
      |-------------+-------+--------+--------+--------+--------+--------|
      |6            |bob    |        |        |        |   xxx  |        |
      |             |-------+--------+--------+--------+--------+--------|
      |             |marc   |   xxx  |        |        |        |        |
      |             |-------+--------+--------+--------+--------+--------|
      |             |mike   |        |   xxx  |   xxx  |        |   xxx  |
      |-------------+-------+--------+--------+--------+--------+--------|
      |7            |bob    |        |        |        |        |   xxx  |
      |             |-------+--------+--------+--------+--------+--------|
      |             |mike   |   xxx  |   xxx  |   xxx  |   xxx  |        |
      |-------------+-------+--------+--------+--------+--------+--------|
      |8            |bob    |        |   xxx  |   xxx  |        |        |
      |             |-------+--------+--------+--------+--------+--------|
      |             |mike   |   xxx  |        |        |   xxx  |   xxx  |
      -----------------------------------------------------------------
```

Recall that PROC LP puts a character string in the macro variable _ORLP_ that describes the characteristics of the solution on termination. This string can be parsed using macro functions and the information obtained can be used in report writing. The variable can be printed on the log with

  %put &_orlp_;   .

That statement will produce

```
STATUS=OK PHASE=3 OBJECTIVE=211000 P_FEASIBLE=YES D_FEASIBLE=YES
INT_ITERATION=1 INT_FEASIBLE=1 ACTIVE=0 ITERATION=0
TIME=129
```

From this you learn, for example, that at termination the solution is integer optimal and has an objective value of 211000.

Example 14: A Multi-commodity Transshipment Problem with Fixed Charges

The following example illustrates a DATA step program for generating a linear program to solve a multi-commodity network flow model that has fixed charges. Consider a network consisting of the following nodes: farm-a, farm-b, farm-c, Chicago, St. Louis, and New York. You can ship three commodities from each farm to Chicago or St. Louis and from Chicago or St. Louis to New York. The following table shows the unit shipping cost for each of the four commodities across each of the arcs. The table also shows the supply (positive numbers) at each of the *from* nodes and the demand (negative numbers) at each of the *to* nodes. The fixed charge is a fixed cost for shipping any nonzero amount across an arc. For example, if any amount of any of the four commodities is sent from farm-c to St. Louis, then a fixed charge of 75 units is added to the shipping cost.

From Node	To Node	Unit Shipping Cost 1	2	3	4	Supply and Demand 1	2	3	4	Fixed Charge
farm-a	Chicago	20	15	17	22	100	100	40	.	100
farm-b	Chicago	15	15	15	30	100	200	50	50	75
farm-c	Chicago	30	30	10	10	40	100	75	100	100
farm-a	StLouis	30	25	27	22	.	.	.	.	150
farm-c	StLouis	10	9	11	10	.	.	.	.	75
Chicago	NY	75	75	75	75	-150	-200	-50	-75	200
StLouis	NY	80	80	80	80	.	.	.	.	200

The program below is designed to take the data in the form given in the table above. It builds the node arc incidence matrix for a network given in this form and adds integer variables to capture the fixed charge using the type of constraints discussed in **Example 8** and **Example 9**. The program solves the model using PROC LP, saves the solution in the PRIMALOUT data set named SOLUTION, and prints the solution. The DATA step can be easily modified to handle larger problems with similar structure.

```
title 'Multi-commodity Transshipment Problem with Fixed Charges';

data network;
   retain M 1.0e6;
   length _col_ $ 22 _row_ $ 22;
   keep _type_ _col_ _row_ _coef_;
   array sd sd1-sd4;
   array c c1-c4;

   input arc $10. from $ to $ c1 c2 c3 c4 sd1 sd2 sd3 sd4 fx;

   /* for the first observation define some of the rows */

   if _n_=1 then do;
      _type_='upperbd';
      _row_='upper';
      output;
      _type_='lowerbd';
      _row_='lower';
      output;
      _type_='min';
      _row_='obj';
```

```
        output;
        _type_='integer';
        _row_='int';
        output;
        end;
_col_='_rhs_';
_type_='le';

    do over sd;                        /* loop for each commodity    */
      _coef_=sd;
      if sd>0 then do;                 /*  the node is a supply node */
        _row_=from||' commodity'||put(_i_,2.);
        if from¬=' ' then output;
      end;
      else if sd<0 then do;            /*  the node is a demand node */
        _row_=to||' commodity'||put(_i_,2.);
        if to¬=' ' then output;
      end;
      else if from¬=' ' & to¬=' ' then do;  /* a transshipment node  */
        _coef_=0;
        _row_=from||' commodity'||put(_i_,2.);
        output;
        _row_=to  ||' commodity'||put(_i_,2.);
        output;
      end;
    end;

    do over c;                         /* loop for each commodity     */
_col_=arc||' commodity'||put(_i_,2.);
if from¬=' ' & to¬=' ' then do;
                                       /* add node arc incidence matrix*/
  _type_='le';
  _row_=from||' commodity'||put(_i_,2.);
  _coef_=1;
  output;
  _row_=to    ||' commodity'||put(_i_,2.);
  _coef_=-1;
  output;
  _type_='  ';
  _row_='obj';
  _coef_=c;
  output;
                               /* add fixed charge variables       */
  _type_='le';
  _row_=arc;
  _coef_=1;output;
  _col_='_rhs_';
  _type_='  ';
  _coef_=0;
  output;
  _col_=arc||'fx';
  _coef_=-M;
  output;
  _row_='int';
  _coef_=1;
```

```
        output;
        _row_='obj';
        _coef_=fx;
        output;
        _row_='upper';
        _coef_=1;
        output;


    end;
    end;

    cards;
a-Chicago    farm-a   Chicago    20 15 17 22     100 100  40   .  100
b-Chicago    farm-b   Chicago    15 15 15 30     100 200  50  50   75
c-Chicago    farm-c   Chicago    30 30 10 10      40 100  75 100  100
a-StLouis    farm-a   StLouis    30 25 27 22       .   .   .   .  150
c-StLouis    farm-c   StLouis    10  9 11 10       .   .   .   .   75
Chicago-NY   Chicago  NY         75 75 75 75    -150 -200 -50 -75 200
StLous-NY    StLouis  NY         80 80 80 80       .   .   .   .  200
;


/* solve the model */

proc lp sparsedata pout=solution  noprint;
run;


/* print the solution */

data;
    set solution;
    rename _var_=arc _value_=amount;
    if _value_^=0 & _type_='NON-NEG';
run;

proc print;
    id arc;
    var amount;
run;
```

The output from this example is shown in **Output 7.19**. The NOPRINT option in the PROC LP statement suppresses the VARIABLE and CONSTRAINT SUMMARY sections. This is useful when solving large models for which a report program is available. Here, the solution is saved in data set SOLUTION and reported using PROC PRINT. The solution shows the amount that is shipped over each arc.

Output 7.19 Multi-commodity Transshipment Problem with Fixed Charges

```
            Multi-commodity Transhipment Problem with Fixed-Charges                    1
            L I N E A R   P R O G R A M M I N G   P R O C E D U R E
                             PROBLEM  SUMMARY

                 Min obj                  Objective Function
                 _rhs_                    Rhs Variable
                 _TYPE_                   Type Variable
                 Problem Density          0.059629

                 Variable Type            Number

                 Non-negative                 28
                 Integer                       7
                 Slack                        31

                 Total                        66

                 Constraint Type          Number

                 LE                           31
                 Objective                     1

                 Total                        32
```

```
            Multi-commodity Transhipment Problem with Fixed-Charges                    2

            L I N E A R   P R O G R A M M I N G   P R O C E D U R E
                             INTEGER ITERATION LOG

  Iter Problem  Condition Objective Branched Value Sinfeas Active
     1      0     ACTIVE 42075.134 Chicago- 34E-5 0.00095    2
     2     -1     ACTIVE 42275.067 b-Chicag  2E-4 0.00061    3
     3     -2     ACTIVE 42350.052 c-StLoui 14E-5 0.00041    4
     4     -3     ACTIVE 42425.042 StLous-N 14E-5 0.00027    5
     5     -4     ACTIVE 42625.014 c-Chicag 13E-5 0.00014    6
     6     -5     ACTIVE 42725.001 a-Chicag  1E-5 0.00001    7
     7     -6 SUBOPTIMAL    42825       .      .       .     6
     8      2 INFEASIBLE 42775.072       .      .       .     3
     9      3     ACTIVE 42650.018 c-Chicag 13E-5 0.00018    3
    10      4     ACTIVE 42725.018 c-Chicag 13E-5 0.00018    3
    11    -10   FATHOMED 42825.005       .      .       .     2
    12     -9   FATHOMED 42750.005       .      .       .     1
```

```
            Multi-commodity Transhipment Problem with Fixed-Charges                    3
            L I N E A R   P R O G R A M M I N G   P R O C E D U R E

                             SOLUTION  SUMMARY

                          Integer Optimal Solution

                 Objective value              42825.000

                 Phase 1 iterations                  24
                 Phase 2 iterations                   8
                 Phase 3 iterations                  15
                 Integer iterations                  12
                 Integer solutions                    1
                 Initial basic feasible variables    29
                 Time used (secs)                    33
                 Number of inversions                 8

                 Machine epsilon                   1E-8
                 Machine infinity      1.7976931349E308
                 Maximum phase 1 iterations         100
                 Maximum phase 2 iterations         100
                 Maximum phase 3 iterations    99999999
                 Maximum integer iterations         100
                 Time limit (secs)                  120
```

```
┌─────────────────────────────────────────────────────────────────────────────────────┐
│           Multi-commodity Transhipment Problem with Fixed-Charges                   4 │
│                                                                                       │
│                    ARC              AMOUNT                                             │
│            Chicago-NY  commodity 1    110                                              │
│            Chicago-NY  commodity 2    100                                              │
│            Chicago-NY  commodity 3     50                                              │
│            Chicago-NY  commodity 4     75                                              │
│            StLous-NY   commodity 1     40                                              │
│            StLous-NY   commodity 2    100                                              │
│            a-Chicago   commodity 1     10                                              │
│            b-Chicago   commodity 1    100                                              │
│            b-Chicago   commodity 2    100                                              │
│            c-Chicago   commodity 3     50                                              │
│            c-Chicago   commodity 4     75                                              │
│            c-StLouis   commodity 1     40                                              │
│            c-StLouis   commodity 2    100                                              │
└─────────────────────────────────────────────────────────────────────────────────────┘
```

REFERENCES

Bartels, R. (1971), "A Stabilization of the Simplex Method," *Numerical Mathematics*, 16, 414–434.

Bland, R.G. (1977), "New Finite Pivoting Rules for the Simplex Method," *Mathematics of Operations Research*, 2, 103–107.

Breau, R. and Burdet, C.A. (1974), "Branch and Bound Experiments in Zero-One Programming," *Mathematical Programming Study*, ed. M.L. Balinski, 2, 1–50.

Crowder, H., Johnson, E.L., and Padberg, M.W. (1983), "Solving Large-Scale Zero-One Linear Programming Problems," *Operations Research*, 31, 803–834.

Dantzig, G.B. (1963), *Linear Programming and Extensions*, Princeton: Princeton University Press.

Garfinkel, R.S. and Nemhauser, G.L. (1972), *Integer Programming*, New York: John Wiley & Sons, Inc.

Greenberg, H.J. (ed.) (1978), "Pivot Selection Tactics," in *Design and Implementation of Optimization Software*, Netherlands: Sijthoff & Noordhoff.

Hadley, G. (1962), *Linear Programming*, Reading, Massachusetts: Addison-Wesley.

Harris, P. (1975), "Pivot Selection Methods of the Devex LP Code," in *Mathematical Programming Study 4*, Amsterdam: North-Holland Publishing Co.

Ignizio, J.P. (1976), *Goal Programming and Extensions*, Lexington, Massachusetts: D.C. Heath and Company.

Murtagh, Bruce A. (1981), *Advanced Linear Programming, Computation and Practice*, McGraw-Hill Inc.

Palmer, K.H. et al. (1984), *A Model-Management Framework for Mathematical Programming*, An Exxon Mongraph, New York: John Wiley & Sons, Inc.

Reid, J.K. (1976), "A Sparsity-Exploiting Variant of the Bartels-Golub Decomposition for Linear Programming Bases," *Harwell Report CSS 20*, A.E.R.E., Didcot, Oxfordshire.

Reid, J.K. (1976), "Fortran Subroutines for Handling Sparse Linear Programming Bases," *Harwell Report AERE-R 8269*, A.E.R.E., Didcot, Oxfordshire.

Taha, H.A. (1975), *Integer Programming*, New York: Academic Press.

Williams, H.P. (1978), *Model Building in Mathematical Programming, 2nd Edition*, H.P. Williams, Wiley Interscience.

The NETDRAW
Procedure

ABSTRACT

The NETDRAW procedure draws a network diagram of the activities in a project. Boxes (or nodes) are used to represent the activities, and lines (or arcs) are used to show the relationships among the activities. Though the description of the procedure is written using project management terminology, PROC NETDRAW can be used to draw any acyclic network. The only information required by the procedure for drawing such a diagram is the name of each activity in the project (or node in the network) and a list of all its immediate successor activities (or nodes connected to it by arcs).

By default, the diagram produced is of line-printer quality. You can use the GRAPHICS option in the PROC NETDRAW statement to obtain a network diagram of high-resolution graphics quality.

Note: you must have SAS/GRAPH software if you want to produce network diagrams of high-resolution quality using the GRAPHICS option.

In addition to sending the output to either a plotter or a printer, you can view the network diagram of the project at your terminal in full-screen mode by specifying the FULLSCREEN option in the PROC NETDRAW statement.

INTRODUCTION

The NETDRAW procedure is designed to draw network diagrams either on a line printer or on any of the graphics devices supported by SAS/GRAPH software. The first step in defining a project is to make a list of the activities in the project and determine the precedence constraints that need to be satisfied by these activities. It is useful at this stage to view a graphical representation of the project network. While the project is in progress, you may want to use the network diagram to show the current status of each activity as well as any other relevant information about each activity.

The ACTNET statement in the NETDRAW procedure is designed to draw activity networks that represent a project in Activity-On-Node format. There are two issues that arise in drawing and displaying a network diagram: the layout of the diagram and the format of the display. The layout of the diagram consists of placing the nodes of the network and routing the arcs of the network in an appropriate manner. The format of the display includes the size of the nodes, the number of character positions between nodes, the color of the nodes and arcs, and the information that is placed within each node. There are several options available in the ACTNET statement that allow you to control the format of the display and the layout of the diagram; these options and their use are explained in detail later in this chapter.

Below is a list of some of the key aspects of the procedure:

- The input data set specifies the activities (or nodes) in the network and their immediate successors. The amount of information displayed within each node can be controlled by the ID= option or by the use of default variables in the data set.
- The procedure uses the node-successor information to determine the placement of the nodes and the layout of the arcs connecting the nodes.
- By default, the procedure produces network diagrams of line-printer quality. You can specify the GRAPHICS option in the PROC NETDRAW statement to obtain high-resolution quality network diagrams. To obtain the full-screen version of the procedure, use the FULLSCREEN (FS) option in the PROC NETDRAW statement.
- The full-screen version of the procedure enables you to move the nodes around on the screen (subject to maintaining the precedence order of the activities) and thus change the layout of the network diagram.
- The positions of the nodes and arcs of the layout determined by PROC NETDRAW are saved in an output data set. This data set can be used again as input to PROC NETDRAW; use of such a data set will save some processing time because the procedure will not need to determine the node and arc placement.
- The network does not have to represent a project. You can use PROC NETDRAW to draw any network that does not have cycles.

- If necessary, the procedure draws the network across page boundaries. The number of pages that are used depends on the number of print positions that are available in the horizontal and vertical directions.
- In graphics mode, the COMPRESS option enables you to produce the network on one page.

SPECIFICATIONS

The following statements are used in PROC NETDRAW:

> **PROC NETDRAW** *options*;
>   **ACTNET** / *options*;

PROC NETDRAW Statement

PROC NETDRAW *options*;

The following options can appear in the PROC NETDRAW statement:

DATA=*SASdataset*
names the SAS data set to be used by PROC NETDRAW. If DATA= is omitted, the most recently created SAS data set is used. This data set contains the network information (ACTIVITY and SUCCESSOR variables) and any ID variables that are to be placed within the nodes.

FULLSCREEN
FS
indicates that the network be drawn in full-screen mode. This enables you to view the network diagram produced by NETDRAW in different scales; you can also move nodes around the diagram to modify the layout.

GOUT=*graphics catalog*
specifies the name of the graphics catalog used to save the output produced by PROC NETDRAW for later replay. See "SAS/GRAPH Graphics Output" in SAS/GRAPH documentation for more details. This option is valid only if the GRAPHICS option is specified.

GRAPHICS
indicates that the network diagram produced be of high-resolution quality. If you specify the GRAPHICS option but you do not have SAS/GRAPH software at your site, the procedure stops and issues an error message.

LINEPRINTER
LP
produces a network diagram of line-printer quality. This is the default.

OUT=*SASdataset*
specifies a name for the output data set that contains the node and arc placement information determined by PROC NETDRAW and used to draw the network. This data set contains all the information that was specified in the DATA= input data set to define the project. If OUT= is omitted, the SAS System still creates a data set and names it according to the DATA*n* convention. See base SAS documentation for more information on SAS files.

ACTNET Statement

> ACTNET / *options*;

The options that can appear in the ACTNET statement are divided into groups according to their functionality and are described under different subsections below.

Variable Lists

The following options specify the variable or variable lists in the input data set that identify the activity (or node), its immediate successors, duration, and any ID information that is to be placed within each node of the network:

ACTIVITY=*variable*

    specifies the variable in the input data set that names the nodes in the network. If the data set contained a variable called _FROM_, this specification is ignored. This specification is mandatory if the data set does not contain a variable called _FROM_.

DURATION=*variable*

    specifies a variable that contains the duration of each activity in the network. This value is used only for display.

ID=*(variables)*

    specifies the variables in the input data set that are to be printed within each node of the network. In addition to the ID variables that are specified, the procedure also prints some additional variables if the NODEFID option is not specified. These are the ACTIVITY variable, the DURATION variable (if the DURATION= option was specified), and any of the following variables that it finds in the input data set: E_START, E_FINISH, L_START, L_FINISH, S_START, S_FINISH, A_START, A_FINISH, T_FLOAT, and F_FLOAT. See Chapter 5, "The CPM Procedure," for a description of these variables.

SUCCESSOR=*(variables)*

    specifies the variables in the input data set that name all the immediate successors of the node specified by the ACTIVITY variable. This specification is ignored if the data set contains a variable named _TO_. At least one SUCCESSOR variable must be specified if the data set does not contain a variable called _TO_.

Layout Control Options

The following options give you some control over the arc-routing algorithm:

HTRACKS=*hnum*

    controls the number of arcs that are drawn horizontally through the space between the nodes. A default value is chosen by PROC NETDRAW on the basis of the maximum number of successors of any node.

VTRACKS=*vnum*

    controls the number of arcs that are drawn vertically through the space between the nodes. A default value is chosen by PROC NETDRAW on the basis of the maximum number of successors of any node.

Format Control Options

The following options enable you to control the format of the display:

BOXHT=*boxht*

specifies the height of the box (in character cell positions) used for denoting a node. If this option is not specified, the height of the box is set to be equal to the number of lines required for printing all of the ID variable values for a given node.

BOXWDTH=*boxwdth*

specifies the width of the box (in character cell positions) used for denoting a node. If this option is not specified, the width of the box is set to be equal to the maximum number of columns required for printing all of the ID variable values for any of the nodes.

NODEFID

indicates that the procedure need not check for any of the default ID variables in the input data set; if this option is in effect, only the variables specified in the ID= option are printed for each node.

NOLABEL

supresses the labels. By default, the procedure uses the first three letters of the variable name to label all the variables that are printed within each node of the network. The only exception is the variable that is identified by the ACTIVITY= option.

XBETWEEN=*xbetween*
HBETWEEN=*xbetween*

specifies the horizontal distance (in character cell positions) between two successive nodes. The value for this option must be at least 3; the default value is 5.

YBETWEEN=*ybetween*
VBETWEEN=*ybetween*

specifies the vertical distance (in character cell positions) between two successive nodes. The value for this option must be at least 3; the default value is 5.

Line-printer and Full-screen Option

The following option specifies characters for the node outlines and connections for the full-screen and line-printer mode of PROC NETDRAW:

FORMCHAR[*index list*]='*string*'

defines the characters to be used for constructing the node outlines and connections in the full-screen and line-printer modes of the procedure. The value is a string 20 characters long. The first 11 characters define the 2 bar characters, vertical and horizontal, and the 9 corner characters: upper-left, upper-middle, upper-right, middle-left, middle-middle (cross), middle-right, lower-left, lower-middle, and lower-right. These characters are used to draw an outline for each node as well as the connecting arcs. The 19th character denotes a right arrow. The default value of the FORMCHAR= option is '|----|+|---+=|−/\<>*', (for more information, see "The Calendar Procedure" in SAS documentation). Any character or hexadecimal string can be substituted to customize the appearance of the diagram. Use an index list to specify which default form character each supplied character replaces; or, replace the entire default string by specifying the full character replacement string without an index list. For example, change the four corners of each node and all turning points of the arcs to asterisks by specifying

```
FORMCHAR( 3 5 7 9 11)= '*****'
```

If you specify

```
FORMCHAR='           ' (11 blanks)
```

a network diagram with no outlines for the nodes (as well as no arcs) is produced. If you have your printout routed to an IBM 6670 printer using an extended font (typestyle 27 or 225) with input character set 216, it is recommended that you specify

```
FORMCHAR='FABFACCCBCEB8FECABCBBB'X
```

If you are printing on a printer with a TN (text) print train, it is recommended that you specify

```
FORMCHAR='4FBFACBFBC4F8F4FABBFBB'X
```

For an IBM PC, it is recommended that you specify

```
FORMCHAR( 1 2 3 4 5 6 7 8 9 10 11 19) = "B3C4DAC2BFC3C5B4C0C1D910"X
```

See "The CALENDAR Procedure" and "SAS Global Options" in base SAS documentation for an illustration of these characters.

Graphics Options

The following options are valid only in conjunction with the GRAPHICS option:

ARROWHEAD=*number*
specifies the length of the arrowhead in character cell positions. The default value is 1.

CARCS=*color*
specifies the color to use for drawing the connecting lines between the nodes.

COMPRESS
indicates that the network is to be drawn on one physical page. This option is valid only in graphics mode. By default, the procedure draws the network, across multiple pages if necessary, using a default scale that allows one character cell position for each letter within the nodes. Sometimes, to get a broad picture of the network and all its connections, you may want to view the entire network on one screen. If the COMPRESS option is specified, PROC NETDRAW determines the scale so that the network is compressed, if necessary, to fit on one screen.

CTEXT=*color*
CT=*color*
specifies the color to use for printing text that appears on the network diagram, including variable names or labels, values of ID variables, and so on. If CTEXT= is omitted, PROC NETDRAW uses the first color in the COLORS= list of the GOPTIONS statement.

DESCRIPTION=*'string'*
DES=*'string'*
specifies a descriptive string, up to 40 characters in length, that appears in the description field of PROC GREPLAY's master menu. If DESCRIPTION= is omitted, the description field contains a description assigned by PROC NETDRAW.

FONT=*name*

specifies the font to use for printing the text on the network diagram. See SAS/GRAPH documentation for a list of fonts. Hardware characters are used by default.

LWIDTH=*width*

specifies the width to be used for drawing the connecting lines between the nodes.

NAME=*'string'*

specifies a descriptive string, up to eight characters long, that appears in the *name* field of PROC GREPLAY's master menu. If you omit the NAME= option, the *name* field of PROC GREPLAY's master menu contains the name of the procedure.

NOARROWFILL

indicates to PROC NETDRAW that the arrowheads should not be filled. By default, the procedure uses filled arrowheads.

PATTERN=*variable*

specifies an integer-valued variable in the input data set that identifies the pattern that is to be used for filling each node of the network. If the data set contains a variable called _PATTERN, this specification is ignored. The patterns are assumed to have been specified using PATTERN statements. If a PATTERN variable is not specified, the procedure uses the first PATTERN statement for non-critical activities, the second statement for critical activities, and the third statement for super-critical activities.

RECTILINEAR

indicates to PROC NETDRAW that the arcs connecting the nodes are to be drawn with rectangular corners. By default, in graphics mode, the procedure uses rounded corners for turns in the arcs, as well as when one arc merges with another.

SEPARATEARCS

separates the arcs to follow distinct tracks. By default, the procedure draws all segments of the arcs along a central track between the nodes which may cause several arcs to merge together. If the SEPARATEARCS option is specified, the procedure may increase the values of the options XBETWEEN= and YBETWEEN= to accomodate the required number of lines between the nodes.

DETAILS

Missing Values

Missing values are not allowed for the ACTIVITY and _X_, _Y_, and _SEQ_ variables. Missing values for the SUCCESSOR and ID variables are ignored.

Input Data Set

There are three typical data sets that can be used with PROC NETDRAW depending on the stage of the project when the procedure is used:

- the ACTIVITY input data set that is used with the CPM procedure. In the initial stages of project definition, it may be useful to get a graphical representation of the project showing all the activity precedence constraints.

- the SCHEDULE output data set (the OUT= data set) produced by PROC CPM. When a project is in progress, you may want to obtain a network diagram showing all the relevant start and finish dates for the activities in the project, in addition to the precedence constraints.
- the NETWORK output data set (the OUT= data set) produced by PROC NETDRAW. Often, you may want to print network diagrams of the project every week (as the project progresses) showing updated information; if the network logic has not changed, it is not necessary to determine the placement and routing of the nodes and arcs every time. You can use the output data set produced by PROC NETDRAW, which contains the positions of the nodes and arcs of the network, update the start and finish times of the activities or merge in additional information about each activity, and use the modified output data set as input to PROC NETDRAW. The new network diagram will have the same layout as the earlier diagram but may contain updated information about the activities. Such a data set may also be useful if you want to modify the layout of the network by changing the positions of some of the nodes. See **Controlling the Layout** for details on how the layout information is used by PROC NETDRAW. If the NETWORK output data set is used, it contains the variables _FROM_ and _TO_, and hence it is not necessary to specify the ACTIVITY= and SUCCESSOR= options. See **Example 7: Modifying the Network Layout**.

The minimum information that is required by PROC NETDRAW from the input data set is the variable identifying each activity in the data set and the variable (or variables) identifying the immediate successors of each activity. In addition, the procedure can use other optional variables in the data set to enhance the network diagram. The procedure uses the variables specified in the ID= option to label each node. The procedure also looks for default variable names in the input data set that are also added to the list of ID variables; the default variable names are E_START, E_FINISH, L_START, L_FINISH, S_START, S_FINISH, A_START, A_FINISH, T_FLOAT, and F_FLOAT. The format used for displaying these variables within each node is described in **Format of the Display**.

If the input data set contains the variables _X_ and _Y_ identifying the x and y coordinates of each node and each turning point of each arc in the network, then this information is used by the procedure to draw the network. Otherwise, the precedence relationships among the activities are used to determine the layout of the network. It is possible to specify only the node positions and let the procedure determine the routing of all the arcs.

Note: if arc information is provided, the procedure assumes that it is complete and correct and uses it exactly as specified.

Layout of the Network

The network layout is determined in two stages. First, the node-successor relationships are used to determine the positions of nodes and the node positions are then used to determine a routing of the arcs. The positions of the nodes and arcs are identified by specifying their x and y coordinates in an imaginary grid. **Figure 8.1** shows a sample grid and explains some of the conventions followed by PROC NETDRAW to determine the node and arc layout. This notation will be useful in later sections describing the output data set and how you can control the layout of the diagram. The asterisks in the figure represent possible positions for the nodes of the network. The arcs are routed between the possible node positions. For example, node A has coordinates ($x=1$, $y=3$) and node B has coordinates ($x=2$, $y=1$). The arc connecting them has two turning points and is completely determined by the two pairs of coordinates ($x=1.5$, $y=3$) and ($x=1.5$,

$y=1$); here, $x=1.5$ implies that the position is midway between the node positions 1 and 2.

PROC NETDRAW sets $x=1$ for all nodes with no predecessors; the x coordinates for the other nodes are determined so that each node is placed to the immediate right of all its predecessors; in other words, no node will appear to the left of any of its predecessors or to the right of any of its successors in the network diagram. The y coordinates of the nodes are determined by the procedure using several heuristics designed to produce a reasonable diagram of the network.

y coord.

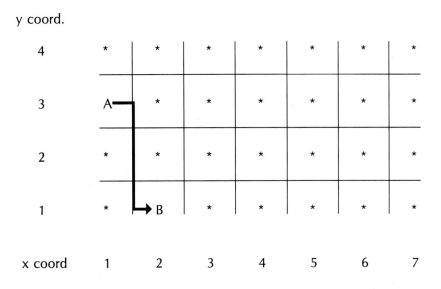

Figure 8.1 Sample Grid and Coordinates for Node and Arc Layout

Note that these coordinates fix only a relative positioning of the nodes and arcs. The actual distance between two nodes, the width and height of each node, and so on can be controlled by specifying desired values for the options that control the format of the display, namely, BOXHT=, BOXWDTH=, and so on. See the following section for details on these options.

Two options, HTRACKS= and VTRACKS=, are available in the ACTNET statement that give you some control over how the arcs are routed. The algorithm used by PROC NETDRAW tries to route the arcs between the nodes so that not too many arcs pass through any interval between two nodes. The value of HTRACKS specifies the maximum number of arcs that are allowed to pass horizontally through any point while VTRACKS specifies the same for arcs in the vertical direction. The default value for both HTRACKS and VTRACKS is the maximum number of successors for any node. See **Example 5:   Controlling the Arc-Routing Algorithm** for an illustration of the use of this option.

Format of the Display

As explained in the previous section, the layout of the network is determined by the procedure in terms of x and y coordinates on an imaginary grid. The distance between nodes and the width and height of each node is determined by the values of the format control options: XBETWEEN=, YBETWEEN=, BOXHT=, and BOXWDTH=. The amount of information that is displayed within each node is determined by the variables specified in the ID= option, the number of default variables that are found in the input data set, and whether the NOLABEL option is specified or not. **Figure 8.2** illustrates the interpretation of the format control options (each of them is assumed to be expressed as number of character positions). The asterisks (as in **Figure 8.1**) represent possible node positions.

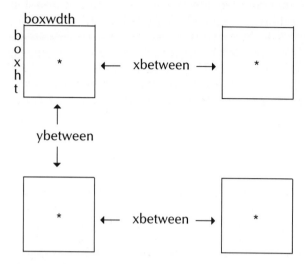

Figure 8.2   Node Positions

The values of the variables specified in the ID= option are placed within each node on separate lines. If the NOLABEL option is in effect, only the values of the variables are written; otherwise, each value is preceded by the name of the ID variable truncated to three characters. Recall from **SPECIFICATIONS** that, in addition to the variables specified in the ID= option, the procedure also prints some additional variables if the NODEFID option is not specified. These variables are printed below the variables listed in the ID option, in pre-determined relative positions within each node (see **Figure 8.3**).

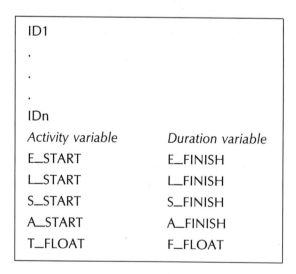

Figure 8.3   Display Format for the ID Variables

The features described above pertain to all three modes of the procedure. In addition, there are options that enable you to control the format of the display that are specific to the mode of invocation of the procedure. For line-printer or full-screen network diagrams, the FORMCHAR= option enables you to specify special boxing characters that enhance the display. For graphics quality network diagrams, you can control the color and pattern used for each node separately by specifying a different pattern number for the variable specified in the PATTERN= option in the ACTNET statement (for details see **Graphics Version**).

By default, all arcs are drawn along the center line between two consecutive nodes. The SEPARATEARCS option, which is available in the graphics version, instructs PROC NETDRAW to draw arcs along separate lines.

If the network fits on one page, it is centered on the page; otherwise, it is split onto different pages appropriately, and each page is drawn starting at the bottom left corner.

Output Data Set

The output data set produced by PROC NETDRAW contains all the information that would be required to draw the network diagram for the given input data. In other words, the output data set contains the node-successor information, all the ID variables that were used in the current invocation of the procedure, as well as variables that contain the coordinate information for all the nodes and the arcs connecting the nodes. The node-successor information used by the procedure is saved in two new variables named _FROM_ and _TO_. This pair of variables contains the values (node, successor) for each pair (activity, immediate successor) specified in the input data set. For each such pair, a sequence of observations is saved in the output data set; the number of observations is equal to one plus the number of turns in the arc connecting the activity to its successor. Suppose that an activity A has two successors, B and C, and the arc connecting A and B is routed as per **Figure 8.1**. **Table 8.1** illustrates the format of the observations corresponding to the two (_FROM_, _TO_) pairs of activities.

Table 8.1   Sample Observations in Output Data Set

FROM	_TO_	_X_	_Y_	_SEQ_	_PATTERN	ID variables
A	B	1	3	0	1	
A	B	1.5	3	1	.	
A	B	1.5	1	2	.	
A	C	1	3	0	1	
		.			.	
		.			.	
		.			.	

For every (node, successor) pair, the first observation (_SEQ_=0) gives the coordinates of the node; the succeeding observations contain the coordinates of the turning points of the arc connecting the node to the successor. The data set also contains a variable called _PATTERN which contains the pattern number that is used for coloring the node identified by the _FROM_ variable. This variable is missing for observations with _SEQ_>0.

Full-screen Version

You can invoke PROC NETDRAW in full-screen mode by specifying FS (or FULL-SCREEN) in the PROC NETDRAW statement. The statement specifications are the same as for the line-printer mode. The full-screen mode offers you a convenient way to browse the network diagram of the project and change the layout of the network by moving the nodes of the network to desired locations. However, you cannot move a node to any position that will violate the precedence constraints that must be satisfied by the node. In other words, you cannot move a node to the left of any of its predecessors or to the right of any of its successors.

The format control options are treated in the same way as for the line-printer version, with some minor changes. It is assumed that the main purpose of invoking the procedure is to gain a general picture of the layout of the entire network and to modify it to some extent. In an effort to display as much of the connections of the network as possible, the initial display on the screen is drawn with only one row and three columns for each node. In other words, the BOXHT=, BOXWDTH=, XBETWEEN=, and YBETWEEN= options are ignored by the procedure in drawing the initial display. However, the full-screen commands supported by PROC NETDRAW enable you to change the scale of the diagram. You can display as much or as little information within each node by invoking the SCALE ROW or the SCALE COL command or both. The SCALE MAX command causes the procedure to display the diagram using the values specified in the PROC statement or the dimensions that would be required to display all the ID information, whichever is larger. The SCALE RESET command returns the scaling to the initial values used for display.

The nodes of the network are color coded depending on whether the activities are normal, critical, or super-critical. The nodes are drawn in reverse-video. By default, the nodes are drawn without an outline; however, there is an OUTLINE command that lets you toggle back and forth between an outlined or non-outlined node. Using an outline for the node is useful if you want to obtain a print of the screen using SPRINT; it helps mark the boundary of each node clearly.

Commands

Table 8.2 lists the commands that can be used from the command line in the full-screen version of PROC NETDRAW.

Table 8.2 Full-screen Commands and Their Purpose

Scrolling	Controlling Display	Changing the Network Layout	Exiting
BACKWARD	OUTLINE	CLEAR	GEND
FORWARD	SCALE	MOVE	END
LEFT			CANCEL
RIGHT			
TOP			
BOTTOM			
VSCROLL			
HSCROLL			

These full-screen commands are explained in greater detail below:

BACKWARD   scrolls toward the top of the network by the VSCROLL amount. BACKWARD MAX scrolls to the top of the network. You can specify the vertical scroll amount for the current command as BACKWARD PAGE | HALF | n.

BOTTOM   scrolls to the bottom of the network.

CANCEL   ends the current invocation of the procedure.

CLEAR   clears any outstanding move commands.

GEND   ends the current invocation of the procedure after drawing the network in graphics mode with the compress option.

END   ends the current invocation of the procedure.

FORWARD   scrolls toward the bottom of the network by the VSCROLL amount. FORWARD MAX scrolls to the bottom of the network. You can also specify the vertical scroll amount for the current command as FORWARD PAGE | HALF | n.

HELP   displays the help screen.

HOME   moves the cursor to the command line.

HSCROLL   sets the amount that information scrolls horizontally when you execute the LEFT or RIGHT command. The format is HSCROLL PAGE | HALF | n. The specification is assumed to be in number of horizontal levels. HSCROLL PAGE sets the scroll amount to be the number of horizontal levels that fit on one screen; HSCROLL HALF is half that amount; HSCROLL n sets the horizontal scroll amount to n levels.

KEYS   displays current function key settings.

LEFT   scrolls toward the left boundary of the network by the HSCROLL amount. LEFT MAX scrolls to the left boundary. You can specify the horizontal scroll amount for the current command as LEFT PAGE | HALF | n.

MOVE   specifies a node to be moved or a place to move a node to. You can specify these in any order. Thus, you can first position the cursor on the node that you want to move, issue the MOVE command, and then position the cursor at a target position and issue the MOVE command again. If the target position is valid, the node is moved. You can also first specify the target position and then indicate the node that is to be moved.

OUTLINE   causes an outline to be drawn around each node in the network. This is useful if you want to print a copy of the screen by using the SPRINT command. The OUTLINE command works like an on/off switch: you can turn it off by entering the command again.

RIGHT   scrolls toward the right boundary of the network by the HSCROLL amount. RIGHT MAX scrolls to the right boundary. You can also specify the horizontal scroll amount for the current command as RIGHT PAGE | HALF | n.

SCALE   controls the scaling of the nodes and space between nodes. The format is SCALE MAX | MIN | RESET | ROW MAX | COL MAX | ROW MIN | COL MIN | ROW n | COL n. The number n denotes the number of character positions. SCALE MIN displays as many nodes on the screen as can fit. SCALE MAX allows as many rows and columns per node as is required to display all the information that pertains to it. SCALE ROW MAX displays the maximum number of rows per node. SCALE COL MAX displays the maximum number of columns per node. SCALE ROW n sets the number of rows per node to n. SCALE COL n sets the number of columns per node to n. SCALE RESET sets the values to be the same as for the initial display. Note that none of these values can be greater than the dimensions of the screen.

TOP   scrolls to the top of the network.

VSCROLL   sets the amount that information scrolls vertically when you execute the BACKWARD or FORWARD command. The format is VSCROLL PAGE | HALF | n. The specification is assumed to be in number of vertical levels. VSCROLL PAGE sets the scroll amount to be the number of vertical levels that fit on one screen; VSCROLL HALF is half that amount; VSCROLL n sets the vertical scroll amount to n levels.

Full-screen Global Commands

Most of the global commands used in SAS/FSP software are also valid with PROC NETDRAW. These commands are described in greater detail in Appendix 2, "Command Reference," in the SAS/FSP User's Guide, Release 6.03 Edition. Some of the commands used for printing screens are described in this section.

SAS/FSP software provides a set of printing commands that enable you to take pictures of windows and to route those pictures to a printer or a file. Whether you choose to route these items directly to a printer queue or to a print file, SAS/FSP software provides you with a means of supplying printing instructions. The following is an overview of these related commands and their functions:

FREE
    releases items in print queue to a printer.

PRTFILE
    specifies file destination for printed items.

SPRINT
    takes a picture of a window.

FREE
    releases all items in the print queue to the printer. This includes pictures taken with the SPRINT command as well as items sent to the print queue with the SEND command. All items in the print queue are also automatically sent to the printer when you exit the procedure, send an item that uses a different form, or send an item to a print file. Items are also sent automatically when internal buffers have been filled.

    If you have routed pictures taken with the SPRINT command to a file rather than to a printer, the file is closed when you execute a FREE command. It is also closed when you send an item that uses a different form, send items to a different print file or to the print queue, or exit the procedure.

Note: any items sent to the same print file after it has been closed will replace the current contents.

PRTFILE [*fileref* | '*actualfilename*' | CLEAR]

specifies a file to which the procedure sends letters or pictures taken with the SPRINT command instead of sending them to the default printer. You can specify a previously assigned fileref or an actual file name.

Specify PRTFILE CLEAR to prompt the procedure to route information once again to the queue for the default printer.

Specify PRTFILE to prompt the procedure to identify the current print file.

SPRINT [NOBORDER] [NOCMD]

takes a picture of the current window exactly as you see it, including window contents, border, and command line. By default, the picture is sent to the queue for the default printer.

By default, both the window border and command line are included in the picture you take with the SPRINT command. You can capture a picture of the window contents that excludes either the window border, the command line, or both. Specify NOBORDER to exclude the border and NOCMD to exclude the command line. Taking a picture of the window contents without the border and command line is a convenient way to print text for a report.

The destination of the picture captured with the SPRINT command is determined by the PRTFILE command. By default, the picture goes to the default printer. Use the PRTFILE command if you want it sent to a file instead. Each time you execute the SPRINT command, the picture you take is appended to the current print file; it does not write over the current file. See the PRTFILE command for further explanation.

Graphics Version

Several options are available in the ACTNET statement to enhance the appearance of the network diagram in graphics mode. These are described in **Graphics Options** in the **SPECIFICATIONS** section. The format control options are also valid in this mode and can be used to control the width and height of each node and the distance between the nodes. These parameters are assumed to denote number of character cell positions. The number of positions available on one page depends on the graphics device that is used; thus, if a plotter is used with large paper, more of the network will be drawn on a single page. Further, you can control the number of character cell positions on a page by changing the values of the global graphics parameters (HPOS and VPOS). Thus, you have a wide degree of control over the amount of information printed on each page of the network diagram.

Another option that is available in Graphics mode to control the appearance of your network diagrams is the specification of a PATTERN variable in the ACTNET statement. If the variable is named _PATTERN, you do not need to use the PATTERN= option; the procedure looks for such a variable by default. You can use this variable to specify the number of the PATTERN statement that is to be used for filling each node of the network. The patterns that can be used with PROC NETDRAW are any of the patterns that can be used for drawing bars (not ones that are used for drawing maps). See SAS/GRAPH documentation for a detailed discussion of PATTERN statements. For a brief description of the

PATTERN statement, see Chapter 6, "The GANTT Procedure." If a PATTERN variable is not specified, the procedure uses the values of the E_FINISH and L_FINISH variables (if these variables exist in the input data set) to determine if activities in the project are normal, critical, or super-critical. The procedure then uses the first PATTERN statement to fill the nodes corresponding to non-critical activities, the second PATTERN statement for nodes corresponding to critical activities, and the third PATTERN statement for nodes corresponding to super-critical activities.

Page Format

As explained in **Format of the Display**, if the network fits on one page, it is centered on the page; otherwise, it is split onto different pages appropriately, and each page is drawn starting at the bottom left corner. If the network is drawn on multiple pages, the procedure numbers each page of the diagram on the top right corner of the page. The pages are numbered starting with the bottom left corner of the entire picture. Thus, if the network diagram is broken into three horizontal and three vertical levels and you want to paste all the pieces together to form one picture, they should be glued in the following manner:

7	8	9
4	5	6
1	2	3

Controlling the Layout

As explained in **Layout of the Network**, the procedure uses the precedence constraints between the activities to draw a reasonable diagram of the network. A very desirable feature in any procedure of this nature is the ability to change the default layout. PROC NETDRAW provides two ways of modifying the network diagram:

- via the full-screen interface
- via the input data set.

The full-screen method is useful for manipulating the layout of small networks, especially networks that fit on a handful of screens. You can use the full-screen mode to examine the default layout of the network and move the nodes to desired locations, using the MOVE command from the command line or by using the appropriate function key. When a node is moved, the procedure reroutes all the arcs that connect to or from the node; other arcs are unchanged.

You can use the input data set to modify or specify completely the layout of the network. This method is useful if you want to draw the network using information about the network layout that has been saved from an earlier invocation of the procedure. Sometimes you may want to specify only the positions of the node and let the procedure determine the routing of the arcs. The procedure looks for three default variables in the data set: _X_, _Y_, and _SEQ_. The _X_ and _Y_ variables are assumed to denote the x and y coordinates of the nodes and all the turning points of the arcs connecting the nodes. The variable _SEQ_ is assumed to denote the order of the turning points. This interpretation is consistent with the values assigned to the _X_, _Y_, and _SEQ_ variables in the output data set produced by PROC NETDRAW. If there is no variable called _SEQ_ in the data set, the procedure assumes that only the node positions are specified and uses the specified coordinates to place the nodes and determines the routing of the arcs corresponding to these positions. If there is a variable called _SEQ_, the procedure requires that the turning points for each arc be specified in the proper order, with the variable _SEQ_ containing numbers sequentially starting with one and continuing onward.

Macro Variable _ORNETDR

The NETDRAW procedure defines a macro variable named _ORNETDR. This variable contains a character string that indicates the status of the procedure. It is set at procedure termination. The form of the _ORNETDR character string is STATUS=xxx REASON=yyy, where STATUS is either SUCCESSFUL or ERROR_EXIT and REASON (if PROC NETDRAW terminated unsuccessfully) can be one of the following:

- CYCLE
- BADDATA_ERROR
- MEMORY_ERROR
- IO_ERROR
- SEMANTIC_ERROR
- SYNTAX_ERROR
- NETDRAW_BUG
- UNKNOWN_ERROR.

This information can be used when PROC NETDRAW is one step in a larger program that needs to determine whether the procedure terminated successfully or not. Because _ORNETDR is a standard SAS macro variable, it can be used in the ways that all macro variables can be used. See the *SAS Guide to Macro Processing, Version 6 Edition* for more details.

EXAMPLES

This section contains eight examples that illustrate several of the features of PROC NETDRAW. In the graphics examples that follow, the color *white* used in the code has been reversed to black in the example output. **Table 8.3** lists the features of these examples.

Table 8.3   Examples Used to Illustrate Features of PROC NETDRAW

Example	Illustrates use of
Example 1	PROC NETDRAW in line-printer format
Example 2	PROC NETDRAW in full-screen format
Example 3	PROC NETDRAW in graphics format

(continued)

Table 8.3   *(continued)*

Example	Illustrates use of
Example 4	the ID= and BOXWDTH= options to control format
Example 5	the HTRACKS= option to control routing of the arcs
Example 6	the PATTERN= option to control node color
Example 7	the output data set produced by PROC NETDRAW to change the node coordinates
Example 8	an input data set to specify node coordinates and subsequent modification of the arc coordinates

Example 1: Printing a Network Diagram

This example illustrates the use of PROC NETDRAW to obtain a line-printer network diagram of the construction project used extensively in the examples in Chapter 5, "The CPM Procedure." The data set EXMP1 (as in Chapter 5) contains the project information. The following program contains two invocations of PROC NETDRAW, one before and one after using PROC CPM to determine the schedule of the project. In the second call to PROC NETDRAW, the duration variable used by PROC CPM is also specified (using the DUR= option) so that the network diagram contains all the information about the project and its schedule. These diagrams use the default values for the FORMCHAR option. You may want to specify FORMCHAR(1 2 3 4 5 6 7 8 9 10 11 19)= "B3C4DAC2BFC3C5B4C0C1D910"X on an IBM PC.

```
data exmp1;
   input task          $ 1-16
      duration
      succesr1 $ 21-35
      succesr2 $ 36-50
      succesr3 $ 51-65;
   cards;
Drill Well          4   Pump House
Pump House          3   Install Pipe
Power Line          3   Install Pipe
Excavate            5   Install Pipe    Install Pump    Foundation
Deliver Material    2   Assemble Tank
Assemble Tank       4   Erect Tower
Foundation          4   Erect Tower
Install Pump        6
Install Pipe        2
Erect Tower         6
;

title 'Construction Project';
proc netdraw data=exmp1;
   actnet / act = task
            succ = (succesr1-succesr3);
run;

proc cpm data=exmp1 date='1jul88'd out=sched;
   activity task;
   duration duration;
   successor succesr1 succesr2 succesr3;
run;
```

```
title2 'Schedule Information';
proc netdraw data=sched;
   actnet / act = task
            dur = duration
            succ = (succesr1-succesr3);
run;
```

Output 8.1   Printing a Network Diagram

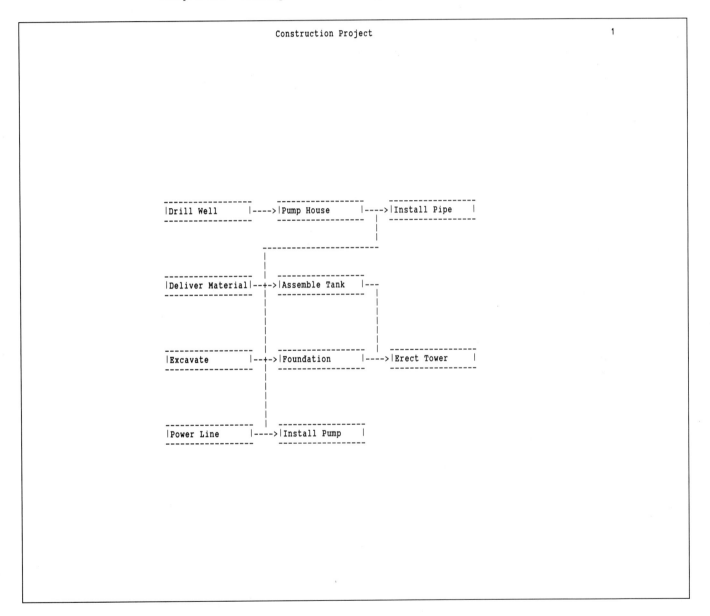

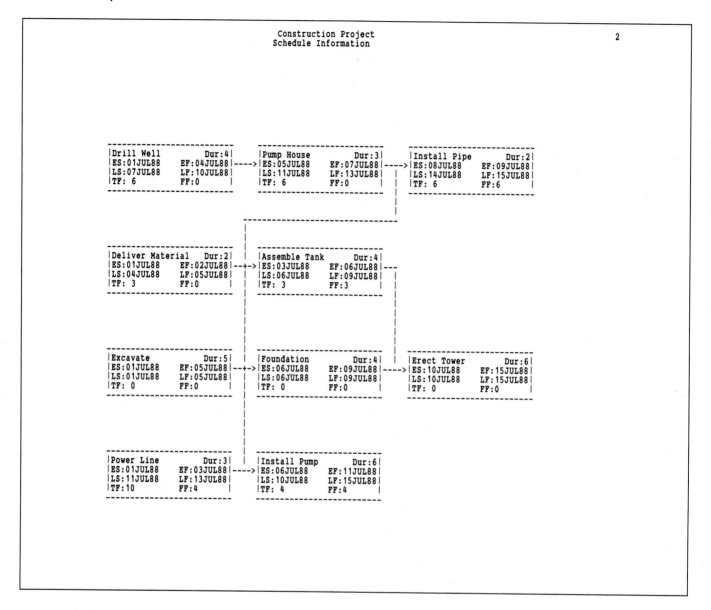

Example 2:   Full-screen Interface

This example illustrates some of the features of the full-screen version of PROC
NETDRAW. The output data set, SCHED, produced by PROC CPM in the previous example, is used again as the input data set for PROC NETDRAW. The procedure is invoked with the FULLSCREEN option, and the FORMCHAR option is
used to specify special characters to be used for drawing the arcs and the arrows.
The initial screen is shown in **Screen 8.1.** The rest of this example shows the
screens produced by issuing various commands in full-screen mode. Each screen
is captioned appropriately.

```
proc netdraw data=sched fullscreen;
   actnet / act = task
           dur = duration
           succ = (succesr1-succesr3)
           formchar(1 2 3 4 5 6 7 8 9 10 11 19)
               = "b3c4dac2bfc3c5b4c0c1d910"x ;
run;
```

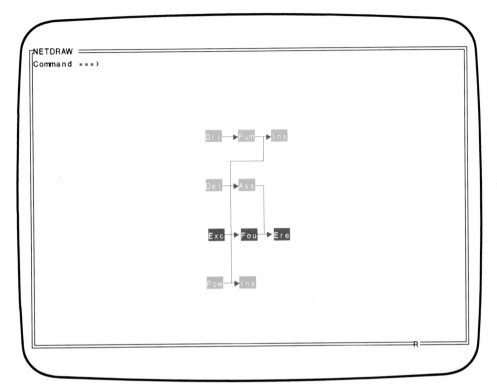

Screen 8.1   Initial Screen

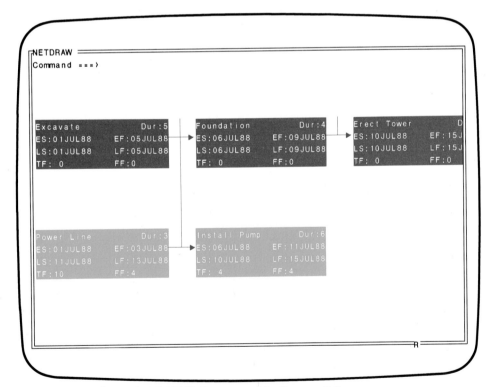

Screen 8.2   After **SCALE MAX** Command in **Screen 8.1**.

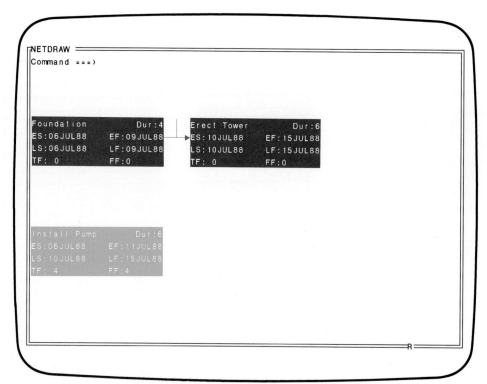

Screen 8.3   After **RIGHT MAX** Command in **Screen 8.2**.

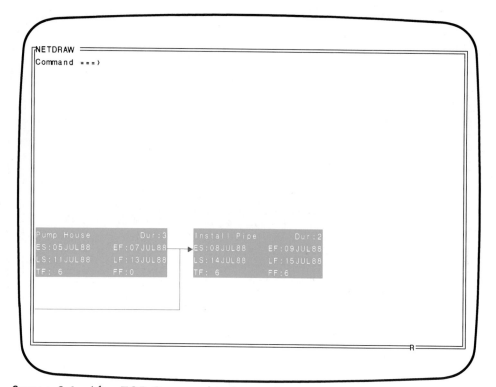

Screen 8.4   After **TOP** Command in **Screen 8.3**.

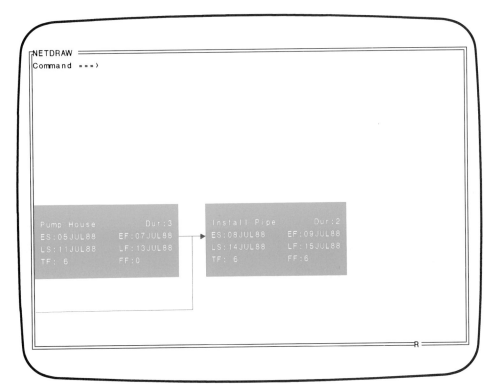

Screen 8.5   After **OUTLINE**; TOP Command in **Screen 8.4**.

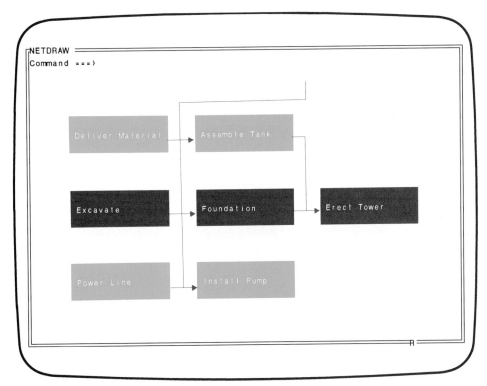

Screen 8.6   After **SCALE COL 16; SCALE ROW 1; BOTTOM** Commands in
Screen 8.5.

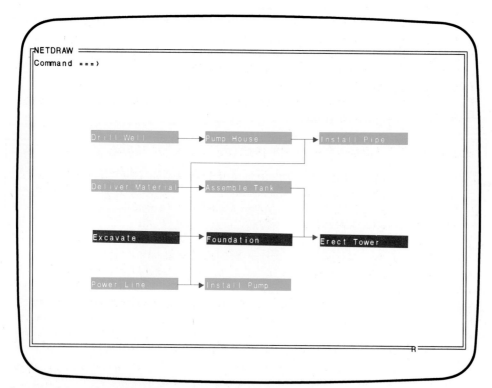

Screen 8.7 After **OUTLINE** Command in **Screen 8.6**.

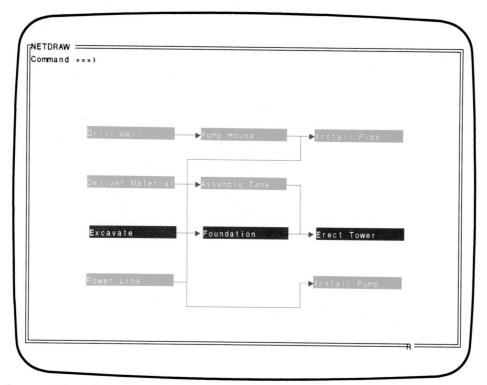

Screen 8.8 After Moving Activity INSTALL PUMP

The last screen is obtained from **Screen 8.7** by issuing a sequence of two commands. First, place the cursor anywhere in the box for the activity that you want to move and issue the MOVE command. (Moving nodes is accomplished more easily by using a function key defined to be MOVE than by writing on the command line.) Then, move the cursor to the desired location for the activity (under ERECT TOWER) and issue the MOVE command again. The procedure responds by moving the node to the specified location and rerouting any arc connected to it. The result is **Screen 8.8**.

Example 3:   Graphics Version of PROC NETDRAW

The same network used in **Example 1** and **Example 2** is drawn here with the GRAPHICS option. As in **Example 1**, the network is first drawn before scheduling with PROC CPM (**Output 8.2**). Note that all the nodes are drawn in the same color as specified by the first PATTERN statement; the color of the arcs is specified by the CARCS = CYAN option. When the SCHEDULE data set produced by PROC CPM is used to draw the network, the activities are colored red or green, depending on whether they are critical or normal, respectively (**Output 8.3**). The procedure uses the values of the E_START and L_START variables to determine if an activity is critical. The first PATTERN statement is used for nodes corresponding to non-critical activities and the second statement is used for critical activities. In the second invocation, the SEPARATEARCS option is used so that the two parallel arcs leading into the activity INSTALL PIPE (one from POWER LINE and the other from EXCAVATE) are drawn along separate tracks instead of along a single track. The COMPRESS option is also used in this case to enable the network to be drawn on a single page.

```
pattern1 c=green v=e;
pattern2 c=red   v=e;

goptions hpos=80 vpos=43;   /* These are the default values for the
                               EGA device driver */

title c=white f=swiss 'Construction Project';
proc netdraw data=exmp1 graphics;
   actnet / act = task font=simplex
            succ = (succesr1-succesr3)
            ctext=white carcs=cyan;
run;

title2 c=white f=swiss 'Schedule Information';
proc netdraw data=sched graphics;
   actnet / act = task font=simplex
            dur = duration
            succ = (succesr1-succesr3)
            compress separatearcs
            ctext=white carcs=cyan;
run;
```

Output 8.2   A Network Diagram of the Construction Project

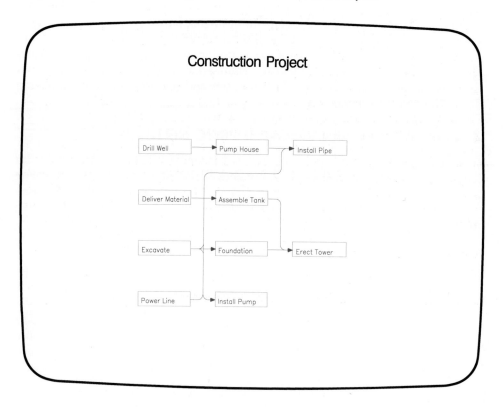

Output 8.3   Schedule Information for the Construction Project

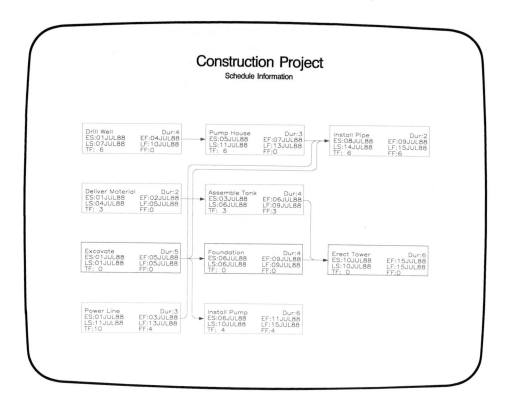

Example 4:   Controlling the Format of the Display

This example uses the data from **Example 1** of Chapter 6, "The GANTT Procedure," and illustrates how you can control the format of the display. PROC
NETDRAW is invoked using the SCHEDULE data set generated by
PROC CPM, so that the activities are color coded according to whether or not
they are critical. Suppose that you do not want to display any of the schedule
information. This example uses the ID= option to control the amount and format
of the information that is displayed within each node. Here, only the activity
name and duration are printed within each node. The NOLABEL option is used
to suppress the printing of the variable names within each node, and the
NODEFAULTID option is used to suppress the printing of any of the default variables that are present in the data set. Even so, the network is too large to fit on
one page and spans multiple pages. The number of pages required to draw the
entire network depends on the values of the global graphics options HPOS and
VPOS. Thus, on a device that has a higher resolution, you can increase the values
of HPOS and VPOS to enable more of the network to be drawn on one page.
The BOXWDTH= option is set to 10, causing some of the activity names to be
truncated. The diagram for this project is shown in **Output 8.4**.

```
data ex  ;
    format activity $20. success1 $20. success2 $20. success3 $20.
                    success4 $20.;
    input activity dur success1-success4;
    cards;
form                 4 pour . . .
pour                 2 core . . .
core                14 strip spray_fireproof insulate_walls .
strip                2 plumbing curtain_wall risers doors
strip                2 electrical_walls balance_elevator . .
curtain_wall         5 glaze_sash . . .
glaze_sash           5 spray_fireproof insulate_walls . .
spray_fireproof      5 ceil_ducts_fixture . . .
ceil_ducts_fixture   5 test . . .
plumbing            10 test . . .
test                 3 insulate_mechanical . . .
insulate_mechanical  3 lath . . .
insulate_walls       5 lath . . .
risers              10 ceil_ducts_fixture . . .
doors                1 port_masonry . . .
port_masonry         2 lath finish_masonry . .
electrical_walls    16 lath . . .
balance_elevator     3 finish_masonry . . .
finish_masonry       3 plaster marble_work . .
lath                 3 plaster marble_work . .
plaster              5 floor_finish tiling acoustic_tiles .
marble_work          3 acoustic_tiles . . .
acoustic_tiles       5 paint finish_mechanical . .
tiling               3 paint finish_mechanical . .
floor_finish         5 paint finish_mechanical . .
paint                5 finish_paint . . .
finish_mechanical    5 finish_paint . . .
finish_paint         2 caulking_cleanup . . .
caulking_cleanup     4 finished . . .
finished             0 . . . .
;
```

```
proc cpm finishbefore date='1sep85'd out=sched4;
   activity activity;
   duration dur;
   successors success1-success4;
run;
proc sort; by e_start;
run;

title c=white f=swiss 'Multi-Story Construction';
title2 c=white f=swiss 'Controlling Display Format';

goptions hpos=120 vpos=80;
pattern1 c=green v=e;
pattern2 c=red    v=e;

proc netdraw data=sched4 graphics;
   actnet / act = activity
            succ = (success1-success4)
            id = ( activity dur )
            nolabel nodefaultid
            boxwdth = 10
            ctext=white font=simplexu
            separatearcs;
run;
```

Output 8.4   Network Diagram Spanning Multiple Pages

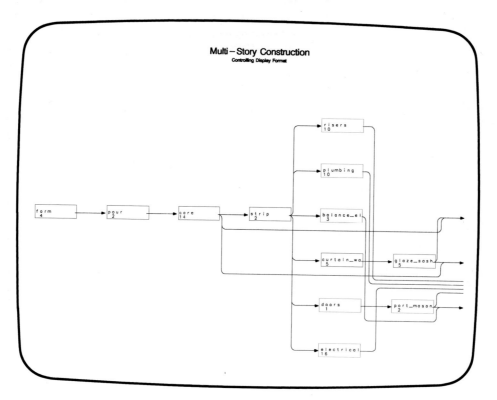

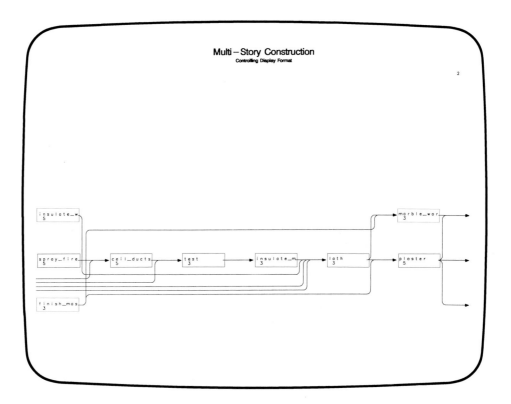

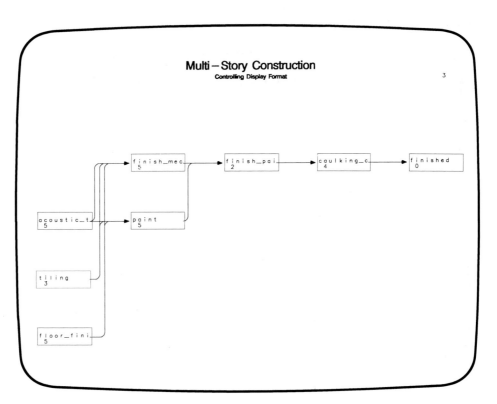

Example 5:   Controlling the Arc-Routing Algorithm

This example illustrates the use of the HTRACKS= option to control the routing of the arcs connecting the nodes. As explained in **Layout of the Network**, the NETDRAW procedure tries to route the arcs between the nodes so that too many arcs do not pass through any interval between two nodes. The default limit on the number of tracks used by the procedure is equal to the maximum number of successors for any node. For the construction project in **Example 3**, this limit is 3. A different routing of the arcs can be obtained by changing the HTRACKS= or VTRACKS= option or both. In this example, PROC NETDRAW is invoked after scheduling the project using PROC CPM, as in **Example 3**, with one change: HTRACKS is set to 1. The resulting network diagram is shown in **Output 8.5**.

```
pattern1 c=green v=e;
pattern2 c=red   v=e;


goptions hpos=80 vpos=43;  /* These are the default values for the
                              EGA device driver */


title c=white f=swiss 'Construction Project';
title2 c=white f=swiss 'Controlling the Network Layout';
proc netdraw data=sched graphics;
   actnet / act = task
            dur = duration
            succ = (succesr1-succesr3)
            compress separatearcs font=simplex
            ctext=white carcs=cyan
            htracks=1;
run;
```

Output 8.5   Controlling the Routing of the Arcs

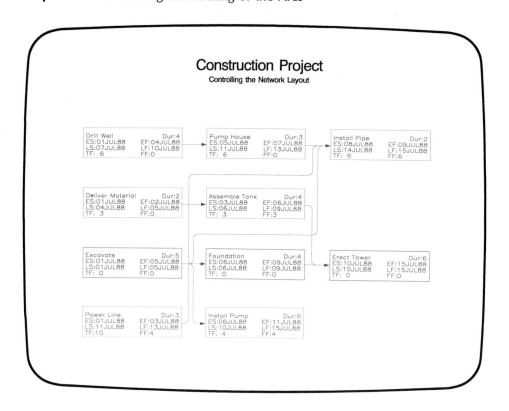

Example 6:   Drawing a Schematic Diagram with PROC NETDRAW

As mentioned in the **INTRODUCTION**, you can use PROC NETDRAW to draw any acyclic network depicting a set of nodes connected by arcs. In this example, a schematic representation of the data flow going in and out of the three procedures (CPM, GANTT, and NETDRAW) is drawn using PROC NETDRAW. (See Chapter 2, "Introduction to Project Management," for a detailed discussion of such a data flow.) The PATTERN= option is used to specify the variable in the data set that identifies the color that is to be used for each node. Nodes representing SAS/OR procedures are colored red, the ones representing output data sets are colored green, and all other nodes (representing the use of other parts of the SAS System) are colored cyan. Three ID variables are used to specify the text that is to be placed within each node. The flow diagram is shown in **Output 8.6**.

```
data dataflow;
input a $ b $ id1 $20. id2 $20. id3 $20. style;
cards;
A B Data Definition:   PROC FSEDIT,      SAS/AF, etc.        2
B C Data Manipulation: Sort, Merge,      Concatenate, etc.   2
B D Data Manipulation: Sort, Merge,      Concatenate, etc.   2
D C                    PROC NETDRAW                          1
C E                    PROC CPM                              1
C F                    PROC CPM                              1
E H                    Resource Usage    Data                3
F G                    Schedule Data                         3
G I Data Manipulation: Sort, Merge,      Subset, etc.        2
G J Data Manipulation: Sort, Merge,      Subset, etc.        2
H K Data Manipulation: Sort, Merge,      Subset, etc.        2
I . Other Reporting    PROC's: PRINT,    CALENDAR, etc.      2
J .                    PROC GANTT        PROC NETDRAW        1
K . Reporting PROC's:  PLOT, CHART,      GPLOT, GCHART, etc. 2
;


title c=white f=swiss 'Data Flow';
title2 c=white f=swiss 'A Typical Project Management System';

pattern1 v=e c=red;
pattern2 v=e c=cyan;
pattern3 v=e c=green;

proc netdraw data=dataflow graphics;
   actnet / act=a succ=b id = (id1-id3)
            nolabel pattern=style
            nodefaultid font=simplex
            ctext=white carcs=cyan
            compress;
   run;
```

Output 8.6   Schematic Representation of Data Flow

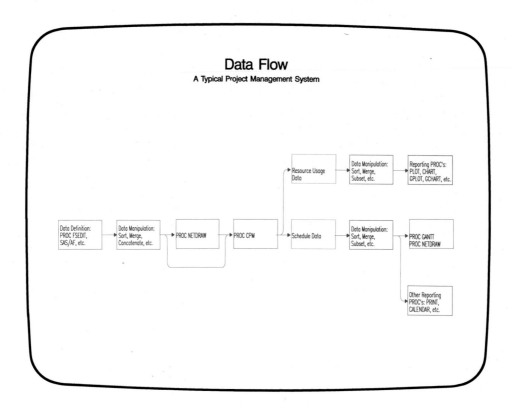

Example 7:   Modifying the Network Layout

This example uses the SURVEY project described in Chapter 2, "Introduction to Project Management," to illustrate how you can modify the default layout of the network. The data set SURVEY contains the project information. PROC NETDRAW is invoked with the graphics option (as in Chapter 2). The network diagram is shown in **Output 8.7**. The output data set produced by PROC NETDRAW (printed in **Output 8.8**) contains the x and y coordinates for all the nodes in the network and for all the turning points of the arcs connecting them.

Suppose that you want to interchange the positions of the nodes corresponding to the two activities, SELECT H and TRN PER. As explained in **Controlling the Layout**, you can invoke the procedure in FULLSCREEN mode and use the MOVE command to move the nodes to desired locations. In this example, the output data set NETWORK produced by PROC NETDRAW is used to change the x and y coordinates of the nodes. A new data set called NODEPOS is created from NETWORK by retaining only the observations containing node positions (recall that for such observations, _SEQ_=0). Further, the _Y_ coordinates for the two activities SELECT H and TRN PER are set to the desired values. The new data set, also printed in **Output 8.8**, is then input to PROC NETDRAW. Note that this data set contains variables named _FROM_ and _TO_, which specify the (node, successor) information; hence, the call to PROC NETDRAW does not contain the ACTIVITY= and SUCCESSOR= specifications. The presence of the variables _X_ and _Y_ indicates to PROC NETDRAW that the data set contains the x and y coordinates for all the nodes. Because there is no variable named _SEQ_ in this data set, PROC NETDRAW assumes that only the node coordinates are given, and uses these node positions to determine how the arcs are to be routed. The resulting network diagram is shown in **Output 8.9**.

```
data survey;
   input id         $ 1-20
         activity   $ 24-31
         duration
         succ1      $ 40-47
         succ2      $ 50-57
         succ3      $ 60-67
         phase      $ 70-78;
   cards;
Plan Survey             plan sur    4    hire per  design q              Plan
Hire Personnel          hire per    5    trn per                         Prepare
Design Questionnaire    design q    3    trn per   select h  print q     Plan
Train Personnel         trn per     3    cond sur                        Prepare
Select Households       select h    3    cond sur                        Prepare
Print Questionnaire     print q     4    cond sur                        Prepare
Conduct Survey          cond sur    10   analyze                         Implement
Analyze Results         analyze     6                                    Implement
;

    title c=white f=swiss 'Conducting a Market Survey';
    title2 c=white f=swiss 'Default Layout';
    pattern1 v=e c=green;

    proc netdraw data=survey graphics out=network;
       actnet / act=activity
               succ=(succ1-succ3)
               id=(id) nodefid nolabel
               carcs=cyan ctext=white font=simplex
               compress;
       run;

    title2 'NETWORK Output Data Set';
    proc print data=network;
       run;

    title2 c=white f=swiss 'Modified Network Layout';
    proc netdraw data=nodepos graphics;
       actnet / id=(id) nodefid nolabel
               carcs=cyan ctext=white font=simplex
               compress;
       run;
```

Output 8.7   Default Network Layout of SURVEY Project

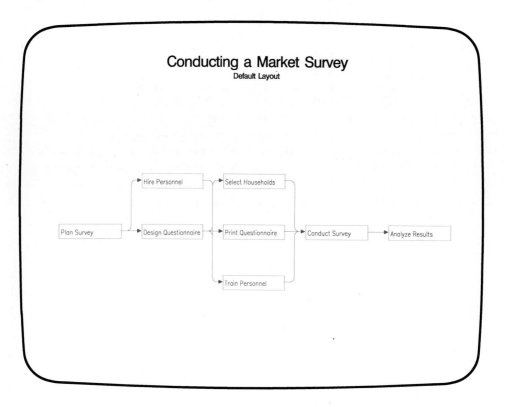

Output 8.8   NETWORK Output Data Set and Modified Node Positions

```
                              Conducting a Market Survey                                    1
                              NETWORK Output Data Set

        OBS    _FROM_     _TO_     _X_    _Y_    _SEQ_    _PATTERN    ID

         1    plan sur   hire per   1.0    2      0         1       Plan Survey
         2    plan sur   hire per   1.5    2      1         .       Plan Survey
         3    plan sur   hire per   1.5    3      2         .       Plan Survey
         4    plan sur   design q   1.0    2      0         1       Plan Survey
         5    hire per   trn per    2.0    3      0         1       Hire Personnel
         6    hire per   trn per    2.5    3      1         .       Hire Personnel
         7    hire per   trn per    2.5    1      2         .       Hire Personnel
         8    design q   trn per    2.0    2      0         1       Design Questionnaire
         9    design q   trn per    2.5    2      1         .       Design Questionnaire
        10    design q   trn per    2.5    1      2         .       Design Questionnaire
        11    design q   select h   2.0    2      0         1       Design Questionnaire
        12    design q   select h   2.5    2      1         .       Design Questionnaire
        13    design q   select h   2.5    3      2         .       Design Questionnaire
        14    design q   print q    2.0    2      0         1       Design Questionnaire
        15    trn per    cond sur   3.0    1      0         1       Train Personnel
        16    trn per    cond sur   3.5    1      1         .       Train Personnel
        17    trn per    cond sur   3.5    2      2         .       Train Personnel
        18    select h   cond sur   3.0    3      0         1       Select Households
        19    select h   cond sur   3.5    3      1         .       Select Households
        20    select h   cond sur   3.5    2      2         .       Select Households
        21    print q    cond sur   3.0    2      0         1       Print Questionnaire
        22    cond sur   analyze    4.0    2      0         1       Conduct Survey
        23    analyze               5.0    2      0         1       Analyze Results
```

```
                        Conducting a Market Survey                           2
                        Modified Node Positions

OBS      _FROM_      _TO_       _X_    _Y_    _PATTERN_   ID

  1      plan sur    hire per     1      2        1      Plan Survey
  2      plan sur    design q     1      2        1      Plan Survey
  3      hire per    trn per      2      3        1      Hire Personnel
  4      design q    trn per      2      2        1      Design Questionnaire
  5      design q    select h     2      2        1      Design Questionnaire
  6      design q    print q      2      2        1      Design Questionnaire
  7      trn per     cond sur     3      3        1      Train Personnel
  8      select h    cond sur     3      1        1      Select Households
  9      print q     cond sur     3      2        1      Print Questionnaire
 10      cond sur    analyze      4      2        1      Conduct Survey
 11      analyze                  5      2        1      Analyze Results
```

Output 8.9   Modified Network Layout of SURVEY Project

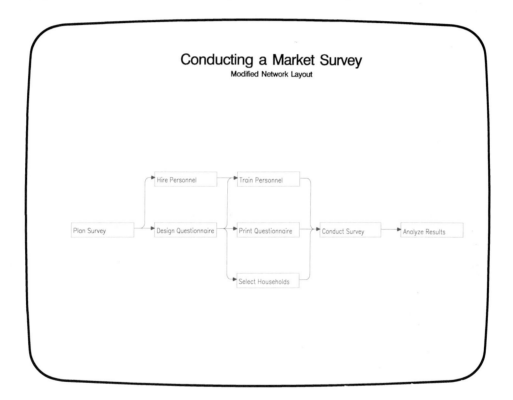

Example 8:   A Distribution Network

This example uses a typical problem in network flow optimization to illustrate how you can use PROC NETDRAW to draw a network by completely specifying all the node positions. Consider a simple two-period production inventory problem with one manufacturing plant (PLANT), two warehouses (DEPOT1 and DEPOT2) and one customer (CUST). In each period, the customer can receive goods directly from the plant or from the two warehouses. The goods produced at the plant can be used to directly satisfy some or all of the customer's demands or shipped to the warehouse. Some of the goods can also be carried over to the next period as inventory at the plant. The problem is to determine how much of the customer's demands in each period is to be satisfied from the inventory at the two warehouses or from the plant and also how much of the production is to be caried over as inventory at the plant. This problem can be solved using PROC NETFLOW; the details are not discussed here. Let PLANT_i represent the production at the plant in period i, DEPOT1_i represent the inventory at DEPOT1 in period i, DEPOT2_i represent the inventory at DEPOT2 in period i and CUST_i represent the customer demand in period i ($i=1$, 2). These variables can be thought of as nodes in a network with the following data representing the COST and CAPACITY of the arcs connecting them.

FROM	TO	COST	CAPACITY
PLANT_1	CUST_1	10	75
PLANT_1	DEPOT1_1	7	75
PLANT_1	DEPOT2_1	8	75
DEPOT1_1	CUST_1	3	20
DEPOT2_1	CUST_1	2	10
PLANT_1	PLANT_2	2	100
DEPOT1_1	DEPOT1_2	1	100
DEPOT2_1	DEPOT2_2	1	100
PLANT_2	CUST_2	10	75
PLANT_2	DEPOT1_2	7	75
PLANT_2	DEPOT2_2	8	75
DEPOT1_2	CUST_2	3	20
DEPOT2_2	CUST_2	2	10
CUST_1	.	.	.
CUST_2	.	.	.

Suppose that you want to draw the above network using PROC NETDRAW and suppose also that you require the nodes to be placed in specific positions. The program below saves the network information along with the required node coordinates in the data set ARCS and invokes PROC NETDRAW to draw the network diagram (shown in **Output 8.10**). The input data set to PROC NETDRAW also contains a variable named NODEPAT that specifies that pattern statement 1 be used for nodes relating to period 1 and pattern statement 2 be used for those relating to period 2. The output data set NETOUT (printed in **Output 8.11**) contains the x and y coordinates for all the nodes as well as for all the turning points of the arcs.

The next part of the example illustrates how you can modify the arc layout by modifying the output data set NETOUT. Two turning points for three of the arcs in the diagram are removed and the y coordinate of a third turning point is changed. The resulting data set (NETIN, also printed in **Output 8.11**) is used as input to PROC NETDRAW to produce the diagram in **Output 8.12**.

```
data arcs;
   input from $  to $  _x_ _y_ nodepat;
cards;
PLANT_1   CUST_1     1  5  1
PLANT_1   DEPOT1_1   1  5  1
PLANT_1   DEPOT2_1   1  5  1
DEPOT1_1  CUST_1     2  6  1
DEPOT2_1  CUST_1     2  4  1
PLANT_1   PLANT_2    1  5  1
DEPOT1_1  DEPOT1_2   2  6  1
DEPOT2_1  DEPOT2_2   2  4  1
PLANT_2   CUST_2     4  2  2
PLANT_2   DEPOT1_2   4  2  2
PLANT_2   DEPOT2_2   4  2  2
DEPOT1_2  CUST_2     5  3  2
DEPOT2_2  CUST_2     5  1  2
```

```
CUST_1       .        3  5  1
CUST_2       .        6  2  2
;

title c=white f=swiss 'Distribution Network';
pattern1 v=e  c=green;
pattern2 v=e  c=red;
proc netdraw data=arcs graphics out=netout;
   actnet / act=from succ=to separatearcs
            pattern=nodepat ctext=white
            compress font=simplex
            carcs=cyan;
   run;


title2 f=swiss 'Output Data Set from PROC NETDRAW';
proc print data=netout;
run;


title2 c=white f=swiss 'Modified Diagram';
proc netdraw graphics data=netin;
   actnet / separatearcs
            ctext=white
            compress font=simplex
            carcs=cyan;
   run;
```

Output 8.10   Distribution Network

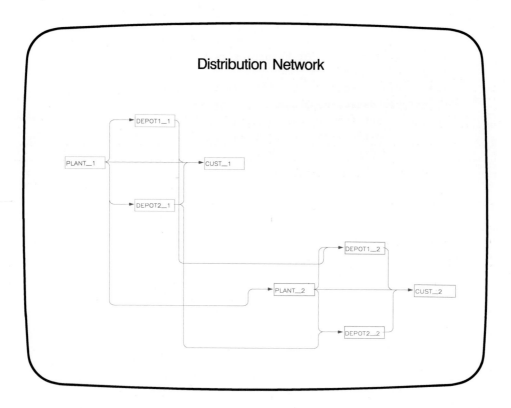

Output 8.11   Output Data Set from PROC NETDRAW

```
                                Distribution Network                                        1
                         Output Data Set from PROC NETDRAW

        OBS     _FROM_        _TO_        _X_     _Y_      _SEQ_     _PATTERN      FROM

         1      PLANT_1      CUST_1       1.0     5.0        0          1        PLANT_1
         2      PLANT_1      DEPOT1_1     1.0     5.0        0          1        PLANT_1
         3      PLANT_1      DEPOT1_1     1.5     5.0        1          .        PLANT_1
         4      PLANT_1      DEPOT1_1     1.5     6.0        2          .        PLANT_1
         5      PLANT_1      DEPOT2_1     1.0     5.0        0          1        PLANT_1
         6      PLANT_1      DEPOT2_1     1.5     5.0        1          .        PLANT_1
         7      PLANT_1      DEPOT2_1     1.5     4.0        2          .        PLANT_1
         8      PLANT_1      PLANT_2      1.0     5.0        0          1        PLANT_1
         9      PLANT_1      PLANT_2      1.5     5.0        1          .        PLANT_1
        10      PLANT_1      PLANT_2      1.5     1.5        2          .        PLANT_1
        11      PLANT_1      PLANT_2      3.5     1.5        3          .        PLANT_1
        12      PLANT_1      PLANT_2      3.5     2.0        4          .        PLANT_1
        13      DEPOT1_1     CUST_1       2.0     6.0        0          1        DEPOT1_1
        14      DEPOT1_1     CUST_1       2.5     6.0        1          .        DEPOT1_1
        15      DEPOT1_1     CUST_1       2.5     5.0        2          .        DEPOT1_1
        16      DEPOT1_1     DEPOT1_2     2.0     6.0        0          1        DEPOT1_1
        17      DEPOT1_1     DEPOT1_2     2.5     6.0        1          .        DEPOT1_1
        18      DEPOT1_1     DEPOT1_2     2.5     2.5        2          .        DEPOT1_1
        19      DEPOT1_1     DEPOT1_2     4.5     2.5        3          .        DEPOT1_1
        20      DEPOT1_1     DEPOT1_2     4.5     3.0        4          .        DEPOT1_1
        21      DEPOT2_1     CUST_1       2.0     4.0        0          1        DEPOT2_1
        22      DEPOT2_1     CUST_1       2.5     4.0        1          .        DEPOT2_1
        23      DEPOT2_1     CUST_1       2.5     5.0        2          .        DEPOT2_1
        24      DEPOT2_1     DEPOT2_2     2.0     4.0        0          1        DEPOT2_1
        25      DEPOT2_1     DEPOT2_2     2.5     4.0        1          .        DEPOT2_1
        26      DEPOT2_1     DEPOT2_2     2.5     0.5        2          .        DEPOT2_1
        27      DEPOT2_1     DEPOT2_2     4.5     0.5        3          .        DEPOT2_1
        28      DEPOT2_1     DEPOT2_2     4.5     1.0        4          .        DEPOT2_1
        29      PLANT_2      CUST_2       4.0     2.0        0          2        PLANT_2
        30      PLANT_2      DEPOT1_2     4.0     2.0        0          2        PLANT_2
```

(continued on next page)

(continued from previous page)

31	PLANT_2	DEPOT1_2	4.5	2.0	1	.	PLANT_2	
32	PLANT_2	DEPOT1_2	4.5	3.0	2	.	PLANT_2	
33	PLANT_2	DEPOT2_2	4.0	2.0	0	2	PLANT_2	
34	PLANT_2	DEPOT2_2	4.5	2.0	1	.	PLANT_2	
35	PLANT_2	DEPOT2_2	4.5	1.0	2	.	PLANT_2	
36	DEPOT1_2	CUST_2	5.0	3.0	0	2	DEPOT1_2	
37	DEPOT1_2	CUST_2	5.5	3.0	1	.	DEPOT1_2	
38	DEPOT1_2	CUST_2	5.5	2.0	2	.	DEPOT1_2	
39	DEPOT2_2	CUST_2	5.0	1.0	0	2	DEPOT2_2	
40	DEPOT2_2	CUST_2	5.5	1.0	1	.	DEPOT2_2	
41	DEPOT2_2	CUST_2	5.5	2.0	2	.	DEPOT2_2	
42	CUST_1		3.0	5.0	0	1	CUST_1	
43	CUST_2		6.0	2.0	0	2	CUST_2	

Distribution Network
Modified Data Set NETIN   2

OBS	_FROM_	_TO_	_X_	_Y_	_SEQ_	_PATTERN_	FROM
1	PLANT_1	CUST_1	1.0	5	0	1	PLANT_1
2	PLANT_1	DEPOT1_1	1.0	5	0	1	PLANT_1
3	PLANT_1	DEPOT1_1	1.5	5	1	.	PLANT_1
4	PLANT_1	DEPOT1_1	1.5	6	2	.	PLANT_1
5	PLANT_1	DEPOT2_1	1.0	5	0	1	PLANT_1
6	PLANT_1	DEPOT2_1	1.5	5	1	.	PLANT_1
7	PLANT_1	DEPOT2_1	1.5	4	2	.	PLANT_1
8	PLANT_1	PLANT_2	1.0	5	0	1	PLANT_1
9	PLANT_1	PLANT_2	1.5	5	1	.	PLANT_1
10	PLANT_1	PLANT_2	1.5	2	2	.	PLANT_1
11	DEPOT1_1	CUST_1	2.0	6	0	1	DEPOT1_1
12	DEPOT1_1	CUST_1	2.5	6	1	.	DEPOT1_1
13	DEPOT1_1	CUST_1	2.5	5	2	.	DEPOT1_1
14	DEPOT1_1	DEPOT1_2	2.0	6	0	1	DEPOT1_1
15	DEPOT1_1	DEPOT1_2	2.5	6	1	.	DEPOT1_1
16	DEPOT1_1	DEPOT1_2	2.5	3	2	.	DEPOT1_1
17	DEPOT2_1	CUST_1	2.0	4	0	1	DEPOT2_1
18	DEPOT2_1	CUST_1	2.5	4	1	.	DEPOT2_1
19	DEPOT2_1	CUST_1	2.5	5	2	.	DEPOT2_1
20	DEPOT2_1	DEPOT2_2	2.0	4	0	1	DEPOT2_1
21	DEPOT2_1	DEPOT2_2	2.5	4	1	.	DEPOT2_1
22	DEPOT2_1	DEPOT2_2	2.5	1	2	.	DEPOT2_1
23	PLANT_2	CUST_2	4.0	2	0	2	PLANT_2
24	PLANT_2	DEPOT1_2	4.0	2	0	2	PLANT_2
25	PLANT_2	DEPOT1_2	4.5	2	1	.	PLANT_2
26	PLANT_2	DEPOT1_2	4.5	3	2	.	PLANT_2
27	PLANT_2	DEPOT2_2	4.0	2	0	2	PLANT_2
28	PLANT_2	DEPOT2_2	4.5	2	1	.	PLANT_2
29	PLANT_2	DEPOT2_2	4.5	1	2	.	PLANT_2
30	DEPOT1_2	CUST_2	5.0	3	0	2	DEPOT1_2
31	DEPOT1_2	CUST_2	5.5	3	1	.	DEPOT1_2
32	DEPOT1_2	CUST_2	5.5	2	2	.	DEPOT1_2
33	DEPOT2_2	CUST_2	5.0	1	0	2	DEPOT2_2
34	DEPOT2_2	CUST_2	5.5	1	1	.	DEPOT2_2
35	DEPOT2_2	CUST_2	5.5	2	2	.	DEPOT2_2
36	CUST_1		3.0	5	0	1	CUST_1
37	CUST_2		6.0	2	0	2	CUST_2

Output 8.12   Modified Diagram of Distribution Network

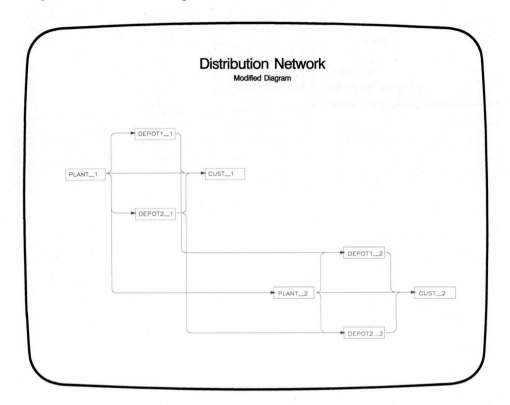

Chapter 9

The NETFLOW
Procedure

ABSTRACT

The NETFLOW procedure solves pure network flow problems and network flow problems with linear side constraints. The side constraints can have coefficients directly related to the arcs of the network as well as others related to variables that have nothing to do with the network (called nonarc variables). This procedure accepts the network specification in a format that is particularly suited to networks. The NETFLOW procedure accepts the side constraints in the same dense or sparse format that the LP procedure uses. Although PROC LP can solve network problems, the NETFLOW procedure generally solves network flow problems more efficiently than PROC LP.

INTRODUCTION

Many linear programming problems have large embedded network structures. Such problems often result when modeling manufacturing processes, transportation or distribution networks, resource allocation, or when deciding where to locate facilities. Often, some commodity is to be moved from place to place, so the more natural formulation in many applications is that of a constrained network rather than a linear program.

Using a network diagram to visualize a problem makes it possible to capture the important relationships in an easily understood picture form. The network diagram aids the communication between model builder and model user, making it easier to comprehend how the model is structured, how it can be changed, and how results can be interpreted.

If a network structure is embedded in a linear program, the problem is a network programming problem with side constraints (NPSC). When the network part of the problem is large compared to the non-network part, especially if the number of side constraints is small, it is worthwhile to exploit this structure in the solution process. This is what PROC NETFLOW does. It uses a variant of the revised primal simplex algorithm that exploits the network structure to reduce solution time.

If a network programming problem with side constraints has n nodes, a arcs, g nonarc variables, and k side constraints, then the formal statement of the problem solved by PROC NETFLOW is

$$\min \mathbf{c}^T\mathbf{x} + \mathbf{d}^T\mathbf{z}$$

subject to:

$$\begin{aligned} \mathbf{F\,x} &= \mathbf{b} \\ \mathbf{H\,x} + \mathbf{Q\,z} \ \substack{\geq \\ =\\ \leq}\ \mathbf{r} \end{aligned} \qquad \text{(NPSC)}$$

$$\begin{aligned} \boldsymbol{\ell} &\leq \mathbf{x} \leq \mathbf{u} \\ \mathbf{m} &\leq \mathbf{z} \leq \mathbf{v} \end{aligned}$$

where

$\mathbf{c}$ is the $a{\times}1$ objective function vector of arc variables (the cost vector)

$\mathbf{x}$ is the $a{\times}1$ arc variable value vector (the flow vector)

$\mathbf{d}$ is the $g{\times}1$ objective function coefficient vector of nonarc variables

$\mathbf{z}$ is the $g{\times}1$ nonarc variable value vector

$\mathbf{F}$ is the $n{\times}a$ node-arc incidence matrix of the network, where $\mathbf{F}_{i,j}$ equals

-1 if arc j is directed toward node i

1 if arc j is directed from node i

0 otherwise.

b   is the nx1 node supply/demand vector, where b_i equals

s   if node i has supply capability of s units of flow

−d   if node i has demand d of units of flow

0   if node i is a transshipment node.

H   is the kxa side constraint coefficient matrix for arc variables, where

$H_{i,j}$ is the coefficient of arc j in the *i*th side constraint

Q   is the kxg side constraint coefficient matrix for nonarc variables, where

$Q_{i,j}$ is the coefficient of nonarc j in the *i*th side constraint

ℓ   is the ax1 arc lower flow bound vector

u   is the ax1 arc capacity vector

m   is the gx1 nonarc variable value lower bound vector

v   is the gx1 nonarc variable value upper bound vector.

The constraints **Fx = b** are referred to as the nodal flow conservation constraints. These state algebraically that the sum of the flow through arcs directed toward a node plus that node's supply, if any, equals the sum of the flow through arcs directed away from that node plus that node's demand, if any. The flow conservation constraints are implicit in the network model and should not be specified explicitly in side constraint data when using PROC NETFLOW. The constrained problems most amenable to being solved by the NETFLOW procedure are those that, after the removal of the flow conservation constraints, have very few constraints. PROC NETFLOW is superior to linear programming optimizers when the network part of the problem is significantly larger than the non-network part.

The NETFLOW procedure can also be used to solve an unconstrained network problem, that is, one in which **H**, **Q**, **d**, **r**, and **z** do not exist.

Side constraints are used frequently in network models in which the amount produced of a particular commodity (the flow through an arc directed from a process node) is proportional to the total amount of raw material (flows through arcs directed toward the node). These are sometimes called proportional constraints. For example, in an oil refinery model, side constraints can be used to specify that for every unit of crude oil that is piped to some plant (node), three-fourths of a unit of gasoline and one-fourth of a unit of diesel fuel are obtained. Similarly, side constraints can indicate the proportions of ingredients that are blended or required to produce an output commodity.

Side constraints are also used in models in which there are capacities on transportation or some other shared resource, or limits on overall production or demand in *multi-commodity*, multi-divisional, or multi-period problems. Side constraints are used to combine the outputs of subdivisions of a problem (either commodities, outputs in distinct time periods, or different process streams) to meet overall demands, or to limit production or expenditures. This method is more desirable than doing separate *local* optimizations for individual commodity, process, or time networks and then trying to establish relationships between each when determining an overall policy if the *global* constraint is not satisfied. Of course, to make models more realistic, side constraints may be necessary in the local problems.

If the constrained problem to be solved has no nonarc variables, then $\mathbf{Q}$, $\mathbf{d}$, and $\mathbf{z}$ do not exist. However, nonarc variables can be used to simplify side constraints. For example, if a sum of flows appears in many constraints, it may be worthwhile to equate this expression with a nonarc variable, and use this in the other constraints. By assigning a nonarc variable a nonzero objective function, it is then possible to incur a cost for using resources above some lowest feasible limit. Similarly, a profit (a negative objective function coefficient value) can be made if all available resources are not used.

If you have a problem that has already been partially solved and is to be solved further to obtain a better, optimal solution, information describing the solution now available may be used as an initial solution. This is called *warm starting* the optimization, and the supplied solution data are called the *warm start*.

Some data can be changed between the time when a warm start is created and when it is used as a warm start for a subsequent PROC NETFLOW run. Elements in the arc variable cost vector, the nonarc variable objective function coefficient vector, and sometimes capacities, upper value bounds, and side constraint data can be changed between PROC NETFLOW calls. See **Warm Starts** in the **DETAILS** section.

Overview

To solve network programming problems with side constraints using PROC NETFLOW, you save a representation of the network and the side constraints in three SAS data sets. These data sets are then passed to PROC NETFLOW for solution. There are various forms that a problem's data can take. You can use any one or a combination of several of these forms.

The NODEDATA= data set contains the names of the supply and demand nodes and the supplies and demands associated with each. These are the elements in the column vector $\mathbf{b}$ in problem (NPSC).

The ARCDATA= data set contains information about the variables of the problem. Usually these are arcs, but there may be data related to nonarc variables in the ARCDATA= data set as well.

An arc is identified by the names of its tail node (where it originates) and head node (where it is directed). Each observation can be used to identify an arc in the network and, optionally, the cost per flow unit across the arc, the arc's capacity, lower flow bound, and name. These data are associated with the matrix $\mathbf{F}$ and the vectors $\mathbf{c}$, $\mathbf{l}$, and $\mathbf{u}$ in problem (NPSC).

Note: although $\mathbf{F}$ is a node-arc incidence matrix, it is specified in the ARCDATA= data set by arc definitions.

In addition, the ARCDATA= data set can be used to specify information about nonarc variables, including objective function coefficients, lower and upper value bounds, and names. These data are the elements of the vectors **d**, **m**, and **v** in problem (NPSC). Data of an arc or nonarc variable can be given in more than one observation.

The CONDATA= data set describes the side constraints and their right-hand-sides. These data are the matrices **H** and **Q** and the vector **r**. Constraint types are also specified in the CONDATA= data set. You can include in this data set upper values or capacities, lower flow or value bounds, and costs or objective function coefficients. It is possible to give all information about some or all nonarc variables in the CONDATA= data set.

An arc is identified in this data set by its name. If you specify an arc's name in the ARCDATA= data set, then this name is used to associate data in the CONDATA= data set with that arc. Each arc also has a default name that is the name of the tail and head node of the arc concatenated together and separated by an underscore character, tail_head, for example. Note: if you use the dense side constraint input format (described later) and want to use these default arc names, you must use only uppercase letters in the node names in ARCDATA.

Supply and demand data also can be specified in the ARCDATA= data set. In such a case, the NODEDATA= data set may not be needed.

The execution of PROC NETFLOW has three stages. In the preliminary (zeroth) stage, the data are read from the NODEDATA=, ARCDATA=, and CONDATA= data sets. Error checking is performed, and an initial basic feasible solution is found. If an unconstrained solution warm start is being used, then an initial basic feasible solution is obtained by reading additional data containing that information in the NODEDATA= and ARCDATA= data sets. In this case, only constraint data and nonarc variable data are read from the CONDATA= data set.

In the first stage, an optimal solution to the network flow problem neglecting any side constraints is found. The primal and dual solutions for this relaxed problem can be saved in the ARCOUT= and NODEOUT= data sets, respectively. These data sets are named in the PROC NETFLOW, RESET, or SAVE statements.

In the second stage, an optimal solution to the network flow problem with side constraints is found. The primal and dual solutions for this side constrained problem are saved in the CONOUT= and DUALOUT= data sets, respectively. These data sets are also named in the PROC NETFLOW, RESET, or SAVE statements.

If a constrained solution warm start is being used, the zeroth and first stages are not performed. This warm start can be obtained by reading basis data containing additional information in the NODEDATA= (also called the DUALIN= data set) and ARCDATA= data sets.

If warm starts are to be used in future optimizations, the FUTURE1 and FUTURE2 options should be used in addition to specifying names for the data sets that contain the primal and dual solutions in stages one and two. Then, most of the information necessary for restarting problems is available in the output data sets containing the primal and dual solutions of both the relaxed and side constrained network programs.

Introductory Example

Consider the following transshipment problem for an oil company. Crude oil is shipped to refineries where it is processed into gasoline and diesel fuel. The gasoline and diesel fuel are then distributed to service stations. At each stage there are shipping, processing, and distribution costs. Also, there are lower flow bounds and capacities. In addition, two times the crude from the Middle East cannot exceed the throughput of a refinery plus 15 units, and one unit of crude mix processed at a refinery yields three-fourths of a unit of gasoline and one-fourth of a unit of diesel fuel. Because there are two products that are not independent in the way in which they flow through the network, a network programming problem with side constraints is an appropriate model for this example (see **Figure 9.1**). The side constraints are used to model the limitations on the amount of Middle Eastern crude that can be processed by each refinery and the conversion proportions of crude to gasoline and diesel fuel.

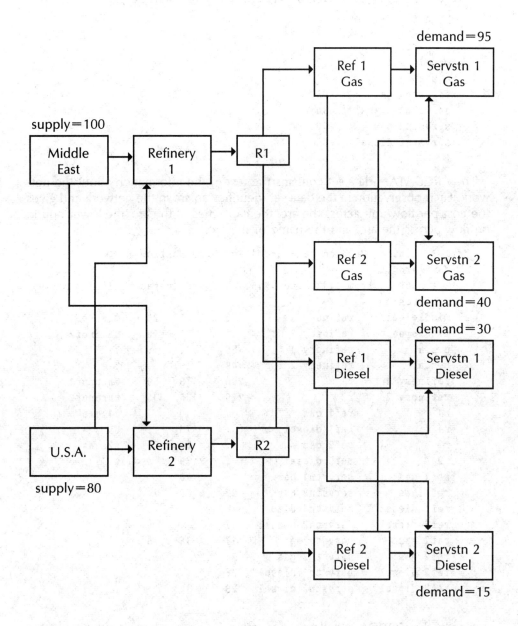

Figure 9.1 Model of a Network Programming Problem with Side Constraints

To solve this problem with PROC NETFLOW, a representation of the model in three SAS data sets is saved. In the NODEDATA= data set you name the supply and demand nodes and give the associated supplies and demands. To distinguish demand nodes from supply nodes, demands are given as negative quantities. For the oil example, the NODEDATA= data set can be saved as follows:

```
title  'Oil Industry Example';
title3 'Setting Up Nodedata = Noded For Proc Netflow';
   data noded;
      input   _node_&$15. _sd_;
      cards;
   middle east      100
   u.s.a.            80
   servstn1 gas     -95
   servstn1 diesel  -30
   servstn2 gas     -40
   servstn2 diesel  -15
   ;
```

The ARCDATA= data set contains the rest of the information about the network. Each observation in the data set identifies an arc in the network and gives the cost per flow unit across the arc, the capacities of the arc, the lower bound on flow across the arc, and the name of the arc.

```
title3 'Setting Up Arcdata = Arcd1 For Proc Netflow';
   data arcd1;
      input   _from_&$11. _to_&$15.   _cost_ _capac_  _lo_    _name_ $;
      cards;
   middle east      refinery 1       63     95       20      m_e_ref1
   middle east      refinery 2       81     80       10      m_e_ref2
   u.s.a.           refinery 1       55     .        .       .
   u.s.a.           refinery 2       49     .        .       .
   refinery 1       r1              200    175       50      thruput1
   refinery 2       r2              220    100       35      thruput2
   r1               ref1 gas         .     140       .       r1_gas
   r1               ref1 diesel      .      75       .       .
   r2               ref2 gas         .     100       .       r2_gas
   r2               ref2 diesel      .      75       .       .
   ref1 gas         servstn1 gas     15     70       .       .
   ref1 gas         servstn2 gas     22     60       .       .
   ref1 diesel      servstn1 diesel  18     .        .       .
   ref1 diesel      servstn2 diesel  17     .        .       .
   ref2 gas         servstn1 gas     17     35       5       .
   ref2 gas         servstn2 gas     31     .        .       .
   ref2 diesel      servstn1 diesel  36     .        .       .
   ref2 diesel      servstn2 diesel  23     .        .       .
   ;
```

Finally, the CONDATA= data set contains the side constraints for the model.

```
title3 'Setting Up Condata = Cond1 For Proc Netflow';
data cond1;
   input
    m_e_ref1 m_e_ref2 thruput1 r1_gas thruput2 r2_gas _type_ $ _rhs_;
   cards;
-2        .        1        .        .        .      >=    -15
 .       -2        .        .        1        .      GE    -15
 .        .       -3        4        .        .      EQ      0
 .        .        .        .       -3        4      =       0
;
```

Note that the SAS variable names in the CONDATA= data set are the names of arcs given in the ARCDATA= data set. These are the arcs that have nonzero constraint coefficients in side constraints. For example, the proportionality constraint that specifies that one unit of crude at each refinery yields three-fourths of a unit of gasoline and one-fourth of a unit of diesel fuel is given for REFINERY 1 in the third observation and for REFINERY 2 in the last observation. The third observation requires that each unit of flow on arc THRUPUT1 equals three-fourths of a unit of flow on arc R1_GAS. Because all crude processed at REFINERY 1 flows through THRUPUT1 and all gasoline produced at REFINERY 1 flows through R1_GAS, the constraint models the situation. It proceeds similarly for REFINERY 2 and the last observation.

To find the minimum cost flow through the network that satisfies the supplies, demands, and side constraints, invoke PROC NETFLOW as follows:

```
proc netflow
   nodedata=noded        /* the supply and demand data */
   arcdata=arcd1         /* the arc description */
   condata=cond1         /* the side constraints */
   conout=solution;      /* the solution */
run;
```

The following messages, which appear on the SAS log, summarize the model as read by PROC NETFLOW and note the progress toward a solution:

```
NOTE: Number of nodes = 14.
NOTE: Number of supply nodes = 2.
NOTE: Number of demand nodes = 4.
NOTE: Total supply  = 180  total demand = 180.
NOTE: Number of arcs = 18.
NOTE: Number of iterations performed (neglecting any constraints) = 7.
NOTE: Of these, 0 were degenerate.
NOTE: Optimum (neglecting any constraints) found.
NOTE: Minimum total cost = 50600.
NOTE: Number of <= side constraints = 0.
NOTE: Number of >= side constraints = 2.
NOTE: Number of iterations, optimizing with constraints = 4.
NOTE: Of these, 0 were degenerate.
NOTE: Optimum reached.
NOTE: Minimal total cost = 50875.
NOTE: The dataset WORK.SOLUTION has 18 observations and 14
      variables.
```

The solution is saved in the SOLUTION data set. It can be printed with PROC PRINT as:

```
proc print data=solution;
   sum _fcost_;
   title3 'Constrained Optimum'; run;
```

Notice that the optimal flow through each arc in the network is given in the variable named _FLOW_, and the cost of flow through each arc is given in the variable _FCOST_.

Output 9.1   Optimal Solution for the Oil Industry Example

```
                                    Oil Industry Example                                      1
                                    Constrained Optimum

                                      S  D
                                      U  E
                         _      _     P  M      _          _   _   _
        _         _      C      C  _  P  A      F          F   A   T      _
        F         T      O      A  L  L  N      L          C   R   N      S
        R         O      S      P  O  Y  D      O          O   C   U      T
        O         _      T      A  _     _      W          S   O   M      A
  O     M                       C              _          T   S   B      T
  B     _                       _                              T  _      U
  S                                                                      S

  1  refinery 1   r1     200   175  50  THRUPUT1  .   .  145.00  29000.00   .   5   2  KEY_ARC    BASIC
  2  refinery 2   r2     220   100  35  THRUPUT2  .   .   35.00   7700.00  29   6   3  LOWERBD  NONBASIC
  3  r1           ref1 diesel  0    75   0        .   .   36.25      0.00   .   8   5  KEY_ARC    BASIC
  4  r1           ref1 gas     0   140   0  R1_GAS .   .  108.75      0.00   .   7   5  KEY_ARC    BASIC
  5  r2           ref2 diesel  0    75   0        .   .    8.75      0.00   .  10   6  KEY_ARC    BASIC
  6  r2           ref2 gas     0   100   0  R2_GAS .   .   26.25      0.00   .   9   6  KEY_ARC    BASIC
  7  middle east  refinery 1  63    95  20  M_E_REF1 100  .   80.00   5040.00   .   1   1  KEY_ARC    BASIC
  8  u.s.a.       refinery 1  55 999999  0            80  .   65.00   3575.00   .   2   4  KEY_ARC    BASIC
  9  middle east  refinery 2  81    80  10  M_E_REF2 100  .   20.00   1620.00   .   3   1  NONKEY ARC BASIC
 10  u.s.a.       refinery 2  49 999999  0            80  .   15.00    735.00   .   4   4  KEY_ARC    BASIC
 11  ref1 diesel  servstn1 diesel  18 999999  0       .  30   30.00    540.00   .  15   8  KEY_ARC    BASIC
 12  ref2 diesel  servstn1 diesel  36 999999  0       .  30    0.00      0.00  12  16  10  LOWERBD  NONBASIC
 13  ref1 gas     servstn1 gas     15    70   0       .  95   68.75   1031.25   .  11   7  KEY_ARC    BASIC
 14  ref2 gas     servstn1 gas     17    35   5       .  95   26.25    446.25   .  12   9  KEY_ARC    BASIC
 15  ref1 diesel  servstn2 diesel  17 999999  0       .  15    6.25    106.25   .  17   8  KEY_ARC    BASIC
 16  ref2 diesel  servstn2 diesel  23 999999  0       .  15    8.75    201.25   .  18  10  NONKEY ARC BASIC
 17  ref1 gas     servstn2 gas     22    60   0       .  40   40.00    880.00   .  13   7  KEY_ARC    BASIC
 18  ref2 gas     servstn2 gas     31 999999  0       .  40    0.00      0.00   7  14   9  LOWERBD  NONBASIC
                                                              ========
                                                              50875.00
```

SPECIFICATIONS

Below are statements used in PROC NETFLOW listed in alphabetical order as they appear in the text that follows.

PROC NETFLOW *options;*
  CAPACITY *variable;*
  COEF *variables;*
  COLUMN *variable;*
  CONOPT;
  COST *variable;*
  DEMAND *variable;*
  HEADNODE *variable;*
  ID *variables;*
  LO *variable;*
  NAME *variable;*
  NODE *variable;*
  PIVOT;
  PRINT *options;*
  QUIT;
  RESET *options;*
  ROW *variables;*
  RHS *variables;*
  RUN ;
  SAVE *options;*
  SHOW *options/qualifiers;*

SUPDEM *variable;*
SUPPLY *variable;*
TAILNODE *variable;*
TYPE *variable;*
VAR *variables;*

Table 9.1 lists the statements according to their functionality.

Table 9.1   PROC NETFLOW: Statements and Descriptions for Use

Function	Statement name
Variable lists of ARCDATA	**CAPACITY** statement
	COST statement
	DEMAND statement
	HEADNODE statement
	ID statement
	LO statement
	NAME statement
	SUPPLY statement
	TAILNODE statement
Variable lists of NODEDATA	**NODE** statement
	SUPDEM statement
Variable lists of CONDATA	**COEF** statement
	COLUMN statement
	RHS statement
	ROW statement
	TYPE statement
	VAR statement
Interactive statements	**RESET** statement
	SAVE statement
	SHOW statement
	CONOPT statement
	RUN statement
	PIVOT statement
	QUIT statement
	PRINT statement

Interactivity

PROC NETFLOW is interactive. You begin by giving the PROC NETFLOW statement. You must specify the ARCDATA= data set. The CONDATA= data set must also be specified if the problem has side constraints. If necessary, you can specify the NODEDATA= data set.

The CONOPT, PIVOT, PRINT, QUIT, SAVE, SHOW, RESET, and RUN statements may be listed in any order and, with the exception of the CONOPT and QUIT statements that can be used only once, may be used as many times as desired.

Use the RESET or SAVE statement to change the names of the output data sets. With RESET, you can also indicate the reasons why optimization should stop, or, for example, indicate the maximum number of iterations that can be performed. PROC NETFLOW then has a chance to either execute the next statement, or, if the next statement is one that it does not recognize (the next PROC or DATA step in the SAS session), do any possible permitted optimization and finish. If no new statement has been submitted, you will be prompted for one. Some options of the RESET statement enable you to control aspects of the primal simplex algorithm. Specifying certain values for these options can reduce the time it takes to solve a problem. Note: any of the RESET options may be specified in the PROC NETFLOW statement.

The RUN statement starts optimization. The PIVOT statement makes PROC NETFLOW perform one simplex iteration. The QUIT statement immediately stops PROC NETFLOW. The CONOPT statement forces PROC NETFLOW to consider constraints when it next performs optimization. The SAVE statement has options that allow you to name output data sets; information about the current solution will be put in these output data sets. Use the SHOW statement if you want to examine the values of options of other statements. Information about the amount of optimization that has been done and the status of the current solution can also be displayed using the SHOW statement.

The PRINT statement makes PROC NETFLOW print parts of the problem. PRINT ARCS makes the NETFLOW procedure produce information on all arcs. PRINT SOME_ARCS limits this output to a subset of arcs. There are similar PRINT statements for nonarc variables and constraints:

```
print nonarcs;
print some_nonarcs;
print constraints;
print some_cons;
```

PRINT CON_ARCS allows you to limit constraint information that is obtained to members of a set of arcs and which have nonzero constraint coefficients in a set of constraints. PRINT CON_NONARCS is the related statement for nonarc variables.

For example, a PROC NETFLOW run might go something like this:

```
proc netflow
    arcdata=dataset
    other options;
  variable list specifications; /* if necessary */
  reset options;
  print statements; /* look at problem */
run;                 /* do some optimization */
  /* suppose that optimization stopped for some reason */
  /* or you manually stopped it */
  print statements; /* look at the current solution */
  save options;     /* keep current solution */
  show options;     /* look at settings */
  reset options;    /* change some settings, like those that */
                    /* caused the optimization to stop */
  run;              /* do more optimization */
  print statements; /* look at the optimal solution */
  save options;     /* keep optimal solution */
```

If you are interested only in finding the optimal solution, have used SAS variables that have special names in the input data sets, and want to use default setting for everything, then the following statement is all you need:

```
proc netflow arcdata=dataset  other options;
```

PROC NETFLOW Statement

PROC NETFLOW *options*;

The options below and the options listed with the RESET statement can appear in the PROC NETFLOW statement.

The options given below can only be specified in the PROC NETFLOW statement and are relevant to the start of the procedure and once specified cannot be changed.

Data Set Options

This section briefly describes all the input and output data sets used by PROC NETFLOW. The ARCDATA=, NODEDATA=, and CONDATA= data sets can contain SAS variables that have special names, for instance _CAPAC_, _COST_, _HEAD_. PROC NETFLOW will look for such variables if you do not give explicit variable list specifications. If a SAS variable with a special name is found and that SAS variable is not in another variable list specification, PROC NETFLOW will determine that values of the SAS variable are to be interpreted in a special way. By using SAS variables that have special names, you may not need to have any variable list specifications.

ARCDATA=*SASdataset*
> names the SAS data set that contains arc and, optionally, nonarc variable information and nodal supply/demand data. ARCDATA= must be specified in all PROC NETFLOW statements.

ARCOUT=*SASdataset*
AOUT=*SASdataset*
> names the output data set that receives all arc and nonarc variable data, including flows or values, and other information concerning the unconstrained optimal solution. The supply and demand information can also be found in the ARCOUT= data set. Once optimization that considers side constraints starts, you will not be able to obtain an ARCOUT= data set. Instead, use the CONOUT= data set to get the current solution. See **The ARCOUT= and CONOUT= Data Sets** in the **DETAILS** section for more information.

CONDATA=*SASdataset*
> names the SAS data set that contains the side constraint data. The data set may also contain other data such as arc costs, capacities, lower flow bounds, nonarc variable upper and lower bounds, and objective function coefficients. PROC NETFLOW needs a CONDATA= data set to solve constrained problems.

CONOUT=*SASdataset*
COUT=*SASdataset*
> names the output data set that receives an optimal primal solution to the problem obtained by performing optimization that considers the side constraints. See **The ARCOUT= and CONOUT= Data Sets** in the **DETAILS** section for more information.

DUALOUT=*SASdataset*
DOUT=*SASdataset*
> names the output data set that receives an optimal dual solution to the problem obtained by performing optimization that considers the side constraints. See **The NODEOUT= and DUALOUT Data Sets** in the **DETAILS** section for more information.

NODEDATA=*SASdataset*
DUALIN=*SASdataset*

names the SAS data set that contains the node supply and demand specifications. You do not need observations in the NODEDATA= data set for transshipment nodes. (Transshipment nodes neither supply nor demand flow.) All nodes are assumed to be transshipment nodes until supply or demand data indicate otherwise. It is acceptable for some arcs to be directed toward supply nodes or away from demand nodes.

The use of NODEDATA= is optional in the PROC NETFLOW statement provided that, if the NODEDATA= data set is not used, supply and demand details are specified by other means. Other means include using the MAXFLOW or SHORTPATH options, SUPPLY or DEMAND list variables or both in the ARCDATA= data set, or the SOURCENODE, SUPPLY, SINKNODE, or DEMAND parameters of the PROC NETFLOW statement.

NODEOUT=*SASdataset*

names the output data set that receives all information about nodes (supply and demand and nodal dual variable values) and other information concerning the optimal solution found by the optimizer when neglecting side constraints. Once optimization that considers side constraints starts, you will not be able to obtain a NODEOUT= data set. Instead, use the DUALOUT= data set to get the current solution dual information. See **The NODEOUT= and DUALOUT= Data Sets** in the **DETAILS** section for a more complete description.

General Options

The following is a list of options you can use with PROC NETFLOW. The options are listed in alphabetical order.

ALLART

indicates that PROC NETFLOW uses an all artificial initial solution (Kennington and Helgason 1980, pg. 68) instead of the default *good path* method for determining an initial solution (Kennington and Helgason 1980, pg. 245). The ALLART initial solution is generally not as good; more iterations are usually required before the optimal solution is obtained. However, because less time is used when setting up an ALLART start, it can offset the added expenditure of CPU time in later computations.

BYTES=*b*

indicates the size of the main working memory (in bytes) that PROC NETFLOW will allocate. The default value for *b* is nearly the number of bytes of the largest contiguous memory that can be allocated for this purpose. The working memory is used to store all the arrays and buffers used by PROC NETFLOW. If this memory has a size smaller than what is required to store all arrays and buffers, PROC NETFLOW uses various schemes that page information between memory and disk.

PROC NETFLOW uses more memory than the main working memory. The additional memory requirements cannot be determined at the time when the main working memory is allocated. For example, every time an output data set is created, some additional memory is required. Do not specify that *b* is the size of all available memory.

COREFACTOR=c

CF=c

allows you to specify the maximum proportion of memory to be used by the arrays frequently accessed by PROC NETFLOW. PROC NETFLOW strives to maintain all information required during optimization in core. If the amount of available memory is not great enough to store the arrays completely in core, either initially or as memory requirements grow, PROC NETFLOW can change the memory management scheme it uses. Large problems can still be solved. When necessary, PROC NETFLOW transfers data from random access memory (RAM) or core that is able to be accessed quickly but is of limited size to slower access large capacity disk memory. This is called *paging*.

Some of the arrays and buffers used during constrained optimization either vary in size, are not required as frequently as other arrays, or are not required throughout the simplex iteration. Let a be the amount of memory in bytes required to store frequently accessed arrays of nonvarying size. Specify the MEMREP option in the PROC NETFLOW statement to get the value for a and a report of memory usage. If the size of the main working memory BYTES=b multiplied by COREFACTOR=c is greater than a, PROC NETFLOW keeps the frequently accessed arrays of nonvarying size resident in main working memory throughout the optimization. If the other arrays cannot fit into core, they are paged in and out of the remaining part of the main working memory.

If b multiplied by c is less than a, PROC NETFLOW uses a different memory scheme. The working memory is used to store only the arrays needed in the part of the algorithm being executed. If necessary, these arrays are read from disk into the main working area. Paging, if required, is done for all these arrays, and sometimes information is written back to disk at the end of that part of the algorithm. This memory scheme is not as fast as the other memory scheme. However, problems can be solved with memory too small to store every array.

PROC NETFLOW is capable of solving very large problems in a modest amount of available memory. However, as more time is spent doing input/output operations, the speed of PROC NETFLOW decreases. It is important to choose the value of COREFACTOR carefully. If COREFACTOR is too small, the memory scheme that needs to be used might not be as efficient as another that could have been used had a larger COREFACTOR been specified. If COREFACTOR is too large, too much of the main working memory will be occupied by the frequently accessed, nonvarying sized arrays, leaving too little for the other arrays. The amount of input/output operations for these other arrays may be so high that another memory scheme might have been used more beneficially.

The valid values of COREFACTOR=c are between 0.0 and 0.95, inclusive. The default value for c is 0.75 when there are over 200 side constraints, and 0.9 when there is only one side constraint. When the problem has between 2 and 200 constraints, c is on the line between the two points (1, 0.9) and (201, 0.75).

DEFCAPACITY=c

DC=c

requests that the default arc capacity and the default nonarc variable value upper bound be c. If this option is not specified, then DEFCAPACITY= INFINITY.

DEFCONTYPE=c
DEFTYPE=c
DCT=c

specifies the default constraint type. This default constraint type is either *less than or equal to* or the type as indicated by DEFCONTYPE=c. Valid values for this option are

LE, le, ≤ for *less than or equal to*
EQ, eq, = for *equal to*
GE, ge, ≥ for *greater than or equal to*.

The values do not need to be enclosed in quotes.

DEFCOST=c

requests that the default arc cost and the default nonarc variable objective function coefficient be *c*. If this option is not specified, then DEFCOST=0.

DEFMINFLOW=m
DMF=m

requests that the default lower flow bound through arcs and the default lower value bound of nonarc variables be *m*. If a value is not specified, then DEFMINFLOW=0.

DEMAND=d

specifies the demand at the sink node specified by the SINKNODE= option. DEMAND= should be used only if the SINKNODE= option is given in the PROC NETFLOW statement and neither the SHORTPATH option nor the MAXFLOW option is specified. If you are solving a minimum cost network problem and the SINKNODE option is used to identify the sink node and if the DEMAND option is not specified, then the demand at the sink node is made equal to the network's total supply.

DWIA=i

controls the initial amount of memory to be allocated to store the **LU** factors. DWIA stands for D^W *initial allocation* and *i* is the number of nonzeros and matrix row operations in the **LU** factors that can be stored in this memory. Due to fill-in in the **U** factor and the growth in the number of row operations, it is often necessary to move information about elements of a particular row or column to another location in the memory allocated for the **LU** factors. This process leaves some memory temporarily unoccupied. Therefore, DWIA=i must be greater than the memory required to store only the **LU** factors.

Occasionally, it is necessary to compress the **U matrix** so that it again occupies contiguous memory. Specifying too large a value for DWIA means that more memory is required by PROC NETFLOW. This might cause more expensive memory mechanisms to be used than if a smaller but adequate value had been specified. Specifying too small a value for DWIA can make time-consuming compressions more numerous. The default value for DWIA= is eight times the number of side constraints.

INFINITY=n
INF=n

is the largest number used by PROC NETFLOW in computations. A number too small can adversely affect the solution process. You should avoid specifying an enormous value for INFINITY= because numerical roundoff errors can result. If a value is not specified, then INFINITY=999999. The INFINITY=n option cannot be assigned a value less than 9999.

INVD_2D

controls the way in which the inverse of the working basis matrix is stored. How this matrix is stored effects computations as well as how the working basis or its inverse is updated. The working basis matrix is defined in the **DETAILS** section. If INVD_2D is specified, the working basis matrix inverse is stored as a matrix. Typically, this memory scheme is best when there are few side constraints or if the working basis is quite dense.

If INVD_2D is not specified, lower (**L**) and upper (**U**) factors of the working basis matrix are used. **U** is an upper triangular matrix and **L** is a lower triangular matrix corresponding to a sequence of elementary matrix row operations. The sparsity-exploiting variant of the Bartels-Golub decomposition (Reid 1975) is used to update the **LU** factors. This scheme works well when the side constraint coefficient matrix is sparse or when many side constraints are nonbinding.

MAXFLOW

MF

specifies that PROC NETFLOW solve a maximum flow problem. In this case, the NETFLOW procedure finds the maximum flow from the node specified by the SOURCENODE= option to the node specified by the SINKNODE= option. PROC NETFLOW automatically assigns an INFINITY=option supply to the SOURCENODE= option node and the SINKNODE= option is assigned INFINITY= option demand. In this way, the MAXFLOW option sets up a maximum flow problem as an equivalent minimum cost problem.

You can use the MAXFLOW option when solving any flow problem (not necessarily a maximum flow problem) when the network has one supply node (with infinite supply) and one demand node (with infinite demand). The MAXFLOW option can be used in conjunction with all other options (except SHORTPATH, SUPPLY= and DEMAND=) and capabilities of PROC NETFLOW.

MAXIMIZE

MAX

specifies that PROC NETFLOW find the maximum cost flow through the network. If both MAXIMIZE and SHORTPATH are specified, the solution obtained is the longest path between the source and sink nodes. Similarly, MAXIMIZE and MAXFLOW together cause PROC NETFLOW to find the minimum flow between these two nodes; this will be zero if there are no nonzero lower flow bounds.

MEMREP

indicates that information on the memory usage and paging schemes (if necessary) will be reported by PROC NETFLOW on the log. As optimization proceeds, you will be informed of any changes in the memory requirement and schemes of PROC NETFLOW.

NAMECTRL=i

is used to interpret arc and nonarc variable names in the CONDATA= data set.

In the ARCDATA= data set, an arc is identified by its tail and head node. In the CONDATA= data set, arcs are identified by names. You can give a name to an arc by having a NAME list specification that indicates a SAS variable in the ARCDATA= data set that has names of arcs as values. PROC NETFLOW requires arcs that have information about them in the CONDATA= data set to have names, but arcs that do not have information about them in the CONDATA= data set can also have names. Unlike a nonarc variable whose name uniquely identifies it, an arc can have several different names. An arc has a default name in the form *tail_head*, that is, the name of the arc's tail node followed by an underscore and the name of the arc's head node.

In the CONDATA= data set, if the dense data format is used, a name of an arc or nonarc variable is the name of a SAS variable listed in the VAR list specification. If the sparse data format of the CONDATA= data set is used, a name of an arc or nonarc variable is a value of the SAS variable listed in the COLUMN list specification.

NAMECTRL is used when a name of an arc or nonarc variable in CONDATA= data set (either a VAR list SAS variable name or value of the COLUMN list SAS variable) is in the form *tail_head* and there exists an arc with these end nodes. If *tail_head* has not already been tagged as belonging to an arc or nonarc variable in the ARCDATA= data set, PROC NETFLOW needs to know whether *tail_head* is the name of the arc or the name of a nonarc variable.

If you specify NAMECTRL=1, a name that is not defined in the ARCDATA= data set is assumed to be the name of a nonarc variable. NAMECTRL=2 will treat *tail_head* as the name of the arc with these endnodes, provided no other name is used to associate data in the CONDATA= data set with this arc. If the arc does have other names that appear in the CONDATA= data set, *tail_head* is assumed to be the name of a nonarc variable. If you specify NAMECTRL=3, *tail_head* is assumed to be a name of the arc with these end nodes, whether the arc has other names or not. The default value of NAMECTRL is three.
Note: if you use the dense side constraint input format, the default arc name *tail_head* will not be recognized (regardless of the NAMECTRL value) unless the head node and tail node names contain no lowercase letters.

RHSOBS=*charstr*
   specifies the keyword that identifies a right-hand-side observation when using the sparse format for data in the CONDATA= data set. The keyword is expected as a value of the SAS variable in the CONDATA= data set named in the COLUMN list specification. _RHS_ or _rhs_ is the default value of *charstr*. If *charstr* is not a valid SAS variable name, enclose it in single quotes.

SCALE=
   indicates that the side constraints are to be scaled so that the largest absolute value of coefficients in each constraint is 1.0. Scaling the constraints is useful when some coefficients of a constraint are either much larger or much smaller than coefficients of other constraints. Scaling might make all coefficients have values that have a smaller range, and this can make computations more stable numerically. Try the SCALE option if PROC NETFLOW is unable to solve a problem because of numerical instability.

SHORTPATH
SP
   specifies that PROC NETFLOW solve a shortest path problem. The NETFLOW procedure finds the shortest path between the nodes specified in the SOURCENODE= option and SINKNODE= option. The cost of arcs are *lengths*. PROC NETFLOW automatically assigns a supply of one flow unit to the SOURCENODE= node, and the SINKNODE= is assigned to have a one flow unit demand. In this way, the SHORTPATH

option sets up a shortest path problem as an equivalent minimum cost problem.

You can use the SHORTPATH option when solving any flow problem (not necessarily a shortest path problem) when the network has one supply node (with supply of one unit) and one demand node (with demand of one unit). The SHORTPATH option can be used in conjunction with all other options (except MAXFLOW, SUPPLY=, and DEMAND=) and capabilities of PROC NETFLOW.

SINKNODE=*sinknodename*
SINK=*sinknodename*

identifies the demand node. SINKNODE= is useful when you specify MAXFLOW or SHORTPATH and need to specify toward which node the shortest path or maximum flow is directed. SINKNODE= also can be used when a minimum cost problem has only one demand node. Rather than having this information in the ARCDATA= or NODEDATA= data set, use SINKNODE= with an accompanying DEMAND= option of this node. *Sinknodename* must be the name of a head node of at least one arc and thus must have a character value. If *sinknodename* is not a valid SAS character variable name, it must be enclosed in single quotes and can contain embedded blanks.

SOURCENODE=*sourcenodename*
SOURCE=*sourcenodename*

identifies a supply node. SOURCENODE=*sourcenodename* is useful when you specify MAXFLOW or SHORTPATH and need to specify from which node the shortest path or maximum flow is directed. SOURCENODE=*sourcenodename* also can be used when a minimum cost problem has only one supply node. Rather than having this information in the ARCDATA= or NODEDATA= data set, use SOURCENODE= with an accompanying SUPPLY= amount of supply of this node. *Sourcenodename* must be the name of a tail node of at least one arc and thus must have a character value. If *sourcenodename* is not a valid SAS character variable name, it must be enclosed in single quotes and can contain embedded blanks.

SPARSECONDATA
SCDATA

indicates that the CONDATA= data set has data in the sparse data format. Otherwise, it is assumed that the data are in the dense format.

Note: if SPARSECONDATA is not specified, all NAME list variable values in ARCDATA are uppercased.

SPARSEP2
SP2

indicates that the new column of the working basis matrix that replaces another column be held in a linked list. If SPARSEP2 is not specified, a one-dimensional array is used to store this column's information, which can contain elements that are 0.0 and use more memory than the linked list. The linked list mechanism requires more work if the column has numerous nonzero elements in many iterations. Otherwise, it is superior. Sometimes, specifying SPARSEP2 is beneficial when the side constrained coefficient matrix is very sparse or when some paging is necessary.

SUPPLY=*s*

specifies the supply at the source node specified by the SOURCENODE option. SUPPLY= should be used only if the SOURCENODE option is given in the PROC NETFLOW statement and neither the SHORTPATH option nor the MAXFLOW option is specified. If you are solving a minimum cost network problem and the SOURCENODE= option is used to identify the source node, and if the SUPPLY option is not specified, then by default the supply at the source node is made equal to the network's total demand.

THRUNET

tells NETFLOW to force through the network any excess supply (the amount by which total supply exceeds total demand) or any excess demand (the amount by which total demand exceeds total supply) as is required. If a network problem has unequal total supply and total demand and THRUNET is not specified, NETFLOW will drain away the excess supply or excess demand in an optimal manner.

TYPEOBS=*charstr*

specifies the keyword that identifies a type observation when using the sparse format for data in the CONDATA= data set. The keyword is expected as a value of the SAS variable in the CONDATA= data set named in the COLUMN list specification. _TYPE_ or _type_ is the default value of *charstr*. If *charstr* is not a valid SAS variable name, enclose it in single quotes.

WARM

indicates that the NODEDATA= or DUALIN= data set and the ARCDATA= data set contain extra information of a warm start to be used by NETFLOW. See **Warm Starts** in the **DETAILS** section.

CAPACITY Statement

CAPACITY *variable*;
CAPAC *variable*;
UPPERBD *variable*;

The CAPACITY statement identifies the variable in the ARCDATA= data set that contains the maximum feasible flow or capacity of the network arcs. If an observation contains nonarc variable information, the CAPACITY list variable is the upper value bound for the nonarc variable named in the NAME list variable in that observation. The CAPACITY list variable must have numeric values. It is not necessary to have a CAPACITY statement if the name of the variable is _CAPAC_, _UPPER_, _UPPERBD, or _HI_.

COEF Statement

COEF *variables*;

The COEF list is used with the sparse input format of the CONDATA= data set. The COEF list can have more than one variable, all of which have numeric values. If the COEF statement is not specified, the CONDATA= data set is searched and variables with names beginning with _COE are used. The number of variables in the COEF list must be no greater than the number of variables in the ROW list.

The values of the COEF list variables in an observation may be interpreted differently than these variables values in other observations. The values can be coefficients in the side constraints, costs and objective function coefficients, bound data, constraint type data, or rhs data. If the COLUMN list variable has a value that is a name of an arc or nonarc variable, the ith COEF list variable is associated with the constraint or special row name named in the ith ROW list variable. Otherwise, the COEF list variables indicate type values, rhs values, or missing values.

COLUMN Statement

COLUMN *variable*;

The COLUMN list is used with the sparse input format of side constraints. This list consists of one variable that has as values the names of arc variables, nonarc variables, or missing values. Some, if not all of these values, also can be values of the NAME list variables of the ARCDATA= data set. The COLUMN list variable can have other special values. Refer to the TYPEOBS and RHSOBS options. If the COLUMN list is not specified in the PROC NETFLOW statement, the CONDATA= data set is searched and a variable named _COLUMN_ is used. The COLUMN list variable must have character values.

CONOPT Statement

CONOPT;

The CONOPT statement has no options. It is equivalent to the RESET SCRATCH statement. The CONOPT statement should be used before stage 2 optimization commences. It indicates that the optimization performed next should consider the side constraints.

Usually, the optimal unconstrained network solution is used as a starting solution for constrained optimization. First finding the unconstrained optimum usually reduces the amount of stage 2 optimization. The unconstrained optimum is nearly always "closer" to the constrained optimum than the initial basic solution determined before any optimization is performed. However, during stage 1 optimization, as the optimum is approached, the flow change candidates become scarcer and a solution good enough to start stage 2 optimization may already be at hand. You should then specify the CONOPT statement.

COST Statement

COST *variable*;
OBJFN *variable*;

The COST statement identifies the variable in the ARCDATA= data set that contains the per unit flow cost through an arc. If an observation contains nonarc variable information, the value of the COST list variable is the objective function coefficient of the nonarc variable named in the NAME list variable in that observation. The COST list variable must have numeric values. It is not necessary to specify a COST statement if the name of the COST variable is _COST_.

DEMAND Statement

DEMAND *variable*;

The DEMAND statement identifies the variable in the ARCDATA= data set that contains the demand at the node named in the corresponding HEADNODE list variable. The DEMAND list variable must have numeric values. It is not necessary to have a DEMAND statement if the name of this variable is _DEMAND_.

HEADNODE Statement

HEADNODE *variable*;
HEAD *variable*;
TONODE *variable*;
TO *variable*;

The HEADNODE statement specifies the variable that must be present in the ARCDATA= data set that contains the names of nodes toward which arcs are directed. It is not necessary to have a HEADNODE statement if the name of the headnode variable is _HEAD_ or _TO_. The HEADNODE variable must have character values.

ID Statement

ID *variables*;

The ID statement specifies variables containing values for pre- and post-optimal processing and analysis. These variables are not processed by PROC NETFLOW but are read by the procedure and written in the ARCOUT= and CONOUT= data sets and the output of PRINT statements. For example, imagine a network used to model a distribution system. The variables listed on the ID statement can contain information on type of vehicle, transportation mode, condition of road, time to complete journey, name of driver, or other ancillary information useful for report writing or describing facets of the operation that do not have bearing on the optimization. The ID variables can be character, numeric, or both.

If no ID list is specified, the procedure forms an ID list of all variables not included in other implicit or explicit list specifications. If the ID list is specified, any variables in the ARCDATA= data set not in any list are dropped and do not appear in ARCOUT= or CONOUT= data sets and PRINT statement output.

LO Statement

LO *variable*;
LOWERBD *variable*;
MINFLOW *variable*;

The LO statement identifies the variable in the ARCDATA= data set that contains the minimum feasible flow or lower flow bound for arcs in the network. If an observation contains nonarc variable information, the LO list variable has the value of the lower bound for the nonarc variable named in the NAME list variable. The LO list variable must have numeric values. It is not necessary to have a LO statement if the name of this variable is _LOWER_, _LO_, _LOWERBD, or _MINFLOW.

NAME Statement

NAME *variable*;
ARCNAME *variable*;
VARNAME *variable*;

Each arc and nonarc variable that has data in the CONDATA= data set must have a unique name. This name is a value of a NAME list variable. The NAME list variable must have character values. See the NAMECTRL= option of the PROC NETFLOW statement for more information. It is not necessary to have a NAME statement if the name of this variable is _NAME_.

NODE Statement.

NODE *variable*;

The NODE list variable, which must be present in the NODEDATA= data set, has names of nodes as values. These values must also be TAILNODE and HEADNODE list variable values. If this list is not explicitly specified, the NODEDATA= data set is searched for a SAS variable with the name _NODE_. The NODE list variable must have character values.

PIVOT Statement

PIVOT;

The PIVOT statement has no options. It indicates that one simplex iteration is to be performed. The PIVOT statement forces a simplex iteration to be performed in spite of the continued presence of any reasons or solution conditions that caused optimization to be halted. For example, if the number of iterations performed exceeds MAXIT1 or MAXIT2 and you issue a PIVOT statement, the iteration will be performed even though the MAXIT1 or MAXIT2 has not yet been changed using a RESET statement.

PRINT Statement

PRINT *options* / *qualifiers*;

The PRINT statement enables you to examine parts or all of the problem. You can limit the amount of information displayed when a PRINT statement is processed by specifying PRINT statement options. The name of the PRINT option indicates what part of the problem is to be examined. If no options are specified, or PRINT PROBLEM is specified, information about the entire problem is produced. The amount of displayed information can be limited further by following any PRINT statement options with a slash character (/) and one or more of the qualifiers SHORT or LONG, ZERO or NONZERO, BASIC or NONBASIC.

Some of the PRINT statement options require you to specify a list of some type of entity, thereby allowing you to indicate what entities are of interest. The entities of interest are the ones you wish to print. These entities might be tail node names, head node names, nonarc variable names, or constraint names. The list is made up of one or more of these constructs. Each construct can add none, one, or more entities to the set of entities to be printed.

ALL
    print all entities that are interesting.

entity
    print the named entity that is interesting.

entity1 - entity2
entity1 -- entity2
    both entity1 and entity2 have names made up of the same character string prefix followed by a numeric suffix. The suffixes of both entity1 and entity2 have the same number of numerals but may have different values. entity1 - entity2 indicates that all entities with the same prefix and suffixes with values on or between the suffixes of entity1 and entity2 are to be put in the set of entities to be printed.

entity1 - CHARACTER - entity2
entity1 - CHAR - entity2
    the numeric suffix of both entity1 and entity2 may be followed by a character string. For example, _OBS07_ - _OBS13_ is a valid construct of the forms entity1 - entity2.

part_of_entity_name:
    all entities that have names that begin with the character string preceding the colon are interesting.

The options below can appear in the PRINT statement.

ARCS
    indicates that you want to have printed information about all arcs.

CON_ARCS (*CONLIST, TAILLIST, HEADLIST*)

is similar to the PRINT SOME_CONS (*CONLIST*) statement, except that instead of displaying information about all arcs that have coefficients in interesting constraints, information about only those arcs directed from a set of interesting tail nodes toward a set of interesting head nodes is displayed. Note: because the two lists are separated by commas, each list must be entered without commas.

CON_NONARCS (CONLIST, NONARCLIST)

is similar to the statement PRINT SOME_CONS (CONLIST), except that instead of displaying information about all nonarc variables that have coefficients in a set of interesting constraints, information about only those nonarc variables in the interesting constraints and belonging to a set of nonarc variables deemed interesting will be displayed. Note: because the two lists are separated by commas, each list must be entered without commas.

CONSTRAINTS

indicates that you wish to have printed information about all constraints.

NONARCS

indicates that information is to be printed about all nonarc variables.

PROBLEM

is equivalent to the statement PRINT ARCS NONARCS CONSTRAINTS;

SOME_ARCS (TAILLIST, HEADLIST)

is similar to the statement PRINT ARCS, except that instead of displaying information about all arcs, only arcs directed from nodes in a set of *interesting* tail nodes to nodes in a set of *interesting* head nodes are included. Note: because the two lists are separated by a comma, each list must be entered without commas.

SOME_CONS (CONLIST)

is similar to the PRINT CONSTRAINTS statement, except that instead of displaying information about all constraints, only those belonging to a set of *interesting* constraints have information printed.

SOME_NONARCS (*NONARCLIST*)

is similar to the PRINT NONARCS statement, except that instead of displaying information about all nonarc variables, only those belonging to a set of *interesting* nonarc variables have information printed.

Following a slash (/), the qualifiers SHORT or LONG, ZERO or NONZERO, BASIC or NONBASIC can appear in any PRINT statement. These qualifiers are described below.

BASIC

only rows that are associated with arcs or nonarc variables that are basic are printed. The _STATUS_ column values for arc are KEY_ARC BASIC or NONKEY ARC BASIC, for nonarc variables NONKEY BASIC.

LONG

all table columns are displayed: the default when no qualifier is used.

NONBASIC

only rows that are associated with arcs or nonarc variables that are nonbasic are printed. The _STATUS_ column values are "LOWERBD NONBASIC" or "UPPERBD NONBASIC".

NONZERO

only rows that have nonzero _FLOW_ column values (nonzero arc flows, nonzero nonarc variable values) are printed.

SHORT
> the table columns are _N_, _FROM_, _TO_, _COST_, _CAPAC_, _LO_, _NAME_, and _FLOW_, or if one SAS variable was specified as being in each of the FROM TO COST CAPAC LO NAME lists, the name of that SAS variable. _COEF_ or the name of the SAS variable in the COEF list specification will head a column when the SHORT qualifier is used in PRINT CONSTRAINTS, SOME_CONS, CON_ARCS, or CON_NONARCS.

ZERO
> Only rows that have zero _FLOW_ column values (zero arc flows, zero nonarc variable values) are printed. The default qualifiers are BASIC, NONBASIC, ZERO, NONZERO, and LONG.

In the oil refinery problem, if you had entered

```
print constraints; run;
```

after the RUN statement, **Output 9.2** would have been produced:

Output 9.2   Printing Information On All Constraints

_N_	_CON_	_TYPE_	_RHS_	_NAME_
1	_OBS1_	GE	-15	M_E_REF1
2	_OBS1_	GE	-15	THRUPUT1
3	_OBS2_	GE	-15	M_E_REF2
4	_OBS2_	GE	-15	THRUPUT2
5	_OBS3_	EQ	0	THRUPUT1
6	_OBS3_	EQ	0	R1_GAS
7	_OBS4_	EQ	0	THRUPUT2
8	_OBS4_	EQ	0	R2_GAS

_N_	_FROM_	_TO_	_COST_	_CAPAC_
1	MIDDLE EAST	REFINERY 1	63	95
2	REFINERY 1	R1	200	175
3	MIDDLE EAST	REFINERY 2	81	80
4	REFINERY 2	R2	220	100
5	REFINERY 1	R1	200	175
6	R1	REF1 GAS	0	140
7	REFINERY 2	R2	220	100
8	R2	REF2 GAS	0	100

_N_	_LO_	_SUPPLY_	_DEMAND_	_FLOW_
1	20	100	.	80
2	50	.	.	145
3	10	100	.	20
4	35	.	.	35
5	50	.	.	145
6	0	.	.	108.75
7	35	.	.	35
8	0	.	.	26.25

_N_	_COEF_	_FCOST_	_RCOST_	_STATUS_	
1	-2	5040	.	KEY_ARC	BASIC
2	1	29000	.	KEY_ARC	BASIC
3	-2	1620	.	NONKEY ARC	BASIC
4	1	7700	3000026	LOWERBD	NONBASIC
5	-3	29000	.	KEY_ARC	BASIC
6	4	0	.	KEY_ARC	BASIC
7	-3	7700	3000026	LOWERBD	NONBASIC
8	4	0	.	KEY_ARC	BASIC

In the oil refinery problem, if you had entered

    print some_arcs(refin:,_all_)/short; run;

after the RUN statement, **Output 9.3** would have been produced:

Output 9.3   Printing Information About Selected Arcs Using The Short
Option

_N_	_FROM_	_TO_	_COST_	_CAPAC_
1	REFINERY 1	R1	200	175
2	REFINERY 2	R2	220	100

_N_	_LO_	_NAME_	_FLOW_
1	50	THRUPUT1	145
2	35	THRUPUT2	35

In the oil refinery problem, if you had entered

    print some_cons(_obs3_-_obs4_)/nonzero short; run;

after the RUN statement, **Output 9.4** would have been produced.

Output 9.4   Printing Information About Selected Constraints Using The Short
and Nonzero Options

_N_	_CON_	_TYPE_	_RHS_	_NAME_
1	_OBS3_	EQ	0	THRUPUT1
2	_OBS3_	EQ	0	R1_GAS
3	_OBS4_	EQ	0	THRUPUT2
4	_OBS4_	EQ	0	R2_GAS

_N_	_FROM_	_TO_	_COST_	_CAPAC_
1	REFINERY 1	R1	200	175
2	R1	REF1 GAS	0	140
3	REFINERY 2	R2	220	100
4	R2	REF2 GAS	0	100

_N_	_LO_	_FLOW_	_COEF_
1	50	145	-3
2	0	108.75	4
3	35	35	-3
4	0	26.25	4

In the oil refinery problem, if you had entered

```
print con_arcs(_all_,r1 r2,_all_)/short; run;
```

after the RUN statement, **Output 9.5** would have been produced.

Output 9.5   Printing Information About Arcs Directed From Selected Tail Nodes Using The Short Option

_N_	_CON_	_TYPE_	_RHS_	_NAME_
1	_OBS3_	EQ	0	R1_GAS
2	_OBS4_	EQ	0	R2_GAS

_N_	_FROM_	_TO_	_COST_	_CAPAC_
1	R1	REF1 GAS	0	140
2	R2	REF2 GAS	0	100

_N_	_LO_	_FLOW_	_COEF_
1	0	108.75	4
2	0	26.25	4

Cautions

When information is parsed to procedures, the SAS System converts the text that makes up statements into uppercase. The PRINT statements of PROC NETFLOW that require lists of entities will work properly *only* if the entities are uppercase in the input SAS data sets.

Entities that contain blanks may also cause problems. The lists of entities consist of constructs that are separated by blanks. For example, the statement to display the arcs directed toward the node named REF1 GAS will not work.

```
PRINT SOME_ARCS(_ALL_,REF1 GAS); run;
```

PROC NETFLOW assumes that REF1 and GAS are two head nodes and that you want displayed arcs directed toward both these nodes (which do not exist). The following will be printed on the SAS log:

```
WARNING: The node REF1 in the list of headnodes in the PRINT SOME_ARCS
         or PRINT CON_ARCS is not a node in the problem. This statement
         will be ignored.
```

To overcome these problems, you must enclose entity names, or parts of names in single or double quotes. For example:

```
print some_arcs (_all_,"ref1 gas");
```

Other examples of using quotes are

```
print some_arcs('lowercase tail','lowercase head');
print some_cons('factory07'-'factory12');
print some_cons('_factory07_'-'_factory12_');
print some_nonarcs("CO2 content":);
```

QUIT Statement

QUIT;

The QUIT statement indicates that PROC NETFLOW is to be terminated immediately. The solution is not saved in the current output data sets. The QUIT statement has no options.

RESET Statement

RESET *options*;

The RESET statement is used to change options after PROC NETFLOW has started execution. Any of the options below can appear in the PROC NETFLOW statement.

The following options fall roughly into five categories:

- output data set specifications
- options that indicate conditions under which optimization is to be halted temporarily, giving you an opportunity to use PROC NETFLOW interactively
- options that control aspects of the operation of the network primal simplex optimization
- options that control the pricing strategies of the network simplex optimizer
- miscellaneous options.

If you want to examine the setting of any options, use the SHOW statement. If you are interested in looking at only those options that fall into a particular category, the SHOW statement has options that will permit you to do this.

The execution of PROC NETFLOW has three stages. In stage zero the problem data are read from the NODEDATA=, ARCDATA=, and CONDATA= data sets. If a warm start is not specified, an initial basic feasible solution is found. Some options of the PROC NETFLOW statement control what occurs in stage zero. By the time the first RESET statement is processed, stage zero will have already been completed.

In the first stage, an optimal solution to the network flow problem neglecting any side constraints is found. The primal and dual solutions for this relaxed problem can be saved in the ARCOUT= and NODEOUT= data sets, respectively.

In the second stage, the side constraints are examined and some initializations occur. Some preliminary work is also needed to commense optimization that considers the constraints. An optimal solution to the network flow problem with side constraints is found. The primal and dual solutions for this side-constrained problem are saved in the CONOUT= and DUALOUT= data sets, respectively.

Many options of the RESET statement have the same name except that they have as a suffix the numeral 1 or 2. Such options have much the same purpose, but option1 controls what occurs during the first stage when optimizing the network neglecting any side constraints and option2 controls what occurs in the second stage when PROC NETFLOW is performing constrained optimization.

Some options can be turned off by the option prefixed by the word *no*. For example, FEASIBLEPAUSE1 may have been specified in a RESET statement and in a later RESET statement, you can specify NOFEASIBLEPAUSE1. In a later RESET statement, you can respecify FEASIBLEPAUSE1 and, in this way, toggle this option.

Output Data Set Specifications

In a RESET statement, you can specify an ARCOUT=, NODEOUT=, CONOUT=, or DUALOUT= data set. You are advised to specify these output data sets early because if you make a syntax error when using PROC NETFLOW interactively, or, for some other reason, PROC NETFLOW encounters or does something unexpected, these data sets will contain information about the solution that was reached. If you had specified the FUTURE1 or FUTURE2 options in a RESET statement, PROC NETFLOW may be able to resume optimization in a subsequent run.

You can turn off these current output data set specifications by specifying ARCOUT=NULL, NODEOUT=NULL, CONOUT=NULL, or DUALOUT=NULL.

If PROC NETFLOW is outputting observations to an output SAS data set and you want this to stop, press the keys used to stop SAS procedures. PROC NETFLOW will, if necessary, wait and then execute the next statement.

ARCOUT=*dataset*
AOUT=*dataset*

> names the output data set that receives all information concerning arc and nonarc variables, including flows and and other information concerning the current solution and the supply and demand information. The current solution is the latest solution found by the optimizer when the optimization neglecting side constraints is halted or the unconstrained optimum is reached.
>
> You can specify an ARCOUT=data set in any RESET statement before the unconstrained optimum is found (even at commencement). Once the unconstrained optimum has been reached, use the SAVE statement to produce observations in an ARCOUT= data set. Once optimization that considers constraints starts, you will not be able to obtain an ARCOUT= data set. Instead, use a CONOUT= data set to get the current solution. See **The ARCOUT= and CONOUT= Data Sets** in the **DETAILS** section for more information.

CONOUT=*dataset*
COUT=*dataset*

> names the output data set that contains the primal solution obtained after optimization considering side constraints reaches the optimal solution. You can specify a CONOUT= data set in any RESET statement before the constrained optimum is found (even at commencement or while optimizing neglecting constraints). Once the constrained optimum has been reached, or during stage 2 optimization, use the SAVE statement to produce observations in a CONOUT= data set. See **The ARCOUT= and CONOUT= Data Sets** in the **DETAILS** section for more information.

DUALOUT=*dataset*
DOUT=*dataset*

> names the output data set that contains the dual solution obtained after doing optimization that considering side constraints reaches the optimal solution. You can specify a DUALOUT= data set in any RESET statement before the constrained optimum is found (even at commencement or while optimizing neglecting constraints). Once the

constrained optimum has been reached, or during stage 2 optimization, use the SAVE statement to produce observations in a DUALOUT= data set. See **The NODEOUT= and DUALOUT= Data Sets** in the **DETAILS** section for more information.

NODEOUT=*dataset*

NOUT=*dataset*

names the output data set that receives all information about nodes (supply/demand and nodal dual variable values) and other information concerning the unconstrained optimal solution.

You can specify a NODEOUT= data set in any RESET statement before the unconstrained optimum is found (even at commencement). Once the unconstrained optimum has been reached, or during stage 1 optimization, use the SAVE statement to produce observations in a NODEOUT= data set. Once optimization that considers constraints starts, you will not be able to obtain a NODEOUT= data set. Instead use a DUALOUT= data set to get the current solution. See **The NODEOUT= and DUALOUT= Data Sets** in the **DETAILS** section for more information.

Options Indicating Conditions under Which Optimization is Temporarily Halted

The following options indicate conditions under which optimization is to be halted. You then have a chance to use PROC NETFLOW interactively. If the NETFLOW procedure is optimizing and you wish optimization to halt immediately, press the CTRL-BREAK key combination used to stop SAS procedures. Doing this is equivalent to PROC NETFLOW finding that some pre-specified condition of the current solution under which optimization should stop has occurred.

If optimization does halt, you may need to change the conditions under which optimization should stop again. For example, if the number of iterations exceeded MAXIT2, use the RESET statement to specify a larger value for MAXIT2 before the next RUN statement. Otherwise, PROC NETFLOW will immediately find that the number of iterations still exceeds MAXIT2 and halt without doing any additional optimization.

ENDPAUSE1

indicates that PROC NETFLOW will pause after the unconstrained optimal solution has been obtained and information about this solution has been output to any current ARCOUT= or NODEOUT= data set. The procedure then executes the next statement, or waits if no subsequent statement has been specified.

FEASIBLEPAUSE1

FP1

indicates that unconstrained optimization should stop once a feasible solution is reached. PROC NETFLOW checks for feasibility every 10 iterations. A solution is feasible if there are no artificial arcs having nonzero flow assigned to be conveyed to them. The presence of artificial arcs with nonzero flows means that the current solution does not satisfy all the nodal flow conservation constraints implicit in network problems.

MAXIT1=*m*

specifies the maximum number of primal simplex iterations PROC NETFLOW is to perform in stage 1. The default value for MAXIT1 is 1000. If *m* iterations are performed and you wish to continue unconstrained optimization, reset MAXIT1 to a number larger than the number of iterations already performed and issue another RUN statement.

NOENDPAUSE1

negates ENDPAUSE1.

NOFEASIBLEPAUSE1
NOFP1

negates FEASIBLEPAUSE1.

PAUSE1=p

indicates that PROC NETFLOW will halt unconstrained optimization and pause when the remainder of the number of stage 1 iterations divided by PAUSE1=p is zero. If present, the next statement will be executed; if not, the procedure will wait for the next statement to be specified. The default value for p is 999999.

FEASIBLEPAUSE2
FP2
NOFEASIBLEPAUSE2
NOFP2
PAUSE2=p
MAXIT2=m

are the stage 2 constrained optimization counterparts of the options described above and having as a suffix the numeral 1.

Options Controlling Aspects of Operation of the Network Simplex Optimization

LRATIO1

specifies the type of ratio test to use in determining which arc leaves the basis in stage 1. When in some iterations, more than one arc can leave the basis. Of those arcs that can leave the basis, the leaving arc is the first encountered by the algorithm if LRATIO1 is specified. Specifying LRATIO1 can decrease the chance of cycling but can increase solution times. The alternative to LRATIO1 is NOLRATIO1, which is the default.

LRATIO2

specifies the type of ratio test to use in determining what leaves the basis in stage 2. When in some iterations, more than one arc, constraint slack, surplus, or nonarc variable can leave the basis. If LRATIO2 is specified, the leaving arc, constraint slack, surplus, or nonarc variable is the one that can leave the basis and is encountered first by the algorithm. Specifying LRATIO2 can decrease the chance of cycling but can increase solution times. The alternative to LRATIO2 is NOLRATIO2, which is the default.

NOLRATIO1

specifies the type of ratio test to use in determining which arc leaves the basis in stage 1. When in some iterations, more than one arc can leave the basis. If NOLRATIO1 is specified, then of those arcs that can leave the basis, the leaving arc has the minimum (maximum) cost if the leaving arc is to be nonbasic with flow capacity equal to its capacity (lower flow bound). If more than one possible leaving arc has the minimum (maximum) cost, the first such arc encountered is chosen. Specifying NOLRATIO1 can decrease solution times, but can increase the chance of cycling. The alternative to NOLRATIO1 is LRATIO1. NOLRATIO1 is the default.

NOLRATIO2

specifies the type of ratio test to use in determining which arc leaves the basis in stage 2. When in some iterations, more than one arc, constraint slack or nonarc variable can leave the basis. If NOLRATIO1 is specified, the leaving arc, constraint slack, surplus, or nonarc variable is the one that can leave the basis with the minimum (maximum) cost or objective function coefficient if the leaving arc, constraint slack or nonarc variable is to be nonbasic with flow or value equal to its capacity or upper value bound (lower flow or value bound), respectively. If several possible leaving arcs, constraint slack, surplus, or nonarc variable have the minimum (maximum) cost or objective function coefficient, then the first encountered is chosen. Specifying NOLRATIO2 can decrease solution times, but can increase the chance of cycling. The alternative to NOLRATIO2 is LRATIO2. NOLRATIO2 is the default.

Options Applicable to Constrained Optimization

The INVFREQ option is relevant only if INVD_2D was specified in the PROC NETFLOW statement; that is, the inverse of the working basis matrix is being stored and processed as a two-dimensional array. The REFACTFREQ, **U**, MAXLUUPDATES, and MAXL options are relevant if INVD_2D was not specified in the PROC NETFLOW statement; that is, the working basis matrix is **LU** factored.

INVFREQ=*r*

recalculates the working basis matrix inverse every INVFREQ iteration. Although a relatively expensive task, it is prudent to do as roundoff errors accumulate, especially affecting the elements of this matrix inverse. The default is INVFREQ=50. INVFREQ should be used only if INVD_2D was specified in the PROC NETFLOW statement.

INTFIRST

In some iterations, it is found that what must leave the basis is an arc that is part of the spanning tree representation of the network part of the basis, (a key arc). It is sometimes necessary to interchange another basic arc not part of the tree (called a *nonkey arc*) with the tree arc that leaves to permit the entire basis update to be performed efficiently. Specifying INTFIRST indicates that of the nonkey arcs eligible to be swapped with the leaving key arc, the one chosen to do so is the first encountered by the algorithm. Otherwise, if INTFIRST is not specified, all such arcs are examined and the one with the best cost is chosen.

The terms *key* and *nonkey* are used as the algorithm used by PROC NETFLOW for network optimization considering side constraints, (GUB-based, primal partitioning, or factorization) is a variant of an algorithm originally developed to solve linear programming problems with generalized upper bounding constraints. The terms *key* and *nonkey* were coined then. The STATUS variable in the ARCOUT= and CONOUT= data sets and the STATUS column in tables produced when PRINT statements are processed will indicate whether basic arcs are key or nonkey. Basic nonarc variables will always be nonkey.

MAXL=*m*

If the working basis matrix is **LU** factored, **U** is an upper triangular matrix and **L** is a lower triangular matrix corresponding to a sequence of elementary matrix row operations required to change the working basis matrix into **U**. **L** and **U** enable substitution techniques to be used to solve the linear systems of the simplex algorithm. Among other things, the **LU** processing strives to keep the number of **L** elementary matrix row operation matrices small. A buildup in the number of these could indicate that fill-in is becoming excessive and the computations involving **L** and **U** will be hampered. Refactorization should be performed to restore **U** sparsity and reduce **L** information. When the number of **L** matrix row operations exceeds MAXL, a refactorization is done rather than one or more updates. The default value for MAXL is 10 times the number of side constraints. MAXL should not be used if INVD_2D was specified in the PROC NETFLOW statement.

MAXLUUPDATES=*m*
MLUU=*m*

In some iterations, PROC NETFLOW must either perform a series of single column updates or a complete refactorization. More than one column of the working basis matrix must change before the next simplex iteration can begin. The single column updates can often be done faster than a complete refactorization, especially if few updates are necessary, the working basis matrix is sparse, or a refactorization has been performed recently. If the number of columns that must change is less than the value specified in the MAXLUUPDATES= option, the updates are attempted; otherwise, a refactorization is done. Refactorization also occurs if the sum of the number of columns that must be changed and the number of **LU** updates done since the last refactorization exceeds REFACTFREQ. The MAXLUUPDATES= option should not be used if INVD_2D was specified in the PROC NETFLOW statement.

In some iterations, a series of single column updates are not able to complete the changes required for a working basis matrix because, ideally, all columns should change at once. If the update cannot be completed, PROC NETFLOW performs a refactorization. The default value for MAXLUUPDATES is 5.

NOINTFIRST

Indicates that of the arcs eligible to be swapped with the leaving arc, the one chosen to do so has best cost. Refer to the INTFIRST option.

REFACTFREQ=*r*
RFF=*r*

specifies the maximum number of **L** and **U** updates between refactorization of the working basis matrix to reinitialize **LU** factors. In most iterations, one or several Bartels-Golub updates can be performed. An update is performed more quickly than a complete refactorization. However, after a series of updates, the sparsity of the **U** factor is degraded. A refactorization is necessary to regain sparsity and to make subsequent computations and updates more efficient. The default value for REFACTFREQ is 50. REFACTFREQ=*r* should not be used if INVD_2D was specified in the PROC NETFLOW statement.

U=*u*

controls the choice of pivot during **LU** decomposition or Bartels-Golub update. When searching for a pivot, any element less than U=*u* times the largest element in its matrix row is excluded, or matrix rows are interchanged to improve numerical stability. The U= option should have values on or between ZERO2 and 1.0. Decreasing the value of the U= option biases the algorithm toward maintaining sparsity at the expense of numerical stability and vice-versa. Reid (1975) suggests that the value of 0.01 is acceptable and this is the default for U=*u*. U=*u* should not be used if INVD_2D was specified in the PROC NETFLOW statement.

Pricing Strategy Options

There are three main types of pricing strategy: PRICETYPEx=NOQ, PRICETYPE x=BLAND, and PRICETYPEx=Q. The one that performs better than the others is PRICETYPEx=Q, so this is the default.

Because the pricing strategy takes a lot of computational time, you should experiment with the options below to find the optimum specification. These options influence the way the pricing step of the simplex iteration is performed. (Refer to **Pricing Strategies** in **DETAILS** for further information.)

```
PRICETYPEx=BLAND
PTYPEx=BLAND

PRICETYPEx=NOQ
PTYPEx= NOQ
PxSCAN= BEST
  PxSCAN=FIRST
  PxSCAN=PARTIAL
  PxNPARTIAL=p

PRICETYPEx= Q
PTYPEx=Q
  PxSCAN=BEST
  PxSCAN=FIRST
  PxSCAN=PARTIAL
  PxNPARTIAL=p
  QxFILLSCAN=BEST
  QxFILLSCAN=FIRST
  QxFILLSCAN=PARTIAL
  QxFILLNPARTIAL=q
  QxFNPART=q
  QSIZEx=q
  Qx=q
  REFRESHQx=r
  REDUCEQSIZEx=r
  REDUCEQx=r
```

Miscellaneous Options

FUTURE1

    signals that PROC NETFLOW must output extra observations to the NODEOUT= and ARCOUT= data sets. These observations contain information about the solution found by doing optimization neglecting any side constraints. These two SAS data sets then can be used as the NODEDATA= and ARCDATA= data sets, respectively, in subsequent PROC NETFLOW runs with the WARM option specified. (See **Warm Starts** in the **DETAILS** section.)

FUTURE2

    signals that PROC NETFLOW must output extra observations to the DUALOUT= and CONOUT= data sets. These observations contain information about the solution found by optimization that considers side constraints. These two SAS data sets then can be used as the NODEDATA= (also called DUALIN=) and ARCDATA= data sets, respectively, in subsequent PROC NETFLOW runs with the WARM option specified. (See **Warm Starts** in the **DETAILS** section.)

NOFUTURE1

negates FUTURE1.

NOFUTURE2

negates FUTURE2.

NOSCRATCH

negates SCRATCH. No optimization considering constraints can occur since the RESET SCRATCH or CONOPT statements were specified.

NOZTOL1

indicates that the majority of tests for roundoff error should not be done. Specifying NOZTOL1 and obtaining the same optimal solution as when the NOZTOL1 option was not specified in the PROC NETFLOW statement, or ZTOL1 was specified, verifies that the zero tolerances were not too high. Roundoff error checks that are critical to the successful functioning of PROC NETFLOW and any related readjustments are always done.

NOZTOL2

indicates that the majority of tests for roundoff error are not to be done during an optimization that considers side constraints. The reasons for specifying NOZTOL2 are the same as those for specifying NOZTOL1 for stage 1 optimization (see the NOZTOL1 option).

SCRATCH

specifies that you do not want PROC NETFLOW to enter or continue stage 1 of the algorithm. Rather than specify RESET SCRATCH, you can use the CONOPT statement.

ZERO1=z

Z1=z

specifies the zero tolerance level in stage 1. If NOZTOL1 is not specified, values within z units of zero are set to 0. Flows close to the lower flow bound or capacity of arcs are reassigned those exact values. Two values are deemed to be close if one is within ZERO1=z of the other. The default value for ZERO1 is 0.000001.

Note: ZERO1 <0.0 or >.0001 is ignored.

ZERO2=z

Z2=z

specifies the zero tolerance level in stage 2. If NOZTOL2 is not specified, values within z units of zero are set to 0. Flows close to the lower flow bound or capacity of arcs are reassigned those exact values. If there are nonarc variables, values close to the lower or upper value bound of nonarcs are reassigned those exact values. Two values are deemed to be close if one is within ZERO2= of the other. The default value for ZERO2 is 0.000001.

Note: ZERO2 <0.0 or >.0001 is ignored.

ZTOL1

indicates that all tests for roundoff error are performed during stage 1 optimization. Any alterations are carried out. The opposite of ZTOL1 is NOZTOL1.

ZTOL2

indicates that all tests for roundoff error are performed during stage 2 optimization. Any alterations are carried out. The opposite of ZTOL2 is NOZTOL2.

RHS Statement

RHS *variable*;

The RHS variable list is used when the dense data format is used. The values of the variable specified in the RHS list are constraint right-hand-side values. If the RHS list is not specified, the CONDATA= data set is searched and a variable with the name _RHS_ is used. If there is no RHS list and no variable named _RHS_, all constraints are assumed to have zero right-hand-side values. The RHS list variable must have numeric values.

ROW Statement

ROW *variables*;

The ROW list is used when either the sparse or dense input format of side constraints is being used. Variables in the ROW list have values that are constraint or special row names. The variables in the ROW list must have character values.

If the dense data format is used, there must be only one variable in this list. In this case, if a ROW list is not specified, the CONDATA= data set is searched and the variable with the name _ROW_ or _CON_ is used.

If the sparse data format is used and the ROW statement is not specified, the CONDATA= data set is searched and variables with names beginning with _ROW or _CON are used. The *i*th ROW list variable is paired with the *i*th COEF list variable. If the number of ROW list variables is greater than the number of COEF list variables, the last ROW list variables have no COEF partner. These ROW list variables that have no corresponding COEF list variable are used in observations that have a TYPE list variable value. All ROW list variable values will be tagged as having the type indicated. If there is no TYPE list variable, all ROW list variable values are constraint names.

RUN Statement

RUN;

The RUN statement causes optimization to be started or resumed. The RUN statement has no options. If PROC NETFLOW is called and is not terminated because of an error or QUIT statement, and you have not used a RUN statement, a RUN statement is assumed implicitly as the last statement of PROC NETFLOW. Therefore, PROC NETFLOW always performs optimization and saves the obtained (optimal) solution in the current output data sets.

SAVE Statement

SAVE *options*;

The SAVE statement can be used to specify output data sets and create observations in these data sets. Use the SAVE statement if no optimization is to be performed before these output data sets are created.

The SAVE statement must be used to save solutions in data sets if there is no more optimization to do. If more optimization is to be performed, after which you want to save the solution, then do one of the following:

- Submit a RUN statement followed by a SAVE statement.
- Use the PROC NETFLOW RESET statement to specify current output data sets. After optimization, output data sets are created and observations are automatically sent to the current output data sets.

The options below can appear in the SAVE statement:

ARCOUT=*dataset*
AOUT=*dataset*
NODEOUT=*dataset*
NOUT=*dataset*
CONOUT=*dataset*
COUT=*dataset*
DUALOUT=*dataset*
DOUT=*dataset*

SHOW Statement

SHOW *options/qualifiers;*

The SHOW statement enables you to examine the status of the problem and values of the RESET statement options. The amount of information displayed when a SHOW statement is processed can be limited if some of the options of the SHOW statement are specified. These options indicate whether the problem status or what category of the RESET options are of interest. If no options are specified, the problem status and information on all RESET statement options in every category is displayed. The amount of displayed information can be limited further by following any SHOW statement options with a slash (/) and one or both qualifiers, RELEVANT and STAGE.

The options below can appear in the SHOW statement.

STATUS
    produces one of the following optimization status reports, whichever is applicable. The warning messages are issued only if the network or entire problem is infeasible.

```
NOTE: Optimization Status.
      Optimization has not started yet.

NOTE: Optimization Status.
      Optimizing network (ignoring any side constraints).
      Number of iterations=17
      Of these, 3 were degenerate
WARNING: This optimization has detected that the network is infeasible.

NOTE: Optimization Status.
      Found network optimum (ignoring side constraints)
      Number of iterations=23
      Of these, 8 were degenerate
```

```
NOTE: Optimization Status.
      Optimizing side constrained network.
      Number of iterations=27
      Of these, 9 were degenerate
WARNING: This optimization has detected that the problem is infeasible.

NOTE: Optimization Status.
      Found side constrained network optimum
      Number of iterations=6
      Of these, 0 were degenerate
```

DATASETS

produces a report on output data sets.

```
NOTE: Current output SAS datasets
      No output datasets have been specified

NOTE: Current output SAS datasets
      ARCOUT=libname.memname
      NODEOUT=libname.memname
      CONOUT=libname.memname
      DUALOUT=libname.memname

NOTE: Other SAS datasets specified in previous ARCOUT=, NODEOUT=,
      CONOUT=, or DUALOUT=.
      libname.memname
                 .
                 .
                 .
```

PAUSE

produces a report on the current settings of options used to make
optimization pause.

```
NOTE: Options and parameters that stop optimization for reasons other
      than infeasibility or optimality
      FEASIBLEPAUSE1=FALSE
      ENDPAUSE1=FALSE
      PAUSE1=999999
      MAXIT1=1000
      FEASIBLEPAUSE2=FALSE
      PAUSE2=999999
      MAXIT2=999999
```

SIMPLEX

produces the following:

```
NOTE: Options and parameters that control the primal simplex network
      algorithm (excluding those that affect the pricing strategies)
      LRATIO1=FALSE
      INTFIRST=TRUE
      LRATIO2=TRUE
      REFACTFREQ=50
      SPARSE=-1
      U=0.1
      MAXLUUPDATES=6
      MAXL=999999
```

PRICING
> produces the following:

```
NOTE: Options and parameters that control the primal simplex network
      algorithm pricing strategies
      PRICETYPE1=Q
      P1SCAN=FIRST
      P1NPARTIAL=10
      Q1FILLSCAN=FIRST
      QSIZE1=24
      REFRESHQ1=0.5
      REDUCEQSIZE1=0.5
      Q1FILLNPARTIAL=10
      PRICETYPE2=Q
      P2SCAN=FIRST
      P2NPARTIAL=10
      Q2FILLSCAN=FIRST
      QSIZE2=16
      REFRESHQ2=0.5
      REDUCEQSIZE2=0.5
      Q2FILLNPARTIAL=10
```

MISC
> produces the following:

```
NOTE: Miscellaneous options and parameters
      ZTOL1=TRUE
      ZERO1=1E-6
      FUTURE1=FALSE
      ZTOL2=TRUE
      ZERO2=1E-6
      FUTURE2=FALSE
```

Following a slash (/), the qualifiers below can appear in any SHOW statement.

RELEVANT
> indicates that you want information only on relevant options of the RESET statement. The following will not be displayed if / RELEVANT is specified:

- Information on noncurrent data sets.
- The options that control the reasons stage 1 optimization should be halted, the options that control the simplex algorithm during stage 1 optimization, if the unconstrained optimum has been reached or constrained optimization has been performed.
- If P1SCAN=BEST or FIRST, P1NPARTIAL is irrelevant.
- If PRICETYPE1=BLAND or NOQ, then the options QSIZE1, Q1FILLSCAN, REFRESHQ1, and REDUCEQSIZE1 are irrelevant.
- If Q1FILLSCAN=BEST or FIRST, Q1FILLNPARTIAL is irrelevant.
- The options that control the reasons stage 2 optimization should be halted, the options that control the simplex algorithm during stage 2 optimization, if the constrained optimum has been reached.
- If P2SCAN=BEST or FIRST, P2NPARTIAL is irrelevant.
- If PRICETYPE2=BLAND or NOQ, then the options QSIZE2, Q2FILLSCAN, REFRESHQ2, and REDUCEQSIZE2 are irrelevant.
- If Q2FILLSCAN=BEST or Q2FILLSCAN=FIRST, Q2FILLNPARTIAL is irrelevant.

STAGE

indicates that you wish to examine only the options that affect the optimization that will be done if a RUN statement is executed next. Before any optimization has been done, only stage 2 options will be displayed if the problem has side constraints and the SCRATCH option of the RESET statement is used, or the CONOPT statement was specified. Otherwise, stage 1 options are displayed. If still optimizing neglecting constraints, only stage 1 options will be displayed. If the unconstrained optimum has been reached and optimization that considers constraints has not been performed, stage 1 options will be displayed and if the problem has constraints, stage 2 options will be displayed. If optimization that considers constraints has been performed, only stage 2 options will be displayed.

SUPDEM Statement

SUPDEM *variable*;

The variable in this list, which must be present in the NODEDATA= data set, contains supply and demand information for the nodes in the NODE list. A positive SUPDEM list variable value *s* (*s*>0) denotes that the node named in the NODE list variable has supply capability of *s* units of flow. A negative SUPDEM list variable value -*d* (*d*>0) means that this node demands *d* units of flow. If a variable is not explicitly specified, NODEDATA= is searched for a variable with the name _SUPDEM_ or _SD_. If a node is a transshipment node (neither a supply nor a demand node), an observation associated with this node need not be present in the NODEDATA= data set. Otherwise, if present, the SUPDEM list variable value must be zero or a missing value.

SUPPLY Statement

SUPPLY *variable*;

The SUPPLY statement identifies the variable in the ARCDATA= data set that contains the supply at the node named in that observation's TAILNODE list variable. If a tail node does not supply flow, use zero or a missing value for the observation's SUPPLY list variable value. If a tail node has supply capability, a missing value indicates that the supply quantity is given in another observation. It is not necessary to have a SUPPLY statement if the name of this variable is _SUPPLY_.

TAILNODE Statement

TAILNODE *variable*;
TAIL *variable*;
FROMNODE *variable*;
FROM *variable*;

The TAILNODE statement specifies the variable that must be present in the ARCDATA= data set that contains the names of tail nodes of arcs. The TAILNODE variable must have character values. It is not necessary to have a TAILNODE statement if the name of the tail node variable is _TAIL_ or _FROM_. If the TAILNODE list variable value is missing, it is assumed that the observation of ARCDATA= contains information concerning a nonarc variable.

TYPE Statement

> TYPE *variable*;
> CONTYPE *variable*;

The TYPE list, which is optional, names the variable that contains keywords that indicate constraint type for each constraint, or the type of special rows in the CONDATA= data set. The values of the TYPE list variable also indicate how, in each observation of CONDATA, the values of the VAR or COEF list variables are to be interpreted and how the type of each constraint or special row name is determined. If the TYPE list is not specified, the CONDATA= data set is searched and a variable with the name _TYPE_ is used. Valid keywords for the TYPE variable are given in the **DETAILS** section. If there is no TYPE statement and no other method is used to furnish type information (refer to the DEFCONTYPE= option), all constraints are assumed to be of the type "less than or equal to" and no special rows are used. The TYPE list variable must have character values and can be used when the data in CONDATA is in either the sparse or dense format. If the TYPE list variable value is a * character, the observation is ignored because it is a comment observation.

TYPE List Variable Values

The following are valid TYPE list variable values. The letters in boldface denote the characters that NETFLOW uses to determine what type the value suggests. You need to have at least these characters. Below, the minimal TYPE list variable values have additional characters to aid you in remembering these values.

The valid TYPE list variable values are

LE
> less than or equal to ($\leq$)

EQ
> equal to ($=$)

GE
> greater than or equal to ($\geq$)

CAPAC
> capacity

COST
> cost

EQ
> equal to

GE
> greater than or equal to

LE
> less than or equal to

LOWERBD
> lower flow or value bound

LO
> lower flow or value bound (**LO**blank)

MAXIMIZE
> maximize (opposite of cost)

MINIMIZE
> minimize (same as cost)

OBJECTIVE
  objective function (same as cost)

RHS
  rhs of constraint

TYPE
  type of constraint

UPPER
  upper value bound or capacity.

The valid TYPE list variable values in function order are

LE
  less than or equal to ($\leq$)

EQ
  Equal to ($=$)

GE
  Greater than or equal to ($\geq$)

COST
MINIMIZE
MAXIMIZE
OBJECTIVE
  cost or objective function coef

CAPAC
UPPER
  capacity or upper value bound

LOWERBD
LO (**LO**blank)
  Lower flow or value bound

RHS
  rhs of constraint

TYPE
  type of constraint.

VAR Statement

  VAR *variables*;

The VAR variable list is used when the dense data format is used. The names of these variables are also names of the arc and nonarc variables that have data in the CONDATA= data set. If the dense format is used and no explicit VAR list is specified, all numeric variables not on other lists are put onto the VAR list. The VAR list variables must have numeric values. The values of the VAR list variables in some observations may be interpreted differently than these variable values in other observations. The values may be coefficients in the side constraints, costs and objective function coefficients, or bound data. How these numeric values are interpreted depends on the value of each observation's TYPE or ROW list variable value. If there are no TYPE list variables, the VAR list variable values are all assumed to be side constraint coefficients.

DETAILS

Input SAS Data Sets

PROC NETFLOW is designed so that there are as few rules as possible that you must obey when inputting a problem's data. Raw data are acceptable. This should cut the amount of processing required to groom the data before it is input to PROC NETFLOW. Data formats are so flexible that, due to space restrictions, all possible forms that a problem's data can be in are not shown here. Try any reasonable form that your problem's data is in; it should be acceptable. PROC NETFLOW will outline what it objects to.

There are several ways to supply the same piece of data. You do not have to restrict yourself to using any particular one. If you use several ways, PROC NETFLOW will check that the data are consistent each time the data are encountered. After all input data sets have been read, data are merged so that the problem is described completely. The order of the observations is not important in any of the input data sets.

The ARCDATA= Data Set

Please refer to the **Overview** and **Introductory Example** for a description of this input data set.

Note: information of an arc or nonarc variable may be specified in more than one observation. For example, consider arc directed from node A toward node B that has cost of 50, capacity of 100, and lower flow bound of 10 flow units. Some observations of ARCDATA= data set may be

```
_TAIL_  _HEAD_  _COST_  _CAPAC_  _LO_
  A       B      50        .       .
  A       B       .       100      .
  A       B       .        .      10
  A       B      50       100      .
  A       B       .       100     10
  A       B      50        .      10
  A       B      50       100     10
```

Similarly, for a nonarc with upperbd=100, lowerbd=10, and objfn coef=50, the _TAIL_ and _HEAD_ values will be missing.

The CONDATA= Data Set

Regardless of whether the data in CONDATA is in the sparse or dense format, a constraint ROW, that has no coefficients with it, will produce a warning message. If a non-arc variable has no constraint coefficients, then a warning will be issued.

Non-sparse input format   If the non-sparse format is used, variables have names of arc and nonarc variables that have data in the CONDATA= data set. Such variables are either specified in the VAR list and have names that can be values of the NAME list variables in the ARCDATA= data set, names of nonarc variables or names in the form *tail_head*. Note: if you intend to use those default arc names, you must specify node names using no lowercase letters. There can be three other variables in the CONDATA= data set, belonging, respectively, to the ROW, TYPE, and RHS lists. The CONDATA= data set of the oil industry example in the **INTRODUCTION** uses the non-sparse data format.

Consider the SAS code that creates a dense format CONDATA= data set that has data of three constraints.

```
data conda1;
    input por_np np_aklds hutt_man tai_ham wgtn_man man_tai type $ rhs;
    cards;
        -0.5      1        .      .        .        .   =      0
          .       .        2      3        .        .   le    80
          1      -3        2      .       -2        4   ge   325
    ;
```

We can use non-constraint type values to furnish data on costs, capacities, lower flow bounds (and, if there are nonarc variables, objective function coefficients and upper and lower bounds). You need not have such (or as much) data in ARCDATA= data set.

```
data conda2;
    input por_np np_aklds hutt_man tai_ham wgtn_man man_tai type $ rhs;
    cards;
        -0.5      1        .      .        .        .   =      0
          10     29        .     16        4       -3   cost   .
          .       .        2      3        .        .   le    80
          50    100        .    120       40        .   capac  .
          1      -3        2      .       -2        4   ge   325
    ;
```

If a ROW list variable is used, the data for a constraint can be spread over more than 1 observation.

```
data conda3;
    input row $ por_np np_aklds hutt_man tai_ham wgtn_man man_tai
        type $ rhs;
    cards;
    row3    .       .     .     .    -2     .     .     .
    row1   -0.5     .     .     .     .     .     =     .
    row2    .       .     .     3     .     .     .    80
    row3    1       .     .     .     .     .     .     .
    row1    .       1     .     .     .     .     =     0
    row3    .      -3     .     .     .     .     .     .
    row3    .       .     2     .     .     .     .   325
    row2    .       .     2     .     .     .     le    .
    row3    .       .     .     .     .     4     ge    .
    ;
```

Using both ROW and TYPE lists, you can use special row names. For example, in observation 2 in the following data set, MY_CAPAC is defined as a capacity special row name. Knowing this, PROC NETFLOW is able to treat the values of the VAR list variables in the last observation as capacities or upper bounds. It should be restated that in any of the input data sets of PROC NETFLOW, the order of the observation does not matter. The fact that the type of the special row MY_CAPAC is read in an observation before observations where MY_CAPAC is a ROW list variable value without a nonmissing TYPE list is convenient. This helps the input data set to be read more quickly, but is not mandatory.

```
data conda4;
    input por_np por_man wgtn_man hutt_man wgtn_nap hutt_nap man_tai
        np_makld taimakld napmakld np_aklds taiaklds napaklds tai_ham
        nap_ham type $ row $ rhs;
```

```
cards;
  10   .   .   .   .   .   .   .   5   .   .   .   .  10   .       my_lo  .
   .   .   .   .   .   .   .   .   .   .   .   .   .   . capac  my_capac  .
   .   .  -2   .   .   .   .   .   .   .   .   .   .   .   .      row3   .
   5   .   .  10   .   .   .   .   5   5   .   .   5   .   .      my_lo  .
  61   . 83   . 78   .   0   . 55   . 40   . 11   . 21 cost   my_cost  .
-0.5   .   .   .   .   .   .   .   .   .   .   .   .   .   =      row1   .
   .   .   .   .   .   .   .   .   .   .   .   .   3   .   .      row2  80
   1   .   .   .   .   .   .   .   .   .   .   .   .   .   .      row3   .
   .   .   .   .   .   .   .   .   .   .   1   .   .   .   =      row1   0
  40  40  40  80  35  50 160   .   .   .   .   .   .  40   .   .  my_capac  .
   .   .   .   .   .   .   .   .   .  -3   .   .   .   .   .      row3   .
   .   .   .   2   .   .   .   .   .   .   .   .   .   .   .      row3 325
  10   .   .  10   .   .   .   .   .   2   .   .   5  10 lowerbd my_lo  .
   .   .   .   2   .   .   .   .   .   .   .   .   .   .  le      row2   .
   .  24   .  58   .  32   .  34   .  75   .  64   .  17   .  .  my_cost  .
   .   .   .   .   .   .   .   4   .   .   .   .   .   .  ge      row3   .
  40  50  40   .  55  50   .  20  65  65  20  50  40  20  35  .  my_capac  .
;
```

Sparse-side constraint input format The side constraints usually become sparse as the problem size increases. When the sparse data format of the CONDATA= data set is used, only nonzero constraint coefficients must be specified. Remember to specify the SPARSECONDATA option in the PROC NETFLOW statement. With the sparse method of specifying constraint information, the names of arc and nonarc variables do not have to be valid SAS variable names.

The CONDATA= data set for the oil industry example is printed below.

```
title 'Setting Up Condata = Cond2 for PROC NETFLOW';
  data cond2;
     input _column_ $ _row1 $ _coef1 _row2 $ _coef2 ;
     cards;
     m_e_ref1  con1  -2    .   .
     m_e_ref2  con2  -2    .   .
     thruput1  con1   1  con3  -3
     r1_gas      .    .  con3   4
     thruput2  con2   1  con4  -3
     r2_gas      .    .  con4   4
     _type_    con1   1  con2   1
     _type_    con3   0  con4   0
     _rhs_     con1 -15  con2 -15
  ;
```

Recall that the COLUMN list variable values _TYPE_ and _RHS_ are the default values of the TYPEOBS and RHSOBS options. Also the default rhs value of constraints (CON3 and CON4) is zero. The third to last observation has the value _type_ for the COLUMN list variable. The _ROW1 variable value is con1 and the _COEF1 variable has the value 1. This indicates that the constraint con1 is *greater than* or equal to type (because the value 1 is *greater than* zero). Similarly, the data in the second to last observation's _ROW2 and _COEF2 variable indicates that CON4 is an *equality* constraint (0 *equals* zero).

An alternative, using a TYPE list variable:

```
title 'Setting Up Condata = Cond3 for PROC NETFLOW';
  data cond3;
     input _column_ $ _row1 $ _coef1 _row2 $ _coef2 _type_ $ ;
```

```
       cards;
        m_e_ref1  con1  -2      .    .  >=
        m_e_ref2  con2  -2      .    .  .
        thruput1  con1   1   con3  -3  .
        r1_gas      .    .   con3   4  .
        thruput2  con2   1   con4  -3  .
        r2_gas      .    .   con4   4  .
        .         con3   .   con4   .  eq
        .         con1 -15   con2 -15  ge
    ;
```

If the COLUMN list variable is missing in a particular observation (the last 2 observations in the data set COND3 above, for instance), the constraints named in the ROW list variables all have the constraint type indicated by the value in the TYPE list variable. It is for this type of observation that you are allowed more ROW list variables than COEF list variables. If corresponding COEF list variables are not missing (for example, the last observation in the data set COND3 above), these values are the rhs values of those constraints. Therefore, you can specify both constraint type and rhs in the same observation.

As in the CONDATA= data set above, if the COLUMN list variable is an arc or nonarc variable, the COEF list variable values are coefficient values for that arc or nonarc variable in the constraints indicated in the corresponding ROW list variables. If, in this same observation, the TYPE list variable contains a constraint type, all constraints named in the ROW list variables have this constraint type (for example, the first observation in the data set COND3 above). Therefore, you can specify both constraint type and coefficient information in the same observation.

Also note that DEFCONTYPE=EQ could have been specified, saving you from having to include in the data that CON3 and CON4 are of this type.

In the oil industry example, arc costs, capacities, and lower flow bounds are presented in the ARCDATA= data set. Alternatively, you could have used the following input data sets:

```
    title3 'Setting Up Arcdata = Arcd2 for PROC NETFLOW';
    data arcd2;
       input _from_&$11. _to_&$15. ;
       cards;
        middle east   refinery 1
        middle east   refinery 2
        u.s.a.        refinery 1
        u.s.a.        refinery 2
        refinery 1    r1
        refinery 2    r2
        r1            ref1 gas
        r1            ref1 diesel
        r2            ref2 gas
        r2            ref2 diesel
        ref1 gas      servstn1 gas
        ref1 gas      servstn2 gas
        ref1 diesel   servstn1 diesel
        ref1 diesel   servstn2 diesel
        ref2 gas      servstn1 gas
        ref2 gas      servstn2 gas
        ref2 diesel   servstn1 diesel
        ref2 diesel   servstn2 diesel
```

```
title 'Setting Up Condata = Cond4 for PROC NETFLOW';
data cond4;
   input _column_&$27. _row1 $ _coef1 _row2 $ _coef2 _type_ $ ;
   cards;
.                                  con1  -15  con2  -15    ge
.                                  costrow    .     .    . cost
.                                    .     . caprow    . capac
middle east_refinery 1             con1   -2    .       .    .
middle east_refinery 2             con2   -2    .       .    .
refinery 1_r1                      con1    1  con3   -3    .
r1_ref1 gas                          .     .  con3    4     =
refinery 2_r2                      con2    1  con4   -3    .
r2_ref2 gas                          .     .  con4    4    eq
middle east_refinery 1             costrow 63 caprow  95    .
middle east_refinery 2             costrow 81 caprow  80    .
u.s.a._refinery 1                  costrow 55    .       .    .
u.s.a._refinery 2                  costrow 49    .       .    .
refinery 1_r1                      costrow 200 caprow 175   .
refinery 2_r2                      costrow 220 caprow 100   .
r1_ref1 gas                          .     . caprow 140   .
r1_ref1 diesel                       .     . caprow  75   .
r2_ref2 gas                          .     . caprow 100   .
r2_ref2 diesel                       .     . caprow  75   .
ref1 gas_servstn1 gas              costrow 15 caprow  70    .
ref1 gas_servstn2 gas              costrow 22 caprow  60    .
ref1 diesel_servstn1 diesel        costrow 18    .       .    .
ref1 diesel_servstn2 diesel        costrow 17    .       .    .
ref2 gas_servstn1 gas              costrow 17 caprow  35    .
ref2 gas_servstn2 gas              costrow 31    .       .    .
ref2 diesel_servstn1 diesel        costrow 36    .       .    .
ref2 diesel_servstn2 diesel        costrow 23    .       .    .
middle east_refinery 1               .    20    .       .    lo
middle east_refinery 2               .    10    .       .    lo
refinery 1_r1                        .    50    .       .    lo
refinery 2_r2                        .    35    .       .    lo
ref2 gas_servstn1 gas                .     5    .       .    lo
;
```

The first observation of COND4 defines CON1 and CON2 as *greater than or equal to* ($\geq$) constraints that both (by coincidence) have rhs values of -15. The second observation defines the special row COSTROW as a cost row. When COSTROW is a ROW list variable value, the associated COEF list variable value will be interpreted as a cost or objective function coefficient. PROC NETFLOW has to do less work if constraint names and special rows are defined in observations near the top of a data set, but this is not a strict requirement. The fourth to ninth observations contain constraint coefficient data. Observations 7 and 9 have nonmissing TYPE list variable values that indicate that constraints CON3 and CON4 are equality constraints. The last five observations contain lower flow data. Observations that have an arc or nonarc variable name in the COLUMN list variable, a non-constraint type TYPE list variable, and a value in (one of) the COEF list variables are valid.

The following data set is equivalent to COND4.

```
title 'Setting Up Condata = Cond5 for PROC NETFLOW';
data cond5;
   input _column_&$27. _row1 $ _coef1 _row2 $ _coef2 _type_ $ ;
```

```
          cards;
           middle east_refinery 1           con1  -2 costrow  63   .
           middle east_refinery 2           con2  -2 lorow    10   .
           refinery 1_r1                       .   . con3     -3   =
           r1_ref1 gas                      caprow 140 con3     4   .
           refinery 2_r2                    con2   1 con4     -3   .
           r2_ref2 gas                         .   . con4      4  eq
           .                                CON1 -15 CON2    -15  GE
           ref2 diesel_servstn1 diesel         .  36 costrow   . cost
           .                                   .   . caprow    . capac
           .                                lorow   .    .     .  lo
           middle east_refinery 1           caprow  95 lorow   20   .
           middle east_refinery 2           caprow  80 costrow  81   .
           u.s.a._refinery 1                   .   .    .      55 cost
           u.s.a._refinery 2                costrow  49   .     .   .
           refinery 1_r1                    con1    1 caprow  175   .
           refinery 1_r1                    lorow   50 costrow 200   .
           refinery 2_r2                    costrow 220 caprow 100   .
           refinery 2_r2                       .  35    .     .  lo
           r1_ref1 diesel                   caprow2  75    .     . capac
           r2_ref2 gas                         .   . caprow  100   .
           r2_ref2 diesel                   caprow2  75    .     .   .
           ref1 gas_servstn1 gas            costrow  15 caprow   70   .
           ref1 gas_servstn2 gas            caprow2  60 costrow  22   .
           ref1 diesel_servstn1 diesel         .   . costrow  18   .
           ref1 diesel_servstn2 diesel      costrow  17    .     .   .
           ref2 gas_servstn1 gas            costrow  17 lorow    5   .
           ref2 gas_servstn1 gas               .   . caprow2  35   .
           ref2 gas_servstn2 gas               .  31    .     . cost
           ref2 diesel_servstn2 diesel         .   . costrow  23   .
          ;
```

If you have data for a linear programming program that has an embedded network, the steps required to change that data into a form that is acceptable by PROC NETFLOW are as follows:

- Identify the nodal flow conservation constraints. The coefficient matrix of these constraints (a submatrix of the LP's constraint coefficient matrix) has only two nonzero elements in each column, -1 and 1.
- Assign a node to each nodal flow conservation constraint.
- The rhs values of conservation constraints are the corresponding nodes supplies and demands. Use this information to create a NODEDATA= data set.
- Assign an arc to each column of the flow conservation constraint coefficient matrix. The arc is directed from the node associated with the row that has the 1 element in it and directed toward to the node associated with the row that has the −1 element in it. Set up an ARCDATA= data set that has two SAS variables. This data set could resemble ARCDATA=ARCD2 above. These will eventually be the TAIL and HEAD list variables when PROC NETFLOW is used. Each observation consists of the tail and head node of each arc.
- Remove from the data of the linear program all data concerning the nodal flow conservation constraints.
- Put the remaining data into a CONDATA= data set. This data set will probably resemble CONDATA=COND4 or COND5 above. .

The sparse-side constraint input format summary   Depending on how you set up your input data set and what variables you choose to use, the following list illustrates possible formats.

- If there is no TYPE list variable in the data set the problem must be constrained and there is no non-constraint data in CONDATA

	COLUMN	_ROWx_	_COEFx_	_ROWy_ (no _COEFy_)
				(may not be in CONDATA)
a1	variable	constraint	lhs coef	+------------------+
a2	_TYPE_ or	constraint	-1 0 1	| |
	TYPEOBS			| |
a3	_RHS_ or	constraint	rhs value	| |
	RHSOBS or .			| constraint or . |
a4	_TYPE_ or	constraint	.	| |
	TYPEOBS			| |
a5	_RHS_ or	constraint	.	| |
	RHSOBS or .			+------------------+

a4 and a5 serve no useful purpose but are still allowed to make problem generation easier.

- If there are no ROW list variables in the data set the problem has no constraints and the information is non-constraint data. There must be a TYPE list variable and only one COEF list variable. The COLUMN list variable has as values the names of arcs or nonarcs and must not be missing values or special row names.

	COLUMN	_TYPE_	_COEFx_
b1	variable	UPPERBD	capacity
b2	variable	LOWERBD	lower flow
b3	variable	COST	cost
.	.	.	.
.	.	.	.
.	.	.	.

- Using a TYPE list variable for constraint data implies the following:

	COLUMN	_TYPE_	_ROWx_	_COEFx_	_ROWy_ (no _COEFy_)
					(may not be in CONDATA)
c1	variable	.	constraint	lhs coef	+------------------+
c2	_TYPE_ or	.	constraint	-1 0 1	| |
	TYPEOBS				| |
c3	_RHS_ .		constraint	rhs value	| |
	or RHSOBS				| |
c4	variable	con type	constraint	lhs coef	| constraint or . |
c5	_RHS_ .	con type	constraint	rhs value	| |
	or RHSOBS				| |
c6	.	TYPE	constraint	-1 0 1	| |
c7	.	RHS	constraint	rhs value	+------------------+

The _COEFx_ values may be missing in which case the constraint is given type data if the observation is in form c4 or c5.

- Using a TYPE list variable for arc and nonarc variable data implies the following:

```
        _COLUMN_      _TYPE_      _ROWx_      _COEFx_   _ROWy_(no _COEFy_)
                                                        (may not be in CONDATA)

        +----------+ +----------+ +----------+          +----------+
    d1  | variable | | UPPERBD  | | missing  | capacity | missing  |
    d2  |          | | LOWERBD  | |   or     | lower flow |  or    |
    d3  |          | | COST     | | special  | cost     | special  |
    d4  |          | | FXDCHRG  | |  row     |   .      |  row     |
    d5  |          | | INTEGER  | | name     |   .      | name     |
    d6  |          | | MULT     | |          |   .      |          |
        +----------+ |          | |          |          |          |
    d7      .        |          | | special  |          |          |
                     |          | |  row     |          |          |
                     |          | | name     |          |          |
                     +----------+ +----------+          +----------+
    d8     variable       .        special   value that     .
                                    row     is interpreted
                                    name    according to
                                            _ROWx_
```

The observation with form d1 to d6 can have ROW list variable values. Observation d7 must have ROW list variable values. The ROW value is put into the ROW name tree so that when dealing with observation d7 or d8, the COEF list variable value is interpreted according to the type of ROW list variable value. For example,

```
    _COLUMN_           _TYPE_         _ROWx_          _COEFx_

        .              UPPERBD        up_row             .
    variable_a         LOWERBD        lo_row          lower flow
    variable_b         COST           co_row          cost
```

Now you can have another observation in the form

```
    _COLUMN_ _TYPE_  _ROW1_ _COEF1_  _ROW2_ _COEF2_  _ROW3_ _COEF3_

    var_c      .     up_row  upval   lo_row  loval   co_row  cost
```

If the TYPE list variable value is a constraint type, and the value of the COLUMN list variable equals the TYPEOBS parameter or the default value _TYPE_, the TYPE list variable value is ignored.

The NODEDATA= Data Set

Please refer to the **Overview** and **Introductory Example** for a description of this input data set.

Output SAS Data Sets

The procedure determines the flow that should pass through each arc as well as the value assigned to each nonarc variable. The goal is that the minimum flow bounds, capacities, lower and upper value bounds, and side constraints are not violated. This goal is reached when total cost incurred by such a flow pattern and value assignment is optimal. The solution found must also conserve flow at each node.

The ARCOUT= data set contains a solution obtained when performing optimization that does not consider any constraints. The NODEOUT= data set contains nodal dual variable information for this type of solution. You can choose to have PROC NETFLOW create the ARCOUT= data set or the NODEOUT= data set and save the optimum of the network or the nodal dual variable values before any optimization that considered the side constraints is performed.

If there are side constraints, the CONOUT= data set can be produced and contains a solution obtained after performing optimization that considers constraints. The DUALOUT= data set contains dual variable information of nodes and side constraints obtained when the solution was obtained after optimization that considered the constraints. CONOUT= and DUALOUT= data sets can be used to save the constrained optimal solution.

The ARCOUT= and CONOUT= Data Sets

The ARCOUT= and CONOUT= data sets contain the same variables. These variables and their possible values in an observation are as follows:

FROM   a tail node of an arc. This is a missing value if an observation has information about a nonarc variable.

_TO_   a head node of an arc. This is a missing value if an observation has information about a nonarc variable.

COST   the cost of an arc or the objective function coefficient of a nonarc variable.

CAPAC   the capacity of an arc or upper value bound of a nonarc variable.

_LO_   the lower flow bound of an arc or lower value bound of a nonarc variable.

NAME   a name of an arc or nonarc variable.

SUPPLY   the supply of the tail node of the arc in the observation.

DEMAND   the demand of the head node of the arc in the observation.

FLOW   the flow through the arc or value of the nonarc variable.

FCOST   flow cost, the product of _COST_ and _FLOW_.

RCOST   the reduced cost of the arc or nonarc variable.

ANUMB   the number of the arc or nonarc variable. Used for warm starting PROC NETFLOW.

TNUMB   the number of the tail node. Used for warm starting PROC NETFLOW.

STATUS   the status of the arc or nonarc.

The variables present in the ARCDATA= data set are present in a ARCOUT= or CONOUT= data set. For example, if there is a variable called TAIL in ARCDATA= and you specified the SAS variable list

```
from tail;
```

then TAIL is a variable in the ARCOUT= or CONOUT= data sets, not _FROM_. Any ID list variables also appear in ARCOUT= or CONOUT= data sets.

The NODEOUT= and DUALOUT= Data Sets

There are two types of observations in the NODEOUT= and DUALOUT= data set. One type of observation contains information about a node. These are called *type N* observations. There is one such observation of this type for each node.

The _NODE_ variable has a name of a node and the _CON_ variable values in these observations are missing values.

The other type of observation contains information about constraints. These are called the *type C* observations. There is one such observation of this type for each constraint. The _CON_ variable has a name of a constraint and the _NODE_ variable values in these observations are missing values.

Many of the variables in the NODEOUT= and DUALOUT= data sets contain information so that this solution may be used to warm start PROC NETFLOW. The variables that will be of most interest to you are _NODE_, _SD_, _DUAL_, _VALUE_, _RHS_, _TYPE_, and _CON_.

The NODEOUT= and DUALOUT= data sets look similar as the same variables are in both. These variables and what the values in an observation of each are:

NODE   Type N: a node name. Type C: a missing value.

_SD_   Type N: the supply (positive) or demand (negative) of the node. Type C: a missing value.

DUAL   Type N: the dual variable value of the node in _NODE_. Type C: the dual variable value of the constraint named in _CON_.

NNUMB   Type N: the number of the node named in _NODE_. Type C: the number of the constraint named in _CON_.

PRED   Type N: the predecessor in the network basis spanning tree of the node named in _NODE_. Type C: the number of the node toward which the arc with number in _ARCID_ is directed, or the constraint number associated with the slack, surplus, or artificial variable basic in this row.

TRAV   Type N: the traversal thread label of the node named in _NODE_. Type C: a missing value.

SCESS   Type N: the number of successors (including itself) in the network basis spanning tree of the node named in _NODE_. Type C: a missing value.

ARCID   Type N: if _ARCID_ is nonnegative, _ARCID_ is the number of the network basis spanning tree arc directed from the node with number _PRED_ to the node named in _NODE_. If _ARCID_ is negative, −_ARCID_ is the number of the network basis spanning tree arc directed from the node named in _NODE_ to the node with number _PRED_. Type C: if _ARCID_ is positive, _ARCID_ is the number of the arc basic in a constraint row. If nonpositive, −_ARCID_ is the number of the nonarc variable basic in a constraint row.

FLOW   Type N: the flow minus the lower flow bound of the arc _ARCID_. Type C: the flow minus lower flow bound of the arc _ARCID_ or lower bound value of the nonarc variable value −_ARCID_.

FBQ   Type N: if _FBQ_ is positive, then _FBQ_ is the subscript in arc length arrays of the first arc directed toward the node named in _NODE_. NETFLOW's arc length arrays are sorted so that data of arcs directed toward the same headnode are together. If _FBQ_ is negative, no arcs are directed toward the node named in _NODE_. Arcs directed toward node i have subscripts in the arc length arrays between FBQ(i) to observation (FBQ($i+1$))-1. Type C: missing value.

VALUE   Type N: missing value. Type C: the lhs value (the sum of the products of coefficient and flows or values) of the constraint named in _CON_.

RHS   Type N: missing value. Type C: the rhs value of the constraint named in _CON_.

TYPE   Type N: missing value. Type C: the type of the constraint named in _CON_.

CON   Type N: missing value. Type C: the name of a constraint.

If specified in variable lists, the variables in the input SAS data sets are used instead of some of the variables above. These variables are specified in the NODE, SUPDEM, RHS, TYPE, and ROW (if there is only one variable in the ROW list) lists and are used instead of _NODE_, _SD_, _RHS_, _TYPE_, and _CON_, respectively.

Loop Arcs

When using the primal simplex network algorithm, loop arcs (arcs directed toward nodes from which they originate) are prohibited. Rather, introduce a dummy intermediate node in loop arcs. For example, replace arc (A,A) with (A,B) and (B,A). B is the name of a new node. B must be distinct for each loop arc.

Multiple Arcs

Multiple arcs with the same tail and head nodes are prohibited. PROC NETFLOW checks to ensure there are no such arcs before proceeding with the optimization. Introduce a new dummy intermediate node in multiple arcs. This node must be distinct for each multiple arc. For example, if some network has three arcs directed from node A toward node B, then replace one of these three with arcs (A,C) and (C,B) and replace another one with (A,D) and (D,B). C and D are new nodes added to the network.

Pricing Strategies

The pricing strategy is the part of the simplex iteration that selects the nonbasic arc, constraint slack, surplus, or nonarc variable that should have a flow or value change, and perhaps enter the basis so that the total cost incurred is improved.

The pricing mechanism takes a large amount of computational effort, so it is important to use the appropriate pricing strategy for the problem under study. As in other large scale mathematical programming software, network codes can spend more than half of their execution time performing simplex iterations in the pricing step. Some compromise must be made between using a fast strategy and improving the quality of the candidate for flow or value change found. It is usually quicker overall to use a fast pricing strategy although more simplex iterations may need to be executed.

The configuration of the problem to be optimized has a great effect on the choice of strategy to use. If a problem is to be run repetitively, experimentation on that network to determine which scheme is best may prove worthwhile. The best pricing strategy to use when there is a large amount of work to do (for example, when a cold start is used) may not be appropriate when there is little work required to reach the optimum (such as when a warm start is used). If paging is necessary, then a pricing strategy that reduces the number of simplex iterations that need be performed might have the advantage. The proportion of time spent doing the pricing step during stage 1 optimization is usually less than the same proportion when doing stage 2 optimization. Therefore, it is more important to choose a stage 2 pricing strategy that causes fewer iterations to be executed.

There are similarities between the pricing strategies when optimizing an unconstrained problem or when constraints are temporarily being ignored and the pricing mechanisms when optimizing considering constraints. To prevent repetition, options and parameters have a suffix or embedded x. Replace x with 1 for optimization without constraint consideration and 2 for optimization with constraint consideration.

There are three main types of pricing strategy: PRICETYPEx=NOQ, PRICETYPE x=BLAND, and PRICETYPEx=Q. The pricing strategy that usually performs better than the others is PRICETYPEx=Q. For this reason, PRICETYPEx =Q is the default.

PRICETYPEx=NOQ

PRICETYPEx=NOQ is the least complex pricing strategy but it is nevertheless quite efficient. In contrast to the specification of PRICETYPEx=Q, a candidate queue is not set up.

The PxSCAN option controls the order in which nonbasic arcs, constraint, slack, surplus, and nonarc variables are searched before one that is eligible for a flow or value change is chosen. If Px SCAN=FIRST, then when a head node is found with at least one nonbasic arc that should have a flow change, the rest of the nonbasic arcs directed toward that node are examined for eligibility to enter the basis. The best of these eligible arcs directed toward this node is selected. If, during stage 2 optimization, no eligible arc is found and there are any non-equality side constraints, the slack and surplus variables of these constraints are tested for their eligibility to enter the basis. If there are any, nonarc variables are then analyzed. After that, arcs directed toward the node with the lowest internal number are examined. This is termed a *wraparound search*.

The scan for entering candidates starts where the last iteration's search left off. For example, if the last iteration's candidate was directed toward the node with internal number i, then the scan starts by examining arcs directed toward the node with internal number $i+1$. If the slack or surplus of constraint i entered the basis in the last iteration, the scan starts by examining the slack or surplus of the constraint with internal number greater than i that has such a logical variable.

If PxSCAN=BEST, all nonbasic arcs and, if optimizing considering the constraints, all slack, surplus, and nonarc variables are examined at each iteration so that the criterion candidate is found to have a flow or value change and perhaps enter the basis.

PxSCAN=PARTIAL is like PxSCAN=FIRST, except that PxNPARTIAL=p eligible flow or value change candidates are examined before the scan is terminated. The criterion candidate is chosen for flow or value change, and the scan in the next iteration resumes where the previous scan left off.

PRICETYPEx=Q

If PRICETYPEx=Q, a queue is set up. Candidates currently on the queue are tested at each iteration and either enter the basis or are removed from the queue. The size of the queue can be specified by using the parameter QSIZEx=q. The default value for QSIZE1 is

```
MIN(100,MAX(24,number of arcs/200))
```

The default value for QSIZE2 is

```
MIN(100,MAX(24,number of arcs and nonarc variables/200))
```

The choice of candidates on the queue eligible for flow or value change is controlled by the PxSCAN option. If you specify PxSCAN=BEST, the best eligible candidate found is removed from the queue. It can sustain a flow or value change and possibly enter the basis. If you specify PxSCAN=FIRST, the first eligible candidate found is removed from the queue, and possibly sustains a flow or value change and enters the basis. If you specify PxSCAN=PARTIAL, PxNPARTIAL=p, then eligible p candidates on the queue are examined and the best of these is chosen to be removed from the queue. When PxSCAN=FIRST or PxSCAN=PARTIAL, the scan of the queue is wraparound.

When the queue is empty, or after QSIZEx times REFRESHQx iterations have been executed since the queue was last refreshed, new candidates are found and put onto the queue. Valid values for the REFRESHQx parameters are between 0.0 and 1.0. The default for REFRESHQx is 0.75. If the scan cannot find enough candidates to fill the queue, the procedure must reduce the value of QSIZEx. If *qfound* is the number of candidates found, the new QSIZEx value is

```
qfound + (( old QSIZEx - qfound ) * REDUCEQSIZEx)   .
```

Valid values of the REDUCEQSIZEx are between 0 and 1 inclusive. The default for REDUCEQSIZEx is 1.0.

QxFILLSCAN can be used to control the scan for new queue members. If QxFILLSCAN=BEST is specified, all nonbasic arcs, constraint slack, surplus and nonarc variables are scanned and the best retained on the queue. If you specify QxFILLSCAN=FIRST, the nonbasic arcs, constraint slack, surplus, and nonarc variables are scanned, but the scan stops when the queue is filled. QxFILLSCAN=FIRST is the default. If you specify QxFILLSCAN=PARTIAL, QxFILLNPARTIAL=q, q head nodes (and the arcs directed toward them), and when doing stage 2 optimization, constraint slack, surplus, and nonarc variables are examined and the best of these are put into the queue. QxFILLNPARTIAL=10 is the default. If QxFILLSCAN=FIRST or QxFILLSCAN=PARTIAL , the scan starts where the previous iteration ended.

PRICETYPEx=BLAND

PRICETYPEx=BLAND is equivalent to PRICETYPEx=NOQ, PxSCAN=FIRST LRATIOx, and the scans are not wraparound. Bland (1977) proved that this pivot rule prevents the simplex algorithm from cycling. However, because the pivots concentrate on the lower indexed arcs, constraint slack, surplus, and nonarc variables, optimization with PRICETYPEx=BLAND can make the optimization execute slowly.

Dual Variables, Reduced Costs, and Status

During optimization, dual variables and reduced costs are used to determine whether an arc, constraint slack, surplus, or nonarc variable should have a flow or value change. The ARCOUT= and CONOUT= data sets have variables called _RCOST_ that contain reduced cost values. In CONOUT=, these variables also have reduced costs of nonarc variables. For an arc, the reduced cost is the amount that would be added to the total cost if that arc were made to convey one more unit of flow. For a nonarc variable, the reduced cost is also the amount that would be added to the total cost if the value currently assigned to that nonarc variable were increased by one.

During the optimization of a minimization problem, if an arc has a positive reduced cost, PROC NETFLOW takes steps to decrease the flow through it. If an arc has a negative reduced cost, PROC NETFLOW takes steps to increase the flow through it. At optimality, the reduced costs of arcs with flow at its lower bound are non-negative; otherwise, the optimizer would have tried to increase the flow, thereby decreasing the total cost. The _STATUS_ of such nonbasic arcs is LOWERBD NONBASIC. The reduced costs of arcs with flow at capacity are non-positive. The _STATUS_ of such nonbasic arcs is UPPERBD NONBASIC. Even though it would decrease total cost, the optimizer cannot increase the flow through such arcs because of the capacity bound. Similar arguments apply for nonarc variables.

The reduced cost is also the amount that would be subtracted from the total cost if that arc was made to convey one less unit of flow. Similarly, a reduced cost is the amount subtracted from the total cost if the value currently assigned to that nonarc variable is decreased by one.

The dual variables and reduced costs can be used to detect whether multiple optimal solutions exist. A zero reduced cost of a nonbasic arc indicates the existence of multiple optimal solutions. A zero reduced cost indicates, by definition, that the flow through such arcs can be changed with zero change to the total cost. (Basic arcs and basic nonarc variables technically have zero reduced costs. A missing value is used for these so that reduced costs of nonbasic arcs and nonbasic nonarcs that are zero are highlighted.)

The range over which costs can vary before the present solution becomes non-optimal can be determined through examination of the reduced costs. For any nonbasic arc with assigned flow equal to its lower bound, the amount by which the cost must be decreased before it becomes profitable for this arc to convey additional flow is the value of its reduced cost. The cost reduction necessary for a nonbasic arc currently assigned capacity flow to undergo a worthwhile flow decrease is the absolute value of its reduced cost. In both cases, this minimum cost reduction changes the reduced cost to zero. Any further reduction promotes a possible basis change.

The reduced cost of an arc (t,h) is

$$rc(t,h) = c(t,h) - \pi(t) + \pi(h)$$

where $\pi(i)$ is the dual value for node i and $c(t,h)$ is the cost of the arc with tail node t and head node h.

If the problem has side constraints and arc (t,h) has nonzero lhs coefficients, then the following term must be subtracted from $rc(t,h)$ (see above):

$$\Sigma_i condual_i \cdot H_{i,(t,h)}$$

where $condual_i$ is the dual variable of constraint i, $H_{i,(t,h)}$ is the coefficient of arc (t,h) in constraint i.

If $d(n)$ is the objective function coefficient of nonarc variable n, the reduced cost is

$$d(n) - \Sigma_i condual_i \cdot Q_{i,(n)}$$

where $Q_{i,(n)}$ is the coefficient of nonarc variable n in constraint i.

The Working Basis Matrix

Let **T** be the basis matrix of NPSC. The following partitioning is done:

$$\mathbf{T} = \begin{bmatrix} \mathbf{A} & \mathbf{B} \\ \mathbf{C} & \mathbf{D} \end{bmatrix}$$

where

- n is the number of nodes
- k is the number of side constraints
- **A** ($n \times n$) nearly entirely comprises node-arc incidence matrix columns. The arcs associated with columns of **A**, called key basic variables or key arcs, form a spanning tree. The data structures of the spanning tree of this submatrix of the basis **T** enable the computations involving **T** and the manner in which **T** is updated to be very efficient, especially those dealing with **A** (or $\mathbf{A}^{-1}$).
- **C** ($k \times n$) are the key arcs' side constraint coefficient columns.
- **B** ($n \times k$) are the node-arc incidence matrix columns of the nontree arcs. The columns of **B** having nonzero elements are associated with basic nonspanning tree arcs.
- **D** ($k \times k$) are the constraint coefficient columns of nonkey basic variables. Nonkey basic variables not only include nontree basic arcs but also basic slack, surplus, artificial, or nonarc variables.

It is more convenient to factor **T** by block triangular matrices **P** and **M**, such that **P** = **T M**. The matrices **P** and **M** are used instead of **T** because they are less burdensome to work with. You can perform block substitution when solving the simplex iteration linear systems of equations.

$$\mathbf{P} = \begin{bmatrix} \mathbf{A} & \mathbf{0} \\ \mathbf{C} & \mathbf{D} \end{bmatrix} \quad \mathbf{M} = \begin{bmatrix} \mathbf{I} & -\mathbf{A}^{-1}.\mathbf{B} \\ \mathbf{0} & \mathbf{I} \end{bmatrix}$$

$\mathbf{D}^{W} = \mathbf{D} - \mathbf{C}\mathbf{A}^{-1}\mathbf{B}$ and is called the working basis matrix.

To perform block substitution, you need the tree data structures of the **A**, also the **C**, **B**, and $\mathbf{D}^{W}$ matrices. Because the **C** matrix consists of columns of the constraint coefficient matrix, the maintenance of **C** from iteration to iteration simply entails changing information specifying which columns of the constraint coefficient matrix compose **C**.

The $\mathbf{A}^{-1}\mathbf{B}$ matrix is usually very sparse. Fortunately, the information in $\mathbf{A}^{-1}\mathbf{B}$ can be initialized easily using the tree structures. In most iterations, only one column is replaced by a new one. The values of the elements of the new column may already be known from preceding steps of the simplex iteration.

The working basis matrix is the submatrix that presents the most computational complexity. However, PROC NETFLOW usually can use classical simplex pivot techniques. In many iterations, only one column of $\mathbf{D}^{W}$ changes. Sometimes it is not necessary to update $\mathbf{D}^{W}$ or its inverse at all.

If INVD_2D is specified in the PROC NETFLOW statement, only one row and one column may need to be changed in the $(\mathbf{D}^{W})^{-1}$ before the next simplex iteration can begin. The new contents of the changed column are already known. The new elements of the row that changes are influenced by the contents of a row of $\mathbf{A}^{-1}\mathbf{B}$ that is very sparse.

If INVD_2D is not specified in the PROC NETFLOW statement, the Bartels-Golub update can be used to update the **LU** factors of $\mathbf{D}^{W}$. The choice must be made whether to perform a series of updates (how many depends on the number of nonzeros in a row of $\mathbf{A}^{-1}\mathbf{B}$) or perform a refactorization.

Flow and Value Bounds

The capacity and lower flow bound of an arc may be equal. Negative arc capacities and lower flow bounds are permitted. If both arc capacities and lower flow bounds are negative, the lower flow bound must be at least as negative as the capacity. An arc (A,B) that has a negative flow $-f$ units can be interpreted as an arc that conveys f units of flow from node B to node A.

The upper and lower value bound of a nonarc variable may be equal. Negative upper and lower bounds are permitted. If both are negative, the lower bound must be at least as negative as the upper bound.

Tightening Bounds and Side Constraints

If any piece of data is furnished to PROC NETFLOW more than once, NETFLOW will check for consistency so that no conflict exists concerning the data values. For example, if the cost of some arc is seen to be one value and as more data are read, the cost of the same arc is seen to be another value, NETFLOW will issue an ERROR message on the SAS log and stop. There is an exception to this. Several values may be given for inequality constraint right-hand-sides. For a particular constraint, the lowest rhs value is used for the rhs if the constraint is of *less than or equal to* type. For a particular constraint, the greatest rhs value is used for the rhs if the constraint is of *greater than or equal to* type.

Reasons for Infeasibility

Before optimization commences, PROC NETFLOW tests to ensure that the problem is not infeasible by ensuring that, with respect to supplies, demands, and arc flow bounds, flow conservation can be obeyed at each node.

- Let IN = the sum of lower flow bounds of arcs directed toward a node plus the node's supply. Let OUT = the sum of capacities of arcs directed from that node plus the node's demand. If IN exceeds OUT, not enough flow can leave the node.
- Let OUT = the sum of lower flow bounds of arcs directed from a node plus the node's demand. Let IN = the total capacity of arcs directed toward the node plus the node's supply. If OUT exceeds IN, not enough flow can arrive at the node.

Reasons why a network problem may be infeasible are similar to those above but apply to a set of nodes rather than for an individual node.

Consider the network illustrated in **Figure 9.2**.

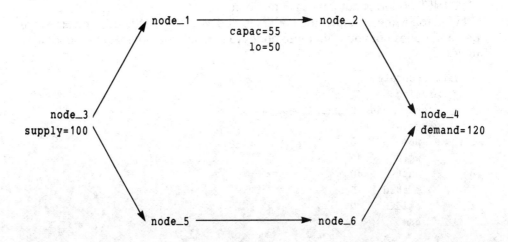

Figure 9.2 An Infeasible Network

The demand of NODE_4 is 120. That can never be satisfied because the maximal flow through arcs (NODE_1, NODE_2) and (NODE_5, NODE_6) is 117. More specifically, the implicit supply of NODE_2 and NODE_6 is only 117, which is insufficient to satisfy the demand of other nodes (real or implicit) in the network.

The lower flow bounds of arcs (NODE_1, NODE_2) and (NODE_5, NODE_6) are greater than the flow that can reach the tail nodes of these arcs, which, by coincidence, is the total supply of the network. The implicit demand of nodes NODE_1 and NODE_5 is 110, which is greater than the amount of flow that can reach these nodes.

When PROC NETFLOW detects that the problem is infeasible, it will indicate why the solution, obtained after optimization stopped, is infeasible. It may report that the solution cannot obey flow conservation constraints and which nodes these conservation constraints are associated with. If necessary, the side constraints that the solution disobeys will also be output.

If stage 1 optimization obtained a feasible solution to the network, stage 2 optimization can determine that the problem is infeasible and note that some flow conservation constraint is broken and possibly that all side constraints are obeyed. The infeasibility messages issued by NETFLOW pertain to why the current solution is infeasible, not quite the same as the reasons why the problem is infeasible. However, the messages highlight *areas* in the problem where the infeasibility can be tracked down. If the problem is infeasible, make NETFLOW do a stage 1 unconstrained optimization. If a feasible network solution is found, the side constraints are where the infeasibility was introduced into the problem.

Missing S Supply and Missing D Demand Values

In some models, you may want a node to be either a supply or demand node but you want the node to supply or demand the optimal number of flow units. To indicate that a node is such a supply node, use a missing S value in the SUPPLY list variable in ARCDATA or the SUPDEM list variable in NODEDATA. To indicate that a node is such a demand node, use a missing D value in the DEMAND list variable in ARCDATA or the SUPDEM list variable in NODEDATA.

Once a missing S or missing D value is found in the input data sets, the THRUNET option is automatically made active.

In the following example, the nodes labeled M_AKLD, AKLD_S, and HAM are demand nodes but you want these nodes to demand the optimal number of flow units.

```
data nodedata;
   missing D;
   input _node_ $ _sd_;
   cards;
       por      50
       wgtn     40
       hutt     80
       m_akld    D
       akld_s    D
       ham       D
   ;
data arcdata;
   input _from_ $ _to_ $ _cost_ _capac_ _lo_ ;
   cards;
       por  np      61  40  10
       por  man     24  40  .
       wgtn man     83  40  .
       hutt man     58  80  .
       wgtn nap     78  35  10
       hutt nap     32  50  .
       man  tai      0 160  .
       np   m_akld  34  20  .
       tai  m_akld  55  65  .
       nap  m_akld  75  65   5
       np   akld_s  40  20   5
       tai  akld_s  64  50  .
       nap  akld_s  11  40  .
       tai  ham     17  20   5
       nap  ham     21  35  10
   ;
proc netflow
   arcdata=arcdata nodedata=nodedata
   arcout=arcout;
proc print data=arcout; sum _fcost_; run;
```

The following messages appear on the SAS log:

```
NOTE: Number of nodes= 10 .
NOTE: Number of supply nodes= 3 .
NOTE: Number of demand nodes= 3 .
NOTE: Total supply= 170 , total demand= 0 .
NOTE: Number of arcs= 18 .
NOTE: Number of iterations performed (neglecting any constraints)=
      17 .
NOTE: Of these, 0 were degenerate.
NOTE: Optimum (neglecting any constraints) found.
NOTE: Minimal total cost= 13640 .
```

The ARCOUT data set is shown in **Output 9.6**.

Output 9.6   The ARCOUT DATA SET

OBS	_FROM_	_TO_	_COST_	_CAPAC_	_LO_	SUPPLY	DEMAND	_FLOW_	_FCOST_	_RCOST_	_ANUMB_	_TNUMB_	_STATUS_	
1	np	akld_s	40	20	5	.	D	5	200	6	11	2	LOWERBD	NONBASIC
2	tai	akld_s	64	50	0	.	D	0	0	9	12	7	LOWERBD	NONBASIC
3	nap	akld_s	11	40	0	.	D	40	440	-49	13	6	UPPERBD	NONBASIC
4	tai	ham	17	20	5	.	D	20	340	-38	14	7	UPPERBD	NONBASIC
5	nap	ham	21	35	10	.	D	35	735	-39	15	6	UPPERBD	NONBASIC
6	np	m_akld	34	20	0	.	D	5	170	.	8	2	KEY_ARC	BASIC
7	tai	m_akld	55	65	0	.	D	60	3300	.	9	7	KEY_ARC	BASIC
8	nap	m_akld	75	65	5	.	D	5	375	15	10	6	LOWERBD	NONBASIC
9	por	man	24	40	0	50	.	40	960	.	2	1	KEY_ARC	BASIC
10	wgtn	man	83	40	0	40	.	10	830	.	3	4	KEY_ARC	BASIC
11	hutt	man	58	80	0	80	.	30	1740	.	4	5	KEY_ARC	BASIC
12	wgtn	nap	78	35	10	40	.	30	2340	.	5	4	KEY_ARC	BASIC
13	hutt	nap	32	50	0	80	.	50	1600	-21	6	5	UPPERBD	NONBASIC
14	por	np	61	40	10	50	.	10	610	16	1	1	LOWERBD	NONBASIC
15	man	tai	0	160	0	.	.	80	0	.	7	3	KEY_ARC	BASIC
									===== 13640					

The optimal demands of nodes M_AKLD, AKLD_S, and HAM are 70, 45, and 35, respectively. For this example, the same optimal solution is obtained if these nodes had demands less than these values (each demands 1 unit) and the THRUNET option was specified in the PROC NETFLOW statement. With the THRUNET option active, when total supply exceeds total demand, the specified nonmissing demand values are the lowest number of flow units that must be absorbed by the corresponding node. This is demonstrated in the following NETFLOW run. The missing D is most useful when nodes are to demand optimal numbers of flow units and it turns out that for some nodes, the optimal demand is zero.

```
data nodedata;
   missing D;
   input _node_ $ _sd_;
   cards;
      por       50
      wgtn      40
      hutt      80
      m_akld     D
      akld_s   -50
      ham        D
   ;
```

```
proc netflow
   arcdata=arcdata nodedata=nodedata
   arcout=arcout;
proc print data=arcout; sum _fcost_; run;
```

The following messages appear on the SAS log:

```
NOTE: Number of nodes= 10 .
NOTE: Number of supply nodes= 3 .
NOTE: Number of demand nodes= 3 .
NOTE: Total supply= 170 , total demand= 50 .
NOTE: Number of arcs= 17 .
NOTE: Number of iterations performed (neglecting any constraints)=
      15 .
NOTE: Of these, 2 were degenerate.
NOTE: Optimum (neglecting any constraints) found.
NOTE: Minimal total cost= 13670 .
```

The ARCOUT data set is shown in **Output 9.7**.

Output 9.7   THE ARCOUT DATA SET

Obs	_FROM_	_TO_	_COST_	_CAPAC_	_LO_	SUPPLY	DEMAND	_FLOW_	_FCOST_	_RCOST_	_ANUMB_	_TNUMB_	_STATUS_
1	np	akld_s	40	20	5	.	50	10	400	.	11	2	KEY_ARC BASIC
2	tai	akld_s	64	50	0	.	50	0	0	3	12	7	LOWERBD NONBASIC
3	nap	akld_s	11	40	0	.	50	40	440	-55	13	6	UPPERBD NONBASIC
4	tai	ham	17	20	5	.	D	20	340	-38	14	7	UPPERBD NONBASIC
5	nap	ham	21	35	10	.	D	35	735	-39	15	6	UPPERBD NONBASIC
6	np	m_akld	34	20	0	.	D	0	0	.	8	2	KEY_ARC BASIC
7	tai	m_akld	55	65	0	.	D	60	3300	.	9	7	KEY_ARC BASIC
8	nap	m_akld	75	65	5	.	D	5	375	15	10	6	LOWERBD NONBASIC
9	por	man	24	40	0	50	.	40	960	.	2	1	KEY_ARC BASIC
10	wgtn	man	83	40	0	40	.	10	830	.	3	4	KEY_ARC BASIC
11	hutt	man	58	80	0	80	.	30	1740	.	4	5	KEY_ARC BASIC
12	wgtn	nap	78	35	10	40	.	30	2340	.	5	4	KEY_ARC BASIC
13	hutt	nap	32	50	0	80	.	50	1600	-21	6	5	UPPERBD NONBASIC
14	por	np	61	40	10	50	.	10	610	16	1	1	LOWERBD NONBASIC
15	man	tai	0	160	0	.	.	80	0	.	7	3	KEY_ARC BASIC

```
                                            =====
                                            13670
```

If total supply exceeds total demand, any missing S values will be ignored. If total demand exceeds total supply, any missing D values will be ignored.

Warm Starts

Using a warm start can increase the overall speed of PROC NETFLOW when it is used repetitively on problems with similar structure. It is most beneficial when a solution of a previous optimization is close to the optimum of the same network with some of its parameters, for example, arc costs, changed. Whether a problem is changed or not, a nonoptimal solution resulting from a previous optimization may be used to restart optimization, thereby saving PROC NETFLOW from having to repeat work to reach the warm start already available.

Time also is saved in the data structure initialization part of the NETFLOW procedure's execution. Information about the previous optimal solution, particularly concerning the size of the problem and a description of the basis spanning tree structure and what is basic in constraint rows is known. Information about which nonbasic arcs have capacity flow and which nonbasic nonarc variables are of their respective upper bounds makes up part of the warm start. Arc data can be placed into the internal arc length arrays in precisely defined locations, in order of ascending head node internal number. It is not necessary to have multiple passes through the data because literals such as node, nonarc variable, arc, constraint, and special row names are defined and meaning is attached to each. This saves a considerable amount of memory as well. None of the pre-optimization feasibility checks need be repeated.

Warm starts also are useful if you want to determine the effect of arcs being closed to carrying flow. The costs of these arcs are set high enough to ensure that the next optimal solution never has flow through them. Similarly, the effect of opening arcs can be determined by changing the cost of such arcs from an extreme to a reasonable value.

Specify the FUTURE1 or FUTURE2 option to ensure additional data about a solution that is to be used as a warm start are output to output data sets. If the FUTURE1 option is specified, extra observations with information on what is to be the warm start are set up for the NODEOUT= and ARCOUT= data sets. The warm start solution in these data sets is a solution obtained after optimization neglecting side constraints. Any cost list variable value in the ARCOUT= data set (and, if there are side constraints, any constraint data in the CONDATA= data set) can be changed before the solution is used as a warm start in a subsequent PROC NETFLOW run. Any nonarc variable data in CONDATA= can be changed at this time as well. New nonarc variables not present in the original problem when the warm start was generated can also be added to CONDATA= before the problem is warm started.

If the FUTURE2 option is specified, extra variables containing information on what will be the warm start are set up for the DUALOUT= and CONOUT= data sets. The warm start solution in these data sets is obtained after optimization that considers constraints has been performed. Part of the warm start is concerned with the constraint part of the basis. Only cost list variable values in the CONOUT= data set can be changed before the solution is used as a warm start in a subsequent PROC NETFLOW run.

If a primal simplex optimization is to use a warm start, the WARM option must be specified in the PROC NETFLOW statement. Otherwise, the primal simplex network algorithm processes the data for a cold start and the extra information is not used.

The ARCDATA= data set is either from a previous run of the PROC NETFLOW ARCOUT= data set with the FUTURE1 option specified (if an unconstrained warm start is used) or from a previous run of the PROC NETFLOW CONOUT= data set with the FUTURE2 option specified (if a warm start obtained after optimization that considers constraints is used).

The NODEDATA= data set is the NODEOUT= data set from a previous run of PROC NETFLOW with FUTURE1 specified if an unconstrained warm start is being used. Otherwise, the DUALIN= data set is from a previous run of the PROC NETFLOW DUALOUT= data set with FUTURE2 specified if the warm start obeys constraints.

You never need to alter the NODEOUT= data set or the DUALOUT= data set between the time they were generated and when they are used. The results would be unpredictable if incorrect changes were made to these datasets, or if a NODEDATA= data set or if a DUALIN= data set were used with an ARCDATA= data set of a different solution.

It is possible, and often useful, to specify WARM and either FUTURE1 or FUTURE2, or both, in the same PROC NETFLOW statement if a new warm start is to be generated from the present warm start.

The extent of the changes done to a primal simplex warm start between the time it was generated and when it was used depends on whether the warm start described an unconstrained or constrained solution. The following list describes parts of a constrained or an unconstrained warm start that can be altered:

- COST list variable values
- The value of an arc's capacity can be changed as long as the new capacity value is not less than the lower flow bound or the flow through the arc.
- Any nonarc variable information can be changed in an unconstrained warm start.
- For an unconstrained warm start, you can alter any side constraint data.

The changes that can be made in constraint data are more restrictive than those for an unconstrained warm start. The lhs coefficients type, and rhs value of a constraint, can be changed as long as that constraint's slack, surplus, or artificial variable is basic. The constraint name cannot be changed.

Example of a Warm Start

The following sample SAS session demonstrates how the warm start facilities are used to obtain optimal solutions to an unconstrained network where some arc cost changes occur or optimization is halted before the optimum is found.

```
                          /* data already in datasets NODE0 and ARC0   */
PROC NETFLOW
    NODEDATA=NODE0 /* if supply_demand info in this SAS data set */
    ARCDATA=ARC0;
                          /* variable list specifications go here      */
                          /* assume that they are not necessary here   */
                          /* if they were, they must be included in    */
                          /* all the PROC NETFLOW calls that follow    */
    RESET
      FUTURE1
      NODEOUT=NODE2  /* these are necessary when FUTURE1 is used  */
      ARCOUT=ARC1;
PROC PRINT
      DATA=ARC1;        /* print out optimal solution              */
PROC FSEDIT
      DATA=ARC1;        /* change some arc costs                   */
DATA ARC2;
   SET ARC1;
      OLDFLOW=_FLOW_;
      OLDFC=_FCOST_;
                          /* make duplicates of the flow and flowcost  */
                          /* variables. If a ID list was explicitly */
                          /* specified, add OLDFLOW and OLDFC to this   */
                          /* list so that they appear in subsequently   */
                          /* created ARCOUT data sets                   */
```

```
PROC NETFLOW
    WARM
    NODEDATA=NODE2
    ARCDATA=ARC2;
  RESET
    MAXIT1=250
    FUTURE1; RUN;
  SAVE
    NODEOUT=SAVELIB.NODE3
    ARCOUT=SAVELIB.ARC3;
                        /* optimization halted because 250 iterations */
                        /* were performed to resume optimization,      */
                        /* possibly in another session (the output     */
                        /* data sets were saved in a SAS library       */
                        /* called SAVELIB)                             */
PROC NETFLOW
    WARM
    NODEDATA=SAVELIB.NODE3
    ARCDATA=SAVELIB.ARC3;
  RESET
    FUTURE1
    NODEOUT=NODE4
    ARCOUT=ARC4;
RUN;
```

If this problem has constraints with data in a data set called CON0, then in each PROC NETFLOW statement above, specify CONDATA=CON0. Between PROC NETFLOW runs, you can change constraint data. In each of the RESET statements, you could specify CONOUT= data set to save the last (possibly optimal) solution reached by the optimizer if it reaches stage 2. You could specify FUTURE2 and DUALOUT= data set to generate a constrained warm start.

```
PROC NETFLOW
    WARM
    NODEDATA=NODE4
    ARCDATA=ARC4
    CONDATA=CON0;
  RESET
    MAXIT2=125      /* optional, here as a reason why optimum  */
                    /* will not be obtained                    */
    SCRATCH         /* optional, but warm start might be good  */
                    /* enough to start stage 2 optimization    */
    FUTURE2
RUN;
    SAVE DUALOUT=DUAL1
    CONOUT=CONOUT1;
                        /* stage 2 optimization halted before optimum*/
                        /* reached. Now you can make cost and nonarc */
                        /* variable objective function coefficient   */
                        /* changes. Then to restart optimization use */
```

```
PROC NETFLOW
    WARM
    CONDATA=CON0    /* NB. NETFLOW reads constraint data only    */
    DUALIN=DUAL1
    ARCDATA=CON1;
  RESET
    FUTURE2
    DUALOUT=DUAL2
    CONOUT=CON2;
RUN;
```

EXAMPLES

The following examples illustrate some of the capabilities of PROC NETFLOW. These examples, together with the other SAS/OR examples, can be found in the SAS sample library.

Example 1:   Shortest Path Problem

Whole pineapples are served in a restaurant in London. To ensure freshness, the pineapples are purchased in Hawaii and air freighted from Honolulu to Heathrow in London. The following network diagram (**Figure 9.3**) outlines the different routes that the pineapples could take. The numbers associated with each arc are the freight cost per pineapple. You can use PROC NETFLOW to determine what routes should be used to minimize total shipping cost.

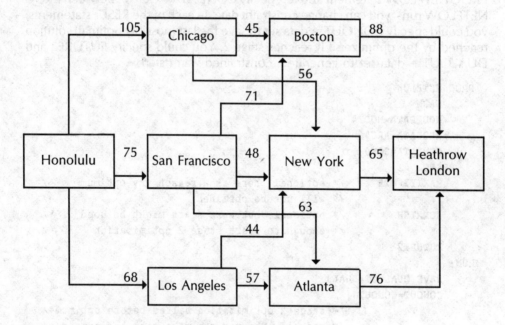

Figure 9.3 Network Model of Possible Paths

The shortest path is the least cost path that all pineapples should use. The SHORTPATH option indicates this type of network problem. The SINKNODE option value HEATHROW LONDON is not a valid SAS variable name so it must be enclosed in single quotes. The TAILNODE list variable is FFROM. Because the name of this variable is not _TAIL_ or _FROM_, the TAIL list must be specified in the PROC NETFLOW statement. The HEAD list must also be explicitly

specified because the variable that belongs to this list does not have the name
HEAD or _TO_.

```
title 'Example 1';
title2 'Shortest Path Problem';
title3 'How to get Hawaiian Pineapples to a London Restaurant';
data aircost1;
   input    ffrom&$13. tto&$15. _cost_ ;
   cards;
Honolulu        Chicago         105
Honolulu        San Francisco   75
Honolulu        Los Angeles     68
Chicago         Boston          45
Chicago         New York        56
San Francisco   Boston          71
San Francisco   New York        48
San Francisco   Atlanta         63
Los Angeles     New York        44
Los Angeles     Atlanta         57
Boston          Heathrow London 88
New York        Heathrow London 65
Atlanta         Heathrow London 76
;
proc netflow
   shortpath
   sourcenode='Honolulu' /* Quotes for case sensitivity */
   sinknode='Heathrow London'
      arcdata=aircost1
      arcout=s_path;
         tail    ffrom;
         head    tto;
proc print data=s_path; sum _fcost_;
title5 'Arcout=s_path';
run;
```

The length at optimality is printed on the SAS log as:

```
NOTE: Shortest path= 177 .
```

Output 9.8 shows you the best route for the pineapples is from Honolulu to Los
Angeles to New York to Heathrow London.

Output 9.8   Arcout=s_path: The Shortest Path

```
                              Example 1                                              1
                         Shortest Path Problem
                How to get Hawaiian Pineapples to a London Restaurant

                             Arcout=s_path
```

O B S	_F_FROM	_T_TO	_COST	_CAPAC	_LO	_SUPPLY	_DEMAND	_FLOW	_FCOST	_RCOST	_ANUMB	_TNUMB	_STATUS	
1	San Francisco	Atlanta	63	999999	0	.	.	0	0	13	9	3	LOWERBD	NONBASIC
2	Los Angeles	Atlanta	57	999999	0	.	.	0	0	.	10	4	KEY_ARC	BASIC
3	Chicago	Boston	45	999999	0	.	.	0	0	4	4	2	LOWERBD	NONBASIC
4	San Francisco	Boston	71	999999	0	.	.	0	0	.	5	3	KEY_ARC	BASIC
5	Honolulu	Chicago	105	999999	0	1	.	0	0	.	1	1	KEY_ARC	BASIC
6	Boston	Heathrow London	88	999999	0	.	1	0	0	57	11	5	LOWERBD	NONBASIC
7	New York	Heathrow London	65	999999	0	.	1	1	65	.	12	6	KEY_ARC	BASIC
8	Atlanta	Heathrow London	76	999999	0	.	1	0	0	24	13	7	LOWERBD	NONBASIC
9	Honolulu	Los Angeles	68	999999	0	1	.	1	68	.	3	1	KEY_ARC	BASIC
10	Chicago	New York	56	999999	0	.	.	0	0	49	6	2	LOWERBD	NONBASIC
11	San Francisco	New York	48	999999	0	.	.	0	0	11	7	3	LOWERBD	NONBASIC
12	Los Angeles	New York	44	999999	0	.	.	1	44	.	8	4	KEY_ARC	BASIC
13	Honolulu	San Francisco	75	999999	0	1	.	0	0	.	2	1	KEY_ARC	BASIC

```
                                                          ===
                                                          177
```

Example 2:   Minimum Cost Flow Problem

You can continue to use the pineapple example by supposing that the airlines now stipulate that no more than 350 pineapples per week can be handled in any single leg of the journey. The restaurant uses 500 pineapples each week. How many pineapples should take each route between Hawaii and London? **Figure 9.4** illustrates the network and unit cost of flow for each arc in the network.

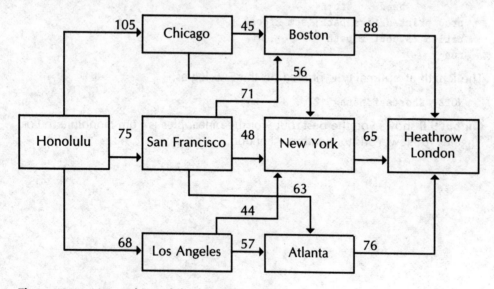

Figure 9.4   Network Model of Possible Paths

You will probably have more minimum cost flow problems because they are more general than maximal flow and shortest path problems. A shortest path formulation is no longer valid because the sink node demands a non-unity number of flow units. All arcs have the same capacity of 350 pineapples. Because of this, the DEFCAPACITY option can be used in ARCDATA=AIRCOST1 rather than CAPACITY list variables, which all have the same value. There is only one supply node and one demand node. These can be named in the SOURCENODE and SINKNODE options.

```
title 'Example 2';
title2 'Minimum Cost Flow Problem';
proc netflow
   defcapacity=350
   sourcenode='Honolulu'  /* Quotes for case sensitivity */
   sinknode='Heathrow London'   demand=500
      arcdata=aircost1
      arcout=arcout1
      nodeout=nodeout1;
         tail    ffrom;
         head    tto;
   set future1;
proc print data=arcout1; sum _fcost_;
title5 'Arcout=arcout1';
proc print data=nodeout1;
title5 'Nodeout=nodeout1';
run;
```

The following notes appear on the SAS log:

```
NOTE: Sourcenode was assigned supply of the total network demand= 500 .
NOTE: Number of nodes= 8 .
NOTE: Number of supply nodes= 1 .
NOTE: Number of demand nodes= 1 .
NOTE: Total supply= 500 , total demand= 500 .
NOTE: Number of arcs= 13 .
NOTE: Number of iterations performed (neglecting any constraints)= 5 .
NOTE: Of these, 4 were degenerate.
NOTE: Optimum (neglecting any constraints) found.
NOTE: Minimal total cost= 93750 .
```

Output 9.9 presents the solutions.

Output 9.9   Solving a Minimum Cost Flow Problem

```
                                    Example 2                                       1
                               Minimum Cost Flow Problem


                                   Arcout=arcout1

                                                                                  S
                               _                S  D           _              _   T
                               C               U  E          F  R           T   A
            F                 _ A              P  M          _ C           A   N  T
            F                 C A              P  A          F C           N   U  U
       O    R         T       O P    _  _      L  N          L O           U   M  S
       B    O         T       S A    L  D      Y  D          O S           M   B
       S    M         O       T C    O  Y         D          W T           B   B
            ─         ─       ─ ─    ─  ─      ─  ─          ─  ─          ─   ─  ─

       1  San Francisco  Atlanta    63 350  0    .    .      0   0     2   9  3  LOWERBD NONBASIC
       2  Los Angeles    Atlanta    57 350  0    .    .    150  8550   .  10  4  LOWERBD NONBASIC
       3  Chicago        Boston     45 350  0    .    .      0   0     4   4  2  LOWERBD NONBASIC
       4  San Francisco  Boston     71 350  0    .    .      0   0     .   5  3  KEY_ARC BASIC
       5  Honolulu       Chicago   105 350  0  500    .      0   0     .   1  1  KEY_ARC BASIC
```

(continued on next page)

(continued from previous page)

```
    6    Boston           Heathrow London    88    350    0      .      500    0       0       22    11    5    LOWERBD  NONBASIC
    7    New York         Heathrow London    65    350    0      .      500    350     22750   -24   12    6    UPPERBD  NONBASIC
    8    Atlanta          Heathrow London    76    350    0      .      500    150     11400    .    13    7    KEY_ARC  BASIC
    9    Honolulu         Los Angeles        68    350    0     500      .     350     23800   -11    3    1    UPPERBD  NONBASIC
   10    Chicago          New York           56    350    0      .       .     0       0       38     6    2    LOWERBD  NONBASIC
   11    San Francisco    New York           48    350    0      .       .     150     7200     .     7    3    KEY_ARC  BASIC
   12    Los Angeles      New York           44    350    0      .       .     200     8800     .     8    4    KEY_ARC  BASIC
   13    Honolulu         San Francisco      75    350    0     500      .     150     11250    .     2    1    KEY_ARC  BASIC
                                                                                       =====
                                                                                       93750
```

```
                                              Example 2                                            2
                                        Minimum Cost Flow Problem

                                          Nodeout=nodeout1

OBS    _NODE_          _SUPDEM_    _DUAL_    _NNUMB_    _PRED_    _TRAV_    _SCESS_    _ARCID_    _FLOW_    _FBQ_

  1    _ROOT_             0          0          9          0         1         0         -1        81       -14
  2    Atlanta            .        -136          7          4         8         2         10       150         9
  3    Boston             .        -146          5          3         9         1          5         0         4
  4    Chicago            .        -105          2          1         3         1          1         0         1
  5    Heathrow London  -500       -212          8          7         5         1         13       150        11
  6    Honolulu          500          0          1          9         2         8        -14         0        -1
  7    Los Angeles        .         -79          4          6         7         3         -8       200         3
  8    New York           .        -123          6          3         4         4          7       150         6
  9    San Francisco      .         -75          3          1         6         6          2       150         2
```

Figure 9.5 illustrates the minimum cost flow through the network.

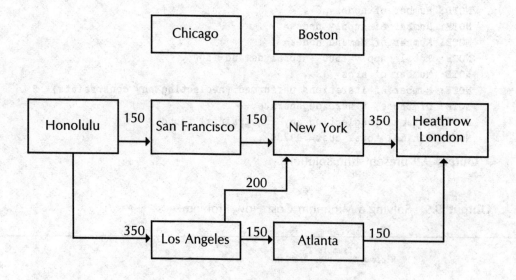

Figure 9.5 Model of a Minimum Cost Flow Solution

Example 3: Using a Warm Start for a Minimum Cost Flow Problem

Suppose now the airlines state that the freight cost per pineapple in flights that leave Chicago has been reduced by 30. How many pineapples should take each route between Hawaii and London? This example illustrates how PROC NETFLOW uses a warm start. **Figure 9.6** shows a minimum cost flow problem.

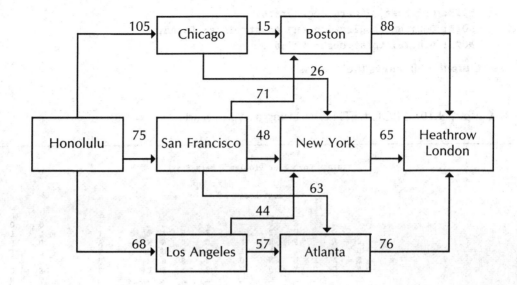

Figure 9.6 Network Model of Possible Paths

In **Example 2**, the SET statement of PROC NETFLOW was used to specify FUTURE1. A NODEOUT= data set was also specified. The warm start information was saved in the ARCOUT1 and NODEOUT1 data sets.

In the following DATA step, the costs, reduced costs, and flows in the ARCOUT1 data set are saved in variables called OLDCOST, OLDFLOW, and OLDFC. These variables form an implicit ID list in the next PROC NETFLOW run and will appear in ARCOUT=ARCOUT2. Thus, it is easy to compare the present optimum and the new optimum.

```
title 'Example 3';
title2 'Minimum Cost Flow Problem - Warm Start';
data aircost2;
   set arcout1;
      oldcost=_cost_;
      oldflow=_flow_;
      oldfc=_fcost_;
      if ffrom='Chicago' then _cost_=_cost_-30;
proc netflow
   warm
      arcdata=aircost2
      nodedata=nodeout1
      arcout=arcout2;
         tail    ffrom;
         head    tto;
proc print data=arcout2; sum _fcost_ oldfc;
title5 'Arcout=arcout2';
run;
```

The following notes appear on the SAS log.

```
NOTE: Number of nodes= 8 .
NOTE: Number of supply nodes= 1 .
NOTE: Number of demand nodes= 1 .
NOTE: Total supply= 500 , total demand= 500 .
NOTE: Number of iterations performed (neglecting any constraints)= 2 .
```

```
NOTE: Of these, 1 were degenerate.
NOTE: Optimum (neglecting any constraints) found.
NOTE: Minimal total cost= 93150 .
```

Output 9.10 shows the results.

Output 9.10   PROC NETFLOW Using a Warm Start

```
                                        Example 3                                                    1
                              Minimum Cost Flow Problem - Warm Start

                                       Arcout=arcout2
```

OBS	FFROM	TTO	COST	CAPAC	LO	SUPPLY	DEMAND	FLOW	FCOST	RCOST	ANUMB	TNUMB	STATUS	OLDCOST	OLDFLOW	OLDFC
1	San Francisco	Atlanta	63	350	0	.	.	0	0	2	9	3	LOWERBD NONBASIC	63	0	0
2	Los Angeles	Atlanta	57	350	0	.	.	0	0	.	10	4	KEY_ARC BASIC	57	150	8550
3	Chicago	Boston	15	350	0	.	.	150	2250	.	4	2	KEY_ARC BASIC	45	0	0
4	San Francisco	Boston	71	350	0	.	.	0	0	26	5	3	LOWERBD NONBASIC	71	0	0
5	Honolulu	Chicago	105	350	0	500	.	150	15750	.	1	1	KEY_ARC BASIC	105	0	0
6	Boston	Heathrow London	88	350	0	.	500	150	13200	.	11	5	KEY_ARC BASIC	88	0	0
7	New York	Heathrow London	65	350	0	.	500	350	22750	-20	12	6	UPPERBD NONBASIC	65	350	22750
8	Atlanta	Heathrow London	76	350	0	.	500	0	0	4	13	7	LOWERBD NONBASIC	76	150	11400
9	Honolulu	Los Angeles	68	350	0	500	.	350	23800	-11	3	1	UPPERBD NONBASIC	68	350	23800
10	Chicago	New York	26	350	0	.	.	0	0	8	6	2	LOWERBD NONBASIC	56	0	0
11	San Francisco	New York	48	350	0	.	.	0	0	.	7	3	KEY_ARC BASIC	48	150	7200
12	Los Angeles	New York	44	350	0	.	.	350	15400	.	8	4	KEY_ARC BASIC	44	200	8800
13	Honolulu	San Francisco	75	350	0	500	.	0	0	.	2	1	KEY_ARC BASIC	75	150	11250
									=====							=====
									93150							93750

Figure 9.7 illustrates the solution to the minimum cost flow problem.

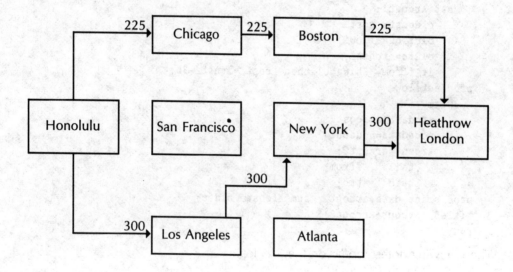

Figure 9.7   Model of a Minimum Cost Flow Problem with a Warm Start

Example 4:   A Multi-commodity, Production, Inventory, and Distribution Problem

Example 4 and **Example 5** use data from a company that produces two sizes of televisions in order to illustrate variations in the way you can use the NETFLOW procedure. The company makes televisions with a diagonal screen measurement of either 19 inches or 25 inches. These televisions are made between March and May at both of the company's two factories. Each factory has a limit on the total number of televisions of each screen dimension that can be made during those months.

The televisions are either distributed to one of two shops, stored at the factory where they were made and sold later, or shipped to the other factory. Some sets can be used to fill back orders from the previous months. Each shop demands a number of each type of TV for the months March through May. The following network (**Figure 9.8**) illustrates the model. Arc costs can be interpreted as production costs, storage costs, back order penalty costs, inter-factory transportation costs, and sales profits. The arcs can have capacities and lower flow bounds.

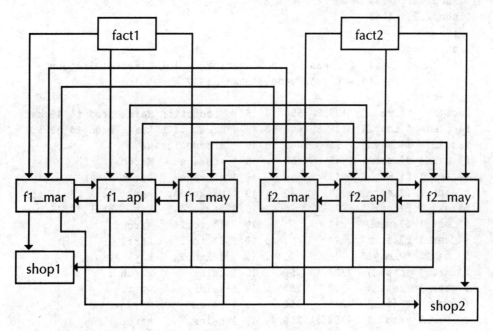

Figure 9.8   Network Model

There are two similarly structured networks, one for the 19-inch televisions and the other for the 25-inch screen TVs. The minimum cost production, inventory, and distribution plan for both TV types can be determined in the same run of PROC NETFLOW. To ensure that node names are unambiguous, the names of nodes in the 19-inch network have SUFFIX _1, the node names in the 25-inch network have SUFFIX _2.

The FUTURE1 option is specified because further processing could be required. Information concerning an optimal solution is retained so it can be used to warm start later optimizations. Warm start information is mostly in variables named _NNUMB_, _PRED_, _TRAV_, _SCESS_, _ARCID_, _FBQ_, and in observations for nodes named _EXCESS_ and _ROOT_, which are in the NODE-OUT=NODE2 output data set. (PROC NETFLOW uses similar devices to store warm start information in DUALOUT= when FUTURE2 is specified.) Variables _ANUMB_ and _TNUMB_ and observations for arcs directed from or toward a node called _EXCESS_ are present in ARCOUT=ARC1. (PROC NETFLOW uses similar devices to store warm start information in CONOUT= when FUTURE2 is specified.)

The following code shows how to save the problem data in a SAS data set and solve the model with PROC NETFLOW:

```
title 'Example 4';
title3 'Multi-Commodity Production Planning/Inventory/Distribution';
data node0;
    input _node_ $ _supdem_ ;
    cards;
fact1_1   1000
fact2_1    850
fact1_2   1000
fact2_2   1500
shop1_1   -900
shop2_1   -900
shop1_2   -900
shop2_2  -1450
;
data arc0;
    input _tail_ $ _head_ $ _cost_ _capac_ _lo_ diagonal factory
          key_id $10. mth_made $ _name_&$17. ;
    cards;
fact1_1  f1_mar_1  127.9   500 50 19 1 production March prod f1 19 mar
fact1_1  f1_apr_1   78.6   600 50 19 1 production April prod f1 19 apl
fact1_1  f1_may_1   95.1   400 50 19 1 production May   .
f1_mar_1 f1_apr_1   15      50  . 19 1 storage    March .
f1_apr_1 f1_may_1   12      50  . 19 1 storage    April .
f1_apr_1 f1_mar_1   28      20  . 19 1 backorder  April back f1 19 apl
f1_may_1 f1_apr_1   28      20  . 19 1 backorder  May   back f1 19 may
f1_mar_1 f2_mar_1   11       .  . 19 . f1_to_2    March .
f1_apr_1 f2_apr_1   11       .  . 19 . f1_to_2    April .
f1_may_1 f2_may_1   16       .  . 19 . f1_to_2    May   .
f1_mar_1 shop1_1  -327.65  250  . 19 1 sales      March .
f1_apr_1 shop1_1  -300     250  . 19 1 sales      April .
f1_may_1 shop1_1  -285     250  . 19 1 sales      May   .
f1_mar_1 shop2_1  -362.74  250  . 19 1 sales      March .
f1_apr_1 shop2_1  -300     250  . 19 1 sales      April .
f1_may_1 shop2_1  -245     250  . 19 1 sales      May   .
fact2_1  f2_mar_1   88.0   450 35 19 2 production March prod f2 19 mar
fact2_1  f2_apr_1   62.4   480 35 19 2 production April prod f2 19 apl
fact2_1  f2_may_1  133.8   250 35 19 2 production May   .
f2_mar_1 f2_apr_1   18      30  . 19 2 storage    March .
f2_apr_1 f2_may_1   20      30  . 19 2 storage    April .
f2_apr_1 f2_mar_1   17      15  . 19 2 backorder  April back f2 19 apl
f2_may_1 f2_apr_1   25      15  . 19 2 backorder  May   back f2 19 may
f2_mar_1 f1_mar_1   10      40  . 19 . f2_to_1    March .
f2_apr_1 f1_apr_1   11      40  . 19 . f2_to_1    April .
f2_may_1 f1_may_1   13      40  . 19 . f2_to_1    May   .
f2_mar_1 shop1_1  -297.4   250  . 19 2 sales      March .
f2_apr_1 shop1_1  -290     250  . 19 2 sales      April .
f2_may_1 shop1_1  -292     250  . 19 2 sales      May   .
f2_mar_1 shop2_1  -272.7   250  . 19 2 sales      March .
f2_apr_1 shop2_1  -312     250  . 19 2 sales      April .
```

```
f2_may_1  shop2_1  -299     250   .  19  2  sales       May    .
fact1_2   f1_mar_2  217.9   400  40  25  1  production  March  prod f1 25 mar
fact1_2   f1_apr_2  174.5   550  50  25  1  production  April  prod f1 25 apl
fact1_2   f1_may_2  133.3   350  40  25  1  production  May    .
f1_mar_2  f1_apr_2   20      40   .  25  1  storage     March  .
f1_apr_2  f1_may_2   18      40   .  25  1  storage     April  .
f1_apr_2  f1_mar_2   32      30   .  25  1  backorder   April  back f1 25 apl
f1_may_2  f1_apr_2   41      15   .  25  1  backorder   May    back f1 25 may
f1_mar_2  f2_mar_2   23       .   .  25  .  f1_to_2     March  .
f1_apr_2  f2_apr_2   23       .   .  25  .  f1_to_2     April  .
f1_may_2  f2_may_2   26       .   .  25  .  f1_to_2     May    .
f1_mar_2  shop1_2  -559.76    .   .  25  1  sales       March  .
f1_apr_2  shop1_2  -524.28    .   .  25  1  sales       April  .
f1_may_2  shop1_2  -475.02    .   .  25  1  sales       May    .
f1_mar_2  shop2_2  -623.89    .   .  25  1  sales       March  .
f1_apr_2  shop2_2  -549.68    .   .  25  1  sales       April  .
f1_may_2  shop2_2  -460.00    .   .  25  1  sales       May    .
fact2_2   f2_mar_2  182.0   650  35  25  2  production  March  prod f2 25 mar
fact2_2   f2_apr_2  196.7   680  35  25  2  production  April  prod f2 25 apl
fact2_2   f2_may_2  201.4   550  35  25  2  production  May    .
f2_mar_2  f2_apr_2   28      50   .  25  2  storage     March  .
f2_apr_2  f2_may_2   38      50   .  25  2  storage     April  .
f2_apr_2  f2_mar_2   31      15   .  25  2  backorder   April  back f2 25 apl
f2_may_2  f2_apr_2   54      15   .  25  2  backorder   May    back f2 25 may
f2_mar_2  f1_mar_2   20      25   .  25  .  f2_to_1     March  .
f2_apr_2  f1_apr_2   21      25   .  25  .  f2_to_1     April  .
f2_may_2  f1_may_2   43      25   .  25  .  f2_to_1     May    .
f2_mar_2  shop1_2  -567.83  500   .  25  2  sales       March  .
f2_apr_2  shop1_2  -542.19  500   .  25  2  sales       April  .
f2_may_2  shop1_2  -461.56  500   .  25  2  sales       May    .
f2_mar_2  shop2_2  -542.83  500   .  25  2  sales       March  .
f2_apr_2  shop2_2  -559.19  500   .  25  2  sales       April  .
f2_may_2  shop2_2  -489.06  500   .  25  2  sales       May    .
;
   proc netflow
         nodedata=node0
         arcdata=arc0;
      set future1
         nodeout=node2
         arcout=arc1;
   proc print data=node2;
   title5 'Nodeout=node2';
   proc print data=arc1; sum _fcost_;
   title5 'Arcout=arc1';
   run;
```

The following notes appear on the SAS log:

```
   NOTE: Number of nodes= 20 .
   NOTE: Number of supply nodes= 4 .
   NOTE: Number of demand nodes= 4 .
   NOTE: Total supply= 4350 , total demand= 4150 .
   NOTE: Number of arcs= 64 .
   NOTE: Number of iterations performed (neglecting any constraints)= 79 .
```

```
NOTE: Of these, 1 were degenerate.
NOTE: Optimum (neglecting any constraints) found.
NOTE: Minimal total cost= -1281110.35 .
```

The solution is given in the NODEOUT= and ARCOUT= data sets. In the ARCOUT= data set, the variables DIAGONAL, FACTORY, KEY_ID, and MTH_MADE form an implicit ID list. The DIAGONAL variable has one of two values, 19 or 25. FACTORY also has one of two values, 1 or 2, to denote the factory where either production or storage occurs, from where TVs are sold to shops, or where TVs are produced to satisfy back orders. PRODUCTION, STORAGE, SALES, and BACKORDER are values of the KEY_ID variable.

Other values of this variable, F1_TO_2 and F2_TO_1, are used when flow through arcs represents the transportation of TVs between factories. The MTH_-MADE variable has values MARCH, APRIL, and MAY, the months when TVs that are modeled as flow through an arc were made. (Assuming that no televisions are stored for more than one month and none manufactured in May are used to fill March back orders.)

These ID variables can be used after the PROC NETFLOW run to produce reports and perform analysis on particular parts of the company's operation. For example, reports can be generated for production numbers for each factory; optimal sales figures for each shop; and how many TVs should be stored, used to fill back orders, sent to the other factory, or any combination of the above for TVs with a particular screen or those produced in a particular month or both.

Output 9.11 is as follows:

Output 9.11   The Nodeout= and Arcout= Data Sets

```
                                        Example 4                                               1

                     Multi-Commodity Production Planning/Inventory/Distribution

                                        Nodeout=node2

 OBS    _NODE_     _SUPDEM_    _DUAL_    _NNUMB_    _PRED_    _TRAV_    _SCESS_    _ARCID_    _FLOW_    _FBQ_

   1   _ROOT_          0        0.00       22         0        11         0          3        166      -69
   2   _EXCESS_     -200        0.00       21        11        10        20         67         10       65
   3   f1_apr_1        .      -79.25        3         6        20         1        -14         30        4
   4   f1_apr_2        .     -188.85       13        19        16         1        -60        535       36
   5   f1_mar_1        .     -127.90        2         1         8         7          1        295        1
   6   f1_mar_2        .     -263.06       12        19        13         1        -59        455       33
   7   f1_may_1        .      -94.25        4         7         3         1        -18        100        8
   8   f1_may_2        .     -131.19       14        18        22         1        -55         25       40
   9   f2_apr_1        .      -90.25        6         8         7         5        -25        245       14
  10   f2_apr_2        .     -198.36       16        19        18         3        -63        320       46
  11   f2_mar_1        .      -88.00        5        10         1         1         12        255       11
  12   f2_mar_2        .     -182.00       15        20        19         8         44        610       43
  13   f2_may_1        .     -110.25        7         6         9         3         20         15       18
  14   f2_may_2        .     -128.23       17        19        12         1        -64         20       50
  15   fact1_1      1000        0.00        1        21         2         8        -65          5       -1
  16   fact1_2      1000        0.00       11        22        21        21        -69          0      -33
  17   fact2_1       850        0.00       10        21         5         2        -66         45      -33
  18   fact2_2      1500        0.00       20        21        15         9        -68        140      -65
  19   shop1_1      -900      199.75        8         2         6         6         21        155       21
  20   shop1_2      -900      343.83       18        16        14         2         57        375       53
  21   shop2_1      -900      188.75        9         7         4         1         32        150       27
  22   shop2_2     -1450      360.83       19        15        17         7         62        120       59
```

Example 4   2

Multi-Commodity Production Planning/Inventory/Distribution

Arcout=arc1

OBS	_TAIL_	_HEAD_	_COST_	_CAPAC_	_LO_	_SUPPLY_	_DEMAND_	_FLOW_	_FCOST_	_RCOST_
1	fact1_1	_EXCESS_	0.00	999999	0	1000	200	5	0.00	.
2	fact2_1	_EXCESS_	0.00	999999	0	850	200	45	0.00	.
3	fact1_2	_EXCESS_	0.00	999999	0	1000	200	10	0.00	.
4	fact2_2	_EXCESS_	0.00	999999	0	1500	200	140	0.00	.
5	fact1_1	f1_apr_1	78.60	600	50	1000	.	600	47160.00	-0.650
6	f1_mar_1	f1_apr_1	15.00	50	0	.	.	0	0.00	63.650
7	f1_may_1	f1_apr_1	28.00	20	0	.	.	0	0.00	43.000
8	f2_apr_1	f1_apr_1	11.00	40	0	.	.	0	0.00	22.000
9	fact1_2	f1_apr_2	174.50	550	50	1000	.	550	95975.00	-14.350
10	f1_mar_2	f1_apr_2	20.00	40	0	.	.	0	0.00	94.210
11	f1_may_2	f1_apr_2	41.00	15	0	.	.	15	615.00	-16.660
12	f2_apr_2	f1_apr_2	21.00	25	0	.	.	0	0.00	30.510
13	fact1_1	f1_mar_1	127.90	500	50	1000	.	345	44125.50	.
14	f1_apr_1	f1_mar_1	28.00	20	0	.	.	20	560.00	-20.650
15	f2_mar_1	f1_mar_1	10.00	40	0	.	.	40	400.00	-29.900
16	fact1_2	f1_mar_2	217.90	400	40	1000	.	400	87160.00	-45.160
17	f1_apr_2	f1_mar_2	32.00	30	0	.	.	30	960.00	-42.210
18	f2_mar_2	f1_mar_2	20.00	25	0	.	.	25	500.00	-61.060
19	fact1_1	f1_may_1	95.10	400	50	1000	.	50	4755.00	0.850
20	f1_apr_1	f1_may_1	12.00	50	0	.	.	50	600.00	-3.000
21	f2_may_1	f1_may_1	13.00	40	0	.	.	0	0.00	29.000
22	fact1_2	f1_may_2	133.30	350	40	1000	.	40	5332.00	2.110
23	f1_apr_2	f1_may_2	18.00	40	0	.	.	0	0.00	75.660
24	f2_may_2	f1_may_2	43.00	25	0	.	.	0	0.00	40.040

OBS	_ANUMB_	_TNUMB_	_STATUS_		DIAGONAL	FACTORY	KEY_ID	MTH_MADE	_NAME_
1	65	1	KEY_ARC	BASIC	.	.			
2	66	10	KEY_ARC	BASIC	.	.			
3	67	11	KEY_ARC	BASIC	.	.			
4	68	20	KEY_ARC	BASIC	.	.			
5	4	1	UPPERBD	NONBASIC	19	1	production	April	prod f1 19 apl
6	5	2	LOWERBD	NONBASIC	19	1	storage	March	
7	6	4	LOWERBD	NONBASIC	19	1	backorder	May	back f1 19 may
8	7	6	LOWERBD	NONBASIC	19	1	f2_to_1	April	
9	36	11	UPPERBD	NONBASIC	25	1	production	April	prod f1 25 apl
10	37	12	LOWERBD	NONBASIC	25	1	storage	March	
11	38	14	UPPERBD	NONBASIC	25	1	backorder	May	back f1 25 may
12	39	16	LOWERBD	NONBASIC	25	.	f2_to_1	April	
13	1	1	KEY_ARC	BASIC	19	1	production	March	prod f1 19 mar
14	2	3	UPPERBD	NONBASIC	19	1	backorder	April	back f1 19 apl
15	3	5	UPPERBD	NONBASIC	19	1	f2_to_1	March	
16	33	11	UPPERBD	NONBASIC	25	1	production	March	prod f1 25 mar
17	34	13	UPPERBD	NONBASIC	25	1	backorder	April	back f1 25 apl
18	35	15	UPPERBD	NONBASIC	25	.	f2_to_1	March	
19	8	1	LOWERBD	NONBASIC	19	1	production	May	
20	9	3	UPPERBD	NONBASIC	19	1	storage	April	
21	10	7	LOWERBD	NONBASIC	19	1	f2_to_1	May	
22	40	11	LOWERBD	NONBASIC	25	1	production	May	
23	41	13	LOWERBD	NONBASIC	25	1	storage	April	
24	42	17	LOWERBD	NONBASIC	25	.	f2_to_1	May	

Example 4   3

Multi-Commodity Production Planning/Inventory/Distribution

Arcout=arc1

OBS	_TAIL_	_HEAD_	_COST_	_CAPAC_	_LO_	_SUPPLY_	_DEMAND_	_FLOW_	_FCOST_	_RCOST_
25	f1_apr_1	f2_apr_1	11.00	999999	0	.	.	30	330.00	.
26	fact2_1	f2_apr_1	62.40	480	35	850	.	480	29952.00	-27.85
27	f2_mar_1	f2_apr_1	18.00	30	0	.	.	0	0.00	15.75
28	f2_may_1	f2_apr_1	25.00	15	0	.	.	0	0.00	45.00
29	f1_apr_2	f2_apr_2	23.00	999999	0	.	.	0	0.00	13.49
30	fact2_2	f2_apr_2	196.70	680	35	1500	.	680	133756.00	-1.66
31	f2_mar_2	f2_apr_2	28.00	50	0	.	.	0	0.00	11.64
32	f2_may_2	f2_apr_2	54.00	15	0	.	.	15	810.00	-16.13
33	f1_mar_1	f2_mar_1	11.00	999999	0	.	.	0	0.00	50.90
34	fact2_1	f2_mar_1	88.00	450	35	850	.	290	25520.00	.
35	f2_apr_1	f2_mar_1	17.00	15	0	.	.	0	0.00	19.25
36	f1_mar_2	f2_mar_2	23.00	999999	0	.	.	0	0.00	104.06
37	fact2_2	f2_mar_2	182.00	650	35	1500	.	645	117390.00	.
38	f2_apr_2	f2_mar_2	31.00	15	0	.	.	0	0.00	47.36
39	f1_may_1	f2_may_1	16.00	999999	0	.	.	100	1600.00	.
40	fact2_1	f2_may_1	133.80	250	35	850	.	35	4683.00	23.55

(continued on next page)

(continued from previous page)

	TAIL	_HEAD_	_COST_	_CAPAC_	_LO_	_SUPPLY_	_DEMAND_	_FLOW_	_FCOST_	_RCOST_
41	f2_apr_1	f2_may_1	20.00	30	0	.	.	15	300.00	.
42	f1_may_2	f2_may_2	26.00	999999	0	.	.	0	0.00	28.96
43	fact2_2	f2_may_2	201.40	550	35	1500	.	35	7049.00	73.17
44	f2_apr_2	f2_may_2	38.00	50	0	.	.	0	0.00	108.13
45	f1_mar_1	shop1_1	-327.65	250	0	.	900	155	-50785.75	.
46	f1_apr_1	shop1_1	-300.00	250	0	.	900	250	-75000.00	-21.00
47	f1_may_1	shop1_1	-285.00	250	0	.	900	0	0.00	9.00
48	f2_mar_1	shop1_1	-297.40	250	0	.	900	250	-74350.00	-9.65

OBS	_ANUMB_	_TNUMB_	_STATUS_		DIAGONAL	FACTORY	KEY_ID	MTH_MADE	_NAME_
25	14	3	KEY_ARC	BASIC	19	.	f1_to_2	April	
26	15	10	UPPERBD	NONBASIC	19	2	production	April	prod f2 19 apl
27	16	5	LOWERBD	NONBASIC	19	2	storage	March	
28	17	7	LOWERBD	NONBASIC	19	2	backorder	May	back f2 19 may
29	46	13	LOWERBD	NONBASIC	25	.	f1_to_2	April	
30	47	20	UPPERBD	NONBASIC	25	2	production	April	prod f2 25 apl
31	48	15	LOWERBD	NONBASIC	25	2	storage	March	
32	49	17	UPPERBD	NONBASIC	25	2	backorder	May	back f2 25 may
33	11	2	LOWERBD	NONBASIC	19	.	f1_to_2	March	
34	12	10	KEY_ARC	BASIC	19	2	production	March	prod f2 19 mar
35	13	6	LOWERBD	NONBASIC	19	2	backorder	April	back f2 19 apl
36	43	12	LOWERBD	NONBASIC	25	.	f1_to_2	March	
37	44	20	KEY_ARC	BASIC	25	2	production	March	prod f2 25 mar
38	45	16	LOWERBD	NONBASIC	25	2	backorder	April	back f2 25 apl
39	18	4	KEY_ARC	BASIC	19	.	f1_to_2	May	
40	19	10	LOWERBD	NONBASIC	19	2	production	May	
41	20	6	KEY_ARC	BASIC	19	.	storage	April	
42	50	14	LOWERBD	NONBASIC	25	.	f1_to_2	May	
43	51	20	LOWERBD	NONBASIC	25	2	production	May	
44	52	16	LOWERBD	NONBASIC	25	2	storage	April	
45	21	2	KEY_ARC	BASIC	19	1	sales	March	
46	22	3	UPPERBD	NONBASIC	19	1	sales	April	
47	23	4	LOWERBD	NONBASIC	19	1	sales	May	
48	24	5	UPPERBD	NONBASIC	19	2	sales	March	

Example 4   4

Multi-Commodity Production Planning/Inventory/Distribution

Arcout=arc1

OBS	_TAIL_	_HEAD_	_COST_	_CAPAC_	_LO_	_SUPPLY_	_DEMAND_	_FLOW_	_FCOST_	_RCOST_
49	f2_apr_1	shop1_1	-290.00	250	0	.	900	245	-71050.00	.
50	f2_may_1	shop1_1	-292.00	250	0	.	900	0	0.00	18.00
51	f1_mar_2	shop1_2	-559.76	999999	0	.	900	0	0.00	47.13
52	f1_apr_2	shop1_2	-524.28	999999	0	.	900	0	0.00	8.40
53	f1_may_2	shop1_2	-475.02	999999	0	.	900	25	-11875.50	.
54	f2_mar_2	shop1_2	-567.83	500	0	.	900	500	-283915.00	-42.00
55	f2_apr_2	shop1_2	-542.19	500	0	.	900	375	-203321.25	.
56	f2_may_2	shop1_2	-461.56	500	0	.	900	0	0.00	10.50
57	f1_mar_1	shop2_1	-362.74	250	0	.	900	250	-90685.00	-46.09
58	f1_apr_1	shop2_1	-300.00	250	0	.	900	250	-75000.00	-32.00
59	f1_may_1	shop2_1	-245.00	250	0	.	900	0	0.00	38.00
60	f2_mar_1	shop2_1	-272.70	250	0	.	900	0	0.00	4.05
61	f2_apr_1	shop2_1	-312.00	250	0	.	900	250	-78000.00	-33.00
62	f2_may_1	shop2_1	-299.00	250	0	.	900	150	-44850.00	.
63	f1_mar_2	shop2_2	-623.89	999999	0	.	1450	455	-283869.95	.
64	f1_apr_2	shop2_2	-549.68	999999	0	.	1450	535	-294078.80	.
65	f1_may_2	shop2_2	-460.00	999999	0	.	1450	0	0.00	32.02
66	f2_mar_2	shop2_2	-542.83	500	0	.	1450	120	-65139.60	.
67	f2_apr_2	shop2_2	-559.19	500	0	.	1450	320	-178940.80	.
68	f2_may_2	shop2_2	-489.06	500	0	.	1450	20	-9781.20	.
									============	
									-1281110.35	

OBS	_ANUMB_	_TNUMB_	_STATUS_		DIAGONAL	FACTORY	KEY_ID	MTH_MADE	_NAME_
49	25	6	KEY_ARC	BASIC	19	2	sales	April	
50	26	7	LOWERBD	NONBASIC	19	2	sales	May	
51	53	12	LOWERBD	NONBASIC	25	1	sales	March	
52	54	13	LOWERBD	NONBASIC	25	1	sales	April	
53	55	14	KEY_ARC	BASIC	25	1	sales	May	
54	56	15	UPPERBD	NONBASIC	25	2	sales	March	
55	57	16	KEY_ARC	BASIC	25	2	sales	April	
56	58	17	LOWERBD	NONBASIC	25	2	sales	May	
57	27	2	UPPERBD	NONBASIC	19	1	sales	March	
58	28	3	UPPERBD	NONBASIC	19	1	sales	April	
59	29	4	LOWERBD	NONBASIC	19	1	sales	May	
60	30	5	LOWERBD	NONBASIC	19	2	sales	March	
61	31	6	UPPERBD	NONBASIC	19	2	sales	April	
62	32	7	KEY_ARC	BASIC	19	2	sales	May	

(continued on next page)

(continued from previous page)

```
63   59   12   KEY_ARC  BASIC     25    1    sales    March
64   60   13   KEY_ARC  BASIC     25    1    sales    April
65   61   14   LOWERBD  NONBASIC  25    1    sales    May
66   62   15   KEY_ARC  BASIC     25    2    sales    March
67   63   16   KEY_ARC  BASIC     25    2    sales    April
68   64   17   KEY_ARC  BASIC     25    2    sales    May
```

Figure 9.9 illustrates the optimal flow through the network.

19-inch Diagonal Televisions

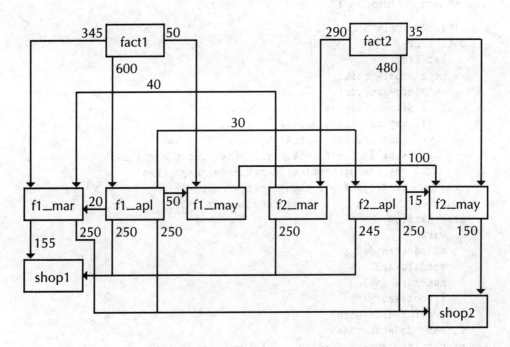

25-inch Diagonal Televisions

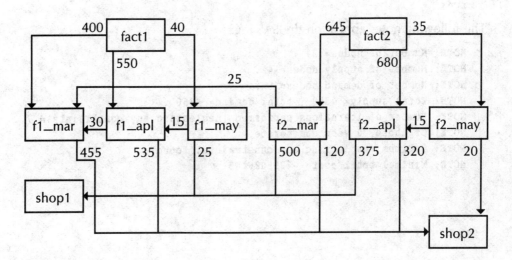

Figure 9.9   Network Model Using the Primal Simplex Network Algorithm

Example 5:   Using a Solution that Neglected Constraints as a Warm Start

This example examines the effect of changing some of the arc costs. The back order penalty costs are increased by twenty percent. The sales profit of 25-inch TVs sent to the shops in May increased by thirty percent. The production cost of 19- and 25-inch TVs made in May is decreased by five percent and twenty percent, respectively. How does the optimal solution of the network after these arc cost alterations compare with the optimum of the original network? If you want to use the warm start facilities of PROC NETFLOW to solve this undefined problem, specify the WARM option. Notice that the FUTURE1 option was specified in the last PROC NETFLOW run.

These SAS statements produce the new NODEOUT= and ARCOUT= data sets shown in **Output 9.12**.

```
title 'Example 5';
data arc2;
   set arc1;
      oldcost=_cost_;
      oldfc=_fcost_;
      oldflow=_flow_;
      if key_id='backorder'
         then _cost_=_cost_*1.2;
         else if _tail_='f2_may_2' then _cost_=_cost_-30;
      if key_id='production' & mth_made='May' then
         if diagonal=19 then _cost_=_cost_-5;
                        else _cost_=_cost_-20;
proc netflow
   warm
   nodedata=node2
   arcdata=arc2
   nodeout=node3
   arcout=arc3;
proc print data=node3;
title5 'Nodeout=node3';
proc print data=arc3 (drop = _status_ _rcost_);
         sum oldfc _fcost_;
title5 'Arcout=arc3';
run;
```

The following notes appear on the SAS log:

```
NOTE: Number of nodes= 21 .
NOTE: Number of supply nodes= 4 .
NOTE: Number of demand nodes= 5 .
NOTE: Total supply= 4350 , total demand= 4350 .
NOTE: Number of iterations performed (neglecting any constraints)= 7 .
NOTE: Of these, 0 were degenerate.
NOTE: Optimum (neglecting any constraints) found.
NOTE: Minimal total cost= -1285086.45 .
```

Output 9.12   Using PROC NETFLOW with a Warm Start

```
                                        Example 5                                            1


                                      Nodeout=node3

 OBS    _NODE_     _SUPDEM_    _DUAL_     _NNUMB_    _PRED_    _TRAV_    _SCESS_    _ARCID_    _FLOW_    _FBQ_

   1   f1_apr_1        .       -64.25        3         1        6         2          4         490       4
   2   f1_apr_2        .      -174.50       13        11       19        20         36         200      36
   3   f1_mar_1        .      -113.55        2         1        8         2          1         290       1
   4   f1_mar_2        .      -248.71       12        19       15         1        -59         455      33
   5   f1_may_1        .       -75.75        4         1        7         3          8          65       8
   6   f1_may_2        .      -117.88       14        17       22         1        -50         335      40
   7   f2_apr_1        .       -75.25        6         3        4         1         14          20      14
   8   f2_apr_2        .      -184.01       16        19       18         2        -63         280      46
   9   f2_mar_1        .       -73.65        5        10        1         1         12         255      11
  10   f2_mar_2        .      -167.65       15        19       20        13        -62         110      43
  11   f2_may_1        .       -91.75        7         4        9         2         18         115      18
  12   f2_may_2        .      -143.88       17        19       14         2        -64         370      50
  13   fact1_1       1000      14.35         1        21        3         8        -65           5      -1
  14   fact1_2       1000       0.00        11        22       13        21        -69           0     -33
  15   fact2_1        850      14.35        10        21        5         2        -66          45     -33
  16   fact2_2       1500      14.35        20        15       21        12        -44         600     -65
  17   shop1_1       -900     214.10         8         2       16         1         21         150      21
  18   shop1_2       -900     358.18        18        16       17         1         57         400      53
  19   shop2_1       -900     207.25         9         7        2         1         32         150      27
  20   shop2_2      -1450     375.18        19        13       12        19         60         235      59
```

```
                                        Example 5                                            2


                                      Arcout=arc3

 OBS    _TAIL_      _HEAD_     _COST_   _CAPAC_   _LO_   _SUPPLY_   _DEMAND_   _FLOW_   _FCOST_   _ANUMB_   _TNUMB_

   1   fact1_1    f1_apr_1     78.60     600      50     1000         .        540     42444.0      4        1
   2   f1_mar_1   f1_apr_1     15.00      50       0       .          .          0         0.0      5        2
   3   f1_may_1   f1_apr_1     33.60      20       0       .          .          0         0.0      6        4
   4   f2_apr_1   f1_apr_1     11.00      40       0       .          .          0         0.0      7        6
   5   fact1_2    f1_apr_2    174.50     550      50     1000         .        250     43625.0     36       11
   6   f1_mar_2   f1_apr_2     20.00      40       0       .          .          0         0.0     37       12
   7   f1_may_2   f1_apr_2     49.20      15       0       .          .         15       738.0     38       14
   8   f2_apr_2   f1_apr_2     21.00      25       0       .          .          0         0.0     39       16
   9   fact1_1    f1_mar_1    127.90     500      50     1000         .        340     43486.0      1        1
  10   f1_apr_1   f1_mar_1     33.60      20       0       .          .         20       672.0      2        3
  11   f2_mar_1   f1_mar_1     10.00      40       0       .          .         40       400.0      3        5
  12   fact1_2    f1_mar_2    217.90     400      40     1000         .        400     87160.0     33       11
  13   f1_apr_2   f1_mar_2     38.40      30       0       .          .         30      1152.0     34       13
  14   f2_mar_2   f1_mar_2     20.00      25       0       .          .         25       500.0     35       15
  15   fact1_1    f1_may_1     90.10     400      50     1000         .        115     10361.5      8        1
  16   f1_apr_1   f1_may_1     12.00      50       0       .          .          0         0.0      9        3
  17   f2_may_1   f1_may_1     13.00      40       0       .          .          0         0.0     10        7
  18   fact1_2    f1_may_2    113.30     350      40     1000         .        350     39655.0     40       11
  19   f1_apr_2   f1_may_2     18.00      40       0       .          .          0         0.0     41       13
  20   f2_may_2   f1_may_2     13.00      25       0       .          .          0         0.0     42       17
  21   f1_apr_1   f2_apr_1     11.00   999999      0       .          .         20       220.0     14        3
  22   fact2_1    f2_apr_1     62.40     480      35      850         .        480     29952.0     15       10
  23   f2_mar_1   f2_apr_1     18.00      30       0       .          .          0         0.0     16        5
  24   f2_may_1   f2_apr_1     30.00      15       0       .          .          0         0.0     17        7

 OBS   DIAGONAL   FACTORY    KEY_ID      MTH_MADE        _NAME_       OLDCOST    OLDFC     OLDFLOW

   1      19         1      production    April       prod f1 19 apl   78.60    47160.00     600
   2      19         1      storage       March                        15.00        0.00       0
   3      19         1      backorder     May         back f1 19 may   28.00        0.00       0
   4      19         .      f2_to_1       April                        11.00        0.00       0
   5      25         1      production    April       prod f1 25 apl  174.50    95975.00     550
   6      25         1      storage       March                        20.00        0.00       0
   7      25         1      backorder     May         back f1 25 may   41.00      615.00      15
   8      25         .      f2_to_1       April                        21.00        0.00       0
   9      19         1      production    March       prod f1 19 mar  127.90    44125.50     345
  10      19         1      backorder     April       back f1 19 apl   28.00      560.00      20
  11      19         .      f2_to_1       March                        10.00      400.00      40
  12      25         1      production    March       prod f1 25 mar  217.90    87160.00     400
  13      25         1      backorder     April       back f1 25 apl   32.00      960.00      30
  14      25         .      f2_to_1       March                        20.00      500.00      25
  15      19         1      production    May                          95.10     4755.00      50
  16      19         1      storage       April                        12.00      600.00      50
```

(continued on next page)

(continued from previous page)

17	19	.	f2_to_1	May			13.00	0.00	0
18	25	1	production	May			133.30	5332.00	40
19	25	1	storage	April			18.00	0.00	0
20	25	.	f2_to_1	May			43.00	0.00	0
21	19	1	f1_to_2	April			11.00	330.00	30
22	19	2	production	April	prod f2 19 apl		62.40	29952.00	480
23	19	2	storage	March			18.00	0.00	0
24	19	2	backorder	May	back f2 19 may		25.00	0.00	0

Example 5   3

Arcout=arc3

OBS	_TAIL_	_HEAD_	_COST_	_CAPAC_	_LO_	_SUPPLY_	_DEMAND_	_FLOW_	_FCOST_	_ANUMB_	_TNUMB_
25	f1_apr_2	f2_apr_2	23.00	999999	0	.	.	0	0.00	46	13
26	fact2_2	f2_apr_2	196.70	680	35	1500	.	680	133756.00	47	20
27	f2_mar_2	f2_apr_2	28.00	50	0	.	.	0	0.00	48	15
28	f2_may_2	f2_apr_2	64.80	15	0	.	.	0	0.00	49	17
29	f1_mar_1	f2_mar_1	11.00	999999	0	.	.	0	0.00	11	2
30	fact2_1	f2_mar_1	88.00	450	35	850	.	290	25520.00	12	10
31	f2_apr_1	f2_mar_1	20.40	15	0	.	.	0	0.00	13	6
32	f1_mar_2	f2_mar_2	23.00	999999	0	.	.	0	0.00	43	12
33	fact2_2	f2_mar_2	182.00	650	35	1500	.	635	115570.00	44	20
34	f2_apr_2	f2_mar_2	37.20	15	0	.	.	0	0.00	45	16
35	f1_may_1	f2_may_1	16.00	999999	0	.	.	115	1840.00	18	4
36	fact2_1	f2_may_1	128.80	250	35	850	.	35	4508.00	19	10
37	f2_apr_1	f2_may_1	20.00	30	0	.	.	0	0.00	20	6
38	f1_may_2	f2_may_2	26.00	999999	0	.	.	335	8710.00	50	14
39	fact2_2	f2_may_2	181.40	550	35	1500	.	35	6349.00	51	20
40	f2_apr_2	f2_may_2	38.00	50	0	.	.	0	0.00	52	16
41	f1_mar_1	shop1_1	-327.65	250	0	.	900	150	-49147.50	21	2
42	f1_apr_1	shop1_1	-300.00	250	0	.	900	250	-75000.00	22	3
43	f1_may_1	shop1_1	-285.00	250	0	.	900	0	0.00	23	4
44	f2_mar_1	shop1_1	-297.40	250	0	.	900	250	-74350.00	24	5
45	f2_apr_1	shop1_1	-290.00	250	0	.	900	250	-72500.00	25	6
46	f2_may_1	shop1_1	-292.00	250	0	.	900	0	0.00	26	7
47	f1_mar_2	shop1_2	-559.76	999999	0	.	900	0	0.00	53	12
48	f1_apr_2	shop1_2	-524.28	999999	0	.	900	0	0.00	54	13

OBS	DIAGONAL	FACTORY	KEY_ID	MTH_MADE	_NAME_	OLDCOST	OLDFC	OLDFLOW
25	25	.	f1_to_2	April		23.00	0.00	0
26	25	2	production	April	prod f2 25 apl	196.70	133756.00	680
27	25	2	storage	March		28.00	0.00	0
28	25	2	backorder	May	back f2 25 may	54.00	810.00	15
29	19	.	f1_to_2	March		11.00	0.00	0
30	19	2	production	March	prod f2 19 mar	88.00	25520.00	290
31	19	2	backorder	April	back f2 19 apl	17.00	0.00	0
32	25	.	f1_to_2	March		23.00	0.00	0
33	25	2	production	March	prod f2 25 mar	182.00	117390.00	645
34	25	2	backorder	April	back f2 25 apl	31.00	0.00	0
35	19	.	f1_to_2	May		16.00	1600.00	100
36	19	2	production	May		133.80	4683.00	35
37	19	2	storage	April		20.00	300.00	15
38	25	.	f1_to_2	May		26.00	0.00	0
39	25	2	production	May		201.40	7049.00	35
40	25	2	storage	April		38.00	0.00	0
41	19	1	sales	March		-327.65	-50785.75	155
42	19	1	sales	April		-300.00	-75000.00	250
43	19	1	sales	May		-285.00	0.00	0
44	19	2	sales	March		-297.40	-74350.00	250
45	19	2	sales	April		-290.00	-71050.00	245
46	19	2	sales	May		-292.00	0.00	0
47	25	1	sales	March		-559.76	0.00	0
48	25	1	sales	April		-524.28	0.00	0

Example 5   4

Arcout=arc3

OBS	_TAIL_	_HEAD_	_COST_	_CAPAC_	_LO_	_SUPPLY_	_DEMAND_	_FLOW_	_FCOST_	_ANUMB_	_TNUMB_
49	f1_may_2	shop1_2	-475.02	999999	0	.	900	0	0.00	55	14
50	f2_mar_2	shop1_2	-567.83	500	0	.	900	500	-283915.00	56	15
51	f2_apr_2	shop1_2	-542.19	500	0	.	900	400	-216876.00	57	16
52	f2_may_2	shop1_2	-491.56	500	0	.	900	0	0.00	58	17
53	f1_mar_1	shop2_1	-362.74	250	0	.	900	250	-90685.00	27	2
54	f1_apr_1	shop2_1	-300.00	250	0	.	900	250	-75000.00	28	3
55	f1_may_1	shop2_1	-245.00	250	0	.	900	0	0.00	29	4
56	f2_mar_1	shop2_1	-272.70	250	0	.	900	0	0.00	30	5
57	f2_apr_1	shop2_1	-312.00	250	0	.	900	250	-78000.00	31	6
58	f2_may_1	shop2_1	-299.00	250	0	.	900	150	-44850.00	32	7
59	f1_mar_2	shop2_2	-623.89	999999	0	.	1450	455	-283869.95	59	12
60	f1_apr_2	shop2_2	-549.68	999999	0	.	1450	235	-129174.80	60	13
61	f1_may_2	shop2_2	-460.00	999999	0	.	1450	0	0.00	61	14
62	f2_mar_2	shop2_2	-542.83	500	0	.	1450	110	-59711.30	62	15
63	f2_apr_2	shop2_2	-559.19	500	0	.	1450	280	-156573.20	63	16
64	f2_may_2	shop2_2	-519.06	500	0	.	1450	370	-192052.20	64	17
									============		
									-1285086.45		

OBS	DIAGONAL	FACTORY	KEY_ID	MTH_MADE	_NAME_	OLDCOST	OLDFC	OLDFLOW
49	25	1	sales	May		-475.02	-11875.50	25
50	25	2	sales	March		-567.83	-283915.00	500
51	25	2	sales	April		-542.19	-203321.25	375
52	25	2	sales	May		-461.56	0.00	0
53	19	1	sales	March		-362.74	-90685.00	250
54	19	1	sales	April		-300.00	-75000.00	250
55	19	1	sales	May		-245.00	0.00	0
56	19	2	sales	March		-272.70	0.00	0
57	19	2	sales	April		-312.00	-78000.00	250
58	19	2	sales	May		-299.00	-44850.00	150
59	25	1	sales	March		-623.89	-283869.95	455
60	25	1	sales	April		-549.68	-294078.80	535
61	25	1	sales	May		-460.00	0.00	0
62	25	2	sales	March		-542.83	-65139.60	120
63	25	2	sales	April		-559.19	-178940.80	320
64	25	2	sales	May		-489.06	-9781.20	20
							============	
							-1281110.35	

Figure 9.10 illustrates the solution to the network problem.

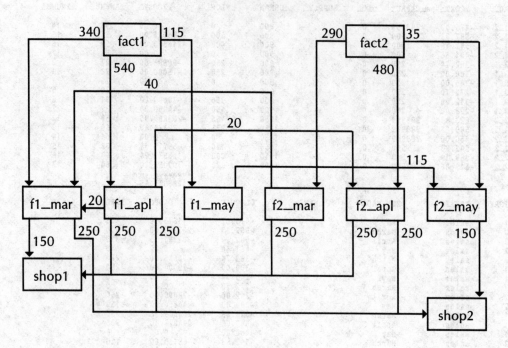

19-inch Diagonal Televisions

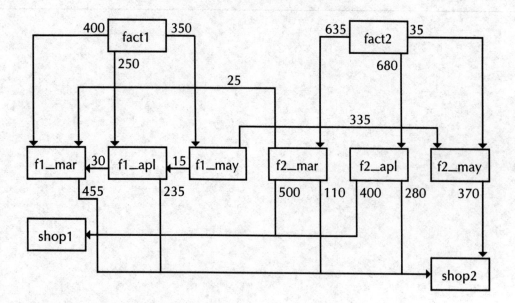

25-inch Diagonal Televisions

Figure 9.10   Optimal Flow through the Network Model

REFERENCES

Bland, R.G. (1977), "New Finite Pivoting Rules for the Simplex Method," *Mathematics of Operations Research*, Volume 2, Number 2 (p. 103–107).

Ford, L.R., and Fulkerson, D.R. (1962), *Flows in Networks*, Princeton, N.J.: Princeton University Press.

Kennington, J.L., and Helgason R.V. (1980), *Algorithms for Networking Programming*, New York: Wiley Interscience, John Wiley & Sons.

Reid, J.K. (1975), *A Sparsity-Exploiting Variant of the Bartels-Golub Decomposition for Linear Programming Bases*, Harwell Report CSS 20, A.E.R.E., Didcot, Oxfordshire, England.

REFERENCES

Chapter 10

The TRANS Procedure

ABSTRACT

The TRANS procedure is used to solve the transportation problem.

INTRODUCTION

The transportation problem is a type of network flow problem. A node of a transportation problem is either a source node or a destination node. Each source node is able to supply a specified number of flow units; each destination node has a demand for a specified number of flow units. Each arc of a transportation problem originates at a source node and terminates at a destination node. Some arcs may have capacities (the maximum amount of flow that they may convey) and lower flow bounds (the minimum amount of flow that the arc may convey). Arcs also have per unit traversal costs, simply referred to as cost (for example, the cost incurred when one unit of flow is conveyed through an arc). **Figure 10.1** shows a transportation problem network having three source nodes and two destination nodes.

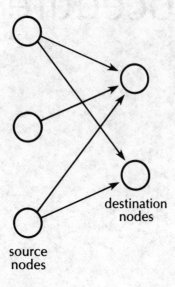

destination
nodes

source
nodes

Figure 10.1   A Transportation Network

The TRANS procedure accepts information about the transportation problem as data and produces a SAS data set that contains the flows that should be conveyed by each arc (the flow between each source and destination node) that minimize the total cost of flow.

Introductory Example

Consider the SAS data set in **Output 10.1**. The SAS code used to create the data set can be found in **Example 1:   Uncapacitated Transportation Network**.

Output 10.1   Uncapacitated Transportation Network

Uncapacitated Transportation Network

OBS	CITY	SUPPLY	ATLANTA	CHICAGO	DENVER	HOUSTON	LOS_ANGE	MIAMI	NEW_YORK	SAN_FRAN	SEATTLE	WASHINGT
1	.	.	50	75	89	8	27	39	64	100	50	8
2	Atlanta	10	20	58	121	70	193	60	74	213	218	54
3	Chicago	150	58	20	92	94	174	118	71	185	173	57
4	Denver	90	121	92	20	87	83	172	163	94	102	149
5	Houston	27	70	94	87	20	137	96	142	154	189	122
6	Los_Ange	80	193	174	83	137	20	223	245	34	95	230
7	Miami	26	60	118	172	96	233	20	109	259	273	92
8	New_York	80	74	71	163	142	245	109	20	257	240	20
9	San_Fran	25	213	185	94	164	34	259	257	20	67	244
10	Seattle	7	218	173	102	189	95	273	240	67	20	232
11	Washingt	15	54	59	149	122	230	92	20	244	232	20

The first observation provides the number of units demanded at each destination node. The SUPPLY column provides the number of units supplied at each source node. If you exclude the first observation and the SUPPLY variable, the remaining values are the cost of shipping one unit between nodes. For example, the per unit transportation cost between Miami and Houston is 96. The transportation problem is solved when the minimum total cost flow between supply points and destination points that satisfies the demand is found. PROC TRANS solves this problem and produces a SAS data set containing the number of units to ship between each supply point and demand point. See **Example 1: Uncapacitated Transportation Network** for the results.

SPECIFICATIONS

The following statements are used with PROC TRANS:

PROC TRANS *options*;
  HEADNODE *variables*;
  SUPPLY *variable*;
  TAILNODE *variable*;

The TAILNODE and SUPPLY statements are required.

PROC TRANS Statement

PROC TRANS *options*;

The options below can appear in the PROC TRANS statement.

Data Set Options

CAPACITY=*SASdataset*
  names the SAS data set that contains the capacity on each arc in the transportation network. These data specify the maximum allowable flow on each network arc. If CAPACITY= is omitted, then the value of the DEFCAPACITY= option is used for each arc in the network.

COST=*SASdataset*
  names the SAS data set that contains the cost, supply, and demand data for the transportation network. If COST= is omitted, the most recently created SAS data set is used.

FLOW= *SASdataset*
  names the SAS data set that contains initial flows. Only arcs that have initial flows need to appear in the FLOW data set. If initial flows that are close to the optimum are supplied, computational time can be saved.

MINFLOW=*SASdataset*
  names the SAS data set that contains the minimum flow data for the transportation network. These data specify the minimum required flow on each arc in the network. If MINFLOW= is omitted, then the value of the DEFMINFLOW= option is used for each arc in the network.

OUT=*SASdataset*
  specifies a name for the output data set. If OUT= is omitted, the SAS System creates a data set and names it according to the DATA*n* convention. See "SAS Statements Used in the Data Set" in base SAS documentation for more information.

Optimization Control Options

DEFCAPACITY=c

specifies the default capacity for the arcs in the network. The default value of c is 99999.

DEFMINFLOW=s

specifies the default minimum flow for the arcs in the network. The default value of s is 0.

DEMAND=d

gives the number of the observation that contains the number of units demanded at each destination node. The default value of d is 1.

MAXIMUM

tells the procedure to maximize rather than minimize the objective function.

NOTHRUNET

tells PROC TRANS to drain away any excess supply (the amount that total supply exceeds total demand) or excess demand (the amount that total demand exceeds total supply). If a transportation problem has unequal total supply and total demand, and you do not specify either THRUNET or NOTHRUNET, then PROC TRANS assumes that the problem is infeasible and does not proceed with the optimization.

THRUNET

tells the procedure to force through the network any excess supply (the amount that total supply exceeds total demand) or any excess demand (the amount that total demand exceeds total supply), as is required. If a transportation problem has unequal total supply and total demand, and you do not specify either THRUNET or NOTHRUNET, then PROC TRANS assumes that the problem is infeasible and does not proceed with the optimization.

HEADNODE Statement

HEADNODE *variables*;

The HEADNODE statement names the destination nodes and identifies variables in the COST= input data set that contain the transportation costs. A value of a HEADNODE list variable in the COST= data set gives the cost of transporting a unit of supply from the source node named in that observation's TAILNODE list to the corresponding destination node. Variables in the MINFLOW=, CAPACITY=, and FLOW= data sets are similarly associated with destination nodes and upper and lower bounds on arc flows.

SUPPLY Statement

SUPPLY *variable*;

The SUPPLY statement identifies the variable in the COST= data set that contains the number of units of supply at each supply node. The SUPPLY statement is required. Values of the SUPPLY variable must be numeric.

TAILNODE Statement

TAILNODE *variable*;

The TAILNODE statement identifies the variable in all input data sets that names each of the source nodes. This variable is included in the output data set. The

TAILNODE statement is required, and the values of the TAILNODE variable must be character.

DETAILS

Missing Values

A missing value in a HEADNODE list variable in the COST= input data set indicates that the arc from that observation's TAILNODE list source node to the corresponding destination node does not exist.

A missing value in the MINFLOW= and CAPACITY= data sets causes the procedure to assign the default capacity or default minimum flow to the corresponding arc, if it exists.

A missing value in the FLOW= data set indicates a zero value if the arc exists.

A missing value in the OUT= data set is used when the arc does not exist.

A missing supply or demand value is interpreted as zero.

Output Data Set

The output data set contains the variables listed in the HEADNODE, TAILNODE, and SUPPLY statements, and an additional variable named _DUAL_. For each observation in the COST= data set that is associated with a source node, the output data set tells you

- the optimal flow between the source and destination nodes
- the name of the source node as given in the TAILNODE variable
- the value of the dual variable associated with that source node.

The demand data specified in the COST= data set are also included in the same observation as they are in the COST= data set. The TAILNODE variable has the value _DEMAND_ in this observation. An observation labeled with the TAILNODE variable taking the value _DUAL_ contains the dual variables at the destination nodes.

Objective Value

If the problem is infeasible, a note to that effect is printed on the SAS log. Otherwise, the value of the objective function, the total cost (the multiple of flow and cost, summed for all arcs) at optimality, is reported on the SAS log.

Demand

The demand at each destination node must be specified. Because there are the same number of destination nodes as there are HEADNODE statement variables, PROC TRANS assumes that the values of the first observation contain the number of units demanded at each destination node. If DEMAND=d is specified in the PROC TRANS statement, then observation d is assumed to contain the number of units demanded at each destination node.

Dual Variables

Let $\pi_i = 1, \ldots, n$ be the dual variable values of the source nodes, $\pi_j = 1, \ldots, m$ be the dual variable values of the destination nodes, and let c_{ij} be the cost of unit flow on the arc between source i and destination j. Then

$$r_{ij} = \pi_i - \pi_j - c_{ij}$$

is the reduced cost of the arc between nodes i and j. This is the amount by which the total cost increases if flow through arc (ij) is increased by one unit. The total cost would decrease by r_{ij} if the flow through arc (i,j) is decreased by one unit. Dual variables are saved in the OUT= SAS data set.

Macro Variable _ORTRANS

On termination, the TRANS procedure defines a macro variable named _ORTRANS. This variable contains a character string that indicates the status of the procedure on termination and gives the objective value at termination. The form of the _ORTRANS character string is

STATUS=xxx **OBJECTIVE=**yyy

where xxx can be any one of the following:

- SUCCESSFUL
- INFEASIBLE
- INFEASIBLE_SUPPLY>DEMAND
- INFEASIBLE_SUPPLY<DEMAND
- MEMORY_ERROR
- IO_ERROR
- SYNTAX_ERROR
- SEMANTIC_ERROR
- BADDATA_ERROR
- UNKNOWN_ERROR.

This information can be used when PROC TRANS is one step in a larger program that needs to identify just how the TRANS procedure teminated. Because _ORTRANS is a standard SAS macro variable it can be used in the ways that all macro variables can be used (see the *SAS Guide to Macro Processing, Version 6 Edition*). One way to print the _ORTRANS variable on the log is illustrated in **Example 1:   Uncapacitated Transportation Network**.

Reasons for Infeasibility

By default, PROC TRANS assumes that all transportation problems have total supply equal to total demand. The THRUNET and NOTHRUNET options allow you to relax this assumption.

Note: if total supply equals total demand, then a transportation problem can be infeasible because either

- nodal flow conservation constraints cannot be met so that the flow into a node plus its supply does not equal the flow out of the node plus its demand
- flow through an arc is either below the arc's lower flow bound or above the arc's capacity.

Balancing Total Supply and Total Demand

When Total Supply Exceeds Total Demand

When total supply of a transportation problem exceeds total demand, PROC TRANS can add an extra destination node (called the excess node) to the problem and set the demand at that node equal to the difference between total supply and total demand. There are two ways that this extra destination node may be added to the transportation network.

Figure 10.2 shows a network in which the NOTHRUNET option is specified. The sum of flows that reach the destination nodes equals the total demand of the transportation problem. For some source nodes, supply may be conveyed through *real* arcs but may also be drained away to the excess node. The supply of each source node is really an upper bound of the number of flow units such a node may actually supply.

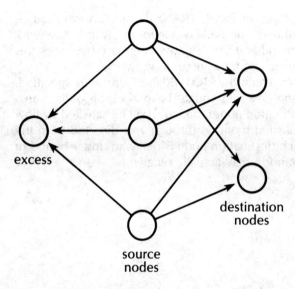

Figure 10.2   Using the NOTHRUNET Option when Total Supply Exceeds Total Demand

Figure 10.3 illustrates a network in which the THRUNET option is used. The sum of flows that reach the destination nodes equals the total supply of the transportation problem.

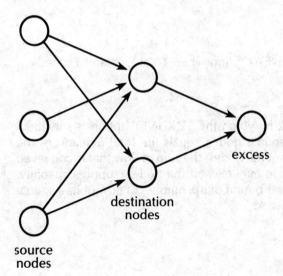

Figure 10.3   Using the THRUNET Option when Total Supply Exceeds Total Demand

For some destination nodes, the amount of flow may exceed that node's demand. The demand of destination nodes is a lower bound of the number of flow units a destination node may demand.

When Total Demand Exceeds Total Supply

When total demand exceeds total supply, PROC TRANS can add an extra source node (the excess node) to the problem. This node is able to supply to the network the difference between total demand and total supply. There are two ways this extra source node may be added to the transportation network.

Figure 10.4 shows a network in which the NOTHRUNET option is specified. The sum of flows that leave the source nodes equals the total supply of the transportation problem. For some destination nodes, demand will be satisfied by flow through *real* arcs and may be satisfied by flows through arcs directed from the excess node. The demand of each destination node is really an upper bound of the number of flow units such a node may actually receive.

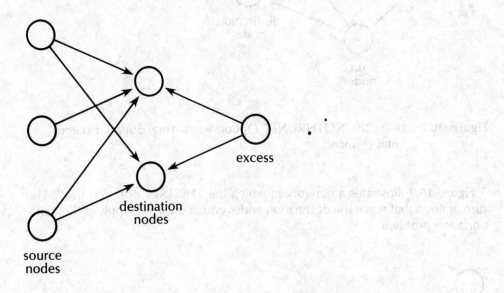

Figure 10.4   Using the NOTHRUNET Option when Total Demand Exceeds Total Supply

Figure 10.5 illustrates a network in which the THRUNET option is specified. The sum of flows that leave the source nodes equals the total demand of the transportation problem. For some source nodes, the sum of flow that is conveyed through arcs originating at that node may exceed the node's supply capability. The supply of source nodes is a lower bound of the number of flow units a source node is able to supply to the network.

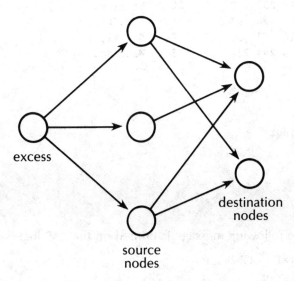

Figure 10.5   Using the THRUNET Option when Total Demand Exceeds Total Supply

Note: if total supply does not equal total demand and either the THRUNET or NOTHRUNET option is specified, PROC TRANS automatically creates the excess node and the arcs incident to it. When the optimization is complete, these ancilliary parts of the network are erased. Information about these parts will not be found in the OUT= SAS data set. However, if you do not specify either the THRUNET or NOTHRUNET option, PROC TRANS will not know how to balance the network, will not begin any optimization, and will determine the problem to be infeasible.

EXAMPLES

Example 1:   Uncapacitated Transportation Network

The transportation problem described in the introduction is solved below. The cost data are stored in a SAS data set; in PROC TRANS you identify the COST variables and the SUPPLY variable. The solution is stored in a SAS data set as shown in **Output 10.2** and printed with PROC PRINT.

```
    title 'Uncapacitated Transportation Network';

data cst;
    input Atlanta Chicago Denver Houston Los_Ange Miami
        New_York San_Fran Seattle Washingt supply city$;
    cards;
 50   75  89    8   27   39   64  100   50    8    .    .
 20   58 121   70  193   60   74  213  218   54   10   Atlanta
 58   20   92   94  174  118   71  185  173   57  150   Chicago
121   92   20   87   83  172  163   94  102  149   90   Denver
 70   94   87   20  137   96  142  154  189  122   27   Houston
193  174   83  137   20  223  245   34   95  230   80   Los_Ange
```

```
 60 118 172  96 233  20 109 259 273  92   26   Miami
 74  71 163 142 245 109  20 257 240  20   80   New_York
213 185  94 164  34 259 257  20  67 244   25   San_Fran
218 173 102 189  95 273 240  67  20 232    7   Seattle
 54  59 149 122 230  92  20 244 232  20   15   Washingt
;

proc trans cost=cst;
    TAILNODE city;
    HEADNODE Atlanta--Washingt;
    supply supply;
run;

proc print;
run;
```

After this program executes, the following message is printed on the SAS log:

```
NOTE: Optimal Solution total = 22928.
```

The job above produces the SAS data set in **Output 10.2**.

Output 10.2 Uncapacitated Transportation Network

```
                          Uncapacitated Transportation Network                                    1
 BS  CITY     ATLANTA CHICAGO DENVER HOUSTON LOS_ANGE MIAMI NEW_YORK SAN_FRAN SEATTLE WASHINGT SUPPLY  _DUAL_

  1  _DUAL_      -71    -33   -105    -48     -165    -109    -20     -179    -186     -20      .       .
  2  Atlanta      10      0      0      0        0       0      0        0       0       0      10     -51
  3  Chicago      30     75      2      0        0       0      0        0      43       0     150     -13
  4  Denver        0      0     87      0        0       0      0        3       0       0      90     -85
  5  Houston       0      0      0      8       19       0      0        0       0       0      27     -28
  6  Los_Ange      0      0      0      0        8       0      0       72       0       0      80    -145
  7  Miami         0      0      0      0        0      26      0        0       0       0      26     -89
  8  New_York      0      0      0      0        0       8     64        0       0       8      80       0
  9  San_Fran      0      0      0      0        0       0      0       25       0       0      25    -159
 10  Seattle       0      0      0      0        0       0      0        0       7       0       7    -166
 11  Washingt     10      0      0      0        0       5      0        0       0       0      15     -17
```

Because the first observation is associated with the demands, the TAILNODE value is _DEMAND_. The second observation has a TAILNODE value of _DUAL_, and the values of the HEADNODE variables are the dual variables at the destination nodes, or the marginal costs of increasing demand at each node.

The third observation contains information associated with the Atlanta source node. The SUPPLY variable has the supply capability of this source node (10 units), and the dual value (−71) for Atlanta is the _DUAL_ variable value in this observation. The values of the HEADNODE variables in this observation give the optimal flow between Atlanta and each destination node. For example, to achieve the minimum cost, you must ship 10 units from Atlanta to Atlanta. No Atlanta units are sent to any other destination. In contrast, the Chicago supply must be sent to four destinations: 30 units to Atlanta, 75 units to Chicago, 2 units to Denver, and 43 units to Seattle.

The variable _DUAL_, the dual variable at the supply nodes, gives the marginal cost of increasing supply at each of those nodes. For example, the marginal cost of increasing supply at Atlanta is −51. This means that a unit increase in supply in Atlanta would decrease total transportation costs by $51.

The macro variable _ORTRANS, defined by PROC TRANS, contains information regarding the termination of the procedure. This information can be useful when PROC TRANS is part of a larger SAS program. For example, this information can be printed on the log using the macro language with the statement:

```
%put &_ORTRANS;
```

The following message is printed on the SAS log:

```
STATUS=SUCCESSFUL  OBJECTIVE=22928
```

Example 2: Capacitated Transportation Network

In this example, the optimal flow is found on a capacitated transportation network. Suppose that there are upper bounds on the amount that can be shipped within each city. This can be interpreted as a limit on the available transportation within the cities. The following SAS program and output show how this capacity constraint is included in the model:

```
title 'Capacitated Transportation Network';

data capcty;
    input Atlanta Chicago Denver Houston Los_Ange Miami
        New_York San_Fran Seattle Washingt city$;
    cards;
10  .   .   .   .   .   .   .   .   . Atlanta
.   60  .   .   .   .   .   .   .   . Chicago
.   .   100 .   .   .   .   .   .   . Denver
.   .   .   10  .   .   .   .   .   . Houston
.   .   .   .   30  .   .   .   .   . Los_Ange
.   .   .   .   .   20  .   .   .   . Miami
.   .   .   .   .   .   75  .   .   . New_York
.   .   .   .   .   .   .   25  .   . San_Fran
.   .   .   .   .   .   .   .   10  . Seattle
.   .   .   .   .   .   .   .   .   10 Washingt
;

proc trans cost=cst capacity=capcty;
    HEADNODE Atlanta--Washingt;
    TAILNODE city;
    supply supply;
run;

proc print;
run;
```

After this program executes, the following messages are printed on the SAS log:

```
NOTE: 10 variables in capacity data set match variables in the
      cost data set.
NOTE: Optimal Solution Total = 24036.
```

The solution printed includes **Output 10.3**.

Output 10.3 Capacitated Transportation Network

```
                        Capacitated Transportation Network                                    1
BS  CITY     ATLANTA CHICAGO DENVER HOUSTON LOS_ANGE MIAMI NEW_YORK SAN_FRAN SEATTLE WASHINGT SUPPLY _DUAL_
 1  _DUAL_      -60     -80    -94    -37    -154   -113     -29    -168    -175      -29       .     .
 2  Atlanta       0       0      0      0       0     10       0       0       0        0      10    -53
 3  Chicago      44      60      3      0       0      0       0       0      43        0     150     -2
 4  Denver        0       0     86      0       0      0       0       4       0        0      90    -74
 5  Houston       0       0      0      8      18      1       0       0       0        0      27    -17
 6  Los_Ange      0       0      0      0       9      0       0      71       0        0      80   -134
 7  Miami         6       0      0      0       0     20       0       0       0        0      26      0
 8  New_York      0       8      0      0       0      0      64       0       0        8      80     -9
 9  San_Fran      0       0      0      0       0      0       0      25       0        0      25   -148
10  Seattle       0       0      0      0       0      0       0       0       7        0       7   -155
11  Washingt      0       7      0      0       0      8       0       0       0        0      15    -21
```

Note that the optimal objective value is greater in the capacitated network (24036) than in the uncapacitated network (22928). Additional constraints can never decrease the objective value of a minimization problem at optimality. Also observe that the flow within Chicago, Miami, and San_Fran are at their limits. The rerouting of flow within these cities accounts for the increase in cost.

Example 3:   Capacitated Transportation Network

Suppose that we place a minimum on the flow within each city. Just as capacity restrictions can be interpreted as limits on available transportation, minimum flow restrictions can be interpreted as requirements to ship minimum quantities on certain routes, perhaps as a result of contractual agreements. The following program adds minimum flow requirements on four routes. Because the MINFLOW= data set contains many missing values, named input mode is used to input the data. The printed solution follows the program.

```
title 'Capacitated Transportation Network';

data minflw;
   input Chicago= Denver=  San_Fran= Seattle= city= $;
   cards;
city=Chicago Chicago=30 San_Fran=40 Seattle=50
city=Denver  Denver=40
;

proc trans cost=cst capacity=capcty minflow=minflw;
   HEADNODE Atlanta--Washingt;
   TAILNODE city;
   supply supply;
run;

proc print;
run;
```

The SAS log contains the following messages:

```
NOTE: 4 variables in minflow data set match variables in the
      cost data set.
NOTE: 10 variables in capacity data set match variables in the
      cost data set.
NOTE: Optimal Solution Total = 31458.
```

The printed solution includes **Output 10.4**.

Output 10.4 Capacitated Transportation Network

```
                          Capacitated Transportation Network                                    1
 BS  CITY      ATLANTA  CHICAGO  DENVER  HOUSTON  LOS_ANGE  MIAMI  NEW_YORK  SAN_FRAN  SEATTLE  WASHINGT  SUPPLY  _DUAL_
  1  _DUAL_       -158     -129     -57     -111        6    -187      -104        -8       24      -104       .       .
  2  Atlanta        10        0       0        0        0       0         0         0        0         0      10    -138
  3  Chicago         0       60       0        0        0       0         0        40       50         0     150    -100
  4  Denver         11        8      71        0        0       0         0         0        0         0      90     -37
  5  Houston         0        0       0        8        0      19         0         0        0         0      27     -91
  6  Los_Ange        0        0      18        0       27       0         0        35        0         0      80      26
  7  Miami           6        0       0        0        0      20         0         0        0         0      26     -98
  8  New_York        8        0       0        0        0       0        64         0        0         8      80     -84
  9  San_Fran        0        0       0        0        0       0         0        25        0         0      25      12
 10  Seattle         0        7       0        0        0       0         0         0        0         0       7      44
 11  Washingt       15        0       0        0        0       0         0         0        0         0      15    -104
```

Note that the optimal objective value is greater in the minimum flow capacitated network than in the capacitated network. Additional constraints can never decrease the objective value of a minimization problem at optimality.

Example 4: An Infeasible Problem

This example shows what happens when the total demand exceeds the total supply. The data from the first example are used with the demand at Atlanta increased to 100 units. Consequently, the demand exceeds the supply by 50 units. When the statements

```
proc trans cost=cst;
   TAILNODE city;
   HEADNODE Atlanta--Washingt;
   supply supply;
run;
```

are executed, the following message is printed on the SAS log:

```
WARNING: Demand exceeds supply by 50 units.
ERROR: The problem is infeasible.
```

However, if the THRUNET option is specified in the PROC TRANS statement, the procedure distributes the supply optimally among the source nodes. In that case, the statements

```
title 'Using the THRUNET Option';

proc trans data=cst THRUNET;
   TAILNODE city;
   HEADNODE Atlanta--Washingt;
   supply supply;
run;

proc print;
run;
```

produce the following message on the SAS log and **Output 10.5**.

    NOTE: Optimal Solution Total = 12910.

The data set in **Output 10.5** is saved by PROC TRANS.

Output 10.5   Using the THRUNET Option

Using the THRUNET Option   1

BS	CITY	ATLANTA	CHICAGO	DENVER	HOUSTON	LOS_ANGE	MIAMI	NEW_YORK	SAN_FRAN	SEATTLE	WASHINGT	SUPPLY	_DUAL_
1	_DUAL_	70	108	54	111	-6	35	124	-20	-20	124	.	.
2	Atlanta	10	0	0	0	0	0	0	0	0	0	10	90
3	Chicago	75	75	0	0	0	0	0	0	0	0	150	128
4	Denver	0	0	89	0	0	0	0	1	0	0	90	74
5	Houston	0	0	0	8	14	5	0	0	0	0	27	131
6	Los_Ange	0	0	0	0	13	0	0	67	0	0	80	14
7	Miami	0	0	0	0	0	26	0	0	0	0	26	55
8	New_York	0	0	0	0	0	8	64	0	0	8	80	144
9	San_Fran	0	0	0	0	0	0	0	32	0	0	25	0
10	Seattle	0	0	0	0	0	0	0	0	50	0	7	0
11	Washingt	15	0	0	0	0	0	0	0	0	0	15	124

REFERENCES

Minieka, E. (1978), *Optimization Algorithms for Networks and Graphs*, New York: Marcel Dekker, Inc.

Papadimitriov, C. M. and Steiglitz, K. (1982), *Combinatorial Optimization Algorithms and Complexity*, Englewood Cliffs, N.J.: Prentice-Hall, Inc.

Using Macro SASMPSXS to Convert from IBM Format to LP Format

This appendix shows you how to use the SAS macro SASMPSXS to convert a mathematical program stored in the CONVERT format as specified in Chapter 4 of the *IBM MPSX Program Description Manual* (number 5734-XM4) to the sparse format expected by the LP procedure. The SASMPSXS macro (a listing is given below), which can be found in the sample library, assumes that the data to be transformed are in a SAS data set called RAW with variables FIELD1 to FIELD6 corresponding to the MPSX format fields. The data set produced by the SASMPSXS macro can be input to PROC LP.

Below, the problem is finding an optimal product mix for a manufacturer that produces four items: a DESK, a CHAIR, a CABINET, and a BOOKCASE. Each item is processed in a stamping department (STAMP), an assembly department (ASSEMB), and a finishing department (FINISH). The time each item requires in each department is given in the input data. Because of resource limitations, each department has an upper limit on the time available for processing. Furthermore, because of labor constraints, the assembly department must work at least 300 hours. Finally, marketing tells you not to make more than 75 chairs, to make at least 50 bookcases, and to find the range over which the selling price of a bookcase can vary without changing the optimal product mix.

The following data show how this example might appear for solution with MPSX:

```
OBS     CARD


 1      NAME            EXAMPLE
 2      * THIS IS DATA FOR THE PRODUCT MIX PROBLEM.
 3      ROWS
 4      N  PROFIT
 5      L  STAMP
 6      L  ASSEMB
 7      L  FINISH
 8      N  CHNROW
 9      N  PRICE
10      COLUMNS
```

11	DESK	STAMP	3.00000	ASSEMB	10.00000
12	DESK	FINISH	10.00000	PROFIT	95.00000
13	DESK	PRICE	175.00000		
14	CHAIR	STAMP	1.50000	ASSEMB	6.00000
15	CHAIR	FINISH	8.00000	PROFIT	41.00000
16	CHAIR	PRICE	95.00000		
17	CABINET	STAMP	2.00000	ASSEMB	8.00000
18	CABINET	FINISH	8.00000	PROFIT	84.00000
19	CABINET	PRICE	145.00000		
20	BOOKCSE	STAMP	2.00000	ASSEMB	7.00000
21	BOOKCSE	FINISH	7.00000	PROFIT	76.00000
22	BOOKCSE	PRICE	130.00000	CHNROW	1.00000
23	RHS				
24	TIME	STAMP	800.00000	ASSEMB	1200.0000
25	TIME	FINISH	800.00000		
26	RANGES				
27	T1	ASSEMB	900.00000		
28	BOUNDS				
29	UP	CHAIR	75.00000		
30	LO	BOOKCSE	50.00000		
31	ENDATA				

A program that converts these data to a SAS data set is shown below. The program expects the data to be in a file with fileref MPSDATA.

```
*------------------------------------------------;
* R_LIST: CONTAINS RAW DATA FOR A LISTING      ;
* RAW:    CONTAINS MODIFIED MPSX FORMAT DATA ;
*------------------------------------------------;

%include sasmpsxs;                      *load sasmpsxs macro;

data raw(drop=card field0)
   r_list(keep=card);
   infile mpsdata;

   input card $char80. @;               *for listing input;
   output r_list;
   input field0 $ 1 @;                  *for skipping comments;
   if field0='*' then return;
                                        *PLACE DATA IN FIELDS;
   input field1 $ 2-3   field2 $ 5-12
         field3 $ 15-22 field4   25-36
         field5 $ 40-47 field6   50-61;

   output raw;

proc print data=r_list;                 *print input data;

%sasmpsxs;                              *invoke sasmpsxs;
```

```
data;                                   *identify objective;
   retain flag 0;                       *and sensitivity rows;
   set prob;

   if      _type_='*ow' then flag=1;
   else if _type_='*ol' then flag=0;

   if flag=1 then do;
      if _row1_='profit' then _type_='max';
      if _row1_='chnrow' then _type_='pricesen';
      end;

proc print;                             *print data in sparse lp format;
run;
```

The DATA step saves the modified MPSX format data in a SAS data set called
RAW, with variables FIELD1 to FIELD6, and saves a SAS data set called R_LIST,
which is used for printing the MPSX input data. In larger problems, you can
remove this code to avoid printing the input data set. At this point, the SASMPSXS
macro is invoked to convert to the sparse PROC LP format. The SASMPSXS macro
places the problem in the output data set called PROB. Then, in a DATA step,
the row named PROFIT is identified as the objective row and the row named
CHNROW is identified as a price change vector. The data set that results from
executing this code is shown here.

OBS	_TYPE_	_COL_	_ROW1_	_COEF1_	_ROW2_	_COEF2_
1	*OW			.		.
2	MAX		PROFIT	.		.
3	LE		STAMP	.		.
4	LE		ASSEMB	.		.
5	LE		FINISH	.		.
6	PRICESEN		CHNROW	.		.
7	FREE		PRICE	.		.
8	*OL	MNS		.		.
9		DESK	STAMP	3.0	ASSEMB	10
10		DESK	FINISH	10.0	PROFIT	95
11		DESK	PRICE	175.0		.
12		CHAIR	STAMP	1.5	ASSEMB	6
13		CHAIR	FINISH	8.0	PROFIT	41
14		CHAIR	PRICE	95.0		.
15		CABINET	STAMP	2.0	ASSEMB	8
16		CABINET	FINISH	8.0	PROFIT	84
17		CABINET	PRICE	145.0		.
18		BOOKCSE	STAMP	2	ASSEMB	7
19		BOOKCSE	FINISH	7	PROFIT	76
20		BOOKCSE	PRICE	130	CHNROW	1
21	*HS			.		.
22		TIME	STAMP	800	ASSEMB	1200
23		TIME	FINISH	800		.
24	*AN	ES		.		.
25		T1	ASSEMB	900		.
26	*OU	DS		.		.
27	UPPERBDD	CHAIR	UP	75		.
28	LOWERBDD	BOOKCSE	LO	50		.

Now, to solve the mathematical program, call the LP procedure:

```
proc lp sparsedata;
   rhs    time;
   range t1;
```

The RHS and RANGE statements are necessary to identify the columns named TIME and T1. Because the SASMPSXS macro uses the variable _TYPE_ and LP identifies the variable _TYPE_ as the default type variable, there is no need for a TYPE statement. Similarly, the macro uses the variable names _COL_, _ROW1_, _ROW2_, _COEF1_, and _COEF2_, which are also recognized by the LP procedure.

L I N E A R   P R O G R A M M I N G   P R O C E D U R E

PROBLEM SUMMARY

Max PROFIT	Objective Function
TIME	Rhs Variable
TYPE	Type Variable
Problem Density	0.678571

Variable Type	Number
Non-negative	2
Lower Bounded	1
Upper Bounded	1
Slack	3
Total	7

Constraint Type	Number
LE	3
Free	1
Objective	1
Total	5

L I N E A R   P R O G R A M M I N G   P R O C E D U R E

SOLUTION SUMMARY

Terminated Successfully

Objective value	8685.714
Phase 1 iterations	0
Phase 2 iterations	2
Phase 3 iterations	0
Integer iterations	0
Integer solutions	0
Initial basic feasible variables	6
Time used (secs)	9
Number of inversions	2

```
Machine epsilon                              1E-8
Machine infinity            1.7976931349E308
Maximum phase 1 iterations                    100
Maximum phase 2 iterations                    100
Maximum phase 3 iterations               99999999
Maximum integer iterations                    100
Time limit (secs)                             120
```

L I N E A R   P R O G R A M M I N G   P R O C E D U R E

VARIABLE   SUMMARY

	Variable					Reduced
Col	Name	Status	Type	Price	Activity	Cost
1	BOOKCSE	BASIC	LOWERBD	76	114.285714	0.000
2	CABINET		NON-NEG	84	0.000	-2.857
3	CHAIR		UPPERBD	41	0.000	-45.857
4	DESK		NON-NEG	95	0.000	-13.571
5	STAMP	BASIC	SLACK		571.428571	0.000
6	ASSEMB	BASIC	SLACK		400.000000	0.000
7	FINISH		SLACK		0.000	-10.857

L I N E A R   P R O G R A M M I N G   P R O C E D U R E

CONSTRAINT   SUMMARY

Constraint			S/S			Dual
Row	Row	Type	Col	Rhs	Activity	Activity
1	PROFIT	OBJECT			8685.714286	-1.000
2	STAMP	LE	5	800	228.571429	0.000
3	ASSEMB	RANGELE	6	1200	800.000000	0.000
4	FINISH	LE	7	800	800.000000	10.857
5	PRICE	FREE			14857.142857	0.000

L I N E A R   P R O G R A M M I N G   P R O C E D U R E

PRICE SENSITIVITY ANALYSIS SUMMARY
Sensitivity Vector CHNROW

```
Minimum Phi              -2.5
Entering Variable        CABINET
Optimal Objective        8400

Maximum Phi              +INFINITY
```

	Variable	------Minimum Phi--------		------Maximum Phi--------	
Col	Name	Price	Reduced Cost	Price	Reduced Cost
1	BOOKCSE	73.500	0.000	+INFINITY	0.000
2	CABINET	84.000	0.000	84.000	-INFINITY
3	CHAIR	41.000	-43.000	41.000	-INFINITY
4	DESK	95.000	-10.000	95.000	-INFINITY
5	STAMP	0.000	0.000	0.000	0.000
6	ASSEMB	0.000	0.000	0.000	0.000
7	FINISH	0.000	-10.500	0.000	-INFINITY

THE MACRO LISTING

```
%macro sasmpsxs;
*----------------------------------------------------------;
* COPYRIGHT (C) 1985 BY SAS INSTITUTE INC., CARY NC        ;
*                                                          ;
*              MPSX CONVERSION MACRO                       ;
*                                                          ;
* CONVERTS AN LP PROBLEM IN THE FORMAT USED BY THE         ;
* MPSX 'CONVERT' ROUTINE TO THAT USED BY PROC LP           ;
* AND THE SPARSEDATA OPTION.                               ;
*                                                          ;
* THE INPUT DATA, WHICH IS IN A SAS DATA SET NAMED         ;
* RAW, SHOULD HAVE FIELDS 1 THROUGH 6 AS DESCRIBED         ;
* IN THE SAS/OR USER'S GUIDE.                              ;
*                                                          ;
*----------------------------------------------------------;
data prob (keep=_type_ _col_ _row1_ _coef1_
                                _row2_ _coef2_);
    length _type_ $ 8 lastname $ 8 _col_ $ 8
           _row1_ $ 8 _coef1_ 8 _row2_ $ 8 _coef2_ 8;
    retain lastname ' ' infinity 7.2e70 intflag 0;


*----------------------------------------------------------;
*          READ THE NAME SECTION                           ;
*----------------------------------------------------------;
    link setraw;
    if field1¬='am' then go to error;
    put 'note: convert ' _row1_ ' dataset.';
    _type_='*'||field1;
    link setraw;
    if field1='ow' then go to rowrd;
                   else go to error;
*----------------------------------------------------------;
*          READ THE ROW SECTION                            ;
*----------------------------------------------------------;
rowrd:_type_='*'||field1; output;
rowlp:link setraw;
    if _row1_='''scale''' then go to errors;
    else if _row1_='''marker''' then go to errorm;
    else if substr(field1,1,1)='d' then go to errord;
    if field1='n' then do;
       _type_='free'; _row1_=_col_; _col_=' ';
       end;
    else if field1='ax' then do;
       _type_='max '; _row1_=_col_; _col_=' ';
       end;
    else if field1='in' then do;
       _type_='min '; _row1_=_col_; _col_=' ';
       end;
    else if field1='g' then do;
       _type_='ge  '; _row1_=_col_; _col_=' ';
       end;
```

```
      else if field1='e' then do;
         _type_='eq  '; _row1_=_col_; _col_=' ';
         end;
      else if field1='l' then do;
         _type_='le  '; _row1_=_col_; _col_=' ';
         end;
      else if field1='ri' then do;
         _type_='pricesen'; _row1_=_col_; _col_=' ';
         end;
      else if field1='ol' then go to colrd;
      else if field1='an' then go to error;
      else if field1='ou' then go to error;
      else if field1='nd' then go to error;
      else do;
         put 'error: field1=' field1' which is an unknown keyword.';
         go to error;
         end;
      output;
      go to rowlp;


*----------------------------------------------------------;
*          READ THE COLUMN SECTION                         ;
*----------------------------------------------------------;
colrd:_type_='*'||field1; output;
collp:link setraw;
      if _row1_='''scale''' then go to error;
      else if _row1_='''marker''' then do;
         if _row2_='''intorg''' then do;
            if intflag=1 then go to errori1;
            intflag=1;
            end;
         else if _row2_='''intend''' then do;
            if intflag=0 then go to errori2;
            intflag=0;
            end;
         else put 'note: marker in column ' _col_ ' ignored.';
         end;
      else if field1='' then do;
         _type_=' '; output;
         if intflag=1 then do;
            _type_='integer';
            _row1_='integer'; _coef1_=1;
            _row2_=' '; _coef2_=.;
            output;
            end;
         end;
      else if field1='hs' then go to rhsrd;
      else if field1='an' then go to error;
      else if field1='ou' then go to error;
      else if field1='nd' then go to error;
      go to collp;
```

```
*-----------------------------------------------------------;
*              READ THE RHS SECTION                         ;
*-----------------------------------------------------------;
rhsrd:_type_='*'||field1; output;
rhslp:link setraw;
      if field1='' then do;
         _type_=' '; output;
         end;
      else if field1='an' then go to ranrd;
      else if field1='ou' then go to bunrd;
      else if field1='nd' then stop;
      go to rhslp;
*-----------------------------------------------------------;
*              READ THE RANGE SECTION                       ;
*-----------------------------------------------------------;
ranrd:_type_='*'||field1; output;
ranlp:link setraw;
      if field1='' then do;
         _type_=' '; output;
         end;
      else if field1='ou' then go to bunrd;
      else if field1='nd' then stop;
      go to ranlp;


*-----------------------------------------------------------;
*              READ THE BOUND SECTION                       ;
*-----------------------------------------------------------;
bunrd:_type_='*'||field1; output;
bunlp:link setraw;
      if field1='lo' then do;
         _type_='lowerbdd'; _col_=row1_; _row1_='lo';
         end;
      else if field1='up' then do;
         _type_='upperbdd'; _col_=row1_; _row1_='up';
         end;
      else if field1='mi' then do;
         _type_='lowerbdd'; _col_=row1_; _row1_='mi';
         _coef1_=-infinity;
         end;
      else if field1='fx' then do;
         _type_='lowerbdd'; _col_=row1_; _row1_='lo';
         lastname=_col_; output;
         _type_='upperbdd'; _col=lastname; _row1_='up';
          end;
      else if field1='fr' then do;
         _type_='unrstrct'; _col_=row1_; _row1_='fr';
         _coef1_=1;
         end;
      else if field1='nd' then do;
         _type_='*'||field1;
         stop;
         end;
      output;
      go to bunlp;
```

```
*-----------------------------------------------------------;
*            READ RAW DATA SUBROUTINE              ;
*-----------------------------------------------------------;
setraw:set raw (rename=(field2=_col_ field3=_row1_
                field4=_coef1_ field5=_row2_ field6=_coef2_));
       field1=left(field1);
       return;
*-----------------------------------------------------------;
*            TERMINAL ERRORS                    ;
*-----------------------------------------------------------;
error:  put 'error: data is not in the expected order.';
        abort;
errors: put 'error: scale is not supported.';
        abort;
errorm: put 'error: this marker is not recognized.';
        abort;
errord: put 'error: defining new rows as linear '
          'combinations of old rows in not supported.';
        abort;
errori1:put 'error: intorg appears before intend in column '
                   _col_ '.';
        abort;
errori2:put 'error: intend appears before intorg in column '
                   _col_ '.';
        abort;
run;
%mend;
```

Index

Your Turn

If you have comments about SAS software or the *SAS/OR User's Guide, Version 6, First Edition*, please send us your ideas on a photocopy of this page. If you include your name and address, we will reply to you.

Please return to the Publications Division, SAS Institute Inc., SAS Circle, Box 8000, Cary, NC 27512-8000.